Politics

Politics

Peter Ferdinand, Robert Garner, and Stephanie Lawson

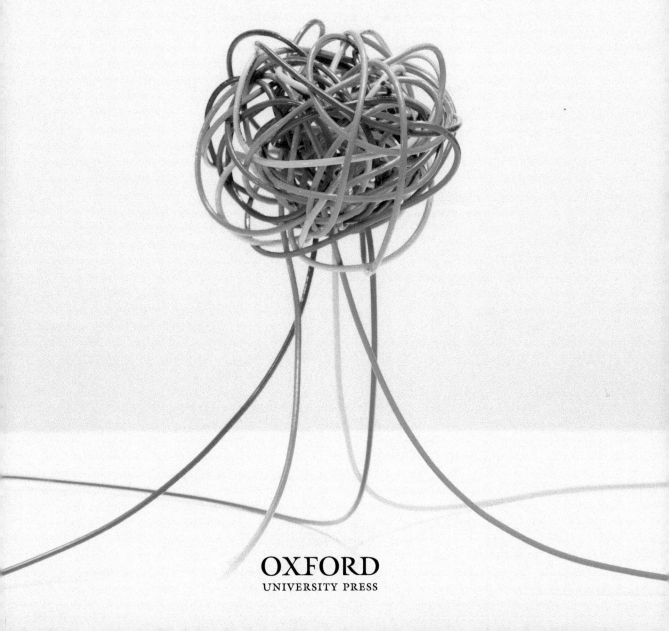

OXFORD

UNIVERSITY PRESS

OXFORD
UNIVERSITY PRESS

Great Clarendon Street, Oxford, OX2 6DP,
United Kingdom

Oxford University Press is a department of the University of Oxford.
It furthers the University's objective of excellence in research, scholarship,
and education by publishing worldwide. Oxford is a registered trade mark of
Oxford University Press in the UK and in certain other countries

© Oxford University Press 2018

The moral rights of the authors have been asserted

Impression: 3

Published in the United States of America by Oxford University Press
198 Madison Avenue, New York, NY 10016, United States of America

British Library Cataloguing in Publication Data
Data available

Library of Congress Control Number: 2017962502

ISBN 978–0–19–878798–3

Printed in Great Britain by
CPI Group (UK) Ltd, Croydon CR0 4YY

Acknowledgements

This is our second book with OUP (the first having run to three editions, plus a Canadian version), and we can continue to say that the help and support we have received from the editorial team has been superb. Particular thanks go to Francesca Walker, who got this project off the ground and coordinated it with great expertise. Throughout, we have owed a debt of gratitude to a number of anonymous reviewers whose constructive criticisms of draft chapters have made the final product that much stronger.

Brief Contents

Contents

List of Boxes

List of Tables

About the Authors

Peter Ferdinand

Peter Ferdinand is Emeritus Reader in Politics and International Studies and former Director of the Centre for Studies in Democratization at the University of Warwick. He is a former Head of the Asia-Pacific Programme at the Royal Institute of International Affairs (Chatham House). He is the author of *Communist Regimes in Comparative Perspective: The Evolution of the Soviet, Chinese and Yugoslav Models* (Harvester Wheatsheaf, 1992), and *Governance in Pacific Asia* (Bloomsbury, 2012). He has edited books on politics and political economy in Taiwan, Central Asia, and Hong Kong, and on the Internet and democracy. His interests are in the politics of Pacific Asia, the former Soviet Union, democratization, political economy, and new rising world powers.

Robert Garner

Robert Garner is Professor of Politics at the University of Leicester. He was previously at the Universities of Buckingham and Exeter. He has published widely in the area of environmental politics in general, and the politics and philosophy of animal rights in particular. His books include *Environmental Politics* (Palgrave Macmillan, 2011), *Animals, Politics and Morality* (Manchester University Press, 2004), *The Political Theory of Animal Rights* (Manchester University Press, 2005), *Animal Ethics* (Polity Press, 2005), and *A Theory of Justice for Animals* (Oxford University Press, 2013).

Stephanie Lawson

Stephanie Lawson is Professor of Politics and International Relations at Macquarie University, Honorary Professor at the Australian National University, and Senior Research Associate at the University of Johannesburg. She has previously held teaching and research positions at the University of New England, the Australian National University, the University of East Anglia, and the University of Birmingham. She is a past President of the Australian Political Studies Association and a Fellow of the Academy of Social Sciences in Australia. She is also the current President of the Pacific Islands Political Studies Association. Her publications span the fields of comparative and international politics, normative theory, and Asia-Pacific studies, on issues ranging from nationalism and ethnic politics to the theorization of democracy and human rights in cross-cultural settings. She has written extensively on politics in the Southwest Pacific more generally and is currently engaged on a research project on the politics of regional identity funded by the Australian Research Council. Her most recent book is *Theories of International Relations: Contending Approaches to World Politics* (Polity Press, 2015).

How to Use This Book

This book is enriched with a number of learning tools to help you to reinforce your knowledge, further your understanding, and develop your ability to think critically.

Reader's Guides

Reader's Guide

This chapter begins by defining the nature of politics, examining what constitutes 'the political', and addressing the question of whether politics is an inevitable feature of all human societies. We also look at the boundary problems inherent in analysing the political and consider whether politics should be defined narrowly, in the context of the state, or whether it is better defined more broadly by encompassing other social institutions. Another

Consolidate your knowledge as you progress through the chapter with Key Points, which summarize the most important ideas and arguments discussed.

Identify the scope of the material to be covered, and what themes and issues you can expect to learn about, with Reader's Guides at the beginning of each chapter.

Key Points

✳ KEY POINTS

- Politics is difficult to define a negative connotations.

- The field of 'the political' enc as a range of values.

Key Concepts

◆◆ KEY CONCEPT 1.2

At its most basic level, sovereign specified territory. It can be embo or, in a democratic system, in 'th by a parliamentary body. In e them. The manifestation of sovere

Deepen your understanding with focused discussions of Key Concepts.

Key Debates

KEY DEBATE 2.3   Th

The state has always been criticiz
as an exploitative institution that
tation of classical Marxism (the
himself) operate with a very sim
sical Marxists. the state is merely

Identify significant controversies and
challenge your preconceptions with Key
Debates boxes, which draw out areas of
conflict and contestation.

Gain insight into the subject area with
important and relevant Key Quotes from
renowned scholars.

Key Quotes

KEY QUOTE 6.2   Th

'Whatever else it may be, national
else the nation may be, it is noth
social space.' (Williams and Smit

'The nation's unique history is em
"homeland", the primeval land o

Key Thinkers

KEY THINKER 8.2

Burke was born in Dublin in 1729
to England in 1750 where he qual
He became an MP in 1776 in a rot
He died in 1797 a rich man with

Contextualize your learning with biographical
information about Key Thinkers in political
analysis.

Develop your ability to connect theory with
the real world with a wide range of Case
Studies from across the world.

Case Studies

CASE STUDY 4.1   M

An interesting illustration of cor
context of the UK Referendum on
was a narrow victory for the leav
quent debate about the role of Pa
Many (on the leave side) argued t

Key Questions

? Key Questions

- What is politics?
- Should politics be seen in a positi
- What is the case for defining politi
- Is politics synonymous with the sta

Review your knowledge and develop your analytical and reflective skills with critical end-of-chapter Key Questions.

Broaden your learning with guided Further Reading, where the authors highlight additional resources you may wish to read, with explanations of why these texts are helpful.

Further Reading

▌▌ Further Reading

Crick, B. (1962), *In Defence of Politi*
This is a classic case for a particular

Dahl, R. (1991), *Modern Political An*
This is a classic account of the study

Glossary terms

Alternative member model A hybrid voting sy: that combines strengths of both majoritarianism and **proportional representation**: votes are cast both for individual candidates within a constituency and for list of candidates from separate parties.

Amoral familism The exaltation of family intere all other moral considerations, originally coined by sociologist Banfiel to describe social relations in Si

Look up and revise key terms, which appear in colour throughout the text and are defined in a glossary at the end of the book.

Make connections across chapters and deepen your understanding of particular topics with marginal cross-references throughout the book.

Marginal cross-references

. While humans certainly on hold that it grossly un-:ompetition, and conflict. ted with the 'end of ideol-) and Francis Fukuyama post-1945 period, liberal

▶ See Chapter 7 for a discussion of human nature.

🔗 Web Links

www.apsanet.org
The American Political Science Association is the majo individuals engaged in the study of politics and govern

Take your learning further with relevant web links to reliable online content.

How to Use the Online Resources

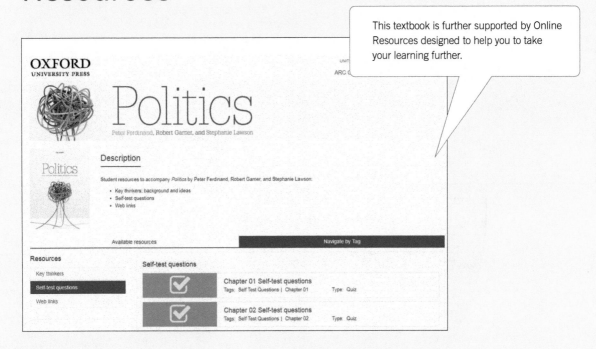

This textbook is further supported by Online Resources designed to help you to take your learning further.

For students:

Multiple-choice questions: Test your knowledge of the chapters and receive instant feedback with online multiple-choice questions.

Web links: Take your learning further with relevant web links to reliable online content.

Flashcard glossary: Revise key terms and concepts from the text with a digital flashcard glossary.

Biographies: Learn more about key thinkers' ideas and backgrounds.

For registered instructors:

Seminar and essay questions: Reinforce key themes from each chapter with suggested seminar and essay questions.

Active learning guidance: Incorporate active learning into your seminars with political scenarios, discussion questions, and teaching notes.

PowerPoint slides: Use the adaptable PowerPoint slides as the basis for lecture presentations or as handouts in class.

Test bank: Assess students' learning with a ready-made test bank, which can be customized to suit your needs.

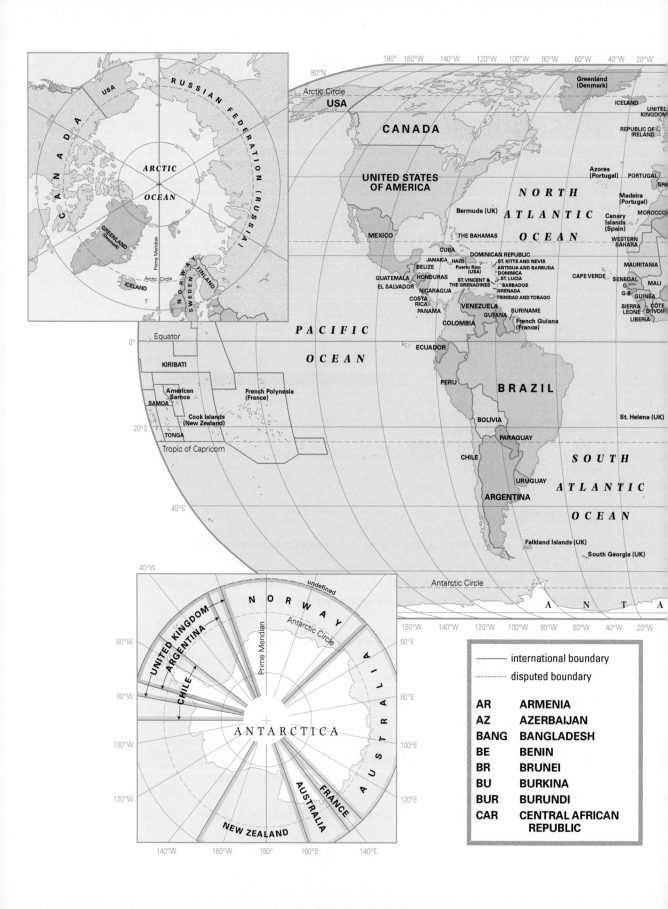

Arctic Circle
USA
ARCTIC
OCEAN
RUSSIAN FEDERATION (RUSSIA)
CANADA
USA
GREENLAND (Denmark)
ICELAND
NORWAY
SWEDEN
FINLAND
Prime Meridian
Arctic Circle

80°N
180° 160°W 140°W 120°W 100°W 80°W 60°W 40°W 20°W
Arctic Circle
USA
Greenland (Denmark)
ICELAND
UNITED KINGDOM
CANADA
REPUBLIC OF IRELAND
UNITED STATES OF AMERICA
NORTH
ATLANTIC
Azores (Portugal)
PORTUGAL
SPA
Bermuda (UK)
Madeira (Portugal)
Canary Islands (Spain)
MOROCCO
MEXICO
THE BAHAMAS
OCEAN
WESTERN SAHARA
CUBA
MAURITANIA
JAMAICA
HAITI
DOMINICAN REPUBLIC
ST. KITTS AND NEVIS
ANTIGUA AND BARBUDA
CAPE VERDE
SENEGAL
MALI
BELIZE
Puerto Rico (USA)
DOMINICA
ST. LUCIA
G-B
GUINEA
GUATEMALA
HONDURAS
ST. VINCENT & THE GRENADINES
BARBADOS
GRENADA
SIERRA LEONE
CÔTE D'IVOIR
EL SALVADOR
NICARAGUA
TRINIDAD AND TOBAGO
LIBERIA
COSTA RICA
VENEZUELA
SURINAME
PANAMA
COLOMBIA
GUYANA
French Guiana (France)
ECUADOR
PACIFIC
Equator
KIRIBATI
OCEAN
PERU
BRAZIL
American Samoa
French Polynesia (France)
SAMOA
St. Helena (UK)
Cook Islands (New Zealand)
BOLIVIA
20°S
TONGA
PARAGUAY
Tropic of Capricorn
SOUTH
CHILE
ATLANTIC
URUGUAY
ARGENTINA
OCEAN
40°S
Falkland Islands (UK)
South Georgia (UK)
Antarctic Circle
A N T A
A N T A R C T I C A

40°W
undefined
160°W 140°W 120°W 100°W 80°W 60°W 40°W 20°W
60°W
NORWAY
Antarctic Circle
60°E
UNITED KINGDOM
ARGENTINA
Prime Meridian
80°W
CHILE
80°E
AUSTRALIA
ANTARCTICA
100°W
100°E
FRANCE
120°W
AUSTRALIA
120°E
NEW ZEALAND
140°W 160°W 180° 160°E 140°E

——— international boundary
·········· disputed boundary

AR	ARMENIA
AZ	AZERBAIJAN
BANG	BANGLADESH
BE	BENIN
BR	BRUNEI
BU	BURKINA
BUR	BURUNDI
CAR	CENTRAL AFRICAN REPUBLIC

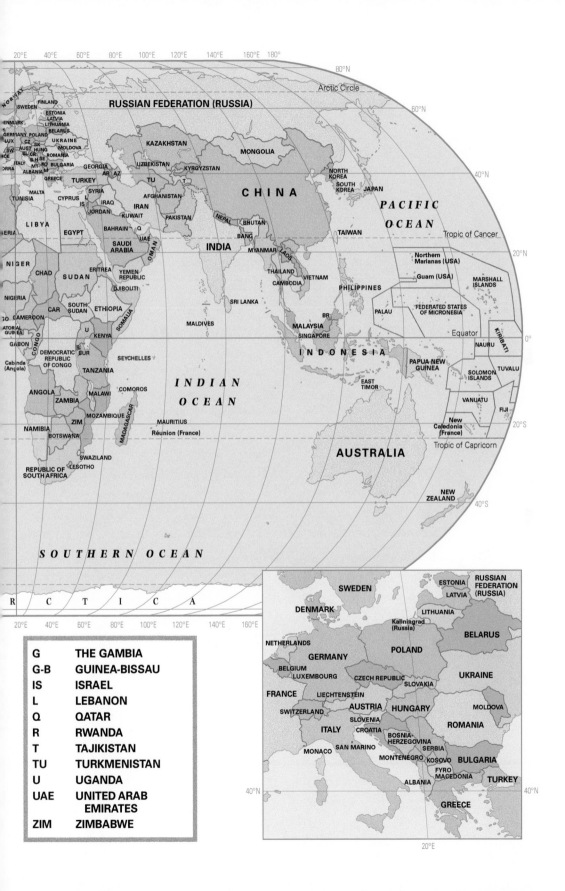

Introduction: The Nature of Politics and Political Analysis

1

- What is Politics?
- Is Politics Inevitable?
- Political Questions
- The Boundaries of the Political
- Politics as Consensus or Conflict?
- The Study of Politics

- Can Politics Be a Science?
- Conclusion
- Key Questions
- Further Reading
- Web Links

Reader's Guide

This chapter begins by defining the nature of politics, examining what constitutes 'the political', and addressing the question of whether politics is an inevitable feature of all human societies. We also look at the boundary problems inherent in analysing the political and consider whether politics should be defined narrowly, in the context of the state, or whether it is better defined more broadly by encompassing other social institutions. Another question concerns whether politics consists essentially in consensual and cooperative behaviour among communities, rather than in violent conflict and war. The chapter then goes on to distinguish between different forms of political analysis—the empirical, the normative, and the semantic—as well as different approaches to the study of politics represented by the deductive and inductive methods. This leads us to consider whether the study of politics can ever be conducted 'scientifically'.

1

What is Politics?

Politics is a many-sided activity that is difficult to reduce to one simple definition. A rather narrow approach would suggest that it consists primarily of activities associated with the governance of the state, including order and security. There is also the conduct of politics between states in the international or global sphere, which is often dealt with in the separate discipline (or sub-discipline) of international relations. Central to the activities in all spheres are the dynamics of power. This is especially so in relation to the distribution of goods. In the words of American political scientist Harold Lasswell (1936), politics is about 'who gets what, when and how'. This also raises questions of value—about what is just and fair in the distribution of goods—which relates in turn to the notion that politics is about producing the conditions for securing human well-being or, as political philosophers put it, for pursuing the 'good life'.

In approaching the question of what politics is and what constitutes the political, it is instructive to look to the etymology of the word. 'Politics' comes to us from the ancient Greek *polis* (from which we also derive 'police', 'policy', and 'polity'). *Polis* is commonly translated as 'city-state', although it is more properly understood as a form of political community encompassing the body of citizens (*polites*), a designated territory, and a set of rules and practices, or constitution (*politeia*), for the conduct of life within the community. The *polis* did not, however, refer to just any political community, but was rather restricted to the particular form that such communities took in the ancient Greek world, in which state and society, which we now tend to treat as distinct entities, were much more of an integrated whole.

Greek philosopher Aristotle (384–322BC) famously described the human as a 'political animal' (*zōon politikon*). Contemporary understandings of this term, however, differ from what Aristotle originally meant. At best, we may use it today to refer to someone active in political life and highly attuned to the dynamics of political activity. At worst, it has a negative connotation, as if being a 'political animal' designates a creature skilled in the arts of political intrigue and subterfuge. But for Aristotle—and this is the key point—it simply meant that humans were, *by nature*, social creatures made for living a common life within the *polis*—the political community. Furthermore, it was only within such a community that *the good life* could be realized.

The task of defining politics is complicated by the fact that politics is often popularly regarded in a pejorative sense, associated with corruption, intrigue, and conflict, as some contemporary understandings of the term 'political animal' indicate. The close association of politics with power, or more especially the abuse of power, compounds the negative associations, as does the perception that many politicians in the contemporary period are only 'in it for themselves'. US President Trump's promise, made during his 2016 election campaign, to 'drain the swamp' of Washington DC initially referred to conflicts of interest created by the political lobbying industry, but the phrase also stands as a more general metaphor, at least for Trump supporters, for almost everything that appears to be wrong at the centre of American politics. This is related to the phenomenon of 'anti-politics', which is discussed further below.

One commentator has noted that the popular association of politics with the apparent pursuit of the material self-interest of politicians in the contemporary period is 'oddly antithetical to its very *raison d'être*'—that is, the realization of the 'collective good' (Hay, 2002: 3). Most contemporary politicians would say that this is actually what motivated them to seek public office in the first place and there is no doubt that many do genuinely believe that it lies at the heart of their calling. The view of politics as essential to the realization of a common or collective good has appeared in the work of political thinkers from the ancient Greeks onwards. In the ancient and pre-modern periods, in addition to Aristotle, political philosophers such as Plato (427–327BC), Cicero (106–43BC), St Augustine of Hippo (354–430), and St Thomas Aquinas (1225–74) all articulated conceptions of the common good and highlighted the task of politics in achieving this. In the Arab/Muslim world, too, philosophers such as Ibn Rushd (1126–98) saw the purpose of government and politics as creating the conditions for the pursuit of the good life, while much of classical Hindu political philosophy in South Asia and the Confucian tradition of thought in East Asia centred on similar themes. The essentially noble purpose of politics is therefore evident in a broad range of philosophical traditions.

In the modern period, political philosophers such as Jean-Jacques Rousseau (1712–78) and John Stuart Mill (1806–73) regarded participation in political life as an honourable activity that ought to be encouraged. In the UK in the 1990s and into the early twenty-first century, politicians such as Tony Blair, Labour Prime Minister from 1997 to 2007, emphasized the strong moral purpose of politics. In the present period, prominent US Congresswoman (Democrat) Nancy Pelosi recalls being taught from an early age that 'politics is a noble calling, that we have a responsibility to other people' (quoted in Marcovitz, 2009: 18). On a slightly different note, it is also interesting to note that, in the ancient Greek world, the term *idiotes* (idiot) referred specifically to a citizen who took no interest in the affairs of the *polis*.

The pejorative critique of politics, however, actually provides a further clue to what politics is about. There is little doubt that politics is associated, among other things, with adversarial behaviour. This is due to the fact that all societies of any complexity are pluralistic and that people inevitably have competing interests and values. Indeed, a popular way of defining politics is that it is the process by which groups representing divergent interests and values manage to make collective decisions. There are two assumptions here. The first is that humans will always have different interests and values and societies of any complexity will contain diversity. It follows that there will always be a need for a mechanism whereby these different interests and values are managed without recourse to violence. The second assumption is that scarcity is also an inevitable characteristic of all societies. Since there is not enough to go around of the goods that people want, there needs to be

⯈ See Chapter 9
for discussion of
political economy.

⯈ See Chapter 7
for discussion of
theories of distributive
justice.

some mechanism whereby these goods are distributed. It is this assumption that underpins the idea, noted above, that politics is about who gets what, when, and how.

Clearly, the way in which economic goods are distributed is crucially important in determining the nature of society and the well-being of those within it. There is also the question of the distribution of goods on a global scale. Here is where economic theories and ideas overlap with those concerning politics to produce the field of political economy, which we examine in Chapter 9. We also examine some competing theories of distributive justice focusing on a particular ordering of economic goods in Chapter 7. For the moment, however, we should note that while economic goods are of great importance, they are not the only ones that humans value. Status is another very important good and, for most people, the granting of an honour, whether by the state or by an organization within civil society, has high prestige value. For even though no monetary gain may be attached to it, honours enhance the sense of self-worth.

The study of politics prior to the twentieth century was very much concerned with a study of values. Political philosophers asked: what is the good life and what is the best kind of society for us to live in? Many different answers have been provided, but, as Stoker (2006: 6) points out, a 'central divide for much of the last two centuries has been between those who prefer liberty over equality and those who prefer equality over liberty'. This, of course, raises the question of the balance between the two. In the present period, there is evidence of a widening gap between rich and poor in many countries—another issue for political economy, as well as for the related debate about values. Of equal importance in the twenty-first century is the conflict between liberty and the value of security—a theme that has become increasingly prominent in the wake of '9/11' and the heightened sense of threat from terror attacks.

So far, we have identified politics and the political as encompassing the institutions of governance and the state, the dynamics of power and the distribution of goods, and values such as liberty, equality, justice, and security. But does this cover the field adequately or should we extend it to include other considerations? We return to these questions shortly, but, for the time being, we consider whether politics is an inevitable feature of human life.

✳ KEY POINTS

- Politics is difficult to define at least partly because it has both positive and negative connotations.
- The field of 'the political' encompasses institutions of governance, as well as a range of values.
- A variety of philosophical traditions highlight the role of politics in producing the conditions for the 'good life'.

Is Politics Inevitable?

If we define politics in terms of the management of differences, conflicts, and scarcity, it does seem to follow that politics is an inevitable feature of all societies. Not all, however, agree with this proposition. For some, such a claim seriously underestimates the possibility of greater social cohesion based around agreement on core values. Politics for Karl Marx (1818–83) is seen in negative terms as a manifestation of class conflict. Political power, as Marx and Engels famously insisted in the *Communist Manifesto* (Marx and Engels, 1848/1976: 105), is 'merely the organized power of one class for oppressing another'. It follows that once that conflict is ended through the overthrow of capitalism, there will be no competing classes. This offers the prospect of a society based on consensus and cooperation in which politics and the state is unnecessary, thus signalling the 'end of politics'. For others, this Marxist vision is unrealistic—'ideal fancy', in Berlin's words (1969: 118). While humans certainly have a great capacity for cooperation, critics of the Marxist position hold that it grossly underestimates other tendencies in human nature—namely, rivalry, competition, and conflict.

▶ See Chapter 7 for a discussion of human nature.

Other, more recent, versions of the 'end of politics' are associated with the 'end of ideology' and 'end of history' theses proposed by Daniel Bell (1960) and Francis Fukuyama (1992), respectively. An argument common to both is that, in the post-1945 period, liberal democratic values gradually assumed a position of dominance across the world. This appeared to be confirmed by the collapse of communism as a viable economic and political system in 1989. While it is true that the Cold War is now a thing of the past, that communism in Russia and Eastern Europe has been dismantled, and that growing affluence in the West has made it more difficult for left-of-centre parties to garner political support, it simply does not follow that we have reached the end of ideology, let alone history.

Another critic of the 'end of politics' theme is Chantal Mouffe, who has challenged what she calls a liberal 'post-political vision' held by those with an overly optimistic view of a globalizing world and who advocate a form of consensual democracy that lies beyond the politics of left and right or any other form of adversarial politics. This approach, she says, not only betrays a complete lack of understanding of what democratic politics is about, but also is dangerous in denying the very nature of 'the political' as a realm for contestation. Her basic argument is that the consensual approach denies the space necessary for the legitimate expression of antagonism: '[A]cknowledging the ineradicability of the conflictual dimension in social life, far from undermining the democratic project, is the necessary condition for grasping the challenge [with] which it is confronted' (Mouffe, 2005: 4). Mouffe is certainly right to question the value of consensus politics in limiting the space for political contestation, but we have to be careful in applying a general label such as 'liberal' to this form of post-politics. *Liberal* democracy is, after all, the principle form of politics in which adversarial, antagonistic behaviour is not only tolerated, but also regarded as 'normal politics' (see Chapter 5).

A cursory glance at the state of world affairs, however, reveals many alternatives to the liberal democratic model. Some share common features with Western liberal democracy in that there are parliaments, elections, political parties, and so on, but there are also significant differences in the way they operate. The post-communist regimes of Russia and Eastern Europe, for instance, operate very differently because of their limited experience of liberal democratic norms. Many East Asian regimes, such as China, Malaysia, and Singapore, have focused on economic development, often at the expense of civil liberties and democratic procedures. China is a one-party state, while in Singapore and Malaysia, although there are a number of political parties, a single ruling party has dominated for decades. Military regimes, often found in Africa, and Islamic regimes, particularly of the fundamentalist variety (as in Iran) that put religious norms before liberty and democracy, highlight the limited application of the 'endist' approaches. As Gamble (2000: 108) points out, '[t]he notion that there are no longer any great ideological issues in the world . . . becomes bizarre in relation to the vast populations . . . in Africa, in Asia, in Latin America and in the former territories of the Soviet Union' who live under regimes that do not subscribe to liberal democratic principles.

There are also many fundamental conflicts in the contemporary world that appear intractable. Some are based on territory, while others are based on political values, with the most insoluble containing elements of both. Here, the uncompromising ideology of nationalism is all too apparent. The Israel/Palestine conflict, in which competing nationalisms make apparently irreconcilable claims, is one such case. And there have been cases in Western Europe where resort to violence has only recently been eliminated, as in Northern Ireland and the Basque country of Spain. Widely divergent views over such issues as multiculturalism and immigration have also generated much conflict.

Gamble (2000) also seeks to challenge what he sees as the pessimistic acceptance in the modern world that humans can no longer influence their destiny. According to this position, the forces of 'bureaucracy, technology and the global market' have led to the 'disenchantment of the world, in which the ability to change that world . . . has been lost, and lost irrevocably' (Gamble, 2000:14). So-called globalization, in particular, appears to signal the end of national autonomy. It no longer matters what allegedly sovereign governments do because we are controlled by global economic forces that no one can alter. As a result, the 'space for politics is shrinking, and with it the possibility to imagine or to realise any serious alternative to our present condition' (Gamble, 2000: 2–3).

Such pessimism is, in part at least, a cause of the alleged 'crisis of politics' seen in declining political participation and the emergence of an 'anti-politics' discourse in Western democracies (Flinders, 2012: 10–15; Heywood, 2013: 443–5). The term 'anti-politics' is now used variously to describe a distrust of career politicians, a rejection of partisan politics as embodied in dominant party systems, a disengagement with mainstream politics or 'politics as usual', and a turn to populism (see Chapter 16). Anti-politics has recently been identified with the 2016 'Brexit' vote in the UK, the campaign for which was spearheaded by the previously marginal UK Independence Party (UKIP), and in the 2016 US presidential election in which Donald Trump gained support from many who saw him as *not* a politician (see Chapter 15).

▶ See Chapter 6 for a discussion of nationalism and multiculturalism.

▶ See Chapters 2, 6, 9, and 19 for a discussion of globalization.

1

Should we really be so pessimistic about contemporary politics and the prospect of positive change? It would be wrong to suggest that there are no constraints, some of them severe, acting upon human will. We may have to deal with the realities of the global market and dehumanizing technologies, but it would be equally wrong to conclude that human agency has no impact. Rather, there is a tension between impersonal forces and human will, a tension 'between politics and fate', that must be recognized and tackled.

✳ KEY POINTS

- Although humans have a great capacity for cooperation, differences in values and interests, as well as the need to manage the distribution of goods, appear to make politics inevitable.
- Different versions of 'endism' proclaim the dominance of liberal democratic values, but this cannot be sustained in the face of ongoing ideological conflicts around the world.
- Contemporary politics in Western democracies appears to have generated much pessimism about the capacity of politics to actually deliver the good life, as reflected in the phenomenon of 'anti-politics'.

Political Questions

We now return to the notion that politics is essentially a mechanism for deciding the distribution of goods and determining which values will dominate. As noted above, if we all had the same interests and values, and there were enough of everything to go around, there would be no need to make such decisions. We could have everything we wanted. Politics is predicated on the assumption that this is not the case. As a result, students of politics ask a number of questions about the decisions that are taken. In the first place, they will ask whether decisions should serve, for instance, the values of justice or liberty, and if so, what do we mean by justice and liberty? Is a just decision one that is made in the interests of the few, the many, or all? Second, students of politics will ask who makes—or should make—the decisions? One person, or a few, or many, or all? Further questions include whether there is anything special about democratic forms of government and whether we have a greater obligation to obey decisions taken in a democratic way than in other ways? These types of question formed the basis of Aristotle's famous sixfold classification of political systems (**see Key Concept 1.1** and **Table 1.1**).

The third main question that students of politics will ask is: why are those making decisions able to enforce them? Here, it is important to make a distinction between power and authority, concepts that are central to politics. We could say that rulers are able to enforce their decisions either because they have the power to do so or because they have the

▶ See Chapter 3 for an exploration of the concepts of power and authority.

❰❱ KEY CONCEPT 1.1 Aristotle's classificatory schema

Aristotle (**see Figure 1.1**) argued that a symbol of good government was the degree to which the rulers ruled in the interests of all and not a sectional interest. As a result, he developed a sixfold classification containing three 'proper' forms of government and three 'deviant' forms of government. His preferred form of government was a monarchy, although he conceded that, in practice, this often degenerated into a self-serving regime. Aristotle regarded democracy as the rule of the poor in their own interests and liable to degenerate into mob rule. However, he also noted that it at least served the interests of the many, rather than the few or one. In this respect, democracy could be seen as the least bad form of government—a sentiment echoed by Winston Churchill many centuries later (Cunningham, 2002: 7).

FIGURE 1.1 Aristotle
© MidoSemsem/ Shutterstock.com

TABLE 1.1 Political systems according to Aristotle

Number ruling	Rulers rule in interest of . . .	
	. . . All	. . . Themselves
One	Monarchy	Tyranny
Few	Aristocracy	Oligarchy
Many	Polity	Democracy

Source: Dahl (1991: 59).

authority to do so. The former implies some form of coercion or sanction—that those with power are able to cause those without power to behave in a way they would not otherwise have done. A regime that relies exclusively on the exercise of power, in the sense described above, is likely to be inefficient and unstable. Such a regime will only survive if it is able to impose coercion continually—a time-consuming and difficult exercise.

On the other hand, if a set of rulers is regarded as possessing legitimate authority, force will not be necessary. Authority, then, may be defined as the product of legitimate power in the sense that rulers are accepted as such by the ruled—they are recognized as having the *right* to exercise power. In a democracy, of course, people also have the right to vote any particular set of rulers out of office if they are dissatisfied with their performance. Thus legitimate power and authority in a democratic system is limited and conditional.

KEY POINTS

- Politics is predicated on the existence of competing interests and values in all societies of any complexity, which prompts questions about how, and by whom, key political decisions are rightfully made.
- Politics involves the exercise of power, but issues of authority and legitimacy moderate the manner in which it is exercised.

The Boundaries of the Political

We have seen that politics is concerned with the management of different interests and values. However, this only takes us so far in a definitional sense, because it does not touch upon boundary problems. Where does politics begin and end? According to Leftwich (1984: 10), this is the 'single most important factor involved in influencing the way people implicitly or explicitly conceive of politics'. For some, politics ought to be defined only in terms of the activities of the state and the public realm, or with a particular type of decision-making based on building compromise and consensus. As a result, institutions other than the state and dispute-resolving mechanisms involving violence or suppression—important as they may be in other ways—are considered to be beyond the scope of politics as such. For others, as we see shortly, this narrow drawing of the boundary misses much of importance that might fairly be described as political.

The state has traditionally been at the centre of much political analysis because it has been regarded as the highest form of legitimate authority in a society. Such authority is embodied in the concept of **sovereignty**, which holds that the state is sovereign in the sense that it is the supreme law-making body within a particular territory. Its formulation is attributed largely to Jean Bodin (1530–96) in France and Thomas Hobbes (1588–1679) in England. Both lived through periods of civil war and both were therefore deeply concerned with problems of order and security. The solution to turbulence and violence within the state was to be found through establishing a supreme political authority—a sovereign power that Hobbes dubbed the 'Leviathan' (**see Key Concept 1.2**). Ultimately, the state has the power of life and death over individuals. In the words of the great German sociologist Max Weber (1864–1920), the state possesses a 'monopoly of the legitimate use of physical force in enforcing its order within a given territorial area' (cited in Gerth and Mills, 1946: 77–8). It can also demand that individuals fight for their country in wars with other sovereign states.

Given these features, the state can be distinguished from the government in the sense that it is a much larger entity, containing not just political offices associated with a government, but also a range of bureaucratic institutions, the judiciary, military, police, and other security agencies. The state can also be distinguished from civil society, which consists of those non-governmental institutions—such as pressure groups, business organizations, and trade unions—to which individuals belong. It is these institutions that provide linkages between the individual and the state.

See Chapters 16 and 18 for a discussion of civil society.

Without doubt, the question of state power and the study of government—its legislative, executive, and judicial functions—occupies a great deal of the political analyst's time. But political analysis requires not just a description of the state and governmental institutions. It also involves the application of political philosophy, which deals with issues such as political obligation. Why should we obey the state? Is there any particular form of the state that we should obey rather than others? What duties or responsibilities do we owe the state? On the other hand, there have always been those—notably Marxist and anarchist thinkers—who have argued that the state is an oppressive institution and therefore ought not to exist (Hoffman, 1995).

See Chapter 7 for a discussion of political obligation.

Those who draw the boundaries of the political in a narrow sense by restricting it to state-related issues have been challenged by others who insist that politics occurs in the

---

❮❯   KEY CONCEPT 1.2   Sovereignty

At its most basic level, sovereignty refers to the supreme political authority within a specified territory. It can be embodied conceptually in a monarch—'the sovereign'—or, in a democratic system, in 'the people' whose sovereignty is usually represented by a parliamentary body. In either case, no other power or authority stands above them. The manifestation of sovereignty in either of these forms is taken to constitute its internal dimension. But it also has an external dimension, for the state itself is considered to be sovereign in relation to other states. This gives rise to the doctrine of state sovereignty, which holds that each state has the right to determine its own internal affairs without interference from any other state. This doctrine is conventionally regarded as having been consolidated in Europe in 1648 through the Peace of Westphalia, which followed a period of prolonged warfare. Sovereignty is therefore conceived as a principle of order between states, as well as within them.

institutions of society below the state. Hay (2002: 3) insists that 'the political should be defined in such a way as to encompass the entire sphere of the social'. Leftwich (1984: 64) substantially agrees, arguing that 'politics is at the heart of *all* collective social activity, formal and informal, public and private, in *all* human groups, institutions and societies'. The term governance, often preferred now to government, reflects this by drawing the boundaries of the governmental process much more widely to include not just traditional governmental institutions, but also inputs from the workings of the market and interest group activity. Indeed, this concurs with everyday discourse, where it is common to hear about politics taking place in business organizations, universities, churches, sport, and the family. Comprehensive political analysis therefore requires that we take account of a range of non-state actors and forces.

Some ideological traditions concur with this wider view of politics. Radical feminists, for instance, see power deriving from patriarchy—meaning literally 'the rule of the father'—in personal relationships and the family, which makes the interpersonal realm acutely political. This is what is meant by the feminist slogan 'the personal is the political'. At a different level, classical Marxists insist that political power derives from dominance in the economic realm. Similarly, whatever its internal divisions, Islamic thought, deriving from religious scriptures, delves into all aspects of the social sphere down to the family, providing normative prescriptions that individuals are meant to follow. To deny the essentially political nature of these dynamics is to therefore offer only a fairly shallow analysis of 'the political' in the contemporary world.

> See Chapter 8 for a discussion of feminism.

It can also be questioned whether the boundaries of the political should stop at the human species. There seems to be a strong case for incorporating at least some species of non-human animals as morally relevant and which therefore ought to have their interests considered in the political process (Garner, 2005). An even more radical position seeks to extend the boundaries of the political to encompass the whole of the natural world—a position designated as dark green ecology (Dobson, 2007).

> See Chapter 8 for a discussion of environmentalism.

There is an apparent danger, however, in expanding the boundaries of the political in the ways suggested above. If we do so, does not politics cease to be a distinctive discipline? How would we distinguish, say, between the work of the sociologist and that of the political analyst? Does not politics, in a very real sense, lose its separate identity? One response by theorist Colin Hay (2002) is that this critique is confusing politics as an arena with politics as a process. For Hay (2002: 27), the distinctiveness of politics lies not in the arena within which it takes place but in 'the emphasis it places on the political aspect of social relations'. This 'political aspect' is then defined in terms of the 'distribution, exercise and consequences of power'. Politics, then, occurs wherever the exercise of power takes place. Of course, Hay is not suggesting that politics explains everything there is to be known, or even the most important things to be known, about social relationships. Other disciplines—sociology, economics, psychology, cultural studies—have important explanatory roles too. 'Though politics may be everywhere,' Hay (2002: 75) continues, 'nothing is exhaustively political.'

1

Politics as Consensus or Conflict?

Another way of approaching boundary issues in defining the scope of politics is by consider-ing the idea that politics is, in essence, the art of resolving conflict peacefully, through com-promise or the building of consensus, whereas the resort to any kind of violence represents a failure of politics. A well-known advocate of this position is Bernard Crick (1962: 18), for whom politics is by far the best way of responding to the problem of order in society. It fol-lows that politics is a 'great and civilizing human activity' associated with admirable values of toleration, respect, and fortitude (Bernard Crick, 1962: 15). This accords with the views noted earlier about politics being a noble pursuit. Crick also sees political rule as concerned with incorporating competing groups in society, in contrast with tyranny and oligarchy, which operate through forcing compliance with the ruling elite. Crick argues further that conciliation is most likely to occur when power is spread widely throughout society so that no one small group can impose its will on others. Unfortunately, politics is too often rejected in favour of violence and suppression. Crick therefore calls for the values of politics to be positively promoted.

Similar arguments have been put forward by Gerry Stoker (2006) and Matthew Flinders (2012). The former argues that politics not only expresses the reality of disagreement and conflict in society, but is also 'one of the ways we know of how to address and potentially patch up the disagreements that characterize our societies without recourse to illegitimate coercion or violence' (Stoker, 2006: 2). For Flinders (2012: 5), likewise, the 'simple essence' of politics is a 'commitment to stability and compromise through social dialogue'. Both Flin-ders and Stoker also argue that much of the present discontent with politics is misplaced. Our expectations are simply too high at a time when politicians appear able to achieve less (Flinders, 2012: 18–35).

It might be best to describe the arguments put forward by Crick, Stoker, and Flinders as representing a particular kind of politics. Crick has been criticized for linking politics too closely with the practices of liberal democracies, where power is commonly assumed to be widely dispersed. It would seem strange indeed if our definition of politics forces us into a position which holds that those countries governed undemocratically by eco-nomic, religious, or military elites are not actually practising politics, but should, as Crick implies, aspire to it. Flinders and Stoker, however, avoid this lack of clarity by explicitly engaging in a defence of *democratic* politics rather than politics per se. Politics, is not absent in undemocratic regimes or in periods of civil or international strife, but takes a different form. If we can only talk about politics in situations when agreements are reached and compromises made, then it would seem to be a very limited activity. In this sense, it is probably sensible to talk of the resort to force and violence and mili-tary conflict as 'politics by other means', as suggested by nineteenth-century Prussian military strategist Carl von Clausewitz. Thus there is a variety ways in which we can ap-proach the issue of defining the political and what it includes and excludes, as illustrated in **Key Quotes 1.3**.

KEY QUOTES 1.3 The nature of politics

'[A political system is] any persistent pattern of human relationships that involves, to a significant extent, control, influence, power or authority.' (Dahl, 1991: 4)

'[Politics is the] art of governing mankind by deceiving them.' (Issac D'Israeli, quoted in Crick, 1962: 16)

'[Politics] can be simply defined as the activity by which differing interests within a given unit of rule are conciliated by giving them a share in power in proportion to their importance to the welfare and the survival of the whole community.' (Crick, 1962: 21)

'Politics is a phenomenon found in and between all groups, institutions (formal and informal) and societies, cutting across public and private life. It is involved in all the relations, institutions and structures which are implicated in the activities of production and reproduction in the life of societies . . . it is not about Government or government alone.' (Held and Leftwich, 1984: 144)

'Politics is designed to disappoint—that is the way that the process of compromise and reconciliation works. Its outcomes are often messy, ambiguous and never final.' (Stoker, 2006: 10)

KEY POINTS

- Defining politics is beset by boundary problems involving disagreement over what is, and what is not, the 'true' field of the political.

- The state, with its sovereign power, is a principal arena of politics, but a broader view sees it as encompassing power relations in social and economic institutions such as the family or the market as well.

- Another way of narrowing the boundary of politics proper is by declaring that resort to coercion and violence lies outside its scope; on the other hand, the resort to force may be seen simply as the pursuit of politics by other means.

The Study of Politics

We can trace not only the vocabulary of politics back to the ancient Greeks, but also the systematic study of politics, at least as it has developed in the West. Despite this long history, politics only became an independent discipline in higher education at the beginning of the twentieth century. Before then, it was subsumed under other academic disciplines such as law, philosophy, and history. The American Political Science Association, the body of professional academics specializing in political studies, was founded in 1903, although its British equivalent, the Political Studies Association, took almost another half-century, being formalized only in 1950 (Stoker and Marsh, 2002: 2). Canada, Finland, India, China, and Japan all had political studies associations before the UK did. There are now over 50 national and regional studies associations affiliated to the International Political Science Association, which was established in 1949 (see http://www.ipsa.org/about-ipsa/history, accessed January 2018).

The teaching of politics has traditionally distinguished between the study of political ideas (sometimes also referred to as political theory or political philosophy), the study of political institutions and processes within states—including comparisons between states (generally referred to as comparative politics)—and politics in the international sphere. The latter was formalized as a separate field of international relations in the immediate aftermath of World War I largely because of a deep concern to develop a specialized body of knowledge focusing on the causes of war and the conditions for peace between states, rather than political relations and issues within states. As noted earlier, this book does not provide a full treatment of international relations, which is often taught in universities as a separate unit of study. It nonetheless touches on a number of issues with global dimensions, including security, political economy, and international organizations. The main focus, however, is on the study of political ideas, institutions, and processes as they occur within the sphere of the state, which contains a mix of conceptual analysis, coverage of the key figures and their ideas in the history of political thought, and discussion of ideologies. The study of these phenomena invites comparisons of the institutions and processes of different states, as well as political history, electoral politics, and public administration, all of which feature in this book.

At another level, the study of politics involves at least three major kinds of political analysis, which are introduced here as an essential background for understanding how we approach issues in the discipline. First, students of politics may engage in normative analysis. This typically asks questions of a valuational kind and seeks to identify what we *ought* to aim for in terms of achieving the good life and the kind of society that will deliver it. These questions lie at the heart of political philosophy rather than the more empirical and positivist style of study, which often goes under the rubric of political *science*. Some see the nineteenth century as the last great age of political philosophy and put its subsequent decline down to the growth of secularism. Dahl (1991: 120) suggests that 'values could no longer be successfully justified by basing them on divinely revealed religious truths'. In addition, the status of philosophy in general had been undermined by virtue of the fact that the senseless destruction of human life in the Holocaust had occurred in what had previously been regarded as the most philosophically sophisticated country in Europe (Horton, 1984: 115).

In academia, a great deal of emphasis was instead placed on empirical political science, although 'analytical' political philosophy, in which the meaning of concepts and the relation between them, remained important. This led to the emergence of behaviouralism, in which skills in quantitative analysis (popularly known as 'number crunching'), particularly in the study of electoral behaviour, became the gold standard. In this intellectual climate, pontificating on what kind of society and polity we ought to have—the very basis of normative analysis—was regarded as unnecessary at best and meaningless at worst.

The decline of normative analysis and the turn to empirical analysis was also partly a product of the rise in status of positivism, an approach that seeks to apply the scientific methodology of the natural sciences to social phenomena (**see Key Concept 1.4**). This approach was associated in particular with French social scientist Auguste Comte (1798–1856), who argued that the scientific stage of history, now upon us, would dominate. An extreme version of positivism was a school of thought known as logical positivism, centring on a group of philosophers known as the Vienna Circle (see Ayer, 1971). For logical positivists, only statements that are empirically verifiable and those that sought to say something about the meaning of concepts and the relations between them are legitimate. Normative statements, making claims of a valuational kind, were regarded as meaningless.

Another factor in the relative decline of normative analysis was the emergence, in the 1950s and 1960s—in the West at least—of 'consensus politics'. What seemed to emerge at this time was widespread agreement on fundamental political principles, accompanied by economic prosperity. There seemed little point in justifying alternative political arrangements when the present ones—based on the mixed economy and the welfare state—appeared to be working so well. This meant that although political parties certainly competed for power and put forward different policy platforms, the political and economic system within which they operated was more or less accepted—by the major parties at least—as the optimal system.

Normative analysis began to make a comeback in the 1960s and 1970s, partly as a result of the decline in consensus politics, itself a product of mounting economic problems, and partly because of the emergence of new and innovative works of political philosophy, most notably Rawls' *A Theory of Justice*, discussed in Chapter 7. Despite this, it should be recognized that a great deal of contemporary political philosophy is much more cautious and tentative than the grand narratives of the past. A number of contemporary political philosophers have noted the discrepancy between the abstract normative work of some

 See Chapter 7 for a discussion of Rawls' work.

<> **KEY CONCEPT 1.4** **Positivism**

Positivism is an approach which holds that science must limit itself to those things that are observable, thereby insisting upon a clear separation between fact and value. At the extreme, positivism—in the form of the doctrine known as logical positivism—holds that only those statements that can be investigated by observation and those that can be examined semantically (as we shall discuss) are worthwhile. Normative questions are regarded as more or less meaningless because they cannot be empirically verified.

political philosophy, in which ideal political and moral principles are advocated, and the difficulty of applying such principles in the non-ideal real world.

What is clear is that normative questions present problems of a peculiar nature for the student of politics. As we see later, empirical facts can play a part in the resolution of normative questions. However, for most scholars, it still remains impossible to derive normative statements merely from empirical facts. This reflected in the famous dictum that it is impossible to derive an *ought* from an *is*. Consider the premise that 'she is old and lonely and her health is frail', followed by the conclusion that 'you ought to help her' (Thomas, 1993: 14). The conclusion does not follow from the premise unless we add another clause along the lines that 'we ought to help those who are old, lonely, and frail'. This, of course, is another normative statement not capable of empirical confirmation.

Given that we cannot resolve normative questions merely by invoking empirical facts, how, then, can we judge the validity of a normative statement? In other words, does this not mean that the logical positivists were right after all—that normative statements are meaningless and attempts to adjudicate between competing values is a worthless exercise? As Dahl (1991: 118) asks, does this mean that asking the question whether democracy is better than dictatorship is equivalent to asking whether 'you like coffee better than tea'? One possible solution is offered by Dworkin (1978: 7–8), who cleverly argues that it is mistaken to regard modern political theories as offering different foundational values. Rather, he suggests, they all have a commitment to egalitarianism in the sense that they all hold that humans are of intrinsically equal value. Even if Dworkin is right, and it might be argued that he overestimates the compatibility between mainstream ideologies such as liberalism and socialism, it still remains the case that other political ideologies clearly do not hold that humans are of equal value. This can lead to the problem of relativism in which statements such as 'slavery is as good as freedom' or 'racism is as good as racial tolerance' cannot be adjudicated. Intuitively, most of us would want to reject this kind of relativism. But it still leaves open the question of how we are to judge between competing political and moral values.

The second type of analysis common to politics is empirical. **Empirical analysis** seeks to identify observable phenomena in the real world with a view to establishing what *is*, rather than what *ought* to be. Empirical analysis, of course, is the basis of the natural sciences. We can observe and record, for example, any number of physical phenomena—such as overnight minimum temperature at a given location, the time at which the sun rises and sets, the speed of light, the boiling point of water at sea level, the number of annual growth rings in a tree—and produce empirical generalizations. Understood in this way, the results of scientific study are objective rather than subjective. In other words, the speed of light is not subject to anyone's preference—it simply is what it is and not what anyone thinks it ought to be. It is not a matter of opinion.

Many *positivist* political analysts have sought to apply the apparently impartial and value-free methods of the natural sciences to the study of political phenomena. As noted above, this has generally taken the form of quantitative analysis, which makes use of statistical data sets. In politics, phenomena such as elections, as well as opinion polls, demographic findings, etc., do indeed lend themselves to statistical analysis. But even if the data produced is largely objective—and this depends on what is selected and measured, and how it is selected and measured—the interpretation of data in politics (and the social sciences more generally) is not straightforward. Operationalizing political or social data—that is, strictly defining the variables to produce factors that can be measured—is much more difficult than in the natural sciences. For example, if one wants to measure how democratic any given political system is, one must first operationalize 'democracy'. As we shall see, democracy is a very hotly contested concept. It is therefore much more difficult than, say, measuring obesity by using a body-mass index calculation, even though the point at which one reaches the value for 'obesity' may also be contested. Apart from the fact that values can and do intrude in the social sciences (as indeed they may in the natural sciences), there are also considerable limits to what knowledge can be acquired through quantifiable data.

The third type of analysis commonly used in politics is semantic analysis, which is concerned with clarifying the meaning of the concepts we use. Many of the key concepts used in politics have no commonly accepted definition and, indeed, have been described as 'essentially contested concepts' (Gallie, 1955/6). 'Democracy', in particular, has encountered enormous difficulty, the more so because it has become such a highly appraisive word. Virtually every country in the world now calls itself a democracy, including the most authoritarian of regimes—the People's Democratic Republic of Korea (that is, North Korea) being a prime example. But, again, most will feel intuitively that if we concede the relativist view that democracy can mean all things to all people, then it really means nothing at all. Defining what we mean by such key terms as democracy, or liberty, or equality is therefore a crucial starting point for political analysis, even if we cannot reach perfect agreement.

In reality, the three forms of political analysis described above are not used independently of each other. As Wolff (1996: 3) notes, 'studying how things are helps to explain how things can be, and studying how they can be is indispensable for assessing how they ought to be'. Thus normative claims are, at least partly, based on empirical knowledge. In the case of Thomas Hobbes, for example, the normative claim that we ought to rely on an all-powerful sovereign to protect us derives from the largely empirical assumption that human nature is so brutally competitive that there is a great risk to our security without the protection of the 'Leviathan'. Conversely, a great deal of empirical analysis presupposes some normative assumptions. This can be seen, in particular, in our choice of investigation. Thus students of politics may, for example, investigate the causes of war and the conditions for peace because it is assumed that war is undesirable and, conversely, that peace is good, and we should therefore try to eliminate war and establish durable peace.

See Chapter 7 for further discussion of Hobbes.

We can now summarize the differences between what might be called empirical/positivist and normative political theory. The starting point for the former is the generation of testable hypotheses concerning political phenomena. An example would be the formulation of a hypothesis which postulates that democracy can only flourish in societies with a market economy and private ownership. This hypothesis can then be tested through an empirical study of actually existing societies. But we should note that this requires making a normative judgement about the political goals that we ought to aspire to. In other words, we need to ask whether a democratic political system or a capitalist economic framework is desirable in the first place.

This raises the further question of whether we can separate political 'theory' from the study of political institutions and processes. We suggest that those who study government without recognition of the key normative questions raised by political philosophers will only produce a partial picture. Systems of government created by human beings are a reflection of normative beliefs. The American Constitution, to give one prime example, is a product of the vision of what the 'Founding Fathers' thought a modern polity ought to be like and the Preamble provides a very clear normative statement of political principle (**see Key Quote 1.5**). Developments since its creation allowing, for example, for universal suffrage reflect modern normative thinking.

In addition to the importance of normative theorizing, it should also be noted that theorizing based on the accumulation of empirical evidence is also a central part of the study of political institutions and processes (Savigny and Marsden, 2011: 5–8). Theories are used in conjunction with empirical work to make sense of the mass of information that political researchers unearth, and to identify and explain relationships between observable phenomena. Knowing about particular political institutions is part of the objective, but locating them within a broader pattern of regularities is equally important and ultimately more productive. These sorts of issues provoke questions such as: why do parties exist? Is it possible to identify general patterns of their interactions? What general principles underlie electoral systems? How can we explain the behaviour of interest groups? And how do we generalize the decisions of innumerable individuals to involve themselves in politics and to do so in particular ways?

A key element of the empirical approach to the study of political institutions and processes is the comparative method. Here, political analysts seek to develop testable generalizations by examining political phenomena across different political systems or historically within the same political system. To take a fairly straightforward example from electoral studies, the proposition that electoral systems using a form of proportional representation tend to produce political and economic instability can be tested by comparing their use with regimes using alternatives such as the first-past-the-post system. A more complex exercise

 KEY QUOTE 1.5   Preamble to the American Constitution

'We the People of the United States, in Order to form a more perfect Union, establish Justice, insure domestic Tranquility, provide for the common defence, promote the general Welfare, and secure the Blessings of Liberty to ourselves and our Posterity, do ordain and establish this Constitution for the United States of America.'

would be needed in attempting an answer to the hypothesis posed earlier—namely, that democracy requires the free market and private ownership. In this case, it is necessary to engage in a comparative examination of different regimes across time and space, so that the relationship between political and economic variables can be better understood. It also requires semantic analysis of the concept of democracy—a term subject to many different definitions, as discussed in more detail in Chapter 4.

Deductive and inductive methods

The foregoing discussion has considered different modes of analysis. Next, we consider two important methods applied in the empirical study of politics. The first is the deductive method, sometimes known as the top-down approach, which starts from a general theoretical proposition and works down to the specific, aiming to test the theory in question by examining the relevant data. The second is the inductive method, which works in the opposite, bottom-up direction, moving from the observation of specific data to general propositions, aiming to generate rather than test theories.

The deductive method

The deductive method is associated with rational choice theories of politics, while the inductive approach is most often associated with behaviouralism.

Rational choice approaches to politics have become an increasingly important branch of the discipline. They are based on the fundamental assumption that humans are essentially rational utility maximizers who will follow the path of action most likely to benefit them. This approach has been used in game theory, where individual behaviour is applied to particular situations. These 'games' reveal how difficult it can be for rational individuals to reach optimal outcomes, not least because of the existence of 'free-riders'—actors who calculate that they can reap the benefits of collective action without paying any of the costs. In political science, the best-known applications can be found in the fields of voting and party competition and in interest group politics.

One problem with the deductive method, as illustrated by rational choice approaches, is precisely that its fundamental assumptions remain just that—assumptions that many regard as simplifications at best and, at worst, entirely inaccurate descriptions of human behaviour. Moreover, rational choice theory is awash with hypotheses about various aspects of the political process, but is short on empirical tests of these hypotheses (Hay, 2002: 39–40). Thus rational choice theory is better able to predict outcomes deriving from certain stated premises than to develop accurate empirical theories of the real world.

The inductive method

As noted above, inductive approaches to politics start with empirical observation from which explanatory generalizations are generated. So whereas deductive approaches deduce theory from first principles, before testing it, inductive approaches generate theory only following observation and generalization. A classic version of inductivism is behaviouralism, which rose to prominence in Western, and particularly American, political studies in the 1950s and 1960s, and which remains especially influential in the US (**see Key Concept 1.6**). The behaviouralists focused on political topics, like voting behaviour, which are readily quantifiable. To give one commonly cited example, empirical data on British voting behaviour during this period produced the generalization that voting is class-based, with the working class tending to vote Labour and the middle and upper classes tending to vote Conservative.

The weaknesses of inductive methods such as behaviouralism mirror those of the deductive method. So while the latter approach is strong on theory, but not on empirical testing, the reverse is true of the former. The inductive approach, in other words, tends to focus more on gathering empirical data than it does on the generation of theory. This traditional form of positivism was famously revised by philosopher of science Karl Popper (1902–94), who argued that rather than generating empirical data from which a hypothesis can be derived, the scientific method should be concerned with seeking to falsify a hypothesis. This has the effect, among other things, of making truth claims temporary—they are only as good as the next successful attempt to refute them. Verification can never be conclusive, but falsification can be. Since Popper, positivists have tended to move away from using the inductive method and have shown more interest in the generation of hypotheses that can be tested and, potentially, falsified or refuted.

Another weakness of the inductive method is that the types of hypothesis generated by inductivism tend not to be explanatory in the sense of offering a causal link between generalizations. Rather, they tend to be merely patterns of statistical correlation (Hay, 2002: 79). Finding correlations between phenomena is not the same as the one explaining

 KEY CONCEPT 1.6   Behaviouralism

Behaviouralism is an approach that developed, particularly in the US, in the post-1945 period. It stresses the importance of the scientific method in the study of social phenomena and seeks to obtain this by objective measurement of the social world. Thus values are to be completely eliminated from social enquiry. The assumption is that human behaviour is capable of being measured in a precise way and that generalizations may be derived from such measurements. Behaviouralism reached the height of its influence in political studies in the 1960s, its proponents being far more likely to use the term 'political *science*' to designate the discipline. Since then, it has been increasingly challenged by those who question the value-free nature of political studies and social enquiry in general. Even so, it remains especially prominent in the discipline in the US and has its adherents elsewhere.

the other. For example, the identification of a statistical correlation between, say, social class and voting behaviour does not, by itself, explain why this correlation exists.

 KEY POINTS

- The study of politics involves three main modes of analysis, empirical, normative, and semantic, although in practice they are not mutually exclusive—we need to know what *is*, before we can talk sensibly about what *ought* to be; similarly, empirical analysis presupposes some normative assumptions.
- Empirical political analysis tends to use either deductive or inductive reasoning. The former is illustrated by rational choice theory; the latter, by behaviouralism.

Can Politics Be a Science?

An important question that follows from the above discussion is whether the study of politics can be, or should aim to be, 'scientific'. To some extent, the answer depends on how we define science, which is itself another exercise in conceptual analysis. If science is defined in terms of the pursuit of 'ordered knowledge based on systematic enquiry', then politics is quite clearly a science (Stoker and Marsh, 2002: 11). Indeed, according to this definition, even normative analysis, provided it is undertaken in a rigorous and systematic way, can be described as scientific. A narrower definition involves applying the methodology of the natural sciences, as attempted in the behavioural approach discussed above. This produces a definition of science as consisting in 'the ability to generate neutral, dispassionate and objective knowledge claims' (Hay, 2002: 87).

The attractions of developing an objective, value-free account of politics through which we can identify the 'truth' about political phenomena are obvious. However, the claims about a science of politics at this more rigid level can be challenged on two main grounds. In the first place, one can question whether the methods of natural science can be readily transferred to a social science such as politics. At a second, more fundamental, level, one can question whether the whole scientific enterprise, in both natural and social settings, stands up to scrutiny in terms of its own assumptions.

At the first level, it is the social elements of politics that are key. Human beings are unpredictable and not amenable to unbending scientific laws in the way that, say, the workings of molecules are in the natural sciences. As Hay (2002: 50) points out, what makes the social sciences qualitatively different from the natural sciences is that the 'former must deal with conscious and reflective subjects, capable of acting differently under the same stimuli, whereas the units which comprise the latter can be assumed inanimate, unreflexive and hence entirely predictable in response to external stimuli'. But here we should note that the same cannot necessarily be said about the organisms studied in biology, a branch of science that also studies very changeable living organisms rather than inanimate phenomena.

The point is, however, that the largely unpredictable and multifaceted behaviour of human beings not only leads us to question the applicability of the 'scientific' method to the field of social and political studies, but also reminds us that social researchers very often face ethical dilemmas in their work, as do scientists working with sentient animals. We cannot treat human, or indeed animal, subjects with the same impunity that many branches of the natural sciences treat inanimate objects. Humans, and animals, can feel emotional and physical distress that researchers in both human and animal science must take into account. Moreover, the prescriptions that might emanate from social research, or which might be derived from it by others, can have important ethical dimensions. An example here would be the implications of social research that leads to claims being made about the importance of race, or gender, in determining intelligence, and therefore moral and political worth. These may be linked to biology as well. All such claims, however, have been shown to be socially contrived or constructed, having no actual basis in biology and rather belonging in the realm of pseudoscience.

See Chapter 6 for a discussion of race and biology in the context of nationalism.

The only way of avoiding the conclusion that a science of society is difficult, if not impossible, because of the unpredictable nature of human beings is to adopt an approach which claims that human behaviour can be determined. As we saw in the case of rational choice theory, however, it is doubtful if assumptions about human behaviour made in such accounts would stand the test of empirical observation. In addition, the study of politics cannot be entirely value-free. As we saw earlier, we impose our own assumptions and norms on our work from the very start of a research project, the choice of which is imbued with our own sense of its importance. But we can also argue that politics *should* be about values and norms.

The core of the scientific project has also been challenged at a more fundamental level. To criticize the social sciences, including the discipline of politics, for not being objective and value-free—and therefore not true sciences—is to assume that there is actually such thing as true value-free science in the first place. As Hay (2002: 87) remarks, the natural scientist, just like the social scientist, is 'socially and politically embedded within a complex and densely structured institutional and cultural landscape which they cannot simply escape by climbing the ivory tower of academe to look down with scientific dispassion and disinterest on all they survey'. This suggests that the practice of science described in the narrow view represents a rather idealized view of the field. Scientists themselves are human and so subjective elements will always be at work in the production of knowledge in their own particular fields. Science is 'therefore by definition a *social* activity attended by all the dynamics characterizing social interaction, including cooperation, competition and conflict' (Lawson, 2016: 3). We might add that there is a lot of politics associated with science, as current debates on the science of climate change indicate only too clearly, giving a very different nuance to the term 'political science'.

1

This idea that scientific knowledge is at least partly socially constructed is the basis of the contemporary 'interpretivist' approach, which has emerged to challenge positivism (see Bevir and Rhodes, 2002). To understand this critique, it is important to grasp the difference between the terms ontology and epistemology. Following Hay (2002: 61), we can say that **ontology** 'relates to *being*, to what *is*, to what *exists*'. In other words, an ontology asks: what is there to know? For our purposes, the key ontological question relates to whether there is a political world 'out there' capable of being empirically observed or whether this 'reality' is, at least to some degree, created by the meanings or ideas we impose upon it. **Epistemology** refers to the task of 'acquiring knowledge of that which exists' (Hay, 2002: 63).

This definitional diversion is important because it enables us to make sense of the fundamental claims being made by those who insist that the study of politics can be a science. Those adopting behavioural or rational choice approaches clearly adopt a foundationalist ontology and a positivist epistemology. A foundationalist ontology consists in an acceptance that a real world exists 'out there' and a positivist epistemology holds that this can be discovered by observation. It is this approach that has been challenged by those writing from an interpretivist standpoint and who challenge, at an ontological level, the very idea that there is an objective reality out there awaiting discovery. It is proposed, instead, that we examine the meanings and interpretations through which humans create realities about politics. From this perspective, then, a 'science' of politics is neither possible nor desirable.

A related issue here is the distinction between 'material realities' and 'ideational realities', and the interaction between the two. This introduces more nuances to debates about ontology and the very nature of 'reality'. A narrow approach to ontology would hold that only things that have a material existence are 'real'. But 'realities' have an existence that go beyond the material insofar as they arise in the realm of the ideational—that is, the realm in which thought processes or ideas produce realities that are not immediately apprehended by the physical senses. If we ask what the material political world actually consists of, we can point to physical objects such as ballot boxes, government buildings, military facilities, and border posts, as well as to particular humans whom we can designate 'prime minister', 'president', 'senator', 'voter', etc. But certain types of box only become ballot boxes by being given that meaning or interpretation, just as someone who becomes a president does so through political processes that cannot be described simply in material terms such as the counting of votes in a ballot box. The *idea* of even having a president, and a state to preside over, is an essential precondition. So although political processes and institutions have material dimensions, these are quite meaningless in the absence of the ideational dimensions produced by humans in social interaction. Thus the reality of the political world can be said to exist 'as a set of relations within a socially created system which runs according to ideas that proceed from the minds of people (agents), who act on those ideas to produce institutions and practices' (Lawson, 2016: 8).

✳ KEY POINTS

- Behaviouralists, in particular, have attempted to devise approaches to the study of politics that employ methods similar to those of the natural sciences.
- This attempt can be challenged, first, by questioning whether the methods of natural science can be transferred to a social science such as politics and, second, by questioning whether any science—natural or social—can ever be entirely objective.
- The nature of 'reality' raises issues of the relationship between the material and the ideational, and the centrality of meaning and interpretation in the study of politics as part of the social world.

Conclusion

This chapter has sought to introduce you to certain basic definitional features of politics, as well as some of the central themes within political analysis. We have not attempted to downplay the difficulty of studying politics, which arises because of the lack of consensus over its meaning and scope. We suggest, however, that having an open mind as to what constitutes the 'political' prevents an undue conservatism which would miss much that is important in the 'real world' of politics. We need also to keep an open mind about *how* we study politics and which methods are appropriate to any given topic within the discipline.

The design of this book also encourages students to think about politics across virtually all regions of the world and therefore to adopt a comparative perspective. So although there is a focus on key issues in politics in the US and the UK, which are analysed largely within a framework of Western political theory, we also discuss issues such as the Islamic understandings of justice, the problems of the African state, the debate over the merits of presidentialism in Latin America and the Philippines, and so on.

Even if you are primarily interested in studying politics within your own country, some knowledge of how politics works in other countries is invaluable to understanding one's own context. So, for example, while Chapter 4 concentrates on theories of democracy developed largely in Western intellectual contexts, Chapter 5 looks at the processes of democratization in a number of different places, including India and China. Similarly, while the treatment of nations and nationalism in Chapter 6 has an initial focus on the development of nationalist ideology in Europe, it draws in examples and case studies from China, Indonesia, and the postcolonial world more generally.

What is vital to the study of politics is that we use consistent, systematic approaches in analysis, whether in the developed or the developing world, so that we can identify similarities and differences in the ways in which apparently similar institutions operate in different contexts. The approach adopted in this book is therefore designed to encourage students to develop a more sophisticated understanding of the similarities and the differences, the strengths and weaknesses. This is all part of the process of studying the conditions under which politics can produce the 'good life', as well as the conditions under which it so frequently fails.

? Key Questions

- What is politics?
- Should politics be seen in a positive light?
- What is the case for defining politics narrowly?
- Is politics synonymous with the state?
- Is politics an inevitable feature of all societies?
- What is the difference between normative and empirical analysis in the study of politics?
- Can politics be a science?
- How can we evaluate between competing normative claims?
- What is meant by inductive and deductive approaches to political studies?
- What is the role of meaning and interpretation in the study of politics?

Ⅲ Further Reading

Crick, B. (1962), *In Defence of Politics* (London: Weidenfeld & Nicolson).
A classic case for a particular interpretation of politics.

Dahl, R. (1991), *Modern Political Analysis* (Englewood Cliffs, NJ: Prentice-Hall).
A classic account of the study of politics by a legendary American academic.

Gamble, A. (2000), *Politics and Fate* (Cambridge: Polity Press).
Like Crick, Gamble seeks to defend politics, but from the perspective of those who would decry the ability of humans to control their destiny.

Hay, C. (2002), *Political Analysis* (Basingstoke: Palgrave).
Cannot be bettered as a comprehensive and accessible account of different approaches to political science. Hard going at times, but worthwhile.

Marsh, D., and Stoker, G. (eds) (2002), *Theory and Methods in Political Science* (Basingstoke: Palgrave).
An extremely useful collection of articles setting out the field.

Savigny, H., and Marsden, L. (2011), *Doing Political Science and International Relations: Theories in Action* (Basingstoke: Palgrave).
A very accessible account of the nature of political analysis, which adopts an issue-based approach in order to make sense of some very complex ideas.

Stoker, G. (2006), *Why Politics Matters* (Basingstoke: Palgrave).
A modern version of Crick's work, which defines politics in terms of consensus and democracy.

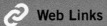 **Web Links**

http://www.apsanet.org
The American Political Science Association (APSA) is the major American professional society for individuals engaged in the study of politics and government.

https://www.psa.ac.uk
The Political Studies Association (PSA) of the United Kingdom, founded in 1950, is the British equivalent of the APSA. Its aim is to develop and promote the study of politics. The site gives details of its activities, including publications and conferences, and contact details for about 40 specialist groups within the Association.

https://www.ipsa.org/
The International Political Science Association (IPSA) was founded in 1949 under the auspices of the United Nations Educational, Scientific and Cultural Organization (UNESCO). The site provides some interesting information on the development of the discipline in an international context.

http://www.hyperpolitics.net
Hyperpolitics is an innovative politics dictionary. It consists of an analytical tool created by Mauro Calise and Theodore J. Lowi that aids students and researchers in building up definitions of political science terms and concepts using conventional and online reference sources.

https://www.keele.ac.uk/depts/por/ptbase.htm
This site provides access to a useful directory of resources maintained by the School of Politics, International Relations and the Environment at Keele University. It includes a listing of web links relating to all aspects of political theory and political philosophy.

 Visit the **Online Resources** that accompany this book to access more learning resources on this topic: www.oup.com/uk/ferdinand/

Politics and the State

2

- The Political Importance of the State
- A Typology of the State
- Theories of the State
- Normative and Empirical Dimensions of the State

- Whither the State?
- Conclusion
- Key Questions
- Further Reading
- Web Links

Reader's Guide

This chapter begins by stressing the importance of the state and sovereignty to the study of politics. An attempt is made to provide an empirical typology of the state, before going on to outline various theories of the state—namely, pluralism, elitism, Marxism, and the New Right. Two key general points about these competing theories are made. First, an organizing theme relates to what each of these theories say about the distribution of power. Second, the theories can be assessed in both empirical and normative terms. Finally, the chapter considers the claim that—predominantly as a result of economic globalization—the state's importance has declined significantly.

The Political Importance of the State

For many centuries, the state has been the dominant form of political organization such that 'no concept is more central to political discourse and political analysis' (Hay and Lister, 2006: 1). It is only a slight exaggeration to say that the state determines how we live and how we die. Virtually all of the land in the world is claimed by a state, of which there are now nearly 200. Indeed, the state's role in the economy and society has increased progressively, particularly since the advent of the 'welfare' state in the post-1945 period.

Despite its political importance, the state is a notoriously difficult concept to define. Some argue that 'the state is not a suitable concept for political theory, since it is impossible to define it' (Hoffman and Graham, 2006: 22). The fact that the state is difficult to define, however, does not seem to be reason enough to refuse to try to define it, unless it is thought that the state does not actually exist, which virtually no one is claiming.

A classic definition of the state is provided by Weber, who regards it as an institution claiming a 'monopoly of the legitimate use of physical force in enforcing its order within a given territorial area'. The state is therefore inextricably linked with sovereignty. Above all, this concept was developed by French political philosopher Jean Bodin (1529–96) and English jurist William Blackstone (1723–80). The idea of the sovereign state denotes its superiority as the highest form of authority in a particular territory. There is, therefore, no higher authority within that territory and, equally importantly, no external challenge to this authority. Sovereign states emerged in the fifteenth and sixteenth centuries in Europe, replacing feudal societies, which shared authority between the aristocracy and the Catholic Church (Tilly, 1975). Subsequent to this, most countries in the world have adopted, often through colonial rule, the sovereign state model, although stateless societies still exist in small communities of people, such as nomadic tribes.

⬛ See Chapter 10 for a discussion of the rise of the European state system.

The usefulness of the concept of sovereignty as a description of political reality, however, is debatable. In constitutional theory, states are sovereign, but, in reality, states have always faced challenges from within and outside their borders, thereby, in practice, limiting their autonomy. In this sense, sovereignty has always been something of a myth. Here, there is a crucial distinction between *de jure* sovereignty, which refers to a legal right to rule supremely, and *de facto* sovereignty, which refers to the actual distribution of political power. As Held (1989: 216) points out: 'Sovereignty has been an important and useful concept for legal analysis, but it can be a misleading notion if applied uncritically as a political idea.' For example, the concept of sovereignty is of little use when discussing the phenomena of so-called failed states, where—as in Somalia—the state is unable to perform the functions of sovereignty.

A Typology of the State

It is important to distinguish between an empirical and a normative account of the state. In the case of the latter, it is asked what the state *ought* to look like. This is the preserve of political philosophers, who ask questions such as how should our rulers be chosen and what ought they to do once in positions of power? We will consider these questions in Chapter 7. This chapter is concerned with an empirical account of the state, which seeks to describe how states are organized and what they do in practice.

An empirical classification of the state is usually organized around the degree to which it intervenes in society and the economy. At one end of this continuum is the so-called night-watchman state in which the state concentrates on ensuring external and internal security, playing little role in civil society and the economy, where the economic market is allowed to operate relatively unhindered. The idea of a night-watchman state was a central characteristic of classical liberal thought and played a large part in shaping nineteenth-century British politics. It sees the state as having a protective role, seeking to uphold the rights—to life, liberty, and property—of individuals against external and internal threats.

See Chapter 10 for a discussion of weak states.

The notion of a minimal state is an ideal type that has probably existed nowhere in reality. The degree, and character, of state intervention in the world today, however, differs enormously. In the so-called developmental state, for instance, there is a strong relationship between state and private economic institutions with the goal of securing rapid economic development. This model has been particularly prevalent in East Asia, where states have developed rapidly since 1945. Japan is the prime example of a developmental state (Johnson, 1995), but the model is also relevant to South Korea and even Malaysia, a so-called illiberal democracy (as we shall discuss).

See Chapter 9 for an exploration of the relationship between the state and economic institutions.

Developmental states should not be confused with social democratic states, which have a broader social and political objective. They are associated with attempts to secure greater social and economic equality, rather than just economic development. For example, one of the criticisms of post-1945 British political and economic development is that Britain adopted a social democrat approach, but neglected the developmental aspect (Marquand, 1988). This failure, it is argued, has hindered the social democratic project because greater social and economic equality is greatly assisted by general economic prosperity, which provides a great deal more resources to redistribute.

States can also be defined in terms of their relationship to democracy or popular control of political leaders. Here, a useful distinction is to be made between liberal democracies, illiberal democracies, and authoritarian regimes (Hague and Harrop, 2007: 7–9). Liberal democracies—such as the US, the UK, and Germany—are characterized by free and fair elections involving universal suffrage, together with a liberal political framework consisting of a relatively high degree of personal liberty and the protection of individual rights. Liberal democracy is now the dominant state form existing in much of the world, in Europe, North and South America, Australasia, Japan, India, and South Africa.

Illiberal democracies—such as Russia and Malaysia—are characterized by elections, but relatively little protection of rights and liberties, and by state control over the means of communication. This creates a situation where there are few constitutional constraints on those in government and where opposition leaders and parties are disadvantaged and, as a result, there are relatively few transfers of power through elections.

Authoritarian regimes can be characterized in terms of the absence of fair elections and therefore the accountability of political rulers. About a third of people in the world live under regimes that can be described as authoritarian—most notably, China, which contains just under 20 per cent of the world's population, and many states in the Middle East. The political elites in such regimes can derive from the military, royalty, or ruling parties, or may merely be individual dictators.

The degree of intervention in the economy and society can vary enormously in authoritarian regimes. At the extreme end is the totalitarian state, so-called because the state intervenes—often through a brutal and oppressive state police—in all aspects of social and economic life, under the guise of a transformative ideology. While liberal state theory postulates the existence of a civil society in which the state intervenes relatively rarely, in totalitarian states civil society is eclipsed. Totalitarianism is very much a twentieth-century phenomenon—associated, in particular, with Nazi Germany, Stalin's Soviet Union, and East Germany—although Iran, since the Islamic revolution in the late 1970s, has a number of totalitarian features.

 KEY POINTS

- However difficult it is to define, the state is undoubtedly a crucial institution for the political analyst.
- Sovereignty is a key defining feature of the state, although it is a concept that, arguably, has greater legal than political importance.
- An empirical account of the state can be distinguished from a normative account.
- It is possible to develop an empirical typology of the state from the minimalist night-watchman state, approximated to by nineteenth-century capitalist regimes, at one end of the spectrum to the totalitarian state of the twentieth century at the other.

Theories of the State

There are various competing theories of the state. These are primarily based on empirical accounts of power distribution. Clearly, it is essential to have an understanding of the concept of power itself, a task that is undertaken in Chapter 3. For now, it is necessary to note that an evaluation of the validity of the empirical theories of the state discussed in this chapter depends, to a large extent, on the way in which the concept of power is defined and operationalized.

The need for an overarching theory of the state emerges from the need to be selective, to have some guide to the choosing of relevant information from the mass of factual evidence that can be unearthed. Choosing a theory of the state constitutes the analyst's criteria for selection and enables him or her to avoid drowning in a sea of information. In this chapter, we will look at four major theories of the state: pluralism, elitism, Marxism, and the New Right. There is another approach to the state put forward by feminists and this is discussed in Chapter 8.

⟩ See Chapter 8 for an exploration of feminism.

2

Pluralism and elitism

By the end of the 1960s, the pluralist approach, associated above all with the work of American political scientist Robert Dahl (1963, 1971), dominated American political science and, by the 1970s, it had become the mainstay of British political science too (see Richardson and Jordan, 1979). It is possible to distinguish between different varieties of pluralism. In the classical pluralist position, society is seen as being composed of thousands of activities that have the effect of creating many different groups of all shapes and sizes. For pluralists, the existence of, often competing, groups is a natural feature of all societies of any complexity. The only way in which these groups can be prevented is through suppression, as they were, for instance, under the old Soviet system.

For pluralists, the role of the state can also be defined in terms of the activities of groups. In this *political* pluralism, the state's role is to regulate and mediate between these groups. Some pluralists see the state as a neutral arbiter in this system, whereas some see it as a group in itself competing against others in society. The outputs of government are the result of group pressure. What governments do will be a mirror image of the balance of power of groups within society (**see Figure 2.1**). It is important to note that pluralists are not saying here that all groups or interests are equal. Rather, pluralists are claiming that there are no predominant classes or interests within society, that all groups are able to make their voices heard in the political process, and that all groups get at least something of what they want.

⟩ See Chapter 16 for a detailed discussion of interest groups.

Power in society for pluralists is diffuse or fragmented. In other words, in a pluralist state, most interest groups will be able to influence public policy outcomes to at least some extent. Dahl defines modern liberal democratic politics in terms of 'minorities rule' rather than majority rule, or polyarchy rather than democracy, to illustrate that politics is based upon the permanent interplay of numerous groups, each constituting a minority. Successful political parties, then, are those that are able to forge a majority coalition of minority groups.

The pluralist conclusion that power is fragmented is based upon a number of related arguments. The first is that the bases upon which power rests are variable—that is, political influence is not dependent upon one particular resource. Rather, there are a variety of important resources—wealth, organization, public support, a group's position in the economy, the ability to exercise, or threaten to exercise, sanctions—which are not the preserve of a small number of groups. For example, a group of key workers such as miners or doctors may not be particularly wealthy or even have public support, but can garner influence through the crucial functions they perform.

Second, even though it may seem that, in a particular issue area, one group or small set of groups is influential, the same groups are not influential in other issue areas. To give a classic example, it has traditionally been argued that the National Farmers' Union (NFU) in Britain is extremely influential within agricultural policy (Smith, 1990: 124–31). There is evidence to suggest that the influence of the NFU has waned now (Grant, 2004: 412–14), but even when the NFU was at the height of its powers, the pluralist position is still upheld, the argument goes, because the NFU was not influential within other areas of policy relating, say, to the economy, education, and health, where other groups are important. Third, more often than not, it is the case that an influential group in a policy arena is challenged by a 'countervailing influence'. In the economic sphere, for instance, the influence of business groups is checked by the role of trade unions.

The position we have just described can be classified as classical pluralism. It is possible to envisage a number of other approaches or theories of the state on a continuum between classical pluralism and classical elitism. The first of these is elite pluralism, sometimes described as democratic elitism. This revision of classical pluralism came about in the late 1950s and early 1960s following a sustained criticism of it. One of the major challengers was American sociologist C. Wright Mills (1956), who argued that power in American society is concentrated in the hands of a powerful elite, dominating the economic, military, and governmental spheres.

See Chapter 4 for a discussion of the elitist theory of democracy.

The pluralist response to this led by Dahl (1958) was to accept that the classical pluralist assumption—that there is widespread participation in decision-making and that groups are themselves internally egalitarian—was misplaced. The existence of political elites, a small group of people playing a disproportionate role in groups, was accepted. Far from undermining the pluralist position, however, scholars such as Dahl suggested that it still existed because these political elites have divided interests and compete with each other to achieve their aims. Politics may be hierarchical, then, but rather than one homogeneous elite group, there are a multiplicity of competing elites (**see Figure 2.2**). Pluralists, for instance, would see business as divided between, say, a financial and a manufacturing sector. Political power for pluralists can be represented diagrammatically, then, by a succession of pyramids and not just one.

Yet further down the continuum between pluralism and elitism is corporatism (**see Case Study 2.1**). Traditionally, corporatism referred to the top-down model in which the state, as in the fascist model, incorporates economic interests in order to control them and civil society in general. This is also the corporatist model, which can be applied to authoritarian states, particularly in Asia. Modern societal or neo-corporatism, on the other hand, reflects a genuine attempt by governments to incorporate economic interests into the decision-making process (Held, 1989: 65). This modern version of societal corporatism shares with pluralism the belief that groups are a crucial part of the political system. Corporatism denies, however, that the competition between groups was as widespread, equitable, and fragmented as pluralists had suggested. Instead, corporatism points to the critical role played by economic elites. Government outputs are a product of a tripartite relationship between elites in government, business, and the trade unions. The insider role of economic elites was sanctioned by the state in return for the cooperation of these key interests in securing the support of their members for government policy.

At the other end of the spectrum from classical pluralism is the ruling elite theory of the state. While classical pluralists hold that Western liberal democracies have diffuse power structures, with a plurality of groups competing to influence the government, ruling elite theory holds that all societies, whatever democratic rhetoric proclaims, are ruled by a single, unified, and self-conscious elite. Whereas the diagrammatical representation of elite pluralism is a series of pyramids, *elitism* can be represented by one pyramid containing an elite and the masses (**see Figure 2.3**).

Elitism is particularly associated with a group of Italian scholars writing at the turn of the twentieth century (in particular, Robert Michels, Gaetano Mosca, and Vilfredo Pareto), although their work was built upon by later, mainly American, writers. The original elitists were concerned primarily with refuting Marx's vision of a future egalitarian society. For them, a ruling elite was an inevitable feature of all complex societies. The elitists claim to have discovered, in the words of Robert Michels, an 'iron law of oligarchy'—that is, in organizations of any complexity, whether they be political parties or interest groups, there will always be a dominant group controlling them. Elites come to dominate because of the resources they can muster, their psychological characteristics, or their position within society. Unlike Marxism, or ruling-class theory, no one resource is necessarily crucial, so that it is possible to conceive of elites based upon military, administrative, and religious factors as much as economic ones.

Later scholarship on elitism came from the US. Unlike the earlier Italian version, modern elitism has ceased to be anti-Marxist and has, instead, become a critique of pluralism. In other words, elitist thinkers such as C. Wright Mills (1956) and James Burnham (1941) have identified empirically the rule of elites, but, rather than regarding this as inevitable or desirable, have argued that it is illegitimate and ought to be challenged.

 CASE STUDY 2.1   **Corporatism in Europe**

Corporatism, or neo-corporatism to be precise, has been particularly prevalent in certain European states. A survey of 18 Western industrialized countries and Japan ranked Austria, Norway, Sweden, and the Netherlands as the top four most corporatist political systems, whereas New Zealand, Canada, the UK, and the US were ranked as the least corporatist and thereby closer to the pluralist model. The same study examined the factors explaining the existence of corporatism, arguing that the influence of social democracy in government is the most important variable, followed closely by the degree of consensus in the political system (Lijphart and Crepaz, 1991).

2

The Austrian system of 'social partnership' remains the most corporatist structure. The so-called *Sozialpartnerschaft* involves the organization of trade unions and employers in the 'big four' institutions: the trade union organization (OGB), and the three chambers established by law with compulsory membership and the power to consider government bills before they are put before parliament. These are the Chamber of Labour (BAK) and the two employer chambers, the Economic Chamber (WKO) and the Chamber of Agriculture (PKLWK). This structure has traditionally been marked by the informality of relationships between the actors (Talos and Kittel, 2002). The key feature is the centralization and hierarchical character of the peak associations of labour and business.

Until the 1970s, corporatism was largely applauded for its economic success. Since then, corporatism has decayed to some extent. A survey of Scandinavian corporatism, for instance, reveals that, since the mid-1970s, there has been a decline in the number of corporatist actors in public bodies and the degree to which governments base decisions on corporatist-style agreements (Blom-Hansen, 2000). Even in Austria, corporatism has begun to weaken. While the structure remains intact, it has less public support, and there is greater opposition from some rank-and-file organizations and a more adversarial relationship between the chambers. As a result, government has become more autonomous, relying less on the peak associations of economic interests (Talos and Kittel, 2002: 44–8).

The form of corporatism we have been describing is shorn of much of the negative connotations of the top-down variety, associated with fascist regimes and authoritarian regimes such as China, which involve the state incorporating key interests in order to control them. Neo-corporatism, by contrast, is seen as a way of incorporating, and modifying, the key interests within civil society. It is argued that it has served a vital aggregation function.

Neo-corporatism has not, however, escaped criticism. In the first place, it is argued that governments tend, in practice, to be unduly influenced by business interests in corporatist arrangements. Even if trade unions are successfully integrated, neo-corporatism is still regarded as less open and democratic than a pluralist system because it is hierarchically organized, with power residing in the hands of economic elites. From the perspective of the New Right, corporatism is condemned for failing to allow the market free rein and thereby acceding to the (it is argued) unrealistic demands of sectional interests.

Marxism and the state

An alternative to elitism is Marxism, or ruling-class theory. Marxism has been a remarkably influential political ideology with, at one time, a large proportion of the world's population living under regimes proclaiming to be inspired by Marx's ideas. Marxism, of course, derives its inspiration from the work of nineteenth-century German thinker Karl Marx (1818–83). Marxism shares with elitism an acceptance of the fact that modern capitalist societies are dominated by a united, self-interested ruling group. Democracy in such societies, therefore, is a sham. Despite elections, the influence of the masses is minimal.

There are, however, two crucial differences between elitism and Marxism. In the first place, unlike elitists, Marxists are very specific about the character of the ruling group in capitalist societies. As we saw, elitists envisage ruling groups with a variety of resources. For Marx, the ruling group in pre-communist societies is always that social group or class which controls the means of production and therefore has economic power. In capitalist society, then, the dominant class is the bourgeoisie and the dominated class is the proletariat (or working class), the latter defined in terms of its non-ownership of the means of production (**see Figure 2.4**).

Marx produced a voluminous and disorganized body of literature, and it has been interpreted in a number of ways. The dominant interpretation of Marx attaches to him the view that it is pointless for the working class to seek emancipation through gaining the vote and winning power through elections. This is not where real power lies. Rather, power lies within the economic sphere of society. In other words, those who have economic power also have political power. The working class, therefore, needs to win power by attacking its source in the economic sphere. Having said that, there is some evidence that Marx was prepared to accept a greater autonomy for the state and that it was not perceived as simply the vehicle of the dominant class. This idea of the 'relative autonomy' of the state was taken up by later Marxists.

The second key difference between elitism and Marxism is that, for the latter, a communist revolution will bring about a truly egalitarian society, one in which a hierarchical society is abolished. By contrast, the earlier elitists argued, in response to Marx, that a hierarchical system of power relations is an inevitable feature of all societies of any complexity and it is a utopian dream to think otherwise. Marx spent very little time describing in detail what this egalitarian society would look like, mainly because of his insistence that the downfall of capitalism would produce such a society, whatever he thought ought to happen.

▶ See Chapter 3 for a discussion of Marxist ideas on state power.

The New Right theory of the state

The New Right theory of the state focuses on how, it is claimed, the state behaves. Its antecedents were liberal free market advocates such as Hobbes, Locke, and Adam Smith (see Chapter 7). The New Right theory challenged the state interventionism that had become standard in post-1945 liberal democracies, centring on the welfare state, the mixed economy, and the use of demand management economic theory developed by John Maynard

2

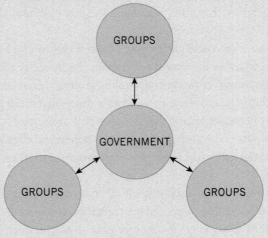

FIGURE 2.1 Pluralist Theory of the State

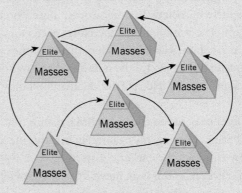

FIGURE 2.2 Elite Pluralism

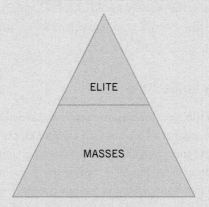

FIGURE 2.3 Elitist Theory of the State

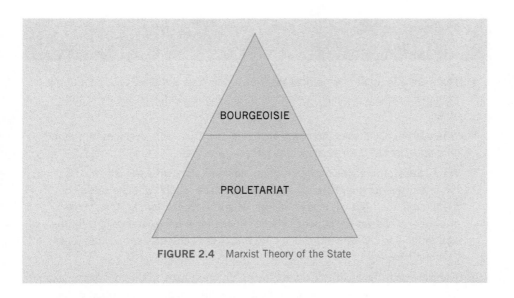

FIGURE 2.4   Marxist Theory of the State

Keynes (1883–1946). Here, the state would seek to increase demand in the economy through public spending on various schemes and these would be reined in when the increased demand threatened to create inflationary pressures.

According to the New Right position, the state has a tendency to expand its activities far beyond what is healthy for society and the economy. In particular, state intervention in the economy is inefficient. Its effect is to prop up unprofitable economic concerns and stifle the emergence of new lean and relevant ones. There are two main forces at work here. The first is external and relates to the demands placed upon it. Here, in a process that is coined the 'economic consequences of democracy' (Britten, 1977), competitive electoral politics encourages politicians to offer ever-increasing benefits in order to attract votes and, once elected, governments then find it very difficult to meet the promises made to individuals and groups, sometimes sailing perilously close to bankruptcy.

See Chapter 4 for a discussion of the alleged economic consequences of democracy.

The second force at work here for New Right thinkers is internal. Here, it is argued—in what has been called the 'over-supply thesis' (Dunleavy and O'Leary, 1987: 117–19)—the state bureaucracy has a tendency to expand because it is in its self-interest to do so (Niskanen, 1971). To increase intervention and 'big' government, bureaucrats will forge relationships with interest groups. Both the bureaucrats and the groups have a vested interest in governments offering more, mainly financial, benefits.

For the New Right, then, the pluralist theory of the state is wrong on two main counts. First, pluralists regard the state as benign, merely reflecting the interests of groups within civil society. By contrast, for New Right thinkers, the state is not neutral, but serves its own interests. Second, the liberal democratic polity does not encourage stability and equilibrium as pluralists suggest. Rather, it has a tendency to lead to governing failure. The end result is 'a hyperpluralism of powerful groups confronting weak governments' (Dearlove and Saunders, 2000: 220).

2

❋ KEY POINTS

- There are a number of empirical theories of the state arranged on a continuum from classical pluralism at one end to ruling elite and Marxist theory at the other.
- Whereas pluralism sees the power structure as diffuse and fragmented, ruling elite and Marxist theories sees it as concentrated.
- The two key differences between ruling elite and Marxism are, first, that, for the latter, the dominant group is always that class which owns the means of production, distribution, and exchange, whereas, for the former, the source of power can be varied. Second, Marxism postulates the existence of a future egalitarian society, whereas ruling-elite theory sees elites as an inevitable feature of all societies.
- The New Right theory of the state offers a different take on the role of the state, focusing on a critique of the collectivist state rather than a description of the distribution of power.

Normative and Empirical Dimensions of the State

We have focused so far in this chapter on the empirical reality of the state. An empirical analysis of a theory of the state would examine the degree to which it reflects the reality of any particular political system. As we shall see in Chapter 3, assessing the empirical adequacy of a theory of the state has a great deal to do with how political power is measured. Here, we should just briefly note that an empirical critique of pluralism would be to say that it exaggerates the extent to which power is fragmented in liberal democratic societies. Indeed, pluralism has been criticized on the grounds that it too readily assumes that groups have a reasonable chance of influencing policy-making, whereas there is strong evidence to suggest that certain interests are much more powerful than others.

▶ See Chapter 3 for a more developed empirical critique of pluralism.

We could engage, too, in an empirical critique of the elitist and Marxist theories of the state. Is it really credible to argue, for instance, that a ruling elite or a ruling class remains entirely untroubled by representative machinery in liberal democracies? Certainly, in addition, one can challenge many, if not all, of the claims made by Marx about the future direction of capitalism, as well as his predictions about how a future communist society would operate (**see Key Debate 2.3**). Indeed, as we shall see in Chapter 8, post-Marxian Marxists did adapt classical Marxism to very different, liberal democratic, circumstances.

▶ See Chapter 8 for a discussion of the development of socialist ideas.

The New Right approach was most influential in the 1970s and 1980s, particularly following the election of Thatcher in Britain and Reagan in the US. As Keynesian ideas were perceived to have failed, neo-liberal ideas came to predominate (see Chapter 9). Ironically, though, the success of political parties and politicians advocating neo-liberal solutions to perceived economic problems does tend to question the demand-side analysis the New Right put forward—that is, the claim that voters will not vote for parties that seek to control public spending and reduce the role of the state has proven wide of the mark.

 KEY DEBATE 2.3   The Marxist theory of the state

The state has always been criticized by anarchist thinkers and is regarded by Marxists as an exploitative institution that ought to be transcended. The dominant interpretation of classical Marxism (the Marxism associated with the writings of Karl Marx himself) operates with a very simplistic definition of politics and the state. For classical Marxists, the state is merely a vehicle for the exercise of power by the dominant class, so that, once classes are abolished, the state itself is abolished or, in the words of Marx's collaborator Fredrich Engels, 'withers away'. A communist society requires no enforcing state because the end of capitalism transforms human nature fundamentally. In other words, once classes are abolished, then conflict between individuals that is significant is a thing of the past.

Many scholars have argued that this is all too simplistic (see Plamenatz, 1963: 351–408).

- In the first place, it is argued that complex societies contain many different sources of division or conflict. Getting rid of classes therefore only ends one source of conflict. Others, based on aspects of life such as religion, culture, or types of work will still exist and will have to be dealt with presumably by an institution such as the state. The experience of the communist states of Eastern Europe backs up this critique of Marxism, for once the constraints of communist control were released, numerous interests, previously suppressed, emerged. As a result, it might be argued too that politics resumed after it had been artificially suppressed.

- Moreover, the transformation of human nature envisaged by Marx, it is argued, is also overly simplistic. There is something in the claim that reducing the level of economic inequality will have an impact on the behaviour of individuals, reducing crime based on acquisitiveness. Marx is justly famous for having pointed this out. However, it is a large step from this to the claim that society can exist effectively without the need for differential rewards as incentives for contributing to it. One of the problems here is Marx's assumption that communism would end material scarcity, which, from the perspective of the twenty-first century, seems remarkably misplaced. As a result of all of these factors, it seems likely that a state would be necessary in a communist regime in order to achieve the desired egalitarian goals. Some would argue that this involves the illegitimate suppressing of the natural urge that individuals have to be different and better than others. Others would argue that this is a necessary price to pay in order to create a fairer and more equal society.

Questions

1. Describe Marx's theory of the state and politics.
2. Critically examine the case for and against Marx's theory of the state.

See Chapter 9 for a discussion of liberal political economy.

According to Dryzek and Dunleavy (2009: 331–3), however, the New Right—or market liberal approach, as they call it—has declined in influence. Issues such as the threat of terrorism—particularly in France and the US—climate change, and the perceived negative impact of globalization on the indigenous working class have emphasized again the need for a strong interventionist approach. Moreover, the financial crisis that erupted in 2008 was, for many, a product of the limited regulation of financial institutions. Trump's election in the US in 2016 reflected this new constituency for a state willing to use its power to correct market failures, to control its borders, and to take a tougher stance on external threats.

In defence of the New Right approach, it seeks to explain the financial crisis in terms of the self-interested vote maximization of politicians who encouraged voters to borrow and spend money with little regard to their ability to pay it back (Minford, 2010). However, the fact that a strong state response—in terms of using tax revenues to bail out failed financial institutions—was an essential rejoinder that has further dented confidence in a market liberal approach. Finally, Dryzek and Dunleavy (2009) note the massively increased technological capacity that makes an efficient state-planned economy more realistic than it was before.

We can distinguish between the functions that the state does play, as a matter of fact, and the functions that it ought to play, as a matter of value. This latter—normative—dimension is the subject matter of Chapter 7. For now, note that the theories of the state discussed above can be considered normatively, as well as empirically. For example, pluralism originated as a normative critique of state monism and a celebration of the wide distribution of power (Nichols, 1994). Indeed, it has been claimed that the empirical pluralists in the US (such as Robert Dahl) 'confused normative claims with empirical reality' (Smith, 2006: 25). In other words, pluralists assumed that they had accurately described the way that American politics operated, whatever the reality, and therefore pluralist theory had the effect of legitimizing the American political system.

There are two main normative critiques that can be made of pluralism. In the first place, it can be argued that the pluralist theory of the state devalues the idea of the general or public interest. Indeed, pluralism almost glories in the differences between people. It therefore accepts as given the rather pessimistic view that society consists of a diverse range of competing, and sometimes hostile, interests. Second, the revised elite version of pluralism might also be criticized from a normative perspective on the grounds that it dismisses the importance of political participation. Thus, instead of accepting the competition between political elites as the best that can be achieved, political philosophers have argued that this is unacceptable from a democratic perspective and that we ought to look at ways in which opportunities to participate can be enhanced.

Elitism, too, can be assessed in normative terms. Ruling-elite theory, as a description of the state, makes no value judgement about the validity of elite rule. From this perspective, classical elitists at least are saying that, whether we like it or not, modern societies are dominated by a ruling elite. Students often confuse this empirical claim for a normative one. Of course, it is possible to justify elite rule on the grounds that the best should rule, uncluttered by the less able masses. Greek philosopher Plato offers just such a scenario, justifying the rule of the so-called philosopher kings. The modern theory of democratic elitism, examined in Chapter 4, is also based partly on a normative claim that elites ought to be left alone to govern because the masses tend to have authoritarian values. According to this position, mass participation in politics tends to result in instability and a climate of crisis (Dye, 2000). In these circumstances, apathy is to be encouraged.

▶ See Chapter 4 for a discussion of the elitist theory of democracy.

The normative character of Marxism, and socialism in general, is very apparent. Marx himself sought to distinguish his 'scientific' version of socialism from what he called the 'utopian' socialism that preceded him. Therefore, Marx claims that the laws of historical development will, whether we like it or not, result in the downfall of capitalism and the creation of a communist state. By contrast, ethical socialists seek to promote socialism and persuade people that it is a desirable form of social organization. Quite clearly, though, Marx does think that communism is a more desirable form of society than capitalism. Indeed, some Marxist scholars think that Marx was much less of a historical determinist than is often claimed and that there is still a role for human agency in effecting change.

▶ See Chapter 8 for an examination of socialism as an ideology.

Finally, the New Right theory also has strong normative underpinnings. Thus state intervention, it is argued, encourages individuals to overly rely on the state to provide welfare support, thereby stifling individual initiative and self-help. Finally, it is also unjust, failing to reward individual effort appropriately. Such claims, of course, are open to challenge. For instance, competing theories of justice argue that need or equality, and not merit, should be the underlying justification for determining the distribution of resources.

▶ See Chapter 7 for a discussion of competing theories of justice.

2

Whither the State?

The state is now under sustained attack as a variety of scholars seek to challenge its utility and very existence. There are empirical and normative dimensions to this debate. From the former perspective, it is suggested that certain modern developments have made the state increasingly redundant. From the latter perspective is the long-standing view that the state is an exploitative institution that ought to be done away with. This derives its major impetus from the ideas of Marx and anarchist thought (**see Key Debate 2.3**).

▶ See Chapter 8 for a critical analysis of socialism and anarchism.

Is the state 'hollowing out'?

▶ See Chapter 7 for a discussion of the impact of globalization on political theory.

The 'hollowing out' thesis (Jessop, 1990) suggests that, in a variety of ways, the state no longer plays the significant role that it used to. The major slant here is the globalization thesis. This is the view that the world has become so economically and politically interdependent that there is little room for manoeuvre for nation-states. To the extent that this is true, there is clearly a gap between the political theory of the sovereign state, articulated at the beginning of this chapter, and the reality of politics in the modern world. Globalization undoubtedly, then, has a significant impact on political studies as an academic discipline. The focus of politics, and particularly political theory, has been on the nation-state. In addition, the dominant tradition in international relations has been the realist tradition, which postulates a state system consisting of individual autonomous and competing sovereign states. Globalization challenges both assumptions.

The issue of globalization will be considered in more detail later in this book. For now, it should be noted that we can adopt empirical and normative approaches to it (Dryzek and Dunleavy, 2009: ch. 14). From an empirical perspective, the major impetus behind globalization is the internationalization of the economy. With the growth of multinational corporations—which have emerged to rival the power of states—and the liberalization of world trade, it is argued, the economic policies of individual states are now determined elsewhere

(Ohmae, 1995). Partly as a result of greater economic interdependence—together with improved communication technology and the emergence of global environmental problems—supranational institutions (whether they be intergovernmental organizations, such as the World Trade Organization, or non-governmental organizations (NGOs), such as Greenpeace) have emerged to challenge further the power of states.

As a result, critics argue, the realist school postulating the key role of sovereign states is time-bound, dating from the Peace of Westphalia in 1648. We are now, it is suggested, in a period of 'new medievalism' where, 'as in medieval Europe, sovereignty is shared among societies that interact in an ongoing way' (Cunningham, 2002: 203; see also Slaughter, 2003: 190). Others argue that the globalization thesis exaggerates the reality: that sovereign states still have a great deal of autonomy and were never, anyway, as self-contained as is often made out (Robertson, 1992) (**see Key Debate 2.4**).

▶ See Chapter 9 for a discussion of the relationship between the state and international economic institutions.

 KEY DEBATE 2.4 Positions in the globalization debate

Globalization may be a highly influential and fashionable subject, but the degree to which it represents reality is highly contested. It is possible to identify a number of positions in the debate.

1. The *hyperglobalist thesis* represents the most 'pure' position. According to this view, the world is now essentially borderless, with economic interests able to move around virtually unencumbered. Indeed, governments are forced to offer incentives (in the form, say, of lower taxes) to encourage investment that might otherwise go elsewhere.

2. According to the *sceptical thesis*, change is less apparent. The ability of economic concerns to move capital and labour across national borders is more difficult than hyperglobalists suggest, not least because of the need for a skilled and able workforce. It is much too premature, therefore, to say that the state is in decline. Indeed, the state since 1945 has expanded its reach and, despite the influence of neo-liberal economics, there is still the expectation, in Europe at least, that the state will be responsible for providing fundamental goods such as health care and education.

3. The *complex globalization thesis* holds a 'halfway house' position. Yes, globalization is happening. In particular, there has been a greater liberalization of trade. Nevertheless, it would be a mistake to claim that the world is now borderless. Rather, the role of the state is now changing economically, as well as politically and socially. There is a much greater need, for example, for the state to share power with international organizations in the global arena, as well as with a variety of actors within civil society.

4. In the *ideational globalization thesis*, even though globalization might not exist in reality, if state actors believe it is happening, then their actions may actually

contribute to making it a reality. In other words, governments may pursue neo-liberal economic policies because they perceive the need to encourage invest-ment, which may otherwise go elsewhere. This will have the effect of undermin-ing the nation-state. According to this position, then, globalization, insofar as it does exist, has a political, and not an economic, cause.

(Adapted from Marsh, Stoker and Hothi, 2006.)

From a normative perspective, it can be argued that the liberation of world markets is a positive development, facilitating greater prosperity. In addition, global problems—such as those concerned with the environment—require global solutions that are beyond the reach of sovereign states (**see Key Debate 2.5**). Finally, it is argued that globalization also facilitates cosmopolitanism, the goal of achieving peace, toleration, and justice in a world where we owe our allegiances to humanity—a form of global citizenship—rather than to partial entities such as the state (Heater, 1999). Others do not see the nation-state as an obstacle to cosmopolitanism and suggest that a system of markets unencumbered by the state is a negative phenomenon, exacerbating inequality in the world and increasing exploitation, particularly in developing countries.

 KEY DEBATE 2.5 **The state and the environment**

Environmentalists have tended to be sceptical about the state's capacity to solve environmental problems. The preferred option for Radical Greens is a decentralized political structure that is anarchistic in character. As many have commented, how-ever, this solution is counter-intuitive given the global character of environmental problems. It has long been appreciated that pollution is no respecter of national boundaries and requires cooperation between states to deal with it. More recently, the international dimension of environmentalism has become more prominent be-cause of the identification of genuinely global problems, such as climate change and ozone depletion. Only global cooperation can hope to solve these problems.

There are a number of approaches to the role of states in international environ-mental politics.

1. Realists argue that the natural condition of relations between sovereign states is one of anarchy. The world's political system is equivalent to Hobbes' state of nature, with each sovereign state seeking to defend its own self-interest, often defined in economic terms, and being extremely suspicious of others. As a result, the prospects for effective international cooperation are bleak.

2. An alternative pluralist or liberal-institutionalist model of international relations devalues the importance of nation-states and emphasizes the coordinating role that can be played by other actors such as international organizations, NGOs, and epistemic communities in the creation and effective implementation of

international environmental regimes (Vogler, 2005). It is argued that this model is a more accurate reflection of reality because—without wishing to question the fact that political sovereignty can provide obstacles for the development of international cooperation or that nation-states remain key actors in international environmental politics—the realist perspective does not sit well with the number of international agreements that have been made and, more to the point, with the fact that at least some of them seem to work reasonably well.

3. For the radical ecology approach, the devalued role of the nation-state suggested by the liberal-institutionalist is not necessarily beneficial for the environment. Indeed, the continuing degradation of the environment, and the difficulty of concluding effective international treaties, may best be explained not by the unwillingness of nation-states to act, but by the role of powerful, globally organized, economic interests and the structure of international capitalism (Paterson, 2000).

4. A fourth approach seeks to re-establish the role of the state as a major player in the environmental debate. The most concerted attempt to develop a normative model for a green state has been provided by Eckersley (2004). She recognizes that hers is a revisionist account, given the distaste for the state that exists in much green political thought. The justification for bringing the state back in is, at least in part, a product of the pragmatic recognition that the state remains the most important form of political organization. According to Eckersley, a green state must:

- facilitate a green public sphere to create greater ecological consciousness;
- be outward-looking, seeking to cooperate with other states to tackle environmental problems; and
- be impeccably democratic, encouraging participation, entrenching environmental rights, and incorporating the interests of non-human nature.

© Peter Macdiarmid/Getty Images

One final point here is that it is not just globalization that represents a threat to the autonomy of the nation-state. In addition, the reality of decision-making is that the state is in partnership with a range of social and economic institutions. Government has now been replaced by governance. Included in those now sharing power with the state are sub-state institutions such as, in Britain, the Scottish and Welsh authorities established by devolution proposals in recent years, as well as the supranational institutions that are the subject of the globalization debate. This overlapping system of governance has been described as neo-medievalism as a result of its similarity to the system of authority in the Europe of the Middle Ages before the emergence of the state.

▶ See Chapter 18 for a discussion of the concept of governance.

Conclusion

In this chapter, we attempted to define the state, before going on to provide empirical typologies of it. We saw that one of the most important typologies of the state centres on the distribution of power. Here, we identified empirical theories of the state on a continuum from the open and diffuse picture painted by classical pluralism to the closed and hierarchical picture painted by elitists and Marxists. These theories can be criticized on empirical grounds—they do not provide an accurate description of how the state is organized—and on normative grounds—they do not provide polities to which we ought to aspire.

Certainly, theories of the state, with the possible exception of Marxism, do not emphasize enough the external constraints operating on the state in the modern world and these globalizing tendencies will be a constant theme of this book. In Chapter 3, though, we will look closely at the concept of power, not least because this will help us to understand how difficult it is to investigate which of the theories of the state is the most accurate description of a particular political system.

? Key Questions

- What is the state?
- Develop a comprehensive typology of the state.
- Compare and contrast the pluralist, elitist, and Marxist theories of the state.
- How far does the American political system exhibit the characteristics of the pluralist theory of the state?
- Is the elitist theory of the state normatively desirable?
- Critically examine the Marxist theory of the state.

- How far is the state a benign institution?
- In the light of 9/11, the global financial crisis, and the growing threat of climate change, the New Right theory of the state is seriously flawed. Discuss.
- Is the state compatible with the protection of the environment?
- Are the state's days numbered?

 ## Further Reading

Dryzek, J., and Dunleavy, P. (2009), *Theories of the Democratic State* (Basingstoke: Palgrave).
Written by two leading political scientists, this is an excellent introduction to competing theories of the state and, indeed, political science in general. It has an excellent chapter on globalization.

Eckersley, R. (2004), *The Green State: Rethinking Democracy and Sovereignty* (Cambridge, MA: MIT Press).
This book is the most comprehensive attempt to theorize what a state conducive to the protection of the environment would look like.

Hay, C. et al. (eds) (2006), *The State: Theories and Issues* (Basingstoke: Palgrave).
This is a very useful book with chapters on various aspects of the debate about the state.

Held, D., Barnett, A., and Henderson, C. (2005), *Debating Globalization* (Cambridge: Polity).
This provides a very useful collection of articles on globalization taking all sides of the debate.

Hoffman, J. (1995), *Beyond the State* (Cambridge: Polity).
This provides a normative critique of the state, while also outlining the different approaches considered in this chapter.

James, A. (1986), *Sovereign Statehood* (London: Allen & Unwin).
This is a detailed conceptual account of sovereignty. Argues that the concept remains useful in understanding modern politics.

Parry, G. (1969), *Political Elites* (London: Allen & Unwin).
This is a relatively old book, but still cannot be bettered for the way in which it expertly surveys the literature on both classical elitism and pluralist versions of elitism.

Savigny, H., and Marsden, L. (2011), *Doing Political Science and International Relations: Theories in Action* (Basingstoke: Palgrave Macmillan).
Chapter 3 of this book contains a useful overview of theories of the state. Case studies applying theories of the state to the credit crunch issue are instructive.

Web Links

https://www.Marxists.org
For Marxist literature.

https://freedomhouse.org/report/freedom-world/freedom-world-2017
Freedom House is an organization that charts the level of freedom provided by states throughout the world.

Visit the **Online Resources** that accompany this book to access more learning resources on this topic: www.oup.com/uk/ferdinand/

Political Power, Authority, and the State

3

- Power and Authority
- Conceptual Questions about Power
- Power and Theories of the State
- Pluralism and Lukes' Three Dimensions of Power
- Interests and Power

- Political Elites
- Marxism and Power
- Feminism and Power
- Conclusion
- Key Questions
- Further Reading

Reader's Guide

This chapter explores the concept of power. It starts by defining power in the context of authority, before going on to discuss the classic threefold typology of authority put forward by German sociologist Max Weber. Some conceptual questions about power are then asked: is it the same as force? Must it be exercised deliberately? Is it a good thing? Can we ever eliminate it? The rest of the chapter is concerned with examining the methodological problems inherent in the measurement of power, particularly in relation to the theories of the state discussed in Chapter 2.

Power and Authority

Power and authority are central concepts in politics. As Hay (2002: 168) states, in only slightly exaggerated terms, 'power is to political analysis what the economy is to economics'. Politics is about competing interests and values, and a key question is what interests and values come out on top in practice. To discover this, we need to know something about power, since those who have power over others can determine which interests and values will be adopted by political decision-makers.

A common way of distinguishing between power and authority is to equate the former with coercion and the latter with consent. Authority, then, is defined here as legitimate power in the sense that rulers can produce acceptance by the ruled not because they can exercise coercion, but because the ruled recognize the right of the rulers to exercise power. Converting power into authority, then, is highly desirable (**see Case Study 3.1**). As Goodwin (2014: 346) points out: 'Where coercion creates obedience at a high cost in manpower and equipment, authority can control both the minds and the behaviour of individuals at a very low cost.'

 CASE STUDY 3.1   **The United States' Supreme Court: authority, power, and legitimacy**

One useful example of the distinction between power and authority is the role of the Supreme Court in the US. The Supreme Court (**see Figure 3.1**) is often said to be the most powerful arm of the American political system because of its established right (of judicial review) to declare actions of the executive and legislative branches to be unconstitutional. This means that the decisions of elected bodies can be overridden by an unelected body. Members of the Supreme Court are chosen by the US President and confirmed by the Senate, but, once appointed, remain as justices for life unless removed for wrongdoing.

It is often asked whether the Supreme Court's apparent power is worrying in a democratic polity. The Court has made many important political decisions relating to such controversial issues as race, abortion, and capital punishment, and yet its members are not elected nor made accountable to the people.

One retort to the claim that the Supreme Court is exercising illegitimate power is to invoke the distinction between power and authority. Thus, it is important to note that the Supreme Court has no army or police force with which to enforce its decisions. In other words, it is unable to exercise power or, at the very least, it has to share power with the executive and legislative branches of the federal government. As a result, in order for its decisions to be accepted without the threat of coercion, the Court relies on its authority. In other words, it has authority, but not power. The Supreme Court would almost certainly lose its authority, and therefore its legitimacy, if it made decisions that are too divorced from public opinion. Supreme Court justices are therefore constrained by the need to remain an authoritative institution in the American polity.

FIGURE 3.1 The US Supreme Court
© MH Anderson Photography/ Shutterstock.com

In terms of the exercise of power, there would seem to be two possible answers to the difficulty of applying coercion. One is to rule through so-called ideological control. In this scenario, rulers are able to maintain control through manipulating the preferences of the ruled so that these preferences reflect the interests of the rulers. Such control—associated with elitist thinkers and Marxist critiques of capitalist society—is much more effective in that it obviates the need for permanent scrutiny and coercion of the ruled. Nevertheless, as we shall see, its validity does depend upon the debatable assumption that individual preferences can be manipulated in such a way.

Some political theorists seek to link authority with philosophy and power with sociological analysis (Barry, 2000: 83). Here, authority is linked with right, with what ought to be, while power is conceived of as an empirical concept, with what is. This distinction, though, is problematic. As we noted above, authority can be a product of manipulation. Or, if one is suspicious of claims that people can be easily brainwashed, it might be argued that people are simply wrong—that they recognize as legitimate the wrong set of leaders.

There is no doubt, for instance, that Hitler had a great deal of authority within German society and yet few would want to claim that we therefore ought to regard the Nazi regime as legitimate. At the very least, we can agree with Goodwin's (2014: 350) assertion that 'a state's authority in the eyes of the people is not necessarily an indicator of its justice'. A linked argument is the case for saying that power is preferable to authority precisely on the grounds that whereas the latter can be based upon manipulation, the former is based on coercion. And, in the case of coercion, it is possible to recognize and act upon it (Goodwin, 2014: 351).

The second answer to the problem of coercion makes no such assumptions about the 'real' interests of the ruled. Rather, it simply asks: how can any set of rulers make themselves legitimate in the eyes of the ruled? In other words, how can rulers convert power into authority? No set of rulers can survive very long without at least some authority. This then raises another question: on what is authority based? The question of when and why political systems are legitimate is a crucial one for political theorists. It is a topic we will focus on in Chapter 7 when we ask what, if anything, makes the state legitimate.

The best-known attempt to come up with an analysis of the basis of authority was provided by Max Weber (Gerth and Mills, 1946). Weber regarded so-called legal–rational authority as the predominant basis for authority in the modern world. To give an example of this, the US President is obeyed not because he is charismatic or because he claims to have a divine right to rule, but because he holds the office of President. We can go further than this. In the modern Western world, and indeed in many other parts of the world now, political institutions are accepted because they are subject to democratic principles. In other words, nowadays, the holder of the office of US President has authority because he is elected. Indeed, the President remains the only part of the American polity whose constituency is the entire American electorate (**see Key Concept 3.2**).

 KEY CONCEPT 3.2   Weber and authority

Max Weber (1864–1920), the German sociologist and social theorist, developed a threefold classification of authority. He recognized that these were ideal types and all societies were likely to contain elements of the three types. An ideal, or pure, type aims at simplifying reality by presenting a logical extreme. It is designed, therefore, to be an explanatory tool rather than a description of reality. Developing ideal types enables the researcher to elicit meaning from what is a very complex reality.

Weber's three ideal types of authority are as follows.

- *Traditional authority*: authority derived from traditional customs and values. A major example would be the principle of the divine right of kings, prevalent in European monarchies, whereby monarchies were said to be ordained by God to rule.

- *Charismatic authority*: authority derived from the personality traits of an individual. This is often associated with the leaders of authoritarian or totalitarian regimes, not least because such charismatic leaders tend to emerge at a time of crisis. This form of authority may be less important in modern liberal democracies where authority tends to be based upon status and not personal qualities. However, charisma still plays some part, being part of a political leader's armoury, particularly now that the media image of leaders is important, even in parliamentary systems such as Britain. Weber regarded charismatic authority as inherently unstable. This is because, since authority rests with an individual and not a set of rules, the death of this individual, or her loss of authority, will immediately lead to instability.

- *Legal–rational authority*: authority derived from the status of an office as part of a system of constitutional rules in a democratic country or a religious document such as the Koran in Islamic regimes.

Weber argued that the modern world exhibits a greater tendency towards legal–rational authority.

3

As Hoffman and Graham (2006: 5–11) rightly point out, although we can define power and authority separately, in practice all governments use both. Even in a **democracy** some exercise of power is necessary. This is not least because decisions taken by a majority (the classic way decisions are taken in a democracy) leave a minority who may be resentful that their view did not prevail. Thus, even though democratic states exercise much more authority than **authoritarian** states, who exercise more power, the former have to exercise power at least some of the time and the latter always have some authority.

See Chapter 4 for a discussion of the problem of majority rule.

To put another spanner in the works, the distinction between authority and power is further clouded by the (likely) possibility that authority is granted to an institution, or an individual, precisely because it has power. It is true that not only do democratic regimes have to exercise power, but also **totalitarian** regimes usually have some degree of authority, even if it is the charismatic authority associated with political leaders such as Stalin and Hitler.

As Heywood (2015: 127–30) points out, the concept of authority is now particularly contentious. Many bemoan the decline of authority, reflecting what they see as the decline of social deference. Conservative thinkers therefore seek to justify its importance, emphasizing the need for people to be led and protected (Scruton, 2001). Those from a liberal perspective, by contrast, while recognizing the importance of authority for social stability, also promote liberty, which can challenge authority.

Conceptual Questions about Power

The meaning of power can be teased out a little further if we consider a number of questions about it.

Is power the same as force?

It is often argued that there is a conceptual difference between power and force or coercion (Barry, 2000: 89–90). Power can be, and usually is, exercised by the threat of force.

However, it might be argued that the actual use of force means that power has failed. For example, the US clearly used a great deal of force in Vietnam, as well as, more recently, in Iraq. However, it palpably failed to gain obedience in the former and it headed the same way in the latter. As Lukes (2005: 70) points out, 'having the means of power is not the same as being powerful'.

Must power be exercised deliberately?

There are some who argue that power must be exercised deliberately. As Bertrand Russell (1872–1970), the great twentieth-century British philosopher, insisted, power is 'the production of *intended* results: the unforeseen effects of our influence on others cannot be called power' (Russell, 1938: 25). The argument here is that it sounds intuitively odd to accord power to someone who has benefited from a situation which that person has not created. Nelson Polsby (1980: 208), the American political scientist, sums this up nicely by using the example of taxi drivers and the weather. Thus taxi drivers, surely benefit when it rains, but they do not cause it to rain. It is merely an unplanned effect of the rain. As Polsby (1980: 209) points out, it is mistaken to regard this as an exercise of power by taxi drivers, since showing that taxi drivers benefit from the rain 'falls short of showing that these beneficiaries created the status quo, act in a meaningful way to maintain it, or could, in the future, act effectively to deter changes in it'; as a result, 'Who benefits? . . . is a different question from who governs?'

This debate is important because it relates to the argument (outlined later) put forward by some Marxists and elitists that the ruling class or elite exercises power not because of its own agency, but because economic structures automatically benefit it and disadvantage others. It is to outcomes that we ought to look then if we want to see the true location of power. Of course, this sits uneasily with the claim that power is about intended effects—about, in other words, agency over structure. Maybe this is merely a matter of semantics. We can dispute that certain structures—the capitalist system, for instance—do inevitably benefit some and disadvantage others. What we cannot do is to dispute the effect of structures that do actually benefit some and disadvantage others. This may not be an exercise of power, if we define power in terms of intended effects, but it is clearly politically significant. Maybe domination, rather than power, is a better word to use in this situation.

Is power a good thing?

Some political thinkers would argue that whether or not power is good depends upon the uses to which it is put. From this perspective, using power to achieve certain desired outcomes is positive. As Lukes (2005: 109) points out, there are 'manifold ways in which power over others can be productive, transformative, authoritative and compatible with dignity'. By contrast, using power to harm others is negative. From a liberal perspective, however, power is always undesirable, because 'every exercise of power involves the imposition of someone's values upon another' (Barry, 2000: 99). This is why liberals recommend limitations on power in the form, for instance, of a separation of powers to prevent one branch of government from exercising too much power.

It is not clear, however, that the exercise of power is necessarily undesirable, whatever the consequences. It is logically possible, for instance, to think of a situation where A might know B's real interests better than B does herself, so that A exercising power over B would be to act in B's interests. An example here would be the relationship between a parent and a child. Liberals could still contend, however, that such a power relationship is illegitimate because, whatever the motive, the exercise of power still infringes the individual's freedom. There are two responses to this. The first is to say that we are faced with a choice between two incommensurable concepts (freedom and intervention for good) and there is no sure-fire way of arbitrating between them. The second is to say that it is logically possible, however unlikely, for A to use her power to insist that B is free. Using the law to abolish human slavery would be a good example of this. It is possible to conceive of someone who wishes to remain in slavery and, in this case, power would be used to make them free.

Can we eliminate power?

A related question is whether it is ever possible for power to be dispensed with. Can a society in which no one exercises power over anyone else exist? Here, the work of French philosopher Michel Foucault (1926–84) is instructive. Foucault is usually taken as offering a challenge to the work of those, such as Habermas (1929–), Marcuse (1898–1979), and Lukes, who, as we shall see later, imply that power is illegitimately exercised and ought therefore to be curtailed. For Foucault, power is ubiquitous, it is everywhere, and power relations between individuals are inevitable.

In his work *Discipline and Punish* (1977), for instance, Foucault argues that the history of legal punishment in France is superficially progressive because extremely violent punishment gave way to regimented incarceration. In reality, however, these are only two ways of achieving the same objective. Both involve power relations and both involve domination. History, for Foucault, then, is 'an endlessly repeated play of domination' (quoted in Hay, 2002: 191). Because power is ubiquitous, there is no possibility of liberation from it, although we can, as Foucault shows, change its focus and implementation. Lukes (2005: 107), who disputes this conclusion (and also denies that Foucault should be interpreted in this way), asks the question raised by Foucault: should we give up thinking 'of the very possibility of people being more or less free from others' power to live as their own nature and judgment dictate?' Foucault answers this in the affirmative. Lukes is less pessimistic.

3

- The concepts of power and authority are usually taken to differ over the issue of legitimacy, the former implying the use or threat of sanctions and the latter reflecting a set of rulers' right to rule.

- A key question for students of politics is the degree to which power is converted into authority. Weber's threefold classification remains the best-known attempt. He argues that modern political authority is legal–rational in nature rather than being based on tradition or charisma.

- Typical questions asked about power, upon which different answers are provided, include whether power is the same as force, whether power can be said to be exercised without the intention of doing so, whether the exercise of power can ever be good, and (a related question) whether we can ever eliminate power relationships.

Power and Theories of the State

We saw in the last chapter that theories of the state centre on the distribution of power. These theories might be used to describe the power structures in different societies. We might be justified, for instance, in claiming that various clearly undemocratic regimes in the world exhibit characteristics equivalent to ruling-elite theory, or even Marxist theory, whereas the liberal democratic regimes in the West are more clearly pluralist-oriented.

The debate about power has applied overwhelmingly to liberal democracies. This is partly because participants in the debate have been Western political scientists, particularly from the US, concerned with analysing liberal democratic political systems. More significantly, it reflects the fact that the power debate has been used to both defend and challenge the claim that political power in liberal democracies is widely spread rather than concentrated. In other words, in non-democratic states, it is assumed that the pluralist model does not apply.

In Chapter 5, we document the existence of authoritarian states, which have survived despite the influence of the democratic ideal. As it is pointed out, however we define them, and whatever their strengths, one thing is for sure: they are not democracies. The point of the Marxist and elitist challenge to the pluralist model is to demonstrate that, despite the democratic rhetoric, the pluralist model is not an accurate description of so-called liberal democracies either.

▶ Chapter 5 documents the existence and character of non-democratic states.

The first observation to make in an analysis of theories of power is that we cannot claim that all of these theories of the state correctly analyse the power structure existing in any one polity. In other words, we cannot claim that a country such as the UK or any other liberal democracy is at one and the same time capable of being explained in Marxist and pluralist terms. A pluralist account of, say, UK politics would look very different from a Marxist account (see the discussion in Dearlove and Saunders, 2000: ch. 9). Having said this, it is possible to argue that, at a micro level, different policy networks within a particular polity exhibit different power structures, some being more open than others (see Smith, 1993, and the discussion in Chapter 14).

Second, we need to ask how we go about determining which of these theories of the state provides a more accurate description of reality in liberal democracies such as Britain or the US. Such a task is enormously difficult, partly because of the problems involved in measuring the exercise of power. These stem largely from the fact that, as we shall see, power has been conceptualized in a number of different ways. These different conceptualizations of power were articulated in a classic account of the concept provided by Stephen Lukes (2005) in a book originally published in 1974.

This became known as the 'faces of power' debate, because Lukes distinguishes between three dimensions or faces of power, himself preferring the third dimension as the most comprehensive. He starts, however, by offering us a definition of power, which, he holds, is widely accepted. This definition is as follows: 'A exercises power over B when A affects B in a manner contrary to B's interests' (Lukes, 2005: 30). This only takes us so far because there is disagreement over the way in which A can act contrary to B's interests.

Pluralism and Lukes' Three Dimensions of Power

The way in which power is conceptualized has a significant bearing on the empirical validity of theories of the state. To see how this is so, let us return to the pluralist theory of the state. Pluralists adopt a decision-making approach to measuring power, which is equivalent to the first dimension of power. The first face of power is where, in Robert Dahl's words, 'A has power over B to the extent that he can get B to do something that B would not otherwise do' (quoted in Lukes, 2005: 16).

This first face of power is otherwise known as the decision-making approach, in that the method used by pluralist researchers is to look at the decisions made and the preferences of those groups involved in decision-making in a particular set of policy domains. It is then suggested that if a group's aims are met or partly met, then they have power (see Hewitt, 1974). If no one group gets its way on all occasions, then the pluralist model is affirmed. The advantage of the decision-making approach utilizing the first face of power is that it is eminently researchable. Indeed, numerous so-called community power studies were undertaken in the US in the late 1950s and 1960s, most of which confirmed the pluralist theory of the state (Dahl, 1963; Polsby, 1980).

Clearly, the decision-making approach could lead to non-pluralist conclusions—that is, it is possible that one group or a small number of groups get their way in the decisions made and the decision-making approach will pick this up. However, critics of pluralism suggest that the pluralist methodology is more than likely to generate pluralist conclusions

(Morriss, 1975). In the first place, the pluralist methodology makes no attempt to rank issues in order of importance. Clearly, some issues are more important than others and it may be the case that an elite group allows other groups to prevail in the lesser issues while ensuring that it gets its way in the more important ones (**see Key Debate 3.3**).

 KEY DEBATE 3.3   The first face of power and its critics

Pluralists typically adopt a decision-making methodology—what Lukes (2005) describes as the first face of power. The decision-making approach is illustrated in **Table 3.1**. This table shows the outcome of four issues on which three groups took positions.

This table shows that all the groups got their way at least some of the time. For example, the decisions taken on Issues 1 and 2 met with the approval of Groups A and B, while Group C achieved its goal on Issue 4. Pluralists would conclude from this that no one group was able to get its way on all issues and that power is therefore widely dispersed.

It is possible that the decision-making approach can generate non-pluralist conclusions. In the example in **Table 3.1**, for instance, it might have been found that Group A got its way on all four issues and Groups B and C lost out. However, the critics of pluralism suggest that the decision-making approach as set out in **Table 3.1** is likely to generate pluralist conclusions.

One of the reasons for this, the critics argue, is that pluralists tend to assume that all issues are of the same political importance as all others. As **Table 3.2** illustrates, this can distort the political reality. What it misses is the possibility that an elite group gets its way on the most important issue or issues, leaving other groups to get their way on the less important ones. Therefore, in the example in **Table 3.2**, Group C gets its way on fewer issues, but yet gets its way on the issue weighted most heavily (Issue 4).

Imagine, for instance, that Groups A and B are trade unions and Group C is a business organization. Further imagine that Issues 1–3 establish for workers an extra 15 minutes' break at various parts of the working day and Issue 4 grants to employers a right to prohibit strike action. Clearly, Issue 4 is much more important for business interests and is a serious restriction on trade unions—yet a pluralist methodology would fail to take this into account as an exercise of power by one group.

TABLE 3.1   The pluralist decision-making approach

	Issue 1	Issue 2	Issue 3	Issue 4	Total
Group A	WON	WON	LOST	LOST	2
Group B	WON	WON	WON	LOST	3
Group C	LOST	LOST	LOST	WON	1

Source: Adapted from Hay (2002: 174), with permission of Palgrave Macmillan.

TABLE 3.2 Pluralism and issue preferences

	Issue 1	Issue 2	Issue 3	Issue 4	Total
Weighting	1	1	1	5	
Group A	WON	WON	LOST	LOST	2
Group B	WON	WON	WON	LOST	3
Group C	LOST	LOST	LOST	WON	5

Source: Adapted from Hay (2002: 177), with permission of Palgrave Macmillan.

Questions

1. What criticisms have been made of the decision-making approach to measuring power?
2. What impact do these criticisms have on the validity of the pluralist theory of the state?

Second, it is assumed that the barriers to entry for groups in the political system are low. In other words, pluralists assume that if a group of people have a case to put or a grievance to express, then it is easy for them to enter the decision-making arena to express it. Clearly, however, this is a dubious assumption. Some groups—such as the unemployed or the homeless—may not have the resources or the expertise to organize effectively even if they want to. Other groups may not bother to organize because they anticipate little success. By focusing on the active groups in the decision-making arena, therefore, pluralists may well miss a range of interests that, for whatever reason, never appear within it.

Moreover, third, there is the related assumption that those issues discussed in the decision-making arena are the most important ones. In other words, it ignores the possibility that an elite group, or indeed a ruling class, can determine what will and will not be discussed. It is here that the second and third faces of power identified by Lukes can be invoked. The second face of power involves what Bachrach and Baratz (1963)—two American political scientists working in the 1960s—described as 'non-decision-making'. Here, an elite group operating behind the scenes can prevent certain issues from ever entering the decision-making arena.

For Bachrach and Baratz, then, power has two faces: the readily observable type, as defined by the first dimension, and a not-so-readily observable realm of non-decision-making. Power, for them, 'is also exercised when A devotes his energies to creating or reinforcing social and political values and institutional practices that limit the scope of the political process to public consideration of only those issues which are comparatively innocuous to A' (Bachrach and Baratz, 1970: 7). Non-decision-making, it is being suggested, usually operates in the interests of the most powerful, who stand to gain most from inaction.

Bachrach and Baratz advocate using both faces of power to gain a more rounded picture of the power structure. The first focuses on decisions actually made. The second is when 'power has the effect of preventing an issue from reaching the point where a decision is required' (Shorten, 2016: 151).

Although undoubtedly difficult, it is possible to identify cases of non-decision-making where issues of importance to some groups have not appeared on the political agenda. A number of empirical studies (Crenson, 1971; Blowers, 1984) have attempted to show how this has occurred. A starting point is to identify covert grievances—grievances that clearly exist, but which are never openly discussed. The next step is to identify the methods employed to prevent issues from appearing on the political agenda. A number of possibilities present themselves. Issues may be excluded because a social movement is denied access to the media, or because its members are bribed and/or victims of intimidation or threats. Equally, they may be excluded because there is consensus among politicians on an issue, therefore denying the electorate a choice. Similarly, issues can be excluded by the use of rules or procedures. In the latter category can be included the common tactic of taking the heat out of an issue by referring it to a legislative committee or, in the British context, a Royal Commission, thereby postponing the need to make a decision.

Another cause of non-decision-making is the so-called law of anticipated reactions. We have already seen how this can impact on a group's decision not to enter the decision-making arena. It can also, however, influence the attitude of decision-makers themselves. A study by American political scientist Charles Lindblom (1977), for instance, argued that business interests hold a privileged position in the decision-making arena because of their position in the economy—that is, governments recognize that businesses can help to deliver desirable economic scenarios—low unemployment and inflation—and, as a result, will always be likely to concede to business demands. This power of business is enhanced even further when governments have to deal with multinational companies, which have the option to take their businesses to another country.

The crucial point here is that business interests do not have to lobby decision-makers or demonstrate on the street to be heard. Pluralist researchers adopting the decision-making approach will not, therefore, identify business interests as one of a number of interests with a stated position. Rather, governments will automatically consider business interests because they anticipate their influence.

The first and second faces of power assume that political actors are aware of their own interests. The second, and much more insidious, way in which an elite group or ruling class can set the political agenda, it is suggested, lies in their ability to shape the demands that groups articulate in the decision-making arena. This is the third dimension of power, or power as 'preference manipulation' (Shorten, 2016: 152; **see Case Study 3.4**). For Lukes (2005: 27), 'A may exercise power over B by getting him to do what he does not want to do, but he also exercises power over him by influencing, shaping or determining his very wants' (**see Key Quote 3.5**). For Lukes, then, the exercise of power may not involve conflict (because individuals who are being dominated are not aware of it). The

CASE STUDY 3.4   Crenson, Lukes, and air pollution

Stephen Lukes, in his now-classic study of power, argues that it is possible to determine empirically cases where individuals can be manipulated so that the wants they express are different from their actual interests. He cites the well-known study by American political scientist Matthew Crenson that looked at air pollution policy in two American cities as an example of how this can be done (Lukes, 2005: 44–8).

Crenson (1971) asks why the issue of air pollution was raised in some American cities, but not in others. He looks in detail at two cities in the state of Indiana. One, East Chicago, introduced air pollution controls in 1949 and the other, Gary, waited until 1962. Crenson's explanation for this is that the latter city was dominated by one powerful steel company whose reputation for power prevented the issue from being raised and, when it was impossible to ignore, influenced the content of the legislation that emerged. It was not just that the industry prevented supporters of pollution control from getting a hearing (an example of non-decision-making), although that was part of the story. In addition, support for pollution controls was weak because, Crenson (1971: 27) claims, there was an element of ideological control too, in which 'local political institutions and political leaders' exercised 'considerable control over what people choose to care about and how forcefully they articulate[d] their cares'.

Lukes argues that Crenson's study reveals a genuine case where the real interests of people are different from the wants they express. As he remarks, 'there is good reason to expect that, other things being equal, people would rather not be poisoned' and yet it appears they were prepared to be (Lukes, 2005: 48).

Using this study in support of the third face of power is, as a number of commentators have noted, enormously problematic. The assumption both Crenson and Lukes make is that it *was* in the interests of people in East Chicago and Gary to have pollution control legislation. Therefore, in Gary, the people articulated their 'real' interests and achieved pollution control legislation, whereas, in East Chicago, they did not. However, this assumption is dubious, to say the least. It could equally be argued that residents of Gary were well aware of the benefits that air pollution legislation might bring, but were equally aware of the economic drawbacks. They were well aware, in other words, that paying the costs of such legislation would make the company less profitable and might lead to redundancies and reduced pay.

It may or may not be the case that pollution control legislation has economic consequences. Arguably, at the level of the individual industrial unit, unemployment and reduced pay would be the result of pollution control, although the benefits to society as a whole (including economic ones) may outweigh these costs. That, however, is little consolation to those whose livelihoods depend upon continued employment at the unit being threatened. This would be the case particularly where, as in Gary, one company dominates the economy.

Questions

1. What is Lukes' third face of power?

2. How far do you agree with Lukes' claim that Crenson's study provides an example of the third face of power in action?

> **Q   KEY QUOTE 3.5   The third face of power**
>
> 'Is it not the most insidious exercise of power to prevent people, to whatever degree, from having grievances by shaping their perceptions, cognitions, and preferences in such a way that they accept their role in the existing order of things, either because they can see or imagine no alternative to it, or because they see it as natural or un-changeable, or because they value it as divinely ordained and beneficial?' (Lukes, 2005: 28)

exercise of power does, though, require 'latent conflict' in the sense that there is a gap 'between the interests of those exercising power and the *real interests*' of those being dominated (Lukes, 2005: 28). Consider this example. Wealthy oil companies regularly fund studies that seek to deny the existence or scale of man-made climate change. These studies, of dubious scientific validity, cloud the judgement of people, thus allowing the oil companies to continue making huge profits from the burning of fossil fuels.

The critique of pluralists here is that they take it for granted that the preferences expressed by individuals and groups are in their interests. No attempt is made by pluralists to ascertain how individuals and groups come to hold the preferences they do. For elitists and Marxists, this is a serious omission, since the ability of dominant groups to exercise ideological control is a key aspect of the exercise of power. By shaping individual preferences—through control over the means of communication and socialization—a ruling elite or class can prevent demands that challenge its interests from ever reaching the political agenda (for example, see the discussion of the power of the media in Chapter 15). In this way, an apparently pluralistic polity—with freedom of association, free elections, and so on—is, in reality, nothing of the sort.

 See Chapter 15 for a discussion of the power of the media.

> **✳   KEY POINTS**
>
> - Determining the empirical validity of the theories of the state discussed in Chapter 1 depends on an analysis of power.
> - Pluralists use what Lukes calls the first face of power, focusing on the decision-making arena.
> - This approach, while capable of producing non-pluralist conclusions, does not, it is argued, provide the complete picture. First, it misses the possibility that a political elite or ruling class can avoid making decisions on certain key issues (the second face of power) and, second, it can ensure that the wants expressed by political actors are not those that will damage the interests of the ruling group.

Interests and Power

Despite the force of their arguments, the critics of pluralism are faced with well-rehearsed methodological difficulties of their own—for if power is exercised in subtler ways, how do we go about measuring it? We saw that it is possible, albeit difficult, to identify non-decision-making, but how do we go about determining if individual preferences have been shaped by dominant forces in society?

The assumption of the third face of power is that one can distinguish between what individuals or groups perceive to be in their interests and what is, in fact, actually in their interests. This requires the researcher to 'discover' the existence of 'objective' interests, which can then be contrasted with the interests that individuals perceive themselves as having. Now, it is not impossible to conclude accurately that someone is acting against their best interests. Imagine, for instance, that the dominant ideology of a university, accepted by all of the students, is that it is necessary to go out drinking the night before an exam on the spurious grounds that this will enhance their performance the following day. Imagine further that the university has shares in a local brewery and that it is likely to further benefit when students fail their exams and have to pay additional fees to resit them. Here, it is possible to conclude that an ideology (accepted by the students) benefits those in power and is not in the interests of the students.

Unfortunately, however, the identification of cases where individuals are clearly acting against their best interests is rarely as simple as that. Take the issue of climate change mentioned above. To qualify as an example of the third face of power, it would have to be shown that action to tackle climate change is in everybody's real interests. An argument could be made, however, that this is not always the case, or not obviously so. It may be, for instance, that action on climate change will significantly damage the economic interests of some people. It may also be the case that although we can admit that climate change will ultimately lead to serious problems, these will mainly affect future generations, so current people can safely ignore the problem. Take, as another example, the issue of smoking (Dearlove and Saunders, 2000: 368). Are we to say that those who continue to smoke, despite being aware of the health problems caused by it, are acting against their own best interests? In some cases, undoubtedly, people would have given up smoking if they had been aware of the damage it was going to cause to their health; others, well aware of the potential health costs, may insist that they want to continue smoking because of other perceived benefits—that it relaxes them, prevents them putting on weight, provides an ice-breaker in social situations—or because they value other things over a long life. In these situations, are we still to say that these people are acting against their best interests?

There is an ever-present danger here of being extremely and unjustifiably patronizing towards individuals: a 'we know best' mentality. In reality, the researcher has to be careful to avoid his or her own subjective preferences from intervening (**see Key Quote 3.6**). For example, imagine that one finds that there is widespread support for the existence of nuclear weapons and the argument that this acts as a deterrent against hostile powers also

> **Q** **KEY QUOTE 3.6** **A critique of the third face of power**
>
> 'The problem (with the third face of power) . . . is the deeply condescending concep-
> tion of the social subject as an ideological dupe that it conjures up. Not only is this
> wretched individual incapable of perceiving her/his true interests . . . But rising above
> the ideological mists is the enlightened academic who from his/her perch in the ivory
> tower may look down to discern the genuine interests of those not similarly blessed.'
> (Hay, 1997: 47–8)

holding nuclear weapons. For the political analyst to argue that this belief is not in the
interests of those holding it requires the imposition of an extremely contentious—and
therefore political—judgement that, for instance, nuclear weapons are expensive and only
encourage other countries to have them too. Others, of course, argue that the nuclear deterrent is in the interests of the people because it helps to maintain peace. Many political
questions are similarly subjective and it is difficult to sustain the view that support for one
value over another constitutes a failure to act in one's own interests. If a poor person, for
instance, prefers freedom over equality, are we to say that person is being manipulated?
Such a position risks illegitimately denying the importance of one particular view of how
society is organized over another.

One innovative critique of the third face of power is provided by Scott (1990). He argues
that researchers tend to confuse willing compliance, suggesting ideological manipulation,
with a political strategy exercised by dominated groups. Such groups may superficially ab-
sorb and articulate the dominant world view of the rulers, but, underneath, a counter-
culture exists that challenges these dominant norms. This kind of strategy, Scott argues,
is apparent in cases of slavery, serfdom, caste domination, and, at a micro level, in relations between prisoners and warders and teachers and students. Lukes (2005: 127–8) does
not challenge the ingenuity of Scott's research, but raises doubts about the correctness of
its interpretation. Scott ignores the public evidence suggesting the willing compliance of
dominant groups in favour of focusing on private transcripts, which, he claims, reveal a deliberate strategy of quiescence. But why should we regard this evidence as more important
than other information suggesting ideological conformity? At the very least, it 'does not
show there is also not widespread consent and resignation' (Lukes, 2005: 131).

Political Elites

Given the difficulty of establishing that real interests are being thwarted, many critics of
pluralism fall back on the existence of political elites. Here, it is argued, if it can be shown
that those occupying the top positions in a variety of institutions have similar social and
educational backgrounds, then this provides evidence of the possibility that a ruling elite

or class does exist. This approach is, superficially at least, a fruitful one. In almost every elite group in a society such as Britain, those occupying the top positions are drawn disproportionately from the middle and upper classes and from those with elite, and expensive, educational backgrounds (in the case of Britain, those with public school and Oxbridge educations). Similarly, C. Wright Mills (1956), in his study of American centres of power, found overlapping social and educational backgrounds.

The problem with the political elite approach is that it arguably does not tell us very much at all about the exercise of power. Common sense tells us that political elites exist, but their existence is not necessarily incompatible with the pluralist position. As we saw in Chapter 2, pluralists accept the existence of elites, but argue that, provided that these elites compete with each other, the basis of the pluralist position is maintained. To demonstrate the existence of a ruling elite or class, we have to establish that there is a coherent, conscious, and conspiratorial group that dominates decision-making.

In other words, establishing the existence of a ruling elite or class requires us to ask two additional questions. First, how far do elite groups share a common set of values and beliefs that is distinct from the rest of society? Second, how far do the aims of elite groups prevail? It is by no means clear that either of these conditions exist in a liberal democracy such as Britain, although the extent to which they do should, in principle, be capable of being researched. The problem is that it requires the type of empirical research of observable phenomena that critics of pluralism have already rejected.

▶ See Chapter 2 for an exploration of pluralists' attitudes towards elites.

3

✳ KEY POINTS

- It is extremely difficult to show conclusively that a political preference is not in the real interests of those who express it.
- Elite background studies do tend to reveal similar patterns of recruitment. However, the existence of a shared social and educational background does not prove the existence of a ruling elite or class.

Marxism and Power

The methodological problems we have identified above are as applicable to Marxist accounts as they are to elitist ones. Marxists, for instance, have emphasized the ability of the ruling class to exercise ideological control over the proletariat. They are therefore subject to the same critique that it is difficult to distinguish 'real' interests from perceived interests.

Marx famously pointed out that 'the ideas of the ruling class are in every epoch the ruling ideas' (McLellan, 1980: 184). As a result of ideological control, the proletariat, for Marxists, are subject to 'false consciousness' and this explains their lack of revolutionary

▶ See Chapter 8 for an exploration of post-Marxian Marxism.

3

fervour. Marx tended to assume that a revolutionary class consciousness would arise spontaneously as a result of objective economic developments. As we shall see in Chapter 8, subsequent Marxists such as Lenin have argued for the need for a revolutionary party to articulate and promote the proletariat's 'real' interests.

The concept of false consciousness is a theme developed by many post-Marxian Marxists. Italian Marxist Antonio Gramsci (1891–1937), for instance (from whom Lukes borrows extensively), emphasized the ability of the ruling class to ideologically manipulate the proletariat through their 'hegemony' and regarded the role of intellectuals as crucial in challenging this domination (Gramsci, 1971). Similarly, neo-Marxist thinker Herbert Marcuse (1898–1979) stressed that the capitalist state creates a situation where a large part of the population are led to believe that the state is benign, if not beneficial, whereas the reality is that the state is exerting power. The evidence for this is provided by those occasions when the state is forced to react violently to public protest (Marcuse, 1964).

Marxists, like elitists, have struggled to explain how it is that the ruling class rules despite the existence of universal suffrage and competitive elections. Marx himself, of course, had not faced this problem as he was writing at a time when suffrage was limited to a small number of wealthy men. Later Marxists, such as Ralph Miliband (1924–94), have tended to fall back on three arguments here (Miliband, 1978). In the first place, they note the similar social and educational backgrounds of state and economic elites. Again, however, this falls prey to the critique outlined above: that such backgrounds do not show conclusively the existence of a cohesive, conspiratorial ruling class.

Second, Marxists such as Miliband argue that business interests represent a particularly powerful interest group. Again, the power of business can be challenged, on pluralist grounds, by noting the countervailing power of non-business interests and also by the state, which Marxists have arguably failed to show always acts in the interests of business. Third, Marxists (as well as elitists) argue that we ought to focus not on the way decisions are made and who is involved in the decision-making arena, but on the outcomes of decision-making. Who wins and who loses from the decisions taken? According to the 'who wins and who loses' position, we only have to look, it is argued, at the inequalities in most societies, including liberal democracies, to see that a particular group benefits. As Westergaard and Resler (1975: 141) state in their classic, Marxist, account of class structure:

> Power is visible only through its consequences: they are the first and the final proof of the existence of power. The continuing inequalities of wealth, income and welfare that divide the population are . . . the most visible manifestations of the division of power in a society such as Britain.

From this, it is assumed that the group that benefits exercises power and therefore that an elitist or Marxist approach is a more accurate description of modern political systems.

We saw earlier in this chapter that it is questionable whether outcomes such as these can be equated with power without the intended actions of a human agent. More specifically, although it is true that a great deal of inequality does still exist in most capitalist societies, it would be wrong to claim that universal suffrage and the coming to power of left-of-centre governments has had no impact on the distribution of resources. The creation of the welfare state and the introduction of free education in modern liberal democracies has undoubtedly improved the lives of many people. Indeed, arguably, the consequences of affluence—not least those relating to the environment—have become as big a problem in the developed world as poverty.

See Chapter 8 for a discussion of the relationship between economic growth and environmental protection.

Marxists counter the argument that the welfare state and other social reforms 'disprove' their central thesis. In the first place, they would argue that the creation of the welfare state was instrumental for the owners of capital because good healthcare and educational provision is essential for a productive workforce. Second, there is the argument that reforms benefiting the working class are made only when social unrest would have been the result had concessions not been made.

Both of these arguments have their problems. In the first place, not all social benefits can be shown to be in the direct interests of the dominant economic class. Some such as, say, measures to improve productivity might be, but it is difficult to see free higher education in subjects in the humanities and social sciences in the same way. Second, the argument that reforms have averted social unrest and even revolution is weak, partly because it is impossible to disprove. We cannot possibly know for sure what the consequences of not granting concessions would have been. Moreover, if the ruling classes are continually making concessions, then the question must be asked: how far do they remain a ruling class?

A more sophisticated Marxist account, which takes account of some of the weaknesses outlined above, is the structural Marxism associated mainly with Greek Marxist Nicos Poulantzas (1936–79), who, in the late 1960s and 1970s, engaged in a sustained debate with Miliband, the exponent of a more traditional Marxism (Poulantzas, 1973, 1976). Poulantzas, a disciple of French structuralist Marxist Louis Althusser (1918–90), moves us from an account based on agency to one based on structure—that is, he argues that benefits in society may be distributed in a particular way not because of the intentional actions of individuals, but because of the structure of the situation. In the economic sphere, capitalists, however kind and philanthropic they may be, are forced to act in particular ways—increasing profit primarily by bringing down wages—if they want to remain in business.

State personnel, too, are forced to act in ways that support the logic of the capitalist system. For Poulantzas, the state is able to act autonomously from the **bourgeoisie**, but this enables it to act in the long-term interests of the dominant class, even if, in some instances, the short-term interests of this class are set aside. Offering concessions to prevent social unrest is one such strategy. Offering free health care and education is not in the short-term interests of the bourgeoisie because paying for it eats into their profits. In the long term, however, the ruling class benefits because of the creation of a healthier, more productive workforce and a climate less likely to result in social unrest.

By emphasizing structure over agency, Poulantzas, it might be argued, still falls foul of the claim that power can only be exercised deliberately. More specifically, he has been criticized for failing to explain why it is that the state behaves in the way he says it does (Hay, 1999). In other words, if the state is not directly controlled by the ruling class, why is it that it still acts in its long-term interests? Even more peculiar: why is it that it has autonomy that is only relative? There is an air of mysticism here, which, perhaps, is the result of not paying enough attention to the attitudes and actions of individuals.

✳ KEY POINTS

- Marxists also emphasize the role of both ideological control and elite background studies, and therefore face similar problems to those seeking to justify a ruling-elite position.

- Marxists also face difficulty in trying to explain how a ruling class can still be said to rule in a liberal democracy where universal suffrage has long been the norm and in which a welfare state now exists.

- Marxists tend to argue that universal suffrage does not dent the power of business interests and that, in any case, much social welfare reform is in the interests of the dominant class.

- The structural Marxism associated with Poulantzas attempts, not always successfully, to deal with these problems. Political actors are forced to act in ways that promote the capitalist system because of the structure of the situation. Moreover, the state acts in the long-term interests of capitalism even though, in the short term, it may seem to damage the interests of the class that is said to rule.

Feminism and Power

➤ See Chapter 8 for a discussion of feminism as an ideology.

So far, we have focused on power relations between groups and classes and between individuals and elites. Feminists would argue that this is to miss the crucial reality of gendered power relations. Liberal feminists, as we will see in a later chapter, critically observe that men tend to dominate the key powerful positions within the public sphere, whether it be in political or business institutions. Radical feminists, on the other hand, argue that it is not power in the state that ought to be the chief focus, but the patriarchal—or male-dominated—character of the private sphere. It is this insight—that the family can be the site of power, oppression, and violence—that is feminism's major contribution to the debate about power.

➤ See Chapter 7 for a discussion of liberal social contract theory and Chapter 8 for a discussion of liberal ideology.

Of particular importance here is Carol Pateman's (1988) notion of a 'sexual contract'. Traditional liberal social contract theory, associated with English political philosophers such as Thomas Hobbes and John Locke, holds that states can only be legitimate if individuals agree to the terms of the state before it is created. Pateman argues that this liberal social contract relies upon an unstated, but essential, sexual contract in which women accept the dominant position of men in return for being protected and cared for. It is men, therefore, who have the power in the public sphere to act on behalf of women. Only when this inequality in the private sphere is tackled, Pateman argues, can the equality, as envisaged by liberal political theorists such as Hobbes and Locke, be realized. The solution cannot come from liberalism, however, because it is an ideology that frowns upon state intervention in the private sphere.

 KEY POINTS

- A feminist theory of power emphasizes gender, rather than classes or individuals.
- For liberal feminists, gendered inequality in the distribution of powerful positions in the public sphere is the chief focus. Radical feminists, on the other hand, emphasize male dominance within the private sphere, which liberal political thought is ill-equipped to tackle.

Conclusion

It is to be hoped that this chapter has been able to demonstrate how crucial the concept of power is to a study of politics. We have seen that semantic, normative, and empirical questions about power abound: what is it? Is it a good thing? How is it distributed? The answers to all of these questions are contested. Answers to the empirical question remain, perhaps, most disputed. Indeed, here, we reached something of an impasse.

On the one hand, we suspect that the conceptualization of power adopted by pluralists, although eminently quantifiable and researchable, is, at the very least, incomplete. On the other hand, the conceptualization of power most favoured by elitists and Marxists, although persuasive, is problematic because it appears unresearchable. This explains why the debate between exponents of competing theories of the state continues. This debate is, perhaps, less intensive than it was 30 years ago and this is partly, at least, to do with the question marks being raised against the efficacy of the state in an increasingly globalized world.

? **Key Questions**

- What is the difference between power and authority?
- Is the exercise of power inevitable?
- Must power always be exercised deliberately?
- Is power the same as force?

- Is power a good thing?
- Design a research project to determine whether the pluralist theory of the state accurately describes the distribution of political power in any one country with which you are familiar.
- Find examples of issues that have been referred to legislative committees or royal commissions. How far do these examples provide evidence of non-decision-making?
- Is power as thought control a viable concept?
- How important is the fact that most political elites in a country such as Britain have similar educational backgrounds?
- Is economic inequality a product of the exercise of power?

 Further Reading

Bachrach, P., and Baratz, M. (1963), 'Decisions and Non-Decisions', *American Political Science Review*, 57: 632–42.
This is a much-cited critique of the pluralist theory of the state which emphasizes the importance of non-decision-making.

Blowers, A. (1984), *Something in the Air: Corporate Power and the Environment* (London: Harper & Row).
This is an interesting British case study relevant to theories of power.

Crenson, M. (1971), *The Un-Politics of Air Pollution* (Baltimore, MD: Johns Hopkins University Press).
This is a study which attempts to put into operation Lukes' critique of the pluralist decision-making methodology.

Dahl, R. (1963), *Who Governs?* (New Haven, CT: Yale University Press).
This is the classic example of the decision-making methodology associated with pluralism.

Lukes, S. (2005), *Power: A Radical View* (Basingstoke: Palgrave Macmillan, 2nd edn).
This is a celebrated account of power. This revised version, first published in 1974, also includes an essay defending it against critics.

Miliband, R. (1978), *The State in Capitalist Society* (New York: Basic Books).
This is the best-known modern defence of the Marxist theory of the state.

 Visit the **Online Resources** that accompany this book to access more learning resources on this topic: www.oup.com/uk/ferdinand/

Democracy

4

Reader's Guide

This chapter explores key aspects of democratic theory. It seeks to define what democracy means, to explore the historical evolution of the term, and to consider the debate between advocates of the protective theory and the participatory theory of democracy. Alleged problems with democracy—relating to majoritarianism, its impact on economic efficiency, and its relationship with desired outcomes—are reviewed. The chapter concludes by considering the new directions democratic theory has taken in recent years. These include associative, cosmopolitan, deliberative, and ecological versions of democracy.

What Is Democracy?

Like many other political concepts, democracy is a term with no precise and agreed meaning. Finding a definitional consensus for democracy is not helped by its emotive connotations. Democracy is a 'good' word. It is almost universally regarded in a favourable light. There are few countries in the world that would want to be labelled undemocratic. Indeed, partly because of the collapse of the old Soviet Union and its satellites, '[a]round two-thirds of all the countries in the world have a basic set of democratic institutions built around competitive elections that enable all adult citizens to choose and remove their government leaders' (Stoker, 2006: 7).

See Chapter 2 for a description of illiberal democracy.

This expansion of competitive elections has led to the growing importance of so-called illiberal democracies or, as they are sometimes called, competitive authoritarian regimes or semi-democracies (Zakaria, 2003; Levitsky and Way, 2002). As we saw in Chapter 2, these are regimes in which, while elections are not blatantly rigged, elected rulers pay little heed to the protection of individual rights (such as free speech) once in power and therefore opposition to rulers, who are able to manipulate electoral outcomes through control of the media and the use of the state apparatus, is difficult. As a result, the turnover of political leaders through competitive elections is small.

See Chapter 5 for an account of the spread of democracy and its different types.

The existence of illiberal democracies, however, raises a conundrum for students of democracy. For, while it is surely stretching the concept to breaking point if we insist that the label 'democratic' can be applied to, say, one-party states—for example in China (which describes itself as a 'democratic dictatorship') or in the old Soviet bloc countries—it is not so clear-cut that we should deny the democracy label to competitive authoritarian states.

It is probably the case that democracy does, justifiably, mean different things to different people; the question is whether there is a core of meaning on which we can all agree. Very basically, democracy refers to a regime whereby political power is widely spread, where power in some way rests with the people. Democracy, then, has something to do with political equality. As Arblaster (2002: 7) points out, this definition is sufficiently vague to allow for a number of interpretations.

Lively (1975: 30) suggests seven possibilities:

1. That all should govern, in the sense that all should be involved in legislating, in deciding on general policy, in applying laws, and in governmental administration.
2. That all should be personally involved in crucial decision-making, that is to say in deciding general laws and matters of general policy.
3. That rulers should be accountable to the ruled; they should, in other words, be obliged to justify their actions to the ruled and be removable by the ruled.
4. That rulers should be accountable to the representatives of the ruled.
5. That rulers should be chosen by the ruled.
6. That rulers should be chosen by the representatives of the ruled.
7. That rulers should act in the interests of the ruled.

Lively (1975: 33–42) argues that possibilities 1–4 are justified in being described as democratic, whereas 5–7 are not. The crucial defining characteristic is accountability. The latter three definitions provide no means whereby the rulers can be removed by the ruled and therefore cannot be defined as versions of democracy. Possibility 7 allows for the inclusion of regimes, such as those subscribing to communism, who claim, despite the lack of competitive elections, to be democratic because the real interests of the many are promoted by rulers who are aiming for social and economic equality (Macpherson, 1966: 12–22).

This claim—that the democratic label can be attached to a regime whose rulers, however they are chosen, govern in the interests of all—is a logical mistake. The outcomes of a political system are separate from the means by which its rulers are chosen. It may be the case, as we will see later, that democracy (in the sense of a political system requiring regular competitive elections) is the most effective way of ensuring that rulers do act in the interests of the ruled. It may also be the case that the achievement of political equality requires a degree of economic equality. Ultimately, though, a benign dictatorship with the interests of her people at heart is not impossible. Many one-party communist states, of course, were far from being benign, arguably precisely because their leaders were not accountable. It is also questionable whether illiberal democracies, where rulers are able to manipulate elections and transfers of power are rare, uphold the accountability rule and can therefore be described as truly democratic. To add an extra layer of complexity, we will see later in the chapter that liberal democracies do not escape criticism from a democratic perspective because of the potential conflict between majoritarian decision-making and the protection of individual rights.

Focusing on the first four of Lively's typology, we are still left with considerable variation. The first two are forms of direct democracy, whereas the latter two are forms of representative democracy. Direct democracy refers to a system whereby the people rule directly. The first definition on Lively's list seems impossible to be realized in anything but a very small-scale society. Even the second raises huge difficulties.

Representative democracy is a more realistic proposition. This is where the people choose others to represent their interests. There can also be stronger and weaker versions of representative democracy. British MPs, invoking great eighteenth-century parliamentarian Edmund Burke (1729–97), for instance, have for long insisted upon their independence from their constituents, so that on at least some issues (mainly moral ones, such as capital punishment and abortion) they vote according to their conscience. Of course, it is debatable how far MPs can remain aloof from their constituents' views without negative consequences befalling them at a future election (**see Case Study 4.1**).

 CASE STUDY 4.1   **MPs, Brexit, and the EU referendum**

An interesting illustration of competing theories of representation occurred in the context of the UK referendum on the European Union. Held in June 2016, the result was a narrow victory for the Leave side of the debate. There has been much subsequent debate about the role of Parliament and MPs in the post-referendum climate. Many (on the Leave side) argued that MPs should simply follow the will of the people. Some even suggested that Parliament should have no role in the implementation of

4

the referendum verdict. Others argued that Parliament should still have the final say, at least on the terms of the exit from the EU, if not the actual decision whether or not to leave. One prominent campaigner took a case to the Supreme Court to establish that Parliament should be involved. Significantly, the vast majority of MPs in both major parties voted to accept the decision to invoke Article 50, allowing the UK to leave the EU, despite the fact that a majority of them supported remaining. The fear of an electoral backlash, particularly against Labour MPs, was the chief reason for the decision not to go against the popular will. This reveals the limited utility of the Burkean model of representation in a democracy with regular elections.

✳ KEY POINTS

- The concept of democracy has a core meaning. It is about popular rule or the rule of the people. This can be interpreted in a wide variety of ways, although some regimes clearly do not exhibit any characteristics of the people having power and others limit it extensively.
- Lively suggests that democracy requires the people to make decisions directly or to choose, and be able to remove, those who make decisions on the people's behalf.

History

Democracy is a Greek term containing two words: *demos*, meaning the citizens within a city-state, and *kratos*, meaning power or rule (Arblaster, 2002: 15). The term was used to describe the practice of the Greek city-states (**see Figure 4.1**). Many contemporary democratic theorists and activists look back to the Greek city-states with great affection, regarding them as providing a participatory model of democracy of which modern liberal democracies fall far short. In actual fact, direct democracy was possible precisely because

FIGURE 4.1 Democracy dates back to the ancient Greek city-states
Phillipp Foltz/ Wikimedia Commons / Public Domain

a considerable number of people—most notably, women, slaves, and foreigners—were excluded and did a great deal of the work that enabled citizens to engage in politics.

For much of its history, democracy has been regarded in a negative light. The Greek philosophers—most notably, Plato and Aristotle—argued that democracy was synonymous with mob rule and a perverted form of government, although the latter regarded democracy as the least bad of the three 'deviant' forms of rule: democracy, tyranny, and oligarchy. Much the same picture applied to successive political thinkers. For instance, neither of the key English political theorists of the seventeenth century, John Locke and Thomas Hobbes, were democrats.

The French and American revolutions

The tide began to turn with the French and American revolutions of the eighteenth century. Both revolutions proclaimed democracy as one of their goals and both were influenced by the writings of French political philosopher Jean-Jacques Rousseau. The Americans endorsed democracy, but were still wary of it. The Founding Fathers of the US Constitution—most notably, James Madison (1751–1836)—were very keen to rid themselves of the absolute monarchy of George III. However, they were equally concerned about the effects of introducing majoritarianism (as we shall see). Majority tyranny was, they thought, the ever-present danger of democracy. As a result, the Founding Fathers created a constitution that set up a directly elected legislature, the House of Representatives, but at the same time checked it by separating power between it and the Senate (the other part of the legislature), the executive branch headed by the President, and the judiciary, headed by the Supreme Court.

The nineteenth-century move towards democracy

By the nineteenth century, democracy was beginning to take on more popular connotations in theory and practice. Many countries began the long and slow road towards universal suffrage. In Britain, successive reforms culminated, by 1918, in universal male suffrage and suffrage for some women and, by 1928, in universal adult suffrage. In theoretical terms, the so-called utilitarian theory of democracy associated with Jeremy Bentham and James Mill was extremely influential (**see Key Concept 4.2**).

As Marxist political theorist C. B. Macpherson (1911–87) pointed out (1977: 23–43), the utilitarian theory was the first attempt to apply democracy to a class-divided capitalist industrial society. This gave rise to liberal democracy, which denotes the linking of democracy with the kind of liberal principles originally associated with the industrial middle class. The linking together of democracy and capitalism raised the crucial question of how to reconcile political equality—the ultimate goal of democracy—with economic inequality. The fear of many property owners at the time was that the arrival of universal suffrage would result in a political programme designed to create greater economic equality, thereby putting their privileged position at considerable risk. Despite the rise of the Labour Party in Britain and similar socialist parties elsewhere, there was no great move towards a socialist political programme. Macpherson (1977: 62), and other left-wing academics such

KEY CONCEPT 4.2   **The utilitarian theory of democracy**

The utilitarian theory of democracy is associated with nineteenth-century British political thinker Jeremy Bentham, who developed the theory in association with his
chief disciple, James Mill. Bentham had initially not been concerned about democracy, feeling that an enlightened despot was just as likely to pursue the utilitarian aim
of the greatest happiness. He came to change his mind after the failure of the British
government to implement any of his schemes of reform.

The utilitarian theory of democracy is based on the premise that democracy is
necessary to ensure that those in government will remain accountable to those they
govern. Bentham and Mill argued that, left to their own devices, members of government will maximize their own pleasure. They will only pursue the greatest happiness
of all if their positions in power are dependent upon it. The function of elections is
therefore a protective device to ensure that the preferences of the people are taken
into account by decision-makers.

as Miliband (1972), argued that this was the product of trade union and Labour Party leaders betraying the revolutionary potential evident within the working class.

In the last 30 years or so, the democratic landscape has been transformed again, with a
doubling of the number of states having competitive elections. This is partly a product of
the collapse of the Soviet bloc and the emergence of independent states in Eastern Europe,
but it has also occurred in Southern Europe (Greece, Portugal, and Spain), Latin America
(for example Venezuela), and parts of Africa (for example Botswana) and Asia (for example
Malaysia). From a democratic perspective, this has undoubtedly been an advance, even
though, as we saw, the democratic credentials of the many illiberal states that have accompanied this wave of democratization can be questioned.

 KEY POINTS

- For much of its history, democracy has been regarded in a negative light.
- The turning point was the French and American revolutions in the eighteenth
  century, after which democracy became a more desirable concept.
- The nineteenth century saw a sustained attempt to achieve universal suffrage in
  practice and to justify it in theory. The utilitarian theory of democracy, associated
  with Mill and Bentham, was really the first attempt to try to justify incorporating democracy into a class-divided society. This raises the question: why did the
  advent of democracy not bring about a more economically equal society?
- In the final quarter of the twentieth century, there was an enormous expansion of
  regimes introducing competitive elections and proclaiming themselves democratic.

The Classical versus the Elitist Theory of Democracy

By the twentieth century, democracy was largely shorn of its negative connotations. In academic political theory, the major dispute in the post-1945 period was over two competing theories of democracy. On the one hand was the elitist theory of democracy (also sometimes called the 'revisionist' or 'protective' theory). This theory is particularly associated with Austrian economist and sociologist Joseph Schumpeter (1883–1950), who articulated his theory in the much-cited book *Capitalism, Socialism and Democracy*, originally published in 1942. Against this is the classical theory of democracy, sometimes also referred to as the 'participatory' or 'developmental' theory (**see Key Debate 4.3**).

Schumpeter was reacting to what he saw as the inevitable role played by elites in modern polities. He therefore recognized the importance of the Italian elitists whom we encountered in Chapter 2. However, far from agreeing with their conclusion that democracy is a sham, Schumpeter argues that democracy can be reconciled with elitism. Schumpeter identifies what he describes as the prevailing classical theory of democracy, which he takes to be a model emphasizing the active participation of citizens in the making of political decisions. This model is associated with the practice of the Greek city-states, and the theories of Rousseau and nineteenth-century British political theorist John Stuart Mill. For Schumpeter, however, this model is both unrealistic and undesirable.

See Chapter 2 for an exploration of elitism.

4

KEY DEBATE 4.3   Advocates of the protective and participatory theories of democracy

Protective theory	Participatory theory
Bentham	Greek city-states
James Mill	Rousseau
Schumpeter	John Stuart Mill
Downs	Cole
	Bachrach
	Pateman

Questions

1. Is it possible to reconcile elitism with democracy?
2. Is participatory democracy politically realistic?

The classical model is unrealistic, Schumpeter argues, because mass participation is not a characteristic of modern democratic societies. Empirically, most people appear happy to leave politics to a class of political elites. The classical model is also undesirable, Schumpeter argues, because, in political matters at least, the masses tend to have little knowledge or interest. Partly because of their indifference to politics, the masses are liable to have authoritarian values and to be seduced by charismatic and dictatorial leaders—a view echoed by Kornhauser (1960). It is no accident that Schumpeter was writing at a time when the rise of fascism in Germany and Italy had brought to power such leaders with the apparent consent, some of it enthusiastic, of a large proportion of the masses. Far from being a threat to democracy, then, elites become the protectors of democracy against the authoritarian values of the masses. Some would argue that the rise of populist leaders, usually from the right, in many European liberal democracies and the election of Trump in the US makes Schumpeter's argument in favour of democratic elitism extremely pertinent (Mather and Jefferson, 2016).

Schumpeter seeks to replace this classical theory of democracy with what he perceives to be a more desirable alternative. In a well-known passage, Schumpeter (1961: 269) redefines democracy as 'that institutional arrangement for arriving at political decisions in which individuals acquire the power to decide by means of a competitive struggle for the people's vote'. What is notable about this definition is that there is no emphasis on participation. Decisions are to be left to a political elite. What makes the system democratic, for Schumpeter, is the competition between elites. The voters in this model do not choose between different sets of policies, but rather simply choose between different teams of leaders, who then decide what policies to carry out.

Schumpeter's account has been built upon by other political scientists. In particular, account has been taken of intermediary groups such as trade unions and business organizations with elites of their own who compete with each other in trying to persuade the political leadership to adopt their policies. Kornhauser (1960) argued that this system of elites safeguards liberal democracies from totalitarian regimes and from 'mass society' in general. Without the various intermediary groups, atomized individuals provide an opportunity for an elite to mobilize them, and this may lead to the overthrow of the existing regime and its replacement by a new elite who may have totalitarian intentions.

This elitist theory of democracy held sway in political science circles for twenty or so years after the end of the Second World War. It was reinforced by the so-called economic theory of democracy, which built on the earlier utilitarian model (**see Key Debate 4.4**). These types of theory can be classified as 'protective' models of democracy, in the sense that they are concerned with ensuring that political leaders are accountable to the wishes of the voters. They are concerned, therefore, with democracy as a means to an end of voter utility maximization.

KEY DEBATE 4.4   **The economic theory of democracy and its critics**

One version of the protective theory of democracy is the so-called economic theory of democracy. This is associated with American political scientist Anthony Downs (1930–), who wrote a hugely influential book on this issue in the late 1950s (Downs, 1957). It is a good example of the use of the rational choice approach to political science.

Downs develops a sophisticated explanatory 'economic theory' of democracy, in which he tries to account for the nature of voter choice and party competition. Downs's theory is labelled economic because it shares certain fundamental principles with economics. In particular, advocates of the economic theory of democracy assume certain characteristics of human behaviour from which the theory is deduced. Humans are regarded as individualistic utility maximizers, whose aim is to achieve benefits for themselves at the least possible cost.

For Downs, the behaviour of politicians and voters is analogous to the behaviour of producers and consumers in the economy.

- Political parties and politicians are equivalent to producers. Just as producers seek to maximize profit, politicians seek to maximize votes. Their only goal is to win power.

- Likewise, just as consumers seek the best buy for their money, voters seek to 'buy' at the cheapest possible price the set of policies that will serve their interests the most. As a result, parties must offer the voters what they want or they will not win enough votes to gain power.

Based on these simple principles, Downs constructs a whole model of competitive party politics. He suggests that voters can be located on an ideological continuum from left to right and that political parties will seek to place themselves at the point where the majority of voters are situated, the vote maximization position.

There have been a number of pertinent criticisms of this model.

- It is overly simplistic. For example, it is inadequate to focus on just one ideological continuum, since that does not take into account the complexities of voter preferences. Moreover, voter choice is not simply about competing ideologies; a crucial dimension of voter choice is voter perceptions of the competence of politicians. This is not easily located on the kind of spectrum Downs uses.

- It is by no means certain that voters and politicians behave in the way that Downs tells us they do.

  - Evidence suggests that at least some voters use their vote in an altruistic way on the grounds of principle rather than merely in their own self-interest.

  - Similarly, to describe politicians as merely vote maximizers is surely too simplistic. Parties may recognize that they have to win votes in order to gain power, but this is different from saying that they have no principles they want to promote.

- Even more devastating for the economic theory of democracy is the evidence which suggests that many voters do not have the level of sophistication that the economic theory demands (Robertson, 1976: 177–81). According to the alternative party identification model, voters choose between parties not on the basis of their perceptions of a party's particular policies, but because they have a long-standing psychological identification with a party. As a result, their support for a party does not change when the party's policies change.

- The economic theory of democracy also finds it difficult to explain why most people bother to vote at all (Barry, 1970: 13–22). For the economic theory, voting is a cost that is only worth paying if the benefits of voting outweigh these costs. Given this, it is only worthwhile voting if the vote makes a difference to the result. The chances of one vote making this amount of difference are minimal.

- The economic theory of democracy takes voter preferences as given. It therefore neglects to consider the possibility that these preferences are shaped by powerful forces in society and not least by the political parties themselves, particularly when they have governmental power (Dunleavy and Ward, 1981).

Questions

1. What is 'economic' about the economic theory of democracy?
2. Do voters and politicians behave in the ways suggested by the economic theory of democracy?
3. Is there any point in voting?

An alternative model can be described as a 'participatory' or 'developmental' model of democracy. This is enshrined in the classical theory of democracy, although this label contains as many differences as similarities. The developmental model is more concerned with democracy as an end in itself—that is, participation is itself enriching. It is not, as for the protective theory, a burden to be undertaken in order to ensure that politicians are accountable. Rather, participation is to be valued for the positive effect it has on individual characteristics. Individuals who participate, it is argued, become more virtuous and intelligent; they understand the need for cooperation and their own self-worth increases, as does their status in the eyes of others.

The antecedents of the developmental model are in the practice of the Greek city-states and the political philosophy of Rousseau, J. S. Mill, and the unjustly neglected British socialist thinker G. D. H. Cole (1889–1959) (Wright, 1979). Support for it began to re-emerge in the 1960s. A new breed of radical democratic theorists began to challenge the elite theory (Bachrach, 1967; Duncan and Lukes, 1964; Pateman, 1970). They argued that, by abandoning the participatory element, the elitist theory of democracy had lost sight of the true meaning of democracy. Any notion of rule by the people had been abandoned. What was needed, then, was the rediscovery of participation in the political process.

Assessing the validity of these competing theories of democracy is a difficult task, not least because the meaning of the concept is disputed. Two observations about these competing models of democracy are particularly important here. One is that if democracy can be defined first and foremost as political equality, then the elite theory of democracy stretches the label to its absolute limits. Schumpeter was, arguably, trying to say that the rule of political elites, albeit in a competitive environment, is, for a variety of reasons, preferable to mass participation in politics. As a result, democracy ought to be limited in the interests of other goals such as stability and efficiency. In other words, Schumpeter is really espousing a mixed form of government combining democracy with other values. The problem is that, by the time Schumpeter was writing, democracy had such positive connotations that it was difficult for him to admit to wanting to limit it.

On the other hand, we can say that advocates of the developmental model must be able to show that their version of democracy is not undesirable and unrealistic, and this, indeed, is what much of the developmental literature seeks to do. For example, advocates of this model would say that political apathy is not inevitable, that people can be encouraged to participate more, and that, once they start, they will improve at it. Some may, perhaps, be less likely as a result to exhibit authoritarian values. Political apathy, they would continue, is partly a product of the lack of participation in decision-making in the working environment. Of great importance to the developmentalists, therefore, is industrial democracy (Pateman, 1970). As Lively (1975: 38) astutely remarks, 'it does not follow from the fact that "classical" democracy does not exist that it cannot ever exist; nor does it force us to redefine democracy, for it might just as well lead us to the conclusion that Western systems are not democracies or are only imperfect democracies'.

Finally, advocates of the developmental model have to show that participation is possible (Arblaster, 2002: 84–5). Here, technological developments would seem to be on their side, offering the possibility of greater involvement in politics through, for instance, the use of the Internet and interactive-TV technology. In a large complex society, the use of referendums, whereby all electors vote on a particular issue, is a direct democratic way of increasing involvement. They are used in many countries, particularly Switzerland and the US, and were used, very successfully, to decide on Scottish independence in 2014 and, more contentiously, the UK's membership of the EU in 2016.

✳ KEY POINTS

- The modern debate has been between exponents of the elite theory of democracy, on the one hand, and the participatory theory of democracy, on the other.

- In the post-1945 period, the elitist theory, associated above all with Schumpeter, held sway. The classical theory, associated with participation and citizen involvement in decision-making, was regarded as undesirable and unrealistic.

- The elitist theory began to be challenged from the 1960s by a new breed of participationists, eager to show the developmental possibilities of greater citizen involvement. The success of their enterprise depends on showing that greater participation is both desirable and realistic.

Problems with Democracy

Unfashionable though it may be, it is nevertheless important to note some arguments that have been made against democracy. Three issues are particularly worthy of consideration. The first of these, the New Right criticism of democracy, we encountered in Chapter 2. Here, it will be remembered, the citizens of democratic political systems are prone to bombard their governments with ever-increasing demands. In turn, these governments have a tendency to try to meet these demands, irrespective of the economic consequences, because they fear the electoral consequences of not doing so. The result is that government becomes overloaded and top-heavy, and may even go bankrupt (Rose and Peters, 1978).

▶ See Chapter 2 for the New Right overload thesis.

Such a scenario was particularly popular in the 1970s, a decade when Western governments appeared powerless in the wake of continual industrial unrest, excessive wage claims (particularly amongst public sector workers), and spiralling public spending. It is perhaps less relevant, however, after several decades in which voters have apparently been able to accept the need for governments to balance the books, even if that results in the austerity measures deemed necessary by free-market politicians.

The second argument challenging the value of democracy relates to the distinction between procedure and outcome. Democracy is a procedure, a method of making decisions, but there is no guarantee that this procedure will produce outcomes that we might desire. This is partly an issue of the role of experts. In a democracy, where political equality is the major objective, the views of experts carry no greater weight that those of ordinary voters. And yet, as Plato argued many centuries ago, there is strong case for the rule of the most able.

The potential discrepancy between procedure and outcome is also partly an issue of values. In other words, we might value a particular goal—for example liberty, equality, a clean environment—but there is no guarantee that a democratic procedure will guarantee the outcome we may desire. We can make two points about this. The first is that most values are contested—that is, for every person who values a more free society, there will be one who values a more equal one. Given this, there needs to be some device to decide which goal, for now at least, predominates. A democratic system would then, of course, give those who lost out the chance to refight, and possibly win, the argument at some time in the future. The second point is that some goals might be so important that we want to insulate them against majority decisions taken in a democracy. It is this issue of majoritarianism that constitutes the third problem with democracy.

▶ See Chapter 7 for an exploration of the state, democracy, and political legitimacy.

As we will see in Chapter 7, many would argue that, to be legitimate, a state must be democratic. This, of course, is why democracy has become such a desirable form of rule. It is regarded in such a positive light because if we have a voice in making the laws under which we live, then they are likely to be in our interests and therefore we get what we want. In other words, we do not lose anything as a result of being in a political community. Democracy, then, has a strong claim to be the political system that would be chosen by people in the state of nature scenario that, as we shall see in Chapter 7, has been an influential device used by social contract theorists.

One of the principal problems with democracy, however, is that we are very rarely going to arrive at unanimous decisions. As a result, democratic government means, in practice, following the view of the majority. There are a number of problems with the majoritarian principle. In the first place, it is well documented that where there are more than two alternatives on which voters can have preferences, then it is difficult to reach a majority decision (Lively, 1975: 14–15). Of course, in practice too, many governments in the UK and presidents in the US are not elected with the majority of votes. This is explained by the use of the first-past-the-post, or plurality rule, electoral system, where the winning candidate merely has to gain more votes than any other candidate. This system is used in the UK, the US, Canada, Jamaica, and India, although most countries now use electoral systems where there is a more proportional relationship between the seats won and the votes cast. This avoids the discrepancies that can occur in countries using plurality rule voting where there are more than two significant parties.

Even if majority rule can be established in practice, it is far from clear that it is the most appropriate political mechanism. For one thing, pure majority rule leaves open the possibility that a government can be elected with majority support, but which then intends to deny the principle of majoritarianism in the future. The best example of this was in Algeria in 1991, when the Islamic Salvation Front won a majority of the seats (although not the votes) in the country's first multiparty elections. With a doubtful commitment to multiparty democracy, the military intervened, cancelling the second round and banning all political parties based on religion. This was then followed by a violent civil war. This raises the question whether it is ever justified, on democratic grounds, to prevent a government with a majority of votes and/or seats from taking power.

Even if the principle of majoritarianism is maintained, however, there is the problem that arises from the fact that some people in every decision made are going to find themselves in a minority. If we accept that democratic decisions are those taken by majority votes, then what happens to those who find themselves in a minority? Do we still expect them to obey the law even though they did not support it and does this not risk the minority being exploited by the majority to the extent that their rights are infringed (**see Case Study 4.5**)?

There are some political philosophers who want to suggest that we cannot expect such people to obey a law that they did not support (see Chapter 7). In practice, of course, we may just have to accept that democracy is not perfect and console ourselves with the thought that at least a majority-rule decision ensures that more people than not are on the winning side. What we can say is that the position of minorities is made much worse if the same people find themselves permanently in a minority. Usually, this does not happen because there are shifting or fluid minorities—that is, everyone can expect to be in a minority from time to time. As a result, the majority in any particular instance is less likely to harm the minority's interests fundamentally because those in the majority know that at some future point they may find themselves in the minority.

See Chapter 7 for a critique of democracy as a source of state legitimacy.

CASE STUDY 4.5 Democracy, rights, and hunting

One interesting example of the potential conflict between the application of majoritarianism and the protection of rights is the debate about hunting in Britain. The hunting community has used a variety of arguments to support the continuation of hunting (**see Figure 4.2**), but one strategy has been to employ the ideals of liberalism and the protection of individual rights. Here, it has been argued that, despite the fact that hunting has been regularly opposed by a majority of British people in opinion polls and a majority of MPs in the House of Commons, it still does not justify a ban because it is illegitimate for a majority to impose its own moral views on the minority. To take such an action is a serious infringement of rights. This rights defence of hunting, however, has so far fallen on deaf ears despite the hunting community's attempt to undermine the legislative ban by appealing to the Human Rights Act 1998.

FIGURE 4.2
© Elle1/ Shutterstock.com

The persecution of a minority is much more likely to take place where there is a permanent majority and a permanent minority. The classic case of this is in Northern Ireland, where traditionally most issues have been decided on ethno-nationalist lines, with Protestants in the majority and Catholics in the minority on key issues. Clearly, such a situation is likely to cause problems and it was the persistent discrimination faced by the minority Catholic community that led to the resurgence of the Troubles in the late 1960s. A form of rule known as **consociational democracy**, involving the sharing of power in divided societies, is one possible solution to this problem of entrenched minorities.

See Chapter 11 for a further discussion of consociationalism.

KEY POINTS

- A number of problems have been noted with democracy, including its alleged tendency to lead to government overload, and the potential conflict between procedure and outcome.

- The issue of majoritiarianism is, perhaps, the most serious problem with democracy. The problem with democracy as a source of state legitimacy is that few, if any, decisions are going to be made unanimously. As a result, the minority are going to have to accept decisions with which they disagree, thereby reducing their freedom.

- Fluid minorities are less of a problem than permanent minorities. The latter are more likely to lead to the oppression of a minority.

New Directions in Democratic Thought

Traditionally, thinking about democracy has been based on a number of assumptions (Saward, 2001). Three are particularly important. The first is that democracy only applies to the political unit of the nation-state—that is, democracy refers to the character of the political institutions in any particular sovereign state. The second is that democracy is principally about the aggregation of preferences—that is, it is assumed that a democratic outcome is one that measures accurately the preferences of the electorate with devices such as elections and referendums. Providing that all adults are allowed to register a preference, the outcome is regarded as a democratic one. Little interest or concern has traditionally been expressed about how these preferences are created in the first place. The third assumption is that the membership of the political community is settled. Debates about the extent of the democratic community have, it is said, been resolved now that universal suffrage has been achieved.

Recent developments in democratic theory challenge all three of these assumptions. In this chapter, we look at four theories that illustrate this change of direction in democratic theory.

Associative democracy

This approach, associated most notably with Paul Hirst (1996), provides an alternative to the state-centric focus of much democratic thought. Associative democracy seeks to reduce the role of the state by advocating the democratic role of voluntary, self-governing associations within civil society. It therefore seeks to provide a 'Third Way' between free-market capitalism and state socialism. The state's role is to be reduced, but decisions are not to be left to the vagaries of the market. Rather, it envisages considerable political participation and decision-making beyond the reaches of the formal state.

Cosmopolitan democracy

The associative theory of democracy challenges the assumption that democracy must be focused on the state. Another, better known, theory that also challenges that assumption is the cosmopolitan theory of democracy. Here, it is suggested (for example by Held, 2006: 304–9) that given that citizens of nation-states are increasingly affected, if not dominated, by forces happening beyond the boundaries of the particular nation-state within which they live, then what matters now is ensuring that global forces are controlled by democratic means. This requires that the international level of inclusion be at the level of the individual and not, or not exclusively, the state. As Weale (2007: 239) points out: 'Just as democracy had to make the transition from the city-state to the nation-state, so it must now make the transition to the international global order.'

An alternative approach to the undemocratic implications of globalization is to 'urge *strengthening* the sovereignty of (democratic) states by defending their internal political structures against external constraint and interference' (Cunningham, 2002: 201). Of course, the cosmopolitan model is based on the assumption that globalization is a reality. This is a position challenged by those holding a realist view of international relations, which still puts the nation-state at the centre of political analysis. It is also based on the principle that state representation is insufficiently democratic. This is because states are unequal in power and influence and therefore, the political influence of individuals varies depending on which nation-state they live in.

Democratic theorists, cosmopolitan democrats argue, should therefore be focusing on ensuring that international institutions are both effective controllers of global developments and that they themselves are under democratic control. A number of institutional arrangements have been suggested. Held (2006: 306), for one, suggests the creation of regional parliaments with the power to make decisions binding in international law and the introduction of referendums across national boundaries. The EU would be a good model of this. Archibugi (1995), similarly, proposes the creation of a Second Assembly within the United Nations, to coexist alongside the General Assembly. Representation would be based on population size, so that the most populated states would get more seats than less populated states. Such a system would therefore allow people from autocratic states to have some democratic representation.

Where the existing sovereign state fits into this model is not clear and, as Hoffman and Graham (2006: 119) point out, this rather undermines the radical force of Held's argument. For them (Hoffman and Graham, 2006: 123), the 'concept of a "cosmopolitan democracy" can only be coherently sustained if the international community ceases to be composed of states'. This, of course, raises the prospect of how realistic cosmopolitan democracy is. Even if it is realistic for the representation of states to coexist with the representation of individuals at the international level, problems remain. Chief among these are the issues of whether a viable international institution of individuals is possible given the scale of representation required and the lack of a common cultural heritage. Added to this is the relevance of such an institution given that institutions representing states are still likely to be necessary if viable international agreements are to be arrived at (Weale, 2007: 239–41).

Deliberative democracy

The third new direction in democratic theory challenges the assumption that democracy is merely about the aggregation of preferences. Deliberative democracy, heavily influenced by the ideas of German philosopher Jurgen Habermas, has become the most written and talked about new theory of democracy (**see Key Debate 4.6**), and there is now an extensive and varied literature on the subject, of which Elstub and McLaverty (2014) provide a comprehensive review. Because of the extent and variety of the literature, it is probably misleading to talk about one account of deliberative democracy. Nevertheless, it is possible to elicit a number of key features shared among a vast majority of the exponents of deliberative democracy.

The first feature is that democracy ought to be defined neither in terms of the aggregation of pre-existing preferences in a vote at elections or in a referendum nor in terms of a reflection of the balance of competing interests within civil society, as the pluralist model has it. Rather, for advocates of deliberative democracy, collective decisions are only legitimate if they are made after reasoned and detailed discussion. Second, it is held that genuinely deliberative arenas ought to be as inclusive as possible, with all points of view and social characteristics represented, and an equal chance to participate offered to all of those who are present. Third, during deliberation, self-interest should be put aside, as should strategic behaviour designed to achieve as much as possible of a pre-existing agenda. Instead, mutual respect of, and empathy for, the arguments of others is encouraged.

Deliberative democracy, then, encourages participants to be open to the views of others, to listen to what they have to say, and to empathize with their point of view. There is a supposed 'moralizing effect' of deliberation (Niemeyer, 2004)—that is, genuine deliberation involves the advancement of arguments by citizens about what is right and in the general or public interest, not about what is in the self-interest of participants. One can contrast genuine deliberation here with the dominance of powerful vested interests that, it is said, is prevalent in traditional interest group politics.

 KEY DEBATE 4.6   **A critique of deliberative democracy**

A number of criticisms have been made of deliberative democracy, as follows.

- It is unrealistic to expect anything other than a small minority to be able to engage in genuine deliberation. To create a universal deliberative system involving everyone is impossible because of time, logistical, and resource constraints. This would seem to mean that we have a choice. We may opt

4

for a genuinely deliberative system that is politically unequal because only a few will be able to take part. It may, for instance, be only political elites, such as professional politicians, who are able to engage in genuine deliberation. The alternative is to maximize participation to enhance political equality through, for instance, increasing the number of referendums held. This would be done, though, at the expense of deliberation. We would therefore seem to be faced with a choice between deliberation and political equality (Parkinson, 2006).

- Some empirical research has found that human beings do not always behave in the way that deliberative democracy theory says they will (Mutz, 2008). There is, for instance, an inability and/or unwillingness to understand complex social, political, and economic issues, and a tendency to follow the dominant majority in group settings, to fit in with the crowd.

- Although there is some evidence from the research of actual deliberative events undertaken that people's views are sometimes transformed, it is—not surprisingly, perhaps—less likely that those with a strong opinion on a topic will change their view on a topic or empathize with the views of others. The implication of this is that deliberation only really works on issues that matter less to people.

- There is evidence that participant's views can be transformed by the provision of information they were not aware of before. It should be pointed out, however, that this can be separated from the deliberation process itself. In other words, one could endeavour to provide comprehensive and balanced information on an issue without requiring those making a decision to then deliberate about it.

- Some political theorists have argued that without some fundamental reforms to the balance of power among competing interests in contemporary liberal democracies, deliberative democracy merely reproduces existing inequalities, advantaging the already powerful. These inequalities are based, in part, on finance, but also go wider, to include the type of communication (rational and formal debate) valued by advocates of deliberative democracy and the possibility of discourse hegemony (Young, 2000).

- The emphasis placed on minimizing difference and conflict in deliberative theory has been criticized by some for unrealistically denying the real purpose of politics, which is predicated on the existence of widely diverse interests and values (Mouffe, 2005).

Questions

1. How does deliberative democracy differ from conventional theories of democracy?
2. Critically examine the claims made for deliberative democracy.

The fourth feature of deliberative democracy is that the inclusive communication and social learning inherent in the deliberative process, it is suggested, leads to better decisions in the sense that they are more informed, more effective, more just, and therefore more legitimate. Finally, and probably most importantly, deliberation, it is argued, increases the possibility of a consensus being arrived at and the transformation of the views of participants. What is important, then, is not what the preferences are at the start of deliberation, but what they are *after* deliberation.

Advocates of deliberative democracy differ about the best site for deliberation. Some focus on the benefits of small-scale so-called mini-publics, such as citizen juries and deliberative polls—the latter involving a small section of the population engaging in debates about an issue and being polled before and after the deliberation in order to see if their views have altered (Fishkin, Jowell, and Luskin, 2002). Other deliberative theorists, by contrast, talk in terms of deliberative political institutions such as legislatures (Steiner et al., 2004) or of a 'deliberative system' within civil society (Dryzek, 2010). Advocates of deliberative democracy differ too over who should do the deliberating. Deliberative participants can be ordinary members of the public or elite policy-makers. They can also be partisans, with a definite view about a topic, or non-specialists with no particular position or vested interest. Deliberative theorists differ in addition over the collective goal of deliberation. Some think that the goal is consensus, where no disagreement between the participants remains, whereas other advocates think that an acceptance of the legitimacy of the procedure is all that matters and the best we can achieve. In the latter camp, Gutmann and Thompson (1996) are particularly notable: they argue that the goal of deliberation is what they call an 'economy of moral disagreement', in the sense that there is a greater acceptance of the terms of difference and disagreement. In other words, differences of opinion are acceptable provided that there is a greater recognition and empathy with the views you disagree with.

Ecological democracy

The fourth and final new democratic theory can be described as 'ecological democracy' because the impetus for it has come mainly from green political theorists who have sought to explore the relationship between the objectives of the environmental movement, on the one hand, and the political process, on the other. They start with the question: should environmentalists be democrats? The conventional answer is that the relationship between environmentalism and democracy is a contingent one: sometimes, the democratic process might produce outcomes that environmentalists are happy with; sometimes, it will not. The relationship between democracy and environmentalism is a contingent one because democracy is a process (a theory of agency) and environmentalism is substantive (a theory of value). There is no guarantee that any particular theory of agency will support a particular theory of value (Goodin, 1992: 168). In the case of the environment, in other words, there is absolutely no guarantee that any particular democratically elected legislature or executive is going to be concerned enough about it to consider prioritizing it above other political issues.

It might be thought that that is all there is to it. Two responses to the contingency conclusion, however, have followed. The first is the suggestion that deliberative democracy is more likely to produce political outcomes favourable to environmental protection (Smith, 2003). The second is the suggestion by some green political thinkers that the membership of the democratic community ought to be expanded. As we saw, with the attainment of universal suffrage this question of who is to be a member of the democratic political community (that is, who counts) was regarded as settled. Some green political theorists, however, question this assumption. They argue that restricting the political community to currently living humans is too limiting because it has the effect of excluding other entities with important interests who are entitled to have these interests represented.

One such important group is future generations. Future generations have important interests that may conflict with ours. For example, we may want to maximize our economic prosperity, but this may cause irreversible problems for generations to come. We might use up all of a particular resource so that there is none left for those not yet born, or we might pollute the planet so that the quality of life for future generations will be much reduced or even non-existent. Even more radical is the claim that democracy is illegitimately anthropocentric—that is, it is too focused on humans. After all, non-humans—animals and nature as a whole—have interests that may conflict with ours. And these interests will be ignored if only humans are members of the democratic political community.

Academic literature has emerged that tries to work out how we might incorporate the interests of the currently excluded. Ingenious schemes have been proposed in which humans act as proxies for future generations and nature, which representatives are allocated some seats in legislative assemblies (Dobson, 1996). An alternative suggestion is for the creation of counter-majoritarian devices designed to impede the will of the majority (Ekeli, 2009). So, for instance, it could be written into a constitution that any legislation has to show that its provisions will not seriously damage the interests of future generations or nature (Hayward, 2005). Other means that have been suggested for helping the political system to incorporate the interests of future generations include giving more political power to the young, on the grounds that the young have a greater interest in the future than older citizens do.

Merely stating that future generations and nature have interests, of course, does not, by itself, justify extending the boundary of the *demos* to include them (**see Key Debate 4.7**). The ecological view of democracy relies upon a particular principle of inclusion. This is the so-called all-affected principle (Goodin, 2007). This is one answer to the so-called boundary problem, or problem of inclusion, in democratic theory, which asks: how do we decide who is to be included in the *demos*? Who is to count as 'the people'? The all-affected principle responds by saying that everyone affected by decisions made has a categorical right to participate in the process of making those decisions.

KEY DEBATE 4.7 A critique of ecological democracy

The ecological theory of democracy is dependent on the validity of the all-affected principle as an answer to the boundary problem in democratic theory. But this is only one answer to the boundary problem. We might, for instance, want to say that inclusion in the *demos* requires significant cognitive capacities. After all, we restrict the franchise to prevent children from voting on the grounds that we do not regard them as sufficiently competent to participate in politics. If we adopt this approach, then it also provides a justification for excluding non-humans from democratic inclusion. That does not mean that we have no moral obligations to non-human animals, but that they do not have a democratic right that their interests be represented.

There are also objections to including future generations within a democratic polity. Can we really know what their interests are? Can we really know all the effects of our actions to make a solid assessment of the impact those actions will have on future generations? How far down the line must we go—one generation? Two? Three? Four? And do all of these generations have the same weight of interest as ours? Should not the interests of currently living humans take precedence over those of future generations? For these reasons and others, some scholars have argued that even if we must take the interests of future generations into account, their interests cannot carry the same weight as ours and should be discounted gradually in line with how far away from us in time they are (Page, 2006).

Questions

1. How should we decide who is to be included in a democratic polity?

2. What are the problems associated with the all-affected principle as an answer to the boundary problem in democratic theory?

 KEY POINTS

- Traditional democratic thinking has been based on a number of assumptions concerning the site of democratic institutions, the measuring of democratic decisions, and the boundary of the democratic community.

- New theories of democracy challenge all of these assumptions.

- The state-centric character of traditional democratic theory and practice is challenged by the associative and cosmopolitan theories of democracy. The aggregative measuring of preferences is challenged by deliberative democracy. The widely accepted limits to the democratic community is challenged by ecological theories of democracy.

Conclusion

We have seen in this chapter that however democracy is defined, it is almost universally feted. When we come to examine its claims to be the most desirable form of rule, however, we come up, in particular, against the problem of what to do with the minority consequences of majoritarianism. The obvious solution to the problem of minorities is to introduce some device protecting their interests. Many political systems, including the US, do just this by including a bill of rights protecting individuals against the majority. In the US, this was included precisely because the Founding Fathers were concerned about the potential dangers of majority rule, or 'majority tyranny' as they called it. The problem here is that it must be questioned how democratic such a bill of rights is. Again, using the Supreme Court in the US as an example, its members are not elected and not removable except under the most extraordinary circumstances.

The protection of some rights—such as the right to free speech, the right to form political associations, and, of course, the right to life—is essential for democracy to function. More pertinently, from the perspective of the subject matter of this chapter, a democratic decision taken with the will of the majority may lead to the sacrifice of negative rights (for example the right to property) in favour of the achievement of more positive ones (for example, the right to free education). Alternatively, the achievement of positive rights may be used as a reason, or as an excuse, for a failure to introduce democracy. For example, in China, the political leadership published a White Paper on democracy in 2005 in which the postponement of democratic reforms was justified partly on the grounds that economic development, and the achievement of better standards of living, were a priority (State Council Information Office, 2005). The upholding of (at least some) rights, then, is not necessarily compatible with democracy. Perhaps our conclusion should be that democracy is not as special as we previously thought and that we should regard other principles, such as the protection of individual rights, as more important (**see Case Study 4.5**).

In many ways, the debate about the implications of majoritarianism might be regarded as rather old-fashioned now. A widespread feeling that modern democratic politics, dominated by money, powerful interests, and the media, is deeply flawed—coupled with the rise of globalization and the ominous threat of climate change—has led to challenges to the central assumptions of traditional democratic theory. Equally, perhaps, it should be asked whether democracy, particularly of the participationist and deliberative variety, is the most appropriate way of dealing with some of the world's most intractable problems. In this context, should not, it might be asked, the role of experts be allowed full rein in order that the interests of the whole planet are put before the self-interested utility-maximizing that passes for electoral choice in much of the democratic world?

? Key Questions

- What is democracy?
- Distinguish between direct democracy, democratic elitism, representative democracy, and deliberative democracy. Which is to be preferred?
- Is democratic elitism a contradiction in terms?
- Is participatory democracy desirable and realistic?
- Is democracy special?
- Is democracy consistent with a class-divided society?
- Discuss the relationship between democracy and majority rule.
- How far should we regard democracy as the ideal way of making political decisions?
- Is cosmopolitan democracy possible and desirable?
- Should democracy only involve humans?

||\ Further Reading

Elstub, S., and McLaverty, P. (2014), *Deliberative Democracy: Issues and Cases* (Edinburgh: Edinburgh University Press).
A current review of the most important contemporary development in democratic theory.

Held, D. (2006), *Models of Democracy* (Cambridge: Polity, 3rd edn).
Probably the best general text on democracy, coupling comprehensive descriptions with astute evaluation.

Macpherson, C. B. (1977), *The Life and Times of Liberal Democracy* (Oxford: Oxford University Press).
A contentious account of the development of democratic thought and practice. Compelling reading.

Shapiro, I. (2003), *The Moral Foundations of Politics* (New Haven, CT: Yale University Press).
An admirably concise account of the answers given by political theorists to the question of political obligation.

Weale, A. (2007), *Democracy* (Basingstoke: Palgrave, 2nd edn).
A sound introduction to the major themes in democratic theory, now in its second edition.

Web Links

http://www.chinadaily.com.cn/english/doc/2005-10/19/content_486206.htm
The full text of the Chinese White Paper on Democracy.

https://www.freedomhouse.org
A useful site that rates countries according to their degree of freedom and democracy.

Visit the **Online Resources** that accompany this book to access more learning resources on this topic: www.oup.com/uk/ferdinand/

Democracies, Democratization, and Authoritarian Regimes

5

- The Spread of Democracy
- Democratization
- Types of Democracy
- Measuring Democracy
- Variety in Democracy
- The Persistence of Authoritarian Regimes

- Conclusion: Smarter Democracy, Deeper Democracy, or towards Democratic–Authoritarian Hybridity?
- Key Questions
- Further Reading
- Web Links

Reader's Guide

Democracy and democratization have long been among the most widely researched and most hotly contested topics in comparative politics. More recently, there has been a resurgence in interest in authoritarian systems, as many have survived the wave of democratization that took place in the 1980s and 1990s. This chapter will first outline the main approaches to analysing democratization. It will then consider different analytical models of democracy and indexes to measure democracy. Then, it will survey the more recent literature on authoritarian systems and why they persist. The final part of this chapter will discuss the challenges that confront democracy in the face of this authoritarian revival.

The Spread of Democracy

According to Freedom House in the US, there were 122 electoral democracies in the world in 2013, which represented 63 per cent of the 195 countries and territories surveyed (Freedom House, 2014). This is an enormous increase compared with the end of the 1980s, when just 41 per cent of 167 states were democracies. The first time that a majority of states in the world were democratic was 1992–93 (Freedom House, 2015). Clearly, the collapse of communist regimes in Eastern Europe and the former Soviet Union (FSU) was the most important factor in this change, but it was not the only one. Replacement of authoritarian regimes by democracies had already started in the 1970s. According to Huntington (1991), there have been three 'waves' of democratization around the world since the nineteenth century (**see Table 5.1**).

The 'third wave' of democratization began in 1974 with the demise of the long-standing authoritarian regime in Portugal, followed by the end of Franco's dictatorship in neighbouring Spain the following year. The World Values survey in 2000 showed that at least 63 per cent of respondents in 79 out of 80 countries agreed with the proposition that 'democracy may have its problems, but it's better than any other form of government'. Nigeria was the sole exception, with only 45 per cent agreeing (Inglehart et al., 2004: tab. E123).

TABLE 5.1 The three waves of democratization

1828–1926	1943–62	1974–
US	Uruguay	Portugal
UK	Brazil	Spain
France	Argentina	Argentina
Switzerland	Colombia	Brazil
Italy	Peru	Philippines
Argentina	Venezuela	Taiwan
	W. Germany	S. Korea
	Italy	Pakistan
	Japan	E. Europe
	India	Former Soviet Union
	Sri Lanka	Mexico
	Philippines	Nigeria
	Israel	S. Africa

Source: Huntington (1991: 16–26).

All of this suggests that democracy has become the predominant legitimate form of state organization around the world.

Democratization

Why do people embrace democracy? According to an important recent study by Welzel (2013), World Values Surveys over more than 20 years show that the aspiration for democracy is part of a more general syndrome of emancipative values—the aspiration to be free from external domination and dependency.

For a discussion of why democracy is regarded as special, see Chapter 4.

Democracy is conventionally held to have originated in ancient Athens in the fifth century BC. Certainly, the term itself came from classical Greek, designating a different form of rule from that of aristocracy or dictatorship. However, Keane (2009) has argued in his magisterial history of democracy that the practice of communities running their affairs through assemblies is much older—up to two millennia older—and can be traced back at least to Persia, India, and the Phoenician Empire. The term 'democracy' may be Western, but the practice has never been exclusively Western.

See Chapter 4 for a further discussion of democracy.

Political science has generated an enormous literature to analyse the global rise of democracy over the last 30 years. Basically, it divides into two types of analysis: first, long-term trends of modernization that create preconditions for democracy and opportunities for democratic entrepreneurs; and second, the sequences of more short-term events and actions of key actors at moments of national crisis that have precipitated a democratic transition—what has sometimes been dubbed 'transitology'. Let us consider these two alternative approaches in turn.

Long-term structural trends (i): economic development

One constantly recurring claim has been that the emergence of democracy is part of a broader pattern of modernization. An influential early example of this approach was Lerner's *The Passing of Traditional Society* (1958), which focused mainly on the Middle East. It suggested that modernization led to increasing convergence of social, economic, and political structures, as well as ways of life. 'Modern' people around the world had more in common with each other than they did with the remaining 'tradition-oriented' sections of their separate societies. And what had driven this transformation, according to Lerner? Primarily, it was economic change.

This sparked one of the most heatedly debated trends in the study of democratization, which continues to the present day: the possible connection between economic development and democratic change. Lipset (1959) argued that the more prosperous a nation, the greater its ability to sustain democracy. Over the last 50 years, this claim has provoked a veritable flood of analyses of evidence for and against. According to Huntington (1991), historical evidence showed that states with a per capita income of at least US$3,000 (in contemporary nominal, not purchasing power parity, terms) were very unlikely to see a successful military overthrow of a democratically elected civilian government. While this did not explicitly equate to a claim that democracy was assured in states with that level of per capita income, it was very suggestive.

Subsequently, Przeworski et al. (2000) qualified the argument by distinguishing between the role of economic development in launching democratization and its role in strengthening democracy once it had been established. They claimed that there was no persuasive evidence of economic development bringing about democratization; only of it strengthening democracy once established. Soon afterwards, however, Boix and Stokes (2003) rebutted this argument with equally weighty statistical evidence to claim that it did bring about democratization. In any case, whichever was true, no one could claim there were no exceptions. India is regularly cited as a counterfactual example to both theories, since it has been a functioning democracy almost continuously since Independence in 1947, despite the fact that even now its per capita income, at around US$1,500, is still below the level predicted to bring democratic stability. On the other hand, Singapore, with a per capita income estimated by the World Bank in 2013 at US$55,183, still is not a democracy. Even if either explanation could claim validation from the trajectories of most democracies in the world, the most that either of them could demonstrate is correlation, not causation. This raises the question of why economic development should lead to democratic change.

Long-term structural trends (ii): the rise of the middle class

Again, it was Lipset (1960) who suggested the first and most influential hypothesis. Economic development depended on the emergence of a middle class whose interests and ambitions led them to challenge traditional elites and demand a share in national affairs, which could only be satisfied by democracy. This was what the history of Western Europe showed. This too has led to a welter of studies that seek to identify and theorize the political aspirations and activities of middle classes in states around the world. For Barrington Moore (1966: 418), the converse also applied in the past to Russia and China: why had they not democratized? As he put it, 'no bourgeois, no democracy'. Historically, he argued, authoritarian rule there had prevented the emergence of an independent-minded bourgeoisie.

Until the third wave of democracy, this supposition seemed generally plausible. To some extent, Huntington's analysis could be said to have updated this approach, since a higher level of development might be assumed to require a more developed middle class too. It still applies. For example, one of the key factors that led to the refashioning of democracy in Turkey under the Justice and Democracy Party (*Adalet ve Kalkinma Partisi*, or AKP) since 2002 has been the material support and encouragement of Muslim small businessmen in the Anatolian heartland (Bugre and SavasKan, 2014).

But Huntington's analysis is not universally valid. It is difficult to argue that the middle classes played the key role in the downfall of the communist regimes of Eastern

Europe and the FSU, or in the Arab Spring. Also, in 'developmental states' (identified in Chapter 1) outside the West, the state has dominated the middle class in directing development. Businesses there tend to be more dependent on the state for finance, contracts, and favours, so they are more cautious about advocating political and economic liberalization for fear of being penalized by government. For example, in China, where even though per capita income in 2013 was calculated by the IMF and the World Bank at US$6,700–6,900, which puts it at the top end of the range when a transition to democracy might be expected, the state continues to dominate the economy and resist democratization (State Council Information Office, 2005; Nathan, 2013; Chen, 2013).

So analysis of the path to democratization in any particular country requires consideration of a wider range of factors.

Short-term explanations: 'transitology'

Other attempts to theorize the reasons for the relative success or failure of democratization have focused on more immediate, short-term factors. The collapse of communist regimes and the rising wave of democratization in the 1990s sparked academic and policy-oriented analysis, which is sometimes called 'transitology'. This sought to identify and disseminate lessons of successful democratic transition after events of a national crisis. Part of its attraction lay in the fact that it offered the hope not only of a smoother, less painful transition for the latecomers to democratization, but also of engineering a successful transition even in states that might lack many of the obvious 'prerequisites' for democracy. In this sense, it was the reverse of the Barrington Moore approach outlined above. Where Moore had suggested that some states were fated to fail at democratization because they had followed the 'wrong' path to modernization, transitology suggested that skilful political statecraft might lead to the triumph of democracy even in the most unfavourable context. Both of these approaches, of course, suffered from over-simplification. Any radical political change is bound to be messy and difficult to control. However, the proliferation of democratic experiments in the 1990s led some to offer a more sophisticated conceptual framework to structure successful transitions to democracy.

The best-known example of this approach is the so-called pacted path to democratization (Karl, 1990). According to this principle, once democratic change is accepted on to the national agenda, all the major political players need to agree on the ground rules for that transition, preferably in the shape of a formal pact. Either implicitly or explicitly, they are also to agree to abide by those rules, even if the final outcome does not favour them. This pact establishes democracy as the only game in town. The prototype for this approach occurred during the transition to democracy in Venezuela in 1958, when the leaders of the three main parties signed the Pact of Punto Fijo committing them to respect the outcome of the forthcoming general election. This inaugurated 40 years of democracy for Venezuela. As it is located in a region not noted for the longevity of democratic regimes, it often came to be presented as a model for successful democratic transition in general, although more recently it has succumbed to populist challenges and social polarization, as we shall see in Chapter 13.

It is true that the essentiality of a 'pact' in ensuring a successful democratic transition can be exaggerated. Democratization has certainly taken place in surprising places without pacts in place, for example in Indonesia after the fall of President Suharto in 1998. Yet successful transitions have taken place in unpropitious circumstances where pacts were in place, while the lack of a 'pact' has scuppered successful democratic transitions. As we can see from **Case Study 5.1**, pacts are easier to recommend in theory than to agree in the midst of a chaotic systemic crisis, with extremists on all sides trying to derail the whole process.

 For the later downfall of liberal democracy in Venezuela, see Chapter 13.

5

 CASE STUDY 5.1 **Pacts and democratic transitions**

For successful 'pact'-based democratic transitions, consider Poland and South Africa. For an example of an unsuccessful, 'pact'-less transition, consider Russia.

Poland

By the end of the 1980s, many felt that no regime in Eastern Europe had less legitimacy than Poland. The military government of President Jaruzelski had ruled since 1981, pre-empting the alternative of a likely Soviet invasion, but it had repressed *Solidarność* (Solidarity, a Polish trade union—**see Figure 5.1**), it was despised by most of the population, it was shunned by the West, and the country was effectively bankrupt. In 1989, the regime and Solidarity finally embarked upon difficult, public round-table negotiations to try to formulate a way out. This lasted three months and eventually they agreed a formula that would allow Solidarity to stand for election to the parliament for the first time, with some seats reserved for it in a (relatively) free and fair election. Until then, the ruling Polish United Workers Party (PUWP) had insisted upon approving all candidates for seats in parliament and took most of them themselves. The PUWP had again reserved 65 per cent of the seats for themselves, but to everyone's surprise Solidarity won all the remaining seats that were contested. Even the Solidarity leaders had not expected this result, let alone the regime. Yet they all accepted the outcome. The PUWP faded away and was dissolved in 1990. Since then, Poland has gone through a political reconciliation and gradual transformation that has turned it into one of the most successful democratizers, despite the initial economic trauma of radical 'shock therapy' through radical market reforms and privatization of state-owned industry. Afterwards, even former communists could find a way back into politics. In 1995, former communist Kwasniewski outpolled the iconic Lech Walesa to become the second president of free Poland. Since it is the largest state in Eastern Europe, Poland's significance for the eventual success of the quiet revolutions in the rest of the region cannot be overstated.

FIGURE 5.1   Solidarność protests in Poland
© Michel Piccaya/ Shutterstock.com

South Africa after the end of apartheid

By the end of the 1980s, few believed in a bright future for South Africa. A pariah racist state shunned by the rest of the world, with increasing violence perpetrated by the regime upon its enemies and vice versa, it seemed destined for a bloodbath. Yet, from the late 1980s, the Boer regime had begun secret talks with representatives of the African National Congress, which led to Nelson Mandela's release from prison in 1990. From then on, the official regime and the black opposition engaged in protracted public negotiations over transition to majority rule. These lasted for three years and were periodically interrupted by brutal violence and murders, with extremists on both sides trying to disrupt the negotiations and harm their enemies. But, in the end, an agreement was reached on a transition that involved an agreement over power-sharing that came into force in 1994.

Russia: a failed and 'pact'-less transition

In Russia, early optimism over democracy in the 1990s has given way to an increasingly authoritarian regime since 2000. Though commentators have offered various explanations, such as the lack of a democratic tradition in Russia and a persisting political culture of deference to a strong state, it can equally well be argued that the failure results from decisions made by the Yeltsin regime during the transition to democracy. The collapse of the communist regime in December 1991 raised hopes abroad that Russia might make as successful a transition to democracy as the states in Eastern Europe. However, in Russia, there was no pact between the key political actors over what should replace communism. President Yeltsin did not believe that the failure of the coup in August 1991 signalled the definitive defeat of the communist opposition. The Communist Party remained by far the strongest political organization in Russia and all the military high command had been party members before 1991. To guard against a communist-military coup, Yeltsin refused to hold new elections to the national parliament in case the democrats lost. This led to two years of wrangling between Yeltsin and the opposition in the existing Supreme Soviet, culminating in Yeltsin's own 'coup' in 1993, when loyal troops shelled the parliament to get the opposition out. Until he resigned in 1999, Yeltsin seemed much more preoccupied either with dismantling the power bases of the communists or with undermining potential rivals than with building robust new democratic institutions. Instead of trying to agree on ground rules with the opposition, he polarized and stigmatized any opposing views. Russia failed to build a democratic system that enjoyed widespread legitimacy. At the same time, Yeltsin introduced radical 'shock therapy' economic reforms that savagely cut the standard of living of most of the population. Given these circumstances, the lack of support for democracy among Russians seemed understandable. In the World Values Survey held at the end of the 1990s, Russia recorded the lowest level of satisfaction with the way in which democracy was developing in their country, with only 7 per cent of respondents declaring themselves 'very' or 'rather' satisfied (Inglehart et al., 2004: tab. E110). Many Russians in turn believed that things would only get better with President Putin in charge.

Nevertheless, it is also important to remember that a successful democratic transition does not guarantee continued democratic success. It is a start and vital, but only a start. In more recent years, both South Africa and Russia have suffered from intensified business and political corruption, allegedly spreading from the top. Now, they resemble each other much more (Dawisha, 2014; Plaut and Holden, 2012).

After a decade, however, the democratization wave of the 1990s began to subside. With it subsided confidence in devising recipes for successful transitions. In 2002, Carothers wrote a provocative critique, 'The End of the Transition Paradigm', in which he remarked that devotees of transitology had applied the formula too simplistically. They had assumed that states in transition were necessarily moving towards democracy, while this was not necessarily the case. External advice needed to be tailored to specific local conditions and to be sensitive to national traditions. For example, in some cases, insisting on early elections might cause greater division than cooperation between social groups.

In January 2014, the issue acquired a new lease of life, at least in part as a response to the worsening situation in the Middle East, where early optimism over the Arab Spring turned into bafflement as one country after another descended into murderous chaos. Instead of a pact, all too often what came to the fore was resentment, recrimination, and revenge over past repression, rather than cooperation for a better future. The same happened in Iraq after 2003 despite, or because of, Anglo-American invasion. Nor was this fate restricted to the Middle East: the earlier 'colour revolutions' in Ukraine and Kyrgyzstan also failed to establish a stable democratic order.

This series of failures testifies to both the complexity of post-authoritarian transitions and the potential benefit of getting them right. While accepting all of Carothers' scepticism about the objectivity of 'transitology' mentioned above, the fate of these regimes demonstrates the costs of failed transitions—human even more than financial. The opportunity for freedom is not in itself enough to ensure democratic success.

These two sections have demonstrated the difficulty in identifying a predominant or set route to democracy. The combination of long- and short-term causes and effects in the democratization of any given country requires sensitive analysis. Any adequate analysis generally requires consideration of both.

5

✳   KEY POINTS

- The aspiration for democracy is part of a broader aspiration for freedom.
- There are two basic approaches to explanations for democratization, focusing on long-term socio-economic change or on the short-term interplay of key political actors at moments of crisis.
- Democratization has long been correlated with economic development and with the rise of the middle class, especially in the West, although there are many exceptions.
- In developmental states, social groups beyond the middle class may be more active in pushing for democracy.
- There is no 'science' of transitions, but evidence suggests that skilful statecraft can facilitate success.
- The most desirable element in a transition is a 'pact' between the key political actors over the ground rules for the new system that all respect.
- However, there is still no guarantee that the collapse of an authoritarian system will lead to democracy.

Types of Democracy

One of the strengths of democracy has been its flexibility—its ability to adapt to a wide range of different circumstances. Athenian democracy was based on direct, regular involvement of the public in all key public decisions, if only involving male citizens. Subsequently, as states got bigger, direct decision-making came to be replaced by representation.

❱ See Chapter 4 for a discussion of representation.

Today, it is difficult to settle on a set of core institutions common to all states that call themselves 'democracies'. In part, this is because of the increasing number of states that claim to be democratic, but different from the liberal West (Zakaria, 1997), such as Iran, Pakistan, Turkey, and now Russia. Even North Korea claims to be a democracy. Partly, it is because the term is used in an enormous variety of ways (Paley, 2002) and partly because academic analysts disagree widely over which systems can meaningfully be classed as de-mocracies—leading to wrangles over 'democracy with adjectives', as Collier and Levitsky (1997) put it (for example liberal democracy, representative democracy, multiparty de-mocracy, populist democracy, etc.).

Keane (2009) has proposed another version of democracy with an adjective: 'monitory democracy'. By this, he means that the key common principle is not how decisions are made nor ensuring choice between candidates for public office (although elections are crucial too), but rather holding officials and governments accountable for their actions—as he puts it, 'putting politicians, parties and elected governments permanently on their toes', which makes it, for him, 'the most complex form of democracy yet' (Keane, 2009: 689). He also commends it as the closest to a universal form in the modern era. Yet, insofar as consultative authoritarian regimes also organize elections and hold officials to account, this approach can blur the distinction between democracies and authoritarian regimes.

An earlier and very influential model of democracy in modern Western industrial societies is Dahl's 'polyarchy'. Extrapolating from his analysis of how local government operated in 1960s New Haven, Connecticut, this focuses on the activity of members of a range of elites who represent wider sections of the population. It aimed to update the traditional notion of representative democracy so that it better reflected the realities of political power in the large states of the late twentieth century. (For details, **see Key Quote 5.2** and for a brief biography, **see Key Thinker 5.3**.)

Q   KEY QUOTE 5.2   Polyarchy

'Polyarchy is a political order distinguished by the presence of seven institutions, all of which must exist for a government to be classified as a polyarchy:

1. Elected officials. Control over government decisions about policy is constitutionally vested in elected officials.

2. Free and fair elections. Elected officials are chosen in frequent and fairly con-ducted elections in which coercion is comparatively uncommon.

3. Inclusive suffrage. Practically all adults have the right to vote in the election of officials.

4. Right to run for office. Practically all adults have the right to run for elective offices in the government, though age limits may be higher for holding office than for the suffrage.

5. Freedom of expression. Citizens have a right to express themselves without the danger of severe punishment on political matters broadly defined, including criticism of officials, the government, the regime, the socio-economic order, and the prevailing ideology.

6. Alternative information. Citizens have a right to seek out alternative sources of infor-mation. Moreover, alternative sources of information exist and are protected by laws.

7. Associational autonomy. To achieve their various rights, including those listed above, citizens also have a right to form relatively independent associations or organizations, including independent political parties and interest groups.'
(Dahl, 1989: 221)

 KEY THINKER 5.3   Robert A. Dahl

Robert A. Dahl (1915–2014) was one of the most influential American political theorists of the twentieth century. He made his name with the book *Who Governs?* (1961), which tackled the question of how American democracy actually worked, as opposed to how it was supposed to work in theory, based upon the practice of power in local government in New Haven, Connecticut. From this, he developed the concept of 'polyarchy', which was presented and widely used as a realistic model of democracy in a large, industrialized society in the twentieth century. All of his later work was devoted to the study of democracy—notably, *Democracy and Its Critics* (1989), and *How Democratic Is the American Constitution?* (2002).

A more widely used term, however, is liberal democracy. There is no complete consensus on the key elements of liberal democracies, but Diamond has provided a useful list of the common features (**see Key Quote 5.4**).

KEY QUOTE 5.4   Liberal democracy

'The deeper level of liberal democracy requires the following:

● Freedom of belief, expression, organization, demonstration, and other civil liberties, including protection from political terror and unjustified imprisonment.

● A rule of law, under which all citizens are treated equally and due process is secure.

● Political independence and neutrality of the judiciary and of other institutions of 'horizontal accountability' that check the abuse of power, such as electoral administration, the audit, and the central bank.

● An open, pluralistic civil society, which affords citizens multiple, ongoing channels for expression and representation of their interests and values, in independent associations and movements and in the mass media as well.

● Freedom of cultural, religious, ethnic, and other minorities to speak their languages, practice their cultures, and express their identities.

● Civilian control over the military.' (Diamond, 2002: 213)

Whether one prefers the term polyarchy or liberal democracy—and there is evidently a lot of overlap—there is no doubt about the need for some kind of analytical distinction between at least two different types of democracy: a minimalist one that consists essentially of just elections, and another, more elaborate version, which displays many more dimensions of popular involvement in public decision-making. More recently, Møller and Skaaning (2013) have gone further and proposed a simple four-stage analytical typology of different types of democracy. This is reproduced in **Table 5.2**. For them, the key difference between polyarchy and liberal democracy is that the latter explicitly requires the rule of law.

The merit of this typology is that it provides a clear and relatively simple framework for assessing the extent of a particular system's democracy. It also embodies an implicit sequencing of stages for deepening democracy. But the next question then is how to 'measure' a country's democracy. How might individual dimensions of democracy be assessed? Can this data be synthesized into an overall assessment? And if this can be done, should it be?

✳ KEY POINTS

- Numerous different models of democracy have been proposed.
- Often, these use Western experiences as a reference point.
- It makes analytical sense to differentiate between different levels of democracy.
- The two most widely used models of developed democracy are polyarchy and liberal democracy.

TABLE 5.2 Typology of democratic regimes

	Competitive elections	Inclusive elections with high integrity	Civil liberties	Rule of law
Minimalist democracy	+			
Electoral democracy	+	+		
Polyarchy	+	+	+	
Liberal democracy	+	+	+	+

Source: Møller and Skaaning (2013). © 2013 National Endowment for Democracy and Johns Hopkins University Press. Reprinted with permission of Johns Hopkins University Press.

Measuring Democracy

There are two common strategies to measure democracy. The first is to assess a particular system along a set of dimensions that constitute what it means to be democratic and then synthesize them into a single score. The best-known example of this is the Freedom House Index, based in the US. This ranking assesses the extent of freedom (rather than primarily democracy) in a country along two fundamental dimensions: political rights and civil liberties. These are then synthesized into an overall assessment.

It is the most comprehensive survey of its kind, now covering 195 countries and 14 territories. It is repeated every year and, as a result, perhaps its greatest strength is the way it charts changes over time. Its data are often used in quantitative academic research to search for correlations with other dimensions of social and economic development.

It is not, however, the only such index. Other similar, albeit less comprehensive indexes, include the Bertelsmann Foundation's Transformation Index, the Economist Intelligence Unit's Democracy Index, and the Polity IV database of political regimes.

Since the focus of each of these indexes is slightly different and since each depends on judgements by analysts, they may come to different assessments of individual countries. Freedom House, for instance, classifies France as fully free and Pakistan as partly free, while Polity IV classifies both as democracies, but not 'complete democracies', unlike, for example, the US, the UK, Germany, Italy, and Spain.

There is a further problem: all of these indexes are compiled in the West. They can create the impression of being superior teachers, marking the 'grades' of non-Western states like pupils. Freedom House is not a politically neutral institution: it deliberately aims to promote democracy—and chiefly American-style democracy—around the world. This, in itself, can antagonize citizens, not to mention governments, of developing countries, who resent the perceived condescension.

Koelble and LiPuma (2008) have forcefully urged the 'democratization of democracy', arguing that the democratizing trajectory of postcolonial states is bound to be different from that of developed countries (though, of course, the US was itself originally a colony). They rejected the possibility of an ahistorical, value-neutral, scientific measurement of democracy, since the starting point for ex-colonies—inequality and entrenched discrimination between ethnic or other communities—still hangs over them in a way that former metropolitan states have never had to confront.

The International Institute for Democracy and Electoral Assistance (IDEA), an institution that promotes democracy internationally, has responded to this line of criticism. It produced a handbook of myriad possible proposals for democratization (Beetham et al., 2002). However, the expectation was that citizens wanting to promote democracy in their country would carry out a 'democratic audit' of their system, identify the most obvious obstacles to democracy, and then set out the most urgent and important recommendations appropriate for reform for them. IDEA has been criticized for not providing a methodologically consistent, sequenced programme for democratization (though it has compiled a great deal of useful comparative data on aspects of democracy around the world). Rather, its main objective was to inspire democracy activists in the field to action. Even if this led to conflicting priorities between countries, it would not matter, since IDEA accepts different trajectories to democracy.

✱ KEY POINTS

- There are two diverging approaches to devising a methodology for measuring a country's democracy.
- The first—and most common—is to compile a standard list of indicators, devise an analytical framework for assessing them, and form a group of experts in one centre to apply the methodology consistently.
- The alternative is to encourage democracy activists in individual countries to come up with their own list of the most urgent areas for democratic or democratization reform, possibly providing them with a checklist of all the things that they might wish to include.
- 'Liberal democracy', as a term, is too suggestive of Western democracy.
- It cannot be assumed that developed democracies have to be 'liberal'.

Variety in Democracy

An early article in the *Journal of Democracy* made a point that is often overlooked in the hunt for quantitative assessment: it is possible for states to be 'differently democratic' (Schmitter and Karl, 1991: 77), even those with consolidated democracies. A recent survey of attitudes to democracy across Europe suggested universal support for liberal democracy (although the practice in some countries fell well short), but also a widespread predilection (especially among lower socio-economic strata) for a 'social democratic' version of democracy that went beyond the liberal. It made social equality and protection against poverty a key expectation, such as is found in the Nordic countries. Though this is not yet a complete reality in most countries, it does suggest the potential for European states to diverge from the liberal democracy of, say, the US in the future (Ferrin and Kriesi, 2016). If so, it would mean different varieties of liberal democracy.

For the moment, Møller and Skaaning have proposed 'liberal democracy' for the most developed form of democracy, but the use of the term inevitably carries overtones of Western superiority, since the typical models of liberal democracy tend to be found in the West. The term is not value-free. It can imply that as democracies develop around the world, they will inevitably converge with those in the West. In the very long run, this scenario may indeed prove correct, but for now it seems premature and contentious.

One country that epitomizes this issue is India, as we shall see in **Case Study 5.5**.

CASE STUDY 5.5   Indian democracy: consolidated—but liberal?

India is unquestionably a consolidated democracy, with a well-established legal system, and it embodies all four characteristics of liberal democracy listed in **Table 5.2**, though to varying degrees. In 2014, 1,766 national or local political parties were registered with the Indian Electoral Commission, so there is no doubt about competitive elections. In the 2014 general election, roughly 540 million people voted—a turnout of 63 per cent (**see Figure 5.2**). Though there are always allegations of vote-buying, the legitimacy of this outcome was not seriously challenged. There are substantial legal protections for civil rights. The courts are active and authoritative, if overworked. In 2015, Freedom House classed India as free, but gave it an overall score of 2.5—the lowest possible composite figure for a state in the 'fully free' category. India is unquestionably a consolidated democracy, but is it a liberal one?

There are two problem areas. The first concerns Indian political culture (that is, the framework of shared understandings within which Indian democracy operates). Implicit in the term 'liberal democracy' are three connotations more associated with the West: equality between individuals, toleration based on individualism, and free-market economics—the sorts of ideas associated with thinkers like John Stuart Mill and Adam Smith. Indian writers such as Chatterjee (2010: 297) have sought to emphasize the deep differences in social values between India and the West: '[C]ommunity has a very tenuous place in the Western liberal theory of civil society and state; in the new political societies of the East, communities are some of the most active agents of political practice.'

While Chatterjee is advocating tolerance in the West for non-Western social values, this could also have darker implications. For example, it could lead to condoning group discrimination and violence. Indian politics, like Indian society, continues to be heavily impacted by local or regional hierarchical caste systems, legitimated by Hindu religious traditions, which segment people into different hereditary groups: 'Discrimination, degradation and violence were written into customary norms of caste relations' (Varshney, 2013: 214). Economic development and democracy have profoundly affected traditional inter-caste relations. Yet violence is still often perpetrated against couples who try to marry across caste lines, as well as against non-Hindus, such as Muslims.

According to Varshney (2013: 114), 'politics since Nehru [the first Indian prime minister] has paid even less ideological attention to the principles of pluralism and tolerance'. For Mohanty (2004: 117), the ethic that has taken over (not surprisingly in a former colony) is *swarajatantra*—that is, self-rule and liberation. A bewildering array of groups—whether ethnic, religious, or regional—pursue their own liberation against others more or less as a zero-sum game, often violently. It does not make for liberal toleration.

As will be outlined in Chapter 13, democracy in India has also led to a bewildering proliferation of political parties. In 2015, there were 1,866 political parties registered with the Electoral Commission and in recent years the total has gone up by about 100 annually. Most of these are regional or local parties rather than national ones and so the effective competition is not quite so extreme—in 2016, there were 'only' 34 parties with seats in the lower house of parliament, the *Lok Sabha*. Nevertheless, they are all ambitious and this leads to raucous competition. All of them produce a cacophony of increasingly extreme demands and promises, vying to establish a distinctive image by outbidding or outshouting the rest. It encourages extremism rather than liberal moderation. The second problem is a consequence of the first. While all Indian citizens are constitutionally equal before the law, not all enjoy equal treatment. To overcome caste discrimination, the Constitution lays down special rights for particular groups of citizens, particularly those from the Scheduled Castes, the Scheduled Tribes, and the Other Backward Classes. This grants them special privileges in terms of state employment and standing for elected office. Even though significant progress has been made in reducing traditional inequality, castes have become interest groups with a kind of veto power to prevent dilution of these rights, so there is unlikely to be much change soon. After an extended exposition of the ways in which the original liberal principles of the founders of the Indian state (who enshrined the principle of equality of all citizens) shifted into acceptance of special treatment for deprived groups on the grounds of backwardness, Bajpai (2011: 293) concludes: 'In many ways India remains a democracy mostly in an electoral sense. Notably, the rule of law is routinely breached, violence and discrimination against religious and caste minorities are common, often aided by state institutions such as the police. Large-scale poverty and economic inequality undercut the equality of political and civil rights.' Thus, on both these counts, it is difficult to apply the term 'liberal democracy' to India.

FIGURE 5.2   Voters in India
© Dipak Shelare/ Shutterstock.com

Scepticism about the appropriateness of the term 'liberal' for India and other democracies is not to question the extent or the depth of their democracy. Rather it is to question the appropriateness of the label itself. A more neutral term would seem preferable that allowed for countries to be 'differently democratic', such as 'consolidated' or 'stable' democracy. Bell (2006) has expressed similar scepticism about the relevance of 'liberal democracy' in East Asia for potential democracies such as Singapore and China, as we shall see in **Key Debate 5.6**. And no doubt the same would be argued about Turkey. Though the ruling AKP presents itself as more liberal than its opponents, it is still conservative rather than liberal in its attitudes towards social values (Axiarlis, 2014). According to White (2003, 2013), liberalism as a doctrine is contentious in Turkey because, for many, it is associated with (aggressive) Western-style secularism, even if imposed by Turkey's own rulers.

5

 KEY DEBATE 5.6   Equality versus elitism in democracy

de Tocqueville (1994: Vol. I, 201–2; Vol. II, 97) on the primacy of equality in democracies:

'Democratic institutions awaken and foster a passion for equality which they can never entirely satisfy... It has been supposed that the secret instinct which leads the lower orders to remove their superiors as much as possible from the direction of public affairs is peculiar to France. This is an error, however; the instinct to which I allude is not French, it is democratic...

I think that democratic communities have a natural taste for freedom... But for equality their passion is ardent, insatiable, incessant, invincible; they call for equality in freedom; and if they cannot obtain that, they still call for equality in slavery.'

Bell (2006: 4, 8, 152, 165–6) on the need to take elitism seriously in designing democracy for East Asia:

'Few, if any, Western liberal democratic theorists in the post-World War II era have sought to learn from the traditions and experiences of East Asian societies... Western liberal democratic theory stands out by its apparent imperviousness to developments in East Asia and elsewhere in the non-Western world...

In the eyes of Singapore elder statesman Lee Kuan Yew, a 'Confucianist view of order between subject and ruler helps in the rapid transformation of society... in other words, you fit yourself into society—the exact opposite of the American rights of the individual'. A modern Confucian society ruled by wise and virtuous elites, that is, can provide the benefits of rapid economic growth and social peace, but it must sacrifice the democratic political rights that make government so difficult in the West...

Confucian political culture places great emphasis on the quality of political rulers. The main task of the educational system is to identify and empower the wise and public-spirited elite, and the common people are not presumed to possess the capabilities necessary for substantial political participation...

A modern-day 'Confucian democrat' is therefore confronted with the dilemma that while West-ern-style democratic institutions do not fully accommodate concerns for the 'rule of the wise', the 'Parliament of Scholar-Officials' idea goes too far in the elitist direction by failing to incorpo-rate any form of political decision-making by the people. The compromise solution may seem obvious at this point: a bicameral legislature, with a democratically elected lower house and a 'Confucian' upper house composed of representatives selected on the basis of competitive examinations.'

The Persistence of Authoritarian Regimes

While the 1990s saw widespread democratization, the period since then has seen a revival of authoritarianism, for example in Egypt and Venezuela. The number of democracies worldwide continued to creep slowly upwards, but many authoritarian regimes that had seemed 'ripe' for democratization stabilized. Kurlantzick (2013) has written of democracy globally as 'in retreat'. A third of states in the world remain authoritarian. Many of their leaders have recovered self-confidence.

Apart from failed transitions, for example in Libya, Syria, Iraq, and Afghanistan, not to mention Russia, two other factors have contributed to this authoritarian revival. The first is the greater level of sophistication of some authoritarian regimes. Shambaugh (2008) has documented the enormous efforts that the Chinese Communist Party put into studying the reasons for the collapse of the other communist regimes and learning lessons to aid its survival.

The second factor is the growing internationalization of the confrontation between democratic and authoritarian regimes. This has been marked by the readiness of some authoritarian regimes to intervene in the internal affairs of others, paralleling the efforts of Western governments to spread democracy. Saudi Arabia, the Gulf States, Venezuela, and Russia have all done this (Vanderhill, 2013).

Over the past 10–15 years, political scientists have begun to pay more attention to au-thoritarian regimes. This can encompass a wide variety of regimes: monarchies, personal dictatorships, military regimes, theocratic regimes, racially or ethnically polarized regimes, and one-party-dominant regimes. What defines them is what they are *not*, rather than what they are—they are *not* democracies (however that may be defined). Devising a single definition for this very heterogeneous group has thus far proved impossible.

Nevertheless, they do have things in common. After reviewing the literature on authori-tarianism, Frantz and Ezrow (2011: 85) point out that regularities appear in different policy outcomes from democracies. Autocracies tend to spend less on social programmes, wages, and environmental policies than democracies. They also tend to attract less foreign direct investment, perhaps because they also tend to be weaker on enforcing property rights. Perhaps not surprisingly, they also offer the greatest opportunities for corruption. Most strikingly, according to Przeworski et al. (2000: 230), dictatorships tend to have higher death rates (but also higher birth rates) than democracies, whatever the level of development. A graphic example of this was in North Korea in the late 1990s, when between 240,000 and 3.5 million people died of starvation out of a total population of 22 million. Nobel-Prize-winning economist Amartya Sen (1999: 7–8) points to the contrast: '[N]o substantial famine has ever occurred in any democratic and independent country with a relatively free press.' Furthermore, according to Geddes et al. (2014), it is possible to distinguish different trends in periods of longevity and different patterns of collapse according to whether the regime was monarchical, personalistic, dominated by a military junta, or controlled by a ruling party.

The research on authoritarian regimes has tended to focus on two distinct, but overlapping, themes of legitimation: (i) how do authoritarian regimes structure their institutions of rule; and (ii) why do ordinary people not challenge authoritarian regimes more?

Authoritarian institutions

Sometimes, authoritarian regimes hold elections to demonstrate their legitimacy, but then one of the puzzles is why people bother to vote when there is no likelihood of it changing the way the country is run. Magaloni (2006) examined the record of the Institutional Revolutionary Party (PRI) in Mexico, which held power from 1929 to 2000, making it one of the longest-lived ruling parties in the world—almost as long as the Soviet Communist Party. It achieved this without resorting to terror. Instead, it held regular national elections and people regularly voted for it because it offered patronage (jobs working for the government or state corporations, such as national oil corporation PEMEX), 'pork' (that is, state largesse for localities that voted for the PRI), and (limited) influence over specific government policies to their supporters (Schedler, 2006: 12–13). So voters could vote to secure benefits, even if they could not change their rulers.

As for how authoritarian systems structure their rule, Gandhi and Przeworski (2007) have argued that those that hold regular elections last longer than those that do not. And, in general, Gandhi (2008) has shown that dictators have an incentive to create institutions to share in policy-making, both as a way of co-opting support, whether from 'insiders' in the regime or key elite groups outside it, and also as a Machiavellian way of exposing real or potential opposition.

Authoritarian regimes sometimes adopt institutions more often associated with democracies to stay in power. In Russia, the Kremlin has created a moderate opposition party, A Just Russia (as well as ruling party United Russia) and a 'social chamber' (in addition to the national parliament) for non-governmental organizations, ostensibly as part of a policy of 'guided democracy' to encourage moderate and constructive new ideas for policy-making and to pre-empt radical opposition. Meanwhile, China has begun experimenting at the local level with its own forms of deliberative democracy (explained in Chapter 4), which were originally devised to strengthen established democracies (**see Case Study 5.7**).

See Chapter 4 for a discussion of deliberative democracy.

In turn, such tendencies complicate the previous categorical distinction between democracies and authoritarian regimes, leading to more hybrid regimes.

CASE STUDY 5.7   China as a hybrid authoritarian system

China is a striking example of a hybrid authoritarian system. The Chinese Communist Party (CCP) has ruled since 1949 and does not allow serious political competition. It brutally suppressed opponents, particularly during the Great Leap Forward (1958–60) and the Cultural Revolution (1966– 69). Since the death of Mao in 1976, it has gradually moved from personal domination by a single leader towards more institutionalized leadership, with no official constitutionally allowed to hold the same leading position for more than ten years. There is significant market freedom and the regime allows private enterprise. Limited competitive elections take place between approved candidates in many villages and townships, and a number of seats in the National People's Congress are reserved for elected representatives from eight 'democratic' parties, though they cannot challenge the leading role of the CCP. However, the regime still controls all key positions in the state apparatus and armed forces, and its members are above the law—they cannot be prosecuted by the legal system unless this has been approved by higher Party officials.

According to the World Bank, China is now an upper-middle-income country with a per capita income of around US$6,560 in 2013, which puts it well within the range where a transition to democracy might take place. Chinese citizens are economically more free than at any point since 1949. There is now a substantial middle class—according to McKinsey, it amounted to around 475 million people in 2012 (Barton, Chen, and Jin, 2013). Moreover, the explosion of the Internet and social media users—in June 2014, there were 632 million reported Internet users in China (CINIC, 2014)—gives citizens much greater opportunities to express views publicly than at any time since 1949, even though the state organizes widespread surveillance of online activity and bans Western search engines and social media sites.

However, widespread demonstrations in favour of democracy were brutally suppressed across the country in June 1989 and the current leader, President Xi Jinping, has reversed the relatively relaxed policies of his predecessor by increasing restrictions on freedom of speech—reportedly, Western democracy is now a taboo subject in Chinese universities (Anderlini, 2015). The 2015 Press Freedom Index of the organization Reporters Without Borders ranked China 176th out of 180 countries (RSF, 2015). Instead, the CCP has mounted an increasingly draconian campaign against official corruption, using language of popular accountability akin to that associated with Keane's 'monitory democracy'. It harps on about the need for social stability and is very wary of an untutored civil society.

At the same time, officials respond to proposals and criticisms from civil society groups to develop better policies, and they use the social media to stimulate citizen responses to individual policy initiatives. In this way, the CCP practises a consultative authoritarianism that encourages and exploits popular support for social stability and sustained improvements in the standard of living (Teets, 2014). This combination of rapid economic growth and stable elite leadership elicits positive responses elsewhere in East Asia (Welsh and Chang, 2015) and in the West too (Berggruen and Gardels, 2013).

Popular acceptance of authoritarianism

It is obvious that terror can subdue peoples, especially if it seems as though any individual, high or low, can be targeted. Frantz and Ezrow (2011: 72) recount the story of Saddam Hussein inviting ministers to contribute ideas on ending the Iran–Iraq War (1980–88) when it was going badly. The minister of health suggested that Saddam should step down temporarily from power to ease negotiations with Iran. For this, he was arrested and executed, and his body was chopped into pieces and returned to his wife in a duffle bag: 'Insecurity, unpredictability, and fear of the unknown . . . all . . . permeated Iraq' (Sassoon, 2012: 128).

However, most authoritarian regimes do not rely exclusively on terror to maintain their rule because it always risks provoking opposition out of despair and even a counter-coup. Even dictators need legitimation, including Saddam Hussein. According to Sassoon (2012: 193), in Iraq: 'Fear played a major role in sustaining the Ba'ath regime for more than three decades, but the party's control of the population was not based only on fear. An elaborate system of rewards and punishments provided a robust framework for the Ba'ath Party's domination.'

Divide and rule—privileging some groups over others—is a technique that has supported dictatorships and empires since at least Roman times. This may involve the use of brutality—for example the military government in Myanmar continued to exploit civil war with minorities in various parts of the country to legitimize its rule with the majority Burmese (Callahan, 2003), as has happened in Syria—but it can also take economic forms. In Malaysia, for instance, the Malay-based regime has practised affirmative action against the minority overseas Chinese to restore Malay domination in the country since 1970 and, for now, still has the backing of grateful Malay middle classes.

✳ KEY POINTS

- The term 'authoritarian regime' can be applied to a very disparate group of states.
- Authoritarian rule can rest on terror, threats, and coercion.
- Authoritarian rulers are also concerned to legitimize their rule.
- The more skilful authoritarian rulers devise institutions to give at least the appearance of involving people outside the core leadership in policy-making, if not of sharing power.
- This can lead to hybrid regimes that have at least some features of democracy.

Conclusion: Smarter Democracy, Deeper Democracy, or towards Democratic–Authoritarian Hybridity?

As authoritarianism has revived, satisfaction with democracy in the West has declined. As Norwegian sociologist Ringen (2007: 41) put it: 'At the moment in history when the standing of democracy in the world is stronger than ever, its standing in the eyes of citizens is weak and probably weakening.' He wrote this before the global financial and the Eurozone crises, which have further shaken confidence in Western governments. Della Porta (2013) has raised the question of whether democracy (at least traditional liberal representative democracy) can be saved at all. Apparently consolidated democracies can crumble—namely, Venezuela (see also Chapter 13). The apparently iconic South Africa is now drifting towards corrupt authoritarianism (Johnson, 2015). And Poland, for all its success in achieving national reconciliation after 1989, has veered more recently towards populist confrontation, with the ruling Law and Justice Party demanding a squaring of accounts with elites who compromised with communism.

Critical questions and challenges multiply. Are democracies too prone to concentrate on short-term issues? Can they devise policies to tackle big long-term challenges, such as climate change (Burnell, 2012)? What about preserving intergenerational equality between older and younger generations over paying for social services? Berggruen and Gardels (2013: 9), for instance, have suggested that more intelligent public governance for the twenty-first century would synthesize, as they put it, Western 'consumer democracy' and Chinese 'meritocratic Confucianism' into 'knowledgeable democracy' with 'accountable meritocracy'. Chapter 15 will argue that citizens are going to find democracy more complex and confusing as they are confronted by conflicting plausible claims over 'alternative' data and 'fake' news in on- and off-line media. This in turn is likely to strengthen the appeal of populism in liberal democracies identified in Chapter 16.

Runciman (2013) agrees with some of these criticisms in his survey of crises that have challenged Western democracies since the early twentieth century. Democracies do find it difficult to take the long view. The time horizon of (most) elected legislators is no longer than the date for their re-election. Yet while democracies may find it difficult to devise long-term plans, and even more difficult to stick to them, he also concludes that democracies are better at coping with complex social and economic changes and adapting to them because they are more pragmatic. Incremental change is what democracies do best. But because they have surmounted difficulties in the past, people in democracies also suffer from what he terms the 'confidence trap'—that is, a refusal to address serious problems until almost too late, believing that they will muddle through again somehow, as they (almost) always have. Casual democratic optimism brings costs, even within established democracies.

As Ringen (2007) suggests, in the end democracy will survive and thrive if its citizens believe that they enjoy a strong sense of freedom and control. This also requires a widespread sense that most of the people share in society's benefits. The recent upsurge of populism in many democracies directed against 'elites' is a reminder of how things can go wrong, even in consolidated, genuinely liberal democracies—an issue to which we shall return in Chapter 16. In other words, democracy needs to sustain the sense of emancipation that was mentioned at the beginning of this chapter. In general, people do not choose to live under authoritarianism if given a real choice, though they may put up with it for the sake of other compensations. As the World Values Surveys show, there is near-universal majority support for the principle of democracy, but the ways in which that principle is implemented vary considerably and that variety is only likely to increase. It certainly is no longer the case that the traditional Western model of liberal, representative, parliamentary democracy inspires deference at home or abroad. New forms of democracy and/or new political actors are needed to revive it. Already a decade ago, the Council of Europe (2004) came up with a list of reforms to restore the confidence of citizens in their democracies in Europe (though few have been implemented). Democratic reformers will try to learn lessons from the experiences of other countries and not just in the West. Local experiments in participatory budgeting in Brazil and India have inspired imitation in Western Europe (Rocke, 2014). Conversely, authoritarian regimes will also sometimes borrow lessons to try to increase their legitimacy without, they hope, losing control. Whether or not that leads to hybrid regimes, it will complicate attempts to differentiate between democratic and authoritarian regimes. So rigorous thinking and consistent use of concepts will be more vital than ever for meaningful analysis and debate.

? Key Questions

- How useful is the term monitory democracy in characterizing modern democracies?
- Is there any point in trying to measure democracy? If so, who should do it?
- What are the limits within which states can be deemed to be 'differently democratic' while still remaining democracies?
- Do the citizens of a liberal democracy have to practise liberal toleration towards each other?
- Will China and Russia become democracies? If so, why and how?
- If India is not a liberal democracy, does that make it an illiberal one (see Chapter 2)? Will India ever become a liberal democracy? What about Turkey?
- Why was there no 'pact' between all the main political actors in Iraq after 2003 and how far does that explain the recurring political chaos there?
- Is there any future in trying to synthesize 'knowledgeable democracy' and 'accountable meritocracy'?
- If they were implemented, how effective would the Council of Europe recommendations be in reviving confidence in democracy?

▐▌ Further Reading

Bell, Daniel A. (2015), *The China Model: Political Meritocracy and the Limits of Democracy* (Princeton, NJ: Princeton University Press).
Raises the question of whether China enables better leaders to rise to the top than Western democracies.

Berggruen, Nicolas, and Gardels, Nathan (2013), *Intelligent Governance for the 21st Century: A Middle Way between East and West* (Cambridge: Polity).
Chapter 5 presents a thought-provoking template for a more intelligent system of governance, attempting to synthesize liberal democracy, deliberative democracy, and meritocratic bureaucracy.

Brooker, Paul (2014), *Non-Democratic Regimes* (London: Palgrave, 3rd edn).
A reliable introduction to the wide range of authoritarian regimes.

Council of Europe (2004), *The Future of Democracy in Europe: Trends, Analyses and Reforms* (Strasbourg).
Includes a list of proposed reforms to restore citizens' confidence in democracy in Europe that are still valid today.

Dahl, Robert A. (1989), *Democracy and Its Critics* (London and New Haven, CT: Yale University Press).
A classic work of debates about the strengths and weaknesses of democracy.

Diamond, Larry (2008), *The Spirit of Democracy: The Struggle to Build Free Societies throughout the World* (New York: Henry Holt).
The sub-title conveys the basic message of this work by one of the US's leading analysts of democracy.

Dobson, William J. (2012), *The Dictator's Learning Curve: Inside the Global Battle for Democracy* (New York: Doubleday).
An American journalist interviews democratization activists in several authoritarian regimes on their experiences.

Keane, John (2009), *The Life and Death of Democracy* (London and New York: Simon & Schuster).
A magisterial account of the evolution of the democratic idea.

Koelble, Thomas A., and LiPuma, Edward (2008), 'Democratizing Democracy: A Postcolonial Critique of Conventional Approaches to the "Measurement of Democracy"', *Democratization*, 15(1): 1–28.
A fundamental critique of Western attempts to measure democracy around the world and effectively a response to Diamond.

Møller, Jørgen, and Skaaning, Svend-Erik (2013), 'Regime Types and Democratic Sequencing', *Journal of Democracy*, 24(1): 142–55.
Presents a clear and well-argued framework for comparative analysis of democratic systems.

Paley, Julia (2002), 'Towards an Anthropology of Democracy', *Annual Review of Anthropology*, 31: 469–96.
An introduction to the enormous variety of ways in which the term 'democracy' is understood and used around the world.

Ringen, Stein (2013), *Nation of Devils: Democratic Leadership and the Problem of Obedience* (London and New Haven, CT: Yale University Press).
Chapters 8 and 9 contain hard-hitting criticisms of British and American democracy.

Saich, Tony (2011), *Governance and Politics in China* (London and New York: Palgrave Macmillan, 3rd edn).
A clear introduction to the Chinese political system and its evolution.

Sassoon, Joseph (2012), *Saddam Hussein's Ba'ath Party: Inside an Authoritarian Regime* (Cambridge: Cambridge University Press).
Provides an eye-opening picture of Saddam Hussein's rule, based on many documents discovered after his death.

Schmitter, Philippe C., and Karl, Terry Lynn (1991), 'What Democracy Is ... and Is Not', *Journal of Democracy*, 2(3): 75–88.
An early and still very relevant discussion of the ways of going about comparative research on democracy.

Varshney, Ashutosh (2013), *Battles Half-Won: India's Improbable Democracy* (New Delhi and London: Penguin/Viking).
A very insightful analysis of one of the oldest democracies outside the West. The first three chapters concentrate on an assessment of Indian democracy.

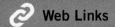 **Web Links**

https://www.freedomhouse.org/report-types/freedom-world#.VAC54GORNbl
The most recent Freedom House annual report on Freedom in the World.

http://www.bti-project.org/bti-home/
The link to the most recent Bertelsmann Transformation Index.

https://www.eiu.com/public/topical_report.aspx?campaignid=DemocracyIndex12
The most recent Economist Intelligence Unit Democracy Index freely available.

http://www.systemicpeace.org/polity/polity4.htm
The Polity IV database.

https://www.idea.int/
The general International IDEA website.

 Visit the **Online Resources** that accompany this book to access more learning resources on this topic: www.oup.com/uk/ferdinand/

Nations and Nationalism

6

- Nations, States, and Nationalism
- The Multinational State and Sub-State Nationalism
- Theories of Nationalism
- Ethnic and Civic Nationalism
- Anti-Colonial Nationalism

- Nationalism and Globalization in the Contemporary World
- Conclusion
- Key Questions
- Further Reading
- Web Links

Reader's Guide

Nationalism is perhaps the most powerful political ideology to emerge in the modern world and is closely associated with the rise of the sovereign state. It is usually taken to be a prime cause of the two twentieth-century world wars. Nationalism later became allied with the decolonization movement in the early post-war period, and then with the processes of new state formation in Eastern Europe and the former USSR following the end of the Cold War, both of which have generally been seen as liberation movements. This chapter explains the concept of the nation, its relationship with the state, and how the phenomenon of nationalism has been theorized, as well as the different forms that nationalism can take. The final section considers how nationalism has been faring in the era of globalization.

Nations, States, and Nationalism

Nationalism has been a subject of much critical discussion in recent years as issues concerning immigration, Brexit, the election of Donald Trump as US President on a populist nationalist platform, and certain anti-globalization movements have been prominent on the political agenda. The importance of such issues for contemporary politics underscores the need to examine very carefully the nature of nationalism as an ideology, its origins, the assumptions underpinning it, and its impact on social and political life. This section is therefore concerned with introducing the essential concepts associated with nationalism and explaining the relationship between them. This provides a basic understanding of the phenomenon, enabling us to better analyse how it works in political life.

Nationalism is widely held to be a product of the modern era—an era that saw the rise of the sovereign state as an institutional structure, while the concept of 'the nation' emerged to signify the body of people who constituted its membership. So although the terms 'nation' and 'state' are often used synonymously, or joined together to produce 'nation-state', they refer to two distinct entities. As we saw in Chapter 2, the state refers essentially to the structure of rule and authority, and the institutions that regulate these, within a particular geographical space. In the global sphere of politics, 'the state' refers specifically to the modern sovereign state, which is recognized as possessing certain rights and duties. This kind of state is distinct from the states that make up a federal system, such as the individual states of which the United *States* of America is composed—or of India, Malaysia, Micronesia, Nigeria, Pakistan, South Africa, Germany, Russia, Canada, Australia, and other countries that form federal systems.

The sovereign state has been given a clear legal definition by the 1933 Montevideo Convention on the Rights and Duties of States. The first Article provides the most succinct understanding of the criteria for a modern sovereign state—namely, a permanent population, a defined territory, and a government capable of maintaining effective control over its territory and of conducting international relations with other states. Thus the state in global politics is envisaged as a *formally constituted, sovereign political structure encompassing people, territory, and institutions.* As such, the state interacts with similarly constituted entities in an international system of states.

Historically, the sovereign territorial state is a product of developments in early modern Europe. Its founding moment is conventionally taken as having occurred following the devastating struggle between Catholic and Protestant forces that ended with the Peace of Westphalia in 1648. This was followed by the consolidation of certain characteristics of the modern state that are central to aspects of contemporary political theory. These characteristics include not only the principle of religious coexistence—providing the basic principles of the secular state, which guarantees freedom of religion—but also the monopoly claims by the state over such matters as declarations of war and the negotiation of peace, diplomatic representation, and the authority to make treaties with foreign powers (Boucher, 1998: 224). The status of the Westphalian Peace as the founding moment of the modern *sovereign* state is a matter of some debate among contemporary scholars (see, for example, Clark, 2005), the finer points of which are beyond the scope of this introductory text.

Like the sovereign state itself, the idea of the nation as we understand it today developed in the modern era. Indeed, its origins lie in the same state-building dynamics that emerged in post-Westphalian Europe, as well as in emergent ideas about democracy, especially through the French Revolution of 1789, which required a distinct body of people—citizens—to constitute a *sovereign people* and which came to be conceptualized as 'the nation'. Although the record of democratic development in Europe remained very patchy until quite recent times, the idea of the nation caught on very rapidly. The subsequent development of the modern state and state system brought together the three prime characteristics of the modern state—*sovereignty*, *territoriality*, and *nationality.*

The term nation derives etymologically from the Latin *natio*—literally, 'birth' or 'to be born', and from which the words 'native', 'nativist', and 'nativity' also derive. It refers specifically to 'a people' rather than a formal, territorial entity or structure of authority, although there are territorial associations. But there is no widely agreed definition of what constitutes 'a people' or 'nation' beyond the fact that it denotes an entity that claims a collective identity, usually grounded in a notion of shared history (preferably a long and glorious one) and a shared culture, which may include language and religion, art, and artefacts. An especially influential formulation of the nation, however, has been provided by Benedict Anderson (2006), who describes it as an 'imagined community', as set out in **Key Quote 6.1**.

> ### Q KEY QUOTE 6.1   Benedict Anderson on the nation as an 'imagined community'
>
> '[The nation] is *imagined* because the members of even the smallest nation will never know most of their fellow-members, meet them, or even hear of them, yet in the minds of each lives the image of their communion . . .
>
> The nation is imagined as *limited* because even the largest of them encompassing perhaps a billion living human beings, has finite, if elastic boundaries, beyond which lie other nations. No nation imagines itself coterminous with mankind . . .
>
> It is imagined as *sovereign* because the concept was born in an age in which Enlightenment and Revolution were destroying the legitimacy of the divinely-ordained, hierarchical dynastic realm . . . [N]ations dream of being free . . . The gage and emblem of this freedom is the sovereign state . . .
>
> Finally, it is imagined as a *community*, because, regardless of the actual inequality and exploitation that may prevail in each, the nation is always conceived as a deep, horizontal comradeship. Ultimately it is this fraternity that makes it possible, over the past two centuries, for so many millions of people, not so much to kill, as willingly to die for such limited imaginings.' (Anderson, 2006: 6–7)

There is also a sense in which members of a nation are believed to share a common ancestry and are therefore linked by biological descent. This is a logical corollary of the notion of a shared history, language, and culture. But the idea that different nations are the product of different biological descent groups further implies that nations are based on 'race'. This kind of thinking was prominent in nineteenth-century Europe, carrying through into the twentieth century and receiving its most extreme expression in Nazi Germany in the 1930s and 1940s, following which the word 'genocide' first appeared in reference to the mass murder of Jews and which was carried out on the basis that people of Jewish descent constituted a 'race', and an 'undesirable' one at that.

It has been argued that nationalism as such is not necessarily inherently racist and has indeed allied itself with other modern ideologies including liberalism, but historically it did give racism the means through which it could become operationalized and many expressions of nationalism have in fact allied themselves with racism (Mosse, 1995: 163). Racism is alive and well in such movements as the so-called Alt-Right (short for 'alternative right'), which rejects mainstream conservatism as being weak, especially on issues concerning 'race'. Many who identify with the Alt-Right harbour anti-Semitic views and a belief in 'White Supremacy', and thus promote a form of racist nationalism that opposes multiculturalism and immigration, while privileging 'white identity'. Alt-Right supporters in the US also tend to support such issues as 'men's rights', oppose gun control, and generally back President Trump's populist policies on economic protectionism and targeted immigration controls on Mexicans and Muslims in particular.

The idea of race as a legitimate way of categorizing people in either biological or social scientific terms, however, has long been discredited. Indeed, it has been argued that it is not actual racial differences that generate racism, but rather 'racism that generates races' (Townley, 2007: 171). As we see later, another approach to the study of nationalism maintains that it is the ideology of nationalism that creates nations and not the other way around. Even so, the terms 'race' and 'racism' remain part of our everyday vocabulary and reflect attitudes and beliefs that are very real in their effects. Many racists, however, attempt to avoid being labelled as such. As one commentator remarks, '[r]acist organizations most often refuse to be designated as such, laying claim instead to the title *nationalist* and claiming that the two notions cannot be equated', although in fact 'the discourses of race and nation are never very far apart' (Balibar, 1991: 37).

The idea of an ethnic group is also close to a racial category and so discourses of race and ethnicity are often closely intertwined. But while 'race' embodies negative connotations, 'ethnicity' often carries positive overtones (Eriksen, 2016: 6). It is therefore more common to find the idea of the nation embracing the concept of ethnicity. The latter term comes to us from the Greek *ethnos*, referring originally to an undifferentiated collectivity (as in a swarm of bees) and commonly used to denote 'a group of people with shared characteristics' (Chapman et al., 2016: 14). This implies common biological descent, as well as a shared culture, both contributing to a social identity invested with various meanings and attributes, which, taken together, are deployed as a marker of difference from other such groups. Some definitions of nation invoke the concept of a common ethnic identity as the prime characteristic and, indeed, the terms are sometimes used almost interchangeably. On the other hand, we may speak of 'multi-ethnic national societies', which, as we see shortly, is now characteristic of most modern states.

Spokespeople for a nation often claim that it has a very long and continuous history, usually in association with a particular territory. As the quotes in **Key Quotes 6.2** indicate, a link to a specific ancestral territory is also a key element in defining the nation, providing it with a spatial foundation and legitimate locale, while also specifying the boundaries between one's own nation and others. To designate it as ancestral is to give it a historic dimension, which strengthens the legitimacy of the territorial claim. *Political* control of a specified territory linked to a specified people constitutes a 'nation-state' and is the ideal that lies at the heart of the ideology of nationalism. In the process of asserting claims to territory, nationalist movements place particular interpretations on spaces or places—interpretations that serve to legitimate claims not just to ownership in an ordinary sense, but also to sovereignty in terms of establishing political power and control over the territory in question.

The focus on territory also invites consideration of the contributions of political geography with respect to how 'landscapes of power' are constructed in the context of nationalism. Landscapes of power involve, among other things, landscapes of control, especially over national frontiers. These are often marked by barriers in the form of walls or fences and sometimes by militarized spaces such as minefields. In virtually all cases, there will at least be checkpoints controlling entry and exit (see, generally, Jones, Jones, and Woods, 2004). Sometimes, the barriers are designed to keep people in rather than out. The infamous Berlin Wall that divided Germany throughout much of the post-war period is one such example and its breach in 1989 still stands as the symbolic moment of the end of the Cold War.

But even as some walls come down, others go up. The best-known contemporary example of at least a threat to build a massive wall of exclusion is US President Trump's call for a barrier of nearly 2,000 miles between the US and Mexico. 'Border security' is also now a stock phrase of politicians in contemporary Australia, where asylum seekers attempting to arrive by boat

KEY QUOTES 6.2   **The territorial dimension of nationalism**

'Whatever else it may be, nationalism is always a struggle for control of land; whatever else the nation may be, it is nothing if not a mode of constructing and interpreting social space.' (Williams and Smith, 1983: 502)

'The nation's unique history is embodied in the nation's unique piece of territory—its "homeland", the primeval land of its ancestors, older than any state, the same land which saw its greatest moments...time has passed but [it] is still there.' (Anderson, 1988: 24)

have been intercepted and incarcerated in offshore facilities. And 'Brexit' was at least partly about stemming the flow of 'foreigners' onto British soil. The steep rise in 'race hate crime' in post-Brexit Britain (Forster, 2016), incidentally, lends credence to the close association between nationalism and racism, although it would be wrong to brand all, or even most, of those favouring the departure from the EU as motivated primarily by racism. Even so, nationalism, at least in the more right-wing versions, generally seeks the exclusion of 'alien' elements from an existing state to safeguard the 'authenticity' of its national character and identity.

Some commentators have endowed the nation with a 'soul' or 'spirit'. Nineteenth-century French scholar Ernest Renan is well known for his pronouncement, 'A nation is a soul, a spiritual principle', constituted by both past and present and representing a 'grand solidarity' that is lived out in everyday life. Interestingly, he went on to note that nations are not eternal, but have a beginning and an end, and that, in Europe: 'They will be replaced, in all probability, by a European confederation' (quoted in Hutchinson and Smith, 1994: 17–18). Renan appears to have anticipated the emergence of the European Union as a political entity transcending all the various European nationalities, although it has scarcely obliterated them and, in the case of the UK, tended to aggravate nationalist sentiments among the English in particular.

The foregoing discussion has sought to clarify the distinctions between state and nation, as well as race and ethnicity, and in the process to specify, more or less, the meaning that each concept has been invested with. This is essential to understanding the political ideology of nationalism. So let us now attempt to provide at least a working statement of what constitutes nationalism. We suggest that *the ideology of nationalism is manifest wherever a group of people conceives of itself as a nation (in one or more of the terms noted above) and then lays claim—usually via an elite—to some kind of political recognition and autonomy, as well as to a specific territory within which 'the nation' is sovereign, preferably in the form of full sovereign statehood.*

Since the early twentieth century, the ideology of nationalism has generally been allied in turn with the apparently democratic principle of national self-determination. In summary, this working statement links the claim to constitute a nation in a sociological sense to a *political* entitlement to statehood underscored by the moral justification embodied in the idea of self-determination. Nationalist ideology, when generalized, therefore supports the claim that each nation is entitled, in principle, to a state of its own. Thus the constitution of the world at large is, ideally, one of separate sovereign nation-states and this provides a standard model for the world. As one commentator has noted: 'Like the Microsoft operating system for personal computers, once nationalism was established as the world standard, every group seeking the benefits of statehood acquired an interest in professing allegiance to and conformity with it' (Mandelbaum, 1999: 21).

Although the principle of a state for each nation as a kind of world standard may seem logical or desirable, most states are in fact multinational. We consider some of the implications of this in the next section. The final concern of this first section, however, is the question of whether there is any real difference between nationalism and patriotism, as set out in **Key Debate 6.3**.

KEY DEBATE 6.3   **Nationalism and patriotism**

Patriotism, in its literal sense, refers to a strong sense of attachment and loyalty to one's homeland, one's *country*. The latter is not the same as the *nation*, and on this basis some commentators believe that patriotism can be distinguished from nationalism simply because the object of devotion and loyalty is, at least technically, different. Patriotism is also often considered to be a milder, less aggressive, form of attachment and loyalty than nationalism, and has been defended as such by a range of prominent thinkers. Take, for example, the following quotation from the famous English author George Orwell (1945/2014)

> By "nationalism"...I mean the habit of identifying oneself with a single nation or other unit, placing it beyond good and evil and recognizing no other duty than that of advancing its interests. Nationalism is not to be confused with patriotism....By "patriotism" I mean devotion to a particular place and a particular way of life, which one believes to be the best in the world but has no wish to force on other people. Patriotism is of its nature defensive, both militarily and culturally. Nationalism, on the other hand, is inseparable from the desire for power...

In contrast, other well-known writers such as Leo Tolstoy argued that patriotism is not only stupid, irrational, and immoral, but also aggressive and dangerous. On this account, patriotism is indistinguishable from nationalism. It is certainly contrary to ideas about 'the higher idea of a brotherhood of man' spoken of by Tolstoy (2017: 75). In contemporary political thought, this notion of 'brotherhood' translates into a doctrine of universal or cosmopolitan morality essential to the conceptualization of human rights.

'Patriotism' may have a literal reference merely to 'country', and therefore be understood simply as 'love of country' and loyalty to it, but can this really preclude one's fellow 'countrymen'? Does not patriotism require defending both country and countrymen? The commitment to 'country' emphasized in patriotism also ties in to the territorial dimensions of nationalism, as discussed earlier in this chapter. As for the emotional aspect, is it really possible to distinguish between patriotic feelings and nationalist ones? Does a patriot wave the flag any less vigorously than a nationalist? It might seem, then, that patriotism provides, at the very least, the bedrock on which a more aggressive style of nationalism may be built. One must also consider Samuel Johnson's (1709–84) famous aphorism that 'patriotism is the last refuge of a scoundrel', suggesting that it lends itself to being manipulated to serve political causes that are less than worthy.

* KEY POINTS

- It is important to recognize that although 'nation' and 'state' are often used synonymously, they refer to two distinct entities. A 'nation' is a people, while the 'state' is a formal authoritative structure embodying sovereign power within a particular geographical space.

- The concept of the nation implies a notion of common biological descent and may therefore be associated with 'race'. In turn, nationalist ideas may be expressed in racist forms, although we must be careful not to simply equate all forms of nationalism with racism.

- Nationalist ideology tends to supports the claim that each nation is entitled to a state of its own and that the constitution of the world is, ideally, one of separate nation-states, as expressed in the principle of self-determination.

- Patriotism is often considered to be a less aggressive and therefore more acceptable form of nationalism, but it is difficult to really distinguish between the two.

The Multinational State and Sub-State Nationalism

However defined, 'nations' are assumed to populate sovereign states and are very often described in singular terms—that is, one state may be assumed to contain one nation. The state of France, for example, is seen as occupied by the 'French nation', Japan, by the 'Japanese nation', Mexico, by the 'Mexican nation', and so on. These examples indicate the commonly accepted conflation of state and people that produces the familiar term 'nation-state', which, again, reflects the principle of national self-determination. However, only a little critical reflection is needed to recognize that the matching of state and nation is seldom so neat and unproblematic. Rather, it is an ideal that has rarely, if ever, been achieved and most states are in fact multinational, multi-ethnic or multicultural (terms that are sometimes used interchangeably). Indeed, there is virtually no state in the contemporary world encompassing a single, homogeneous nation. The 'French nation' is historically founded on a plurality of language groups with separate identities—identities that survive to the present day despite the strongly assimilationist character of the French state. Japan is often described as a 'pure' nation-state, but it has an indigenous minority—the Ainu—and also encompasses the people of Okinawa and residents of Korean descent, many of whom do not identify as Japanese and therefore maintain distinct identities. Mexico has a dominant *Mestizo* population of mixed Spanish/European/indigenous descent, along with a number of minorities including African-Mexicans, as well as groups that identify as wholly indigenous and whose diversity is reflected in the fact that they speak around sixty indigenous languages between them.

Until recently, Iceland could claim to be the only truly homogeneous country in the world, with almost 100 per cent of the population possessing in common all the ingredients that constitute a 'nation'—the same language, religion, history, culture, ethnicity, common biological descent, etc. The latter in particular is rare enough to make Iceland, along with some other key factors, the ideal subject for studies in population genomics (which involves comparing DNA sequencing of different populations). Recent immigration, however, means that some 13 per cent of a current population of around 330,000 people were not born in Iceland, introducing a novel element of multiculturalism to the country (Jakobsson and Halfdanarson, 2016: 2). This is likely to increase further over time.

Many states are more obviously made up of several 'nations' and are therefore multinational states. These have been defined generally as 'states that contain one or more national minorities coexisting with a national majority that has historically been the backbone of the state' (Máiz, 2000: 35). A prime example is the contemporary British state, as illustrated in **Case Study 6.4**.

 CASE STUDY 6.4   The multinational British state

The contemporary British state is formally known as the United Kingdom of Great Britain and Northern Island. It was created by three acts of union between England and three other entities—Wales (in 1536), Scotland (in 1707), and Ireland (in 1801). Ireland achieved effective independence in 1922 as the Irish Free State—later the Republic of Ireland—encompassing 26 of the 32 Irish counties, with the remaining six comprising Northern Ireland and remaining part of the UK. The sectarian divide between Catholics and Protestants in Northern Ireland has seen decades of civil strife. England, always the culturally and politically dominant entity, is home to approximately 85 per cent of a total UK population of around 65.5 million, followed by Scotland, with around 5.3 million, Wales, with just over 3 million, and Northern Ireland, with almost 2 million.

The Scottish, Welsh, and Northern Irish sub-state national entities are commonly understood to have descended from the native population that existed in Britain at the time of the Roman occupation, the latter lasting for almost 500 years from AD43 until the early fifth century. Thereafter, waves of settlers from northern Germany and southern Denmark—the Angles, Saxons, and Jutes—formed the basis of a dominant Anglo-Saxon population, which in due course became English (although containing as well a mixture of native Celts or Britons due to intermingling over the centuries). Today, the Scottish, Welsh, and Northern Irish are often referred to as the 'Celtic fringe', a term that one commentator has described as a 'perfect verbal symbol of their marginal status in the minds of the English' (Heyck, 2002: 43). In response to perceived marginalization in an English-dominated state, each of these entities has undergone national cultural revivals and national assertiveness, leading in turn to political recognition via devolution. Devolution is a term indicating the establishment of sub-national assemblies in Northern Ireland and Wales and a parliament in Scotland, which enjoy varying degrees of self-government.

In 2014, the Scottish 'nation' voted on whether or not to establish Scotland as a sovereign state (**see Figure 6.1**), with the 'no' vote coming in at around 55 per cent. In the same year, the Cornish also received recognition as a distinct national minority within Britain and not merely an appendage to the English nation. There is much speculation about a further Scottish referendum on independence in the wake of the Brexit referendum in which 62 per cent of Scottish voters supported remaining in the EU, the largest 'remain' vote of any of the four sub-national entities. Should Scotland achieve independence in a future referendum, it could theoretically join the EU in its own right.

6

All of these national sub-groups within the UK are now multilayered, especially since immigration over the centuries has brought millions of people of different 'nationalities' to the British Isles, thereby producing the 'multicultural' (as well as 'multinational') Britain of the contemporary period. In the post-war period, the most significant sources of migrants into the UK have been the West Indies and South Asia, and about 13 per cent of the population is now 'non-white' (noting that 'white British' is the official ethnic category of the majority population).

Immigration from other European countries has also had some impact, although perhaps not as significant as some might expect. In 2015, around 3.2 million people living in the UK were citizens of another EU country, amounting to about 5 per cent of the UK population. But, at the same time, an estimated 1.2 million people born in the UK were living in other EU countries, making the net figure much lower (https://fullfact.org/immigration/eu-migration-and-uk/, accessed January 2018).

Views about the impact that immigration has had on British national culture and identity vary, as debates during the Brexit campaign in particular indicated. But evidence suggests that, in the final analysis, immigrants do integrate, while at the same time making a positive contribution to local culture, as well as to economic growth and development, as they have done for much of the past 2,000 years—and noting that the Anglo-Saxon forebears of the English population were themselves immigrants from other parts of Europe (see http://www.parliament.uk/pagefiles/10493/LLN%20 2010-023%20ImmigrationFP.pdf, accessed January 2018).

FIGURE 6.1 Campaigners in the Scottish independence referendum of 2014
Jonathan Mitchell/Atlas Photo Archive/ Photoshot/ Age Fotostock

Former British settler colonies such as the US, Canada, Australia, and New Zealand are now among the most multinational states in the world today. These states have a history of empire and mass migration, both of which are aspects of globalization. But if we look to places like Nigeria, India, and Russia, it is also evident that these states are made up of many different groups speaking different local languages and possessing different cultural practices. Even relatively small states can be incredibly diverse. Papua New Guinea, for example, has a population of just over 7 million, yet there are more than 850 different languages spoken and each language group could theoretically consider itself to be 'a nation'.

Nonetheless, states are still widely assumed to contain singular nations and, although most states are acknowledged as containing many more than one, the identity of the state will to some extent be equated with a dominant majority. Thus, in the US, Canada, and Australia, a dominant white English-speaking majority constitutes a mainstream and the 'national identity' of each tends to be built around their values. This is also true of New Zealand, although it is tempered by an official biculturalism, which has given a much stronger profile to indigenous Māori people in formulations of national identity. In Canada, there has been resistance to the dominance of the Anglophone majority from the Francophone province of Quebec, to the point where secession to form a separate sovereign state very nearly succeeded in 1995, with a referendum on the matter failing by the narrowest of margins. The idea of the nation here—and in most other cases where a separate national identity is strongly asserted in a political context—is related very closely to the culture concept: 'We are a nation because we have a culture', said a Francophone student from Montreal (quoted in Handler, 1988: 39).

The largest multinational state in the world, in terms of population, and one of the most complex, is China, the subject of **Case Study 6.5**.

CASE STUDY 6.5   Nations and nationalism in China

China has a population of around 1.39 billion people, with a total land area of just under 9,400,000 square kilometres, making it the largest unitary state in terms of both population and land area. (Russia, a federal state, has the largest land area, followed by Canada and the US, also both federal.) But while the population possesses citizenship of the People's Republic of China (PRC)—that is, the Chinese state—does this mean that they form a single nation as *a* people? In addressing this question in relation to some of the key elements of nationhood—language, ethnicity, a myth of common descent, territory, and shared culture or civilization—we can see just how complex the issue of nationality is.

The ethnic category of 'Han Chinese', derived from an early population that occupied the Yellow River valley and about which there is a popular myth of common descent from a 'Yellow Emperor', constitutes about 92 per cent of the total population of the PRC. There is therefore some sense in which one can identify 'Han ethnicity' as characterizing the vast majority of the Chinese population and providing the foundations of a Chinese nation. People designated as Han Chinese, however, do not necessarily speak the same language, at least as a first language. In fact, there is enormous linguistic diversity throughout China and if a common language is an element of 'nation-ness', it is difficult to speak of the Chinese as constituting a single nation. But states can work to create a national language as part of a 'nation-building' project. A standardized form of the Beijing dialect of Mandarin has been adopted as the national or standard language (*putonghua*), although it is only one of ten recognized languages of the Sino-Tibetan or Sinitic family of languages spoken within China, each of which in turn has many variations (Chappell, 2016: 3). There is a standardized written form for Chinese languages, again devised at the level of the state, meaning that the same script is used for virtually all the different verbal forms, thus enhancing a measure of uniformity and therefore a sense of sameness.

Different approaches to nationalism, one conservative and one modernist, have produced quite different interpretations of the issue of language within China. Both approaches see language as 'an instrument of thought, a form of national culture, and a depository of traditional ideas, values, beliefs and practices' (Guo, 2015). And both see language as essential in transmitting 'cultural Chineseness' and consolidating national identity. But rather than maintaining language in traditional forms, the political, modernist perspective has promoted transformation and standardization in order to contribute to effective state-building 'and the creation of a new, modern China that is economically prosperous and politically and militarily strong' (Guo, 2015). While Han Chinese predominate, the Chinese state also officially recognizes 56 minority ethnic groups (although some are internally diverse—that is, they actually contain more than one ethnic group). China's linguistically and ethnically diverse population reflects the fact that the contemporary Chinese state is founded on an empire incorporating numerous and varied cultural groups first unified under the Qin dynasty more than 2,000 years ago and consolidated under the succeeding Han dynasty.

Contemporary China also encompasses Tibet and the Tibetans, who have a distinct national identity grounded largely in Tibetan Buddhism, as well as their own political history, but who were incorporated into the PRC in the 1950s. The increasing presence of Han Chinese, together with decades of repressive PRC rule and the refusal of the latter to acknowledge the legitimacy of Tibet's spiritual leader, the Dalai Lama, has worked to foster a much stronger sense of Tibetan nationalism than might otherwise have been the case. But Chinese nationalism, which maintains that Tibet is an integral part of the Chinese state, clearly has a preponderance of political/military power behind it to enforce its claims to the people and territory. Simmering resentment and outbreaks of public unrest are likely to continue as two nationalisms—Chinese and Tibetan—continue to confront each other.

Another notable case concerns the Uyghur people, who make up around half of the population of China's north-western Xinjiang region—otherwise called Uyghuristan or

East Turkestan by separatists. Uyghurs are mainly Muslim, speak their own Uyghur language, and maintain a Turkic identity that links them to other Central Asian people. The region is bordered by Russia, Kazakhstan, Kyrghizstan, Tajikistan, Afghanistan, Pakistan, India, and Mongolia, giving it considerable strategic significance. Like Tibet, it has a distinctive political history. It was incorporated into the Chinese Manchu empire in the 1870s by force, at which time it was given the name Xinjiang, meaning 'new frontier'. With the exception of two brief periods of independence in the 1930s and 1940s, Xinjiang has been ruled from Beijing ever since. Discrimination against Uyghur people, for example in state employment, as well as religious repression, has fanned Uyghur nationalism and alienated Uyghur people from the Chinese state. Chinese authorities have attempted to link Uyghur nationalism, and periodic episodes of violence, to international Islamic terrorism. This has justified further repression, which in turn simply strengthens Uyghur separatist sentiments (see Clarke, 2014). As with the Tibetan case, this hardly serves the PRC's desire to strengthen a broader sense of Chinese national unity and solidarity among its diverse peoples.

Taiwan, which China claims as an integral part of the Chinese state under the 'One China' principle, is a different case again. Its dominant population belong to the category of Han Chinese, although it has an indigenous minority of just under 2 per cent. The fact that its main population is categorized as Han is used by the Chinese state to legitimate its claims, while also, of course, claiming the territory as Chinese. But Taiwan has a complex political history. It was not always part of the old Chinese Empire and indeed it was ruled by imperial Japan from 1895 to 1945. After the Second World War, it came under the formal control of the Republic of China (ROC), led by the Chinese Nationalist Party under Chiang Kai-Shek. However, China's Communist Revolution followed in 1946 and Mao Zedong soon succeeded in establishing the PRC in mainland China, while Chiang, who still claimed to represent 'China' in the form of the ROC, withdrew to Taiwan, setting up a separate political administration there that continues to this day and which gives Taiwan de facto sovereign status.

Taiwan's separate political status, which has now endured for around 70 years, and the fact that it has a non-Chinese indigenous population—which supporters of Taiwanese nationalism say has contributed to a distinctive culture in Taiwan—have been asserted as the basis for a separate national identity for Taiwanese people generally. This identity gathered strength from the late 1980s, when Taiwan began a process of democratization, thus sharpening the sense of political difference with mainland China. As one commentator on the Taiwanese case suggests, identity comes down to a matter of politics, although it is no less 'real' or authentic as a result (Brown, 2004: 2).

In more general terms, it has been suggested that although China obviously regards itself as a 'nation-state' in the present period, the idea of 'nation' in this compound term does not accurately reflect the sense of the Chinese self:

> China has existed within roughly its present borders for two thousand years, and only over the last century has it come to regard itself as a nation-state. The Chinese, in constantly making reference to what they describe as their 5,000-year history, are aware that what defines them is not a sense of nationhood, but of civilization. In this context, China should not primarily be seen as a nation-state but rather a civilization-state. (Jacques, 2012: 12)

The phenomenon of the multinational state and of sub-state nationalism also highlights the issue of 'nations without states'. This is a constant theme in any discussion of nationalism in the contemporary era, in which processes of state-making have created minorities within many, if not most, modern states. The examples discussed so far in this chapter clearly illustrate this issue—Scots, Québécois, Tibetans, and so on may all be considered nations without states, or at least without states of their own. Another relevant instance occurs where minority groups have become divided between several countries by historic processes of state-making. The Kurds, for example, are considered to be a distinct ethnic group (or nation) that is spread among contiguous regions of south-eastern Turkey, northern Syria, northern Iraq, and western Iran. The Kurds constitute a minority in each of these states, but the project of Kurdish nationalism seeks to unify all groups within these regions in a unitary state of independent Kurdistan. There is little likelihood, however, of this coming about in the foreseeable future. Palestinians form another notable example of a nation without a state. Although there is a Palestinian Authority and over 130 UN member states recognize a de facto Palestinian state, Palestinian people and their territory (split between Gaza and the West Bank, with some land also appropriated by Israel for Jewish settlements) lack the essential criteria for statehood, which will only come about with agreement from Israel. That prospect is unlikely in the foreseeable future due to seemingly intractable disputes over land, water, and the status of Jerusalem and holy sites, among other things.

✳ KEY POINTS

- Despite the ideal of a world in which states are matched neatly with homogeneous nations, almost every state in the world is in fact multinational.

- In most multinational states, there is a dominant majority and 'national identity' tends to be built around their values, as illustrated by the centrality of England and the English to the British state, of the Han Chinese to the Chinese state, of the Jews to the Israeli state, and so on.

- China also stands as a prime example of a contemporary multinational state reflecting the legacy of centuries of empire.

Theories of Nationalism

Various theoretical approaches to the nation have revolved around issues concerning the longevity of the nation as a recognizable entity in the human history. One approach sees nations as perennial phenomena, meaning that they have existed since 'time immemorial'. Of course, not all nations can claim such longevity—and nations come and go, as Renan remarked—but it is the phenomenon of the nation itself, rather than any particular version of the nation, that is claimed to be perennial. This approach tends to support an assumption that nations are naturally occurring phenomena, as distinct from artificially constructed communities. As with most theoretical approaches, there are mild versions and stronger ones. A mild version, dubbed 'perennialism', would not go much further than the claim outlined above, pointing simply to various instances of nations throughout both ancient and modern history, from, say, the Spartans and Athenians of ancient Greece to Native American nations like the Iroquois Confederacy in what is now upper New York State, to the Welsh, Scots, Irish, English, and Cornish, who, along with later arrivals, make up contemporary Britain. Perennialism acknowledges that nations come and go, and can be made and remade, but will always exist in some form or another, with or without a state. But a perennialist standpoint generally falls short of 'naturalizing' the nation—that is, of holding that nations are 'given by nature'.

'Primordialism' represents a stronger version of this thesis, viewing the phenomenon of the nation, and of national belonging, as essentially natural to human organization in an organic, almost biological sense, such as in the 'herd instinct', reflecting the deepest aspects of 'human nature' and therefore part of our essential being from the start of human existence. The literal meaning of 'primordial', according to the *Oxford English Dictionary*, is 'of, relating to, or existing from the very beginning of time; earliest in time; primeval; primitive; (more generally) ancient, distant in time' and which 'constitutes the origin or starting point from which something is developed or derived, or on which something else depends, fundamental, basic, elemental' (quoted in Özkirimli, 2010: 49). It follows that nationalists who draw on primordialist themes tend to emphasize the longevity of their particular nation, its very antiquity constituting a sense of grandeur and inspiring awe and reverence in its members, in turn feeding and strengthening a fundamental emotional attachment and loyalty, which can be activated and drawn on as and when required in certain political contexts.

Some scholars have identified other variants of the general perennialist/primordialist thesis set out above. Anthony D. Smith (2000) notes that one can also discern culturalist and socio-biological approaches. The first is associated with the work of anthropologist Clifford Geertz, who emphasized the extent to which culture, as a 'web of meaning', is inevitably involved in the subjective interpretation of a group's assumed primordial essence; thus 'primordial attachments rest on perception, cognition and belief' (Smith, 2000: 22). The socio-biological approach was pioneered in the work of sociologist Pierre van den Berghe (1978), who emphasizes evolutionary themes in theories of human sociability and related notions of biological descent and kinship. The core of his argument lies in the claim that ethnocentrism, a sense of racial belonging, together with the tendency to nepotism in social practice, are based on kinship ties, which are driven in turn by an objective evolutionary imperative to ensure that one's genes are passed on not simply by one's direct descendants, but by the wider kinship group to which one is biologically related.

Sociobiology has had less of an impact in studies of nationalism, perhaps because its rationalist premises are less likely to be invoked by actual practitioners of nationalism than those involving emotion and sentiment. Cultural anthropologists have also been highly suspicious of biological explanations, which they tend to associate with theories of race, and therefore racism. Concepts of culture, however, are just as likely to be used as the basis for racism in contemporary discourses, perhaps even more so than ideas based on biology (see Lawson, 2006).

Despite the rejection of the premises of socio-biology, notions of kinship and related-ness have a significant presence in the work of leading theorists of nationalism. Anthony D. Smith, for example, has pioneered 'ethno-symbolism' as a theory of nationalism underpinned by culturalist assumptions, but which nonetheless takes kinship (understood as biological relatedness) as a key attribute of the nation. Smith first highlights what he sees as the ultimate importance of the memories, values, symbols, and myths emanating from the assumed 'ethnic past' of a group that regards itself as a nation. Without these, says Smith, nationalism as an ideology would be powerless. But it also requires a link with kinship as well as with territory, as set out in **Key Quote 6.6**.

Smith's ethno-symbolist approach is a response to 'the need to understand the "inner world": of ethnicity and nationalism through an analysis of symbolic elements and subjective dimensions', which he says provides a more complete and balanced account of how ethnicity and nationalism take shape, especially with respect to their subjective dimensions (Smith, 2009: 23, 26). At the same time, it is a direct, critical response to another influential approach to the study of nationalism: modernist theory.

The modernist approach is associated, first and foremost, with the work of philosopher and social anthropologist Ernest Gellner (1925–95), who links nationalist thought with a distinctive mode of social and cultural organization embodied in modernity, which has represented a decisive rupture with older forms of organization. Whereas nationalism might be seen by some as the political expression of particular nations, Gellner argued that it is the other way around. Nations are a product of nationalism: 'Nationalism is not the awakening of nations to self-consciousness; it invents nations where they do not exist' (Gellner, 1964: 168). Even though some pre-existing differentiating markers are required in the construction of the nation, Gellner's analysis held that claims to the antiquity of nations in general, or of any nation in particular, were essentially false. Thus nations were

---

Q KEY QUOTE 6.6 Anthony D. Smith and ethno-symbolism

'What makes these myths, values, symbols and memories so attractive and potent is their invocation of presumed kinship and residence ties to underpin the authenticity of the unique cultural values of the community. In this sense, the ethnic community resembles an extended family or rather a "family of families", one which extends over time and space to include many generations and many districts in a specific territory. This sense of extended kinship, of "kith and kin", attached to a particular "homeland", underlies the national identity and unity of so many modern nations and endows their members with a sense of kin relatedness and immemorial continuity.'
(Smith, 1998: 46)

conjured into being through an ideology, distinctly modern in its origins, which sought to identify a particular group with a particular territory in order to invest it with sovereign statehood and the political power and status that goes with it. Following on from this is the 'normative nationalist principle', which Gellner identifies as the political principle 'which holds that the political and national unit should be congruent' and which, by implication, requires cultural unity between rulers and ruled (Gellner, 1983: 1, 125).

There have been many critics of Gellner's position on the modernity of nations and their invention via the ideology of nationalism, with various scholars seeking to posit the existence of nations well before the modern period by pointing to cultural precedents. The rejoinder from the modernist perspective, however, is that the identification of certain elements, such as consciousness of a shared cultural, religious, territorial, or linguistic identity, which were certainly present in various times and places before the advent of the modern era, does not constitute the essence of nationalism. Rather, 'its essence is a theory of political legitimacy' (O'Leary, 1988: 55)—a theory expressed in the normative nationalist principle.

Further important work from a modernist perspective has been carried out on the role of the state in the emergence of nationalism, for it is the modern state that gives institutional expression to political legitimacy as embodied in the nation. A key contribution has been made by John Breuilly (1993: 1), who emphasizes that nationalism is primarily a form of politics—that politics is, first and foremost, about power and that power in the modern world is principally about control by the state. Another point to note here is that the emergence of the modern state in Europe also saw a transition in the status of people from merely subjects of a monarch to citizens of a state with all the rights and duties that go with that status. This is also seen as integral to the development of modern democracy in which sovereignty became vested in the people—that is, the 'nation'—rather than in the person of the monarch (Lawson, 2006: 109). In constitutional monarchies, such as in Britain, the monarch is still known as 'the sovereign', but this designation is purely symbolic.

✳ KEY POINTS

- The primordialist approach assumes not only that nations may be found throughout human history from 'time immemorial', but also that they are naturally occurring phenomena.

- Ethno-symbolism is a theory of nationalism underpinned by culturalist assumptions incorporating memories, values, symbols, and myths, as well as the 'blood ties' of kinship (understood as biological relatedness) as a key attribute of the nation.

- Modernism takes nations to be the product of nationalism—an ideology that emerged only in the modern era as the sovereign state idea emerged.

Ethnic and Civic Nationalism

The theorization of nationalism has also involved the identification of many different kinds of nationalism. These range from cultural nationalism, linguistic nationalism, ethnic nationalism, indigenous nationalism, religious nationalism, romantic nationalism, diasporic or long-distance nationalism, and expansionist nationalism to civic nationalism, liberation nationalism, pan-nationalism, anti-colonial nationalism, and postcolonial nationalism, among other possible formulations. Many of these overlap—for example religious, linguistic, cultural, and ethnic nationalisms share certain features. Others transcend some of the givens of regular nationalist formulations—for example pan-nationalisms (such as Slavic nationalism) and diasporic or long-distance nationalisms (for example Jewish nationalism, where adherents do not necessarily reside in, and often do not wish to reside in, Israel, but participate from afar). These forms necessarily rise above the territorial dimension even as they hark back to a land or region of ancestral origin. It is also notable that Jewish nationalism contains elements of cultural, religious, linguistic, romantic, and ethnic nationalism. Sorting out typologies of nationalism is therefore a complex task. Here, we consider just two broad types—ethnic nationalism and civic nationalism. These are often placed in opposition to each other, mainly because the latter appears to contradict some of the key notions contained in forms of nationalism associated with ethnicity.

Ethnic nationalism is a phenomenon that attracted considerable attention at the end of the Cold War, especially as the old Soviet Union and Eastern bloc fell apart under the apparent onslaught of 're-awakened' ethnic nationalisms, which many interpreted in primordialist terms as representing a 'natural' reaction by long-suppressed ethnic communities. The case of the break-up of Yugoslavia represents a prime example of how ethnicity became highly politicized to the extent that civil war erupted and ended only with the establishment of new state entities on the supposed basis of ethnic identity. As we have seen, ethnicity combines elements of shared history, heritage, and ancestry, which often includes common religious, linguistic, or other cultural ties. When politicized, these provide the essential ingredients for a movement aimed at establishing the legitimacy of a particular named group. Thus ethnic groups in the former Yugoslavia designated Serbs, Croats, Albanian Muslims, and so on, either struggled to assert supremacy over others or struggled to resist the impositions of a rival group by establishing a claim to political autonomy based on ethnic identity. This led, eventually, to the establishment of new states based conceptually on the normative nationalist principle. In the case of Serb ethnic nationalism, one study found that 'violent conflict along ethnic cleavages [was] provoked by elites in order to create a domestic political context where ethnicity is the only politically relevant identity' (Gagnon, 1994–95: 132). This suggests that ethnicity, under such circumstances, becomes a resource in the hands of political elites seeking to obtain positions of power via nationalist appeals that aim not only to invest one's own ethnic group with a certain political legitimacy (and by implication themselves as leaders), but also to delegitimize 'ethnic Others'.

In contrast, civic nationalism assumes, in principle, the equal political legitimacy of any citizen or group of citizens within the state regardless of their identity, ethnic or otherwise. The civic concept of 'the nation' is therefore an open one, in that membership depends only on a person's status as a citizen and citizenship is, in principle, available to people regardless of their ethnic identity. The political values underpinning such practices are usually associated with those of liberal democracy and include secularism as the basis of religious freedom and tolerance. What unites citizens is acceptance of these principles as the basis for common membership within a state, notwithstanding inevitable political disagreement in the policy sphere.

States that operate formally along the lines of such principles, however, often fall short in practice. As noted previously, national identity in contemporary multicultural states such as the US, the UK, Australia, and Canada is generally configured around a white Anglophone majority, which has created a dominant culture reflecting its own values. Even when multiculturalism is official policy, minorities obviously can and do face discrimination, often in subtle ways. Moreover, none of these states offer easy admission to anyone wanting to join 'the nation' as a citizen.

The French state espouses another version of civic nationalism. It treats all citizens as equally French regardless of ethnic origin, or cultural or religious affiliation, but is strongly assimilationist in expecting citizens to fully embrace its republican values regardless of their own cultural background. One may ask whether this is much different from expectations in the officially multicultural Anglophone states, where pressures to assimilate are also present, and all are expected to embrace the state's liberal democratic values and institutions.

✳ KEY POINTS

- Ethnic nationalism, which aims at establishing the legitimacy of a particular named group, combines and politicizes elements of shared history, heritage, and ancestry, which often include common religious, linguistic, or other cultural ties.
- Civic nationalism assumes, in principle, the equal political legitimacy of any citizen regardless of their ethnic identity and therefore that membership is, in principle, available to virtually anyone who accepts the values of the state.

Anti-Colonial Nationalism

The third variety of nationalism to be considered here is anti-colonial nationalism. This phenomenon began to emerge in the colonized world (or more specifically, those parts of the world colonized by Europeans) after the First World War, taking practical form in the widespread movement for decolonization in Africa, Asia, and the Pacific that followed the Second World War. Although directed against European domination, anti-colonial nationalism drew much of its inspiration from certain European liberal-democratic ideas about justice, human rights, and especially national self-determination. These ideas had been absorbed by students from the colonial empires—especially those educated in Europe and the US, as well as from the more liberal missionaries active in the colonies— and were further encouraged by European socialists and Labour figures of the time (Neuberger, 2006: 516).

There is also a sense in which colonialism created the very identities on which many anti-colonial nationalist movements came to be based. Most states on the African continent today are based squarely on boundaries established by colonial powers, which brought together many different ethnic groups in a single political unit where no such unit had existed before. This was achieved through the doctrine of *uti possidetis juris*, which held that the territorial boundaries of postcolonial states should follow those of the former colonial state, the purpose being to minimize territorial disputes (Saltford, 2003: 8). This doctrine held firm throughout most of the decolonization process in Africa and elsewhere.

One author notes that Ghana faced the problem of 'reconciling an anticolonial national ideology that claimed continuity with precolonial indigenous culture with the fact that the modern national polity was successor to the colonial state, relying no less on the continued subordination of a diversity of indigenous societies' (Mock, 2012: 152). In other cases, sub-state identities were also created under colonial rule, some of which were to become highly problematic in later years. The presence of 'Hutus' and 'Tutsis' in Rwanda, for example, are said to be the result of colonial manipulations of identity and rest on no genuine ethnic differences at all (Brown, 2000: 161). Yet they came to acquire such power *as* identities that one of the late twentieth century's worst genocides, when up to 1 million Tutsis were massacred by Hutus over a period of just 100 days in 1994, was based on the politicization of perceptions of meaningful differences between the two categories.

In Asia, a prime example of how a national identity was forged out of the highly disparate elements that made up the colonial state is Indonesia. In place of the Dutch East Indies, the idea of 'Indonesia'—and of 'Indonesians'—developed in the context of a concerted effort by indigenous intellectuals and activists in key positions to articulate a unitary vision of a unified independent state along the lines of one people, one language, one *bangsa* (nation), where there was, in reality, a considerable diversity of ethnic groups, languages, and cultural practices throughout the archipelago. The success of *bangsa Indonesia* grew out of aligning the myriad identities of sub-state ethnic groups in opposition to Dutch rule rather than attempting to impose a single cultural template. This made anti-colonial nationalism more territorial than ethnic or cultural (Reid, 2010: 110). Much of the strength of Indonesian nationalism today comes from the accommodation of ethnic differences within the state, although there is no question that this has limits when it comes to some minorities, and there have been serious separatist movements in Aceh and West Papua. Also, the security forces have played a much greater role in enforcing and maintaining national unity and order within the state than in safeguarding it from external threats. More generally, it is notable that the early themes of anti-colonial nationalism have resonated throughout the seven decades or so of Indonesian independence and remain an important sub-text of contemporary nationalism, which continues to 'draw heavily on the terminology and symbols of the anti-colonial struggle' (Aspinall, 2015: 76).

The postcolonial world has seen many instances of sub-state nationalist conflict arising between various groups in the aftermath of independence, some seeking either a form of autonomy within the state or complete secession to create an entirely new, independent state. But it was firmly resisted both by those in control of postcolonial states, as well as by the international community. While the struggle for independence from (European) colonial masters was seen as heroic, the struggle for independence on the part of minorities who felt trapped in the new states was not (Pavković and Radan, 2016: 2). The only secessionist movement to succeed during the entire Cold War period was Bangladesh, which split from Pakistan in 1971. Pakistan, originally consisting of West Pakistan and East Pakistan (now Bangladesh), had itself been created in the process of decolonization in 1947 for the purpose of establishing a Muslim-majority state separate from Hindu-majority India. But West Pakistan's attempt to dominate and subordinate East Pakistan sparked resistance, resulting in a violent war of liberation to establish the new state of Bangladesh.

The most recent example of secession is South Sudan, which formally split from Sudan in 2011 after years of violent confrontations. As in the original split between India and Pakistan, religion was a key element, with Muslims predominating in the northern part of Sudan and Christians in the south, but where some also adhere to indigenous belief systems. The creation of South Sudan as a sovereign state, however, has scarcely resolved other problems within the country, with yet another civil war, based partly on ethnic differences, developing in the aftermath of independence as South Sudanese government and opposition groups failed to forge a peaceful political path ahead. As of 2017, a brittle peace prevails, but some 13,000 UN peacekeeping troops remain stationed in the country. South Sudan ranks second on the 'Fragile State' Index (previously known as the 'Failed State' Index) after Somalia. What these and other cases show are the extraordinarily difficulties associated with 'nation-building', as explained in **Key Concept 6.7**, although these difficulties have not been confined to the former colonial world, as the case of the former Yugoslavia attests.

Like all varieties of nationalism, it is clear that anti-colonial nationalism is a complex phenomenon with many different facets, although it shares in common with other varieties a political project entailing the creation of a sovereign state. But as we have seen, it is

KEY CONCEPT 6.7   **Nation-building**

Nation-building entails a deliberate political project of inculcating a common national identity among a diverse citizenship. It has typically been applied to new states formed in the process of decolonization, whose leaders perceived the importance of strengthening cohesion and forging a common sense of purpose among otherwise disparate groups.

equally clear that there is rarely just one single, identifiable, 'nation' involved in the process of state creation, or in the transformation of a colonial state into a new sovereign state, but rather a plurality of groups, each of which may in time make a claim to the right of self-determination in a sovereign state of its own.

 KEY POINTS

- Anti-colonial nationalism is generally directed against European domination, although historically it drew much of its inspiration from certain European liberal-democratic ideas—especially the right to national self-determination.
- Anti-colonial nationalism shares in common with other varieties a political project entailing the creation of a sovereign state and has just as often required a project of 'nation-building' in an attempt to forge a single national group out of a diverse population.

Nationalism and Globalization in the Contemporary World

When the United Nations was established in 1945, it had just 51 members. By 1980, that number had tripled, due largely to decolonization. Following the end of the Cold War and the creation of many new sovereign states in Eastern Europe and the former USSR, the number grew again, reaching 189 by the end of the century. With the addition of South Sudan in 2011, membership is now 193. Each state claims some basis in nationality and so the trend over the last seven decades or so appears to reflect a strengthening of the basic principle of nationalism—that nations should have their own states and that states should be based on nations. If that principle were carried through to its logical conclusion, however, there would seem to be no end to the establishment of new states, for there are potentially hundreds of 'nations' that could claim sovereign status. As we have also seen, there is a large category of 'nations without states', or at least nations without a state specifically of its own. Many have already staked a claim, with separatist/independence movements active in such places as Quebec in Canada, Bougainville in Papua New Guinea, West Papua in Indonesia, Scotland in the UK, Catalonia in Spain, and so on. Of course, it remains to be seen just how many of these movements will eventually succeed in creating a new state based on their conception of a legitimate nation.

At the same time, trends in globalization—a process involving political, social, cultural, and economic dynamics transcending both nation and state—are sometimes thought to be countering the impact and influence of nationalist movements. Although globalization, as a historic phenomenon, may be seen as occurring over a very long period, the idea only gained currency following the end of the Cold War, even amid the flurry of new nation-state formation at the time. One well-known globalist, Kenichi Ohmae, opined that the traditional nation-state model was in terminal decline and would be replaced by more efficient and meaningful regional conglomerations held together by economic and commercial interests and populated by consumers, rather than by citizens sharing common ethnic or cultural attributes. A few years later, another commentator, Michael Mandelbaum, joined the discussion, but was less certain about when, if ever, the nation-state would give way to another model. Their views are expressed succinctly in **Key Quotes 6.8**.

Views such as those of Ohmae and Mandelbaum prompt further questions about what would replace nation-states as units of both political organization and community belonging, which provide a whole range of functions. The capacity of nation-states, or at least the governments in control of them, to utilize their resources to prosecute large-scale warfare, not to mention the mass murder of their own citizens, has been demonstrated only too

---

Q KEY QUOTES 6.8 **Kenichi Ohmae and Michael Mandelbaum on the decline of the nation-state**

'The nation state has become an unnatural, even dysfunctional, unit for organizing human activity and managing economic endeavor in a borderless world. It represents no genuine, shared community of economic interests; it defines no meaningful flows of economic activity. In fact, it overlooks the true linkages and synergies that exist among often disparate populations by combining important measures of human activity at the wrong level of analysis.' (Ohmae, 1993: 78)

'The eclipse of the nation-state has been regularly foretold; now, as in the past, the state is not on the verge of withering away. But its once overweening and still formidable powers are plainly, if slowly and unevenly, declining. It is possible that they may someday diminish to the point at which the borders of sovereign states will have no more significance than those of American postal zones, and the bitter twentieth-century conflicts over borders will seem as distant and puzzling as the theological disputes that provoked battles and persecutions in medieval Europe do to us.' (Mandelbaum, 1999: 26)

clearly throughout the modern period. Various forms of nationalism have driven many of these episodes, or have at least been a major factor. Even those states imbued with a more civic national consciousness are not immune.

But after nearly three decades of intensive globalization in the post-Cold-War period, it seems that the nation-state idea is gaining in strength rather than weakening under its pressures. Some may well read this shift as a reaction against globalization, as exemplified by the apparent appeal of the populist nationalism purveyed by Donald Trump, as explained in **Key Concept 6.9**. This was expressed throughout his campaign, as well as in his 'America First' inaugural address, which promised a strong shift to economic protectionism through which a 'new national pride will stir our souls, lift our sights, and heal our divisions' (Trump, 2017). But neither globalization nor nationalism have had their day and, even though the forces underpinning each may appear contradictory, both are likely to continue to coexist for a long time to come.

 KEY POINTS

- Although it is often assumed that globalization undermines the nation-state idea, nation-state creation in the era of globalization following the end of the Cold War almost rivals that of the decolonization era.
- Globalization and nationalism are both powerful forces and will almost certainly continue to coexist, albeit in tension, for a long time to come.
- Populism and nationalism appear to have combined in a backlash against globalization in the contemporary period.

 KEY CONCEPT 6.9   Populist nationalism

It is commonly believed that we live in an era in which 'populism' and 'nationalism' have combined to produce a backlash not only against globalization, but also against domestic policies on such matters as immigration and multiculturalism. Populism is generally understood as embodying an appeal by certain political elites to the 'ordinary person', whose essential rights and interests have allegedly been ignored by other parties. In the context of nationalist debates about 'keeping foreigners out' and 'protecting jobs at home', populism combines with such nationalist sentiments to produce a powerful political discourse that leads many to seek an alternative to the kind of 'politics as usual' represented by more mainstream politicians or parties, whose policies tend to cluster around the centre ground of politics. Contemporary populist nationalists are generally associated with right-wing politics, but there is no reason to assume that left-wing politics is immune.

Conclusion

Nationalism is a highly complex ideology exhibiting many different facets and forms, but in virtually all cases resting on some particularistic conception of the nation and its legitimate territorial domain and involving a strong orientation to the modern sovereign state. Certainly, whatever their historic status and the manner of their formation, nations are seen as integral to, and indeed constitutive of, the modern state. This is as true of 'multinational states', where a dominant sector of the population generally dictates national interests and values, as it is of more homogeneous states. The 'nation-state' is therefore set to endure as a category in global political order for the foreseeable future, even though the constitution of particular nations and the political claims made in their name remain deeply contested. As for the ideology of nationalism, it is likely to remain a powerful force at various levels of politics even as other forces seem to undermine it from time to time.

6

? Key Questions

- What constitutes a nation, on the one hand, and a state, on the other?
- Is there a real difference between a nation and an ethnic group?
- What is meant by the term 'imagined community'?
- In what sense is nationalism a 'modern' ideology?
- Which theoretical approach to nations and nationalism do you find most compelling and why?
- What is the difference between ethnic nationalism and civic nationalism?
- What are the main features of anti-colonial nationalism?
- Is 'nation-building' an issue only for the former colonial world?
- Is nationalism under serious challenge from globalization or is it the other way around?
- How do you see the future of nations and nationalism?

 ## Further Reading

Breuilly, John (ed.) (2013), *The Oxford Handbook of the History of Nationalism* (Oxford: Oxford University Press).
This book comprises a significant collection of essays by leading scholars of nationalism, global in scope and with much historical depth. It looks at different forms taken by nationalist ideology from Europe to the Middle East, Asia, and the Americas.

Herb, Guntrum H., and Kaplan, David H. (eds) (2008), *Nations and Nationalism: A Global Historical Overview* (Santa Barbara, CA: ABC-Clio).
A comprehensive work, presented in four volumes, this collection provides another detailed coverage of the phenomenon of nationalism around the world, starting with the French Revolution and taking the reader through to the early twentieth century.

Hobsbawm, E. J. (1992), *Nations and Nationalism since 1780: Programme, Myth, Reality* (Cambridge: Cambridge University Press, 2nd edn).
A classic work on nations and nationalism by a leading historian, this work also starts with the French Revolution, ending with an analysis of the end of the Cold War and its implications for nationalism, mainly in Europe and the former USSR.

Rÿser, Rudolph C. (2012), *Indigenous Nations and Modern States: The Political Emergence of Nations Challenging State Power* (New York: Routledge).
This is a more specialized study, looking at the phenomenon of what the author calls 'bedrock nations'—indigenous people whom many once thought would be absorbed and assimilated by modern societies, but whose identities have survived to take up a role as assertive political actors in many contemporary states.

Spencer, Phillip, and Wollman, Howard (eds) (2005), *Nations and Nationalism: A Reader* (New Brunswick, NJ: Rutgers University Press).
Another interesting collection of essays by key commentators on the subject matter, providing an overview of the origins, different types, and concepts of nationalism, issues such as race, gender, and ethnicity, and the impact of globalization and migration, as well as debates about citizenship and self-determination.

 Web Links

https://plato.stanford.edu/entries/nationalism/
The online Stanford Encyclopedia of Philosophy provides an excellent scholarly account of the ideology of nationalism, including moral debates.

http://www.the-american-interest.com/2016/07/10/when-and-why-nationalism-beats-globalism/
A contemporary commentary on the nationalism/globalism debate and why nationalism seems to be on the rise.

https://nationalismstudies.wordpress.com/
Website of the Association for the Study of Ethnicity and Nationalism, based at the London School of Economics and Political Science.

https://blog.oup.com/2016/12/nationalism-brexit-identity-referendum/
Oxford University Press blog site discussing the role of nationalism in the Brexit vote.

 Visit the **Online Resources** that accompany this book to access more learning resources on this topic: www.oup.com/uk/ferdinand/

The Ideal State

7

- Political Theory and Normative Analysis
- Justifying the State
- Consent and Democracy
- The Social Contract
- The General Will
- Utilitarianism
- Liberalism, Liberty, and the State
- Marxism and Communitarianism
- The Just State
- Political Theory beyond the State
- Anarchism and the State
- Conclusion
- Key Questions
- Further Reading
- Web Links

Reader's Guide

This chapter is concerned with articulating the basics of political philosophy. Most political philosophy is normative in character. A key question that political philosophers engage with is what makes the state legitimate, or what is the ideal state we ought to be striving for. To answer this question, we can focus on either procedures or substantive outcomes. In the former, the way in which the state comes about, or the way in which the state makes decisions, provides the grounds on which to judge the state's legitimacy. Here, we examine the issues of consent and democracy. In the latter, it is what the state does that is the basis for assessing its legitimacy. Here, we consider a range of possible answers that political philosophers have given. These include security, the protection of natural rights, the general will, the pursuit of happiness, community, liberty, and justice. There are two caveats to the chapter's preoccupation with the state. The first is the Marxist and anarchist claim that the state can never be legitimate. The second is the claim that political philosophy's focus on the state is inappropriate, given the increasing interconnectedness of the world and the state's declining power.

Political Theory and Normative Analysis

This chapter is concerned with articulating the basics of political philosophy or political theory, which terms are used interchangeably. The traditional approach of political philosophers is normative—that is, they are not preoccupied with asking how states are organized, or how much freedom is allowed for individuals within the state, or other questions that political scientists might ask. Rather, they are concerned with asking how the state *ought* to be organized and how much freedom *ought* individuals be granted.

This chapter is unmistakable normative in tone, but we can make at least three caveats to the claim that this is what political philosophy ought primarily to be about. In the first place, a great deal of political philosophy consists of semantic analysis, in which the meaning of key political concepts is explored. Second, some political theorists promote political realism as an alternative (Rossi and Sleat, 2014). This approach suggests that political philosophy should distance itself from normative analysis in order to distinguish itself from moral philosophy. Instead, it ought to focus on specifically political values such as order, stability, conflict, authority, and interests (themes that are covered extensively in this book).

Finally, some political theorists now seek to distinguish between ideal and non-ideal theory. Here, a number of contemporary political philosophers have noted the discrepancy between the abstract normative work of some political philosophy, in which ideal political and moral principles are advocated, and the difficulty of applying such principles in the non-ideal real world. John Rawls' theory of justice, discussed below, is often taken to be the classical example of an ideal theory. As he writes (Rawls, 1971: 9), 'the nature and aims of a perfectly just society is the fundamental part of the theory of justice'.

Advocates of so-called non-ideal theory are not claiming simply that political pragmatism should prevail over normative political philosophy, but rather that any political philosophy that does not take account of the non-ideal world in which it is attempting to influence and address is normatively deficient (Farrelly, 2007). In other words, it is being claimed that normative political principles, such as those present in many theories of justice, are not logically independent from questions relating to non-ideal constraints, whether they concern unsympathetic social, economic, or historical circumstances, moral disagreement, or human nature. This boils down to the well-known moral principle that 'ought implies can'. As Farrelly (2007: 845) points out, 'there is some conceptual incoherence involved in saying "This is what justice involves, but there is no way it could be implemented"'. In other words, a valid theory of justice must be relevant to the eradication of at least some current injustices.

Justifying the State

Needless to say, it is difficult to cover in one book, let alone one chapter, the ground covered by centuries of philosophizing about politics. One useful way of undertaking this unenviable task is to focus on the answers given to one simple question: how can the state be justified? Or, to put it another way, what makes the state legitimate? What, that is, is the ideal state that we would recommend for humans to live under? Answers to this question represent the core of political philosophy, which has as its fundamental aim the identification of the ideal polity and the good society. This question is related to an important preoccupation of political philosophers, the idea of political obligation, which considers what, if any, grounds there are for obeying the state. The task of considering why we should obey the state is important because of its compulsory nature. If we join a voluntary organization, such as a pressure group or a church, we have to accept the rules of that organization, but if we do not like them, we have the option of leaving. For most of us, we do not have the same option when it comes to the state. Some people may be able to go and live somewhere more to their liking, but for most people, that is not an option—and it is certainly not an option to live in a stateless society. Most of us do not have a choice when it comes to accepting the laws of the state, or at least if we choose not to obey the state, then we can expect sanctions to be applied against us.

Consent and Democracy

So, what does make a state legitimate? Here, it is useful to make a distinction. To answer our question, we can focus on either procedures or substantive outcomes. In the former, the way in which the state comes about, or the way in which the state makes decisions, provides the grounds on which to judge the state's legitimacy. In the latter, it is what the state does that is the basis for assessing its legitimacy.

In terms of procedure, one of the most popular ways of legitimizing the state is to say that if we consent to it, then we are obliged to obey it. This principle derives principally from John Locke, the seventeenth-century English political philosopher, who argued that since we have a natural right to freedom, only our consent can justify political power being exercised over us. Of course, we then have to ask: what precisely is it that counts as consent? Political philosophers have got themselves into a bit of a muddle trying to answer this question. Most notoriously, Locke argued that consent need not be expressly given, in the sense that someone has to actually formally register their consent. Instead, Locke argued, consent can also be given tacitly, in the sense that it does not require a formal act. Locke (1690/1988: 177) argues, then, that if an individual lives under a particular political jurisdiction, gaining the benefits—whatever they may be—of doing so, then that person can be said to have consented to political rule.

Clearly, this is problematic, not least because for most people there is little choice but to live where they are. Political philosophers tend to argue, therefore, that consent must be expressed. Moreover, it must be continuous, since no subsequent generation can be bound by the consent of their predecessors. But how is this to be achieved? One suggestion is that voting serves this function (Singer, 1973)—that is, that when we vote, irrespective of the outcome, we accept (or consent to) the political order under which we live. This clearly provides an option not to consent—by not voting or spoiling a ballot paper. It follows logically that those who do not choose to vote are withholding consent and are not then obliged to obey the state. The obvious problem here is that those who vote are not primarily, if at all, knowingly consenting to the political system. Likewise, many who fail to vote clearly do so for reasons other than registering their lack of consent. Moreover, even if we choose not to vote, we will be forced by the state to obey laws in any case, so non-voting has no purchase in this regard. Voting, by itself, then, is not an express act of consent and incurs the same problem as residence (Hyams, 2015: 12–13).

For some political philosophers, consent through mere voting is not enough to make a state legitimate. Instead, we only have an obligation to obey the state if we accept the outcome deriving from our vote. This is important, it is argued, because only if we get what we want from decisions made will we remain as autonomous as we were before a political community was created. If a decision is made with which we profoundly disagree, maybe because it does not serve our interests well, then being obliged to go along with it limits our autonomy (or sphere of freedom). As a result, for political philosophers such as Robert Paul Wolff (1970), the only legitimate kind of society is one that preserves individual autonomy and this, for Wolff, is an anarchist society, a society without government (see below for a discussion of anarchism).

The importance attached to maximizing our autonomy helps us to explain why democratic forms of government are regarded as politically desirable. Democracy seems to offer us the ideal grounding for political obligation because if we make the laws under which we live, then they are likely to be in our interests and therefore we get what we want. In other words, we do not lose anything as a result of being in a political community. As we saw in Chapter 4, however, democracy is associated with majority rule. It is very rare for unanimity to break out when a political decision is made. According to the position associated with Wolff, those who find themselves in a minority are not obliged to accept the law—and because there is no solution to the majority rule problem, no government can ever be legitimate, requiring everyone to be obligated to it. If we were able to discover a way of ensuring that the outputs of the state are unanimously approved, the political obligation problem identified by Wolff would be solved. One such attempt—centred on the general will—is examined below.

✱ KEY POINTS

- With some caveats, political philosophy has been traditionally concerned with normative analysis.
- A key question political philosophers have sought to answer is: why, if at all, is the state legitimate?
- From the perspective of procedures, consent and democracy have been regarded as two legitimizing devices. Both, however, are problematic.

● The problem with democracy as a source of a political obligation is that few, if any, decisions are going to be made unanimously. As a result, the minority are going to have to accept decisions with which they disagree, thereby reducing their freedom.

The Social Contract

The second way of determining what makes the state legitimate is to focus on outcomes. Is there something that the state ought to do if we are to owe allegiance to it? A classic means of determining what the role of the state ought to be is provided by the liberal social contract tradition. This is particularly associated with the work of seventeenth-century liberal political thinkers Thomas Hobbes (1588–1679) and John Locke (1632–1704). The social contract tradition is based around the idea of an imaginary state of nature, where individuals exist without government. In other words, it is argued that in order to find out what form of government is justified and why, we should try to consider what life would be like without the state. Social contract theorists envisage individuals coming together to decide the nature of the political system under which they will live. This approach was also adopted by a twentieth-century liberal political philosopher, John Rawls, whose ideas we will consider later in the chapter. This contract is hypothetical—that is, social contract theorists are not suggesting that this contract was ever made in practice. Rather, they are suggesting what individuals *ought* to have agreed to if they were in a contractural situation.

Despite using the same social contract methodology, Hobbes and Locke provide very different versions of an ideal state. Much of the difference revolves around the issue of human nature, a key variable in political thought (see Plant, 1991: ch. 1). Hobbes famous-ly paints a picture of human nature as egotistical and competitive. Without government, life is very insecure. Indeed, in a well-known phrase, life in the state of nature, for Hobbes (1651/1992: 186), is 'solitary, poor, nasty, brutish and short'. As a result, a political system is necessary in order to impose order and ensure security both from the risk of external threat and from the threat of internal conflict. The ideal political system for Hobbes, then, is an all-powerful sovereign, which Hobbes describes as the *Leviathan* (**see Figure 7.1**).

John Locke, writing a little later, appears to be much less pessimistic about human nature and the ability of human beings to rub along without undue conflict. Because there are no immediate security considerations for Locke (1690/1988), individuals should choose to live under political rule only when it protects what individuals have in the state of nature. For Locke, individuals have natural rights, given by God, and these natural rights ought to be protected by the state (**see Key Concept 7.1**). Locke promotes what became known as negative rights. These rights—to life, liberty, and property—are rights against societal and state interference.

▶ For Hobbes' influence on international theory, see Chapter 17.

FIGURE 7.1   Hobbes' Leviathan
Library of Congress / Wikimedia Commons /
Public Domain

◀▶ KEY CONCEPT 7.1   Natural rights

It is common to make a distinction between natural rights and legal rights. Legal rights are those that exist within a particular society at a particular time. They are simply statements, then, of what the existing law is and what rights the state will protect. Natural rights, on the other hand, are rights that humans are said to possess irrespective of the particular legal and political system under which they live. These are said to derive from natural law, a higher law, handed down from nature or God. In a more secular age, what were previously described as natural rights have been renamed as human rights (Woods, 2014).

Modern liberal thinkers, writing particularly after 1945, have argued for the existence of positive rights. These are rights to things, such as free education and health care, which are enshrined in the United Nations Convention on Human Rights, established in 1948. These positive rights have the potential to conflict with the negative rights promoted by Locke. In particular, the right to own property can conflict with other, more positive, rights and some political thinkers writing particularly from a Marxist perspective have criticized Locke for seeking to defend a possessive individualism that justifies selfishness, greed, and vast inequalities (Macpherson, 1962).

The General Will

We said earlier that there is one potential solution to the problem of majoritarianism and the consequent loss of autonomy. This is the idea of the **general will**. The general will has been a popular theme in political philosophy but it is particularly associated with eighteenth-century French philosopher Jean-Jacques Rousseau (1913). For Rousseau, general will can be contrasted with the selfish, particular, wills of individuals. It is tantamount, then, to the common good, something that is in the general interest of the community—that is, in the collective interests of society. This general will, then, amounts to more than the sum of particular wills. Rather, it is a genuine collective will, irrespective of the particular wills of members of the community. Rousseau holds that if the state pursues this common or general interest—and not particular interests—then we have an obligation to obey it. Hegel adopts a very similar theory, whereby the state pursues the common interest, thereby transcending the particular interests pursued by families and by **civil society**.

Rousseau's arguments are more complex than has been suggested so far. We can coax them out by looking at what might be regarded as a key problem with his theory. We might respond to Rousseau and other advocates of the general will by asking: what is so good about it? Why are we obliged to accept it? Why should I not be selfish and encourage the state to pursue a programme that is in my own selfish interests? We might answer by saying that we ought to obey the general will because it is the right and moral thing to do. The problem with this is that some people may deny the importance of this moral edict and say, 'I'm still not going to obey the general will because, on this occasion at least, it is not in my interests to do it'. It is at this point that Rousseau's argument becomes a little more complex and contentious, for he wants to claim that not only should we promote the general will, but also this is what we really want to do. He even goes as far as to say that if we are forced to accept the general will, then we are being forced to be free (Rousseau, 1913). We are being forced to be free because we are being forced to accept what we really want to do.

Rousseau's theory is heavily dependent on the very existence of a community's collective will. Some political theorists suggest that that idea is a fiction. Of course, if this is the case, it becomes a potentially dangerous doctrine, open to abuse by a dictator who justifies tyrannical measures on the spurious grounds that they are in the 'public' or 'collective' interest (Talmon, 1952). Here, critics have been particularly scathing about the implications of Rousseau's claim that it is legitimate to force someone to be free. This aspect of Rousseau's theory relies on a particular conception of freedom, which we will consider below.

For now, if we accept that Rousseau is right and that we all do really want to pursue the general will, it is important to recognize that he has found a solution to the loss of autonomy that political philosophers such as Wolff find so problematic about the state. For Rousseau, a political system that we can all accept because we want to does not require us to sacrifice any of our autonomy. Rousseau (1913: 191) sets out his task as follows:

The problem is to find a form of association which will defend and protect with the whole common force the person and goods of each associate, and in which each, while uniting himself with all, may still obey himself alone, and remain as free as before. This is the fundamental problem of which the social contract provides the solution.

Rousseau's answer is that we can all obey a political system that pursues the general will and remain as free as we were before, because the general will is what we all want. In other words, what the state wants to do, if it pursues the general will, can be unanimously accepted as representing the will of all.

✳ KEY POINTS

- The liberal social contract tradition, represented most notably by Hobbes and Locke, provides different reasons to justify the state, the former focusing on security; the latter, on the protection of natural rights.
- If Rousseau is right that we always really want the state to promote the general will, he has solved the problem of political obligation. This is because even if we oppose the general will, we can be forced to follow it, which is tantamount to being forced to be free. Our allegiance to the state therefore makes us as free as we were before a political community was created.

Utilitarianism

⏩ See Chapter 4 for a description of the utilitarian theory of democracy.

Another influential account of state legitimacy is the philosophy known as **utilitarianism**. The utilitarian theory of the state is associated with the work of British political thinker Jeremy Bentham (1748–1832). Bentham (1948) argues that the key to judging the effectiveness of a government is the degree to which it promotes the greatest happiness, or, as he sometimes put it, the greatest happiness of the greatest number. Happiness, for Bentham, is associated with pleasure. Insofar as governments do maximize happiness, then they are valid; if they fall short of this goal, then they are not. The state should therefore stop individuals causing pain to others through a rigorous system of punishment. Moreover, the state also has a paternalistic role to ensure that individuals do pursue what is in their best interests and therefore maximize their own happiness. Bentham came to think that only if they are accountable to the electorate will rulers seek to maximize the happiness of all, rather than their own happiness. This forms the basis of the utilitarian theory of democracy.

The chief advantage of utilitarianism as a general ethical theory, as well as a guide to political action, is that it is flexible enough to justify the attainment of what most would regard as important social goals. By focusing on the happiness of the community, rather than the protection of individual rights, it is able to sanction the kind of collective goals associated with the welfare state. On the downside, utilitarianism—or at least the classical version associated with Bentham—has been criticized for its aggregative character (**see Key Debate 7.2**).

 KEY DEBATE 7.2 **Rights versus utilitarianism**

Traditionally, the two dominant approaches to ethics have been rights and utilitarianism. Until relatively recently, it was utilitarianism that held sway, but since the Second World War, rights theory has made a significant comeback. The following points should be borne in mind when considering the merits of the two approaches.

- Utilitarianism is a secular theory. It therefore 'does not depend on the existence of God, or a soul, or any other dubious metaphysical entity' (Kymlicka, 2002: 11). Earlier versions of rights tended to have such a religious overtone.

- By focusing on the consequences of an action and not the motives of those responsible, utilitarians ask us to consider those who are affected by it. This would seem to be a laudable goal.

- On the other hand, utilitarianism is intuitively mistaken in assuming that there is nothing amiss in an action taken for malicious motives that inadvertently produces a desirable outcome. Imagine, for instance, that I attack someone and severely injure them. All things being equal, most would want to condemn my behaviour. However, imagine too that it was subsequently discovered that my action prevented that person from continuing on his way where someone else was waiting with the intention of killing him. Suddenly, it is not certain, on utilitarian grounds, that my action ought to be condemned after all.

- Conversely, it seems odd to condemn an action taken for the best of motives that produces undesirable consequences. Imagine, for instance, that I am teaching a group of students in a very hot room. I take pity on them by opening the window in order to let more air in and, as a result, a wasp flies in and stings one of the students, who subsequently dies. Most would argue that I ought not to be blamed for this, particularly if I did not know that the student in question was allergic to wasp stings. However, because it is only concerned about consequences, a utilitarian analysis would hold that my action was morally reprehensible.

- Utilitarianism 'provides a clear and definite procedure for determining which acts are right or wrong' (Brandt, 1992: 113). By contrast, rights theory struggles with what to do in situations where rights conflict. For example, should the right to free health care or education be more important than the right to the fruits of one's own property?

7

- Utilitarianism is flexible enough to justify the attainment of what most would regard as important social goals. It is therefore more flexible and less individualistic than rights. On the other hand, as a deontological theory, rights theory, unlike utilitarianism, seeks to protect individuals whose fundamental interests cannot, under normal circumstances, be sacrificed in order to promote the general welfare (Dworkin, 1978). It therefore avoids the aggregative consequences of utilitarianism, thereby ensuring that individual interests cannot be sacrificed for some greater good. As a result, 'it avoids the very counter-intuitive solutions to questions of distributive justice' that utilitarianism offers (Carruthers, 1992: 27). In Jones' words (1994: 62): 'There is no end to the horror stories that can be concocted to illustrate the awful possibilities that utilitarianism might endorse.' The persecution of a racial minority in the interests of a racist majority is one such example among many other possibilities.

Questions

1. What are the implications of adopting a utilitarian approach to public policy?
2. What criticisms can you make of a political discourse based on rights?

 KEY POINTS

- A utilitarian position argues that the state is legitimate insofar as it maximizes happiness.
- Utilitarianism's emphasis on consequentialism is challenged by rights discourse, which seeks to protect individuals whatever the consequences for the general welfare.

Liberalism, Liberty, and the State

The classical liberal theory of the state, which is closely associated with pluralism, holds that the state ought to remain neutral as between different conceptions of the good. A liberal society's function, Arblaster (1984: 45) suggests, 'is to serve individuals, and one of the ways in which it should do this is by respecting their autonomy, and not trespassing on their rights to do as they please as long as they can do so without harm to others'. This harm principle, associated with J. S. Mill, is central to the liberal emphasis on freedom and toleration. It is also the central theme of John Rawls' later work, as laid out in his *Political Liberalism* (1993).

So, what is the case for regarding freedom as a desirable objective that the state should uphold? Before we can examine this question, we need to define what we mean by freedom.

This is necessary because, like many other political concepts, freedom—or liberty (the terms are used interchangeably here)—is a difficult concept to define. Like democracy, part of the problem is that freedom is regarded as a 'good' concept, one that all governments should pursue. The reality, however, is that there may be good grounds for limiting freedom to pursue other goods that are valued.

The most oft-cited definitional distinction is between negative and positive varieties of freedom. This distinction is particularly associated with Oxford political theorist Isaiah Berlin (1909–97). Berlin famously argued, in an article first published in 1958, that these represent the two main, and distinct, conceptions of freedom. The negative conception is concerned with the question, 'What is the area within which the subject . . . is or should be left to do or be what he is able to do or be, without interference by other persons?', while the positive conception is concerned with the question, 'What, or who, is the source of control or interference that can determine someone to do, or be, this rather than that?' (Berlin, 1969: 121–2.) Therefore, Berlin seeks to distinguish between the area of control, emphasized by negative liberty, and the source of control, emphasized by positive freedom. The ability of individuals to be self-governing, then, is crucial for advocates of the latter.

Berlin's purpose in making this distinction was primarily to defend negative liberty against advocates of the positive version. Indeed, he was violently opposed to the latter version, seeing it as an enemy of real freedom. This was because he argued that self-government usually involved the argument that genuine freedom requires that the 'real' (rational or moral) self be established over the 'actual' self. Berlin emphasized the illiberal implications of this move.

A useful way of understanding these two different versions of freedom is to consider what might count as a constraint on our freedom. Perhaps the most obvious constraint on our freedom is when we are *physically coerced* by others. Here, we are unfree when others physically constrain us from doing what we want to do. This is the classic formulation of negative freedom. Some political theorists would also want to say that our freedom can be limited by a lack of *rationality* or *morality*. In other words, the constraint here is not other people, but ourselves. This is the classic formulation of positive freedom. Only rational or moral behaviour, then, can be truly free. In other words, we are free insofar as we behave morally or altruistically, acting in accordance with the common interest, or what Rousseau (as we saw above) describes as the general will. Conversely, we are unfree insofar as we behave immorally or selfishly.

This view, that freedom is linked to morality, is a central feature of one version of the so-called positive theory of liberty. The main advocate is Jean-Jacques Rousseau. The credibility of this approach to freedom depends on the validity of the assertion that what we really want to do is to behave morally, and insofar as we do not behave morally, we are not doing what we really want to do. We become unfree, therefore, if we behave selfishly because ultimately we do not want to be selfish. It is in this sense that Rousseau can argue that we can be 'forced to be free'.

In response to the attempt to link freedom with morality, we might want to say that it seems to confuse two very different values. There may be a case when it makes sense to say that we can be freed from our desires—as in the case of, say, a paedophile who genuinely wants to behave in a different way. However, this requires a recognition from the individual himself that his behaviour is unacceptable, coupled with a desire to change it. The notion of forcing someone to be free goes further than this by arguing that someone can be coerced into behaving differently. There may be a case for saying that this is justifiable and indeed the state does intervene (as in the case of paedophiles) to try to change behaviour. However, it seems more appropriate to say in such cases that the state is imposing society's moral standards on individuals not in order to make people freer, but on the grounds that the moral principle is important enough to justify sacrificing freedom for.

Another constraint that can illustrate the difference between positive and negative notions of freedom relates to *economic impediments*. If we regard freedom as merely the absence of externally imposed physical coercion, we would seem to be saying that freedom is best achieved if the state and society leave people largely to their own devices. Some political thinkers argue, however, that, by intervening in the lives of individuals, the state can do a great deal to increase freedom. In other words, an individual is not really free to develop as a human being and enjoy freedom if she does not have enough to eat or a roof over her head. By intervening to provide at least a basic standard of living below which individuals cannot fall, then the state can play a positive role in increasing the freedom of individuals to make something of their lives.

As with grounding freedom on notions of rationality and morality, however, it might be argued that advocates of this version of positive liberty are confusing liberty with other values—that is, preventing poverty, homelessness, and unemployment might be justified for a whole host of reasons, but these reasons are not the same as freedom. Clarity, it might be argued, demands that we should say that state intervention limits freedom in order to secure greater economic equality.

The preliminary work having been done, we can now attempt to discover how far freedom is a desirable objective, and one that the state ought to promote and uphold. One of the best-known defences of freedom was put forward by British political philosopher John Stuart Mill. His essay *On Liberty*, originally published in 1859, is divided into two parts. In the first, he seeks to argue the case for the maximum possible freedom of thought and discussion. Even if an opinion being expressed is palpably false or hurtful to the sensibilities of others, Mill argues that it still should not be censored. True beliefs, he argues, will gain in vigour when they have to be upheld against objections and false beliefs are more likely to be seen as such if they are open to public challenge. Mill strongly believes, too, that freedom of thought and expression is a means to social progress. Society, in other words, will be stronger if a wider variety of opinions and lifestyles are tried and tested.

In the second part of the essay, Mill seeks to argue the case for freedom of action. Here, Mill makes the well-known distinction between self- and other-regarding actions. This is the so-called **harm principle**. Only those actions that harm others (affecting them adversely) should be prevented by public opinion or the state. Self-regarding actions are not to be interfered with. We are entitled to warn of the dangers of pursuing a particular self-regarding path, but we cannot, according to Mill, physically restrain someone. Mill is very clear, here, that actions which others find offensive, but which do not cause them physical or financial harm, are not to be seen as other-regarding. Mill's thoughts on liberty have been very influential in determining the nature of state intervention in modern liberal societies. Laws legalizing homosexuality between consenting adults in many liberal democratic states, for instance, owe much to Mill's distinction between self- and other-regarding actions (**see Case Study 7.3**).

In formulating a critique of Mill, it is crucial, first, to note how his arguments for freedom are strongly influenced by the utilitarian framework of his thought. Thus he argues for maximizing freedom of thought and discussion on the grounds that it will lead to social progress, through the development of greater knowledge. Likewise, Mill advocates freedom of action partly on the grounds that he thinks that humans are the best judges of what they want to do and partly because he thinks that making people free to choose what to do with their lives would be character-forming. In both cases, Mill is making the claim, then, that freedom makes humans happier.

It is by no means clear, however, that social progress will result from maximizing freedom of thought and discussion. Mill was arguably much too optimistic that, in the marketplace of ideas, rationality and truth will prevail. It seems equally possible that the truth will need to be protected against its enemies. On utilitarian grounds, too, it is not clear that freedom of thought and discussion will always promote happiness. One can readily think of cases where withholding the truth from someone may be in their best interests.

Much of the debate about Mill has focused on his arguments for freedom of action. Here, it is regularly argued that the distinction between self- and other-regarding actions is unsustainable (**see Case Study 7.4**). Surely, it is suggested, there are few, if any, actions that affect the actor alone? Others have challenged Mill's view that actions which others find offensive, but which do not cause them physical harm, should be regarded as self-

 CASE STUDY 7.3 The Wolfenden Report

In the 1950s, at a time when homosexual acts were illegal in the UK, the government set up a departmental committee, under Sir John Wolfenden, to consider both homosexual offences and prostitution. Wolfenden's influential report, published in 1957, put forward the argument that 'homosexual behaviour between consenting adults in private be no longer a criminal offence'. The grounds for this recommendation, derived from Mill, was that such acts were self-regarding. Despite the recommendations of the report, however, it was not until July 1967 that homosexuality was finally decriminalized in England and Wales.

CASE STUDY 7.4   Smoking and liberty

The contemporary debate about smoking illustrates the difficulty of delineating the boundaries of freedom of action. The British government's proposal for a total ban on smoking in pubs and clubs came into force in July 2007. The main philosophical justification for the ban is that smoking harms those who are forced to passively inhale the smoke of others. This is a principle associated with J. S. Mill, who would argue that smoking in private, where no one else will be harmed, is legitimate.

If it can be established that passive smoking is harmful, which it seems it can, then the application of Mill's other-regarding principle would seem to be clear-cut. Of course, it might be argued that non-smokers choose to frequent places, such as pubs and clubs, where others smoke—but if smoking is allowed in all pubs and clubs, as it was in Britain, then the choice of those who do not smoke is severely constrained. Moreover, the health risks of those who work in places where people smoke are even greater because of the amount of time they are exposed to smoke.

There are two criticisms of Mill's harm principle that do not challenge the smoking ban, but rather suggest that it does not go far enough. The first is the argument that even smoking in private can, in most circumstances, harm others. This relates to the oft-stated criticism of Mill's harm principle that it is difficult to distinguish between self- and other-regarding actions. Thus is it not the case that smoking, even in private, potentially harms others? If I become ill through smoking, as is likely, then this will impact upon family members, who will be harmed—financially and emotionally—by my death or incapacity. Similarly, my ill-health will have wider financial consequences for the health service that has to treat me and the social benefit system that has to sustain me if I am unable to work.

The second criticism is the point that even if we can denote an action as being self-regarding, there are good grounds for suggesting that the state ought to intervene to stop individuals from harming themselves. This is the paternalistic critique of liberal-inspired freedom. Here, society and the state might step in to prevent me from engaging in an activity that they have good reason to believe will harm me. My health and well-being may, then, not be served by liberty and indeed my happiness might be enhanced by restricting my freedom. In terms of smoking, it might be argued that the state should intervene on paternalistic grounds to ban it on the grounds that to do so will, in the long run at least, improve the health of those who choose to smoke and thereby increase levels of happiness.

regarding. Certainly, a utilitarian (as Mill claimed to be), committed to maximizing happiness in society, would have to take into account behaviour that others find offensive (whether written, said, or acted upon), but which does not directly harm them physically or financially. Such actions would have to be weighed against the benefits of allowing them to continue. This is highly relevant in an era when there have been many cases where religious sensibilities have been injured by, for example, the publication of blasphemous caricatures of religious beliefs. This was highlighted in 2015 in the context of the terrorist attack in Paris on the staff of *Charlie Hebdo*, a French satirical weekly magazine. Very few would want to argue that the magazine's negative depiction of the prophet Muhammad justified such a brutal attack. On the other hand, it is very difficult to argue against the claim that the depiction caused great offence and upset to many people (Smits, 2016: 150–68).

Mill, of course, is putting forward a liberal theory of freedom, justifying limited state intervention and maximizing personal autonomy. This has been very influential in shaping the modern liberal theory of the state, with its emphasis on neutrality and moral pluralism. It should be noted, however, that Mill was equally aware of the poverty and squalor evident in nineteenth-century England and the consequences of this for the enjoyment of freedom. Indeed, he recognized the challenge and, to some extent, the value of the socialist critique of liberalism that was emerging towards the end of the century. Mill can therefore be located on the cusp between the old classical liberalism and the new liberalism emphasizing social reform that came to dominate British politics.

 See Chapter 8 for a discussion of the difference between classical and new liberalism.

7

> ✳ **KEY POINTS**

- J. S. Mill argues for maximizing freedom, only actions that are other-regarding being suitable for state or societal intervention.
- A number of problems with Mill's formulation are evident. In particular, there is a case on the grounds of maximizing happiness, or paternalism, or the pursuit of knowledge, for limiting areas of freedom that Mill would regard as sacrosanct.
- The relationship between freedom and equality is a complex one, with those on the left arguing that equality is not necessarily a constraint on freedom.

Marxism and Communitarianism

The socialist—more specifically, the Marxist—critique of the liberal theory of freedom centres on the impact of the inequality, seen as the natural consequence of a capitalist economy. In the best-known Marxist account, Cohen (1979) points to the freedom to own property, and the resulting unequal ownership of property, as providing severe limitations on freedom for those who do not own property. In liberal capitalist regimes, the right to deprive others of the use of one's own property is a central feature. According to this approach, then, the freedom of the proletariat is necessarily constrained and only when property is collectively owned can freedom be enhanced. For classical Marxism, as we have seen, the state is merely the means by which one—economic—class exploits another. The

See Chapters 2 and 3 for a further discussion of the Marxist theory of the state.

7

state, for Marx, is therefore an illegitimate institution because it underwrites exploitation. The ideal political framework for Marxists, therefore, is a post-capitalist communist society in which the state's exploitative function is removed.

For much of its history, the major ideological opponent of liberalism came from the left—from Marxism, in particular. In more recent years, however, the liberal theory of the neutral state has been challenged by a body of thought known as communitarianism. The label 'communitarian' embraces a wide variety of views. In general, communitarian thinkers seek to re-establish the state as an institution with a role to play in uniting society around a set of values. This contrasts greatly with the liberal insistence that the state should allow a plurality of belief systems to exist (**see Key Debate 7.5**).

In many ways, the antecedents of communitarianism are those political philosophers, such as Jean-Jacques Rousseau (1712–78) and Georg Friedrich Hegel (1770–1831), who suggested that the state and morality are inextricably linked. Thus, for Rousseau, the state should be judged by the degree to which it upholds the general will. As we saw, this is the will that binds people together and can be contrasted with the selfish or partial will existing within everyone.

 KEY DEBATE 7.5 **Communitarianism versus liberalism**

Since the 1970s, communitarianism has provided a more potent ideological challenge to liberalism than conservatism and socialism. Defining the basic thrust of communitarianism is difficult because of the disparate nature of its adherents, coming from the right and left of the political spectrum. The essence of the communitarian approach is an attack on what is perceived to be the asocial individualism of liberalism. This attack is both methodological and normative (Avineri and de-Shalt, 1992: 2).

- Methodologically, communitarians argue that human behaviour is best understood in the context of the social, historical, and cultural environments of individuals. Thus 'it is the kind of society in which people live that affects their understanding both of themselves and of how they should lead their lives' (Mulhall and Swift, 1996: 13).

- Some communitarian writing suggests that the basis of the communitarian critique of liberalism is the normative assertion that liberal theory accurately reflects liberal society and therefore ought to be transformed. Others suggest, methodologically, that liberal theory misrepresents the reality of modern societies, where social ties are more important in determining the belief systems of individuals than liberal theory has realized (Walzer, 1990).

Normatively, communitarians emphasize the value of communal existence and the importance of being bound together by a shared vision of the good promoted by a perfectionist state—part of a tradition that can be traced back to Aristotle—on which particular emphasis is placed by MacIntyre (1985).

Questions

1. What is the communitarian critique of liberal political thought?
2. Evaluate the communitarian case against liberalism.

✳ KEY POINTS

- One of the key debates in modern political theory is that between the liberal and the communitarian theories of the state.
- Liberalism upholds a version of moral pluralism, whereas communitarianism seeks moral uniformity. The antecedents of the communitarian position reside in the attempts, by political philosophers such as Rousseau and Hegel, to justify obedience to a state promoting the general will.

7

The Just State

Another way of determining the legitimate state is to argue that it must be just. Justice is yet another one of those political concepts that is difficult to define. Very basically, justice requires us to give to others what they are due or entitled to. This contrasts with charity. It may be morally good for us to contribute to a charity, but we are under no obligation to do so. In the modern world, justice is a distributional concept—that is, it is concerned with how different resources—wealth, income, educational opportunities, and so on—ought to be distributed. It is a concept, then, that implies that resources are scarce, for if we had more than enough resources to go around, there would be no need to agonize over who should have them.

A distinction can be made between procedural justice and social justice. In the former case, justice involves the following of rules, irrespective of the outcomes, whereas the latter is more concerned about outcomes. Modern theories of social or distributive justice have identified a number of criteria that we might consider as guides to distribution (Miller, 1976: 24–31). We could say that resources ought to be distributed according to *need*, or *desert* (or *merit*), or a principle of pure equality. All theories of justice must involve equality, in the sense not that resources ought to be distributed equally, but that there ought to be consistency of treatment. This involves equality before the law and the principle that equals ought to be treated equally.

Beyond this formal principle of equality, we can adopt various principles of distributive justice. We may decide, for example, to adopt a theory of justice based on need. This is particularly associated with socialism, as in the slogan 'from each according to his ability, to each according to his needs'. Even in modern liberal democracies, however, the existence of a welfare state amounts to a recognition that meeting needs is just, although such societies also adopt desert or merit as a criteria for the distribution of resources once basic needs are met. A meritocratic theory of justice advocates distributing resources to those who display some merit and therefore deserve to be rewarded. It is associated with liberalism. Merit can include a natural talent or it can refer to someone's propensity for hard work or a general contribution to society. A contemporary take on the desert principle can be found in the literature on luck egalitarianism (Barry, 2006). According to this position, the causes of inequality should be distinguished, so that those who are unequal because of bad luck ought to be compensated, whilst those who are unequal because of their own lack of hard work or poor choices should not be.

A desert-based theory of justice, then, regards it as just to differentially reward talent and hard work. It recognizes the social advantages of encouraging the development and employment of talent through the deployment of incentives. It is linked to the principle of equal opportunity. If we intend to reward talent or hard work, it would seem unjust for an individual to start out with a structural disadvantage. It therefore would seem to demand educational and welfare opportunities for all to allow for the creation of a level playing field.

The best-known contemporary account of justice is John Rawls' *A Theory of Justice*, published to much acclaim in 1971. Indeed, his lengthy book is regarded as the most important work of political philosophy published since the end of the Second World War. Rawls' account can be divided into two. First, there is the *method* he uses to arrive at his principles of justice; second, the *principles* themselves. In terms of the method, Rawls (1921–2002) (**see Figure 7.2**) draws from the long-neglected social contract tradition associated with Hobbes and Locke (discussed above). He seeks to devise a method for arriving at principles of justice to which everyone can consent. Rawls' answer to this is to devise a hypothetical situation in which, he argues, there will be unanimous support for particular principles of justice.

FIGURE 7.2 John Rawls
Photo by Frederic REGLAIN/Gamma-Rapho
via Getty Images

Rawls asks us to imagine a so-called original position in which individuals meet and decide how they want their society to be organized. In this original position, the members will be under a 'veil of ignorance'—that is, they will have no idea what their own position in society will turn out to be. They do not know if they will be rich or poor, black or white, male or female, disabled or able-bodied. Rawls also assumes that individuals in the original position will be self-interested, wanting the best for themselves. Finally, he also suggests that they will desire what he calls primary goods, such as wealth, good health, education, and so on.

In the second part of the theory, Rawls outlines the principles he thinks will derive from individuals in the original position. There are two (Rawls, 1971: 302):

1. Each person is to have an equal right to the most extensive total system of equal basic liberties compatible with a similar system of liberty for all.
2. Social and economic inequalities are to be arranged so that they are both:
   (a) to the greatest benefit of the least advantaged . . . and
   (b) attached to offices and positions open to all under conditions of fair equality of opportunity.

Rawls adds that (1) (the liberty principle) has priority over (2), and (2) (b) (the fair opportunity principle) has priority over (2) (a) (the difference principle). This means, for example, that one cannot sacrifice liberty in order to achieve economic improvement, thereby ruling out slavery, where it is conceivable that individuals could have a relatively high degree of welfare, but no liberty.

Rawls' work has generated a huge literature (see, for instance, Daniels, 1975; Wolff, 1977; Kukathas and Pettit, 1990). It is useful to distinguish between criticisms of his method, on the one hand, and his principles, on the other. In the former case, it has been questioned whether people in the original position would have produced the principles of justice at which Rawls arrives. His central claim is that, because they do not know where they will end up in the social strata, individuals behind the veil of ignorance will be conservative, in the sense of being unwilling to take risks. It is not clear, however, that people in the original position would choose the kind of risk-averse strategy Rawls suggests (Wolff, 1996: 177–86) where we try to ensure that the worst possible scenario is as good as possible.

In terms of Rawls' principles of justice, he has been criticized from the left and the right. From the left, it has been argued that his difference principle is not as egalitarian as it seems (Wolff, 1977). Suspicions are aroused, in particular, by the priority given to liberty. From the right, his major critic has been American philosopher Robert Nozick (1938–2002). Nozick, writing from a libertarian perspective—heavily influenced by John Locke—in which the minimal state protecting property rights is the ideal, puts forward a procedural theory of justice—that is, he regards the way in which property is acquired as the key principle of justice and not the outcome of this acquisition. It is therefore a historical and not an end-state theory, in which 'past circumstances or actions of people can create differential entitlements or differential deserts to things' (Nozick, 1974: 155). Provided that an individual's acquisition of property is fair, then she has a just entitlement to it. Nozick regards any attempt to redistribute property (defined in a wide sense to refer to anything possessed by an individual), even through taxation, as unjust.

Nozick therefore regards Rawls' end-state theory—that inequality is justified only when it benefits everyone and in particular the worst-off—as illegitimate. For Nozick, any attempt to enforce patterns of justice, such as an end-state principle seeking to meet need, results in an illegitimate restriction of liberty. Left to their own devices, people's actions will always disrupt a particular pattern. Intuitively, one might doubt that the consequences of Nozick's principles are just. It could, for instance, result in such inequalities that the poorest members of society are at risk of starvation. His attack on taxation as a form of forced labour can be regarded as an exaggeration. Moreover, it can be argued, as we saw earlier in the chapter, that redistributing resources actually increases liberty because it increases choices for the poor (Wolff, 1996: 194–5).

Nozick is part of a tradition (including Hobbes and Locke) that regards a minimal, or night-watchman, state as the ideal. This classical liberal position advocates a minimal state in order to maximize freedom. A modern version of this justification is provided by a group of thinkers and political actors known as the New Right. The political popularizers of the New Right were leaders such as Thatcher and Reagan, but the academic ballast was provided by political economists such as Friedrich von Hayek and Milton Friedman, as well as political philosophers such as Robert Nozick.

The New Right challenged the state interventionism that had become standard in post-war liberal democracies, centring on the welfare state, the mixed economy, and the use of demand management economic theory developed by John Maynard Keynes (1883–1946). For the New Right school of thought, state intervention is counter-productive. It encourages individuals to overly rely on the state to provide welfare support, thereby stifling individual initiative and self-help. It is also inefficient, propping up unprofitable economic concerns and stifling the emergence of new lean and relevant ones. Finally, it is also unjust, failing to reward individual effort appropriately.

7

▶ See Chapter 8 for a discussion of liberalism.

✳ KEY POINTS

- Justice is a distributional concept. What political theorists have mainly disagreed about is the criteria for distributing resources.

- Distributing resources based on desert takes account of incentives, but considerable state intervention would seem to be necessary in order to facilitate the equality of opportunity that the principle demands.

- Rawls' theory of justice has been criticized for the method he uses to arrive at his principles of justice and the principles themselves.

- Rawls' principles of justice have been criticized from the left and the right. From the left, he is not regarded as egalitarian enough; from the right, he is too egalitarian.

- Robert Nozick has provided the best-known critique of Rawls from the right. He argues that the kind of redistribution that Rawls calls for is illegitimate. Individuals should be entitled to hold the property they own without intervention from the state, provided that they have acquired it fairly.

Political Theory beyond the State

Since the sixteenth century, political theory has been associated with—and has helped shape the character of—the nation-state. One fundamental question for students of politics now is the degree to which politics now exists beyond the state at a higher supranational level. In other words, it is now arguably the case that the focus of politics has begun to shift because, in a practical sense, we are living in a world that is becoming increasingly interdependent, where the forces of so-called globalization are placing increasing constraints on what individual so-called sovereign states can do on their own. It follows, of course, that the challenge to the modern state from the forces of globalization, discussed in various places in this book, questions not only the sovereign state, but also political theory itself, which grew up to theorize it. At the extremes, we could defend to the hilt the state-specific nature of much political thought by denying the claims made by advocates of globalization. Conversely, we could accept these claims and render the dominant state-specific school of political theory redundant. What is certain is that political theorists will increasingly have to grapple with the impact of globalization. Indeed, this is already beginning to happen. The case for cosmopolitan theories of democracy, for instance, was considered in Chapter 4, and cosmopolitan, or global, theories of justice are equally prevalent in the literature now.

To put cosmopolitan theories of justice into context, it should be noted that Rawls and Nozick, although different in many ways, limited their terms of reference to the sovereign state. Limiting a discussion of justice to the internal affairs of wealthy Western states, however, seems trivial, given the staggering inequalities between different parts of the world—particularly given the oft-made claim that the rich states in the North are at least partly responsible for the poverty in the South. This has led political theorists to develop theories of justice that are global in scope (**see Case Study 7.6**).

This so-called cosmopolitan approach to justice is based on the principle that our loyalties ought to be with human beings as a whole, rather than only those who happen to live within the boundaries of the state within which we reside. This idea, that human beings are equal members of a global citizenry, has a long history in political thought, but the growing inequality between the North and the South in recent decades, and the greater recognition

CASE STUDY 7.6 **Climate change and justice**

Cosmopolitan theories of justice seek to impose a duty on individuals and states either to act positively to end injustices in the world or, at the very least, to refrain from acting so as to cause harm. Both practices feature in the politics of climate change. Cosmopolitans insist that rich industrialized countries should desist from continuing to burn fossil fuels at the rate they currently are. Equally, since these countries are held responsible for climate change, they are also obliged, it is argued, to assist those states in the developing world that have not been responsible for causing climate change, but which are least able to deal with its consequences (Caney, 2008). Despite intensive international negotiations over the past two decades or so, neither outcome has materialized to the degree that many cosmopolitan theories of justice would advocate.

Having said that, in the initial treaty designed to tackle global warming—the Kyoto Protocol—no CO_2 reduction targets were set for developing countries partly in recognition that it was the responsibility of the developed countries—because of their past responsibility for climate change—to take action and partly because developing countries refused to accept any reduction targets. In addition, in subsequent negotiations, the developing countries have agreed to reductions in greenhouse gas emissions, but only in the context of a complex system of financial and technology transfer from the richer parts of the world to the poorer.

of this inequality, has made questions surrounding global justice 'one of the great moral challenges of the age' (Linklater, 2008: 555).

There is little agreement on what our moral obligations should be to those outsiders who do not belong to our community. At the extreme end, Singer (2002) puts forward the principle of unlimited obligation whereby we (in the rich North) are obliged to help others (in the poor South) even to the point of seriously eroding our own standards of living. A less extreme position is to apply Rawls' principles on a global scale, thereby justifying a greater degree of redistribution between the rich and the poor parts of the world (Beitz, 1979; Pogge, 1989). All cosmopolitan theories of justice, it should be noted, are vulnerable to the charge, often put forward by exponents of non-ideal theory, that they are putting forward principles that are unrealizable.

 KEY POINTS

- The traditional state focus of political theory has been challenged by globalization.
- Political philosophers have increasingly turned their attention to global cosmopolitan theories, most notably in the area of justice.

Anarchism and the State

It would be odd if we did not include, in a chapter on the ideal state, a consideration of the position of the anarchist strand of political thought, which denies that there can ever be an ideal state. We have left anarchism until the end of this chapter because, although it has an impeccable intellectual pedigree, it is extremely questionable whether anarchism has had any lasting impact, or is capable of having any impact, on the development of modern politics.

Anarchism dates back to the nineteenth century. It has a number of varieties, although Goodwin (2014: 134) is probably right to say that the primary link is with the socialist tradition. Thus anarchists such as Proudhon (1809–65), Bakunin (1814–76), and Kropotkin (1842–1921) were all involved in practical socialist politics within the Socialist International, engaging in debate, and regularly falling out, with Marx, the dominant intellectual figure within it. One of the first anarchist thinkers, William Godwin (1756–1836), was an exponent of the liberal individualist school of anarchism, but this is particularly associated with a group of twentieth-century American thinkers—most notably, Murray Rothbard (1926–95).

Despite the many differences between anarchists, they share an abhorrence of the state, which they regard as an illegitimate, even criminal, type of organization illegitimately exercising force over individuals and society, and reducing the liberty of the people. Obviously, this simple principle raises many questions. In the first place, there is a question mark over what anarchists are actually opposing: is it just the state, or is it the state, government, and any form of authority structure? Clearly, if the latter, then anarchism does rely on an optimistic view of human nature. In fact, anarchist thinkers differ here, with some holding that human nature is intrinsically good, and others holding that it is socially determined and therefore can be shaped by the social and political environment. Whatever the exact form of the theory, anarchists all tend to argue that an anarchist society will be one in which the people will be morally correct, doing what is required of them.

Even assuming that human nature is generally good, anarchists still face problems. How are the functions of the state to be performed? One answer, some anarchists suggest, is that the free market could take on this role. One problem here is the inequality likely to result if the market is responsible for providing functions such as education and health care. Another is the authority deficit likely to follow from a private police force responsible for tackling crime and social deviancy. For socialist and communist anarchists, similarly, it is unlikely that their egalitarian objectives can be met without a body, such as the state, to ensure they come about. Moreover, if an authority structure is necessary to provide egalitarian outcomes, it will, of course, be counter to the anarchist argument that this will reduce freedom.

Hoffman (1995) tries to rescue anarchism. He argues that the anarchist mistake was to regard the state and the government as synonymous, whereas this is to confuse force and constraint. The state exercises force, and this is what anarchists are opposed to, but government, while inevitably requiring constraints, is not an institution exercising force. Therefore, 'to link the state and government as twin enemies of freedom is to ignore the fact that stateless societies have governments, and that even in state-centric societies, the role of government is positive and empowering'. It follows then that 'without a distinction between state and government it is impossible to move beyond the state' (Hoffman and Graham, 2006: 259). This does not, however, entirely let anarchists off the hook. This is because government, without a state, relies on authority, since it has no means of force to ensure its decisions are obeyed. This rather takes us back to square one—that is, how will such a society deal with those who refuse to accept the authority of the government?

Compared with the other traditions of political thought we have considered in this chapter, anarchism would appear to have had little influence on modern politics. Strong anarchist movements existed between the 1880s and the 1930s, and anarchists briefly held power during the Spanish Civil War (Vincent, 1995: 117). Since then, there have been anarchist tendencies present in 1960s counter-culture, student protests, and, more recently, in environmental and anti-globalization movements. It has remained a peripheral ideology, however, tainted—however unjustly—with the charge that it is a recipe for confusion and chaos.

✳ KEY POINTS

- Anarchism is primarily an offshoot of socialism.
- Anarchists share an abhorrence of the state, but this principle raises many difficult questions that many argue anarchists cannot effectively answer.
- Anarchism has had relatively little influence on modern politics.

Conclusion

The main function of this chapter has been to aim to give a sense of the major themes within political philosophy. Until recently at least, the chief preoccupation of political philosophers has been to ask how, if at all, the state can be legitimized. This is another way of asking: what is the most desirable political system? Two ways of answering this question—based on procedures and substantive outcomes, respectively—have been explored. This preoccupation with the state faces two main challenges. In the first place, for some—anarchist—thinkers, no state form is legitimate. Anarchists' abhorrence of the state is based on its corrupting influence, which undermines a human being's tendency to be morally upstanding. This basic principle, however, raises more questions than it answers. For instance, who is to perform the functions of the state? How are the egalitarian aspirations of the dominant socialist strand of anarchism to be achieved without authority structures to enforce it? If there is a need for some authority structure—as some anarchists recognize—can this be consistent with the claim that this will inevitably lead to a loss of freedom?

The second challenge has come from the impact of globalization. This has questioned, empirically, the political importance of the state, and has led political theorists to seek to apply political concepts such as freedom and justice globally. Our greater knowledge of different cultures—enabled by technological developments, which now give us a clearer picture of how different societies operate, and by increasing mobility, leading to the emergence of multicultural communities—makes us more circumspect about the value of freedom and what practices should be regarded as legitimate restrictions on freedom. Likewise, there are increasing calls for the principle of justice to be applied globally to address the shocking inequalities between different parts of the world. These developments provide important challenges to political theorists—challenges with which they have only recently begun to grapple.

? Key Questions

- Which normative theory of the state do you find most convincing?
- Is democracy special?
- Are we obliged to obey decisions taken democratically?
- In the wake of the threat of terrorism, should we regard security as more important than liberty?
- How effective is the communitarian critique of liberalism?
- What constraints exist on our freedom?
- Should smoking be banned?
- Should we maximize freedom of thought and expression?
- How should we distribute resources in our society?
- How viable is a cosmopolitan theory of justice?

▌▌▌ Further Reading

There are many very good introductory texts on political philosophy. The best are:

Heywood, A. (2015), *Political Theory* (London: Palgrave, 4th edn).

MacKinnon, C. (ed.) (2015), *Issues in Political Theory* (Oxford: Oxford University Press, 3rd edn).

Miller, D. (2003), *Political Philosophy: A Very Short Introduction* (Oxford: Oxford University Press).

Shorten, A. (2016), *Contemporary Political Theory* (London: Palgrave).

Smits, K. (2016), *Applying Political Theory: Issues and Debates* (London: Palgrave, 2nd edn).

Swift, A. (2014), *Political Philosophy* (Cambridge: Polity Press, 3rd edn).

Wolff, J. (2016), *An Introduction to Political Philosophy* (Oxford: Oxford University Press, 3rd edn).

Classic texts that students ought to try to read include:

Berlin, I. (1969), *Four Essays on Liberty* (Oxford: Oxford University Press).

Hobbes, T. (1651/1992), *Leviathan* (Cambridge: Cambridge University Press).

Locke, J. (1690/1988), *Two Treatises of Government* (Cambridge: Cambridge University Press).

Marx, K., and Engels, F. (1848/1976), *The Communist Manifesto* (Harmondsworth: Penguin).

Mill, J. S. (1972), *Utilitarianism, On Liberty, and Considerations on Representative Government* (London: Dent).

Rawls, J. (1971), *A Theory of Justice* (Cambridge, MA: Harvard University Press).

Rousseau, J. (1913), *The Social Contract and Discourses* (London: Dent).

🔗 Web Links

http://www.political-theory.org
On political theory in general, see the homepage of the 'Foundations of Political Theory' section of the American Political Science Association (APSA). Among other things, it will give you access to a wide range of key journals.

https://www.Marxists.org
For Marxist literature.

http://www.ucl.ac.uk/Bentham-Project
This, the website of the Bentham Project at University College London, is the best source on Bentham.

https://www.utilitarian.net/jsmill/
This is a useful site on Mill.

https://plato.stanford.edu/entries/original-position/
On Rawls.

 Visit the **Online Resources** that accompany this book to access more learning resources on this topic: www.oup.com/uk/ferdinand/

Ideologies

8

Reader's Guide

After outlining the general characteristics of an ideology this chapter considers, a range of ideologies. These can be divided into two. Traditional ideologies were shaped by the Enlightenment, either, in the case of liberalism and socialism, adopting its key principles or, in the case of conservatism and fascism, railing against them. Each of these ideologies cannot be understood outside the economic, social, and political environment in which it emerged. Traditional ideologies have had an extraordinary impact on the development of world politics in the last two centuries. More contemporary ideologies—most notably, environmentalism and feminism—are less optimistic about the ability of ideologies to construct an overarching explanation of the world, and also respect difference and variety. This is a product of social and economic change that has brought into being a number of powerful identity groups based on gender, culture, and ethnicity, and raised question marks over the environmental sustainability of current industrial practices.

Traditional and Contemporary Ideologies

This chapter focuses in detail on a range of political ideologies. Ideologies are central to this whole book because they help to shape the domestic and international political landscape. Many of the themes within them will be familiar because ideologies contain a collection of political ideas, many of which we have examined in previous chapters of this book.

To the extent that ideologies provide a guide to political action, they have had a crucial impact on our world. Sometimes, such as the atrocities committed in the name of communism and fascism, this impact is negative. At other times, such as the influence of social democracy on the creation of the welfare state, this impact can be—in many people's eyes at least—positive (**see Case Study 8.1**).

Ideologies can be usefully divided into traditional and more contemporary types. Traditional ideologies are associated with the school of thought known as the Enlightenment (**see Key Concept 8.2**). Liberalism and socialism emerged as embodiments of the Enlightenment, whereas conservatism and fascism sought to challenge its assumptions. Anarchism is another example of the former, while nationalism is, in some versions at least, an example of the latter. These two ideologies are considered in separate chapters.

 Nationalism is covered in Chapter 6, while anarchism is covered in Chapter 7.

8

The second part of the chapter moves on to examine more contemporary ideologies that challenge the claims of the traditional ideologies. Contemporary ideologies, explored in this chapter, should be seen in the context of growing scepticism about the utility of Enlightenment ideologies. Postmodernism offers the most fundamental challenge to this modernism. Some modern feminist thought also rejects monolithic value systems and seeks to promote the differences between men and women as politically important. The politics of difference is also explored in the context of multiculturalism, an antidote to the ethnic nationalism

> ### 📖 CASE STUDY 8.1   The importance of ideologies: Grenfell Tower
>
> Ideologies have a crucial role in understanding and interpreting the human world. To illustrate this, consider the catastrophic fire at Grenfell Tower, a residential tower block in London, in June 2017. Ideologies shaped—and can arguably explain—this event. The decision to build a high-rise tower block in the first place, for instance, was the result of post-war housing policy that was heavily influenced by social democracy. The fire itself may have been caused by deregulation and a shrinking of the resources available to the state—both ideas associated with economic liberalism. Finally, the fire, and the subsequent treatment of the surviving residents—the vast majority of whom were poor and from ethnic minorities, including a sizeable proportion of women—might be regarded as an illustration of the explanatory power of intersectional feminism, which points to the links between race, capitalism, and gender, and their capacity to produce and perpetuate systems of oppression and class domination.

KEY CONCEPT 8.2   Enlightenment

A seventeenth- and eighteenth-century intellectual and cultural movement that emphasized the application of reason to knowledge in a search for human progress, the Enlightenment was both a cause and an effect of the decline in the authority of religion. The influence of the Enlightenment was felt in many disciplines, in both arts and sciences. In politics, it is associated with the attempt to model political institutions around a set of abstract rational principles. The French Revolution is often regarded as the highlight of the Enlightenment. Its chief critic within political philosophy was Edmund Burke (1729–97), who railed against the Enlightenment in his violent attack on the French Revolution.

discussed in Chapter 6. Another contemporary ideology, environmentalism, incorporates the growing scepticism about the human ability to master and control nature. Finally, the idea of the dominance of liberal values in the world is clearly at odds with the political and social importance of religious fundamentalism, based on a belief system very different from the largely secular Enlightenment ideologies looked at in the first part of the chapter.

What Is an Ideology?

The term 'ideology' was first used at the time of the French Revolution at the end of the eighteenth century by Antoine Destutt de Tracey (1754–1836). He used the term to denote a rationalistic science of ideas, which could be discovered in the same way as truths in the natural sciences. The normative character of ideology, however, quickly became apparent to others. For some, the word 'ideology' has a pejorative or negative meaning. In contemporary popular usage, for instance, 'ideologue' is often used to denote someone with an uncompromising devotion to a set of ideas irrespective of their utility, or as simply an extremist. Marx is the best-known political thinker who defined ideology in negative terms. He used the term to mean a set of ideas that is false, deliberately designed to obscure reality in order to benefit a particular class in society. Marx's aim was to contrast ideology with the truth that his 'scientific' socialism was designed to reveal (Marx and Engels, 1846/1970).

Others would regard Marxism itself as a classical example of an ideology. To so define Marxism, we need a more neutral or descriptive definition of the term. Here, an ideology might be defined as a set of ideas designed to provide a description of the existing political order, a vision of what the ideal political order ought to look like, and a means, if necessary, of transforming the former to the latter. An ideology therefore contains empirical, normative, and semantic elements. The key point is that the ideologies discussed in this chapter represent competing world views—that is, they offer different ways of seeing the world, what the problems are, and how we should solve them.

A number of other features of ideologies are worth noting. First, ideologies are more often than not action-oriented in the sense that they seek to promote a particular social and political order for which they urge people to strive. Second, it is sometimes said that ideologies are less rigorous and sophisticated than 'proper' political philosophy. In reality, as Vincent (1995: 17) points out, 'ideological themes can be found on a continuum from the most banal jumbled rhetoric up to the most astute theorizing'.

Third, it is often said that the twentieth century in particular can be regarded as the age of ideologies in the sense that regimes based on particular ideological traditions—communism and fascism—wreaked havoc during this century. However, it is more appropriate to say that the twentieth century was the age of ideologies with which liberalism—which had tended to dominate in the West up to that point—profoundly disagreed. The liberal critique of fascism and communism as ideologies is a reflection of a tendency among some liberals to regard liberalism as somehow above the ideological fray. As Goodwin (2014: 39) points out: 'Liberalism appears as a necessary truth, the basis of reality, rather than as one political ideology among many.'

Fourth, as well as containing empirical and normative elements, ideologies also seek to combine concepts that political philosophers, as we have seen, will look at individually. An attempt can be made to identify the core characteristic of a particular ideology, but this is difficult, if not impossible, because all ideologies have different strands or schools and sometimes there is considerable overlap between one ideology and another, such as when we talk about liberal versions of feminism or social democratic versions of socialism. Ideologies are, then, in the words of Festenstein and Kenny (2005: 4), 'internally pluralistic, contested, complex, and overlapping'.

One way out of this problem is to adopt the approach suggested by Freeden (1996). In a major study of the concept of political ideology, Freeden recommends identifying the morphology of an ideology. By this, he means it is possible to distinguish between concepts at the core of an ideology from those that are further away from the centre and those that are at the periphery.

One final general point about political ideologies is worth making in this introductory section: it is important to recognize that ideologies reflect, as well as shape, the social and historical circumstances in which they exist. To give an illustration of this, the two main ideologies since the nineteenth century have been liberalism and socialism. It was no accident that these ideologies emerged at the time of the Industrial Revolution and reached their zenith in the nineteenth century. In the first place, both liberalism and socialism reflected the optimism of the time—a time when it was thought that there was nothing that human beings could not understand rationally and achieve politically and economically. Human beings could be masters of all they surveyed. This optimism derived from the dominance of so-called Enlightenment thinking. Second, liberalism and socialism became dominant ideologies because they were associated with new social groupings created by the Industrial Revolution. Liberalism was largely promoted by the industrial middle class and socialism was promoted by, or in the interests of, the industrial working class.

✱ KEY POINTS

- To the extent that ideologies provide a guide to political action, they have had a crucial impact on the world.
- Traditional ideologies were shaped by the Enlightenment and seek to offer competing ways of understanding the world.
- Contemporary ideologies challenge the metanarrative character of traditional ideologies. (A metanarrative tries to give a totalizing, comprehensive account of various historical events and social and cultural phenomena, based upon an appeal to universal truth or universal values.)
- For some, 'ideology' has a pejorative meaning; others adopt it as a more neutral term.
- Ideologies are action-oriented and comprise a combination of concepts.
- It is usually possible to identify the core concepts of an ideology, but all ideologies have disputed meanings.
- Ideologies reflect, as well as shape, the social and historical circumstances in which they exist.

8

Liberalism

Liberalism is an important ideology because it has been the dominant political tradition in the West for many centuries. As such, it is considered throughout this book, particularly in Chapter 7, and therefore receives a relatively limited treatment here. It is s a term that came into common usage in the nineteenth century, when a party of that name emerged under the leadership of William Gladstone (1809–98), British prime minister on four separate occasions. Liberalism, and the values associated with it, however, has had a much longer history. The origins of liberalism are often traced to the rise of a capitalist political economy—in particular, as a defence of private property. The individualistic political philosophy of Hobbes and Locke is crucial here (Macpherson, 1962).

Liberalism is difficult to pin down, not least because of its longevity and the fact that it has gone through a variety of different formulations. A key division is between classical liberalism, on the one hand, and the new social liberalism, on the other. The classical tradition—drawing, in particular, on the economic theory of Adam Smith (1723–90) and the social theory of Herbert Spencer (1820–1907)—emphasizes that the state's role should be limited to ensure internal and external security and to ensure that private property rights are enforced. It is partly justified on the grounds that the market is the most effective means of meeting human needs. There is also a moral dimension in that a limited state maximizes freedom and rewards those who work hardest.

⯈ See Chapter 7 for a discussion of the contribution made by Hobbes and Locke to the development of liberal political thought.

⯈ See Chapter 9 for a discussion of liberal political economy.

Classical liberalism began to be questioned towards the end of the nineteenth century, as the extent of poverty began to be recognized and socialist ideas emerged as an alternative. From within the liberal tradition, a new emphasis on social reform began to emerge, associated with thinkers such as T. H. Green (1836–82), L. T. Hobhouse (1864–1929), and J. A. Hobson (1858–1940). This new liberalism saw a much more positive role for the state in correcting the inequities of the market, but it was argued that far from reducing liberty, this actually increased it by creating greater opportunities for individuals to achieve their goals. It influenced the direction of the British Liberal Party politics, the Liberal government elected in 1906 carrying through a range of social-reforming measures, including old-age pensions.

The new liberalism came to dominate the political landscape for much of the twentieth century, although largely under the auspices of social democratic parties. In turn, however, a revised version of classical liberalism emerged to challenge it in the 1970s under the guise of the New Right and right-wing governments, particularly in Britain and the US, were elected on programmes that were, in part, influenced by the classical liberal agenda. The academic ballast for this popular political movement was provided by thinkers such as Hayek and Nozick, whose ideas we have already touched upon in this book.

▶ See Chapter 7 for Nozick's critique of Rawls' theory of justice.

8

Liberal thought

The core meaning of liberalism can be found in the concepts of liberty, tolerance, individualism, and a particular kind of equality. Liberty is *the* concept right at the centre of liberal thought—'the primary value in the liberal creed', as Goodwin (2014: 46) puts it. For some liberal thinkers, liberty is seen as an intrinsic good; for others, such as J. S. Mill, it is a means to an end in the sense that its value is in the possibilities for self-development it produces.

▶ See Chapter 7 for a discussion of the distinction between positive and negative liberty.

The classical liberal tradition emphasizes negative liberty. Freedom is about removing external constraints. The new liberal tradition emphasizes positive liberty, whereby the state can remove obstacles to freedom. In emphasizing the collective role of the state, the new liberalism has been accused of abandoning 'true' liberalism by relegating the role of the individual. In its defence, advocates of the new liberalism argue that liberty can only be maximized through the enabling role of the state.

▶ See Chapter 7 for discussion of the liberal social contract tradition and anarchist thought.

A corollary of liberty is the liberal focus on the individual. As exemplified by the social contract tradition of Hobbes and Locke, the individual is prior to society. The notion of rights is prominent in liberal thought precisely because of the prominence given to individuals. Individuals ought to be protected against society and the state, as seen in J. S. Mill's classic defence of individual liberty. At its extreme level, individualism denies the state's right to intervene in any aspect of the life of the individual. As we have seen, even the classical version of liberalism sees some role for the state and therefore extreme libertarianism is best located in anarchist thought.

The liberal focus on the individual stems from the belief that individuals are rational and able to determine their own best interests, which they will always pursue. Thus, in the economic realm, individuals, according to the classical liberal position at least, are best left to their own devices as consumers and producers. The 'hidden hand' of the market will then ensure that economic utility is achieved.

The prominence of the individual in liberal thought involves the downgrading of the community. The community is merely an aggregate of individuals with competing interests and values. There is no room for regarding the community as a unified entity, as in the political philosophy of those such as Hegel and Rousseau. The distinction between the community and the individual is the source of the modern debate between liberals and communitarian thinkers. Communitarians criticize the liberal social contract tradition, which envisages humans in a pre-social state. For communitarians, political principles must be derived from actual existing societies that provide identity and meaning for individuals.

See Chapter 7 for a discussion of communitarianism.

The liberal approach to equality is distinctive. Liberals regard individuals as of equal value, but they do not accept equality of outcome. Rather, the liberal position is characterized by equality of opportunity, whereby fairness is ensured because individuals—in theory, at least—starting from the same position are rewarded for their efforts. Of course, the free market does not allow for genuine equality of opportunity because individuals do not start out in life from the same position. Some inherit advantages gained by their antecedents. It might be argued that the state intervention advocated by the new liberals actually makes equality of opportunity more of a reality. The introduction of free education and health care, in particular, has the effect of equalizing life chances.

✱ KEY POINTS

- Liberalism is the dominant political tradition in the West.
- Liberalism has its classical and social-reforming strands.
- The core concept of liberalism is liberty, with the classical tradition emphasizing negative liberty and the social-reforming tradition emphasizing positive liberty.
- The prominence of the individual in liberal thought involves the downgrading of the community.
- Liberals advocate equality of opportunity rather than equality of outcome.

Socialism

Socialism is an ideology, like liberalism, that is a child of the Industrial Revolution, being associated with the emergence of an industrial working class. Socialism has been associated with working-class parties, but it differs from mere trade unionism in the sense that it seeks to transform society in cooperative and egalitarian directions. Somewhat ironically, indeed, many of the advocates of socialism have in fact been middle class.

Historical development

The historical development of socialism pivots around the giant figure of Karl Marx. The pre-Marxian socialists have often, following Marx himself, been described as utopian. Three thinkers—Claude-Henri Saint-Simon (1760–1825), Charles Fourier (1772–1837), and Robert Owen (1771–1858)—are usually regarded as the founders of socialism. Marx regarded these thinkers as utopian in the sense that they regarded socialism as ethically desirable, but had no contextual historical analysis of the possibilities of bringing about political change. Marx, by contrast, developed what he called a 'scientific' socialism, which not only argued that socialism was ethically desirable, but also attempted to explain the historical conditions that would bring it about.

See Chapter 2 for a discussion of Marxist ideas on the state.

Marx's ideas have had a huge impact on the development of socialism and, indeed, on world politics in general. Lenin and the Bolsheviks revised his ideas to suit Russia's circumstances and, after the Russian Revolution in 1917, the Soviet state (which, accurately or not, claimed to be based on Marxist ideas) was created. This historical event—coupled, perhaps, with the failed German Revolution of 1918–19—resulted in the division of world socialism into two camps: on the one hand, communism, centring on the so-called Third International of world communist organizations; on the other, social democracy.

The revisionists, whose leading exponent was Eduard Bernstein (1850–1932), sought to revise Marxism in light of contemporary circumstances. In most central and western European countries, this revisionist Marxism, later restyled social democracy, predominated. Marxism had less influence in Britain, where more moderate socialist organizations had always dominated. From 1917, Marxists (at least initially) looked to Russia for their inspiration.

Means and ends in socialist thought

As we have seen, all ideologies are a collection of ideas and it is often difficult to pinpoint core and peripheral ideas in their morphologies. Socialism, above all ideologies, would seem to have the largest number of competing varieties. As a result, it is tempting to use the word 'socialisms' rather than 'socialism', the former being the title of a well-known book on the subject (Wright, 1996).

In order to understand the key divisions within the socialist tradition, it is useful to distinguish between *means* and *ends*—that is, between the methods that socialists have thought appropriate to achieve their objectives and the end goals or objectives. In terms of means, the key distinction has been between revolutionary and evolutionary socialism. In the revolutionary camp, we need to make a further distinction. There are those, most notably Marx, who tended towards the assumption that a revolution would be a popular uprising. On the other hand, there are those, such as Lenin (**see Figure 8.1**), whose preference was for a coup involving a disciplined band of revolutionaries. It was Lenin's advocacy of a disciplined party—the Bolsheviks—which created the structure that, after the 1917

FIGURE 8.1 Vladimir Lenin, who played a leading role in the Russian Revolution
© Everett Historical/ Shutterstock.com

Russian Revolution, became the Communist Party, a **political party** that dominated the Soviet Union for decades.

Evolutionary socialism has been the main alternative to revolution. It is based on the belief that, with universal suffrage, socialism can be achieved through political democracy. It assumes, therefore, that the state can be responsive to working-class interests once enfranchised. This formed a central part of the division of socialist thought after the Russian Revolution.

Socialists, too, disagree about the ends of socialism. Two dimensions to this are most apparent. First, some socialists see a crucial role for the state in a socialist society, whereas others envisage a decentralized communal society, more akin to anarchism. The second dimension of socialism's ends concerns the balance between public and private ownership of the means of production. Within socialist thought, there is a continuum with complete public ownership at one end of the spectrum and relatively little at the other. This debate has been central to socialist debate within the West. Socialists have also differed over the form that public ownership should take, with the state corporation model challenged, particularly since the 1960s, by more decentralized forms involving workers' cooperatives and even a market socialism model (Miller, 1990).

⟩ See Chapter 7 for a discussion of the anarchist theory of the state.

Key socialist principles

Behind these differences of means and ends, it is possible to identify a number of core socialist principles. The first of them is *a particular view of* human nature. Socialists tend to have an optimistic view of human nature, which, they suggest, is capable of being shaped by social, economic, and political circumstances. Liberals and conservatives tend to regard human beings as selfish, individualistic, and materialistic. Socialists, on the other hand, regard such behaviour as socially conditioned rather than innate. A socialist society would promote values of cooperation, fellowship, and compassion, thereby shaping the values of its citizenry.

The second core socialist principle is *equality*. For many, equality is the defining feature of socialism. Unlike liberals, socialists are more likely to advocate equality of outcome. This is partly because socialists see inequality not so much as resulting from differences of ability, but in terms of an individual's location in a social structure. Educational attainment, in particular, is seen by socialists as a classic example of inequality at work, since it is heavily influenced by social class. Equality of outcome is promoted by socialists, too, because they have a less pessimistic view of human nature. For liberals, inequality is necessary in order to provide incentives. For socialists, on the other hand, human nature can be moulded to the point where individuals would be willing to work for the good of society irrespective of the lack of material incentives available.

The third core principle of socialism is *community and cooperation*. There is an emphasis in socialism on what humans can achieve collectively rather than individually. Therefore, there is an emphasis on the achievement of collective, rather than individual, goals through cooperation. Community is linked to the other two core socialist values in the sense that common ownership and equality are obvious ways in which communal values can be furthered.

Socialism, authoritarianism, and utopia

Many have suggested that the socialist vision is utopian. The word utopia, originally coined by Thomas More in the sixteenth century, is a play on two Greek words translated as good and nowhere. 'Utopian' therefore refers to a 'good society that is nowhere' or, to put it another way, a society that is incapable of realization. This leads to the question of whether socialism is similarly unrealizable.

Liberals, and especially conservatives (see below), brand utopias as unrealistic and unrealizable, and suggest that socialism comes into this category. According to this argument, socialists develop utopian visions of a better society in which human beings can achieve genuine emancipation and fulfilment as members of a community. The problem, however, is that such a society demands too much of its citizens. This might be acceptable if its effects are benign, but, so the argument continues, to maintain such an egalitarian society inevitably results in an authoritarian state, which has to continually intervene to prevent differential levels of talent and effort from eroding the socialist distribution of goods (Popper, 1962).

Such a critique is directed at the Soviet style of communism, whose overbearing state was, it is argued, a direct product of socialist ideas. Whether or not this critique is justified, it is clear that the authoritarian label cannot be attached to the social democratic variety of socialism, which, in any case, draws from liberalism as much as it does from Marxian varieties of socialism. Even then, as we saw in Chapter 7, there is a libertarian critique of redistributive versions of liberalism that claims that it illegitimately infringes liberty.

✳ KEY POINTS

- A dominant figure within socialism is Karl Marx, who described his socialism as scientific as opposed to the utopian variety of those socialists who preceded him.

- At the turn of the twentieth century, socialism divided into two camps, with the communists on one side and the revisionists (later to be social democrats) on the other.

- To classify different varieties of socialism, it is useful to distinguish between means and ends.

- Core socialist principles include an optimistic view of human nature, equality of outcome, and community and cooperation.

- Some argue that socialism is utopian and has authoritarian tendencies.

Conservatism

Elements of conservative thought can be found throughout history. However, conservative thought received its greatest fillip as a response to the Enlightenment tradition. Whereas liberalism and socialism bought into the progressive and rationalistic values of the Enlightenment, conservatism provides a negative response to it. The classic text here is Edmund Burke's (1729–97) vitriolic attack on the French Revolution of 1789, first published in 1790 (Burke, 1790/1968) (**see Key Thinker 8.3**).

Conservative political movements have not been ideologically uniform. In much of Europe, for example, they have historically been anti-liberal, reactionary, and authoritarian, whereas in Britain, conservatism has been tinged with liberalism. The nineteenth-century Conservative Party was notable for the social-reforming administrations of Peel and Disraeli, and later, following the creation of the post-1945 settlement by the British Labour Party, the Conservative Party largely accepted the dominance of social democratic ideas. Following the breakdown of the social democratic consensus in the 1970s, however, the Conservative Party became heavily influenced by the New Right. A similar shift to the right was noticeable in the US, with the election of President Ronald Reagan in 1980.

KEY THINKER 8.3   Edmund Burke (1729–97)

Burke was born in Dublin in 1729. After studying at Trinity College in Dublin, he moved to England in 1750, where he qualified as a lawyer before settling on a career in politics. He became an MP in 1776 in a rotten borough, before winning a seat in Bristol in 1775. He died in 1797, a rich man with an estate of some 600 acres in Buckinghamshire.

Burke's fame emerged from his writing and speeches on important political issues of his day. He is best known for his vitriolic best-selling attack on the French Revolution (Burke, 1790/1968), but he also wrote and spoke on the British constitution, and the relations between Britain and India and the American colonies. There is a much-discussed apparent contradiction in Burke's writings in the sense that he opposes the French Revolution, but supports the American Revolution and the Indian opposition to British colonial rule. Some put this down to an unstated fear that the French Revolution threatened the emerging capitalist class in Britain (Macpherson, 1980). Others argue that there was no inconsistency, since Burke was applying his political principles in a logical way. Thus he was opposed to the French revolutionaries because they were overthrowing an established order on the grounds of abstract rational principles. On the other hand, he supported the Americans and the Indians because they were seeking to uphold long-held traditions against the encroachment of the British.

See Chapter 7 for a discussion of the New Right theory of the state.

With its emphasis on the unconstrained free market, the New Right had more in common with classical liberalism than conservatism. Certainly, the ideological character of Thatcher's leadership was inimical to the pragmatism of conservative thought. However, the New Right also embodied a number of traditional conservative values—such as law and order, respect for authority, and the importance of traditional values—and the Thatcher governments were prepared to use the state to enforce them. This ideological mix was described by one British academic commentator as 'the free economy and the strong state' (Gamble, 1994).

In the US, so-called neo-conservatism has been more successful in challenging traditional conservatism. This has combined a brand of social authoritarianism with nationalism to create a reactionary movement that has had a large impact on the direction of US domestic and foreign policy, particularly under the presidency of George W. Bush. Similar traits appear in the platform of Donald Trump, although his brand of populism (particularly his isolationism) is difficult to reconcile with neo-conservatism. The major intellectual adherent of neo-conservatism in foreign policy has been political thinker Leo Strauss (1899–1973). Strauss, with a Zionist background, argued that the US should fight tyranny wherever it was found. Initially, this took the form of recommending a strong line against the Soviet Union, but since its collapse the attention of 'neo-cons' has turned to the threat from religious fundamentalism, seen as a challenge to conservative values. The intervention in Iraq and Afghanistan can be seen as a product of neo-conservative ideas.

Conservative thought

Determining the nature of conservative thought is not easy, not least because it tends to claim to be non-ideological, preferring practical principles and pragmatism over abstract reasoning. As a result, conservative thinkers have been reluctant to set out their position in a reasoned and codified fashion, since to do so would be to engage in an exercise that they themselves condemn. This has been problematic, however, for, taken literally, the word 'conservatism' suggests a desire to conserve, which has reactionary overtones. Conservatives therefore risk being accused of merely seeking to defend the status quo in order to defend existing privilege and power. This is unfortunate because conservatism can be seen as an ideology where 'certain fundamental convictions have been identified which constitute a distinct political standpoint' (Goodwin, 2014: 180).

Pride of place among these convictions is an *aversion to rationalism*. This rationalism was very much a product of the Enlightenment. It celebrated the ability of human beings to construct societies on the basis of rational principles such as—in the French Revolution—'liberty, equality, and fraternity'. There was no limit to the progress possible in human societies. For Michael Oakeshott (1901–90), a notable twentieth-century conservative, a rationalist 'stands . . . for independence of mind on all occasions, for thought free from obligation to any authority save the authority of reason' (Oakeshott, 1962: 1). It was the rationalist temper of the French Revolution that Burke so savagely attacked.

A number of other conservative values derive from this attack on rationalism. In the first place, the *conservative model of society is organic rather than mechanical*. In other words, society cannot be taken apart and rearranged like the parts of a machine. Rather, society is a little-understood, complex, and interdependent organism. To change one part may have an unpredictable and undesirable impact on other parts. Burke is not saying that no change is ever permissible, but that it should be gradual and moderate, taking care to preserve what is valuable in the organism.

The second conservative value to derive from anti-rationalism is *human imperfection*. Conservatives are sceptical about the human capacity to fully understand their social and political environment. At the very least, collective wisdom of the past and present is preferable to the abstract reasoning of a few. We should therefore, as far as possible, stick with what we know. This scepticism about human capacities follows through into the conservative *advocacy of hierarchy*. As Plato recognized, effective self-government is a myth: some are innately more capable of governing than others. This is the reason behind Burke's well-known justification of MPs retaining autonomy from their constituents.

> **KEY POINTS**
>
> ● Conservatism is a reaction to the Enlightenment tradition of political thought.
>
> ● The New Right has liberal and conservative elements.
>
> ● The underlying principles of conservatism are an aversion to rationality, an organic view of society, human imperfection, and a preference for hierarchy.

Fascism

Unlike the other ideologies we have discussed in this chapter, fascism is a twentieth-century phenomenon. It is particularly associated with the relatively short-lived, and terrifying, regimes led by Mussolini (1883–1945) in Italy and Hitler (1889–1945) in Germany in 1925–43 and 1933–45, respectively (**see Figure 8.2**). Indeed, for some commentators, fascism is regarded as a distinctly inter-war phenomenon (Trevor-Roper, 1947). Others disagree with this limitation (Kitchen, 1976) (**see Case Study 8.4**). More attention has been paid to the causes of the rise of fascism than its ideological character. Fascism is seen, for instance, as a product of particular political and historical circumstances, or as a product of a flawed human psychology, or of moral decay (Vincent, 1995: 145–50).

FIGURE 8.2   Fascist leaders Benito Mussolini and Adolf Hitler in 1938
© Everett Historical/ Shutterstock.com

CASE STUDY 8.4   Neo-Nazism

There has been a large number of neo-Nazi organizations and movements in the post-Second World War period, although, for obvious reasons, its adherents rarely use that term. Their goal has been to revive the ideology of national socialism, or some variant of it. The neo-Nazi phenomenon exists in many parts of the world including the US and many European countries, including, most notably, Austria, Russia, Belgium, Croatia, and France. It has even emerged in Germany, particularly after reunification in the 1990s, despite the extensive programme of denazification after 1945. Even Israel has not been immune as immigrants from the former Soviet Union, some of whom do not identify as Jews, have exported extreme right-wing views.

There was little overt neo-Nazi activity in Europe until the 1960s. Since then, neo-Nazis have engaged in a number of common activities. Some have competed in elections; Holocaust denial has been common, or at least it has been suggested that it needs to be contextualized with the human rights abuses of the allies; Nazi regalia has been promoted; attempts have been made to gain support in student organizations; and violence, against immigrants, Jews, and Muslims has been common and this has sometimes involved murder. While their activities are often shocking and newsworthy, the membership of neo-Nazi organizations remains small, although, particularly since the financial crash in 2008, radical right-wing parties, some of whom might be described as fascist, have had some electoral success (Mudde, 2007; Schain et al., 2002).

Fascism represents an extreme form of nationalism and authoritarianism. Unlike other forms of nationalism, however, fascism is accompanied by a wider set of ideas. Some of these ideas are distasteful and implausible. In addition, fascism rejects abstract intellectualizing in favour of action, instinct, and emotion, and as a result there are few intellectual works on which to rely, the principal exceptions being those of Italian fascist Giovanni Gentile (1875–1944) and Hitler's *Mein Kampf* (1926/1969), the latter being of some use in explaining the character of the ideology. An added difficulty of studying fascism is that the Italian variety is different in significant respects from the German, not least in the latter's treatment of race and its greater extremism, and there is a case, therefore, for considering Nazism as a distinct ideological phenomenon.

Despite these caveats, it would be a mistake to regard fascism as non-ideological. It is best understood in terms of its oppositional mentality. Fascism is, above all, anti-Enlightenment. It therefore opposes Enlightenment ideas such as liberalism, democracy, reason, and individualism. It is also profoundly anti-Marxist. Certain elements of fascism are similar to conservatism, in particular the focus on the organic state, but fascism is also revolutionary and, in the case of Germany at least, also racist and nationalistic. Fascism's opposition to liberalism and individualism stems from the belief that it is the community that creates individuals—that, without it, they are nothing. It is therefore opposed to the liberal position that humans can be envisaged living in a pre-social state. Rather, their identity is forged through membership of a community.

▶ See Chapter 2 for a discussion of the elite theory of the state.

Accompanying the social nature of individuals is an authoritarianism that consists of the elite view whereby some individuals are regarded as superior to others and thereby fitter to rule than others. The masses are regarded as largely ignorant, needing to be led by an elite and particularly by one all-powerful leader, a *Führer* or *Duce*. Italian fascists, in particular, were influenced by the elite theory of the state we encountered in Chapter 2. As we saw, elite thinkers such as Pareto, Mosca, and Michels regarded elite rule as inevitable. This was largely put forward as an empirical theory with limited normative overtones. What elite theory did, however, was to provide a justification for the fascist belief in the inevitability of hierarchy and the herd-like character of the masses.

Fascism's totalitarian tendencies make it an extreme form of authoritarianism. In fascist theory, it is the state that confers meaning upon individual lives and, as a result, individuals should be subservient to it. This provides a justification for the totalitarian state, in which the individual is subsumed in the state's greater goal, largely achieved through technological means. In Italy, in particular, the role of corporations was, theoretically at least, to provide the means whereby society—and particularly employer and employee organizations—were to be incorporated into the state.

▶ See Chapter 6 for a discussion of ethnic nationalism.

In German fascism, in particular, this emphasis on inequality and hierarchy took on a racial character, with the German Aryan race regarded, as a result of the adoption of various pseudoscientific theories, as superior to other racial groups—particularly Jews and people of colour. A belief in the German nation, or *Volk*, fed into a militant, aggressive, and expansionist nationalism. The goal of nationalism was therefore to establish the 'master race' across the globe, by a process of natural selection drawn from social Darwinism, putting into servitude, or eliminating, 'inferior' races in the process. War and conflict was seen as inherently virtuous and character-building, as well as serving the goal of racial superiority.

✱ KEY POINTS

- Fascism is anti-democratic, anti-liberal, and totalitarian.
- Fascists reject abstract intellectualizing in favour of action.
- Fascism is best understood in terms of its oppositional mentality.
- Central fascist themes are the emphasis on the state's role in creating meaning for individuals and an elitist view of humans. In Germany, the belief in the superiority of some humans took on a racial dimension.

Contemporary Ideologies

Contemporary ideologies have been much less ambitious and much less certain than the traditional variety discussed so far. It is easy to see why these new ideologies—such as feminism and environmentalism—have become more important in recent years. Unlike the nineteenth century, there is now much greater scepticism about the ability of human beings to master the world. In this sense, the influence of the Enlightenment has begun to wane. We are now much more cautious about universal ideologies that proclaim to understand the world and know how to put it right.

Underpinning this contemporary analysis of politics and ideology is the theory of postmodernism. Postmodernism is not an ideology so much as it is a critique of ideologies, or at least of particular types of ideology. Thus some of the major accounts of ideologies (Vincent, 1995; Heywood, 2007; Goodwin, 2014; Hoffman and Graham, 2006) do not have separate chapters on postmodernism. Postmodernism is a label given to a wide variety of theorists in a wide variety of disciplines, not just in the social sciences, but also in art, architecture, and cultural studies. It is also associated with a wide variety of academics and authors, although perhaps the two with the biggest impact on political theory have been Michel Foucault (1926–84) and Jacques Derrida (1930–2004). It is difficult to provide one all-embracing definition of postmodernism as it contains so many different emphases and nuances. At the very least, the postmodern attitude points out the necessary limitations in the project to master the nature of reality. It is therefore a direct challenge to the modernist approach.

The modernist approach, influenced by the Enlightenment, is essentially a belief in the omnipotence of reason, a confidence in the ability of reason to penetrate to the essential truth of things and to achieve progress, and a foundationalist ontology which argues 'that a real world exists independently of our knowledge of it' (Stoker and Marsh, 2002: 11). We saw earlier that, with the exception of conservatism, this confidence was present in post-Enlightenment ideologies, and principally liberalism and socialism. Postmodernism represents a challenge to this confidence. It suggests that the search for ultimate answers is a futile exercise as the world is too fractured and too diverse for grand explanatory schemes or theories. Instead, difference and variety are celebrated. Moreover, an anti-foundationalist ontology is promoted whereby the world cannot be objectively observed, but is socially constructed in a variety of ways.

For some postmodernists, the approach represents merely the description of a historical period that comes after modernity. Therefore, it is not a normative theory as much as a signpost to where the world is heading in a more fractured and uncertain way. The postmodern age is also equated with the end of a theory of knowledge—that is, postmodernists are accused of adopting a relativistic attitude arguing that all knowledge claims, all political and moral commitments, are redundant. Clearly, such a position is antithetical to much of what we have been trying to do in the opening few chapters of this book, for a postmodernist of this ilk would reject the effort to put a rational case for democracy or freedom, or to decide between the liberty claims of liberalism against the equality claims of socialism. As such, postmodernism has been criticized for being overly destructive. As Hay (2002: 217) points out, 'by confining itself to deconstruction postmodernism never risks exposing itself to a similar critique by putting something in place of that it deconstructs'. In other words, postmodernism is criticized for its oppositional nature. In Gamble's words (2000: 116), it offers 'no guidance as to what should be done about all the modernist processes which are in full flow'.

✱ KEY POINTS

- Contemporary ideologies challenge the metanarrative character of traditional ideologies, while traditional ideologies are regarded by their critics as too homogeneous and certain in their orientation.
- Contemporary ideologies are influenced by postmodernism.
- The postmodern attitude points out the necessary limitations in the project of trying to master the nature of reality.
- There is a celebration of diversity and difference.
- Postmodernism has been criticized for being overly destructive without offering any guidance to action.

Feminism

Feminism starts from the empirical claim that women are disadvantaged in a variety of ways. It has been common since the 1980s to divide feminism into liberal, socialist/Marxist, and radical strands, although since then feminism has further fragmented into a number of different, sometimes cross-cutting, categories. As a result, 'feminists are profoundly and at times bitterly divided, not only over political priorities and methods, but also over goals' (Bryson, 1999: 5).

Liberal feminism

So-called first wave feminism, in the late nineteenth and early twentieth centuries, was characterized by its liberal character. The position of liberal feminism is that women ought to have the same liberal rights as men in the public sphere, where equality is demanded in the worlds of politics, education, and work. Two early key texts of liberal feminism advocating political and legal rights for women are Mary Wollstonecraft's *A Vindication of the Rights of Women*, and J. S. Mill's *The Subjection of Women*, originally published in 1792 and 1869, respectively. A modern statement of liberal feminism is provided by Betty Friedan (1963).

There is no doubt that substantial ground has been made in securing greater equality for women in the public arena. Women have legal and political rights in Western liberal democracies. Thus, after ferocious campaigning by the suffrage movement, women in Britain were granted the vote in 1918 and on the same terms as men in 1928. Other liberal democracies have followed suit. In the workplace, too, legislative initiatives against sex discrimination, such as the British Equal Pay Act 1970, have helped to equalize male and female pay and working conditions. Marriage laws, too, are much more enlightened, women no longer being regarded as essentially the property of men.

Without doubt, too, however, greater strides are needed in both the workplace and political arena. Women's representation in the political arena, for instance, still lags far behind that of men. Of course, there is the wider question of whether the adequate representation of women's interests requires that the legislature and executive mirrors exactly the gender composition of the wider society. On the one hand, it might be argued that the feelings and interests of women may be better understood and attended to if their interests are represented by other women (Phillips, 1995). On the other hand, it might be questioned whether women need to be represented by other women, particularly given that all politicians in liberal democracies face potential electoral defeat if it is thought they have not represented the electorate's interests. Moreover, to ensure that legislatures mirror the wider society in terms of gender composition requires a great deal of electoral engineering, such as the introduction of women-only shortlists for parliamentary seats. To do so, however, is to impose constraints on electoral choice, which many would regard as undesirable.

▶ See Chapter 12 for further discussion of representation in legislatures.

In the workplace, despite equal pay legislation, women's average earnings remain less than men's. The revelation, in July 2017, that there is a significant gender pay gap among employees of the BBC is testimony to this. More generally, there is a preponderance of women in part-time and low-paid employment, and many women do the types of job that tend to be valued less. Moreover, women remain the primary carers and are disadvantaged, and often deeply psychologically affected, by their enforced absence from work (Friedan, 1963). As a result of this continued inequality, some feminists argue for the introduction of measures such as positive discrimination (an example from the political realm would be the introduction of quotas for parliamentary candidates, as mentioned above) designed to redress the unfair competition between men and women.

Liberal feminists, however, still regard the state as the 'proper and indeed the only legitimate authority for enforcing justice in general and women's rights in particular' (Jaggar, 1983: 200). This will be achieved, they argue, through the elimination of sexist attitudes in society, through education, and by putting pressure on the state applied through interest representation and political parties.

Radical feminism

The 'second wave' of feminism, dating back to the 1960s, has been characterized by its radical strand. There are a variety of different interpretations of radical feminism, but they all share the position that the exploitation of women is more central and universal than liberal feminists think, and is not merely a product of inequality in the public realm. The crucial point is the identification of a 'patriarchal' basis to society not just, or most importantly, in the public realm, but also in private family life and in relationships between men and women at all levels of society (**see Key Quote 8.5**). Patriarchy means literally 'rule by the father'. For radical feminists, men's oppression of women, therefore, is all-pervading (Millett, 1971). Radicals thus argue that 'it is not equality that women should want, but liberation' (Hoffman and Graham, 2006: 329).

The importance that radical feminists attach to power relationships within the private sphere clearly puts it at odds with liberal feminism. From a liberal perspective, the state's role ought to be limited to the public sphere, whereas the private sphere remains a sphere of personal choice and individual freedom. For radical feminists, such an ideology leaves the source of men's power untouched. Thus the focus on the state by political theorists has been heavily criticized by feminists (Pateman, 1988).

Some radical feminists emphasize the sexual repression of women under patriarchy—that women have been effectively 'castrated' by the patriarchal culture, which demands that they be passive and submissive creatures. This was the theme of Germaine Greer's book, *The Female Eunuch*, published in 1970. Women have also suffered death and physical mutilation at the hands of a patriarchal society, not least in the practice of female infanticide in China and India and the female genital mutilation that is still widespread in many parts of the world. Unlike Marxist feminists (to be discussed later in this chapter), radical feminists regard patriarchy as an independent explanatory variable and not as a product of the organization of economic classes in the capitalist system. This gender-based sphere of domination, radical feminists argue, is largely ignored by conventional political theory's focus on the state. As Pateman (1989: 3) points out, 'the public sphere', in conventional political theory, 'is assumed to be capable of being understood on its own, as if it existed sui generis, independently of private sexual relations and domestic life'. By upholding patriarchal domination in families and civil society, the state therefore contributes to gender-based oppression.

 KEY QUOTE 8.5   Kate Millett on patriarchy

'What goes largely unexamined, often even unacknowledged . . . in our social order, is the birthright priority whereby males rule females . . . It is one which tends moreover to be sturdier than any form of segregation, and more rigorous than class stratification . . . However muted its present appearance may be, sexual dominion obtains nevertheless as perhaps the most pervasive ideology of our culture and provides its most fundamental concept of power.' (Millett, 1971: 25)

8

Race, class, and feminism

A number of feminist criticisms have been made of this radical strand. Perhaps the most important critique is that radical feminism has a tendency to ignore the oppression of women based on race and class. In terms of the former, it has been argued that feminism has universalized the experiences of white (usually middle-class) women, thereby neglecting the specific oppression that women of colour have been subject to. There needs, therefore, to be a greater recognition of the particular experiences of black women, whose life experiences cannot be merely subsumed under one all-encompassing feminist critique (hooks, 1981).

In terms of class, Marxist and socialist feminists put a different slant on women's exploitation (Mitchell, 1971; Barrett, 1988). The reality of capitalism is that, for both men and women, working life is equally exploitative, particularly for working-class women whom, they argue, feminists often ignore. For both men and women, therefore, socialist feminists argue for a transformation of society so that working lives become more amenable and domestic lives cease to have an economic function. Marxist feminists, in particular, are much less sanguine than the liberal strand about the possibilities of women's position improving through focusing on the state, because the state's function is to uphold the capitalist system, which, in turn, is ultimately responsible for the exploitation of women (McIntosh, 1978). Both black and socialist feminists emphasize the intersectionality of race, capitalism, and gender, and their capacity to produce and perpetuate systems of oppression and class domination (Crenshaw, 1989).

The fragmentation of feminism

In recent years, there has been enormous fragmentation within feminist thought. Disputes have occurred, for instance, over the significance of biological differences, with some (Firestone, 1972) regarding these differences as the source of women's oppression, while others (Pateman, 1989) deny this, some seeking to recapture the importance of motherhood from a feminist viewpoint and others seeking to emphasize the importance for women to be able to choose not to be mothers. Some feminists have violently opposed pornography (Dworkin, 1981), while other, liberal, feminists have sought to reclaim it for women (McElroy, 1995). Feminists have also differed over the character of political structures, with some wanting separatist, non-hierarchical political structures, while others reject this oppositional stance and seek to build alliances with other social groups and participate in conventional political structures even though they are male-dominated.

Some feminists have sought to make alliances with postmodernism (Assiter, 1996). Postmodernism, superficially at least, would seem to be a strange bedfellow of feminism, as the former would reject the latter's attempt to universalize a theory that explains the subordination of women. As a result, some prefer to see feminist thought as an offshoot of Enlightenment modernism.

However, postmodernism does offer something of value to feminists. In the first place, it emphasizes difference and variety, which suits feminism's attempt to shift attention away from the public to the private realm. Similarly, postmodernism facilitates celebration of the differences between men and women, allowing women's separate roles, and values, to be regarded as equally important. It also allows an appreciation of the differences among women based on their class, race, and culture. A postmodern feminism therefore recognizes the difficulty of developing one approach with which to challenge a patriarchal society.

Current position

As indicated, the utility of feminism has been damaged by internal ideological debates and general fragmentation. Further problems have been caused by the hostile political environment feminists have had to operate in since the 1980s (Heywood, 2007: 251–2). Some have argued, in the light of gains made by women, that radical feminism seeks to go too far. As a result, there has been a backlash against the women's movement (Faludi, 1991). Despite this, political and economic inequalities based on gender are still widespread in liberal democracies and elsewhere, and whilst this exists feminism clearly still has an important role to play.

KEY POINTS

- Feminism starts from the assumption that women are unequal to men, subject to subordination at best and to oppression at worst.
- Feminism is best divided into liberal, socialist, and radical strands.
- Liberal feminism seeks to achieve the same rights for women as are possessed by men in the public sphere.
- Significant progress has been made in the securing of liberal rights for women, although this should not be exaggerated.
- Socialist feminists insist that more attention should be placed on working-class women whose plight is inextricably linked to the existence of the capitalist system.
- Radical feminism seeks to focus attention on patriarchal relationships in the private sphere.
- Feminist thought has undergone a great deal of fragmentation, with differences evident over motherhood, pornography, political strategy, and the value of postmodernism.

Environmentalism

Concern for the natural environment is not a new phenomenon. Legislation designed to control pollution, for instance, dates back to the nineteenth century and there are probably earlier examples than this. As a distinctive issue, however, the environment did not really exist until the 1970s and it did not become a mainstream issue for another decade. The rise of environmentalism is partly a consequence of the existence of severe objective environmental problems: the effects of air pollution, the use of pesticides in agriculture, the depletion of non-renewable resources, the extinction of many species of plants and animals, and the more recent problems of ozone depletion and climate change. A number of international gatherings—those at Stockholm in 1972 and the Earth Summit at Rio 20 years later being the most symbolic—helped to establish the state of the environment as a key issue of our time, albeit one that rarely has an impact on national elections. Such has been the impact of humans on the environment that geologists have now suggested that a new 'Anthropocene' epoch in planetary history is upon us (Crutzen and Stoermer, 2000). This marks a change from a period in which humans adapted to changes in their natural environment to a period in which humans are directly responsible for altering the environment and, in the process, degrading it.

Ideologically, environmental thought can be divided into two main categories. On the one hand is the reformist approach (sometimes described as 'light green' or 'shallow' environmentalism). On the other is the radical ('dark green' or 'deep') approach. For some political theorists, only the latter can be properly described as an ideology (Dobson, 2007). To distinguish the two, one might refer to the former as environmentalism and the latter as ecologism. Environmentalism can be seen, then, as a single-issue concern not necessarily inconsistent with a range of ideologies, whereas ecologism is a separate ideology with a set of distinct ideas. The differences between the two can be illustrated if we examine their major characteristics.

The economic realm

One major distinction between reformist and radical accounts is their approach to economic growth. Radical greens see economic growth as incompatible with environmental protection. The aversion to economic growth is partly a normative claim that individuals will lead much more fulfilled lives in a non-materialistic society. It is primarily, however, an empirical claim that there are natural limits to growth and that, unless production and consumption levels and population size are reduced to sustainable levels, economic and political collapse will be the result.

This empirical claim received its impetus from a report by a group of American scientists published as *The Limits to Growth* (Meadows, 1972). The report was based on a series of computer runs that factored in potential solutions to a range of environmental problems, while growth in the other variables stayed the same. At each step, the authors argued, the solution did not solve the need for a cut in economic growth to forestall environmental

8

degradation. Their conclusion was that if we fail to cut economic activity, then the point of no return will be reached not far into the current (twenty-first) century.

There have been many criticisms of the *Limits to Growth* report (Martell, 1994: 33–40). Not least it has been suggested that there is no necessary trade-off between economic growth and environmental protection. This reformist challenge is based on the assertion that provided that growth is sustainable, then it is permissible from an environmental perspective. Sustainable development is therefore the centrepiece of a reformist alternative. There have been numerous definitions of sustainable development, the best known defining it as development that 'meets the needs of the present generation without compromising the ability of future generations to meet their own needs' (World Commission on Environment and Development, 1987).

Sustainable development is notoriously vague, or at least lacking in detail. A more precise formulation is the principle known as ecological modernization (Hajer, 1997), which suggests a number of ways in which growth can be sustainable. First, growth need not necessarily occur through the use of non-renewable resources such as coal and gas. Second, the production of environmental goods—such as catalytic converters for cars or scrubs removing the pollution from power stations—can itself be a source of economic growth. Finally, it is argued that environmental damage is not cost-free economically, so that protecting the environment can be consistent with economic growth.

The philosophical realm

Reformists (and indeed all of the ideologies encountered in this chapter) adopt an anthropocentric view of the world—that is, this ethic is human-centred. Humans are regarded as having intrinsic value and non-humans have only extrinsic value. For exponents of anthropocentrism, the value of non-human nature is extrinsic to us. We protect the environment, in other words, because it is in our interests to do so and not because we think that nature has any worthwhile interests of its own. Some radical greens, on the other hand, adopt what has been called an ecocentric ethic (Leopold, 1949; Fox, 1995; Eckersley, 1992). This position accords intrinsic value to both humans and to non-human parts of nature. In other words, nature has moral worth independently of human beings (**see Key Debate 8.6**).

The political realm

There is now a considerable body of green political thought (Dobson, 2007). We have seen earlier in this book that green thinking has influenced our thinking about concepts such as justice and democracy. For reformists, environmental solutions can coexist with existing political structures. By contrast, radicals argue that in order for environmental objectives to be achieved, it is necessary for far-reaching social and political change.

There is a division of opinion, however, on what change is necessary. In the so-called survivalist literature, principally evident in the 1970s, there is an authoritarian strain (Hardin, 1968;

KEY DEBATE 8.6   Justifying an ecocentric ethic

The difficulties of justifying an ecocentric ethic philosophically are considerable. For many philosophers, sentience—or the capacity to experience pain and pleasure—is the key benchmark for moral standing. It is easy to see why damaging the interests of a human or an animal matters to her, but it is more difficult to see why damaging a tree matters to the tree. We can clearly negatively affect a tree's interests, but, following Frey (1983: 154–5), it does not seem sensible to talk about wronging the tree. Thus polluting a river is to harm it, but since the river only has extrinsic value for those sentient beings who benefit from it, it is only they who can be wronged by polluting the river.

The key question would seem to be whether establishing an ecocentric ethic is important in terms of protecting the environment. Increasingly, green thinkers argue that there are sufficient prudential grounds for protecting nature (Barry, 1999). To give an example, we should protect forests not because forests have intrinsic value, but because it is in our interests to do so—not least because they provide crucial sinks for carbon dioxide and therefore help to control rises in the temperature of the planet.

Questions

1. What is a non-anthropocentric ethic?
2. Why should we protect the environment?

Heilbroner, 1974; Ophuls, 1973; Shearman and Wayne-Smith, 2007). Most radical greens now advocate decentralized, small-scale, self-sufficient, anarchist-type communities linked together by loose authority structures (Schumacher, 1973; Bookchin, 1971). Despite their ability to reduce or eliminate large-scale industrial production, to enable people to be closer to nature, and to facilitate political participation and social cohesion, the environmental utility of these loose alliances has been questioned by some green thinkers (Goodin, 1992). At a time when international agreements are seen as essential for effective environmental protection and yet difficult to achieve in the existing state system, the ability of a diverse range of small self-governing communities to ensure effective coordination is, at the very least, problematic.

See Chapters 4 and 7, respectively, for an exploration of the relationship between environmentalism and democracy and justice.

A distinct ideology?

It needs to be asked, finally, how far radical environmentalism or ecologism represents a distinct ideology, separate from the other ideologies we have considered. A quick glance at the literature reveals that a number of traditional ideological positions have sought to claim environmentalism for themselves. Thus there are works of eco-socialism (Pepper, 1993), eco-liberalism (Wissenburg, 1993), and eco-feminism (Mellor, 1997). There is even an attempt to claim the green label for fascism (Bramwell, 1989).

On the other hand, the existence of separate green political parties throughout the world suggests that ecologists regard their position as distinct. Clearly, the limits to growth position adds an extra dimension to political thinking. In particular, it challenges the shared optimistic vision that liberals, socialists, and Marxists have about the ability of humans to master their environment for their own infinite economic ends. Similarly distinct is the ecocentric ethic adopted by some radical greens. All traditional ideologies are incorruptibly anthropocentric in orientation, regarding the natural world as a resource for humans to exploit.

Ecology is less distinct, however, in its political orientation. Here, it borrows from other traditions of thought—from the authoritarian implications of Hobbes' Leviathan to the participatory democracy of Rousseau and the lack of hierarchy advocated by anarchism. Insofar as these political positions are recommended for the achievement of environmental objectives, there is a case for saying that they are being used in distinctive ways, but, as we have seen, there is no one favoured political position for ecologists.

 KEY POINTS

- The rise of environmentalism has been, partly at least, the product of severe environmental problems.
- Environmental thinkers can be divided into radical and reformist camps.
- In economic terms, the radicals support a limit to growth, while the reformists advocate a version of sustainable development.
- In philosophic terms, the radicals hold an ecocentric ethic, while the reformists hold an anthropocentric ethic.
- In political terms, radicals advocate far-reaching change, while the reformist position can coexist with a variety of ideological positions.
- In its economic and philosophical/ethical guises, there is a case for saying that environmentalism is a distinct ideology, but this is less clear-cut in terms of political structures.

Multiculturalism

Multiculturalism has emerged as a direct challenge to those nationalists who desire to create distinct states based on ethnicity and the traditional model of citizenship, associated above all with the work of T. H. Marshall (1950), which emphasized the need to 'promote a . . . common national identity among citizens' (Kymlicka, 2002: 327). By contrast, multiculturalism seeks to advocate pluralistic states based on many different religious, cultural, and ethnic identities. The term 'multiculturalism' was first used as recently as the 1960s in Canada, as a result, in particular, of growing demands among the French-speaking community in Quebec who reject the Anglophone domination of the Canadian state. By the 1970s, multiculturalism had become official government policy (Tierney, 2007). The two key questions we will consider here are, first, what is the correct ideological location for multiculturalism and, second, is it a positive or negative phenomenon?

Multiculturalism and ideology

Initially, before the 1990s, multiculturalism was seen by political theorists as particularly aligned with communitarianism. As we saw in Chapter 7, communitarianism, by focusing on group rights and community cohesion and identity, is a direct challenge to the liberal focus on the autonomous individual. As Kymlicka (2002: 337) points out: 'Communitarians . . . view multiculturalism as an appropriate way of protecting communities from the eroding effects of individual autonomy, and of affirming the value of community.' To this end, Kymlicka (1995) sought to develop a theory of group rights. These include rights of self-governance (for national, territorially concentrated, minority populations, such as the Inuit in Canada), 'polyethnic' rights to allow minority groups to preserve their distinctive ways of life, and representative rights to correct the under-representation of minority or disadvantaged groups in education and public and political life.

> **See Chapter 7 for a discussion of communitarianism.**

This opposition between multiculturalism and liberalism might strike the reader as somewhat odd. After all, the liberal emphasis on the neutral state, the reluctance of liberals to countenance interfering in competing conceptions of the good (seen most notably in the later political philosophy of John Rawls), and the liberal focus on the protection of minority rights would seem to equate liberalism with multiculturalism. This is particularly the case when one considers that liberalism emerged as a defence of religious toleration. It is not surprising, therefore, that, since the 1980s, liberals have sought to accommodate multiculturalism.

However, this accommodation presents problems for liberals. There is a potential conflict between liberal values and the upholding of minority cultural rights when the latter involves the infringing of individual rights. It would be odd, for instance, for liberals to sanction illiberal practices such as forced marriages, confining women to the home, and, even worse, female genital mutilation, all issues that have troubled feminists, as well as removing children from public education and apostasy (the practice of preventing individuals from rejecting a particular faith). Moreover, the use of a group right against behaviour from others that might offend can conflict with freedom of expression, a central canon of liberalism.

One way out of this dilemma for liberals is to offer limited support for multiculturalism, affirming it only when it does not involve the infringement of individual rights (Kymlicka, 2002: 340–1). Rawls (1993) essentially does this by arguing that liberals can only accept a 'reasonable pluralism', thereby not forcing it into a position where it is has to accept the moral legitimacy, say, of slavery. Kymlicka (1995) wants to go further than Rawls in a multicultural direction by arguing that the degree to which we should expect different cultures to assimilate depends upon how the minority group's position is established. Thus, refugees, and those who have chosen to emigrate should be prepared to assimilate, whereas in the case of indigenous national minorities who have not chosen to be cultural minorities, such as Indigenous Australians and the Native American tribes, more effort should be made to permit differentiated rights, even when they conflict with liberal principles.

While we may think that Kymlicka's principle has a great deal of validity, it is somewhat arbitrary, and it is debatable how far it remains consistent with liberal values. Others either reject multiculturalism or reject liberalism. The best example of the former is

8

political theorist Brian Barry (2001), who has doubts about the value of multiculturalism because it is a threat to liberal values. On the other hand, some political theorists argue that a convincing multiculturalism must go beyond the liberal objection to the infringement of individual rights, since the liberal multiculturalism of those such as Rawls and Kymlicka is heavily weighted towards liberalism. Parekh (2000), for instance, argues that we should adopt a much more pluralistic morality and be prepared to jettison liberalism when it conflicts with multiculturalism. This has the effect of offering a separate ideological status for multiculturalism, separate from liberalism and communitarianism.

Is multiculturalism a good thing?

A related question is whether multiculturalism is a positive principle that we ought to adopt. This has become an issue of some political saliency, particularly in the context of 9/11 and the Islamic terrorism in Britain and France carried out by its own citizens. Multiculturalism has been challenged primarily because of a concern for social unity and a feeling that it is 'corrosive of long-term political unity and social stability' (Kymlicka, 2002: 366). It is for this reason that France, among European states, practises the most insistent policy of assimilation, which has caused particular controversy in the case of the wearing of religious dress. In addition, as we have indicated, the danger of moral pluralism is that it allows for the potential infringement of individual rights.

In defence of multiculturalism, it offers a solution to the inevitable cultural diversity present in modern societies. There is 'remarkably little evidence' that multiculturalism leads to social conflict. Indeed, it might be regarded as a force for social inclusion, since allowing minority cultural groups to practise their differences is more likely to make them feel positive towards, and included within, the society in which they live (Kymlicka, 2002: 367). Moreover, cultural diversity brings a richness to otherwise homogeneous lives, encourages toleration of difference, and allows individuals to generate a sense of belonging. Rejecting different approaches to life, as some liberals would seem to be doing, also suggests an arrogance and infallibility that many argue is not justified.

✳ KEY POINTS

- Multiculturalism seeks to promote pluralistic states based on many different religious, cultural, and ethnic identities.
- Multiculturalism was initially aligned with communitarianism, but was later adopted by liberals.
- The liberal advocacy of multiculturalism is problematic because of the need to sanction practices within minority cultures that are illiberal.
- Some, writing from outside the liberal tradition, argue that liberalism ought to be sacrificed in favour of multiculturalism.

● Multiculturalism has been attacked for its divisive nature and the potential for the infringement of liberal principles. Others defend it as one means of accommodating diversity and the richness diversity brings.

Religious Fundamentalism

Religion is not ideological insofar as it remains a private concern among individuals and groups. It becomes ideological if it seeks to organize political principles along religious lines and seeks political influence or power in order to achieve it. There are, of course, many instances in world history of religion playing a political role, not least the European conflicts between Catholics and Protestants in the sixteenth and seventeenth centuries.

Since then, however, many societies, influenced by the Lockean principle of religious toleration, have separated the church from the state, not least in the US, where this is enshrined in the Constitution. In these secular regimes, religion becomes a private pursuit not impinging on the public realm and the state remains neutral between competing faiths, provided that the practices of any one of them do not infringe the rights of any citizen, and even then there may be exceptions. Despite this, there are many contemporary examples of conflicts centring, at least to some extent, on religion, such as Northern Ireland (between Protestants and Catholics), particularly in the 1970s, Iraq (between Shi'a and Sunni Muslims, a strand of the latter morphing into ISIS, the so-called Islamic State of Iraq and Syria), and Darfur in the Sudan (between Muslims and Christians). As Goodwin (2014: 445) states, 'religious differences have, for millennia, led to a waste of human life and to the undermining of the imperatives of human toleration'.

The fundamentalist religious strands, which became current in the twentieth century, are ideological precisely because they do seek to enter the political realm. To be a fundamentalist is to be convinced of the truth of the doctrine one is professing (in the case of religious fundamentalism based on an interpretation of a sacred text) and to seek to ensure that these truths are adopted by the state, even by the use of force and violence. Such is the publicity given to it that, when we think of religious fundamentalism, the Islamic variety comes easily to mind. Indeed, scholar Samuel Huntington (1996) argued, in a controversial study, that we are now faced by a 'clash of civilisations' in which societies upholding Western values are under attack from non-Western civilizations and particularly those dominated by Islam.

An important caveat needs to be made about fundamentalism in general, and religious fundamentalism in particular. Most Muslims, Christians, and Jews are tolerant and peaceable and are content to allow for religion to remain separate from politics. All religions—Christianity, Islam, Judaism, Hinduism, Sikhism, and even Buddhism—have their fundamentalist elements, although, by and large, they remain in a minority (Heywood, 2007: 281). Therefore, it is preferable, as one critique of Huntington has suggested, to talk about a clash between fundamentalist Muslims and fundamentalist Christians rather than a 'clash of civilisations' (Ali, 2002).

The characteristic of Islamic fundamentalism is its desire to create a theocracy (a regime based on religious principles). It is undoubtedly a potent religious force, particularly in Africa and the Middle East, receiving a fillip when the Shah of Iran was deposed by an Islamic funda-

See Chapter 17 for more on ISIS and the security situation in Iraq and Syria.

8

mentalist regime led by Ayatollah Khomeini in 1979. Following on from the Muslim Brotherhood, formed in Egypt in 1928, a number of new militant Islamic groups have emerged, most notably ISIS, and Boko Haram in Nigeria, to add to Al-Qaeda (literally 'the base'), formed by Osama bin Laden in Afghanistan in 1988 and held responsible for the attacks on the Twin Towers in New York and the Pentagon in Washington on 11 September 2001 (9/11).

In some senses, Islamic fundamentalism is opposed to modernity. Thus it is virulently anti-democrat and morally conservative, regarding modern Western values as corrupt and licentious. Nevertheless, it is 'best described . . . as a modern movement opposed to modernity' (Hoffman and Graham, 2006: 397). This is because Islamic fundamentalists (and those of the Christian variety too) have not been slow in using modern communication devices, such as the Internet, to propagate their cause and mobilize support. It is noticeable, too, that an Islamic regime such as Iran is fully prepared to use the benefits of scientific research, as in the case of nuclear weapons technology, to defend itself against perceived threats from the West.

As with all fundamentalist groups, the certainty of belief of Islamic fundamentalist groups is infectious and leads to a 'capacity to generate activism and mobilize the faithful' (Heywood, 2007: 289), although it is also true that its strength derives from social and economic circumstances, often coupled with the mistakes of existing non-fundamentalist elites. Thus, rightly or wrongly, it has been claimed that the Islamic terrorist threat has been largely provoked by the response of the US and its allies.

Given that Christianity is the world's biggest religion, it would be surprising if it did not have a fundamentalist element. Christian fundamentalism is particularly associated with the Christian New Right that emerged in the US in the 1970s. It has sought to campaign for conservative moral values—particularly against the rights given to particular social groups, such as people of colour, feminists, and the gay rights movement—and against abortion. Christian fundamentalists have sometimes resorted to violence, particularly against the staff and clients of abortion clinics, and sometimes against the intrusion of the public sector in general, such as in the Oklahoma bombing in 1995.

KEY POINTS

- Religion becomes ideological if it becomes embroiled in politics.
- Religious fundamentalism can be characterized by its intention of organizing politics along religious lines.
- Not all Muslims are fundamentalists, and fundamentalism occurs in all religions and, arguably, in all ideologies.
- Religious fundamentalists, of the Muslim and Christian varieties, are anti-modernist in the sense of being morally conservative and, in the case of the former, anti-democratic too, but they are also modernist in the sense that they utilize modern communication media and campaigning strategies.

Conclusion

The traditional ideologies described in this chapter have exercised an extraordinary influence on world politics, not always in the way their adherents intended. Indeed, such has been the negative impact of at least some of the ideologies discussed that, since the middle of the twentieth century, political theorists have been much more circumspect about offering the kind of overarching interpretations of the world, or 'metanarratives', that ideologies traditionally offered.

Contemporary ideologies represent a challenge to the state. This is seen first in the greater emphasis on the supranational dimension observed, in particular, in environmentalism, multiculturalism, and religious fundamentalism (Hoffman and Graham, 2006: 317–18). All have been impacted on by the phenomenon of globalization, a central theme of this book. The new ideologies are also a product of social and economic change, centring in particular on the decline of class as a major fault line in world politics. Finally, environmentalism is a product of the objectively deteriorating state of the natural environment, coupled with rising affluence. All of this has resulted in an ideological world that, while more dynamic and pluralistic, is less sure of itself and more open to change.

? Key Questions

- How would you distinguish between traditional and contemporary ideologies?
- Does new liberalism develop or depart from classical liberalism?
- Is socialism utopian and/or authoritarian?
- To what extent can conservatism be considered an ideology?
- Did fascism die with Hitler and Mussolini?
- Has feminism achieved its objectives?
- What does feminism say about the state?
- Is there a distinct ideology of environmentalism?
- Is multiculturalism consistent with liberalism?
- Under what circumstances does religion become ideological?

||| Further Reading

Bellamy, R. (2000), *Rethinking Liberalism* (London: Pinter).
This is a collection of essays by a noted scholar on the development of liberal thought.

Bryson, V. (2003), *Feminist Political Theory: An Introduction* (Basingstoke: Palgrave, 2nd edn).
This is an excellent introduction.

Dobson, A. (2007), *Green Political Thought* (London: Unwin Hyman, 4th edn).
This is the standard introduction to the subject.

Freeden, M. (1996), *Ideologies and Political Theory* (Oxford: Oxford University Press).
This is a monumental work that not only covers ideologies in depth, but also offers an innovative way of thinking about them.

Goodwin, B. (2014), *Using Political Ideas* (Chichester: John Wiley & Sons, 6th edn).
This is an excellent, well-established introduction to the ideologies discussed in this chapter.

Gray, J. (2003), *Al Qaeda and What It Means to Be Modern* (London: Faber & Faber).
This is a typically incisive account of religious fundamentalism by a key thinker.

Kymlicka, W. (2002), *Contemporary Political Philosophy* (Oxford: Oxford University Press, 2nd edn), ch. 8.
This covers, in summary form, the multicultural debate in which the author is a key participant.

Moussalli, A. (ed.) (1998), *Islamic Fundamentalism* (Reading: Ithaca Press).
This is a good collection of articles by leading experts in the field.

O'Sullivan, N. (1976), *Conservatism* (London: Macmillan).
This is a well-regarded account of conservative thought.

Wright, A. (1996), *Socialisms* (London: Routledge, 2nd edn).
This reflects well the diversity of socialist thought.

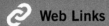 **Web Links**

http://www.kirkcenter.org/burke/edmund-burke
On Edmund Burke's conservatism.

http://plato.stanford.edu/entries/nationalism/
On nationalism.

http://www.anarchistfaq.org
On anarchism.

http://www.ipu.org/wmn-e/classif.htm
For information on women's political representation.

http://www.erraticimpact.com/~ecologic/
For a list of environmental links.

https://plato.stanford.edu/entries/multiculturalism/
An analysis of multiculturalism.

 Visit the **Online Resources** that accompany this book to access more learning resources on this topic: www.oup.com/uk/ferdinand/

Political Economy: National and Global Perspectives

9

- The Study of Political Economy
- The Age of Mercantilism
- The Rise of Liberal Political Economy
- Marxism and Critical IPE
- The Post-War International Economic Order
- The North–South Gap

- Globalization and Regionalization in the Post-Cold-War World
- Financial Crises in the Global System
- Conclusion
- Key Questions
- Further Reading
- Web Links

Reader's Guide

In providing an overview of the field of political economy, this chapter adopts a historical, comparative, and international perspective, which enables an appreciation of how ideas, practices, and institutions develop and interact over place and time. It looks at important theories such as Marxism, liberalism, and economic nationalism, and significant issues including the interaction of states and markets, the nexus between wealth and power, and issues in the wider global economy, including the North–South divide. The final section discusses the twin phenomena of globalization and regionalization, and the way in which these are shaping political economy at the global level and challenging the traditional role of the state. An underlying theme of the chapter is the link between economic and political power.

The Study of Political Economy

Political economy is a field of study that lies at the intersection of politics and economics, while incorporating insights from a number of other disciplines—sociology, history, and law in particular—and which is concerned primarily, although not exclusively, with the relationship between states and markets. In this context, it is also concerned with the distribution of wealth and the nature of economic power. It has both national and international dimensions, although these are deeply intertwined and it is virtually impossible to talk about a 'national economy' in isolation from wider global political and economic dynamics.

Political economy has its intellectual origins in the work of such figures as Adam Smith (1723–90) and Karl Marx (1818–83), who established what we now call classical political economy. Marx is obviously a founding figure in the socialist tradition and he in fact coined the term 'classical political economy' to describe the bourgeois mode of production, but the 'classical' label now refers most often to liberal thinkers in the field who, in addition to Smith, include William Petty (1623–87), Thomas Malthus (1766–1834), David Ricardo (1772–1823), and John Stuart Mill (1806–73). Despite certain differences, these liberal thinkers shared a belief in the efficacy of the 'free market', understood as free trade in goods and services, unimpeded by government interference, or with perhaps just minimal regulation, and mediated only by the forces of supply and demand.

Before the twentieth century, 'political economy' was used as a synonym for what we now refer to as economics. Since then, the field of economics has developed along the lines of a social science dominated by an approach known as 'neo-classical economics'. This approach has sought to establish a distinctive and separate profile for a discipline of economics within the social sciences and, by so doing, to marginalize the implications of historical and sociological factors, as well as to separate the realm of economics from politics and, by implication, from political interference, as explained in **Key Concept 9.1**.

 KEY CONCEPT 9.1   **Neo-classical economics**

Neo-classical economics is based on the search for immutable laws of human economic behaviour and interaction. These are assumed to emanate from an essentially rational human tendency to maximize individual self-interest. Translated into the sphere of institutions such as the market and the firm, neo-classical economics further assumes that free markets behave rationally to produce the greatest measure of economic efficiency, as opposed to any central planning mechanism that may be imposed by government. The rationality of firms is expressed first and foremost in their profit-seeking behaviour.

The neo-classical approach is also said to underpin the doctrine of neo-liberalism, which has attracted much attention in recent years. This concept is discussed in a later section, but for the moment we should note that the term denotes the reassertion of the value of older liberal ideas in the contemporary context. Neo-liberalism generally holds that 'free markets in which individuals maximize their material interests provide the best means for satisfying human aspiration, and that markets in particular are to be preferred over states and politics, which are at best inefficient and at worst threats to freedom' (Crouch, 2011: vii). Neo-liberalism also strongly advocates deregulation of private sector economic and financial activity and austerity in fiscal policy. The latter refers to the way in which governments raise revenue—mainly through taxes—and how they use the proceeds not only to provide public goods, but also to control macro-economic conditions, including the demand for goods and services. Thus neo-liberalism consists in a 'free market ideology based on individual liberty and limited government that [connects] human freedom to the actions of the rational, self-interested actor in the competitive marketplace' (Jones, 2014: 2).

Critical approaches to contemporary political economy repudiate the idea that economics can be separated from politics. Equally, they reject any notion that the study of politics can be carried out without reference to economics. Market relations, says one commentator, are political constructions and are recognized as such by a political economy approach. Further, political economy poses some essential questions 'about power relations and the (in)equality of capitalism's distributive consequences' (Clift, 2014: 1).

Some schools of liberal economic thought—notably, Keynesian economics—also stand in contrast with neo-classical economics and neo-liberal ideology in that the political regulation of the market is seen as essential if economic stability is to be maintained, especially in view of the fact that markets are not actually 'self-correcting', as neo-classical economists would have us believe. In times of recession and stagnation, Keynesian economics further holds that government spending plays a crucial role in stimulating economic activity. We further consider the impact of Keynesian economics, as well as aspects of neo-liberalism, later in this chapter.

Although the study of political economy has had an international dimension from its earliest days, the addition of the word 'global' or 'international' to 'political economy' scarcely occurred before the 1970s. This has changed significantly as the study of global politics has expanded well beyond political and strategic relations between governments to encompass many other concerns, from the global environment to the global economy. There is now a well-established field of international political economy (IPE). So, just as the study of political economy challenges the notion that economic life can be analysed separately from social and political life, so too must it challenge the domestic–international divide. As suggested earlier, it must therefore look not just to the national sphere, but also to the comparative and global dimensions of the subject matter.

As with politics more generally, it is also the case that political economy cannot confine itself simply to the structural study of institutions or organizations, but must also take account of the norms, values, and interests that they reflect. Furthermore, any arrangement of national and global systems of production, distribution, and exchange reflects a mix of values and must therefore be understood neither as divinely ordained nor as the fortuitous outcome of mere chance, but rather as 'the result of human decisions taken in the context of manmade institutions and . . . self-set rules and customs' (Strange, quoted in Balaam and Veseth, 2005: 5).

It has been noted above that many studies in political economy take the state and the market to be the two main entities involved. As Gilpin (1987: 8) puts it, 'the parallel existence and mutual interaction' of these entities work to create 'political economy'. The state embodies political forces, while the market, famously cast as 'the invisible hand' by Adam Smith, is defined as 'a coordinating mechanism where sellers and buyers exchange goods and services at prices and output levels determined by supply and demand' (Cohn, 2005: 7).

The relationship between states and markets is often depicted as one of permanent tension, since the efforts of state actors are primarily concerned with preserving **sovereignty** and political unity, on which state power relies, while markets are assumed to thrive on openness and the absence of barriers to trade. The tension is well illustrated by some of the difficulties following the 2016 vote on EU membership in the UK. Leaving the European Union may well enhance the sovereignty of the British state (although not necessarily its political unity), but it is by no means certain that the UK will be better off in terms of trade—an issue raised again later in this chapter.

At another level, the relationship between states and markets may be seen as complementary because state action is required to protect property rights, provide infrastructure, and regulate transactions. In turn, where an economy is thriving, which it seems more likely to do where trade barriers are minimal, there is often a proportional strengthening of national political and military power (Cohn, 2005: 7). These are among the issues discussed in the next section.

 KEY POINTS

- Political economy sits at the intersection of politics and economics, as well as incorporating other interdisciplinary insights, and has national and international dimensions.
- Studies in political economy focus mainly on states and markets, with the relationship between these consisting in a tangle of complex interactions and involving important dynamics of power and wealth.

The Age of Mercantilism

Mercantilism (from the Latin for 'merchant') is a form of economic **nationalism** aimed at building state power. It emerged in European economic and political thought in the seventeenth century, initially from a cluster of ideas and policies concerning the balance of trade (Miller, 1991: 335). The basic premise of classical mercantilism is that national wealth and military power form a virtuous circle: wealth enhances military power vis-à-vis other states (and in early modern Europe this often meant superior naval power); substantial wealth is acquired through trade; trade is protected by naval power; the wealth generated by trade further enhances naval capacity—and so on. The relentless pursuit of trade is therefore justified by its positive contribution to national strength.

The catch-cry of the mercantilist, however, was not *free* trade, but national *protectionism*, which was the logical accompaniment to its basic principles. Mercantilism therefore acquired the characteristics of a nationalist discourse, which, in a post-feudal age of state-building in Europe, resonated with other ideas about national greatness. It also went hand in hand with justifications of colonialism. In addition, the grounds for legitimate warfare were enlarged to encompass commercial and market considerations (Watson, 2004: 3).

Mercantilism was at odds with emergent liberal ideas in both economics and politics more generally. Conservative economic historians depicted mercantilism as *rightly* subordinating economic to political considerations of national interest. This was in line with their belief in 'the subordination of the individual to the state and to the exaltation of vigorous nationalism characteristic of mercantilism' (Viner, 1949: 4). Friedrich List (1789–1846), an early nineteenth-century defender of mercantilism, rejected the 'cosmopolitical' world view of economic liberals, which assumes peaceful relations in a politically stable environment. List argued that political economy must start instead from the premise that relations between states are inherently conflictual. It follows that nationalist rivalries produce the major dynamics with which political economy must grapple. It follows that 'true political science' must see a world characterized by free trade as 'a very unnatural one' (List, 1991: 54).

Mercantilist thinking declined following the rise of liberal thought, but enjoyed a resurgence from the late nineteenth century on into the early twentieth century, when nationalism was rife. Liberal ideas supporting free trade suffered a proportionate decline. But this situation was not to last. Cohn (2005: 71) writes that the extreme nationalism and trade protectionism of the inter-war period, and their association with the Great Depression, as well as the experience of the Second World War, gave liberal economic principles a boost in the post-war period.

An interesting question now is the prospect of a new age of mercantilism as more political leaders adopt nationalist and anti-globalization postures. In the wake of Brexit and an increase in support for right-wing nationalist populism in places such as France, EU Commission President Jean-Claude Juncker (2017) declared that EU members could not afford to revert to isolationism and protectionism: 'I can see no scenario whatsoever in which economic nationalism can be consistent with the idea of Europe or the prosperity of its people.'

Economic nationalism has also made a significant comeback in the US under the Trump presidency (**see Figure 9.1**). Donald Trump's strongly nationalist inaugural address incorporated a direct reference to mercantilist policies, as illustrated in **Key Quote 9.2**. Much of his rhetoric has been directed against China and Mexico, both of which have trade

FIGURE 9.1   Donald Trump
© Joseph Sohm/ Shutterstock.com

surpluses with the US and which he therefore sees as having benefited at the expense of the US. But, as one source notes, the US 'has invested more than $90 billion in Mexico, millions of American jobs are tied to trade with the southern neighbor, and rising wealth in Mexico has actually curbed immigration from that country' (Bartash, 2017). The extent to which Trump's economic nationalist platform is implemented, and its consequences, remains to be seen. One widely anticipated outcome of protectionist policies is inflation, due to the likelihood of a sharp rise in the price of consumer goods, and there would be numerous flow-on consequences in other parts of the US economy, as well as globally. For the time being, we can only watch this space.

 KEY QUOTE 9.2   Trump on protectionism

'From this day forward, a new vision will govern our land.

From this moment on, it's going to be America First.

Every decision on trade, on taxes, on immigration, on foreign affairs, will be made to benefit American workers and American families.

We must protect our borders from the ravages of other countries making our products, stealing our companies, and destroying our jobs. Protection will lead to great prosperity and strength.' (White House, 2017)

KEY POINTS

- Mercantilism is a form of economic nationalism that bases its theory of political economy on certain balance-of-trade principles aimed at enhancing state power.
- Mercantilism opposes the ideology of the free market, favouring a strong state that not only provides security, but also is actively involved in the economy by promoting protectionist measures.
- Mercantilist thinking is evident in the policies of President Trump, as well as in some elements of Brexit.

The Rise of Liberal Political Economy

By the late eighteenth century, liberal political economy had displaced mercantilism in prominence due largely to the influence of Adam Smith, David Ricardo, and other liberal intellectuals. Smith's free-trade ideas were based on the division of labour, economic interdependence, and the notion that states in an unregulated global economy would find a productive niche based on absolute advantage. This meant that each state would find the greatest benefit in producing specialized goods most efficiently and trading these with other states, who would do the same.

These ideas were further refined by David Ricardo (1772–1823), who expanded Smith's insights by introducing the concept of *comparative* advantage, a key concept in international trade theory. Ricardo (1821: 99) stated that: 'The same rule which regulates the relative value of commodities in one country, does not regulate the relative value of the commodities exchanged between two or more countries.' This suggests that even if one state has no absolute advantage in the production of any particular good, it can at least specialize in the production and export of those it can produce with a relative advantage (Cohn, 2005: 92).

In the contemporary period, it has been argued that Ricardo's theory of comparative advantage no longer holds in a world where capital, rather than being largely confined within national boundaries, now moves freely to wherever returns are highest, relative to risk. Labour, too, is much more mobile than in Ricardo's day. Even so, his theory of comparative advantage has influenced generations of economists and remains a cornerstone of trade theory to this day, especially in terms of critiques of protectionism (Carbaugh, 2016: 33).

Another important concept underpinning early liberal political economy was laissez-faire (literally, 'let be'), meaning that the state should allow free rein to *individual initiative, competition, the pursuit of self-interest, and the invisible hand of market forces*—all classic elements of liberal political economy. While the pursuit of self-interest may seem attuned only to selfish individual ends, Smith and other liberals believed that the sum of such individual actions adds to overall wealth and prosperity for the community.

9

Liberalism thus described is a theory of the individual *in* society rather than a theory of individual self-regarding action without reference to a wider social sphere. But because liberal theorists were opposed to mercantilist state practices, and to the abuse of state power more generally, liberal thought acquired a distinct anti-statist hue. Even so, most versions of liberalism recognize the state as essential for the organization of political life, as well as for legislation to protect rights, especially property rights, keeping law and order and providing essential infrastructure where the private sector cannot.

Early classical liberals also came up with the notion of 'homo economicus'. As described by Mill (1844/1972: 144), the phrase 'presupposes an arbitrary definition of man, as a being who inevitably does that by which he may obtain the greatest amount of necessaries, conveniences, and luxuries, with the smallest quantity of labour and physical self-denial with which they can be obtained in the existing state of knowledge'. But he added a critical note: 'Political Economy . . . reasons from *assumed* premises . . . which might be totally without foundation in fact' and so 'are only true . . . *in the abstract*' (Mill, 1844: 144–5, emphasis original).

Despite Mill's caveat, many have taken the nature of homo economicus as a truism. A much more recent commentary describes homo economicus as 'a selfish, single-minded creature: her sole concern is the minimization of cost and the maximization of her own utility. Economists assume that she is fully informed at all times, makes no mistakes, and is able to instantaneously make complex optimization decisions' (Kim, 2014). While Mill's account was much more nuanced, the latter appears to accord more fully with contemporary neo-liberal thinking, although defenders of the latter may dismiss it as a caricature.

Under the influence of John Maynard Keynes (1883–1946), another strand of liberal thought emerged to challenge the assumptions of traditional liberal economic theory. In 1926, Keynes produced a pamphlet entitled *The End of Laissez-Faire* in which he declared that the ideology underpinning the pet doctrine of classical economics—that is, that the unfettered pursuit of individual self-interest in the economic realm inevitably worked for the greater good of society—simply could not be deduced from basic economic principles. Keynes argued that while markets provide *some* of the mechanisms for governing human life, the state must take responsibility for others, and the key to a prosperous, successful society was in finding the balance (Keynes, 1926; Barnett, 2013: 144).

Keynesian theory therefore incorporated a more expansive view of the role of government in the economy. Keynes also believed that the sum of rational individual actions did not always add up to a rational outcome at the collective level, making it important for the state to regulate and make adjustments. Certainly, to treat 'the market' as the infallible source of all wisdom was a mistake. In a major work, first published in the wake of the Great Depression, Keynes highlighted the importance of understanding aggregate demand (total spending in the economy) and, where necessary, the role of governments in maintaining stable business cycles and forestalling 'boom and bust' episodes (Keynes, 1936). Keynes is therefore widely regarded as the key founding figure in macro-economic theory and the use of both fiscal and monetary policy (the latter referring to control of money supply and interest rates by central banks) to moderate adverse economic circumstances.

The post-war global economic order reflected many Keynesian ideas, which were supported in the US by John Kenneth Galbraith (1908–2006), who was a key figure in presenting a liberal case for state involvement in economy and society. But he also maintained a critical stance on simplistic market fundamentalism: 'The notion that [the market] is intrinsically and universally benign is an error of libertarians and unduly orthodox conservatives' (Galbraith, 1984: 39–42). Galbraith's groundbreaking work, *The Affluent Society,* first published in 1958, also sought to explain how and why so much wealth accumulated in the private sector in the US, and why so little made its way into the public sector (Galbraith, 1998)—a situation that remains in need of explanation today.

Galbraith was influenced directly not only by Keynes' ideas, but also by the profound misery he witnessed during the Great Depression. He was a keen supporter, and indeed promoter, of the 'New Deal' introduced by President Franklin D. Roosevelt to alleviate the plight of millions of destitute Americans through such measures as public works to boost employment, supporting agricultural prices, creating new mortgage markets, shortening the working week, and regulating securities, among other things (Rauchway, 2008: 1). New Deal ideas continued to impact policy choices for many years, including the post-war era, when the Bretton Woods system was adopted as a mechanism for underpinning stability in the global economy, as discussed below.

Galbraith also introduced the phrase 'conventional wisdom', his account of which is highly pertinent to the study of the power of ideas in politics and economics, as set out in **Key Concept 9.3**.

A series of political and economic crises from the 1970s saw the decline of Keynesian ideas and the concomitant rise of what we now call neo-liberal ideas, which echo the fundamentals of classical economy. A key figure in the rise of neo-liberalism was Austrian-born economist Friedrich von Hayek (1899–1992), an implacable opponent of state intervention in the economic sphere and of socialist planning, which he regarded as tantamount to slavery. In his classic work *The Road to Serfdom,* first published in 1944, Hayek wrote that economic power 'centralized as an instrument of political power . . . creates a degree of dependency scarcely distinguishable from slavery' (Hayek, 2001: 150).

Although earlier thinkers had generated ideas about the 'spontaneous order' of social and economic life, of which the 'invisible hand' is an important manifestation, Hayek refined those ideas. He began by contrasting the superiority of the spontaneous order generated by the sum of knowledge arising from individual interactions and practices, on the one hand, with the necessarily limited knowledge possessed by a central governing authority on the other. The latter, he argued, produces a 'made order', which is, by definition, artificial and therefore inferior. The framework within which the more 'natural' spontaneous order is accomplished, and its knowledge transmitted, is the *market* (see Petsoulas, 2001: 19–20).

Another key figure in the rise of neo-liberalism was Milton Friedman (1912–2006), best known for his approach to monetary policy in which key elements of Keynesian theory were rejected in favour of an emphasis on the role of money (Friedman, 1968). Friedman's doctrine of 'monetarism' attracted followers in the US Federal Reserve Bank ('the Fed')

9

KEY CONCEPT 9.3   'Conventional Wisdom'

Observing first that while familiarity may breed contempt in some areas of human behaviour, Galbraith noted that familiarity in the field of social ideas is the touchstone of acceptability. Ideas which achieve a degree of general acceptability invariably acquire stability, becoming in due course 'the Conventional Wisdom'. The only thing that really brings about a change in the conventional wisdom is not in the first instance a genuinely new set of ideas, but rather the march of events. Galbraith illustrated this by reference to the Great Depression, noting the strength of conventional wisdom concerning the absolute necessity of maintaining a balanced budget even in a time of truly devastating depression. At that time, he said, a balanced budget would have meant increasing tax and reducing public expenditure. 'Viewed in retrospect, it would be hard to imagine a better design for reducing both the private and the public demand for goods, aggravating deflation, increasing unemployment, and adding to the general suffering' (Galbraith, 1998: 14).

Nonetheless, President Hoover, in the early 1930s, had maintained the 'absolute necessity' of bringing in a balanced budget as 'the most essential factor to economic recovery'. Almost every economist of the time agreed. Galbraith went on to note that in fact the budget (thankfully) never was actually balanced during the depression, or came anywhere near it. But it was not until around 1936 that the acceptability of deficit budgeting during such times began to take hold, due in large measure to the 'march of events' of the depression itself, and subsequently to the articulation of Keynes's ideas about the need for stimulus provided by public spending and other measures in such circumstances.

and elsewhere, and seemed to prove useful for a time, but was ultimately abandoned. But he was more popularly known for his advocacy of free-market ideology, which verged on absolutism.

A leading contemporary economist, Paul Krugman (2007), has suggested that Friedman 'slipped all too easily into claiming both that markets always work and that only markets work' and appeared unable to acknowledge not only that markets could go wrong, but also that government intervention could serve some useful purposes. This, says Krugman (2007), 'contributed to an intellectual climate in which faith in markets and disdain for government often trumps the evidence'. Further, many developing countries were enticed into opening up their capital markets—despite warnings about the possibility of being exposed to financial crises: 'When the crises duly arrived, many observers blamed the countries' governments, not the instability of international capital flows' (Krugman, 2007).

As with most 'isms', the term 'neo-liberalism' is contested. It has also been associated with an array of quite different political figures (**see Figure 9.2**), from Margaret Thatcher and Tony Blair in the UK, to Ronald Reagan and George W. Bush in the US, and to Boris Yeltsin and Jiang Zemin in Russia and China, respectively, among others (Steger and

FIGURE 9.2   Ronald Reagan and Margaret Thatcher have been associated with neo-liberalism
© ZUMAPRESS.com/ Keystone Pictures USA/ Age Fotostock

Roy, 2010: x). What unites these otherwise diverse figures is a commitment to a doctrine calling for the privatization of state resources and assets, and the deregulation of financial and other institutions, in the belief that this will produce the conditions under which the market can operate most efficiently and on a self-regulating basis. This is very far not only from the socially oriented liberalism of Keynes and Galbraith, which supported robust state institutions and a well-regulated form of 'welfare capitalism', but also from the classical liberalism of Adam Smith and David Ricardo (see Harvey, 2007: 20). One author sets out what he sees as the core assumptions of the doctrine (**see Key Quote 9.4**).

The discussion in this chapter suggests that liberalism, as an ideology or economic doctrine, cannot be reduced to any one consistent approach. While there are obviously common elements that unite liberal thinkers, such as a belief in individual freedom, there are also many tensions. Looking to the broader question of capitalism, with which liberal thought is firmly aligned, studies in comparative political economy have identified distinctive types or varieties of capitalism in different countries. There is not the space to look at these in any detail, but we can at least note that one influential work on the subject identifies two basic varieties in modern liberal states: 'liberal market economies', exemplified by the US, which rely on hierarchies within firms and competitive markets (and which is often seen as the standard model); and 'coordinated market economies' with non-liberal characteristics, exemplified by Germany and Japan, which rely on non-market forms of coordination, including negotiation, collaboration, and bargaining (see Howell, 2003: 103–4). Another

KEY QUOTE 9.4   The essence of neo-liberal political economy

'Neoliberalism is in the first instance a theory of political economic practices that proposes that human well-being can best be advanced by liberating individual entrepreneurial freedoms and skills within an institutional framework characterized by strong private property rights, free markets and free trade. The role of the state is to create and preserve an institutional framework appropriate to such practices. The state has to guarantee, for example, the quality and integrity of money. It must also set up those military, defence, police, and legal structures and functions required to secure private property rights and to guarantee, by force if need be, the proper functioning of markets. Furthermore, if markets do not exist (in areas such as land, water, education, health care, social security, or environmental pollution) then they must be created, by state action if necessary. But beyond these tasks the state should not venture. State intervention in markets (once created) must be kept to a bare minimum because, according to the theory, the state cannot possibly possess enough information to second-guess market signals (prices) and because powerful interest groups will inevitably distort and bias state interventions (particularly in democracies) for their own benefit.' (Harvey, 2007: 2)

variety is welfare capitalism, promoted by social liberals such as John Maynard Keynes and J. K. Galbraith. There is also the phenomenon of state capitalism—often associated with socialism—a leading practitioner of which is said to be China and which is clearly non-liberal (*Economist*, 2012).

 KEY POINTS

- Classical liberalism generally holds that the sum of rational, self-interested, individual actions adds to overall wealth and prosperity, while the role of the state must be restricted to the provision of essential infrastructure, security, and certain public goods that cannot be provided by the market.

- Social liberals in the tradition of Keynes and Galbraith see a much more important role for the state in guiding and regulating the economy and for producing the necessary conditions for human well-being. They also critique the idea that the sum of rational individual actions necessarily produces a rational collective outcome nor is the market seen as an infallible source of wisdom.

- Neo-liberalism once again asserts the benefits of deregulation, the free play of market forces, and minimal government intervention in the economic sphere.

- Capitalism is usually associated with liberalism, but there are non-liberal forms as well.

Marxism and Critical IPE

Karl Marx (**see Figure 9.3**), along with his collaborator Friedrich Engels (1820–95), stands at the head of a tradition of political economy that provides a thoroughgoing critique of capitalism and the ideologies underpinning it. Chapter 3 introduced the theme of power in Marxist theory, explaining ideology, hegemony, and the way in which ruling classes maintain control and promote the legitimacy of capitalism. Marx's notion of ideology as 'false consciousness' is especially important in analysing how the interests of any ruling class are presented as natural, inevitable, and desirable even for subject classes. This masks the deeper 'truth' about domination and subordination. Here, we should also note the Marxist emphasis on the role of the bourgeoisie, generally defined as a merchant and/or propertied class wielding essential economic power. A key difference between conservative approaches to economics, which take the capitalist system as given, and the Marxist tradition of critique is that while the former simply assume that politics and society barely even exist (although that can scarcely be said of social liberals such as Keynes and Galbraith), a Marxist approach is much more thoroughly embedded in the social and political relations underscoring the economic sphere.

▶ See Chapter 8 for a discussion of Marxism.

FIGURE 9.3   Karl Marx
© Everett Historical/ Shutterstock.com

Marx's economic theory involves the critical analysis of such issues as the role of labour in producing surplus value, and thus profit, and associated issues in productivity and wages. More generally, the theory is concerned to critique the crises produced in capitalism. Marx pays particular attention to the social and political circumstances in which economic development takes place and through which economic institutions emerge, and is exemplified through his method of historical materialism. This explains human development in general, including 'class struggle'—a term that highlights the essential conflict of interests between workers and the ruling class. Historical materialism is especially concerned to expose how capitalism came to dominate production on a global scale.

It is important to note at the outset that although Marx places the *production* of the basic material necessities for sustaining life at the centre of his theory, this does not make it a form of economic reductionism—that is, it does not reduce the explanation of all social phenomena to an economic cause. On the contrary, Marx is concerned to show that production is as much a social and political process as an economic one. It follows that the *mode of production* constitutes the central dynamic and organizing mechanism in society and, as a consequence, holds the key to historical change. Marx's preface to *A Contribution to the Critique of Political Economy*, first published in 1859, illustrates the extent to which he views the material realities of the human condition as mediating the whole approach people take to existence. This, in turn, forms the basis for what is called Marx's 'materialist conception of history', as set out in **Key Quote 9.5**.

Elsewhere, Marx wrote of a fallacy propagated by defenders of capitalism and liberal political economy that the mode of production is 'encased in eternal *natural* laws independent of history, at which opportunity bourgeois relations are then quietly smuggled in as the inviolable *natural* laws on which society in the abstract is founded' (Marx, 1848, emphasis added). This highlights the 'naturalization' of ideas, and hence of power, by ruling classes and resonates with the idea that the political structure of society always reflects 'the prevailing class interests and is never independent of them' (Morrison, 2006: 132).

Q   **KEY QUOTE 9.5**   **Marx's historical materialism**

'In the social production of their existence, men inevitably enter into definite relations which are independent of their will, namely relations of production appropriate to a given stage in the development of the material forces of production. The totality of these relations of production constitutes the economic structure of society, the real foundation, on which arises a legal and political superstructure and to which correspond definite forms of consciousness. The mode of production of material life conditions the general process of social, political and intellectual life. *It is not the consciousness of men that determines their existence, but their social existence that determines their consciousness.*' (Reproduced in Medema and Samuels, 2013: 395, emphasis added)

Italian intellectual Antonio Gramsci (1891–1937) developed some of these ideas further in his theorization of hegemony, while also downplaying the more materialist aspects of Marxism. He observed that ruling classes maintain power and control, even in the absence of constant coercive force, because they made prevailing inequalities seem natural, inevitable, and even right. This highlights the importance of *cultural power* in controlling 'hearts and minds' and in maintaining systems of domination. It resonates with the Marxist conception of ideology as false consciousness, but clearly focuses more on the consensual nature of support for hegemony. It also chimes with Galbraith's notion of conventional wisdom.

Gramsci's ideas have had a significant impact on leading figures in the field of IPE such as Robert W. Cox, whose approach—generally labelled neo-Gramscian—focuses on the nature of hegemony and its mechanisms of domination and subordination, coercion, and consent. Cox, like Galbraith, invites us to view existing patterns of thought, as well as material arrangements, with a critical eye and to reject methodologies that constrain the capacity to think outside the parameters of conventional theory. He proposes a 'new political economy', which suggests that we should not simply accept the global economic or political order as it is, with all its inequities, but rather question how it came into being and how it might be transformed into one that is more just and equitable (Cox, 1981).

More recent approaches in critical political economy, while not abandoning class as a key category through which subordination occurs, pay much more attention to issues of race and gender, although neither of these categories have been considered 'mainstream' issues in political economy. Yet studies of poverty provide incontrovertible evidence that race (or ethnicity) and gender are key factors when it comes to social, economic, and political disadvantage.

On race, there is no question that racial oppression pre-dated capitalism, but that the globalization of capitalism and the establishment of the European empires in particular coincided with the rise of the slave trade in the Americas and genocidal campaigns against indigenous populations in various locations (O'Hara, 2014: 427). But it is also evident that capitalism can, under varying circumstances, erode racism, as the relative success of many middle-class African Americans in the contemporary period shows (O'Hara, 2014: 430). The US-based Institute for Research on Poverty (2014) reported that the poverty rate among black Americans decreased from 41.8 per cent in 1966 to 26.2 per cent in 2014, although it is still more than twice that of white Americans, on 12.7 per cent. With respect to gender, another US-based organization notes that more than half of all children living below the poverty line are in families headed by women, that two-thirds of minimum wage earners are women, and that one in seven women lives below the poverty line (End Poverty Initiative, 2015).

Another study highlights the fact that international labour migration is a massive industry with significant race and gender dimensions. It rests on wage inequalities between source and destination countries caused by highly uneven development

9

(Goss and Lindquist, 1995: 317). The other side of the coin is the search by transnational corporations for ever-cheaper sources of labour. Countries providing low-cost labour are ideal bases for manufacturing industries. While supporters of the system see this as bringing benefits to the poor on the grounds that any job is better than no job, its critics see it as perpetuating and profiting from relations of exploitation.

 KEY POINTS

- The Marxist tradition of critique is embedded in the social and political relations underscoring the economic sphere. It emphasizes in particular the extent to which the political structure of society reflects the interests of ruling classes and is never independent of them.

- Critical IPE questions how the world economy came into being, what interests support it (and are supported by it), and how it might be transformed. It is more sensitive to issues of race and gender, as well as class, and incorporates a wider range of institutions in its analysis.

- Class, race, and gender remain relevant in a global sphere where low-cost labour migrates or, alternatively, where manufacturing industries locate themselves in countries providing cheap and more easily exploited labour.

The Post-War International Economic Order

As the Second World War drew to an end, plans for a new international economic order to free up access to markets and raw materials were developed alongside those for new international political institutions. Delegates meeting in 1944 at Bretton Woods, New Hampshire, were also concerned to institute a system that stabilized exchange rates and avoided recreating the conditions that had triggered worldwide depression in the inter-war years. However, contending national interests challenged pure liberal principles and the system that emerged reflected many compromises: '[U]nlike the economic nationalism of the thirties it would be multilateral in character; unlike the liberalism of the gold standard and free trade, its multilateralism would be predicated on domestic interventionism' (Ruggie, 1998: 72–3).

Institutionally, the result was the establishment of three major bodies collectively dubbed the 'Bretton Woods institutions'. These were the International Monetary Fund (IMF), the International Bank for Reconstruction and Development (IBRD)—later called the World Bank—and the General Agreement on Tariffs and Trade (GATT), which was signed in 1947 as an interim measure until the architecture for a more permanent institution could be worked out. It took until 1995 to establish the World Trade Organization

(WTO) (see Wilkinson, 2000). The WTO is now the only global international organization dealing with rules of trade between nations.

One of the success stories in the early post-war years was the work of the IBRD in Europe, in which the US played a major role. Fearing communist influence in a badly damaged Europe, where millions of people were struggling, US strategy was, as we have seen earlier, to contain that influence partly by rebuilding the economies of Western Europe via the Marshall Plan. From 1948 to 1952, up to US$13 billion in US aid was distributed in ways compatible with securing Europe as a major trading and security partner.

In the meantime, the IMF was charged with maintaining a stable exchange rate mechanism and balance of payments regime although it did little in its first few years due to the focus on European reconstruction, as well as the rebuilding of Japan and aid packages to Greece and Turkey, also funded largely by the US. In the late 1950s and 1960s, the IMF's involvement in supplying credits increased, especially as decolonization progressed, and it became a major player in developing economies. The US continues to dominate both the IMF and the World Bank, a reflection of its early role in global financial institutions as the major supplier of funds, despite its having become one of the world's largest debtor nations in the present period (see Brinded, 2016).

Although the Bretton Woods institutions remain an important part of international economic architecture, a breakdown nonetheless occurred in the exchange rate mechanism. By the early 1970s, the US was faced with rising imports and a significant trade imbalance. Huge dollar outflows providing liquidity for the global economy, although contributing to the US's considerable prosperity, could not be sustained. Increased interdependence and the recovery of the European and Japanese economies, along with vastly increased financial flows, made it almost impossible to control currency values, producing adverse dynamics (see, generally, Spero and Hart, 1997: 16–21). In 1971, the US abandoned the dollar gold standard and raised tariffs on imports.

Other industrialized countries reacted by strengthening protectionism themselves. This flew in the face of GATT principles supporting free trade, thus hampering reforms. Further trouble was in store with rising inflation, commodity shortages, unaccustomed floating currencies, and then the 'oil shocks' of the mid-1970s when oil producers quadrupled the price of oil in a year, with multiple consequences for the global economy, including recession.

By the early 1980s, in the wake of both global economic developments and the fiasco of the Vietnam War, the status of the US as the world's leading economic and military powerhouse seemed in decline (Keohane, 2001). The global recession hit most countries hard and the US was no exception. Liberal economics was identified by more conservative commentators as the culprit. One US-based commentator, William R. Hawkins, deployed the term 'neo-mercantilism' in proposing a form of economic conservatism based more squarely on national interest and dismissing the 'utopianism' of liberal economists' visions of world order based on free-trade principles (Hawkins, 1984: 25–39).

9

Five years later, however, the collapse of communism and the apparent triumph of liberal democracy, capitalism, and free-market ideology saw a new world order proclaimed by liberal triumphalists, sweeping all before it in a wave of optimism about the global future. It also gave a major boost to the neo-liberal ideas promoted by figures such as Milton Friedman, discussed earlier, although, as we shall see shortly, the onset of the global financial crisis (GFC) in 2008 severely tested these ideas.

 KEY POINTS

- The Bretton Woods system emerged after the Second World War as a compromise between liberalism and nationalism. Although the system is said to have collapsed by the early 1970s, the IMF, the World Bank, and the WTO still underpin contemporary global economic governance.

- Following world recession in the 1970s, neo-mercantilism enjoyed a revival, but the end of the Cold War saw a triumphant liberalism reassert global economic openness as the basis for a prosperous new world order, although that is now being challenged by various proponents of economic nationalism such as US President Trump.

The North–South Gap

By the mid-1970s, the rising protectionism of key industrialized states influenced by neo-mercantilist ideas, in addition to soaring energy costs, inflation, and increasing indebtedness, led to calls for a New International Economic Order (NIEO). Its proponents called for meaningful reforms in aid, foreign investment regimes, the terms of trade, financial arrangements including loans, and a fairer overall monetary system. In the 1960s, developing countries had formed the Group of Seventy-Seven (G77) in the wake of the UN Conference on Trade and Development (UNCTAD) to lobby as a bloc in global forums, especially the United Nations and the GATT. It had limited success. Neither the oil-producing nations who formed their own Organization of the Petroleum Exporting Countries (OPEC) nor the countries of the industrialized North were prepared to contemplate significant concessions to ease the burden of poorer countries.

In the meantime, the World Bank and IMF promoted structural adjustment programmes for poor, underperforming countries. Inspired by neo-liberal economic orthodoxies, these included the privatization of state-owned industries and resources, deregulation, strict limitations on public spending, and other austerity measures. Loans were made conditional on governments implementing such measures. The result in many cases was to limit access to health care, education, and public utilities even further without significantly improving overall economic performance or alleviating poverty.

The policy measures imposed by the World Bank and IMF—both based in Washington, DC—became known as the 'Washington Consensus', a term originally indicating adherence to a set of broad policy measures, which, in addition to privatization and deregulation, included public sector reform, tax reform, fiscal discipline, trade liberalization, property rights, and interest rate and exchange rate reforms. The way in which these were interpreted and implemented is often seen as reflecting the thoroughgoing market fundamentalism supported by neo-liberal ideology, which, in the wake of capitalism's triumph in the Cold War, seemed unchallengeable (see Williamson, 2009). The 'consensus' appeared to have crumbled by the early 2000s in the wake of evidence that showed poorer economic performance under the policy measures imposed (World Bank, 2005: 34–6), and what remained of it was extinguished by the GFC of 2008.

The spectacular economic growth achieved by China and India in recent years has maintained broad faith in market principles among many policy-makers. However, the gap between rich and poor in these countries has been widening, rather than narrowing, as the wealth created through economic growth has by no means trickled down to alleviate the poverty of millions. This suggests that while capitalism as an economic system certainly generates wealth, it does not distribute it effectively or equitably, thus indicating a crucial role for both governments and international organizations like the UN.

With respect to global inequalities, the UN adopted a set of 'Millennium Development Goals' (MDGs) in 2000, with 2015 set as the year by which the number of people living in extreme poverty would be halved—a goal requiring significant funding commitments from richer countries. A 2005 World Summit reaffirmed the MDGs and committed additional funding, although progress in many areas remained disappointing. Another five years on, a UN report indicated that very little had changed, especially in sub-Saharan Africa. Although there had been some growth before the GFC, this event hit the poor particularly hard, slowing progress significantly. More generally, the report set out a position on the role of both states and markets, which envisaged a more proactive role for the former than neo-liberal ideology suggests (**see Key Quote 9.6**).

Since that report, there has been more optimism about achieving the MDGs. By the time of the twentieth anniversary of the UN's World Summit for Social Development in

KEY QUOTE 9.6 States, markets, and global poverty reduction

'Experience has shown that economic growth alone is necessary, but not sufficient, to greatly reduce poverty in its many dimensions. Indeed, the mixed record of poverty reduction calls into question the efficacy of conventional approaches involving economic liberalization and privatization. Instead, Governments need to play a developmental role, with implementation of integrated economic and social policies designed to support inclusive output and employment growth as well as to reduce inequality and promote justice in society.' (UN, 2010: iii)

2015, reports were much more upbeat. While acknowledging that progress had been uneven in some areas, it was noted that there had been a general decline in world poverty. The UN has refreshed the MDG project with a post-2015 development agenda called the '2030 Agenda for Sustainable Development', which promises to continue efforts in key areas of concern such as poverty and hunger alleviation, combating disease, improving opportunities for youth, and environmental protection (http://www.un.org/millenniumgoals, accessed August 2017).

 KEY POINTS

- The North–South gap generates serious international political, economic, and social problems, and although some markets thrive on the disparities, few actually defend it as fair or just.

- Some programmes inspired by neo-liberal economic thinking and formulated by the World Bank and IMF, such as structural adjustment programmes, have been criticized for compounding the problems.

Globalization and Regionalization in the Post-Cold-War World

If globalization is defined in terms of 'the acceleration and intensification of mechanisms, processes, and activities . . . promoting global interdependence and perhaps, ultimately, global political and economic integration' (Roach, Griffiths, and O'Callaghan, 2014: 140), then it is impossible to separate globalization from the study of IPE. Indeed, some analyses focus almost exclusively on the economic dimensions of the phenomenon, positing global market forces as the central dynamic: 'The world economy has internationalized its basic dynamics, it is dominated by uncontrollable market forces, and it has as its principle economic actors and major agents of change truly transnational corporations that owe allegiance to no nation-state and locate wherever on the globe market advantage dictates' (Hirst and Thompson, 1999: 1).

Because globalization involves deepening trends in interconnectedness that transcend state boundaries and controls, it also challenges the traditional view of international order based on independent sovereign states. Even relatively strong developed states are seen as losing their autonomy and a fair measure of regulatory capacity. But what this means for the capacity of states to deliver a reasonable measure of prosperity and protection in terms of human security to their citizens is a particularly vexed question in the global South, where, as we have seen, structural adjustment programmes have had a negative impact on state capacity. Further, the 'market' is not geared to anything but producing profits, and a strictly economistic approach to explaining and understanding the dynamics of globalized markets cannot address issues of justice, either within or between states.

A major focus in recent years has been on the tax-avoidance strategies of multinational corporations, which many states have been unable to tackle effectively. A 2017 report estimated global revenue losses to be in the order of US$500 billion annually and noted that the most significant losses occurred in low- and lower-middle-income countries, as well as across sub-Saharan Africa, Latin America, the Caribbean, and South Asia (Cobham and Jansky, 2017: 1). Corporations such as Google, Microsoft, Apple, Amazon, Starbucks, Gap, and IKEA have been identified as costing alone the EU tax revenue up to US$76 billion a year (Chew, 2016).

There have also been significant revelations about the extent of offshore tax havens used by the super-rich, including celebrities, business-people, sports stars, politicians, and public officials from around the world, as well as fraudsters, money launderers, and dealers in illicit goods. The 'Panama Papers'—which refers to some 11.5 million files leaked in April 2016 from the database of the world's fourth largest offshore financial services provider, Mossack Fonseca, based in Panama—have revealed details of tax havens and offshore companies set up to hide the assets of political, business, and other figures from Russia, China, the US, the UK, and dozens of other countries. As the US Justice Department launched an enquiry in April 2016 into widespread international tax-avoidance schemes, then US President Obama said that 'the leak from Panama illustrated the scale of tax avoidance involving Fortune 500 companies and running into trillions of dollars worldwide' (Neate, 2016). Offshore schemes are not necessarily illegal, but they do offer ways and means of hiding assets from public scrutiny, as well as simply avoiding paying tax, and thereby holding back vast sums that could otherwise be used for public goods—schools and colleges, hospitals and health services, roads and bridges, environmental projects, and so on.

Another aspect of global economic development that has attracted significant attention over the last two decades is the enormous growth in some Asia-Pacific economies and the prospects for a 'Pacific Century'. Despite the setbacks of a regional financial crisis in the late 1990s and some fallout from the 2008 GFC, the Asia-Pacific boom is continuing apace, with the growth of China and India attracting particular attention. But what has been especially interesting about developments in the region is the extent to which many states, or rather their governments, have been proactive in creating the conditions for growth in the global economy. It has therefore hardly been a case of states versus markets, but rather states *promoting* markets as part of a broader developmental strategy.

State governments have also been active agents in the promotion of regionalization. This is a complex integrative process incorporating cultural and social dimensions, as well as political and economic ones, although, as with globalization, the primary dynamic of regionalization is usually seen to be economic. However, many regionalizing processes have an important security dimension as well. For example, the Association of Southeast Asian Nations (ASEAN), one of the longest-standing regional organizations outside Europe, was founded primarily for the purpose of securing regional peace in the Cold War period and has only lately been concerned with economic issues.

9

Although some have seen regionalization as leading to the consolidation of rival trading blocs that threaten global multilateralism, others see it as perfectly compatible with global integration (Haggard, 1997: 20). Indeed, in some parts of the world, it is regarded as a means of participating more effectively in a globalized economy by creating opportunities for economic growth via free trade and other arrangements within a regional framework. Regionalization on this account is part of the broader globalization process itself rather than a negative reaction against it.

Regionalization is proceeding apace in Africa, the Middle East, in the areas covered by the former USSR, South Asia, South East and East Asia, and the Pacific and Caribbean. There are also organizations covering huge swathes of the globe. The Asia-Pacific Economic Cooperation (APEC) forum, for example, has grown from an initial 12 participants in 1989, to a current membership of 21, comprising Australia, Brunei, Canada, Chile, China, Hong Kong, Indonesia, Japan, Malaysia, Mexico, New Zealand, Papua New Guinea, Peru, Philippines, Russia, Singapore, South Korea, Taiwan, Thailand, the US, and Vietnam. Its 'region' reaches halfway round the world, with its member countries being home to around 2.8 billion people and their economies representing approximately 57 per cent of world gross domestic product (GDP) and 47 per cent of world trade (see https://www.apec.org/About-Us/About-APEC, accessed January 2018).

While regionalization is clearly occurring in most parts of the world, the extent to which it has become institutionalized varies considerably. It is usually held to be most advanced, but by no means complete, in Europe. The EU itself has been a long time in the making: almost five decades passed from the time of the founding of the European Movement in 1943 to the Maastricht Treaty of 1992. But Brexit is no doubt a substantial setback for the European project, and perhaps for Britain itself. At the time of writing, however, the future of both Britain and the EU in a post-Brexit world is unclear and it will take several years before the consequences can be properly assessed. In the short term, the value of the British pound has dropped significantly, falling to a 31-year low against the US dollar by January 2017, while major global banks such as Goldman Sachs and JP Morgan are planning on shifting many of their operations and staff to Ireland or Germany. Job losses in the UK have a number of effects, including the fact that thousands of highly paid jobs in the financial sector contribute both to consumer spending, as well as to HM Treasury through the higher taxation rates such employees pay (Davies and MacAskill, 2017). The European Banking Authority and the European Medicines Agency, based in Canary Wharf in London, employ just over 1,000 staff between them. A recent media report also noted that important EU agencies will shift their operations and staff, and that there will be plenty of willing takers around the EU area:

> The banking and medicines agencies are seen as the first spoils of Brexit by the 27 remaining members of the EU. About 20 countries are expected to enter the bidding process . . .

> There will be fierce competition to attract the agencies' highly skilled employees, their families and the business that comes with them.

> This includes 40,000 hotel stays for visitors each year. (BBC, 2017).

Other indicators show that UK economic growth was the slowest in the EU area in the first quarter of 2017 and that inflation was up due to the low value of the pound. But the good news is that there have been no signs of recession, at least in the short term.

Brexit aside, there are other ongoing financial problems in Europe, including a sovereign debt crisis triggered partly by the GFC, but revealing additional problems within the Eurozone, especially in Greece. 'Sovereign debt' refers simply to money owed by governments and a crisis occurs when governments cannot meet loan repayments or interest. Bailouts by other financial institutions, such as the IMF, are usually conditional on governments adopting austerity measures in public sector spending. In Greece, this led to significant social and political unrest as public spending cuts deepened and unemployment rose, triggering further concerns about 'financial contagion' affecting not only the Eurozone, but US financial institutions as well. It is interesting to note that financial giant Goldman Sachs, a key player in the GFC, had helped the Greek government to cheat on European rules designed to restrain irresponsible financial behaviour by disguising its borrowings (Balzli, 2010). Apart from illustrating the high level of interdependence produced by both globalization and regionalization, the Greek case in particular, including the crisis of 2015 that nearly precipitated 'Grexit' (the Greek exit from the Eurozone), illustrates the extent to which both governments and financial institutions require constraints.

Experiments in regional integration in other parts of the world are generally far less institutionalized and there is little evidence elsewhere of a willingness to compromise or 'pool' sovereignty to enhance integration, a factor that has been key to the EU's success. While states in other regions may cooperate closely on a range of matters, integration is fairly superficial. National sovereignty is jealously guarded by many states, some of which were still colonies only a generation ago and which cling tenaciously to an almost absolute principle of non-interference in their 'sovereign affairs', especially when it comes to matters of human rights.

In summary, although regional schemes have existed for decades and despite Brexit, the general trend towards strengthening regionalization in the post-Cold-War period is clear. It is driven primarily by economic factors, but virtually all of the regional associations aspire to closer social and political ties as well. The other observable pattern is the continuing development of an overarching tripolar economic system based on the 'macro-regions' of Europe, North America, and Asia—the principal powerhouses of the global economy. Seen from this perspective, globalization and regionalization are indeed complementary dynamics in the global economy. We have also seen, however, that while globalization and regionalization may well be complementary in nurturing processes of economic liberalization, they may also be complementary in undermining the economic role and functions of the nation-state. Trade liberalization and financial deregulation are all about easing state-imposed restraints even though state actors are, in many cases, responsible for macro-economic policy allowing such developments.

Outside the academy, dissent and critique emanates from broad social movements manifest in 'anti-globalization' protests—now regular occurrences at various global or

See Chapter 18 for a discussion of social movements, including anti-globalization groups.

regional forums. Most participants are peaceful protesters gathering under the banners of various non-governmental organizations, with concerns ranging from labour rights to environmental issues, consumer protection, peace advocacy, and so on. Others are self-described anarchists, whose tactics range from civil disobedience to violence, mainly against commercial property and security personnel. An early manifestation of 'global protest' was the 'Battle for Seattle' in November 1999, when around half a million demonstrators converged on a WTO ministerial meeting. Since that time, the security costs of hosting meetings has risen substantially, peaking with the G8 and G20 meetings held in Canada in 2010, which brought together leaders of the world's richest nations, at a staggering reported cost of US$1.4 billion, most of which was spent on security (Field, 2011). In comparison, the G20 held in Brisbane in 2014 cost a relatively modest US$400 million (http://www.news.com.au/finance/economy/g20-summit-brisbane-2014-was-it-all-worth-it/story-e6frflo9-1227124910998, accessed January 2018). However, in addition to the cost of providing security, the destruction of property during riots at the G20 meeting in Hamburg in 2017, where up to 100,000 protesters gathered, is likely to run to about €12 million (http://www.presstv.ir/Detail/2017/07/19/528963/Germany-Hamburg-G20-protests-rioting-damages-millions, accessed January 2018).

While anarchists—who are, by definition, anti-statist—get most of the media attention, many of the protesters are concerned with issues that have actually been the traditional preserve of the state, and see the processes of globalization and regionalization as undermining the rights and interests of ordinary people in a variety of ways. As mentioned above, these include labour rights and consumer protection, as well as environmental issues. This has prompted much debate on the role of the state and indeed the future of sovereignty in a globalizing world. The role of the state has also come under scrutiny again in the wake of the GFC, which we consider in the final section.

✳ KEY POINTS

- Globalization and regionalization are complex integrative processes driven predominantly by a liberal economic logic, while incorporating social and political dimensions.

- Some critical IPE approaches welcome the openings provided by globalization for new social movements, while remaining critical of adverse economic consequences for marginalized groups.

- Both globalization and regionalization have been seen as undermining the traditional role of the state—an unwelcome development from the perspective of traditional leftist perspectives concerned with the negative impact on state provision for social protection and for Keynesians alarmed at the weakening role of government in regulating the economy.

Financial Crises in the Global System

From the Great Depression of the inter-war period to the GFC of 2008 and subsequent crises in the Eurozone, the global economic system has been subject to significant fluctuations in its fortunes. The GFC followed a period of rapid growth in the US and the development of increasingly complex financial products. The latter involved the securitization of high-risk loans, mainly in the form of sub-prime mortgages that had encouraged people with insufficient means to buy into a fast-rising housing market. From around 2006, interest rates started to climb and many could not meet repayments, precipitating an increase in bank foreclosures. With an avalanche of defaults, the 'housing bubble' burst. Financial institutions were left holding significantly devalued assets and from early 2007 a number faced collapse. One of the largest investment banks, Lehman Brothers, declared bankruptcy in September 2008. Institutional failure created a liquidity crisis and loans for thousands of businesses, as well as mortgages, became increasingly difficult to obtain. When banks stop lending, precipitating a 'credit crunch', the economy contracts, unemployment rises, and recession sets in.

The spate of financial institutional failure also saw massive government bailouts. By early 2009, financial institutions, as well as the car industry in the US, had been propped up by a government commitment of a staggering US$12.2 trillion (*New York Times*, 2009). The idea that markets are efficient self-regulators and perform best when left alone by governments now seemed ludicrous. The 'efficient market hypothesis' was declared dead at a meeting of the World Economic Forum in Davos in January 2009. Former US Federal Reserve Chairman Alan Greenspan had previously admitted that he had made a big mistake by 'assuming that banks' self-interest would prevent them doing anything that would threaten their own survival' (Wighton, 2009). Homo economicus, 'that cool calculator of self-interest . . . would not have been so incautious in protecting his wealth' (McDonald, 2009: 249).

Heavy exposure to the high-risk strategies of US loan schemes saw a number of European economies hit very hard. The UK banking industry was badly mauled and government bailouts followed. In Iceland, three major banks failed and had to be nationalized, bringing the Icelandic economy itself to the brink of collapse. Icelandic banks had also attracted significant investments from other European institutions, including pension funds, lured by what seemed to be attractive interest rates in fairly safe investments. By 2010, a sovereign debt crisis in the Eurozone emerged, with Greece, Portugal, Spain, Italy, and Ireland the hardest hit.

Of course, a 'global' crisis generally means just that and we have noted already the adverse impact on poverty reduction measures in the global South. Interestingly, one advanced industrial economy—Australia—did escape recession, as explained in **Case Study 9.7**.

There have been numerous commentaries and critiques of the GFC and its impact on the global economy, probing both proximate and deeper causes, as well as looking at lessons learnt. Well-known financier and businessman turned liberal philanthropist Hungarian–American George Soros has provided a sharp commentary on economic theory in the wake of the crisis, which also has implications for how we view the 'science' of politics (**see Key Quote 9.8**).

CASE STUDY 9.7   Australia and the GFC

In 2008, when the GFC struck economies around the world, Australia's economy proved the most resilient. At the time, Australia had a population of 21.25 million and a GDP of almost US$50,000 per capita. It had enjoyed a substantial period of economic growth attributable to a decade-long commodities boom, favourable terms of trade, and an immigration programme bringing skilled workers in particular into the country. Unemployment was at a 30-year low, although inflation was relatively high, at 4.2 per cent. Australian commodities are often emphasized, but the service sector in fact made up around 65 per cent of the economy. The budget surplus for 2008/09 was projected to be just over AU$27 million.

As the GFC wrought havoc in other advanced economies, a combination of factors kept the Australian economy on a stable footing. These included: continued strong commodity exports to China; continued population growth through immigration; prudential regulation of financial institutions, meaning relatively very low levels of 'toxic debt', which meant that banks maintained a high credit rating; a well-timed announcement by the Labour government that it would guarantee bank deposits and keep credit flowing; a cut in interest rates by the Reserve Bank; and a fiscal stimulus package, which included direct payments to households and a boost to the housing sector, as well as public spending on infrastructure—the latter a typically Keynesian strategy (Tanner, 2009). There was no talk of austerity, but rather the opposite.

Since then, Australia's deficit has risen, due partly to falls in the demand for commodities. As of mid-2017, the budget deficit was predicted to be almost AU$30 billion for the 2017/18 year, but net debt remains low by international standards and Australia retains a 'AAA' credit rating. At the same time, Australia broke a world record when it celebrated continuous economic growth (that is, with no technical recession) for almost 30 years. Despite these figures, Australia has experienced very slow wages growth, the gap between rich and poor has widened, and an ageing population poses problems for the future—all issues affecting most other advanced economies in the present period.

 KEY QUOTE 9.8   George Soros on 'the anatomy of a crisis'

'Economic theory has modeled itself on theoretical physics. It has sought to establish timelessly valid laws that govern economic behavior and can be used reversibly both to explain and to predict events. But instead of finding laws capable of being falsified through testing, economics has increasingly turned itself into an axiomatic discipline consisting of assumptions and mathematical deductions . . .

Rational expectations theory and the efficient market hypothesis are products of this approach. Unfortunately they proved to be unsound. To be useful, the axioms must resemble reality . . . rational expectations theory was pretty conclusively falsified by the crash of 2008 which caught most participants and most regulators unawares. The crash of 2008 also falsified the Efficient Market Hypothesis because it was generated by internal developments within the financial markets, not by external shocks, as the hypothesis postulates.

The failure of these theories brings the entire edifice of economic theory into question. Can economic phenomena be predicted by universally valid laws? I contend that they can't be, because the phenomena studied have a fundamentally different structure from natural phenomena. The difference lies in the role of thinking. Economic phenomena have thinking participants, natural phenomena don't. The thinking of the participants introduces an element of uncertainty that is absent in natural phenomena. The uncertainty arises because the participants' thinking does not accurately represent reality . . .

We really have to rethink our view of the financial markets quite profoundly; recognizing that instead of perfect knowledge and perfect information our understanding is inherently imperfect and that applies to market participants and regulators and social scientists alike.' (Soros, 2010)

9

 KEY POINTS

- The GFC was the latest in a series of 'boom and bust' episodes in the global capitalist economy, the first of which was the Great Depression of the late 1920s and early 1930s, which also started in the US.

- Both the Great Depression and the 2008 GFC illustrate the phenomenon of financial 'contagion', made possible by the interconnectedness of a globalized economy, although the case of Australia illustrates that domestic economic policy and circumstances still matter.

- The GFC tested neo-liberal approaches to the relationship between states and markets in advanced industrialized economies and found them wanting. Even so, the tenets of neo-liberal economics appear to remain firmly entrenched as 'conventional wisdom'.

Conclusion

The proper study of politics at either the national or global levels entails due attention to the relationship between states and markets, between political and economic power, and the impact of these on the quality of human life. Liberal perspectives appear to have dominated, although there are varieties of liberal thought, just as there are varieties in any broad ideology. There is certainly a significant difference between the liberalism of Keynes and Galbraith and that of contemporary neo-liberals. More generally, it appears that globalization, aided by the revolution in transport, communications, and other forms of technology, has produced a thoroughly interdependent world characterized by a global market for goods and services.

The twin phenomena of globalization and regionalization both reflect and support a liberal view of world order. Critical approaches to political economy at both national and global levels, however, urge attention to the vested interests that lie behind the liberal world order and the injustices they mask. The experience of the GFC has served to reinforce critiques of the latter, but despite what appear to be the abject failings of unregulated banking and financial markets—what Galbraith would have called the 'march of events'—neo-liberalism remains the dominant economic ideology of the early twenty-first century.

? Key Questions

- In what sense does classical mercantilism see national wealth and military power forming a virtuous circle?
- How does liberal theory justify the pursuit of economic self-interest?
- How relevant is class analysis to contemporary political economy?
- How do gender-sensitive studies contribute to political economy?
- What are the main features of critical political economy and how does it add to traditional Marxist perspectives?
- What does the North–South gap tell us about justice and injustice in the global economy?
- What is meant by the terms 'structural adjustment' and 'good governance', and how do they reflect liberal political and economic principles?
- What are some of the main concerns expressed through the 'global protest' movement?
- Are globalization and/or regionalization genuine threats to the future of the nation-state as the foundation of world order?
- What does the 2008 global financial crisis tell us about the relationship between states and markets, and the nature of homo economicus?

Further Reading

Amoore, Louise (ed.) (2005), *The Global Resistance Reader* (London: Routledge).
This book claims to be the first comprehensive account of the exponential rise of transnational social movements in opposition to the financial, economic, and political hegemony of major international organizations such as the WTO, World Bank, and IMF, with discussion of conceptual issues, substantive themes, and case studies.

de Lombaerde, Philippe, **and Schulz, Michael** (eds) (2009), *The EU and World Regionalism: The Makability of Regions in the 21st Century* (Farnham: Ashgate).
This is a comparative study of how region-building in one location influences other such projects. The EU occupies centre place in the analysis as the longest standing and most influential experiment in regionalization.

Hancké, Bob (ed.) (2009), *Debating Varieties of Capitalism: A Reader* (Oxford: Oxford University Press).
The study of IPE is, in many ways, the study of capitalism, and this reader explores the complex debates surrounding the phenomenon and the institutions through which it operates.

Jones, Daniel Stedman (2012), *Masters of the Universe: Hayek, Friedman and the Birth of Neo-Liberal Politics* (Princeton, NJ: Princeton University Press).
This is a highly readable, but nuanced, account of two of the most influential figures in political economy in recent years and the enormous impact their ideas still have even in the face of evidence contradicting them.

Waligorski, Conrad P. (2006), *John Kenneth Galbraith: The Economist as Political Theorist* (Lanham, MD: Rowman & Littlefield).
This is a comprehensive analysis of Galbraith's political economy within the framework of debates between liberal and conservative theories and controversies, which provides keen insights into the content and nature of American political thought about a whole range of values from equality, individualism, and democracy to the legitimate role of government and the structure of modern capitalism.

 Web Links

http://www.brettonwoods.org/page/about-the-bretton-woods-institutions
A good brief summary of Bretton Woods institutions, with links to other parts of the Bretton Woods website.

http://www.iisd.org
Website of the International Institute for Sustainable Development, which contains wide-ranging information on the developing world.

http://www.oecd.org

The website of the Organisation for Economic Co-operation and Development (OECD) is an invaluable source of statistical data, as well as more general discussion of current developments in the global economy.

https://europa.eu/index_en.htm

This is the (English-language) gateway to the EU website, which contains an enormous amount of information. Note that all the regional organizations mentioned in this chapter have websites that are easily found with a search engine.

https://www.wto.org

The site of the World Trade Organization, with information on its history, purpose, and functions, as well as many useful documents and data sources.

 Visit the **Online Resources** that accompany this book to access more learning resources on this topic: www.oup.com/uk/ferdinand/

Institutions and States

10

- Institutions
- States
- The Rise of the European State
- The Spread of the European State System
- The Modern State

- Strong States and Weak States
- Conclusion
- Key Questions
- Further Reading
- Web Links

Reader's Guide

This is the first in a series of chapters that change the focus of analysis to domestic institutions. Political scientists spend a great deal of time analysing the behaviour of institutions and theorizing about them. All the social sciences do. This chapter will first introduce you to the concept of institutions and to different factors that structure political behaviour. Then, it will present the multifaceted concept of the state. After that will come a brief historical account of the ways in which the European type of state and the European state system spread around the world between the seventeenth and twentieth centuries. This will lead on to a discussion of the modern state and some of the differences between them—strong states, weak states, and democratic states—before offering a conclusion.

Institutions

Institutions are essentially regular patterns of behaviour that provide stability and predictability to social life. Some are informal, in that they have no formally laid-down rules—the family, social classes, kinship groups, and such. Individuals internalize 'codes of behaviour' from them as a result of socialization, by example or out of conviction. Others are more formalized, having codified rules and organization—governments, parties, bureaucracies, legislatures, constitutions, and law courts. Institutions structure the behaviour of individuals and groups. In that sense, they are constraints. On the other hand, they serve as resources for the knowledgeable, who navigate their way through them to achieve desired outcomes. Thus institutions are both constraints and resources.

Students of politics tend to concentrate more upon formal institutions, which form political systems. This is especially true of those who work on Western political systems, where such institutions dominate political life. They try to identify the regular processes of change that are intrinsic to the system itself or to parts of it. Sometimes, they claim to have identified regularities that can be elevated to the level of 'laws', as in the natural sciences. One example, to which we shall return in Chapter 13, concerns **Duverger's Law**. This stated that first-past-the-post electoral systems produce two-party systems. At the same time, however, political studies also focus on the environment in which these systems are situated. Any political system may be buffeted by pressures arising either in the society surrounding it, or in the international arena. This may lead to disruption or even breakdown, in the form of revolutions—but in most cases, states adapt to these challenges. Political scientists attempt to identify regular patterns of adaptation as a way of generalizing more widely about the behaviour of political institutions.

See Chapter 13 for a discussion of Duverger's Law.

As Steinmo (2001: 7555) put it: 'Institutions define the rules of the political game and as such they define who can play and how they play. Consequently, they ultimately can shape who wins and who loses'.

It is, however, important to also grasp the relationship between political institutions and the surrounding environment of other political, social, and economic forces. We will use a simplified version of structuration theory, originally formulated by Giddens, to clarify these relationships. He distinguished between 'system', 'structure', and 'structuration' (Giddens, 1979: 66). We will adapt the term 'system' to mean 'political system'. We will use the term 'structure' to mean 'political institution'. And **structuration** will refer to the complex of factors that both constrain and also provide resources for changes in the operation of institutions and the system as a whole. These can range from levels of economic development, through regional or class group activity, to the behaviour of individual political actors. In studies of politics, as in the social sciences more generally, it is rarely the case that big events or changes can be attributed to a single factor. What caused the American Revolution? Or the Russian Revolution? Most political decisions are the product of the interaction of several factors. It is the relative weight of these factors that determines the specific outcome. Thus explanation of causation is a matter of judgement.

At this point, it is important to introduce another basic distinction from the categories used in studies of politics to explain political events: 'structure' versus 'agency'. Here, what is meant by 'structure' is the impact of the particular configuration of institutions. To what extent did they determine the outcome, or at least predispose a particular outcome? Sometimes, this is presented in terms of 'path-determined' outcomes. The contrast is with 'agency'—that is, the effect of choices and actions by one or more agents, whether individuals or groups of them. Since politics is a social activity, it is very rarely the case that a particular political outcome was absolutely determined by structure alone. Did the American Revolution have to happen and succeed? Would it have done so without George Washington? Did the Russian Revolution? Would it have done so without Lenin? Nor is it the case that agents have complete freedom: their options are always constrained by structures of one kind or another.

 See Chapter 9 for an exploration of the relationship between the state and economic institutions.

 KEY POINTS

- Institutions play a vital role in structuring political behaviour.
- Political, economic, and social factors all provide structuration in political life and determine particular outcomes.
- 'Structure' and 'agency' perform complementary and contrasting functions in determining outcomes.

10

States

Chapter 2 outlined the concept of the **state**, as well as some of its ambiguities. Let us recall the definition that was given there: 'the state is sovereign, its institutions are public, it is based upon being legitimate, it is in the business of domination, and it covers a particular territorial area'. To this, let us add one other characteristic that will be elaborated more in Chapter 11. In addition to their monopoly on the means of violence, states—especially modern states—also claim a monopoly on law-making. Pre-modern societies evolved binding rules for their members through a variety of means: edicts of rulers, clan or family traditions, religious prescriptions, and so on. They also often allowed a variety of agencies to enforce them. Modern states, however, claim the sole right to formulate laws and they insist that state courts enforce them.

 See Chapter 2 for a discussion of the state.

At its most general, the state becomes a synonym for the structure of rule and authority within a particular geographical area. It is abstract: 'In some important senses, the state is more an idea held in common by a group of people, than it is a physical organism' (Buzan, 1991: 63). We talk of the nation-state, the welfare state, and so on.

Yet there is another, more limited and more concrete, use of the term. This is used to designate the apparatus of institutions and individuals who are responsible for managing public affairs. It includes executives, legislatures, courts of justice, the armed forces, and central and local officials. This apparatus also collects revenue to pay for the services that it provides, whether through taxes or other forms of contributions. This use of the term is easier to grasp, but the overlap between the two levels of meaning of the term 'state' complicates the individual's relationship with the state. As Edelman (1964: 1) wrote over 50 years ago: 'The state benefits and it threatens. Now it is "us" and often it is "them". It is an abstraction, but in its name men are jailed or made rich on . . . defense contracts, or killed in wars.' Commentators may alternate between the two and it is important always to keep this in mind. Most of this chapter will concentrate on the more organizational features of the state, although you should not forget the broader usage of the term. The rest of this chapter will focus first on the rise of the European state and then on its proliferation across the world with the spread of the European state system. After that will follow a discussion of the modern state, and then of strong and weak states.

In more distant times, there was a much greater variety of forms of rule in tribes and small communities around the world. The antecedents for European ideas on government are to be found in writings from classical Greece and Rome, including the idea of democracy, and they were revived during the Renaissance after centuries of oblivion. However, the modern European state emerged gradually between the seventeenth and nineteenth centuries. And then, as we shall see, it spread to other parts of the world. Although there certainly were alternative forms of rule in other parts of the world that preceded it, such as the imperial system of classical China, modern states in other parts of the world display key features that make them more similar to the European model than to their own historical predecessors.

10

KEY POINTS

- The term 'the state' is used in a great variety of ways, some concrete and some abstract. This makes detailed analysis difficult and contentious.

The Rise of the European State

See Chapter 2 for an exploration of different theoretical conceptions of the state.

The first thing to note is the growth of state capacity over the last three centuries—a key fact that has already been mentioned in Chapter 2. In Chapter 2, we introduced you to the theoretical concept of the state. Here, we will focus more upon its historical evolution. As Tilly (1990: 96) put it, over the last 1,000 years, the European state has evolved from being a wasp to being a locomotive. By this, he meant that the state has evolved from a small inconvenience to the people that it ruled to become a powerful driver of social and economic development. The origins of the modern state are to be found in Europe as it emerged between the seventeenth and the nineteenth centuries. Up until then, it was impossible to separate the personality of the state from the personality of the ruler. The ruler used personal appointees as officials to run the affairs of state. The ruler was also responsible for paying them, and although some states did impose taxes, a great deal of the upkeep of officials came from the ruler's own property and income. A salaried bureaucracy began to emerge, and one of its most important functions was to collect and administer taxes. Gradually, what emerged was a system for extracting taxes from broader sections of property owners, especially to pay for the most expensive state activity, which was warfare. As Tilly (1975: 42) put it: 'War made the state and the state made war.' But protracted wars risked bankrupting a monarch. Time and again, the need to raise funds for fighting drove governments to devise new ways of raising money. The UK introduced income tax in 1799 to pay for the war against Napoleon. The US did so in 1861 to pay for the effort of the civil war. Gradually, this capacity, allied with access to a modernizing and industrializing commercial economy and a large rural population, enabled some states to dominate others (Tilly, 1990: 15). They in turn became the models with which others had to deal and, if possible, surpass.

The French Revolution transformed the powers of the state, as it introduced a level form of taxation for all its citizens and the principle of the modern mass army. This enabled the French, for a while, to dominate continental Europe. Britain was forced to emulate it so as to resist it. By the beginning of the nineteenth century, as Hegel recognized, the bureaucracy itself had become the state, elevating itself high above and separate from the rest of society (van Creveld, 1999: 143). This was a decisive development. First, what was expected from state officials was a primary loyalty to the state and the public good, rather than to any individual monarch or section of society. Then, second, they evolved rules and patterns of administration that further separated them from the rest of society. Later, Weber publicized the importance of the new bureaucratic form of public administration: impersonal, rule-based, goal-oriented activity, with promotion of officials exclusively based on merit and performance. He made it into an ideal type of social organization, which he identified, not without misgivings, as part of a process of ever-growing rationalization of social life. He emphasized the technical superiority of bureaucratic over any other form of organization. Subsequent commentators have coined the term 'Weberian' public administration to denote this type of organization.

In addition, in the eighteenth and nineteenth centuries, the economic and military might of the dominant European powers, reinforced by superior technology, enabled them to develop empires overseas. This spread the European type of state to other continents through colonies, albeit in a cut-down version. Sometimes, a private agency took over public functions. In India, for example, individual behaviour was traditionally regulated by caste associations rather than by the state. And the state had little power to levy taxes: 'Politics was thus consigned to the realm of spectacle and ceremony. No concept of a state, an impersonal public authority with a continuous identity, emerged: kings represented only themselves, not enduring states' (Khilnani, 2004: 20). Therefore, when the British arrived, the East India Company could start raising its own funds for public services

10

See Chapter 14 for a discussion of theories of bureaucratic policy-making.

without competing with the existing state authorities. In Burma, what made the colonial state different was also the concern of the new rulers with the growth of trade—something the traditional rulers had ignored (Taylor, 2009: 70). Administration in colonies was always more rudimentary than in the metropolitan countries, but even if it was a pale shadow of the original, it was still a recognizable copy.

The power of the model can be seen in the response of a state such as Japan. While the imperial European powers imposed their systems on the peoples that they colonized, not all territories became colonies, although most did. Japan was an exception (**see Case Study 10.1**).

Turkey is another of the few examples of the territories that did not become a Western colony, but which adopted Western forms of rule so as to compete with the West. By the nineteenth century, the Ottoman Empire was in decline and, significantly, it was the military that took the lead in looking to the West for ideas and models of reform so that Turkey could compete. It was military considerations that drove increasingly radical reforms of the state in the nineteenth and twentieth centuries. This culminated in the rise of Ataturk as president of a secular republic in 1923, who pushed through a full separation of state and religion that was modelled primarily upon principles of laicism borrowed from France (Starr, 1992: 8–15).

 CASE STUDY 10.1   **The modernization of the Japanese state**

Japan had cut itself off from the outside world for 300 years when, in 1854, American Commodore Perry led a number of warships into Tokyo Bay and demanded that Japan open up to international trade. The Japanese had no ships that could challenge the Americans and they were forced to agree. This set in train a whole series of transformations of Japanese society and the state as the Japanese sought to modernize, so that they could compete with the West and make Japan 'rich and strong'. This led to the imposition at first of a more authoritarian system of rule, with the restoration to more effective power of the Meiji Emperor in 1868. The government swelled into a much larger civilian bureaucracy that could develop resources for the state. It sent representatives abroad to learn more about the political, legal, and technological strengths of the West, so that the best could be transplanted to Japan. The traditional class of independent warriors—the samurai—were forced to serve the state, either by becoming officials or officers in the new national army. In 1890, the first Japanese Constitution came into force, which set limits (albeit ambiguous ones) on the powers of the Emperor. This also established a parliament and an independent judiciary. All of these reforms transformed Japan. From a backward and introverted nation, it gradually became a recognizably modern state that by 1895 was able to defeat its biggest regional rival, China, and by 1904–05 was the first non-European state to win a war against a European imperial power—Russia. Japan then developed its own empire. Within a few decades, Japan had exploited the new state to expand its national might in a process that had taken European nations centuries.

10

After independence, the former colonies took over these state apparatuses and also the institutions that they had established. Whether it was the former Spanish colonies in Latin America during the nineteenth century, or the former British, French, German, and Italian colonies in the twentieth century, the newly independent states largely adopted the same basic attributes of rule and the same apparatus of institutions, even though they also in other respects usually expressed a forthrightly anti-imperialist ideology. Most importantly, they also adopted and often developed the bureaucratic machine that extracted resources from the people to pay for government. In some cases, the innovation of the separation between ruler and officials that had earlier marked the rise of the modern state was now reversed. In what have been called patrimonial states, some rulers came to use the state to extract resources from the rest of society for their own benefit. This practice has been associated with African states, although it is not exclusive to that region. Critics of the Putin regime in Russia, for example, allege that it too is a kleptocratic state (Dawisha, 2014).

As the European states grew stronger, gradually new institutions were devised to try to prevent them from becoming too despotic. Legal principles were established that would also constrain rulers, particularly through constitutions. Finer (1997) emphasized two events that were crucial in this respect: the American Revolution and the French Revolution. For him:

> [T]he transcendent importance of the American Revolution is that it demonstrated for ever that quality of the Western European government we have called 'law-boundedness'. Here is a government which draws its powers from and can only act within a framework of fundamental law—the Constitution—which is itself interpreted by judges in the ordinary courts of the country. Could law-boundedness go further, could it receive a more striking affirmation? (Finer, 1997: 1485)

From this followed six innovations, as can be seen from **Case Study 10.2**.

It was the American Constitution that introduced the formal principle of 'separation of powers'. To some extent, this evolved from practice in Britain, which had had a constitutional monarchy since 1689 and which had been extolled by Montesquieu (1689–1755) in his work *On the Spirit of Laws* of 1748, a strong influence upon many of the framers of

---

 CASE STUDY 10.2 **The governmental innovations of the American Revolution**

1. The deliberate formulation of a new frame of government by way of a popular convention
2. A written constitution
3. A bill of rights enshrined within it
4. Guaranteed protection for these rights through judicial review
5. The separation of powers along functional lines
6. The division of powers between the national and the state governments
   (Finer, 1997: 1485)

the American Constitution. However, whereas in Britain and in other states in continental Europe, the basis for the different houses of parliament was social class—for example the House of Lords and the House of Commons—the distinction in the American Constitution was entirely abstract and functional—the House of Representatives and the Senate. It was a more democratic form of institutionalization, which assumed that all citizens were equal and subject to the same laws.

At the time, the combination of new institutions and principles was an experiment. No one knew whether they would all work together. However, the American Constitution has proved a model and a starting point for all subsequent writers of constitutions.

Then, only just over a decade later, another revolution further transformed the theory and practice of government:

> The French Revolution is the most important single event in the entire history of government. The American Revolution pales beside it. It was an earthquake. It razed and effaced all the ancient institutions of France, undermined the foundations of the other European states, and is still sending its shock-waves throughout the rest of the world. (Finer, 1997: 1517)

The governmental legacy of the French Revolution can be summarized in four main points (**see Case Study 10.3**).

As can be seen from this list, not all of the points can be reconciled with each other. The French Revolution celebrated the Rights of Man making all men equal and at the same time inaugurated an era of populist dictatorship. Although the Revolution had a universal appeal, France became the prototype nation-state, with nationalism as its core political ideology, and it provoked a backlash among other peoples, especially in the German states, which led to the creation of nation-states throughout Europe in the nineteenth century. And although it preached universal harmony, it also devised a new form of military

10

 CASE STUDY 10.3　**The governmental legacy of the French Revolution**

1. The Declaration of the Natural Rights of Man and the Citizen established the legal basis for the sovereignty of the democratic state, based upon the General Will.

2. Nationalism—It laid down the national unity of all French citizens and their primary obligation of loyalty to it. The Napoleonic Wars spread the doctrine throughout Europe and provoked a matching response from the peoples of other nations.

3. Citizen armies—In the defence of the Revolution, the French state mobilized far more citizens to fight on its behalf than had ever been seen in Europe, which forced its enemies to compete.

4. Neo-absolutism—The rise of the Committee of Public Safety was followed by the Napoleonic dictatorship. (Finer, 1997: 1538–66)

organization—the mass citizen army—which became the model for military organization throughout Europe. Yet, in their different ways, these diverse elements became the precursors for various forms of modern government not just in Europe, but also throughout the world. Both modern democracies and dictatorships, rule by law and by force, were prefigured by the French Revolution. Thus, although the French Revolution began as an attempt to create checks upon the absolutist monarchy, it instituted new forms of state activity that led to far greater intrusion in the lives of ordinary people than ever before. In that sense, as Finer (1997: 1566) puts it: '[A]ll four [of these elements] are still alive, working like a leaven throughout the globe. In that sense the revolution is a Permanent Revolution. Nothing was ever like it before and nothing foreseeable will turn this Revolution back.'

 KEY POINTS

- A crucial importance in the development of the European state was the separation of state officials from personal servants of the ruler.
- Another crucial development was the separation of the state from the rest of society through institutionalization and bureaucratization.
- Warfare was a catalyst for increasing the raising of funds for the state from society and increasing the state's reach.
- The American and French revolutions developed modern principles of government.
- This led to the invention of institutions to check the power of the state.

10

The Spread of the European State System

States today have two sets of roles or functions. The first consists of functions that they exercise towards their own populations. The second is those that they perform towards other states. States 'recognize' each other and, by doing so, confer an additional degree of legitimacy.

The rise of the European state also transformed the international system. We will outline it here because it explains the spread of the European type of state across the world. The modern European state system is normally taken to have resulted from the treaties that established the Peace of Westphalia in 1648 and ended the Thirty Years War. This led to the paradigm of a:

> . . . European state . . . [that] was a sovereign, territorially delimited political unit, facing other similar units, each striving for supremacy but never achieving it owing to their rapidly adopted skill of forming combinations that would defeat such a purpose, that is, the techniques of the 'balance of power' first developed by the Italian city-states in the fourteenth and fifteenth centuries. (Finer, 1997: 1306)

◗ See Chapter 1 for discussion of the concept of sovereignty.

In subsequent centuries, Europeans spread their patterns of inter-state behaviour around the world as they built up empires, first in South America, then North America, Africa, and Asia (**see Figure 10.1**). Western concepts of state sovereignty differed from traditions in other parts of the world in two respects. First, they were based upon formal legal principles. Second, they insisted upon the sovereignty of a state running uniformly throughout territory within prescribed boundaries. In Africa, by contrast, authority and rule were more fluid. According to Clapham (1996: 29):

> African [states] formed islands of relatively settled government beyond which stretched deserts, forests or zones of progressively impoverished savannah which a strong ruler would seek to control but from which a weak one would retreat. Dissident or defeated groups could strike out into the borderlands to conquer or establish kingdoms of their own.

Likewise, in South East Asia, traditional understandings of state sovereignty focused more upon the mystical power of the ruler at the centre of the state, which radiated outwards, like a force-field or like a cone of reflected light. Thus the power was weaker the further that one went from the centre, until it ran up against a stronger force-field from another state (Suwannathat–Pian, 1988: 29). In both continents, states were defined by their capitals rather than by their perimeters. Therefore, traditional rulers concentrated more upon maintaining and strengthening the power at the centre and they paid less attention to what was happening on the periphery (Anderson, 1990: 21–36).

Western states imposed stronger boundaries on their territories and insisted upon undivided sovereignty right up to those borders. They drew much firmer borders, imposing

10

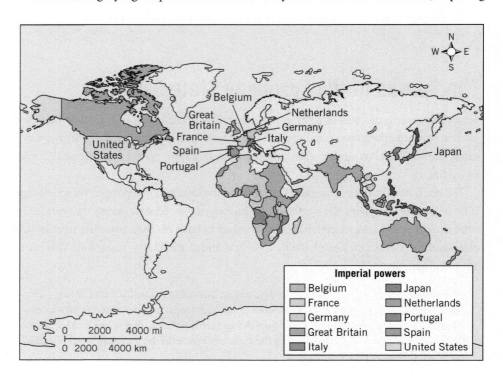

FIGURE 10.1
Imperial powers, 1900

them, often arbitrarily, upon peoples that they colonized. This was particularly true of South America and sub-Saharan Africa. The consequences of this for state legitimacy and viability are still with us today. One of the most extreme examples was the partition of the South Asian subcontinent in 1947. When it became clear that the leader of the Muslims there—Jinnah—could not reach an agreement with Nehru, the leader of the Indian National Congress, about the future shape of India, the British appointed a judge to determine the border between the future India and Pakistan. Though he had never been to India before, he was given just six weeks to do the job. The movements of millions of people from one part of the subcontinent to the other, and the violence that accompanied them, still poison Indo-Pakistan relations.

When these colonies became independent, they usually took over the existing legal framework and these borders, reasserting the latter's inviolability. After independence, they then tried to build modern nation-states, attempting to forge nations out of citizens on the European model. Thus, in many parts of the world, it has been the state that has created the nation, whereas in Europe it has often been the nation that has created the state.

 KEY POINTS

- The European type of state spread to lands on other continents.
- War and colonial expansion were the key elements in it doing so.
- This also led to the emergence of a European-type system of states around the world.

10

The Modern State

Today, the state has become the universal form of political organization around the world. Currently, 193 states are members of the United Nations, ranging in size from China, with a population of over 1.3 billion, to Tuvalu, with a population estimated at 12,000. In area, they range from Russia, with over 17 million square kilometres, to Monaco, with an area of 2 square kilometres. A third set of functions performed by a state relates to its relations with other states. States have to manage relations with each other through diplomacy, and they have to devise defence policies to protect their territory and their people against attacks from outside. Equally importantly, states recognize each other as legitimate rulers over defined areas of territory and, in this way, they reduce the anarchy that exists, at least potentially, at the global level because of the lack of a global government. This diplomatic recognition provides reassurance against attack, although it is not an infallible guarantee. On the other hand, it also means that states expect their counterparts to interact with them in familiar and predictable ways. Bureaucratic agencies in one state that deal with the outside world—and in an era of globalization this is increasingly the case—expect to find equivalent agencies in other states. This strengthening international society contributes to the proliferation of government agencies in individual states.

There is no doubt about the national importance of state apparatuses—given the growing share of state expenditure in individual countries' gross domestic product (GDP), as can be seen from **Table 10.1**. This charts their growth, particularly since the end of the Second World War. Figures on the size of government bureaucracies tell the same story, as seen in **Table 10.2**, even though there are great differences between the practices of countries over whom they count as state officials. Some states have been proportionately much bigger than these three.

How, then, do we generalize what states are and what they do? One way is to focus upon their origins and sources of legitimation. Stepan has proposed a distinction between what he terms 'nation states' (for example France, Sweden, Japan, and Portugal) and 'state

TABLE 10.1   Growth of general government expenditure in selected countries, 1870–2015 (% GDP)

General government for all years	About 1870	1913	1920	1937	1960	1980	1990	1996	2015
Australia	18.3	16.5	19.3	14.8	21.2	34.1	34.9	35.9	36*
Austria	10.5	17	14.7	20.6	35.7	48.1	38.6	51.6	51.6
Canada			16.7	25	28.6	38.8	46	44.7	41.1
France	12.6	17	27.6	29	34.6	46.1	49.8	55	56.6
Germany	10	14.8	25	34.1	32.4	47.9	45.1	49.1	43.8
Italy	13.7	17.1	30.1	31.1	30.1	42.1	53.4	52.7	50.3
Ireland			18.8	25.5		48.9	41.2	42	28.7
Japan	8.8	8.3	14.8	25.4	17.5	32	31.3	35.9	39.5
New Zealand			24.6	25.3	26.9	38.1	41.3	34.7	40*
Norway	5.9	9.3	16	11.8	29.9	43.8	54.9	49.2	48.8
Sweden		10.4	10.9	16.5	31	60.1	59.1	64.2	50.2
Switzerland	16.5	14	17	24.1	17.2	32.8		39.4	33.9
United Kingdom	9.4	12.7	26.2	30	32.2		39.9	43	42.8
United States	7.3	7.5	12.1	19.7	27	31.4	32.8	32.4	37.6

* 2014 figure.

Source: Tanzi and Schuknecht (2000: 6–7); OECD (2017), General government spending (indicator). doi: 10.1787/a31cbf4d-en (accessed September 2017).

TABLE 10.2 Size of government bureaucracies, selected years

	1821	1985*
Germany	23,000**	855,000
UK	27,000	1,065,000
US	8,000	3,797,000

* Central government civil servants only   ** Prussia only
Source: Finer (1997: 1624).

nations' (for example Belgium, Canada, India, Spain, and Ukraine) (see **Table 10.3**). The differences between them are explained in **Key Debate 10.4**. But it is worthwhile considering a third type of state that does not otherwise fit easily into this typology— namely, Islamic states—because Islam postulates a higher authority than that of any state, even one composed of Islamic believers—that is, the divine will. From that perspective, states are more transient entities, since they should ultimately unite into a worldwide community of believers. So **Key Debate 10.4** also presents a synopsis of key features of such states.

A second approach to analysing and comparing states is functionalist. This focuses upon the different types of function that they perform. Gill (2003) has suggested that there are three basic types of internal role performed by the modern state. The first is that of the state as partisan. In other words, the state operates on the basis of, and pursues, its own interests, or at any rate values to which it wants all its citizens to subscribe. This may be reinforced by a Weberian state bureaucracy, with its own structure and procedures that resist pressures from the rest of society. This would be typical of authoritarian regimes, for example Putin's Russia. Or the rulers prescribe some ideological goal for all their citizens, for example communism or Islam. Other goals or values are banned, or at least stigmatized.

The second role is that of the state as guardian. Here, the state stabilizes and, where necessary, rebalances society in a way of which society itself is incapable. Therefore, the state is essential for social stability. This could be because of fundamental conflict in society that threatens to tear it apart. Examples of this would be federal or consociational political systems, which have been designed to counter fundamental cleavages in society and to which we shall return in more detail in Chapter 11. Or it could take the form of a developmental state already mentioned in Chapter 2, as in East Asia, where the state directs the development of society and the economy in what it regards as a path of development that is in the national interest (for example industrialization and economic modernization).

The third type of role is the state as instrument. Here, the state operates primarily as a tool in the hands of some group or groups in society at large. This could take the form of

See Chapter 14 for a discussion of bureaucratic policy-making.

See Chapter 2 for a description of the developmental state.

KEY DEBATE 10.4   Nation-states, state-nations, and Islamic states

Nation-state policies stand for a political-institutional approach that attempts to match the political boundaries of the state with the presumed cultural boundaries of the nation . . . By contrast state-nation policies stand for a political-institutional approach that respects and protects multiple but complementary sociocultural identities . . . State-nation policies involve crafting a sense of belonging (or "we-feeling") with respect to the state-wide political community, while simultaneously creating institutional safeguards for respecting and protecting politically salient sociocultural diversities. (Stepan, Linz, and Yadav, 2011: 4–5)

TABLE 10.3   Ideal types of nation-state and state-nation

	Nation-state	State-nation
Pre-existing conditions: sense of belonging/'we-feeling'	Attachment to one major cultural civilizational tradition, which largely corresponds to existing state boundaries	Attachment to more than one cultural civilizational tradition within existing boundaries, possibly of an existing state
State policy: cultural policies	Unity in oneness: homogenizing cultural identity, especially one official language	Unity in diversity: recognition and support for more than one cultural identity, including more than one official language, within one state
Institutions: territorial division of power	Unitary states or symmetrical federations	Federal or asymmetrical unitary states, accepting state multilingual areas
Politics: ethno-cultural or territorial cleavages	Not very salient	Salient, recognized, and democratically managed
Politics: autonomous or secessionist parties	Autonomist parties are normally excluded from coalitions; secessionist parties are outlawed or marginalized	Autonomist parties can be included in coalitions at the centre and govern in federal units; non-violent secessionist parties can participate in the democratic process
Citizen orientation: political identity	Single identity in state and cultural nation	Multiple, but complementary, identities
Citizen orientation: obedience/loyalty	Obedience to state and loyalty to nation	Multiple state identities and identification with multiple institutions

Source: Stepan, Linz, and Yadav (2011: 8). © 2011 The Johns Hopkins University Press. Reprinted with permission of Johns Hopkins University Press.

10

Islamic states

Islamic states, or states with predominantly Muslim populations, amalgamate many features of these two types. They accept diversity of cultural and linguistic policies, and historically they have recognized the need for special administrative arrangements for religious and ethnic minorities, but they are suspicious of secessionism. They have practised tolerance rather than toleration (Krämer, 2015: 179–84). The state expects loyalty and obedience. It bans the conversion of Muslims to other religions, while encouraging the conversion of other believers to Islam. Even though numerous separate states have been created in the Middle East, their legitimacy has been periodically challenged by the supranational values of Islamic religion and of the aspiration for a global community of believers, the *umma*. From this perspective, sovereignty belongs only to God (Allah), rather than to people, or any group of them. Legitimacy comes ultimately from divine sources rather than from any particular territory: 'Islamic government draws its principles, laws, and practices from the shari'a' (Shahin, 2015: 72).

This marks a basic difference from both nation-states and state-nations in the rest of the world. Both of these other types are fundamentally contested in the Islamic world. In Islamic political thought, 'the state is never considered in terms of a territorialized nation-state: the ideal is to have a power that would rule over the entirety of the *umma*, the community of the faithful, while actual power is exercised over a segment of the *umma*, whose borders are contingent, provisional, and incomplete' (Roy, 1994: 13). The long-term ambition is to restore the concept of a 'caliphate' as both precedent and future ideal—that is, a single Islamic state ruled by a caliph (a 'deputy of God') for all Muslims, as originally existed in the Islamic world immediately after the death of the Prophet. Radical movements to create new Islamic states, such as the Muslim Brotherhood, so-called ISIS (Islamic State in Syria, Iraq, and the Levant), and Hezbollah, aim to merge existing states (such as Syria, Iraq, and Lebanon) and destroy the state boundaries imposed by colonial powers in the early twentieth century as a step towards one overarching caliphate. Such an enterprise is, however, bedevilled by the fundamental division in the Islamic world between Sunni and Shi'a (Muslim Brotherhood and ISIS are predominantly Sunni, while Hezbollah is Shi'a), by persisting ethnic and other divisions, and by the need at least for now to interact with other states. Attempts to establish Islamic states have ended in failure, but according to Roy (1994), the ideal of an Islamic caliphate does not die either.

Based on: Roy (1994), Krämer (2015), Shahin (2015).

Questions

1. Are nation-states only to be found in the developed world?
2. Are state-nations only to be found in the developing world?
3. Are there any examples of state-nations becoming nation-states?
4. How different are explicitly Islamic states such as Iran from other types of state?

10

a genuine liberal democracy, where the people are in control of the state's actions. Alternatively, it could be a state that is controlled by a particular section of society, for example a particular ethnic group or 'big business', or it could even be a patrimonial state, where political actors take advantage of state power to enrich their clients. One much-debated theory of the state, Marxism, views the capitalist state precisely as an agent of the dominant economic class(es) in society—that is, the capitalists, who exploit the workers (the proletariat). As Marx and Engels put it in the Communist Manifesto of 1848: 'The executive of the modern state is but a committee for managing the common affairs of the whole bourgeoisie.' Here, the state is just a tool.

In practice, any modern state performs a combination of all three roles. Most state bureaucracies operate to some extent on the basis of their own codified procedures and institutions, which are intended to resist outside turbulence. Most states do develop some perspective on the desirable path of development for that society and attempt to mobilize resources to achieve it, and most states are to some extent responsive to groups outside themselves. Dictators such as President Suharto of Indonesia favour 'loyal' businessmen who do their bidding and in return enjoy special favours. Thus what is important is the balance between these three types of role in particular states. Are they *predominantly* partisans, guardians, or instruments?

India exemplifies the complexity. After independence, the new state approved a constitution that declared India to be a socialist state, which is still in force. Critics of the state today also complain about Indian civil servants being deaf to the concerns of ordinary people. From both of these perspectives, the state is 'partisan'. On the other hand, India is also a federal state that seeks to preserve national unity between linguistically fairly disparate, geographically distant, and socially and religiously hierarchical communities, where partition from Pakistan in 1947 destroyed any sense of subcontinental identity. So, in this respect, the state is a 'guardian'. And, at time of writing, the government of Prime Minister Modi is much more concerned to promote the interests and concerns of the Indian business classes. So, in this respect, it is acting more as an 'instrument' of business. Indeed, as this example shows, the problem is made even more complex because the balance between the three functions of any state may change over time, as it has in India.

 KEY POINTS

- The state in the West today is larger than at any time in history.
- A basic ideal-type distinction is between 'nation-states' and 'state-nations'.
- States with large Islamic populations amalgamate the two types, and are also overshadowed by the traditional ideal of a single Islamic caliphate.
- The modern state can act predominantly either as partisan, as a guardian, or as an instrument.

Strong States and Weak States

This list of state functions, internal and external, suggests that the modern state has become more powerful than at any time in its history. According to historian A. J. P. Taylor (1965: 1): 'Until August 1914, a sensible, law-abiding Englishman could pass through life and hardly notice the existence of the state, beyond the post office and the policeman.' All this was changed by the First World War. There is no doubt that the twentieth century witnessed the most extreme manifestations of state power that the world has ever seen, in the form of what some analysts characterized as totalitarian systems, such as Hitler's Germany and Stalin's Russia. Even though state control was never as completely total as the term might imply and there still remained pockets of resistance, there was no doubt about the aspiration of their leaders for total control or the spread of institutions to try to achieve it. Now that the archives of some of these states are open, it is possible to gain a clearer perspective on the size of such states. For example, at the time of its collapse in 1989, the German Democratic Republic had what has been described as a 'honeycomb' state, in which perhaps a sixth of the adult population were involved in one way or another in the state's 'micro-systems of power'. Over 91,000 were full-time employees of the secret police alone by the time the state collapsed—a ratio of 1 to every 180 people in the population and the highest for any former communist state (Fulbrook, 2005: 236, 241). Yet however strong and all-powerful they looked, most of these regimes have now collapsed.

These were extreme versions of the modern state. As the powers of the state have increased in the twentieth century, so too have the expectations of what it can perform. Manow and Ziblatt (2015) have written of the 'layered' nature of the modern state in the more developed world. These states now perform much more varied functions than the military and basic economic ones of earlier centuries. Rotberg (2004) has provided a long list of the political goods or functions that a modern state might be expected to provide its citizens. Typically, the most important are:

1. human security;

2. predictable, recognizable, systematized methods of adjudicating disputes and regulating both the norms and the prevailing mores of a particular society or polity;

3. freedom to participate in politics and to compete for office, respect, and support for national and regional political institutions, such as legislatures and courts, tolerance of dissent and difference, and fundamental civil and human rights.

However, there are many others also expected by citizens, including medical and health care, schools and educational institutions, roads, railways, harbours and other elements of physical infrastructure, communication networks, money and a banking system with a national currency, a beneficent fiscal and institutional environment within which citizens can pursue personal entrepreneurial goals and potentially prosper, space for the flowering of civil society, and methods of regulating the sharing of the environmental commons (Rotberg, 2004: 2–3). If we look at states in the developed world, we can usually find that they

10

perform these functions to the satisfaction of their citizens, even if not perfectly. They are 'strong' or 'robust' states.

It is also important to remember that not all states today are like that. Most states in the developing world have only established some of the 'layers'. Some layers they may reject, whilst some states ('developmental' states—see Chapter 2) have built layers of state intervention to accelerate economic development that more 'developed' states may have abandoned or never even employed. In general, states in the developing world have lower levels of resources. A large part of the explanation for this lies in the fact that states in the developed world have built up a wide array of social services—on average, states in the Organisation for Economic Co-operation and Development (OECD) devote about 21 per cent of GDP to this. States in the developing world in general are only beginning to do the same. But it also reflects the much greater difficulty that states in the developing world experience in trying to collect taxes. As of 2013, only 800,000 people out of a Pakistani population of 180 million were paying taxes (CNN, 2013). In India, only 27 million people were paying income tax in 2016—that is, 2 per cent of the population (McCarthy, 2017). Where general government expenditure in almost all European states is equal to at least 40 per cent of GDP, in Indonesia it is only around 15 per cent and in India it is about 20 per cent. Many states are clearly weak. Chabal and Daloz (1999: 1) have argued that the state in Africa is 'not just weak, but essentially vacuous, with virtually none meeting the Weberian criteria'. Bayart (1993: 258) amplified this by saying that in most states of sub-Saharan Africa:

> The frontiers of the state are transgressed, the informal sector is a canker on the official economy, taxes are not collected, poaching and undisciplined exploitation of mineral resources becomes endemic, weapons circulate, resettled villages split up, the people appropriate the legitimate use of force to themselves and deliver summary justice, delinquency spreads, businesses suffer from languor induced by underproductivity, delays and absences.

Table 10.4 contains a list of the 20 'weakest' states according to *Foreign Policy* magazine in 2007 and 2017.

Case Study 10.5 presents the story of Somalia, which has been effectively a territory without a central state since 1991. This makes it the territory with the longest such experience in modern times. How did this happen? As Hobbes was quoted as saying in Chapter 1, this should be a region where life is 'solitary, poor, nasty, brutish and short'. Is this actually the case?

See Chapter 7 for more on Hobbes and the social contract tradition.

Thus, even though the structures of modern states are fairly similar, they vary considerably according to their capacities. This raises the questions of what makes a state strong and, conversely, what makes it weak. It is possible to identify a series of factors.

Clearly, one is size. Although China enjoys the same international legal status as Monaco, in practice there is an enormous difference in their respective capacities to pursue their goals in the world.

Another factor is the strength of the economy. As the largest economy in the world, the US possesses the capacity to finance a high level of domestic public services and respond to the preferences of its people. By contrast, a poor state such as Burma (Myanmar) is much less capable of providing a wide range of adequate services for its people.

TABLE 10.4   Ranked list of the 20 weakest states in 2007 and 2017

Rank	2007	2017
1.	Sudan	Somalia
2.	Iraq	Central African Republic
3.	Somalia	Yemen
4.	Zimbabwe	Sudan
5.	Chad	Syria
6.	Ivory Coast	Democratic Republic of the Congo
7.	Democratic Republic of the Congo	Chad
8.	Afghanistan	Afghanistan
9.	Guinea	Iraq
10.	Central African Republic	Haiti
11.	Haiti	Guinea
12.	Pakistan	Nigeria
13.	North Korea	Zimbabwe
14.	Burma	Ethiopia
15.	Uganda	Guinea Bissau
16.	Bangladesh	Burundi
17.	Nigeria	Pakistan
18.	Ethiopia	Eritrea
19.	Burundi	Niger
20.	East Timor	Ivory Coast

Source: Fund for Peace (http://fundforpeace.org/fsi/decade-trends/)

A third factor is military might. Again, the US, as the only remaining military super-power, can do far more than other states to protect its people and territory, as well as to pursue foreign policy goals, although its failures in Iraq suggest that there are more limits to this power than were previously supposed.

So far, we have looked primarily at external factors in estimating the strength of states, but equally important are domestic ones. First, there is the issue of legitimacy. If a state

CASE STUDY 10.5 **Somalia as a failed state**

Unlike many postcolonial states, especially in sub-Saharan Africa, Somalia does not suffer particularly from ethnic heterogeneity nor are most of its boundaries much disputed, though Somalis have also traditionally resided in what are now Ethiopia, Kenya, and Djibouti. Occupying territory as large as France, it has a population estimated in 2007 at 9.1 million—that is, only roughly 15 per cent of the French. However, all Somalis believe they are descended from a common ancestor. The main divisions between Somalis are based upon clans and sub-clans rather than separate ethnicity. In addition, some commentators on Somalia have also stressed the strong-minded individualism of nomadic herdsmen, who view authority with suspicion. The colonial and postcolonial states have all been suspended above the rest of society, only partially integrated into it.

In 1960, the post-independence state was formed from former British and Italian colonies. In 1969, power was seized by General Siad Barre after the assassination of the last civilian president. Barre attempted to create a modern state by suppressing traditional clan ties, but gradually the army fragmented along clan lines. Barre's regime became notoriously corrupt and its domestic support shrank to his own clan.

In 1991, Barre was overthrown by his former intelligence chief, Mohamed Farah Aidid, which then provoked a bloody civil war between rival militias. Initially, the conflict was confined within the country, but hundreds of thousands of people died either from the ferocious fighting or subsequent starvation. In 1993, the UN, and primarily the US, attempted to impose a peace that would mark a new role in peace-making in the post-Cold-War era, with Operation Restore Hope. They were initially welcomed into the capital, Mogadishu, but after a few months their unsuccessful attempts to arrest the most prominent warlord, Aidid, led to widespread civilian casualties and united Somalis against outsiders. Even the Red Cross had to be protected. Mogadishu was devastated by withering American firepower and retaliation (Peterson, 2000). The deaths and mutilation of American servicemen in the events popularized in the film *Black Hawk Down* turned American popular opinion against the intervention and the UN later withdrew. Since then, Somalis have largely been left to their own devices.

There is no central authority in Somalia. In 2003, Kenya took the lead in organizing a conference that established a transitional federal government, but little progress has been made in its national legitimacy. In late 2006, forces from Ethiopia intervened to frustrate a movement for unity on the basis of Islamic courts.

Menkhaus (2007: 86–7) writes of 'a loose constellation of commercial city-states and villages separated by long stretches of pastoral statelessness'. *De facto*, one part of the country (Puntland) has declared autonomy, while another (Somaliland) in the north is effectively independent. The only effective administrations are at the local level and public services (education, health care, welfare) have collapsed. Clans and sub-clans defend their interests using traditional customary interclan practices of recompense for injuries or damage received by their members instead of relying upon state justice, but heavily armed militias can still demand resources, largely with impunity. Yet average life expectancy is estimated, in the CIA's *World Factbook*, at 52 years (though no statistics are very reliable)—higher than in many other African countries and about the same as in Nigeria. Somaliland is supposedly as safe as anywhere in the Horn of Africa. It has even established a rudimentary democratic system with elections and political parties. Insecurity is certainly a major problem in the country—perhaps 500,000 people have been killed and there are estimates of 2 million Somali refugees abroad, a fifth of the population. Sporadic civil war continues, driving refugees abroad and periodically emptying the capital, Mogadishu (**see Figure 10.2**).

The traditional economy of trade in herds of cattle is flourishing as compared with the pre-1991 period, since the state cannot extract usurious taxes (Little, 2003). Private enterprise has found ways of providing services such as the transfer of money within and outside the country despite the lack of banks. Businessmen also buy off militiamen to provide security for their trade, so there is no state monopoly on the means of violence. Mobile phone companies prosper, while the landline service decays. The private sector has taken over the supply of public services where quick profits are possible (for example running ports, airports, electricity supply, but not public sanitation). Transnational corporations such as Total and GM have found ways of doing business in the country despite the lack of a stable institutional and legal system. Somalis abroad remit back home anywhere between US$500 million and $1 billion per year, which bolsters the domestic economy, especially in the cities.

FIGURE 10.2   Somalia has been effectively a territory without a central state since 1991
© hikrcn/ Shutterstock.com

Somalis have found ways of coping with the lack of a state, which they regard as 'an instrument of accumulation and domination, enriching and empowering those who control it and exploiting and harassing the rest of the population' (Menkhaus, 2007: 86–7). Yet they are disadvantaged because they cannot protect their maritime resources, having no navy, and they cannot defend their businesses against foreign discrimination. Saudi Arabia, previously the largest importer of Somali cattle, banned them because the country could no longer provide a veterinary service to prevent the spread of disease. The insecurity in urban areas has prevented any significant investment in infrastructure or industry. And in 2010–11 Somali pirates captured more ships despite increased international naval patrols and began to operate much farther away from the coast.

lacks the consent to rule on the part of its people, then it is bound to be potentially weak, because it will need to rely more upon force to achieve acquiescence. This could be the result of dissension over its borders. Many postcolonial states have international frontiers that were imposed more or less arbitrarily, with the frequent consequence that ethnic or tribal communities straddle borders and refuse to think of themselves as citizens of at least one of the states where they are found and wish to establish their own homeland, or it could be the result of challenges to the dominant ideology of the state. Ultimately, what brought down the regimes in Eastern Europe and the former Soviet Union was the lack of support for the official ideology of communism. And some states are bedevilled by the legacies of overlapping layers of different historical colonizers. Syria, for example, was a much larger entity in the Ottoman Empire, but then had its current borders fixed by the British and the French after the First World War. Syrian leaders have never fully accepted the change and now the country has sunk into murderous civil war. Without that shared sense of popular legitimacy and accepted borders, states are brittle, however superficially strong they may look. They are vulnerable to new challenges because they lack flexibility and are slow to adapt.

A second crucial factor in the strength of states is the robustness of the state institutions themselves. To what extent can they withstand turbulence from the rest of society? Bayart (1993) and Chabal and Daloz (1999) repeatedly emphasize the weakness of many African states as the result of the interpenetration of state, society, and the economy. Individual African politicians expect to use the state to become rich as a way of impressing others and redistributing resources to their 'clients': 'Rich men are powerful and powerful men are rich' (Chabal and Daloz, 1999: 52). Ethnic and tribal communities expect 'their' representatives, whether democratically elected or even lowly officials in the government bureaucracy, to channel resources to them, because if they do not do so, no one will. Thus state institutions in Africa are far less robust than those in the West, because they do not stand above or apart from society in the same way. The structuration provided by the rest of the society outweighs the capacity for autonomous, rule-based behaviour on the part of the bureaucracy. The institutions are not really institutionalized and the African state is more easily penetrated by outside forces as a result—at least for the moment. The emergence of robust African states may in part be simply a matter of time—the time that it takes for political ideas and political behaviour to adjust to the still relatively new state units. Van Creveld (1999: 306) reminds us that, in the nineteenth century, newly independent states in South America suffered similar fragility. Colombia had 30 civil wars, Venezuela had 50 revolutions, and Bolivia, 60. According to Coronil (1997: 76) on Venezuela, at the beginning of the twentieth century:

 See Chapter 13 for a case study on Venezuela.

> [T]he state was so weak and precarious as a national institution that its stability and legitimacy were constantly at risk. Without a national army or an effective bureaucracy, in an indebted country that lacked a national road network or an effective system of communication, the state appeared as an unfulfilled project whose institutional form remained limited to localized sites of power with but partial dominion over the nation's territory and sway over its citizens.

We shall see in Chapter 13 that it does not look like this now. From this, it might be argued that maybe, in time, African states will also acquire greater robustness.

To some extent, this section has identified fundamental disparities between the state in the developed world and the state in the developing one today. In general, European states and the US are strong, while those in the developing world are weaker. All of the weak states listed in **Table 10.4** are former Western colonies. General theorizing about the state by Western political scientists has tended to focus on the issues associated with the strong. Recently, however, the problems of weakening states in the developed world have begun to attract more attention. Increasing globalization is beginning, but still only just beginning, to recast this debate. States in the developed world are now increasingly exercised by the erosion of their sovereignty, for example by multinational corporations and other transnational actors and forces (Marsh et al., 2006: 176). The erosion has not yet reached anything like the same level as in the developing world. Nevertheless, there seems to be a spreading slow decline in the autonomy of the state in different parts of the world. To that extent, the vectors of state capabilities in different parts of the world are beginning to converge again.

10

✳ KEY POINTS

- There is an enormous range in the capabilities of states in different regions of the world.
- Some states are at best 'quasi' states (Jackson, 1990).
- States need legitimacy and robust institutions to be strong.
- Globalization has a growing impact on limiting state capabilities around the world.

Conclusion

This chapter has set the framework for the next six chapters. These will explore various dimensions of the state, whether as organization or as structures of authority. It has also illustrated the great disparity in capabilities between some states and others. The next four chapters will focus upon the most important institutions of states, while the following two will deal with broader forces that provide structure to the context of political life.

? Key Questions

- What is a nation-state? Does it matter whether the nation or the state came first? Are nation-states stronger than state-nations?

- Does the state require moral authority to enjoy domestic legitimacy?

- According to **Table 10.1**, the French state takes a much bigger proportion of national GDP than the American state. Does that make the French state the more powerful of the two?

- Is state capacity simply a function of the level of economic development, or is it simply a function of longevity and habituation? Does the Venezuelan state have greater capacity than the South African?

- Is there a strong state in sub-Saharan Africa?

- How far can theories of the modern Western state (see Hay, Lister, and Marsh, 2006) be applied to states in the developing world?

- Is the UK now a nation-state or a state-nation? What about Canada?

- Did internal dissension or external destabilization play a bigger role in destroying the Somalian state?

- How would you try to strengthen a weak state in the developing world? Would democracy help?

- Is Pakistan a failed state (see Lieven, 2011)? Can the outside world do anything about it?

- Are some states simply too weak and/or too arbitrarily constructed to justify continued international recognition? Should the international community simply let them disintegrate? What would be the consequences?

- Is the state entering a period of decline? How would you measure its effectiveness compared with earlier periods?

▐▌ Further Reading

Buzan, Barry (1991), *People, States and Fear* (London: Harvester International, 2nd edn), esp. ch. 2.
A much-read study that considers both the internal and external roles of the state.

Chabal, Patrick, and Daloz, Jean-Pascal (1999), *Africa Works: Disorder as Political Instrument* (Oxford: International Africa Institute, in association with James Currey).
A vivid account of the distinctive features of states in Africa.

Feldman, Noah (2008), *The Fall and Rise of the Islamic State* (Princeton, NJ: Princeton University Press).
A sophisticated introduction to the history of the Islamic state and its contemporary evolution.

Fergusson, James (2013), *The World's Most Dangerous Place* (Boston, MA: Da Capo Press).
A journalist's account of life in Somalia.

Fukuyama, Francis (2011), *The Origins of Political Order: From Prehuman Times to the French Revolution* (London: Profile Books).
A magisterial account of the origins of states in various continents.

Gill, Graeme (2003), *The Nature and Development of the Modern State* (Basingstoke: Palgrave).
A good survey of theories of the state in the aftermath of the collapse of communism.

Hay, Colin, Lister, Michael, and Marsh, David (eds) (2006), *The State: Theories and Issues* (Basingstoke: Palgrave).
A collection of articles that discuss contemporary issues in theories of the Western state.

Leftwich, Adrian (2004), 'Theorizing the State', in Peter Burnell and Vicky Randall (eds), *Politics in the Developing World* (Oxford: Oxford University Press), 139–54.
An attempt to extend theories of the state to the developing world.

Lieven, Anatol (2011), *Pakistan: A Hard Country* (New York: Public Affairs).
A sympathetic and well-informed analysis of a troubled state whose fate is often linked to security in the West.

Van Creveld, Martin (1999), *The Rise and Decline of the State* (Cambridge: Cambridge University Press).
A sweeping historical survey of the rise and spread of the Western state.

Wood, Graeme (2016), *The Way of the Strangers: Encounters with the Islamic State* (London: Allen Lane).
An account of the aims and justification of the Islamic state by ISIS.

 Web Links

http://www.pbs.org/ktca/liberty
Devoted to the American Revolution.

http://chnm.gmu.edu/revolution/
Devoted to the French Revolution.

http://www.magnacartaplus.org
Contains links to many human rights documents.

http://fundforpeace.org/fsi/
The most recently updated list of fragile (formerly failed) states.

http://www.china.org.cn/english/2005/Oct/145718.htm
The Chinese 2005 White Paper on Political Democracy.

 Visit the **Online Resources** that accompany this book to access more learning resources on this topic: www.oup.com/uk/ferdinand/

Laws, Constitutions, and Federalism

11

- Law and Politics
- Constitutions
- Fundamental Rights
- Constitutional Courts and Judicial Review
- Legal Adjudication of Political Problems

- Federalism, Consociational Democracy, and Asymmetrical Decentralization
- Conclusion: Growing Legalization of Political Life
- Key Questions
- Further Reading
- Web Links

Reader's Guide

This chapter will first discuss the importance of constitutions in determining the basic structure of the state and the fundamental rights of citizens that they establish. It will raise the question of whether the Universal Declaration of Human Rights is Western-centric. Then, as a reminder that the rule of law may not always be interpreted uniformly, we shall explore different ways in which states may attempt to realize justice in applying the law, focusing in particular on differences between Islamic and Western practice. Next, we shall consider the importance of constitutional courts. After that, we shall turn to the institution of federalism as a way of containing the powers of the state and of managing diverse societies. Then, we will look at consociationalism as an alternative approach to managing such diversity. We will conclude with a brief discussion of the increasing legalization of political life.

Law and Politics

Chapter 7 emphasized the power of the modern state and attempts to control it. According to Finer (1997), one of the main Western innovations in the theory of the state was the introduction of the 'law-bounded state', although Bonnett (2004: 5) argues that it was only towards the late nineteenth century that the idea of the West being a law-governed society came to be widely accepted. In other words, the decisions of the ruler(s) had to be codified and published so as to impose limits on the exercise of arbitrary power and to provide predictability in public affairs. Zakaria (1997:27) concurs: 'For much of modern history, what characterized governments in Europe and North America and differentiated them from those around the world, was not democracy but constitutional liberalism. The "Western model" is best symbolized not by the mass plebiscite but the impartial judge.'

The spread of Western conceptions of law around the world is a consequence of the spread of Western ideas of the state. Previously, in traditional societies in other parts of the world, authoritative rule-making was not seen as the exclusive domain of political rulers. Binding rules on human conduct could emerge from a variety of sources, such as, clans or tribes and religious authorities. Although these rules may not have been specifically called 'laws', they had the same force. Because there was no single source of authority for these rules, there existed a kind of norm-creating pluralism. Moreover, traditional societies in Africa and Asia were inclined to prefer to achieve order through internalized harmony and self-regulation, rather than formal legal adjudication (Menski, 2006: 547).

Gradually, however, Western states arrogated to themselves exclusive responsibility for issuing such rules as laws and they also codified them for the sake of consistency of application. Then, as legislatures became more common, law-making became their primary function. Gradually, these practices spread around the world as Western states did. They were associated with the 'civilizing mission' that Western states set for themselves. This monopoly on legislative activity is another essential feature of the modern state. A further refinement is that states often claim as well that the legitimacy of binding rules for society depends upon approval by the legislature. Sometimes, this is described as legal positivism (that is law is what the state says it is). Other types of rule lack this legitimacy and so lack the same degree of authority. It has become widely accepted as normal in Western states. As Twining (2000: 232) put it:

> [O]ver 200 years Western legal theory has been dominated by conceptions of law that tend to be monist (one internally coherent legal system), statist (the state has a monopoly of law within its territory), and positivist (what is not created or recognised as law by the state is not law).

It is perhaps best exemplified in the principle of secularism in France, where the civil state authorities assert their precedence over all competing sources of rule-making authority, especially religious ones. Ataturk was heavily influenced by this example in the reforms that he introduced in the 1920s, which asserted Turkish state supremacy over Islamic religious authorities. There, the state's Directorate of Religious Affairs controls the mosques by employing all Muslim clerics on salaries and subjecting them to an administrative hierarchy, which supervises their pronouncements. The most striking demonstration of the state's claim to authority was the announcement in 2008 that it would seek to establish which of the Prophet's sayings, or *hadith*, were genuine.

The extent to which this claim to legal monism has become accepted can be seen in the UK in the heated opposition to the Archbishop of Canterbury's lecture in 2008, which raised the possibility of the state accepting principles of shariah law in regulating family life of Muslims in the UK. He did not actually propose that a system of parallel law should be established; merely that some principles of shariah law might be incorporated into state law. Nevertheless, it was widely taken as challenging the dominant assumption of the primacy of state-approved and state-codified law. In fact, states in other parts of the world do allow greater legal pluralism. India, Pakistan, and Bangladesh, for example, do allow different religious communities the right to establish their own rules to regulate matters of faith and family rules; so legal pluralism does exist and it may spread further in the future as a result of globalization. For the moment, Western states still claim a monopoly on the making of law. Lieven (2011), however, explains why the state legal system in Pakistan still attracts widespread discontent, because it is more unwieldy, more bureaucratic, and more expensive than traditional and religious legal systems.

There is a close connection between legal and political systems. It can be said of the law that its primary concern is the 'authoritative allocation of values in society'. Creating laws to regulate human conduct (legislation) has been one of the most basic functions performed by states since earliest times. This is 'rule by law'. For laws to be legitimate (to be accepted by citizens), states have established rules of procedure that are themselves legitimate and have to be followed. They have to be approved in legislatures, a subject to which we shall return in Chapter 12. Almost all states have legislatures, although their powers and procedures may vary widely.

There is a second function performed by law. It determines what is criminal behaviour, it prescribes punishments for criminals, and it provides impartial rules for binding adjudication in disputes. This is often encapsulated, especially in the West, in the concept of the rule of law. This goes further than rule by law. It means that everyone in a society, whether ruler, minister, or ordinary citizen, is expected to obey the law. At least in theory, everyone is equal before it. Bingham (2011) identified eight elements in the rule of law (**see Key Concept 11.1**).

As enshrined in the American Constitution (**see Figure 11.1**) and repeated widely in other constitutions since then, the legal system is a check upon the exercise of power by the

11

‹ › KEY CONCEPT 11.1   List of requirements for the rule of law

(a) The law must be accessible, intelligible, clear, and predictable.

(b) The laws should apply equally to all.

(c) Public officials should exercise their functions fairly, not unreasonably, and for the purpose originally intended.

(d) The law must adequately protect fundamental human rights.

(e) Means must be provided to settle civil disputes without prohibitive cost or inordinate delay.

(f) Trial procedures should be fair.

(g) States must comply with international legal obligations (Bingham, 2011).

FIGURE 11.1 The US Constitution

U.S. National Archives and Records Administration/ Wikimedia Commons/ Public Domain

executive. One essential prerequisite for it to perform that function is independence from the state, in the sense that the state accepts that judges are free to determine the merits of legal cases irrespective of the consequences for state administration. Although an impartial legal system is a check upon the freedom of manoeuvre of legislators and therefore of the majority in a democracy, the rule of law is one of the essential elements of what Western states call good governance, a topic to which we shall return in Chapter 14. It is certainly an integral feature of liberal democracy. We shall return to the adjudication function of legal systems and their relationship with political systems towards the end of this chapter.

 See Chapter 14 for a discussion of good governance.

Constitutions

The term 'constitution' can be used in two different ways, one general and one narrower. In the broad sense, it denotes the overall structure of a state's political system. King (2007) provides a broad definition (**see Key Quote 11.2**).

This can also be expanded to cover a nation's political culture, as when people talk about a particular decision being contrary to the nation's 'constitution'—that is, it may infringe the 'spirit' of the constitution rather than its precise terms.

The second, narrower, use of the term 'constitution' refers to a specific document that lays down the basic institutions of state and procedures for changing them, as well as the basic rights and obligations of its citizens. It also serves as the basic source of national law, so that individual laws and legal codes are expected to conform to it. It is, or should be, the core of the legal system. For most states, this is a demanding requirement, which requires continual monitoring and, usually, a special constitutional court that can adjudicate whenever there seems to be a conflict. Islamic states in addition require the harmonization of divinely inspired, avowedly universal shariah law with national, civil, more secular codes. For an example of an attempt to devise an Islamic constitution, see Moten (1996: appx B). For the more practical difficulties of a constitutional court (in this case, in Egypt) trying to cope with these problems, see Lombardi (1998). This could be contrasted with the existing constitutions of Iran and Saudi Arabia.

In practice, the difference between the two uses of the term 'constitution' is not nearly as wide as it used to be. Only three states—the UK, New Zealand, and Israel—now do not have

11

Q KEY QUOTE 11.2 King on constitutions

'. . . the set of the most important rules and common understandings in any given country that regulate the relations among that country's governing institutions and also the relations between that country's governing institutions and the people of that country.' (King, 2007: 3)

a written constitution. The last 30 years have seen an enormous surge in constitution-writing around the world. At least 81 states introduced new constitutions, while a further 33 carried out major constitutional reform. In many cases, this was a consequence of the collapse of communism and the independence of many states in the former Soviet Union and former Yugoslavia—but it also included Saudi Arabia (which adopted a constitution in 1992), Algeria (1989, amended 1996), and Morocco (1996). Therefore, legitimate patterns of political behaviour became both more transparent and also more regularized. Still, as King (2007) reminds us, no state includes all of even the most fundamental elements of the political system in a single written document. For example, virtually no state establishes a particular electoral system in its constitution, yet this is a vital element in determining how power can change hands.

 See Chapter 12 for discussion of different types of electoral system.

In addition to the details of specific constitutions, you should also bear in mind the related notion of constitutionalism. This can mean two things. It can encapsulate a normative outlook on the political values embodied in a particular country's constitution (that is doing things according to its 'spirit'), or it can mean a broader normative standpoint—making the observance of constitutions the most fundamental principle of political life. At its most extreme, this could mean that constitutions, once codified, should remain inviolate. In practice, no state makes this an absolute principle. Constitutions do change. They are amended or even replaced. However, states generally make it very difficult by insisting upon special procedures for changing them, so that such change takes place without haste and after due reflection. This notion of the special status of constitutions in general is part of constitutionalism. Respect for the primacy of the Constitution remains a core element of the American political system. The same is true of continental Europe, where the memory of disastrous dictatorships accentuated the attractiveness of a robust constitutional order. Western advice on good governance to developing countries regularly stresses the importance of constitutionalism and the rule of law.

11

✳ KEY POINTS

- Common usage of the term 'constitution' is ambiguous. It can mean either a legal document and/or a pattern of rule.
- Constitutions may embody aspirations for future patterns of rule, as well as regulating how that rule should be exercised now.
- Constitutionalism is a normative doctrine giving high priority to the observance of a constitution's provisions and making it effective.

Fundamental Rights

One of the basic features of constitutions is that they usually contain a list of fundamental rights of citizens. The first lists of civil rights were contained in the American Constitution and the list of the Rights of Man from the French Revolution. Though, more recently, the United Nations adopted in 1948 a Universal Declaration of Human Rights, the fact that the notion of human rights first emerged in Western countries has led rulers of non-Western states to claim that it is inappropriate for non-Western societies, particularly when they are criticized by Western governments for failing to respect them. This is illustrated by **Key Debate 11.3**.

 KEY DEBATE 11.3 **Are human rights a 'Western' construct?**

In the aftermath of the Second World War, the newly created United Nations attempted to establish a better world that would never revert to the injustice and conflict of the past. It adopted the Universal Declaration of Human Rights in 1948, which declared in Article 1 that 'all human beings are born free and equal in dignity and rights'. Article 2 goes on to add that everyone, without exception, is entitled to these freedoms and rights (for more details, **see Key Debate 19.3**). However, Article 29(2) clarifies that limitations on the exercise of these rights can only be tolerated 'for the purpose of securing due recognition and respect for the rights and freedoms of others and of meeting the just requirements of morality, public order and the general welfare *in a democratic society*' (emphasis added). In other words, even though not all founding states of the UN were democracies in the Western sense (such as the USSR), most were, and the Universal Declaration of Human Rights does assume the standards and perspective of (predominantly Western) democracy.

Subsequently, that perspective has been challenged by newly independent colonies and state socialist regimes (such as China), which all instinctively mistrust Western pretentions to establish the basic standards of international political morality. But, more recently, Islamic states and peoples have also begun more openly to assert alternative principles of international morality. For their perspective on human rights, let us consider the Cairo Declaration on Human Rights in Islam (1990) and the Arab Charter on Human Rights (updated 2008), which are coloured by their distinctive religious traditions and national experiences of colonization from the West. The first ten Articles of the Cairo Declaration are devoted to the principles of religious morality underlying human life. The first Article declares that all human beings are united by submission to God and that 'all men are equal in terms of basic human dignity and basic obligations and responsibilities, without any discrimination on the grounds of race, colour, language, sex, religious belief, political affiliation, social status or other considerations'. Article 6 specifies that 'woman is equal to man in human dignity, and has rights to enjoy as well as duties to perform; she has her own civil entity and financial independence, and the right to retain her name and lineage'. However, it adds that 'the husband is responsible for the support and welfare of the family'. Article 10 prohibits attempts to convert people to another religion or atheism. Article 11 prohibits slavery, humiliation, oppression, and exploitation, and specifically prohibits colonialism as 'one of the most evil forms of enslavement'. The rest of the Articles

11

specify rights to free movement, work, property, a clean environment, medical and social care, and privacy. According to the Cairo Declaration, all individuals are equal before the law, but shariah law is the sole source of authority over what constitutes crime and punishment. The Declaration ends with three Articles that specify shariah law as the basic framework for interpreting all these rights and emphasize that everyone has the freedom to express opinions provided that they are not contrary to its principles.

The Arab Charter on Human Rights repeats most of these rights, but without specifying shariah law as the basic framework for interpreting them. It also adds (Article 24) that individuals have the right to take part in political activity, to stand for election, and to freedom of association and peaceful assembly, provided that this is compatible with restrictions 'necessary in a democratic society in the interests of national security or public safety, public health or morals, or the protection of the rights and freedoms of others'. It draws no distinction between the rights of men and women. In that respect, it traces a more moderate line between the two previous positions, appealing to secular, as well as religious, Arab states. It converges more with the UN Declaration and accepts the perspective of democracy. It repeats the caveat of possible restrictions on the enjoyment of those rights for the sake of national security, public order, and public morality. But redress for citizens who allege violation of human rights may still be trickier than in the West, especially in explicitly Islamic states that incline more towards the Cairo Declaration. The enjoyment of human rights greatly depends upon the operation of a state's legal system and how it understands the rule of law.

Questions

1. Compare these three documents. How significant are the differences?

2. Is there any sense in which the rights enshrined in the Universal Declaration of Human Rights are less complete than those in either of the other two documents?

3. Is there a significant Western bias in the Universal Declaration of Human Rights?

In the twentieth century, constitutions have often gone beyond purely 'political' rights to include broader social rights. These additions usually relate to welfare provisions, but they may also specify other conditions as well. For example, many states (especially those with Catholic or Islamic societies) lay particular emphasis upon the family as the basic unit of society and assign to it a privileged position. The Universal Declaration of Human Rights was an early exemplar of this trend of establishing social rights. It includes additional specific political rights that were not mentioned in the Rights of Man. It lays down that every individual has: the right to freedom of thought, conscience, and religion, including the right to change them (Article 18); the right to freedom of opinion and expression, including the freedom to receive and impart information and ideas through any media and regardless of frontiers (Article 19); and the right to freedom of peaceful assembly and association (Article 20). In addition, it lays down a number of social rights as well. Everyone has the right to social security (Article 21), to work and equal pay for equal work (Article 23), to rest and leisure, with reasonable limits on working hours (Article 24), to a standard of living 'adequate for the health and well-being of himself and of his family' (Article 25), to education (Article 26), and to participation in the cultural life of the community (Article 27). In theory, all states that have accepted the Universal Declaration of Human Rights have also committed themselves to observing it, whether or not its provisions are specifically incorporated into their constitutions.

At least in principle, these rights are 'justiciable' within individual states—that is, citizens should be entitled to go to law to seek redress if they feel that any of these rights are being infringed by their government. This depends upon the willingness, and the resources, of individual citizens to pursue their own claims in the courts. More recently, a further trend has emerged, especially in the US and Catholic states, which is support for the 'right to life'. In other words, citizens can take up the right of someone else—in this case, as yet unborn—and so prevent abortions.

What is clear from this extension of rights is that they leave a great deal of room for judicial interpretation. The various welfare and cultural rights do not lend themselves to simple 'yes' or 'no' adjudication. They leave open the question of amount or degree. Is a citizen of a developing country entitled to the same degree of welfare as one in Europe? What level of health care? Of education? It leaves open the question of the relative priorities of every sovereign government. Should the courts become involved in determining the levels of welfare spending, as opposed to other claims on the budget? This is a particularly sensitive issue in democracies. Even in the case of the more 'political' rights, such as freedom of expression and association, where a 'yes/no' adjudication by the courts is more likely, recent experience has shown that these too may increasingly have to be balanced against other public priorities. For example, the right to freedom of expression may have to be weighed against the 'right' to public security, as in the examples of government restrictions to prevent incitement of hatred or terrorism.

Thus, although the twentieth century has seen a dramatic expansion in the range of rights to which citizens are supposedly entitled, there is still scope for individual legal systems to come up with a great variety of interpretations. All of this explains why in democracies, perhaps even more than in authoritarian regimes, the court system is increasingly limiting the freedom of manoeuvre of elected governments. This is true even of Britain, which did not have a Charter of Human Rights of its own, but since 1998 has subscribed to the European Convention on Human Rights, as laid down in the Human Rights Act 1998. The British government announced in 2016 that Britain's departure from the EU will mean that the British Supreme Court will once again become the supreme arbiter of human rights in the UK, rather than the European Court of Justice, but it also claims that this will not in any way diminish the protection now afforded to those rights.

Increasingly, constitutions of nation-states contain not only provisions regulating the operation of specific institutions, but also aspirations about the direction in which their respective political systems are expected to develop. This has always been a feature of constitutions of states in Latin America, but it is increasingly prominent in Europe and also in Islamic societies. Insofar as they contain provisions that are not yet realized, then they also allow greater scope for the courts to contribute to the realization of those aspirations. In that sense, they allow for greater legalization of the political process. In fact, they will contribute to it.

KEY POINTS

- Over the last two centuries, there has been an increasing number of universal rights.
- They have expanded from political freedoms to rights to welfare, cultural protection, and cultural respect.
- There is a potential clash between the enforcement of rights by courts and the sovereignty of parliament.

Constitutional Courts and Judicial Review

Chiefly because of the sensitivity of the issues that they are called upon to determine, all states have a constitutional court of some kind. As we shall see, this is particularly true of federal states where constitutional guarantees to subnational units are a crucial reassurance that their interests will not be repressed. Some courts may be called by that name specifically. Others may assume that role as part of a wider range of judicial functions. In most countries, those who serve on these courts are either trained and experienced lawyers, or academic lawyers. France is something of an exception, however, in that its Conseil constitutionnel has more limited powers. It can only pass comment on a law in the short period of time between its approval in parliament and its promulgation. Once promulgated, a law in France cannot be changed, except by parliament, and it is not required that a member of the Conseil be a lawyer—sometimes, they are distinguished politicians. At present, out of ten members, one is a former president of the republic, four more are politicians, and three are former civil servants. Only two are lawyers, although others have studied law.

One trend that has become more evident in recent years has been the readiness of courts in the US and the UK to challenge government decisions through judicial review, on the grounds that fundamental rights have been infringed or that administrators have failed to observe due process. While this has often been regarded at the very least as embarrassing or irritating for governments, the courts have justified this intrusion by the need to ensure that human rights have been duly observed, even those of condemned criminals. This appears to be a tendency that is spreading to other countries (for example India). There, too, the courts have gradually increased their propensity to expand the scope for judicial comments on the executive's observance of constitutional rights, but they are less assertive than courts in the US and Europe in requiring the executive to comply and come up with policies of redress. So far, according to Shankar (2010), they have limited themselves to expressing views and leaving the questions of what, if anything, to do about them to politicians and voters. But, according to Rajamani and Sengupta (2010: 88), the Supreme Court has gradually come to play a much more assertive role:

> At the behest of public-spirited individuals, the Court has passed (and continues to pass) orders inter alia to protect the Taj Mahal from corrosive air pollution, rid the Ganges of trade effluents, address air pollution in Delhi and other metropolitan cities, protect the forests and wildlife of India, and clear cities of their garbage. The phenomenon of potentially endless judicial oversight in public interest cases cannot but lead to the conclusion that the judiciary is merely substituting judicial governance for executive governance in areas highlighted by public interest litigants.

Because of the opacity of the system for appointments to the higher reaches of the judiciary in India, Godbole (2009: 22) has claimed that the Supreme Court is 'the world's most powerful judiciary'. France, again, is an exception. There, the state takes the view that challenges to the constitutionality of potential human rights abuses are better raised in parliament, which has the duty of holding the government to account, than by the courts. British judges shared this view until the 1970s, but do so no longer (King, 2007: 115–49).

KEY POINTS

- States establish special courts, or legal arrangements, to safeguard constitutions.
- There is an increasing tendency to appeal for executive policy-making to be subject to standards laid down by judicial review.

Legal Adjudication of Political Problems

As the quotation from Zakaria (1997) indicated, the legal framework of the state is extremely important for politics in the West—Europe, as well as the US. Most European states pride themselves on the robustness and impartiality of their legal systems. The EU places great store on legal propriety in its decisions and decision-making processes. This makes for greater involvement of lawyers and legal arguments in policy debates. For example, German participation in the euro was considered by the German Constitutional Court, and the scope for intervention by the European Central Bank is significantly constrained by the Court's decision irrespective of the economic arguments. In the UK, the question of whether Parliament needed also to formally approve the decision to apply to leave the EU after the 2016 referendum was determined by the Supreme Court. And the movement to make state administration more efficient by replacing government departments with arm's-length agencies as part of the New Public Management reforms (to which we shall return in Chapter 14) has meant that accountability for the performance of these agencies has moved towards the courts and away from parliaments.

Within the general trend of creeping legalization of political life, there remains considerable scope for variation in the interpretation and implementation of even universal human rights by the courts of different nations. This is not only because of the interests, or self-interest, of particular nation-states, but also because of different approaches to the ultimate objective of the justice that legal systems are expected to dispense. Approaches to the function and purpose of law also vary from one country to another. Concern and respect for the law are not exclusive to the West. As Montada (2001: 8037) put it, 'the concern for justice seems an anthropological universal, but it takes many faces, because there are divergent views on what is meant by the term and how it is realized in particular legal jurisdictions'. Let us outline four basic differences, which revolve around different interpretations of the meaning of 'justice'.

The first can be summarized as a kind of legal positivism. The law of a particular country is neither more nor less than the sum of the laws that it has established. It can be summed up by a common phrase used by French lawyers: *La loi est la loi*. This means that the wording of each individual law as approved by parliament, as well as the whole legal code, is sacrosanct. It is inappropriate for judges to seek to enquire whether any particular law is phrased inadequately. Their task is simply to enforce it.

This approach to constitutional issues is replicated in France's former colonies, but it resonates more widely too. In pre-modern China, there was a school of legal thinking called the Legalists. Their main concern was to ensure that the Chinese obeyed the law. As long as they did, this would ensure order and harmony in society and prevent **anarchy**. The Legalists were not especially interested in 'justice' except insofar as an orderly society was also a just one. It was order and harmony that was just, not necessarily any particular law. They wanted to deter law-breaking, as that would be unjust. To this end, extreme punishments were 'just', however brutal for the individual law-breaker, as they would ensure justice for the rest of society. This was rule by law, but it was aimed at making people fear rulers and officials. It was law for deterrence.

A second approach to the social function of law was typified by communist states. Here the function of law was subordinated to some higher, non-legal goal: communism itself. Universal human rights were of lesser concern, except in the indefinite future, even if such states' constitutions specifically upheld them. Judges had to be members of the Communist Party, which meant that they had to defer to the Party leadership. So appeals to the courts to defend the human rights of political dissenters were bound to fail. And still in China today officials of the Communist Party can only be prosecuted for criminal offences after the Party leadership has agreed. Thus, although in China there is increasing talk of 'rule of law' replacing 'rule by men', there is still a long way to go, at least by Western standards.

A third approach to law and society can be seen in Islamic states. In general, there is no doubt about the traditional importance of justice and the law there. According to Rosen (1989: 74): 'Everywhere one encounters in Islamic life the idea of justice.' For Lewis (2005: 39), 'the traditional Islamic ideal of good government is expressed in the term "justice" ' and according to Hallaq (2005: 193), 'if ever there was any pre-modern legal and political culture that maintained the principle of the rule of law so well, it was the culture of Islam'. However, insofar as this rule of law existed, it was more because of practice, rather than because of the explicit separation of the powers of rulers and judges, as in the West. It was because both rulers and judges were supposed to defer to the revealed law of the shariah. In general, rulers appointed and could dismiss judges. There was no notion of ordinary people having rights vis-à-vis their rulers, unless the latter broke divine law.

On the other hand, the state did not claim the same monopoly over law-giving as Western states do. Laws were mainly formulated by legal scholars, not by rulers, and there are four equally respected schools of legal scholarship to which Sunni judges could belong (the Hanafi, Maliki, Shafi'i, and Hanbali). The traditions of these schools could lead to different decisions in particular cases, especially commercial ones. People could choose their lawyers according to the type of decision they would be likely to make in a particular dispute. Moreover, there was not the same insistence upon consistency between the decisions of judges and upon binding precedents. Judges much more frankly tried to do justice according to the particular circumstances of an individual case, rather than forcing the facts to fit a set of orthodox decisions. There was no systematic codification of legal precedents. Therefore, traditionally in Islamic societies there was a tendency for political monism, but legal pluralism, whereas in the West we find the obverse: a greater tendency towards political pluralism and legal monism, with legal systems expected to deliver consistent authoritative verdicts.

By contrast, the fourth approach to legal justice—what we can loosely term the Western approach—places greater stress upon procedural justice. This means making sure that verdicts are similar and more consistent in similar sets of circumstances. It requires a greater legal bureaucracy to ensure consistency of verdicts, with one or two higher layers of appeal courts, as well as ministries of justice to administer them. It also risks delivering verdicts that are less well tailored to individual circumstances. However, it does provide greater predictability about likely outcomes to court cases. Gradually, the Western approach spread more widely around the world in the nineteenth and twentieth centuries. It was part of the spread of the Western state that was described in Chapter 7 and it also contributed to it, because the state took the responsibility of codifying laws and creating the judicial apparatus to achieve this. Again, one of the best examples is Japan. As the Japanese state sought to respond to challenges from the West in the second half of the nineteenth century, it sent scholars to Europe to study alternative national legal systems, particularly

See Chapter 10 for a discussion of the rise of the Western-type state.

Britain, Germany, and France, and to present comparative reports on the respective merits of different legal codes. In the end, Japan turned to the principles of German administrative law to provide the basis of its new code of administrative law, while it looked to Germany and France for the principles of commercial law. Turkey responded in similar ways as it sought to withstand the challenge to its own empire from Europe. From the 1870s onwards, Turkey too began to produce legal codes that grafted Western legal principles and the organization of justice onto its own well-established forms of jurisprudence and courts, and these were then spread throughout its empire in the Middle East. Civil courts assumed greater authority over religious ones. Gradually, the state assumed control of the legal process as it embarked on Western-style modernization.

Although the Western legal practices and norms have spread around the world, this does not mean that they have become universal and fully consistent. The decision in 2007 of President Musharraf of Pakistan to 'correct' the Supreme Court by dismissing most of the judges and replacing them with more pliant ones was a striking example of persisting differences. Even more striking was the decision of the Turkish government to dismiss at least 2,700 judges in the aftermath of the failed coup attempt in 2016.

In addition, we should remember that other elements in the context of national legal systems may also have a significant bearing on the way law is practised. Epp (1998), for instance, has shown how the pursuit of civil rights in a number of states with quite similar legal frameworks—the US, India, the UK, and Canada—has varied considerably according to the legal infrastructure of individual countries. In particular, what matters is the availability of public resources to help poorer litigants to pursue cases. Litigants in the US and Canada find this much easier than in the UK or India. The consequence is that there has been a much stronger movement to pursue rights-related cases in North America, with Canada in particular undergoing what Epp (1998: 156) describes as 'a vibrant rights revolution' since 1960. He explains this in part by the adoption in 1982 of the Charter of Rights and Freedoms, but also in part by a growing support structure for legal mobilization (advocacy organizations, government aid for litigants, lawyers, and legal scholars who changed the previous prevailing conservative mindset of the legal system) (Epp, 1998: 195–6). The availability of resources for litigation has an important impact upon the pursuit of rights. What this shows is that there is a close connection between a country's legal system and the evolution of its political system. The two interact with and impact on each other.

Even the simple fact of the number of lawyers that are qualified in a country will have a big impact on the place of law in a nation's public life and therefore on citizens' ability to have recourse to law. The US has almost 1 million qualified lawyers, which represents about 0.3 per cent of the population. This reflects a society that is prone to litigation, but the availability of lawyers no doubt also contributes to it. The UK has half that proportion, Germany has a quarter, and France, an eighth, while Japan and India have only roughly a twenty-fifth. No doubt this also played a part in the limited pursuit of rights in India that Epp mentioned above. These figures explain the widespread perception that the Japanese are very reluctant to go to law and to the courts when they have a problem. They try to find alternative ways of resolving disputes. Yet they would all be said to practise the rule of law.

This section has argued that a whole range of factors contributes to a variety of interpretations of the rule of law in the practice of legal systems in different regions of the world.

 KEY POINTS

- Orientations on appropriate functions for legal systems have traditionally varied from country to country and this can lead to variation in the practice of the 'rule of law'.
- This can lead to different interpretations of even universal rights.
- There is a distinctive emphasis in Western jurisprudence on realizing procedural justice through greater consistency and bureaucratic organization.

Federalism, Consociational Democracy, and Asymmetrical Decentralization

One form of state where the law has always played a prominent role in the political process is federalism. This is because federal states are explicitly designed to protect the rights of the constituent parts. Legal guarantees are essential this. Determining the respective rights of the national and state governments and the institutions to implement them requires legal arguments and ensures the constant involvement of lawyers. American politics demonstrates this most graphically, where issues of 'states' rights'—that is, which level of government is fundamentally responsible for public policy in a particular field—regularly overshadow debates over the content of policy (for example where should the issue of women's rights to abortion be decided?). But the US also demonstrates another key feature of federalism.

The American Constitution was explicitly designed to restrain the power of the state. One way, as we have seen, was through the establishment of checks and balances, with the threefold division of power between executive, legislature, and judiciary. There was, however, a second way. This was through the establishment of a federal system. The territorial decentralization of power, it was hoped, would further obstruct any possible oppression. Ever since then, federalism has been touted as a solution to the risks of potential dictatorship. The importance of this idea can be seen in the federal constitution that was imposed upon West Germany after the Second World War. It was intended to undermine the remaining roots of Nazi dictatorship and it has justified the hopes that were placed upon it. These institutions have taken root in the German political system and have made Germany a reliable democratic partner in the heart of Europe.

11

In general, what is federalism? According to Robertson (1993: 184):

'Federalism' is now used to describe such a form of government, in which power is constitutionally divided between different authorities in such a way that each exercises responsibility for a particular set of functions and maintains its own institutions to discharge those functions. In a federal system each authority therefore has sovereignty within its own sphere of responsibilities, because the powers which it exercises are not delegated to it by some other authority.

What this definition emphasizes is the constitutionally backed equality between the national government and the federal units for responsibility for performing particular functions. It reassures the federal units or states that their decisions cannot be overridden by some higher authority. It is a protection against a domineering centre or worse.

To provide substance for that protection, federal systems usually establish two institutions. First, there is normally a two-chamber parliament, with the upper chamber composed of representatives from the states. The latter are given specific powers to ensure that their constitutional prerogatives cannot be legislated away without their consent. Second, there is usually a constitutional court to rule upon the constitutionality of legislative proposals, again aimed at reassuring the states that they cannot be coerced into submission. But some federal states are more preoccupied than the US about the dangers of excessively strong powers granted to states within a federation ultimately leading to secession. So in India, for example, whilst the first minister of each state is elected, there is also a governor who is appointed by the president in Delhi. That minister is charged with coordinating policies with the national capital and can be dismissed by the president—as has occasionally happened. So federalism in India has a more centralizing dimension than in, say, the US.

Lastly, we should note that the EU—also a federal state—is very different. There, the (unicameral) European Parliament is effectively a third chamber, standing above, or rather alongside, the national parliaments of the member states. And the European Court of Justice, while it does have a constitutional character, is primarily concerned with ensuring consistent interpretation of European law across all the member states, rather than supporting individual states who complain of excessively centralizing policies coming from Brussels. Here, the federal state is more explicitly concerned with laying a path to a more powerful European state in the future, although European policy-makers have sought to reassure sceptics by espousing the countervailing principle of subsidiarity—that is, that policies should be implemented at the most appropriate level, whether it be the federation, the nation-state, or local government. But this is a principle of administration rather than one of fundamental rights. The persisting Eurozone financial crisis has thrown the conflicting centralizing versus decentralizing pressures into sharp relief (Wyplosz, 2015).

Generally, however, since the American Revolution, federalism has been called upon to provide a constitutional framework for states facing two other challenges. The first is simply territorial size. Most federal states occupy a large area. As can be seen from **Table 11.1**, seven of the ten largest states in the world by area are federations. Of course, many of them are heterogeneous in terms of population, but size is also an important issue. Here, Australia is the paradigmatic example. The federation there was originally created in

TABLE 11.1   Federalism among the ten largest states in the world, by territory

State	Federal/Unitary
Russia	F
Canada	F
US	F
China	U
Brazil	F
Australia	F
India	F
Argentina	F
Kazakhstan	U
Sudan	U (but decentralized)

1900 to allow significant devolution of power to individual states because of the difficulties of trying to run the whole country from Canberra, given the communications technologies that were available at that time. Diversity of population was not a significant factor in the decision.

In most cases, however, federalism has been proposed to provide guarantees for minority communities—usually ethnically based—that they will be able to preserve their particular way of life, their culture, their language, their religion, etc., or at least that there will be no political challenge to them. Because of this, as can be seen from **Table 11.2**, federations vary considerably in size, some being very small indeed.

TABLE 11.2   List of federations

Argentina	Germany	Russia
Australia	India	St Kitts & Nevis
Austria	Iraq	Switzerland
Belgium	Malaysia	United Arab Emirates
Bosnia and Herzegovina	Mexico	US
Brazil	Micronesia	Venezuela
Canada	Nepal	Nigeria
Comoros	Ethiopia	Pakistan

The experience of federations is, of course, not always positive. There is quite a long list of those that have disintegrated, some disastrously. The collapse of the USSR has been described by President Putin as one of the greatest disasters of the twentieth century, while that of the former Yugoslavia unleashed the greatest conflict in Europe since the Second World War (**see Case Study 11.4**). Even where federations have survived, some have still gone through bloody civil wars , for example Nigeria in the 1960s or the US in the 1860s. The experience of Belgium, which in 2007 went for over 150 days without a national government and then in 2010–11 for a further 589 days, also suggests that they are not always capable of decisive national decision-making. So federations are not automatically capable by their very existence of preventing violent conflict and/or dissolution or of providing effective government. Yet it can be argued that a prime cause of the collapse of the USSR and Yugoslavia was the lack of the legal support and the rule of law without which constitutional provisions of any kind are more vulnerable. It was not the constitutional provisions themselves. On the positive side, Stepan (2004: 441) declared: 'Every single long-standing democracy in a territorially based multilingual and multinational polity is a federal state'—though, as we shall see shortly, this is not entirely true. Some multilingual states (such as Spain) practise asymmetric decentralization, rather than formal federalism, to recognize the special status of certain parts of the country. And Suberu (2004: 328) has maintained that, despite the civil war, 'federalism has long been recognized as the indispensable basis for Nigeria's identity and survival'.

CASE STUDY 11.4   The collapse of the former Yugoslavia

Yugoslavia was created at the end of the First World War as a state for South Slavs to prevent the return of imperial powers to treat them as colonies. However, between the wars it was bedevilled by enduring enmity between the two largest ethnic communities, the Serbs and Croats. In the Second World War, it was dismembered under Axis control and hundreds of thousands were killed in fratricidal conflict.

After Liberation, largely by the communist partisans under Tito, the Yugoslav state was restored, this time as a federation. Even the ruling Yugoslav Communist Party was divided into separate federal units. The six federal republics (Serbia, Croatia, Slovenia, Bosnia–Herzegovina, Macedonia, and Montenegro) had equal representation in the federal government, and after 1974 the two autonomous regions of Kosovo and Vojvodina in Serbia were granted only slightly less. Yugoslavia was by far the most genuinely federal communist state. In 1963, it created the only constitutional court in the communist world. For a long time, the memory of the blood-letting during the war, a political culture that exalted the shared heroism of the partisan resistance, the pride in a Yugoslav road to socialism based upon workers' self-management, and the threat of foreign intervention, as well as Tito's own robust leadership, all helped to preserve national unity. Despite occasional challenges to the leadership—in 1968 a new generation of Croat leaders tried to introduce a more liberal set of policies, but were rejected by Tito—Yugoslavia stayed united and prosperous until he died in 1980.

Afterwards, however, the state ran into increasing difficulties. There was no cohesion in the national leadership. Tito had avoided naming a successor and he had created a federal system with a collective presidency, where the leader of each of the federal republics acted as head of state for just one year in rotation. He had emphasized the need for national decision-making on the basis of 'consensus' (that is, unanimity). After he was gone, each republic leader put the interests of their own republic above that of the state as a whole. The national economy fragmented increasingly into republic units. Inter-republic trade actually declined. Inflation continued to increase throughout the 1980s. The national leadership agreed remedies in Belgrade and then refused to implement them when the leaders returned to their republic capitals. No one was prepared to make sacrifices for the good of the country as a whole. Popular dissatisfaction grew. All the nationalities, even the Serbs, the largest one, felt that they were the losers within the federation. Trust disintegrated across the country.

Then, in 1987, heir apparent to the Serbian leadership Slobodan Milošević made a speech at an event commemorating the 600th anniversary of the defeat of the Serbs at the hands of the Ottoman Turks in Kosovo. He made an unexpected appeal for Serbs to stand up for their rights and vowed that Belgrade would back them. This provoked an emotional response across Serbia, which he then tried to turn into a movement to restore decisive national government under his leadership. Large numbers of Serbs were mobilized to march on Montenegro, and then Slovenia, to bring them to heel. In turn, this provoked apprehension in the other republics about resurgent Serbian chauvinism. The constitutional court proved ineffective. The collapse of the communist regimes in Eastern Europe exacerbated the sense of crisis. Partly to forestall similar developments in Yugoslavia and partly to keep Milošević at bay, the leaders of the communist parties in Croatia and Slovenia began to call for multiparty elections.

In turn, this provoked Milošević to send the federal army into Slovenia and Croatia to try to bring them to heel or, if that failed, to establish a greater Serbia that could protect all Serbs against a repeat of the genocide that they had suffered in the Second World War. With that, he launched a civil war that became the biggest conflict in Europe since the Second World War and destroyed the state of Yugoslavia.

(For a discussion of various explanations for the collapse of the former Yugoslavia, see Ramet, 2005.)

11

Yet, in the 1970s, the idea that federalism was the naturally most appropriate solution to the problems of division in deeply divided societies was challenged by the theory of consociationalism, which was initially introduced in Chapter 4. This was based upon the experience of a few small states with deep multi-ethnic and multi-confessional cleavages, largely in Europe, which had achieved intercommunal harmony and cooperation without a

▶ See Chapter 3 for an introduction to consociational democracy.

formal federal system. The first example of this to be cited was the Netherlands. The key to its success was attributed not to formal constitutional arrangements or legalism, but rather to iterated patterns of cooperation between elites in sharing power, which generated and reinforced mutual trust. According to Lijphart (1977), there are four main characteristics of consociational democracies (**see Key Concept 11.5**).

In fact, some of the other states that were later adduced as examples of the same practice ran into serious problems. Consociationalism, no more than federalism, is no automatic guarantee of social harmony. Not all of these difficulties were domestically caused. Lebanon, for instance, was destabilized by conflict between Israel and the Palestinians living in Lebanon. Cyprus was destabilized by Turkish invasion. Nevertheless, since this model was usually applied to small states in general, this made them more vulnerable in the case of outside intervention. In fact, most sets of consociational arrangement have proved relatively short-lived, and not just because of external intervention. Only the Netherlands has remained faithful to the model. This has suggested that the model may be more appropriate as a temporary solution to societies that have recently suffered from major division or conflict. It can help to stabilize the state through increased trust between communities, before some transition to a more permanent set of arrangements.

It is also the case that some states practise both federalism and consociationalism (for example India, Belgium, and Malaysia). The two sets of arrangements are not necessarily mutually exclusive and Lijphart (2001) contends that this combination has been a key factor in India's democratic achievements.

One last development should be noted. This concerns new state practices in managing their centre–periphery relations around the world. This is a greater willingness to consider flexibility in arrangements between some states or provinces and the centre that is not offered to all those units. States no longer feel that they have to make an exclusive choice

11

 KEY CONCEPT 11.5 **Features of consociationalism**

- Government by grand coalition—that is, governments including deputies from the parties representing all of the main communities, which usually requires that they hold far more than a bare majority of seats in parliament

- Segmental or subcultural autonomy—that is, each ethnic or confessional community being responsible for administering policies in specific policy areas that affect them

- Proportional representation in the electoral system, which makes simple majoritarian rule very unlikely, and proportionate representation in the distribution of posts in government bureaucracies, the distribution of public funds, and so on

- Agreement on minority vetoes for certain types of legislation

between either unitary or federal systems. They sometimes devise hybrid combinations. This can be called asymmetric decentralization or asymmetric federalism, and the general principle can be found in both federal and unitary states. A particularly striking example is Spain, which has granted much more extensive self-governing powers to some of the regions or 'autonomous communities', such as Catalonia, the Basque Country, Galicia, and Andalusia, than to the other 13, although Catalan political scientist Colomer (2007: 80) still calls the Spanish state 'the clearest case of failure . . . to build a large nation-state in Europe'. The same principle has been applied in the UK, with varying powers granted to the Scottish, Welsh, and Northern Irish assemblies. More recently, the Scottish Nationalist Party has advanced the quasi-federal argument that the UK should not be able to leave the EU without majorities in favour in all four constituent parts of the kingdom. France, where the state has traditionally been very preoccupied with constitutional equality and the dominance of Paris, has granted greater autonomy to Corsica than to other *départements*. All of these are still formally unitary states. Federal states display the same tendency for hybridity. The Soviet Union for decades distinguished between federal republics, autonomous republics, autonomous regions, and autonomous districts, all of which had different sets of powers from the more 'orthodox' provinces. Pakistan allows greater self-rule to the north-west frontier region and the federally administered tribal areas as compared with Punjab or Sindh. This means that other states that are confronted by challenges of great ethnic or religious cleavages can draw upon a much wider range of possible precedents to demonstrate flexibility. In many ways, the old distinction between federal and unitary states has disappeared, as similar kinds of asymmetrical relationships are introduced into both of them.

11

  KEY POINTS

- Federalism has a dual role as a check on centralized government and as a way of managing profound social diversity.

- Federations may collapse without appropriate legal structures or widespread popular support.

- Consociationalism is an alternative approach to handling social diversity, relying on elite cooperation rather than legal formalism.

- Consociationalism may be understood more broadly as a more consensual form of rule than majoritarianism and can be combined with federalism.

- There is an increasing use of asymmetric arrangements to handle diversity in both federal and unitary political systems, which erodes the differences between them.

Conclusion: Growing Legalization of Political Life

This chapter has highlighted four things. The first is the importance of constitutions as fundamental institutions that structure political systems. By establishing the basic principles for political life, they channel the political behaviour of all the inhabitants of a state in various directions and, equally importantly, prevent some other forms of political behaviour, and they help to provide greater transparency about the ways in which public decisions are made.

Second, constitutions need a developed legal system to give life to the provisions that they contain. Without some kind of accompanying rule of law, constitutions may be flouted by government or they may be undermined, as the example of Yugoslavia shows.

Third, this still allows for different approaches by which legal systems attempt to achieve justice. Emphases vary from one state to another and this will also mean that interpretations of universal human rights will to some extent vary from one country to another.

Fourth, federalism as a form of government does help to prevent excessive concentration of powers in a nation's capital. It can also help to provide reassurance to some minorities that their interests will not be overridden by larger communities. It can promote harmony in heterogeneous states marked by deep cleavages. However, it is not the only structure that can achieve this. Consociationalism offers an alternative approach to the same challenge, although it has tended to succeed only in smaller states and then over a more limited period of time. More recently, unitary states have shown greater flexibility in devising new forms of decentralization that take account of the regional differences and vary the rights that they offer to particular communities. In this way, the boundaries between federal and unitary states are becoming more blurred.

Last, there is a trend underlying the argument of this chapter—that is, the expanding role played by law in social life. The extent to which law plays a central role in the political process varies considerably from one state to another. It is certainly more pronounced in the developed world, especially the US. However, the trend is much more widely evident. Pakistan is but one example. The attempt by President Musharraf in 2007 to curtail the independence of the Supreme Court provoked concerted resistance from lawyers as a whole, with widespread popular support.

There are two dimensions to this trend. It encompasses, first, a growing tendency to devise legal frameworks to regulate an increasing number of dimensions of social behaviour within individual states and, second, an expansion of international legal activity to support globalization (Buxbaum, 2004; Lieberman, 2001). We have already mentioned the increased use of judicial review in the US and most European states. The change in the growing salience of law and legal processes is striking in the case of a state such as China, which, at the beginning of its reforms in the early 1980s, had only 200 lawyers and now has around 300,000. The increase in the number of trained lawyers certainly marks a change in the direction of the rule of law, even if China is still a long way from practising it in the same way that the West does. This trend does make for greater checks upon the power of the state and the executive branch of government—but it also makes politics more complicated and more difficult for non-lawyers to understand. Dahl (2001: 115) has remarked that the American system 'is among the most opaque, confusing, and difficult to understand' among Western democracies. At roughly the same time in a survey of public opinion in the Trilateral countries (the US, Japan, and Western Europe), King (2001: 91–3) concluded:

> The American people have lost confidence in their government because they have ceased to understand it . . . The American political system was probably hard for most ordinary people to understand when it was first designed in the 1780s . . . it has become even more complicated since then.

The checks on the power of the state may be greater, but is politics becoming more opaque and more esoteric, increasingly confined to a more limited political 'class'? This is an issue to which we shall return in Chapters 12 and 13. It also has contributed to the rise of populism and the election of Donald Trump, as discussed in Chapter 16.

? Key Questions

- Visit https://www.constituteproject.org/ and find the longest and shortest constitutions in the world. What would you expect to be the consequences for the operation of the political systems of these two states? How different are they likely to be?

- What is the most absurd constitutional provision that you have come across? Does it deserve the special status?

- If accepted, what difference would the Archbishop of Canterbury's proposals on the adoption of shariah legal principles make to the relationship between the state and law in the UK?

- Britain has no written constitution. What difference does that make as compared with the political arrangements and practices of any other state with which you are familiar?

- Should the UK become a federal state?

- Are the French right to resist the expansion of judicial review in political life and to leave constitutional challenges largely to parliament?

- Assess Dahl's arguments about the weaknesses of the American Constitution. Is there any likelihood of them being remedied?

- What are the main differences between federalism in Canada and the US?

- What are the main differences between federalism in the EU and the US?

● If federalism does indeed weaken the power of the government, does it make weaker states in the developing world too weak? What is the evidence from Nigeria, India, Brazil, and/or Pakistan?

● Do the autonomous communities of Catalonia and the Basque Country in unitary Spain have greater powers for self-government than the federal *Länder* in Germany?

● Are federalism or consociationalism viable solutions to the internal conflict in Iraq?

● If the rule of law is a good thing, does that mean that the more laws a state has, the better?

 Further Reading

Amoretti, Ugo M., and Bermeo, Nancy (eds) (2004), *Federalism and Territorial Cleavages* (Baltimore, MD: Johns Hopkins University Press).
An account of the ways in which federalism can manage territorial divisions within states.

Bingham, Tom (2011), *The Rule of Law* (London: Penguin).
A readable account of the principles inherent in the rule of law from Britain's former senior Law Lord.

Burgess, Michael (2006), *Comparative Federalism: Theory and Practice* (London: Routledge).
A recent account of the theory of federalism.

Dahl, Robert A. (2001), *How Democratic Is the American Constitution?* (New Haven, CT: Yale University Press).
A study of weaknesses of the American Constitution, including the great difficulty of changing it.

Hueglin, Thomas, and Fenna, Alan (2015), *Comparative Federalism: A Systematic Enquiry* (Toronto: University of Toronto Press).
An excellent comparative study of federalism in Canada, Germany, the US, and the EU.

Ibeanu, Okechukwu, and Kuna, Mohammad J. (2016), *Nigerian Federalism: Continuing Quest for Stability and Nation-Building* (Sebastopol, CA: Safari).
A recent, well-informed analysis of the evolution of federalism in Nigeria.

King, Anthony (2007), *The British Constitution* (Oxford: Oxford University Press).
A recent authoritative study of the British 'constitution' in the broad sense.

Lane, Jan-Erik (1996), *Constitutions and Political Theory* (Manchester: Manchester University Press).
An examination of the relationship between constitutions and political theory.

Lieven, Anatol (2011), *Pakistan: A Hard Country* (New York: Public Affairs).
Chapter 3 contains an insightful account of the reasons for popular preferences for non-state legal adjudication.

Lijphart, Arend (1999), *Patterns of Democracy: Government Forms and Performance in Thirty-Six Countries* (New Haven, CT: Yale University Press).
States the case in favour of big coalition government, including consociationalism, as a more consensual and ultimately more effective form of rule.

Menon, Anand (2006), *Comparative Federalism: The European Union and the US in Comparative Perspective* (Oxford: Oxford University Press).
A stimulating comparison of the EU and the US as federal states.

Mitra, Subrata K., and Pehl, Malte (2010), 'Federalism', in Niraja Gopal Jayal and Pratap Bhanu Mehta (eds), *The Oxford Companion to Politics in India* (New Delhi and Oxford: Oxford University Press), 43–60.
A very good survey of the evolution of Indian federalism since Independence, set against the general principles of federalism.

Souza, Celina (2014), *Constitutional Engineering in Brazil: The Politics of Federalism and Decentralization* (London: Palgrave Macmillan).
An interesting account of the way in which political leaders in Brazil debated the best way to decentralize the Brazilian state under democracy.

Wyplosz, Charles (2015), 'The Centralization–Decentralization Issue' (Brussels: Directorate-General for Economic and Financial Affairs, EU Commission Discussion Paper 14) (https://publications.europa.eu/en/publication-detail/-/publication/b0865d0b-8907-11e5-b8b7-01aa75ed71a1/language-en, accessed January 2018).
A discussion of the options open to the EU in terms of centralization versus decentralization in the context of possible solutions to the Eurozone financial crisis.

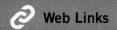 **Web Links**

https://www.constituteproject.org/
A site offering connections to all the constitutions that are online.

http://rowanwilliams.archbishopofcanterbury.org/articles.php/1137/archbishops-lecture-civil-and-religious-law-in-england-a-religious-perspective
The text of the Archbishop of Canterbury's lecture.

http://www.un.org/en/documents/udhr/
The text of the Universal Declaration of Human Rights.

http://www.refworld.org/docid/3ae6b3822c.html
The text of the Cairo Declaration on Human Rights in Islam.

https://www.cartercenter.org/resources/pdfs/peace/democracy/des/revised_Arab_charter_human_rights.pdf
The text of the 2008 update of the Arab Charter of Human Rights.

 Visit the **Online Resources** that accompany this book to access more learning resources on this topic: www.oup.com/uk/ferdinand/

Votes, Elections, Legislatures, and Legislators

12

- The Voting Paradox
- Elections
- Functions of Legislatures
- Types of Legislature
- The Structure of Legislatures
- Legislators
- Conclusion
- Key Questions
- Further Reading
- Web Links

Reader's Guide

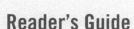

This chapter will first explain some of the basic issues involved in assessing the operation of voting and electoral systems. Then, it will survey the functions of legislatures. It will also discuss the growing practice of measures to establish quotas to increase gender equality in legislative recruitment. It will present a classification of legislatures based upon their capability to stand up to the executive branch of government. After that comes a basic introduction to the internal structure of legislatures: the choice of single or double chambers, and the role of parliamentary committees. Then, it will deal with trends in the backgrounds of members of parliament in various countries, specifically focusing upon the criticism that they constitute a 'political class'.

The Voting Paradox

Voting is a mechanism for making collective decisions. It is also intended to be a means for ensuring that the majority preference for a candidate or a policy is reflected in the ultimate decision. It is possibly the most basic element of any democracy. Yet it is subject to two basic paradoxes. The first is that the huge number of citizens in any modern state means that no individual's vote is likely to make the difference between two or more choices. This makes it potentially 'irrational' for any individual to bother to vote at all. Yet without votes, democracy—or at any rate representative democracy—is not possible. This helps to explain why, although we argued in Chapter 5 that democracy is associated with values of freedom and liberation and although voter turnout in national democratic elections generally remains quite high, some states make it compulsory (for example Argentina, Australia, Brazil, Cyprus, and Singapore).

The second paradox concerns the difficulty of relying upon votes to determine the objective preferences of the public. This is due to the mathematical problem known as the Arrow impossibility theorem, which asserts that when a group of people are asked to make one choice as their preference between three or more alternatives, it is impossible to conclude that one particular outcome is the one 'most preferred' unless over 50 per cent all vote for it. Let us see an example from **Table 12.1** that illustrates this, where people are choosing between three alternatives (A, B, C).

None of the three alternatives wins a majority of first choices, but if we just count first choices, then C wins, with 10 votes out of 22. If the first two choices are counted equally, then B wins, with 18 votes out of 44. However, it might be fairer to give extra weight to first choices over second ones, since that would reflect more genuine strength of preference. Suppose first choices are given two points and second choices are given one. In that case, A wins, with 24 points out of a possible 66.

We can see that all three possibilities could win, depending on the counting system used, without the actual votes changing at all. None of the options ever achieved a majority of the total votes or points available, whichever system was being used, so it would be impossible to conclude that the general preference was 'clearly' in favour of one particular option. As you can easily imagine, this problem gets worse with a greater number of

TABLE 12.1   Hypothetical distribution of votes

No. of voters	First choice	Second choice	Third choice
8	A	B	C
4	B	A	C
6	C	B	A
4	C	A	B

alternative choices, whether they are candidates or policy options. This means that the determination of preferences depends upon the particular procedure chosen for assessing the votes. Any procedure chosen is a compromise between theory and practicality. It also explains why referendums are usually reduced to a choice between two possible alternatives. In that way, even though it might seem to artificially constrain the choices that are being voted upon, it will result in an unambiguous outcome.

Therefore, the choice of method for assessing votes is crucial and really can alter the outcome. To give one famous example, Riker (1982: 227–32) showed that when Lincoln won the presidential election in 1860 against three rivals, different methods of assessing the votes that are used in various parts of the world today could easily have led to either of two others winning. If that had happened, then the American Civil War might never have occurred and world history might have developed along quite different lines.

More recently, votes have been used to estimate the strength of commitment of voters to particular public policy choices. How strongly do people prefer one option as compared with another? Public choice theory has developed a whole range of techniques derived from micro-economic theory for estimating likely public preferences. These all rest on the same assumption as has dominated economics—that is, that voters, like economic actors, are fundamentally rational beings who base

© Denis Kornilov/ Shutterstock.com

their vote upon calculation of the likely benefits and costs to them of any particular decision that they have to approve. It is an assumption that offers the prospect of predictability in politics. The majority of voters will support proposals that bring them greater benefit than losses, so political leaders need to formulate proposals that will appeal to those interests. From that perspective, political success is about devising a winning calculus of benefits.

Yet it is not clear that voters exclusively behave in ways that maximize their self-interest. Caplan (2007) has written of the 'rational irrationality' of politics. He argues that voters generally fail to appreciate how their economic interests are most likely to be served, because their instincts conflict with the rational recommendations of economic theory. His conclusion is that economists should stress even more the importance of preferring markets to determine provide goods, public goods included, over government provision, in the hope that public understanding will follow.

And a third set of perspectives focuses upon ethnographic analysis of actual voter behaviour. These illuminate the fact that people often vote for reasons of self-expression rather than self-interest. Even though, in any large polity, no individual's vote is likely to be the one that makes the crucial difference between two policy choices and so it might be thought irrational for individuals to bother to vote, they do so because it strengthens their sense of being citizens equal with one another and reminds public officials of their obligations of democratic accountability. This is true even in India, the largest democratic polity in the world.

The contrasting positions are exemplified in **Key Debate 12.1**.

KEY POINTS

- The method chosen for assessing votes plays a crucial part in determining the outcome.
- Votes can be used to calculate the strength of voters' rational preferences.
- The act of voting may also express emotional commitment and a sense of self-worth.

Elections

Elections are methods of assessing preferences through votes. They are vital to democracy. According to Article 12 of the Universal Declaration on Democracy adopted by the Inter-Parliamentary Union in 1997: 'The key element in the exercise of democracy is the holding of free and fair elections at regular intervals enabling the people's will to be expressed.'

KEY DEBATE 12.1 **Can voter behaviour be explained on the basis of rationality?**

Downs (1957: 36–7) on rational voting:

'In order to plan its policies so as to gain votes, the government must discover some relationship between what it does and how citizens vote. In our model, the relationship is derived from the axiom that citizens act rationally in politics. This action implies that each citizen casts his vote for the party he believes will provide him with more benefits than any other . . .

Given several mutually exclusive alternatives, a rational man always takes the one which yields him the highest utility *ceteris paribus*, i.e., he acts to his own greatest benefit.'

Caplan (2007: 195, emphasis original) on 'irrational voting':

'The optimal mix between markets and government depends not on the absolute virtues of markets, but on their virtues compared to those of government. No matter how well you think markets work, it makes sense to rely on markets *more* when you grow pessimistic about democracy . . .

Above all, I emphasize that voters are irrational. But I also accept two views common among democratic enthusiasts. That voters are largely unselfish, and politicians usually comply with public opinion . . .

Thus, when the public systematically misunderstands how to maximize social welfare—as it often does—it ignites a quick-burning fuse attached to correspondingly misguided policies. This should make almost anyone more pessimistic about democracy.

The striking implication is that even economists, widely charged with market fundamentalism, should be more pro-market than they already are. What economists currently see as the optimal balance between markets and government *rests upon an overestimation of the virtues of democracy*. In many cases, economists should embrace the free market in spite of its defects, because it still outshines the democratic alternative.'

Banerjee (2014: 144–68) on the reasons Indian citizens give for voting:

'Indian citizens have plenty of reasons to be dissatisfied with the performance of governments and they do not hold politicians in great esteem either. Why then do they bother to vote? And why do poor people vote more than middle-class ones? And why does 80 per cent of the population prefer a democratic albeit inefficient system to an authoritarian one?'

An ethnographic survey identified a wide spread of motivations: resignation or inertia, instrumentality, loyalty, protest vote, affectivity or emotional commitment, peer pressure, voting for citizenship, and voting for recognition.

Indian citizens, especially those who otherwise felt ignored by the state, were clearly motivated to vote to remind the state of the importance of the sovereignty of ordinary people in a democratic country. As some put it, politicians might hold power for five years at a time, but for the 15 days of campaigning, the voter was the king. Often people remarked that they felt important during the elections, because the powerful people who were usually remote and inaccessible had to come to them during a campaign, shake their hand and ask them how they were doing . . . For those members of society who belonged to the lowest sections . . . this momentary glimpse of being valued was hugely important.'

12

This debate demonstrates that the notion of rational voting behaviour, while a plausible hypothesis, is difficult to operationalize and subject to various interpretations, because voters have a wide range of interests and differing rationales for their ways of assessing them.

Questions

1. Do you intend to vote in the next national election? What about other students in your class? Why, or why not? And what considerations would determine your vote?

2. Should voting in national elections be made compulsory? What about in local elections?

3. Should we expect the same considerations to structure voting behaviour in the US and in India?

For electoral systems, there are two basic alternative principles underlying them, although there are several sub-variants. These are summarized in **Key Concept 12.2**.

The first basic type is the simple **plurality**, first-past-the-post majority system. This has the advantage of simplicity. At least in theory, it allows voters to choose individual candidates rather than party representatives. It also tends to be biased in favour of producing governments with larger majorities, at the expense of more representative reflections of public opinion. This can allow governments to be more decisive. It can also facilitate a

---

 KEY CONCEPT 12.2 **Types of electoral system**

- Majoritarian systems (first-past-the-post)
  - Single-member plurality systems (UK, US, India)
  - Two-round system (France)
  - Alternative vote (Australia)
  - Block vote (Singapore, Syria)
- Proportional representation (PR)
  - Party list (Netherlands, Israel, Brazil)
  - Single transferable vote (Ireland)
- Hybrids (Germany, Russia, Japan, Scottish Parliament, Welsh Assembly)

strong opposition and broadly based parties. It disadvantages extremist parties. On the other hand, it can exclude minorities and it can have the effect of restricting the number of women representatives. Also, in many constituencies, it can lead to a large number of 'wasted' votes for a candidate who has no realistic chance of being elected, thereby discouraging those voters from voting at all (Reynolds, Reilly, and Allis, 2007: 36–7). The figures from the last four British general elections are striking. In 2005, the Labour Party won the election with 35.2 per cent of the vote and 356 MPs. In 2010, the Conservative Party gained 36.1 per cent of votes, but only 306 seats (that is, more votes and fewer seats). In 2015, the Conservatives gained 36.9 per cent of votes and 331 seats (that is, even more votes than Labour in 2005, but still 25 fewer seats). In 2017, the Conservatives' share of the vote soared to 42.4 per cent, but they still won fewer seats (318) than Labour did in 2005. Similarly, in the Indian general election of 2014, the Hindu nationalist BJP Party won an outright majority with only 30 per cent of the votes (**see Case Study 12.3**).

Variants of this system can include multi-member constituencies, where voters either have as many votes as the required number of successful candidates, in which case this can produce even stronger majorities if people vote consistently for the same party, or they

 CASE STUDY 12.3   The Indian general election in 2014

The Indian general election in 2014 marked a turning point in Indian politics. Prior to the election, widespread expert expectations were that national politics would continue to suffer from paralysis caused by an 'inevitable' coalition government, with 35 parties contesting seats in the lower house of parliament, the Lok Sabha. However, with widespread voting on the basis of caste or regional identity rather than policies, the nationalist BJP Party, under Narendra Modi, won a stunning victory. For the first time since 1984, a party in India won an outright majority, gaining 282 seats out of 543. It also evidenced the possibility of first-past-the-post systems delivering majorities on a minority vote: the BJP won 52.9 per cent of seats with only 31.3 per cent of the vote. This was also the first time that the BJP had ever won more votes than the main opposition Indian National Congress (INC). Allied parties gained a further 61 seats. Their previous total combined with the BJP was 159 seats. Voter turnout was also very high, at 66 per cent, with voting spread over five weeks in different parts of the country.

In its electoral campaign, the BJP exploited widespread dissatisfaction with the ineffectiveness of the outgoing INC-led coalition, especially in its handling of the economy. The Party also made effective use of social media to popularize the image of its leader, Narendra Modi (Wyatt, 2015).

The BJP still faces considerable challenges in getting its legislation passed. Nevertheless, its triumph serves as a reminder of the way in which free elections, however imperfect, can bring about radical change in government without provoking the overthrow of the system.

12

have only one vote, in which case candidates can be elected with as little as 20 per cent of the vote, undermining their legitimacy. (An up-to-date list of countries practising these and all of the other alternative systems mentioned for their national legislatures can be found at https://www.idea.int/data-tools/data/electoral-system-design, accessed January 2018.)

The alternative principle is **proportional representation (PR)**, where the priority is to ensure an adequate representation of the range of public opinion, irrespective of whether it strengthens or weakens the cohesion of government that results from it. This can be important for new democracies in creating a wide sense of ownership of the system. It reduces the number of 'wasted' votes and favours minorities, but also encourages parties to spread their appeal beyond their core districts. It may contribute to greater stability of policy and make coalition agreements more visible, as is argued by Lijphart. On the other hand, it is more likely to lead to coalition governments and to fragmentation of the party system, with small parties able to negotiate a disproportionate say in policy-making—see the scathing condemnation of the effects of proportional representation in Israel by Asa-El (2008) later in this chapter. Holding coalition governments to account for individual decisions is more difficult under proportional representation (Reynolds, Reilly, and Allis, 2007: 58–9).

> See Chapter 11 for more on Lijphart and consociational democracy.

Since first-past-the-post and proportional representation systems tend to produce different kinds of outcome, each of which has much to commend them, a more recent trend has been for countries to adopt hybrids such as the **alternative member model**, with some seats elected on the basis of a simple majority and some on the basis of proportional representation. Germany, Japan, New Zealand, and Russia, for example, have all gone down this route, though a British referendum rejected it in 2011.

One alternative intermediate system is to hold two rounds of elections in constituencies where the first round does not produce an absolute majority. In the second round, the candidates are reduced to the two most successful alternatives, which prevents strategic voting and ensures that there is no doubt about the preference of the majority. France does this, as do many of its former African colonies, as well as Iran and several former republics of the Soviet Union.

Altogether, of the main types of electoral system, 70 states in the world have list proportional representation, 47 have first-past-the-post (plus 22 with two-round elections), and there are 21 hybrids (Reynolds, Reilly, and Allis, 2007: 32).

Colomer (2004) has argued that electoral change around the world has tended to take place in the direction of increasingly inclusive formulas, leading to fewer risks for the parties involved. This has meant a much greater tendency for electoral reform to move from majoritarian to mixed or proportional systems, rather than the reverse. His explanation is party self-interest: when threatened by challenges from newcomers, parties prefer to minimize the risk of complete extinction, which would be far greater under majoritarianism than by agreeing to a more PR-based system. This would offer greater opportunities for survival, albeit in somewhat reduced numbers of representatives elected (Colomer, 2004: 4, 58; Farrell, 2001: chs 7, 8). Dunleavy (2005) has argued that this process is now under way in Britain. The 2010 election showed that hung parliaments could happen in Britain, in part because increasing numbers of parties are winning seats. The same happened in 2017 for the opposite reason, as the Conservatives and Labour gained ground at the expense of the minor parties. However, the referendum in 2011 on the voting system reconfirmed popular preference for the majoritarian system and the two major parties still hanker after the majority that the majoritarian system might deliver for them.

 KEY POINTS

- The two main alternative voting systems widely used are first-past-the-post and proportional representation.
- Their outcomes tend to have different virtues: stronger government versus more representative government.
- There are hybrid or intermediate alternatives that attempt to mitigate the disadvantages of theoretically purer systems.
- Voting systems have a big impact upon party systems.

Functions of Legislatures

Norton (2013: 4) has pointed out a fundamental paradox about legislatures in the modern world: 'On the one hand, legislatures are in decline, yet on the other they are ubiquitous.' At present, there are 263 parliamentary chambers in 189 countries. This means that a little under a third of countries have two chambers. If we bear in mind the sub-national elected bodies that determine policies for more restricted areas, there are thousands of elected bodies around the world. It is no wonder that legislative studies is one of the oldest branches of political science. Within this potential diversity, there is a paradox about the main object of the studies. Gamm and Huber (2002: 313) present it clearly: 'The scholarly world of legislative studies is, overwhelmingly, a world that studies the US Congress. And the study of Congress tends to be the study of the postwar House of Representatives.' Yet this chapter will illustrate much of the diversity from around the world, not just the US.

Legislatures are crucial institutions in any political system, but above all in democracies. A democracy would be inconceivable without a parliament. They are vital elements in the structures of power within the state and they usually, though to varying degrees, act as checks upon the freedom of manoeuvre of the state executive. Without legislatures, power in the modern state would be highly concentrated and potentially oppressive. They are essential in upholding constitutions because they can publicize attempts to subvert them and they can support the courts if the executive attempts to undermine or suspend them.

There are two ways of presenting a comparative overview of legislatures, as indeed is the case for most political institutions. One way is to focus upon the functions that they perform.

See Chapter 10 for a discussion of strong states and weak states.

12

In that sense, they, or the actors who devised them, are responding to a perceived need in the political system. The second way is to concentrate upon institutional arrangements that are common, so as to show their similarities and differences (in this case, debating chambers, standing committees, how members of staff run their offices and handle links with constituents, and so on). We shall largely concentrate on the former type of exposition—the functional—but in Chapter 14 we will examine one particular institutional issue: the differences between parliamentary and presidential political systems and their respective merits.

The functions of parliaments can be divided into three broad groupings. First, there are the representational functions, where parliaments either represent the views of citizens or are representative of particular groups in society. Second, there are governmental functions: legislatures contribute to forming governments, formulating policy, ensuring the accountability of government for its actions, and enhancing government communication with citizens. Third, there are procedural functions that determine the procedures under which legislatures do their work (Olson, 1994).

Representation

See Chapter 10 for a discussion of the rise of the European state system.

12

The original function of parliaments in Europe was to provide a forum where different classes in society could express their views to the monarch on matters of public concern. Their role was purely consultative. There was no sense that parliaments could decide policy, let alone impose their will on monarchs. Gradually, however, they acquired greater authority as rulers saw fit to consult them when needing to raise taxes for public works, most importantly for raising armies. Thus not only did the European state grow in response to the needs of war, as suggested in Chapter 10, but also parliaments did so as a means of constraining the ability of monarchs to make war.

Inherent in parliaments, therefore, is the notion that they are representative of wider society. To be legitimate they have to 'represent' the people. However, over time, different dimensions of possible representativeness have been proposed. In practice, these are difficult to reconcile, not least because the composition of parliaments is also inevitably intertwined with the electoral system on which they are based. So states with different histories and different national priorities may arrive at different institutional solutions to the same problem.

Does representation mean that deputies should be numerically representative of particular sections of society, as were originally the Houses of Lords and Commons in the UK? Should the numbers of women representatives roughly correspond to the number of women in the population as a whole? What about ethnic minorities? One perspective on this is offered by Jacobson (1997). He points out that in, the US Congress, the black and Hispanic population is under-represented, though the disparity between share of population and share of representatives is not as great as in the case of women—but Jacobson (1997: 2007) condones this with a different slant on representation: 'Congress is probably quite representative of the kinds of people who achieve positions of leadership in the great majority of American institutions. What it does produce is a sample of local elites from a remarkably diverse nation.' Election to Congress is certainly an elite achievement, and so it would be both more appropriate and realistic for members of Congress to be representative of elites rather than the population as a whole. This was not, however, an explicit objective of the Founding Fathers. Rather, it is a rationalization.

A more recent trend has been to actively seek to make the composition of legislators correspond more exactly to the basic structure of the population as a whole. Most obviously, this has concerned the proportion of women in parliaments.

In that respect, communist regimes were more 'representative' than states in the West because members of their parliaments were statistically fairly representative of broad sections of society. However, in recent years, there has been an active movement around the world to increase the proportion of women in national legislatures in democracies. There are now at least 40 countries that have introduced quotas for women representatives in legislatures, while in a further 50 countries political parties have adopted quotas for women candidates for election (Dahlerup, 2005: 145). At present, there is still a long way to go before such quotas will be achieved, for reasons that Matland (2005) and Dahlerup (2005) have discussed. Nevertheless, it is likely to increase pressure for measures to be adopted to raise the recruitment of people from other groups in society that are also regularly underrepresented. In that case, at least in democracies, legislatures will undergo major transformation in the coming decades.

See Chapter 13 for a discussion of party systems.

Or should 'representation' rather refer, as suggested in Chapter 3, to the role of deputies in expressing the views of their constituents? In that case, the personal characteristics of individual deputies are less important. Representation is then taken to be an expressive function. Whoever is a member of parliament expresses views on behalf of others. That person is understood to be a channel of communication to those in authority. This leaves open the question as to how far a representative is obliged simply to express the views of a larger community of citizens and how far that representative has the freedom to express personal opinions or come to individual judgements. In practice, representatives will always have some freedom to do the latter, but, as we have seen in Chapter 4, the view that they are positively entitled to exercise their individual judgement is associated with Edmund Burke and with the practice of the House of Commons (**see Key Quote 12.4**).

See Chapter 4 for a discussion of representative democracy.

12

Some other parliamentary systems adopt a more restrictive view and enshrine the principle of recall, whereby electors can 'recall' their representatives, or rather delegates, either to be replaced or to face re-election for failure to adequately represent the views of their constituents. Sometimes, this is referred to as the 'trustee' system (representatives are the trustees of their electors). This is a principle instituted by the French National Assembly after the Revolution. It subsequently became part of the socialist tradition, so that deputies in communist and some socialist states such as China and Cuba are liable to recall if a significant number of their electors conclude that the deputy has failed to carry out the mandate. Such a provision would guard against deputies elected on a one-party ticket subsequently moving to another party without

> ### Q KEY QUOTE 12.4   Burke on the relationship between an MP and his constituents
>
> 'Certainly, Gentlemen, it ought to be the happiness and glory of a Representative, to live in the strictest union, the closest correspondence, and the most unreserved communication with his constituents . . . But, his unbiased opinion, his mature judgement, his enlightened conscience, he ought not to sacrifice to you; to any man, or to any set of men living . . . Your Representative owes you, not his industry only, but his judgement; and he betrays, instead of serving you, if he sacrifices it to your opinion.
>
> Parliament is not a *Congress* of Ambassadors from different and hostile interests; which interests each must maintain, as an Agent and Advocate, against other Agents and Advocates; but Parliament is a *deliberative* Assembly of *one* Nation, with one Interest, that of the whole; where, not local Purposes, not local Prejudices ought to guide, but the general Good, resulting from the general Reason of the whole. You chose a Member indeed; but when you have chosen him, he is not Member of Bristol, but he is a Member of *Parliament*.' (Burke, 1996: 68–9, emphasis original)

resubmitting themselves to the electorate for approval. Populist regimes too are attracted by this idea because they are wary of representatives frustrating the 'sovereign will' of the people (see Chapter 16).

On the other hand, many states enshrine the principle of parliamentary immunity to protect the right of deputies to speak out without fear of prosecution or threat of libel proceedings for what they may say in parliament. This also means that, occasionally, individuals will seek election as a way of preventing, or at any rate postponing, prosecution for some criminal act. In the 2014 Indian general elections, for example, a third of all deputies elected to the Lok Sabha had criminal records or pending prosecutions; for a fifth, this involved serious crimes such as murder, kidnapping, and robbery. In fact, acquiring a reputation for doing whatever it takes to promote the interests of constituents (for example against the national government), even if it involves criminality or consorting with criminals, can powerfully mobilize voters in India (Vaishnav, 2017)—as it used to do in Italy.

Another key question is: who are a particular deputy's electors? In general, most parliaments enshrine the principle of a direct link between an elected representative and a particular district within the country. There are a few exceptions (for example Israel, Peru, and the Netherlands) where voters in a single national constituency choose between the lists of candidates offered by different parties, so that those elected accurately represent the national preferences of the people. This ensures that members of parliament are proportionately representative. On the other hand, critics of the Israeli system have alleged that this proportionality has exacerbated the difficulties of forming a government, since it concedes excessive power to small parties, which makes executive policy-making extremely fraught. According to Amotz Asa-El (2008), a former editor of the *Jerusalem Post*:

Israel maintains the most extreme model of the proportional electoral system and the results are nothing short of disastrous. This system has been depleting Israel's political energies for decades: it radicalised the territorial debate, debilitated the economy, obstructed long-term planning, derailed government action, distracted cabinets, diverted budgets, weakened prime ministers, destabilised governments, enabled anonymous and often incompetent people to achieve positions of great influence and responsibility and blurred the distinctions between the executive and legislative branches of government. Perhaps most crucially, it has led talented, accomplished, moral and charismatic people to abandon the political arena.

We have already discussed the relative merits of plurality versus proportional representation systems. What is important to note here is the effect of the combination of a solely national constituency, proportional representation, and a low threshold for parties to be allowed to take up seats: they only need to win 2 per cent of votes to do so in Israel, though it should be remembered that the Netherlands has the lowest threshold in the world, at 0.67 per cent, and the same fragmentation and polarization does not seem to occur there. According to Asa-El (2008), an essential element in reform will be the linking of at least some Knesset seats with specific constituencies within Israel. This will increase the incentives for representatives to focus on local issues that are of concern to voters. At present, its members allegedly pay scant attention to the type of local issues that are the staple of constituency politics in other countries. On the other hand, in Israel, a wide range of minority views are represented in parliament. If nothing else, this does avoid the risk of neglecting the views of minorities that are not geographically concentrated in a few places so that their local representatives have to listen to them.

For most states, the connection between an individual representative and the people whom (s)he represents in a territorial constituency is regarded as an essential contribution to the legitimacy of parliament. This is held to be so even though it may lead to other distortions in the way in which the people's overall views are represented. However, this raises another set of questions. Is there an optimal size for a constituency? How similar in size should they be? Further, who should be responsible for redrawing constituency boundaries as population concentrations change? Most European states assign this responsibility to public officials, but in the US the boundaries of districts for the House of Representatives are determined by incumbents (though California has recently transferred this power to an independent commission). This no doubt contributes to the fact that between 80 and 90 per cent of House races are won by incumbents. This has favoured the Republicans at least there, because their supporters are more 'efficiently' distributed across various kinds of constituencies, where Democrats are more concentrated into urban areas (McCarty, Poole, and Rosenthal, 2009; Jacobson, 2013).

The size of constituencies, and the redrawing of their boundaries to reflect demographic changes in their population so as to ensure rough parity between different constituencies, is always a highly contentious issue. In England, the maximum disparity in size between parliamentary constituencies is roughly two to one—largely because of the unique size of

12

the Isle of Wight (Boundary Commission for England, 2007: 482–3). Otherwise, it would be a great deal more even. In Wales, there is only a disparity of one-and-a-half times, but in Scotland, it is three-and-a-half times, because of a special requirement that the Orkney and the Shetland Islands form distinct constituencies. The effect of this is to create even greater disparity within Britain as a whole. The disparity between the Isle of Wight and Na h-Eileanan an Iar (a constituency in the Outer Hebrides) is roughly five to one. To reduce it, the Conservative government in 2015 announced its intention to cut the number of constituencies from 650 to 600 for elections from 2018 onwards.

In Japan, by the end of the 1970s, urban areas had nearly four times as many eligible voters as rural areas in elections to the lower house of the parliament, the Diet. Since then, the disparity has been halved by redrawing boundaries to roughly the same level as England. But for the upper house, the House of Councillors, there is still a disparity of over five times between different prefectures (Stockwin, 1999: 128–9).

One of the most extreme manifestations of this problem is in the US Senate, where there is an even greater disparity between states over the number of eligible voters, though there is greater equality between House districts. The US Constitution grants two senators to each state of the union, irrespective of size. The consequence is that now Wyoming, the state with the smallest population, has the same number of senators as California, the state with the largest population, even though California's population is 72 times larger. Even though the cumulative effect of this principle is that smaller (often more rural) states have a disproportionate impact on Senate voting, because together they can mobilize a much greater proportion of votes there than their combined populations would warrant, there is no prospect of this being changed, because to do so would require a constitutional amendment and the smaller states can muster enough votes to prevent it.

KEY POINTS

- Members of parliament represent wider society, most often through the means of territorial districts.
- Part of their legitimacy is based upon the assumption that they are also representative of society.
- The extent and ways to which they are 'representative', however, is contentious and varies from one state to another.
- The introduction of quotas to increase recruitment of women in parliament may lead to measures to do the same for other groups under-represented there.

Apart from the responsibility of forming governments, parliaments have three other functions: formulating legislation, ensuring governmental accountability, and forming public opinion.

Legislation

An alternative term for parliament is legislature (that is, the supreme law-giver in society). It is the national legislature that determines the final shape of laws, although, as we saw in Chapter 11, in most states this is now qualified by the need to respect international legal conventions; in many, by the practice of judicial review. To some extent, this legal function also helps to explain the relative frequency with which elected representatives have been trained as lawyers. In the US, which reserves a very prominent role for the law in public affairs (as we saw in Chapter 11), roughly 40 per cent of House members were lawyers in the mid-1990s, while the equivalent figure for senators was 54 per cent (Jacobson, 1997: 207). In 2015, 14 per cent of British MPs were lawyers, representing a slight increase in the average of 11–12 per cent elected over the previous 30 years, but in 1979 and 1983, roughly 15 per cent were lawyers (Hunter and Holden, 2015; McGuinness, 2010).

See the discussion in Chapter 11 on the growing legalization of political life.

In practice, however, it is the executive that is the chief initiator of legislation. According to Olson (1994: 134), there is a common experience around the world that 90 per cent of new legislation originates in the executive, rather than in parliament, and that 90 per cent of that is adopted. Thus, in India, the national parliament has not passed a single private member's bill since 1968 (Pai and Kumar, 2014: 17). This phenomenon is true even of the US, where the executive cannot, on its own, introduce proposed new legislation into Congress; it needs to find sympathetic members of the House or Senate to do so. The picture is more complicated for members of the European Union (EU), where member states have to introduce national legislation to give force to decisions agreed in Brussels. According to a report from the House of Commons Library (Vaughne, 2010), roughly 6.8 per cent of all statutes and 14.1 per cent of all statutory instruments passed by the UK Parliament had a role in implementing European obligations, but the proportion rose to around 50 per cent for legislation 'with a significant economic impact', above all in agriculture. It also commented that, for other EU members, the proportion ranged from 6.3 per cent to 84 per cent, though directly comparable statistics were not available. Of course, national parliaments in the EU also approve a lot of regulations that are not technically new legislation, but which represent an updating (and sometimes expansion) of legislation passed in the past. All this means that, today, national legislatures primarily respond to initiatives that originate elsewhere.

See the discussion in Chapter 11 of legal adjudication in political life.

12

Ensuring accountability

Parliaments, especially in democracies, hold the government to account for its actions. This is particularly important as a way of ensuring that governments honour the commitments that they made to the public when seeking election. It strengthens the incentive for credible commitments and hence increases the chances of a government being replaced at the next election for failure to keep its promises. But even in authoritarian regimes where this is unlikely, parliaments can hold executives to account. According to Olson (1994: 143–4), even under authoritarianism it is difficult for the executive always to control the legislature. He cites as examples the growing activism of the Brazilian Congress under military rule in the 1970s and 1980s, and of the Sejm under martial law in Poland in the 1980s. Another example is China. There, the National People's Congress only meets for two weeks per year and thus performs more of a symbolic function as far as legislation is concerned. However, in recent years, it has become an increasingly vocal critic of the policies of individual ministries, while refraining from criticizing the government, and therefore the regime, as a whole. In particular, it has cast votes condemning inadequate government action to deal with issues such as corruption and crime. Thus simply having parliaments can strengthen trends towards democracy over time.

It should be noted, however, that parliaments are not the only institutions that hold the executive to account. In most states, the media also perform this role, whether or not they are explicitly recognized by the state, as we shall see in Chapter 15. Also, within the executive, there are institutions that keep a check on what other executive agencies do—what O'Donnell (2003) called 'horizontal accountability', which he contrasted with the 'vertical accountability' performed by parliaments. Examples of such agencies are audit offices, such as the National Audit Office in the UK, which check on government spending. In practice, all of these institutions contribute to the accountability of government and they often cooperate with each other.

Formation of public attitudes

A fourth function of legislatures is to contribute to the formation of public opinion and often to set the agenda for public debate. This is an expansion of the role of representing the views of the people to government. Here, parliaments take the lead in forming public opinion, as well as providing a forum. Obviously, in an era of mass communications in which the media play such a role in informing the public about issues of the day, the role of parliaments in this respect is more circumscribed than it was in the nineteenth century, when debates in parliament were reckoned to set the agenda for public debate. Nevertheless, there are issues—for example moral ones, such as abortion, or environmental ones, such as genetically modified foods—where parliamentary debates play a key role in forming public opinion, although the line between parliament forming public opinion and representing it becomes fuzzy. Debates in parliament and in parliamentary committees are regularly reported in the media. In North America, the C-Span and CPAC cable networks are devoted full-time to coverage of the US Congress and Canadian parliament. Some parliaments, such as the Bundestag and the Dutch and Scottish Parliaments, have attempted to take advantage of new communications technologies such as the Internet to stimulate public debate over current affairs. This was an attempt to develop a more reflexive approach to policy-making in society at large—the sort of deliberative democracy discussed in Chapter 4—although it seems to have had only limited success.

Another way in which parliaments can stimulate public debate in politics can be observed in Sweden. There members of parliament regularly meet with advisory commis-

▶ See Chapter 4 for a discussion of deliberative democracy.

12

sions to formulate legislative proposals. This acts as a constraint on both the executive and the sovereignty of parliament, but it does help to ensure a wider range of views are involved in the legislative process, which should lead to better legislation (Olson, 1994: 135).

 KEY POINTS

- Today, parliaments mostly respond to initiatives for policy that originate from elsewhere in the political system—primarily, the executive.
- Parliaments provide a means for holding governments to account for their election promises.
- Parliaments also provide a forum for national debate.

Procedural

There are also three procedural functions that legislatures perform.

Ritualizing conflict

Parliamentary activities help to ritualize conflict. They function on the basis of debate (that is, the expression of differing views). To that extent, they legitimize diversity of views and its expression. In the Iranian parliament, for instance, though access to it is restricted to religious parties because secular ones are banned, what would otherwise be in danger of being condemned as factionalism conducted by dissident groups acquires greater respectability or legitimacy (Baktiari, 1996). Critics of democracy sometimes allege that parliaments exacerbate divisions in society by providing opportunities for dissenting opinions to be expressed. It is true that Westminster-type parliaments formalize the role of official opposition to the government. This often, it is alleged, forces the parties not in government into excessive confrontation, further exacerbated by the seating arrangements that have the government and opposition facing each other at a distance of a little over two swords' lengths. In some states such as Taiwan, national legislators exploit the media coverage of their debates to establish a partisan image that will help their chances of re-election, for example occasionally throwing lunch boxes at each other to dramatize the differences between them and their opponents to attract TV attention.

A response to this is that all societies have a plurality of opinions on any issue and parliament only reflects that. As far as seating arrangements are concerned, a more common arrangement is for the members of parliament to be arrayed in a semi-circle facing the speaker in a debate, as in European parliaments and the US Congress. Where dissension is particularly extreme, parliaments can help to resolve disputes that might otherwise take a more violent turn. In that sense, they 'routinize' conflict, and even though members of parliaments sometimes use parliamentary debate to rouse public opinion in pursuit of

12

extremist goals, it does not mean that parliaments by nature manufacture conflict. Often, they can tame its excesses.

Partisanship

Although it occasionally happens that independent members are elected to parliament, in the overwhelming majority of cases legislators represent political parties, as well as territorial constituencies. Even in the Chinese National People's Congress, where roughly two-thirds of deputies are members of the Chinese Communist Party, the remaining third have to be approved by the Party and are expected to support the regime. Unlike the judiciary, members of parliament are expected to hold partisan ideologies that structure their overall views on political issues and priorities. This fact reinforces the role of parliaments as debating chambers out of which better legislation emerges.

Transparency

Parliaments are generally committed to openness, to publicizing issues and policies. A parliament that kept its deliberations secret would make no sense—as was the case with the Supreme Soviet in Stalin's time. It would have purely symbolic value. Although debates in parliaments in authoritarian regimes may publish only edited versions of debates, rather than full transcripts, they still contribute to some extent to the publicizing of important issues. They make policy-making somewhat more open. The publication of verbatim transcripts of all their deliberations obviously does this even more. All this contributes to the more open resolution of disagreements in society and thus to its stability. However, this is a problem in societies that are most accustomed to more traditional, possibly more consensual, styles of decision-making. It certainly comes as a shock to politicians who are more used to negotiating deals only behind the scenes. The greater openness can be used to embarrass politicians. It upsets and changes political culture, as any Chinese or Arab leader will acknowledge.

 12

> **KEY POINTS**
>
> - Parliaments assume diversity of opinions and ritualize political disputes.
> - They assume that legislators have partisan opinions.
> - They also contribute to open policy-making and dispute resolution.

Types of Legislature

As will be obvious, legislatures vary considerably not only in their powers, but also in their relations with the surrounding political and societal structures. Mezey (1990) produced an influential typology of legislatures to try to identify the range of their possible operations, which is still regarded as relevant today (Marschall, 2015). He proposed a fivefold classification based upon the principle of the capacity of a legislature to stand up to the executive.

1. *Active* legislatures, such as the US Congress, which is at the centre of the political system and genuinely does have the power to say 'no' to the president as often as it feels necessary.

2. *Reactive* legislatures, such as the House of Commons, as well as such parliaments as those of France, Germany, India, Sweden, and Japan—Here, the legislature has less power to withstand the government, but it can set firm parameters within which the government has to act and it can impose sanctions on a government that infringes them.

3. *Vulnerable* legislatures, such as the Philippines—Here, the legislature is much more pliant, in part because of local political culture that tolerates, or at any rate acquiesces, in legislators pursuing their own material interests. In Italy, the legislature has been more vulnerable because of the difficulties of forming stable coalition governments.

4. *Marginal* legislatures, such as Pakistan, Peru, Nigeria, and Russia under Putin—While these legislatures do perform important legislative functions, they enjoy much more tentative support from social elites. At times, the executive has decided that it can do without the legislature and the latter has been unable to resist.

5. *Minimal* legislatures—Here, the examples primarily came from communist states, which met rarely and served the purposes more of symbolizing national unity and regime legitimacy than of exercising any check upon the government. This is still largely true of the National People's Congress in China and the Vietnamese National Assembly.

12

More recently, Fish and Kroenig (2011) have offered a quantitative comparison of the relative powers of parliaments around the world, based upon their formal powers vis-à-vis the rest of the political system. The strongest and weakest parliaments are listed in **Table 12.2**—but note that these scores were calculated before more recent major political changes in Libya, Myanmar, and Turkey.

In general, they show that the most powerful parliaments tend to be found in Europe, while the least powerful ones are in the Middle East.

Lastly, we should mention a parliament of a special type—namely, the European Parliament. This is an institution in evolution, just as the EU itself is. Originally a mainly consultative institution composed of delegates from the parliaments of the member states, it has developed a life of its own, with members elected directly from each member state. In general, it has equal powers of legislation with the European Council of Ministers, who represent the individual member states (though there are some areas where one or the other has primacy). In that sense, the two institutions could be seen as a special kind of

TABLE 12.2   The strongest and weakest parliaments around the world

Strongest		Weakest	
Germany	0.84	Bhutan	0.22
Italy	0.84	Chad	0.22
Mongolia	0.84	Jordan	0.22
Czech Republic	0.81	Qatar	0.22
Macedonia	0.81	Bahrain	0.19
Bulgaria	0.78	Oman	0.16
Croatia	0.78	North Korea	0.13
Denmark	0.78	Libya	0.13
Latvia	0.78	Saudi Arabia	0.09
Lithuania	0.78	Turkmenistan	0.06
Netherlands	0.78	UAE	0.06
Turkey	0.78	Myanmar	0
UK	0.78	Somalia	0

Note: 1 = all-powerful; 0 = powerless.
Source: Fish and Kroenig (2011: 756–7).

bicameral. And, under the Lisbon Treaty, the European Parliament approves the composition of the European Commission and can dismiss it with a vote of no confidence. However, this power is relatively limited, in that the Commission is also responsible to the individual member states, who ultimately have to agree upon its overall finances. The president of the Parliament is a member of the troika of officials who represent the EU to outsiders, along with the presidents of the Commission and Council of Ministers. Its members in general want to expand its powers vis-à-vis the Commission, but the Commission is not accountable to the Parliament in the way that executives are in national democracies, though the Parliament can certainly embarrass the Commission by publicizing issues where it disagrees. It has been suggested that one way forward for the EU would be to see the Parliament as part of a tricameral European legislature, where the other two chambers would be the Council of Ministers and the parliaments of the member states (Cooper, 2013), though this would be an extremely complex and potentially cumbersome body. Others speculate about the evolution of the EU into a more conventional presidential or parliamentary system (Marschall, 2015), but either is still a very distant prospect.

KEY POINTS

- Legislatures can be classified according to the extent to which they can impose their will upon the executive.
- The factors that contribute to this capability derive both from internal factors and the broader political and social context.
- The European Parliament is a special type of transnational legislature, the functions and powers of which are slowly evolving.

The Structure of Legislatures

Now let us turn to two structural features of the way in which parliaments work.

Unicameral/bicameral

As mentioned at the beginning of this chapter, roughly a third of parliaments around the world have two chambers. Thus one major issue in establishing a parliament concerns whether to have one (unicameralism) or two (bicameralism) chambers. As of 2017, there were 77 bicameral parliaments (40 per cent) and 116 unicameral ones (60 per cent) (IPU, 2017). In practice, there is enormous variety in the arrangements that individual nations make to order the relations between two chambers where this occurs. As of the late 1990s, out of 61 second chambers only 19 were composed exclusively of directly elected members. Fifteen were hybrids, with mixed memberships of the directly elected and the nominated, while the remaining 27 contained no directly elected members (including the House of Lords). Within these three subcategories, there is still room for enormous variety in the ways in which the second chambers are constituted (for details, see Patterson and Mughan, 1999: 6–7). Within this variety, it is possible to identify four sorts of factors underlying them. The first is tradition. In the past, two chambers allowed for the separate representation of different sections of society—usually, the aristocrats in one and the ordinary people in the other. They have generally survived even in the context of a modernizing society, though Denmark took the decision to abolish its upper chamber in 1953 and Sweden did the same in 1959.

The second reason for an upper house often has to do with federalism. The places in it are set aside for representatives from the next lower level of government. This serves as a guarantee to them that their wishes will not be ignored by the national government. It reassures them that they do not need to contemplate leaving the union.

The third reason is the likelihood that it will lead to better representation of minorities. This is especially important in a large and diverse state like India, though even then there are huge problems. In the Indian upper house (the Rajya Sabha), the ratio of seats to voters is 1:200,000 (Sivaramakrishnan and Joshi, 2014: 107).

See Chapter 11 for a discussion of federalism.

12

The fourth reason is the expectation that it will lead to better legislation (Tsebelis and Money, 1997). This is explained in two ways. On the one hand, there is the rationale of efficiency in terms of legislation. The need for legislation to be scrutinized in two chambers, rather than one, should lead to it being better fit for purpose—what Patterson and Mughan (1999: 12–16) call the principle of 'redundancy'. It allows for a second opinion on the best form of a particular law. The other reason for expecting better legislation is that the need for legislation to satisfy two chambers increases the likelihood that the final outcome will better approximate to the wishes of the population at large (which may be difficult to determine definitively given the difficulties of establishing societal preferences, as suggested by the Arrow impossibility theorem, as discussed earlier in this chapter, especially if the two chambers have been elected or selected according to different principles or at different times). Both principles resonate with the concern expressed in 1788 by Madison in *Federalist Papers 62* about the need to prevent overhasty, too subjective legislation.

According to Tsebelis and Money (1997: 4–5), the existence of one or two chambers of parliament makes little difference to the relations between the legislature and the executive, but it obviously does affect the legislative process. This largely depends on the specific powers of the two chambers and the rules that they adopt for regulating the process by which they achieve agreements. Most constitutions give greater powers to one chamber than to the other, especially where control of the government budget is concerned. This obviously determines the way in which the two houses achieve compromise in cases of disagreement. Italy is the exception that proves the rule: there, the Senate and the Chamber of Deputies have co-equal powers. This obviously complicates the negotiation of agreements, adding to the paralysis of Italian government, although it has been successful in preventing the return of a fascist dictatorship, as it was intended to do. Prime Minister Renzi called a referendum in 2016 to try to give greater power to the Chamber of Deputies, but it was rejected, in what was interpreted as a vote against the political establishment, and he resigned.

But even where one chamber is more powerful than the other, the need to find compromises still regularly affects the final version of laws. Even if one chamber lacks the power to veto proposals (as does the UK's House of Lords at present), the process of trying to achieve compromise will affect at least some legislative outcomes. The mechanism used to achieve this compromise will also affect the outcome: is it a joint committee of both houses, or does a bill have to be considered by full sessions of each chamber? And, in both cases, what kind of majority is needed? All this makes a difference.

Committees

On average, the UK's House of Commons has sat for about 150 days per year since 1945 (House of Commons Library, 2016). During 2000–10, the Indian parliament sat for around 73 days per year (Pai and Kumar, 2014: 14). In general, members of parliament often spend more time in parliamentary committees than in the debating chamber. This is because most of the detailed consideration of proposed legislation is carried out in ad hoc committees convened to consider particular bills. In addition, most parliaments also establish permanent committees to effect regular scrutiny of the workings of individual ministries—though India only began to do this after 1993. They often interrogate ministers and senior officials, and sometimes hold inquiries into particular issues of policy that the members think worthy of consideration or reconsideration. As some of the committee members may have long experience of parliament and government, they may be very knowledgeable about particular policy areas, in which case they can embarrass ministers, or even the government as a whole. For legislators from parties not in government, this can be a very useful way of weakening the popularity of the party or parties in power and thereby establishing their own credibility as alternatives. It is also another way of parliament fulfilling its functions of the formation of public opinion and the visibility of policy-making. However, beyond that, parliaments differ considerably in their committee arrangements. Some parliaments, such as the German and Swedish, allow these parliamentary committees to propose legislation to the house as a whole, whereas this cannot happen at Westminster. In France, there are a few, large, permanent committees that divide into ad hoc committees to consider specific bills.

 KEY POINTS

- Bicameralism may offer the prospect of better legislation that corresponds more closely to the preferences of the population, but it is more time-consuming.
- The procedures for resolving disagreements between two chambers will affect the particular legislative outcomes.
- Most parliamentary work is done in committees of the legislature.

12

Legislators

Now let us turn to some common features of those securing election as legislators. In democracies, as has been explained above, there is a presumption that members of parliament are representative of the population at large. This is true in only the most general terms, for most people obviously do not stand for election to parliament. In general, legislators tend to be male, better educated than the average citizen, and to come from the middle class (even if they represent socialist parties).

In fact, commentators have remarked on a growing tendency in Western states for the emergence of a political 'class'. The term was originally coined at the end of the nineteenth century by Gaetano Mosca, the Italian political scientist who was mentioned in Chapter 1. By this he meant, as Oborne (2007: 24) explains, a group that is 'self-interested, self-aware and dependent for its economic and moral status on the resources of the state'. However, according to Oborne, it did not fit the reality of that time very well, because there were significant external checks upon political figures and because the resources of the state were not so easily bent to serve them. Now, however, he argues: 'The Political Class has won its battle to control Britain . . . In an unannounced takeover of power, the public domain has been seized by the Political Class' (Oborne, 2007: 310). Nor is this argument made about Britain alone. Rizzo and Stella (2007) have made much the same claim about Italian politics, where they stigmatize 'an oligarchy of insatiable Brahmins'. As we shall see in Chapter 16, populist 'anti-politicians' across Europe have increasingly sought to exploit the term 'political class' as a way of discrediting rivals.

Academics, as well as journalists, have begun to make use of the same concept. Borchert (2003: 6), for instance, introduced the term in a study of most OECD countries and explained it as meaning the political class that 'lives off politics' and acts as a 'class for itself'. Actually, as Borchert emphasizes (2003: 16), the concept is bound to be fuzzy at the edges when applied to individual countries. It is clear that it includes legislators and elected members of lower-level public councils, as well as employees of political parties—but should it apply to judges who are publicly elected, as in the US and Germany? Also, what about party nominees on the boards of state-owned companies in many states of Europe? Clearly, therefore, it will be difficult to achieve full comparability.

▶ See the discussion in Chapter 10 on strong states and weak states.

Nevertheless, this term has analytical utility and potentially much wider comparative application. As we have already seen in Chapter 10, accounts of politics in African states also typically emphasize the widespread pursuit of politics for the purposes of making money (Bayart, 1993; Chabal and Daloz, 1999). So the term could be used as the basis for wider comparative studies. What Borchert and his colleagues also highlight is a more recent phenomenon specific to OECD democracies—namely, the emergence of a category of political professionals who are skilled in the arts of winning elections, whether as candidates or working for candidates, and who have never had another career. In earlier periods, members of parliament included a much higher proportion of people for whom politics was their second or third career, people who had had a wider experience of life, which they then brought to their legislative activity. This is no longer so common and it is now often regarded as a defect.

This trend is not uniform and it has national specifics in the way in which it operates. In Japan and Ireland, for instance, a surprisingly high proportion of members of the national parliament are the children of older legislators who used to hold the same constituency. In Japan, the figure had risen to 28 per cent of deputies to the Lower House of the Diet in 2003 (Usui and Colignon, 2004: 408–9); in Ireland, the figure remained fairly constant between 22 and 25 per cent between 1992 and 2002, and the proportion of candidates from 'political families' went up for the principal parties in the 2011 election (Gallagher et al., 2003: 114; Gallagher and Marsh, 2011: 65). This certainly suggests class-like characteristics, but does not seem to be replicated in other countries, though there certainly are individual cases of parliamentary seats passing from father to child in other countries. The income of political professionals varies considerably from one country to another. To some extent, that reflects different degrees of self-interest on the part of politicians in different countries.

If this trend towards increasing professionalization of political careers is regarded as problematic, it remains doubtful whether any specific measures can be proposed to reverse or change it. Sutherland (2004) suggested that an alternative would be random selection of individuals for service in parliaments, just as juries are chosen, arguing that it is especially appropriate for British conditions. Actually, this approach resembles the one adopted in the short-lived Paris Commune of 1871, which then had a great influence on the world socialist movement. The Bolsheviks in Russia initially attempted to establish something similar in October 1917, but the rapid onset of civil war then undid it. It still has iconic significance for some socialists. Nevertheless, while it certainly might seem fairer, it is not clear that this would preserve legislative professionalism or that it would, in practice, enable parliament to stand up to a much more experienced government. A succession of inexperienced members of parliament would make it easy for the executive to mislead them or conceal things from them.

 KEY POINTS

- There is an increasing trend of professionalization of political representatives.
- Some have alleged that this has already led to the emergence of a 'political class'.

Conclusion

Finally, let us consider the regard in which parliaments are held by their citizenry. It might be expected that parliaments elected by the people would enjoy broad popular support, especially in democracies with free and fair elections, yet the World Values Surveys suggest differently. To some extent, democratic citizens are more suspicious of their representatives. In the most recent round carried out in 60 countries in 2010–14, there was an enormous range of answers to the question on the confidence that people had in their parliament, as can be seen from **Table 12.3**.

What this shows is a tendency for people in countries in the developing world to have greater confidence in their parliaments than citizens in the developed world. Often, it is the case that people in authoritarian systems have greater confidence in their parliament than do citizens in democracies. The World Values Surveys also asked questions about confidence in other institutions. Overall, the average around the world for those with confidence in parliament was lower than that for national governments (46 per cent) and the press (43 per cent), but more than political parties (29 per cent).

While this does not suggest a great challenge to the existence of parliaments, it does suggest widespread scepticism about either how parliaments or how politicians operate, or both. Arora (2003: 36) has remarked on the public image of the Indian parliament being 'at a very low ebb'—and this for a country where the World Values Survey showed a relatively high

12

TABLE 12.3   Confidence in parliaments*

Uzbekistan	85	Turkey	54
Qatar	85	Germany	44
China	77	Japan	20
Singapore	76	US	20
Bahrain	72	Romania	15
Malaysia	69	Peru	12
Kazakhstan	67	Poland	11
Rwanda	65	Slovenia	6
Azerbaijan	64	**Average**	**38**
Philippines	60		

* Proportion of respondents in various countries answering 'a great deal of confidence' or 'quite a lot of confidence' to the question 'How much confidence do you have in parliament?'
Source: http://www.worldvaluessurvey.org/WVSOnline.jsp, V117 (accessed August 2017).

level of public confidence, at 57 per cent. At the same time, we should also bear in mind Norton's (1998: 190) comment on legislatures in Western Europe. He observed that the fundamental relationship between the legislature and the executive is determined by factors external to the legislature—the constitution, the political culture, the state of the economy, and so on. Therefore, when people criticize parliaments, they are often in reality complaining about something else. Mainwaring (2006) concluded something similar from a series of studies of the legislatures in the five Andean states of Bolivia, Colombia, Ecuador, Peru, and Venezuela. He and other collaborators chose this region because it has a particularly low level of public confidence in parliaments by world standards, as well as those of Latin America—and this was despite the fact that all the countries in the region had experienced a widening and deepening of representation over the previous 30 years. His conclusion was that this lack of confidence was primarily the result of popular perceptions of broader deficiencies in the political system as a whole. The economies had failed to develop and so had standards of living. There were also serious problems with corruption. Thus the popular lack of confidence in legislatures reflected a deeper dissatisfaction with the failure of the political system as a whole to deliver a better quality of life to the people. While it is true that sovereign parliaments in democracies have, in principle, the power to change government in ways that the people want, they may not, in practice, be able to achieve the changes that people would want. Institutions such as the judiciary or the military, even if corrupt, may resist political pressure. Thus assessments of legislatures are inseparable from assessments of the political system as a whole. Almost all of these Andean states can be included in the category of 'weak states' presented in Chapter 10: 'Better state performance is key to promoting greater confidence in the institutions of representative democracy and greater satisfaction with democracy' (Mainwaring, 2006: 331). Policy implementation is as important as policy formulation. Chapter 14 will go on to consider ways in which states formulate policies.

? Key Questions

- What are the relative strengths and weaknesses of the various alternative means of assessing votes, for example simple plurality, the Borda count, the Condorcet count, and approval voting? (See Saari, 2001.)
- How typical are Indian election practices of those held in democracies around the world?
- How threatening for democracy is the emergence of a 'class' of 'professional' politicians in the UK? Can anything be done to prevent it?
- How useful is the term 'political class' in comparing the politics of different states?
- What should be the powers and functions of a reformed House of Lords as a second chamber? Why has producing a long-term replacement for the old House of Lords proved so difficult?
- Does a second chamber of parliament make it more likely that laws better reflect the preferences of the whole population? Are there any circumstances in which it might not?
- How representative should a legislature be of the citizens of a given country? In what ways?
- Where would you fit the European Parliament in Mezey's typology?
- Should criminals be barred from standing for election? Would it be undemocratic?
- Assess the arguments in favour of special measures to increase gender equality among members of parliament. Should the same arguments be applied to other groups in society currently under-represented?
- How far does it matter if there is great disparity in the size of constituencies electing representatives to the same legislature? Why?
- Are citizens in democracies more critical of their representatives? Why?
- Why do individuals stand for election to public office in democracies? Would you? Given all the disparagement, is it worth the aggravation?
- How far should parliaments seek to lead public opinion, and how far should they simply follow and represent it?
- How do you explain the greater public confidence in legislatures in many authoritarian regimes than in democracies?

Further Reading

Ballington, Julie, and Kazam, Azza (eds) (2005), *Women in Parliament: Beyond Numbers* (Stockholm: International IDEA, revised edn), (https://www.idea.int/publications/catalogue/women-parliament-beyond-numbers-revised-edition?lang=en, accessed January 2018).
An international discussion of ways in which the number of female legislators could be increased.

Banerjee, Mukulika (2014), *Why India Votes?* (New Delhi: Routledge).
Based on recent ethnographic fieldwork on how elections are conducted in the world's largest democracy.

Corbett, Richard, Jacobs, Francis, and Neville, Darren (2016), *The European Parliament* (London: John Harper, 9th edn).
The standard introduction to the European Parliament.

Cowley, Philip, and Ford, Robert (eds) (2014), *Sex, Lies and the Ballot Box: 50 Things That You Need to Know about British Elections* (London: Biteback).
A fascinating collection of summarized academic articles on what election analyses tell us about the practice of British politics.

Crewe, Emma (2015), *The House of Commons: An Anthropology of British MPs at Work* (London: Bloomsbury).
An ethnographic study of what it is like to be a British MP today.

Farrell, David M. (2011), *Electoral Systems: A Comparative Introduction* (Basingstoke: Palgrave, 2nd edn).
A very approachable introduction to the various types of electoral system.

Fish, M. Steven, and Kroenig, Matthew (2011), *The Handbook of National Legislatures: A Global Survey* (Cambridge: Cambridge University Press).
A mine of information about legislatures around the world.

Jacobson, Gary C. (2012), *The Politics of Congressional Elections* (New York: Longmans, 8th edn).
An authoritative account of the evolution of election issues in the US.

Mehra Ajay, K., and Kueck, Gert W. (eds) (2003), *The Indian Parliament: A Comparative Perspective* (Delhi: Konark).
Presents aspects of politics and procedure in the Indian Parliament from a European perspective.

Mosca, Gaetano (1939), *The Ruling Class* (New York: McGraw-Hill).
A classic of political analysis.

Norton, Philip (ed.) (1998), *Parliaments and Governments in Western Europe* (London: Cass, two vols).
An authoritative compendium of material on various European legislatures.

Oborne, Peter (2007), *The Triumph of the Political Class* (London: Simon & Schuster).
A political columnist's indictment of the political class in Britain.

Reynolds, Andrew, **Reilly, Ben, and Allis, Andrew** (2007), *Electoral System Design* (Stockholm: International IDEA).
Details the considerations that should underlie the choice of electoral system, especially for regimes in transition to democracy.

Sutherland, Keith (2004), *The Party's Over: Blueprint for a Very English Revolution* (Exeter: Imprint Academic).
A radical proposal for the random selection of members of Parliament.

Tsebelis, George, **and Money, Jeannette** (1997), *Bicameralism* (Cambridge: Cambridge University Press).
Presents the issue of two chambers from an academic perspective.

Vaishhav, Milan (2017), *When Crime Pays: Money and Muscle in Indian Politics* (London and New Haven, CT: Yale University Press).
A path-breaking study of corruption and criminality among elected Indian representatives.

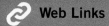 **Web Links**

http://www.ipu.org/parline-e/parlinesearch.asp
An International Parliamentary Union database on structure and working of parliaments around the world.

http://www.ipu.org/english/parlweb.htm
A link to websites of national parliaments.

https://www.idea.int/gender/index.cfm
The International IDEA website on democracy and gender issues.

http://boundarycommissionforengland.independent.gov.uk/
The gateway to the work of the Boundary Commission for England.

http://www.bcomm-scotland.independent.gov.uk/
The gateway to the work of the Boundary Commission for Scotland.

http://bcomm-wales.gov.uk/?lang=en
The gateway to the work of the Boundary Commission for Wales.

http://www.pippanorris.com
This includes links to many databases on British constituencies.

 Visit the **Online Resources** that accompany this book to access more learning resources on this topic: www.oup.com/uk/ferdinand/

Political Parties

13

- Parties
- The Emergence of Parties
- Functions of Parties
- Typologies of Political Parties
- Types of Party outside the West
- Party Systems

- Problems Facing Parties
- Conclusion
- Key Questions
- Further Reading
- Web Links

Reader's Guide

This chapter will look at political parties: why they emerged, how they can be classified, what functions they perform, how they interact, and, finally, what are the challenges facing them today.

Parties

One of the paradoxes about democracies is that, on the one hand, there is near-unanimity on the indispensability of political parties. They are almost ubiquitous, even in authoritarian regimes. The Universal Declaration on Democracy included, in Article 12, 'the right to organize political parties and carry out political activities' as one of the 'essential civil and political rights' (Inter-Parliamentary Union, 1997)—yet a strict public-choice approach to politics would question the logic of their existence. From this perspective, individuals only rationally form groups to pursue their interests when they can be sure that the benefits that they are likely to obtain are greater than the costs of membership. This is only likely to be the case for small groups where the share of benefits that any individual member can obtain in the case of success will be larger. For big organizations such as political parties, especially at the national level, the benefits that any individual member is likely to gain are bound to be minuscule, while the costs of membership are still significant. Thus it is irrational for people to join parties. They should only form (small) interest groups.

Then, too, criticism is often levelled at parties because they allegedly create and exacerbate divisions in society rather than help to mitigate them. This is particularly the case where political parties exclusively represent specific ethnic communities. But, more generally, Achen and Bartels (2016) have argued that political parties appeal to competing group identities in society, structure them politically, and make them partisan, thereby hindering national cooperation. In Britain, this is termed 'tribal' politics. As we shall see from **Case Study 13.3**, this kind of argument underlay the attempt in Uganda to do without parties after years of ethnically based civil war. The same argument is repeated by the leaders of the People's Republic of China to justify the leading role of the Communist Party, as they keep reminding their citizens of the chaos that China suffered in the 1920s and 1930s, when regional warlords fought over national power.

Carothers (2006: 4) expands on what he terms the 'standard lament' about political parties in various countries where he has done research:

1. Parties are corrupt, self-interested organizations dominated by power-hungry elites who only pursue their own interests or those of their rich financial backers, not those of ordinary citizens.

2. Parties do not stand for anything: there are no real differences among them. Their ideologies are symbolic at best and their platforms vague or insubstantial.

3. Parties waste too much time and energy squabbling with each other over petty issues for the sake of meaningless political advantages rather than trying to solve the country's problems in a constructive, cooperative way.

4. Parties only become active at election time when they come looking for your vote; the rest of the time you never hear from them.

5. Parties are ill-prepared for governing the country and do a bad job of it when they do manage to take power or gain places in the national legislature.

13

KEY POINTS

- Parties are a vital element in modern political systems, especially democracies.
- Despite this, the rationality of party membership can be questioned.
- Parties generally suffer from low public esteem and are often associated with corruption.

The Emergence of Parties

Historically, there were two phases in the development of political parties. Originally, they emerged within the parliaments of the first democracies as groups of independently elected representatives who needed to find ways of cooperating in passing legislation. These were caucus parties—loose organizations of like-minded representatives. Then, later, parties became involved in the process of trying to structure the vote in popular elections. For most countries, these two stages were combined, because the model of parties was imported from abroad at the same time as parliaments. For them, parties had to structure both the popular vote and also the workings of parliament, but in the case of party pioneers, such as Britain and the US, it is possible to separate the two stages.

There is an alternative way of theorizing the emergence of parties that goes beyond the purely chronological. This concentrates on the previously unfulfilled functions that parties emerged to perform. In this approach, historical description and more abstract logic are intertwined. It seeks to explain the systemic needs that parties had to fill. This approach is most common in the US, so let us consider how it is used to explain the emergence of parties there.

Why did parties initially emerge in Congress? This was because the task of finding a new coalition each time a proposed bill was being considered for legislation was extremely time-consuming, especially if it involved sounding out the views of each representative afresh. Forming blocs of relatively like-minded representatives simplified the negotiating process and also enlarged the influence of individual members over legislation. It was easier for groups of members to have an impact because, together, they were more likely to have the casting vote over a particular bill than would individual members. They could extract greater concessions in the terms of the bill, or alternatively they could more effectively trade concessions over one bill for advantages over another—what, in the US, is called 'log-rolling'. Because legislation is an iterative process, group commitments encouraged greater confidence that commitments would be honoured than those of individuals. It was easier to hold groups of legislators to their word than it was for individuals and thus to penalize those who broke it. Thus relatively coherent groups of legislators provided greater predictability for other legislators or groups of them as negotiators. This crucial role of parties in structuring and facilitating the business of parliaments should always be remembered because, as we shall see, even if today there seems greater reluctance on the part of individuals to become committed rank-and-file party members, thus provoking doubt about the future role of parties in society, their function in structuring the work of parliaments is unlikely to disappear.

The importance of this point can be seen in the very fact that they emerged in the new US Congress after Independence, when the American Founding Fathers had a distinct antipathy to any kind of party or faction, which they regarded as incompatible with real democracy. In his 1787 *Federalist Paper No. 10*, Madison attacked 'factions', because they could oppress or exploit the people as a whole. He defined 'faction' as:

> . . . a number of citizens, whether amounting to a majority or a minority of the whole, who are united and actuated by some common impulse of passion, or of interest, adverse to the rights of other citizens, or to the permanent and aggregate interests of the community.

By the Third Congress (1793–94), like-minded legislators had begun to form groups to smooth the passage of bills. Even in the circumstances where Congress only met for one or two months per year and therefore had a tiny legislative load compared with today, so that the problems of log-rolling were small, this predictability was still a key benefit (Aldrich, 1995: 68–96).

Later, parties began to form outside Congress as a way of mobilizing support for candidates, first in presidential and then in local elections. Aldrich argues that the first time this happened was in 1828, with the emergence of the Democratic Party in support of General Andrew Jackson. The effectiveness of the Party was first shown in the fact that he won this election, where he had lost in 1824. Moreover, he did so on the basis of a turnout that increased from 30 per cent of the electorate to over 50 per cent, so party organization motivated supporters to vote. Then, when opponents followed suit by organizing the Whig Party (though it only lasted for about 25 years), the combined effect of these two parties could be seen in a turnout rate of over 78 per cent in 1840. The emergence of mass parties both changed the course of elections and also stimulated greater interest in politics in general, at least as measured by turnout. Thus they strengthened democracy (Aldrich, 1995: 97–125).

Since then, political parties have gone through several mutations. The next was the emergence of mass parties between the second half of the nineteenth and the first half of the twentieth centuries. The effectiveness of the American parties, as well as the lessons of growing party democracy in Britain, made political parties a vital element in the extension of democracy elsewhere in Europe and, later, further afield. In addition, industrialization overturned traditional patterns of authority relations and drove increasing numbers of people into growing urban areas, where parties could more easily mobilize support. All the political issues associated with industrialization provided the matter for a new, more popular democracy in which mass parties became the norm and where the franchise was extended to include all men, and then all women. This was the era when party membership was highest. This period also entrenched a key social divide as the basis for a great deal of political activity (that is, that between capital and labour). While not all party systems revolved around this division, many did.

To cope with this at times exponential increase in party members, and to ensure greater coordination both in their activities and also those of party-elected representatives, the number of full-time party officials increased. While it brought greater professionalism to the internal workings of political parties, it also complicated the practice of democracy in internal decision-making in parties. How much weight should be given to the views of ordinary party members as opposed to those of party officials? Should they all be treated as equal? Could they be?

After the Second World War, parties in Europe evolved further towards what have been termed 'catch-all' parties—that is, parties that devote less attention to ideology and more to strategies to win over the median voter, who would make the crucial difference in a general election, even though it might mean appealing to voters who would instinctively support a different party. The consequence of this change has been to strengthen the hand of the party leadership that would be needed to make these strategic decisions. An early indication of the change came in West Germany in 1959, when the Social Democratic Party renounced Marxist ideology and committed itself to a market economy and liberal pluralism.

More recently, European and American parties have, it has been argued, undergone a further mutation as they turned into cartel parties that seek to exploit their access to state resources to solidify their pre-eminence and discourage newcomers (Katz and Mair, 1995, 2009; **see Key Debate 13.1**). They are also often seen by critics as contributing to the emergence of a distinct political class.

⯈ See Chapter 12 for a discussion of the emergence of a 'political class'.

 KEY DEBATE 13.1   Modern 'catch-all' versus cartel parties

Democracies need parties, yet today parties in Western democracies are losing members and generally find it increasingly difficult to attract adequate resources to operate (see also Chapter 4). Should they operate as 'catch-all' parties that continue to rely solely on voluntary contributions from citizens, although in practice this may involve disproportionate obeisance to wealthy individuals and large corporations who expect policy favours in return? Or should they seek funds for their public service from the state as a kind of cartel? Either choice could be interpreted as a form of, or at least a tendency towards, corruption. This could also be presented as a choice between 'American' and 'European' party practices, and judgement in part also depends upon your view of the state: does it embody a higher moral character (the predominant European view), or is it no different from other large organizations that pursue their interests at the expense of the rest of society (a view prevalent in American political culture)? See also Chapter 10.) Is state-funding of political parties a necessary evil in the modern era or the beginning of a slide towards the alienation of politicians from the public and potentially the downfall of democracy itself?

The implications for modern party behaviour and party leadership are sketched in **Table 13.1**, particularly the two right-hand columns. Which type would you favour?

13

TABLE 13.1 Katz and Mair on different types of party

Characteristics	Mass party	Catch-all party	Cartel party
Time period	1880–1960	1945–	1970–
Principal goals of politics	For or against social reform	Social amelioration	Politics as profession
Basis of party competition	Representative capacity	Policy effectiveness	Managerial skills, efficiency
Pattern of electoral competition	Mobilization	Competitive	Contained
Nature of party work and campaigning	Labour-intensive	Labour- and capital-intensive	Capital-intensive
Main source of party's resources	Members' contributions	Wide variety of contributions	State subventions
Relations between ordinary members and party elite	Bottom-up: elite accountable to members	Top-down: members are cheerleaders for elite	Stratarchy, i.e. mutual autonomy
Character of membership	Large and homogeneous; actively recruited on basis of class identity; emphasis on rights and obligations	Membership open to all; rights emphasized, but not obligations; membership marginal to individual's identity	Members as individuals valued for contributing to legitimizing myth; blurred distinction between members and non-members
Party channels of communication	Party had its own	Party competes for access to non-party channels of communication	Party gains access to state-regulated channels of communication
Position of party between civil society and state	Party represents sections of civil society	Party is broker between civil society and state	Party becomes part of state
Representative style	Delegate	Entrepreneur	Agent of state

Source: Katz and Mair (1995: 18).

As party membership has declined, this has strengthened the authority of the party machine, which in turn has become increasingly professional in its handling of all the media alternatives for putting its message across. Aldrich has particularly focused on this evolution in the case of the two American parties since the 1960s. Where, previously, the parties were dominated by local party machines such as that of Mayor Daley in the Democratic Party in Chicago and careers of elective office holders were made through the party machine, now parties have turned into organizations of media-savvy professionals ready to serve the needs of whichever candidates emerge to prominence. Thus the parties have become candidate-centred rather than machine-centred (Aldrich, 1995).

This historical outline of the emergence of the modern party suggests that analysis of any modern party can usefully be divided between its activities in three arenas: (i) the party-in-government (including parliament); (ii) the party-in-the-electorate (its strategies for winning popular support and votes); and (iii) the party's internal organization (Aldrich, 1995). All parties that seek election have to establish their own synthesis of these three roles, but the political system in which they operate, the policy goals that they set themselves, and the attitudes of ordinary citizens towards them all provide **structuration** for the particular synthesis that they evolve. All of this determines their particular interpretation of intra-party democracy.

 KEY POINTS

- The first parties emerged to structure the work of legislatures.
- Later phases of development were mass parties to structure the votes of electors, catch-all parties to win more votes irrespective of ideological appeal, and cartel parties more dominated by party professionals.
- All parties seeking electoral success have to balance three sets of roles vis-à-vis government, the electorate, and their own internal professionals.

13

Functions of Parties

Modern **political parties** are protean organizations performing an extremely wide range of functions in the pursuit of political power. Ware (1996: 5) has provided the following definition: 'A political party is an institution that (a) seeks influence in a state, often by attempting to occupy positions in government, and (b) usually consists of more than a single interest in the society and so to some degree attempts to "aggregate interests".'

In general, they perform seven functions, irrespective of whether they operate in democracies or authoritarian regimes. These are listed in **Key Concept 13.2**.

KEY CONCEPT 13.2   Functions of political parties

- Legitimation of the political system
- Integration and mobilization of citizens
- Representation
- Structuring the popular vote
- Aggregation of diverse interests
- Recruitment of leaders for public office, thus facilitating (normally) non-violent choice between individuals
- Formulation of public policy, facilitating choice between policy options

The balance between these functions varies according to the type of state. Not all parties perform all of these functions. In democracies, parties have a more prominent role in providing choice between individual political actors and between policies—indeed, in performing most of the last six functions. Authoritarian regimes place more emphasis upon the second function—though their interpretation of integration and mobilization implies more of a top-down, rather than bottom-up, process—and the last three functions. For example, Greene (2007) has shown how the Revolutionary Institutional Party (PRI) in Mexico used its control over state resources to hamstring potential rival parties, making it one of the longest-lived ruling parties in the world. Meanwhile, the Chinese Communist Party, with nearly 89 million members in 2016, continues to allocate members to key positions throughout the state (McGregor, 2010; Shambaugh, 2008). However, while it may be almost unthinkable for democracies to exist without political parties (for an exception that proves the rule, see the example of Uganda in **Case Study 13.3**), what is striking is the wide variety of states than contain them. Most states today, not just democracies, contain political parties. The only significant group of exceptions has been many Islamic states, although even Iran has political parties. Even communist regimes, which never tolerated challenges to the leading role of the Communist Party, organized regular elections at all levels of the state as a way of re-engaging the commitment of their citizens to the goals of the regime and also of demonstrating claims to popular legitimacy to the rest of the world. Authoritarian regimes too, such as South Korea between the 1960s and the end of the 1980s, have devoted considerable resources to holding regular elections and mobilizing support for the ruling parties, even though there was never a realistic possibility of political alternatives winning power.

Thus legitimation of the political system, whatever its basic structure, remains the single most common function of political parties. The only exceptions are parties that seek to overthrow the existing political system—especially those that seek violent revolution rather than change through the ballot box.

13

CASE STUDY 13.3 **Uganda as a no-party state**

Uganda is a rare example of a state that has attempted to practise democracy without political parties.

Since independence in 1962, Uganda has gone through civil war, genocide, and revolution. It was originally put together as a colony by Britain from a variety of former tribal kingdoms and principalities. There was no tradition of democracy and, in the less than 70 years of colonial rule, Britain only began to introduce it in the last few years. Milton Obote was elected the first Ugandan president, but democratic values did not develop among the newly elected parties. Uganda effectively became a one-party state from 1964, but Obote was overthrown by Idi Amin in 1971, who declared himself president for life. Gradually, the country slid into tyranny, chaos, violence, and economic collapse. In 1979, he was overthrown and Obote was reinstalled as president. This time, he attempted to restore a multiparty system, but the party leaders refused to cooperate with each other and violence returned. Between 1971 and 1986, an estimated 1 million people died.

When the National Resistance Movement took over the country under Yoweri Museveni, he declared that the country needed a fresh political start. Political parties would be banned because they institutionalized division and antagonism in the country, as shown by the experience of 1979–86, where what was needed was unity. The new regime would try to inculcate the spirit of unity, mutual tolerance, and democracy through the dissemination of the principles that had underlain the practice of the resistance movement. This would also be better in keeping with African traditions of tribal consultation.

The Constitution adopted in 1995, after nearly a decade of military and transitional rule, allowed for either a multiparty political system or a democratic 'movement political system', but although political parties were not banned, the regime prevented them from organizing openly. Party representatives had to stand for election to parliament as individuals. Instead, the regime focused its efforts at democratization on local resistance councils. However, armed groups in the north still challenge the authority and the democracy of the government in Kampala.

The Constitution laid down a limit of two five-year terms on any president. As Museveni's second term drew towards its close, the regime began to float the idea of a third term. This provoked unease both at home and among foreign governments that gave aid. In the end, a referendum was held, which approved the change to a multiparty democracy. Thus the reintroduction of open political parties was a response to both domestic and external pressure. However, in the general election called in early 2006, Museveni won a clear majority, despite opposition allegations of electoral irregularities. The Supreme Court upheld the outcome by a vote of four to three. Critics alleged that little changed in the way the country is ruled. As of 2015, 29 political parties were registered with the Ugandan Electoral Commission. President Museveni is still in power.

13

The ways in which parties perform these roles depend upon three things: (1) the constitutional framework within which they operate; (2) the particular national system of elections; and (3) the technologies of communication available to them.

 See Chapter 11 for a discussion of federalism.

1. As we have already seen in Chapter 11 from the constitutional distinction between federal and non-federal regimes, the degree of central authority in a state has a key impact upon the organization of political parties. The relative powers of a party's central apparatus and local organizations to some extent reflect the relative powers of the corresponding government authorities.

2. Countries with primaries to select candidates for election to major offices have to organize their activities on a different timetable from that of other countries.

 See Chapter 15 for a discussion of the impact of the media on politics.

3. As television and advertising have become more powerful, parties have turned to them increasingly to get their messages across rather than relying upon more personalized direct contact with party activists, even though this has greatly inflated their costs. Now the rise of the Internet is beginning to offer new possibilities for much more personalized canvassing, with candidates contacting voters individually to respond to their particular concerns. It can even facilitate new parties—as we shall see in Chapter 16 in the case of the Five Star Movement in Italy.

✳ KEY POINTS

- Parties perform an extremely wide range of functions in political systems.
- These are structured by the constitutional framework of the political system, the national system of elections, and the technologies available to them for communicating with voters.

13

Typologies of Political Parties

Political scientists develop typologies of political parties to try to think more systematically about their activities and to make more meaningful comparisons. Within the discipline of political science, the European experience of party life has, for a long time, dominated such classifications. For example, von Beyme (1985: 29–158) formulated a very influential typology based primarily upon the programmatic orientation of primarily European parties— that is, their ideologies and the goals that they set for themselves if in power (though it has been expanded here to include the category of Islamic parties) (**see Table 13.2**).

These more general programmes make them distinctively different from interest groups, which certainly wish to influence government decisions, but not to take part in government themselves. It should be noted that there is still considerable variation between parties with similar general programmatic orientation in different states.

TABLE 13.2 A typology of political parties, based on von Beyme (1985)

Type	Orientation
Liberal or radical	Such parties stand for equal legal and political rights, as well as free trade.
Conservative	Such parties tend to support traditional forms of social relations, including hierarchy. They often appeal to nationalism as well. Recently, however, some conservative parties have veered towards more radical, neo-liberal, free-market economic policies.
Christian democracy	Developed after the Second World War as a way of trying to find a third, Catholic-influenced, way between liberalism and socialism. While it endorsed more traditional authority relations, preferring women to stay at home and raise children, it accepted a significant role for state-provided welfare.
Socialism or social democracy	Such parties advocate workers' control of the means of production. Usually, they have had close connections with their trade union movement and many were affiliated to the Socialist International. They also advocate state welfare systems. However, unlike communist parties, they accept the need to maintain market economies, even though they would prefer some form of planning too.
Communism	These parties were inspired by the Russian Revolution of 1917 and sought to spread the communist alternative to socialism based upon the teachings of Marx and Lenin. They were affiliated to the Communist International (Comintern) in Moscow. Such parties were also distinguished by their organizational doctrine of unconditional loyalty to the party ('democratic centralism') and strict party discipline.
Regional parties	These parties stand for the interests of particular regions of countries and often want, whether overtly or covertly, to establish their own states. There has been a surge of popularity for these parties in Europe over the last 20 years. Possibly the most successful has been the Lega Nord in Italy, which has occasionally participated in national coalition governments.
Environmental parties	These appeared more recently, initially emerging from interest groups such as Friends of the Earth. Typically, they win support from younger and middle-class voters and tend to be sceptical of free-market economic policies. They advocate consensus-based decision-making and social justice.
Nationalist parties	These certainly flourished in former colonies, as the new regimes sought to establish their national values. The end of the Cold War removed some alternative poles of political organization, allowing freer rein for nationalists, for example in Eastern Europe and the former Soviet Union. Because such parties' ideology is based upon a concept of the whole nation, as opposed to the interests of a part of it (e.g. a class), they aspire to a hegemonic position in the political system, which can make cooperation difficult with other parties.
Islamic parties	Islamic political parties are relatively recent developments, because of the authoritarian nature of many Islamic regimes in the Middle East. In Iran, however, all parties represented in the Majles (Parliament) are Islamic, representing a fairly wide spread of opinions. Like nationalist parties, Islamic parties seek to speak for the whole of society rather than the interests of a part of it and therefore they too aim for a hegemonic position in the political system.

Source: Based on von Beyme (1985: 29–158).

13

However, while it is important never to forget the importance of ideas and ideology in distinguishing between political parties, it is increasingly difficult to use such categories to differentiate between parties in different regions of the world, particularly since the end of the Cold War. The collapse of communism in the former Soviet Union and Eastern Europe undermined the international appeal not only of communism, but also of socialism. Global ideologies have tended to give way to ones more specific to national traditions and political cultures. And, even inside Europe, Christian Democracy is no longer so important politically: perhaps its most powerful exponent, the Italian Christian Democratic Party was dissolved in 1994 in the aftermath of a massive corruption scandal and its former members migrated to various other parties.

So Gunther and Diamond (2003: 173) formulated an alternative typology that was intended to be more universal, which can be seen in **Table 13.3**. It is based primarily upon the ways in which, and the extent to which, parties organize themselves. This means that the lower down the table we go, the more organized they are.

TABLE 13.3 Gunther and Diamond's typology of political parties

Basic category	Variants	Sub-variants
Elite-based	Traditional local notables (esp. nineteenth century)	
	Clientelistic	
Electoralist	Personalistic	
	Catch-all	
	Programmatic	
Movement	Left-libertarian	
	Post-industrial extreme right	
Ethnicity-based	Exclusive ethnic	
	Congress/coalition movement	
Mass-based	Religious	Denominational
		Fundamentalist
	Nationalist	Pluralist
		Ultranationalist
	Socialist	Class-/mass-based
		Leninist

Source: Based on Gunther and Diamond (2003: 173).

Types of Party outside the West

DeSouza and Sridharan (2006) accepted the Gunther and Diamond typology to provide the basic structure for their analysis of Indian political parties. And ideologies do still play a role in Indian politics, albeit somewhat different ones from those of von Beyme. Varshney (2002: 55) has identified three 'master narratives' underlying Indian politics in the twentieth century, which also differentiate political parties: (i) secular nationalism; (ii) religious nationalism; and (iii) relations and struggles between caste groups in Hinduism. Vaishnav (2017: 136–7) expands on the way this operates:

> While ideology of a programmatic sort is virtually absent, it is present in a very different (non-economic) sense. Across political parties, caste, religion, and language all represent cleavages in society that have acquired ideological import over time. In diverse societies, the practice of ethnic politics revolves around concepts like 'dignity', 'honor', 'justice', and 'inclusion'. Although they do not operate on a conventional left–right spectrum, these notions do contain substantive content.

Yet Vaishnav (2017: 136) also argues that, in practice, 'ideology is largely an afterthought in Indian politics'. While political activists marshal ideas to win support, more pragmatic considerations govern their actions and those of potential supporters. So whilst the Hindu BJP party defeated the secularist Indian National Congress (INC) in 2014, winning an absolute majority, which certainly had a strong ideological dimension, this had as much to do with the dynamic leadership of Narendra Modi of the BJP contrasting with the lacklustre campaign led by the latest scion of the Nehru–Gandhi-dominated INC, Rahul. The BJP seemed to offer the prospect of more benefits for more people because of its more business-friendly policies. Money matters at least as much in Indian politics as it does in the US. Parties are vehicles for winning power and getting access to mechanisms for redistributing resources, so they engage in all sorts of activities, including (not very covert) corruption to win votes. Criminal prosecutions are no bar to public office either. A fifth of deputies elected to the Lok Sabha in 2014 declared that they were the object of serious criminal prosecutions and, if convicted, would be liable to lengthy jail time (Vaishnav, 2017: x).

One other feature of the Indian party system should also be noted: the proliferation of parties, as their backers seek to win power at the local level, even if they are ineffective as national parties. This is a strengthening trend. During the first two decades after independence, the INC dominated electoral politics at the national, as well as the state, levels, although the toleration in Delhi of local party bosses meant that it was a fairly decentralized organization. But, in recent decades, political fragmentation has gathered momentum. In 2015, 1,866 political parties were registered with the Electoral Commission and 464 parties contested the 2014 general election. Of these, 34 actually won seats in the Lok Sabha.

On the face of it, this is a puzzle, since India has a first-past-the-post electoral system, and Duverger's Law (see Chapter 12) suggests that this should encourage two-party national politics, not fragmentation. But Sridharan (2010) explains that the key intervening

13

variable is the fact of India's federal system. There is indeed a discernible tendency towards bi-party outcomes in most of the states of India, but the two main parties differ from one state to another. In many cases, these are parties concentrated in one state. Consequently, at the federal level, coalitions involving regional parties have become a regular feature of national politics. Though it has a majority on its own in parliament, the BJP government under Modi has included a few non-BJP ministers as a way of preserving relations with partners in certain localities.

The phenomenon of party proliferation and political fragmentation is fairly common, especially in large states with diverse populations. In Brazil, a state with 26 federal units, there are 35 registered parties and 22 of them held seats in the lower house of parliament in 2016. Yet in Mexico, another federal state with 31 units, where democracy has become consolidated since 2000 when the candidate of the National Action Party (PAN), Vicente Fox, became the first president from outside the Institutional Revolutionary Party (PRI) since 1929, politics continues to be dominated by the three parties that were established well before 2000—the two just mentioned and the Party of the Democratic Revolution (PRD). So while general explanations can be offered for party fragmentation around the world, there are always exceptions.

Elischer (2013: 26–42) also accepts the Gunther and Diamond typology as the starting point for his analysis of African political parties, but amends it so as to make it less Euro-centric and more appropriate for comparative research across other regions of the world. He argues that the differentiation between two different types of elite-based party based upon different historical periods in which parties emerged makes no sense in the context of twenty-first-century African politics. The same is true for the two 'movement'-based party variants, since they are based upon post-industrial values, which are premature for an Africa that is largely still yet to industrialize. He proposes replacing the congress/coalition variants of ethnicity-based parties with 'multi-ethnic alliance' and 'multi-ethnic catch-all' variants (which also replaces the catch-all variant of electoralist parties, since, in his view, all African parties are, to some extent, ethnically based). And he also dismisses the pluralist and ultra-nationalist sub-variants of movement-based parties, since they are more or less identical to the exclusive-ethnic and multi-ethnic categories.

The resulting version is presented in **Table 13.4**.

TABLE 13.4 Typology of African political parties

Party type
Mono-ethnic
Ethnic alliance
Ethnic catch-all
Programmatic
Personalistic

Source: Elischer (2013: 39).

At the same time, Booysen's (2011) detailed study of the African National Congress (ANC), in power since 1994, can serve as a reminder of the difficulty of locating many parties precisely within such frameworks in general. This is partly because of the wide range of functions that a long-time ruling party comes to perform and partly because its activities evolve with different leaders. The party sees itself as a multi-ethnic alliance, representing all the citizens of South Africa. At the same time, to use Gunther and Diamond's categories, its leadership tries to maintain the tradition of the disciplined Leninist style of organization that it had to develop to survive in its struggle against apartheid. As a programmatically socialist party, it prides itself on its ties to 'the masses'—and it still wins large majorities in general elections and it is the only national mass party in South Africa. It could be seen as 'personalistic' in that its appeal has been heavily buttressed by the personal leadership of Nelson Mandela, Thabo Mbeki, and Jacob Zuma—although that attraction has been gradually declining, in large part because it has also become more 'clientelistic', and corrupt, especially under Zuma. Booysen herself identifies its most basic identity as a 'party-movement' rather than a ruling party. All of this is a reminder of the provisional nature of such classificatory assessments.

 KEY POINTS

- Typologies facilitate more systematic comparison between party activities.
- They vary according to the primacy accorded to different basic features
- More research needs to be done in overcoming Eurocentric categories in establishing valid typologies for parties across different regions of the world.
- Giving due weight to all the dimensions of a party's activities, so as to synthesize them and fit it into a general typology, is a matter of fine judgement.

13

Party Systems

Any state with more than one political party also has a party system. Sartori (1976: 44) defined these as 'the system[s] of interactions resulting from interparty competition'. These interactions are affected by: (1) the nature of the political system as a whole; (2) the pattern of basic cleavages in society that underlie the differentiation between parties; and (3) the channels open for competition between the parties (primarily, the electoral system, though not exclusively—for example uneven availability of campaign funding to individual parties can also significantly affect electoral outcomes).

1. Clearly, the constitutional nature of the state has a fundamental impact upon the competition between parties because parties have to operate according to its rules. Parties have to operate rather differently in liberal democratic regimes, where electoral

success does lead to changes of government, from more authoritarian regimes where the rulers will not contemplate electoral overthrow and where opposition parties, if tolerated, have to be much more circumspect in their criticisms. It also matters whether a regime is presidential or parliamentarian.

2. The pattern of relations between political parties is in part determined by the fundamental cleavages in society. These are based on social history. The original version of this as it applied to politics in Europe was formulated by Lipset and Rokkan (1967). They concluded that there were four fundamental cleavages that had structured the rise of the new mass parties in Europe either towards the end of the nineteenth century or in the first quarter of the twentieth. Since then, these 'frozen' cleavages have remained the basis of West European party systems. These cleavages were: (i) centre versus periphery—that is, the competing claims of different communities within the same state for power both at the centre and in regional authorities (sometimes, these were also based upon different linguistic communities, but not necessarily); (ii) state versus church, which was particularly important in Catholic states where a significant part of the challenge to the Church's temporal powers was mounted by anticlerical liberals and radicals; (iii) land versus industry, in that the growth of industrialization and of industrial capitalists posed a challenge to more traditional rural elites; and (iv) owner versus worker—that is, the rise of capitalism also pitted the interests of the new industrial workers against those of their employers. All Western European states were affected to varying degrees by these divisions, but the outcome differed in terms of actual party representation.

3. The electoral system also affects the system of political parties. A political science classic, Duverger's *Political Parties* (1964) argued that first-past-the-post electoral systems tend to produce two-party systems—what later became known as Duverger's Law. By contrast, he argued, proportional representation tends to produce multiparty systems. While these are more generalizations than uniform 'laws' (in the past, for example, Venezuela had proportional representation and also a two-party system), there is no doubt about the logic of the argument.

Given these structuring factors, most typologies of party systems focus upon the number of parties contained in them. One version gives the following fourfold classification (Ware, 1996: 159):

1. Predominant party systems, where one party occupies a dominant place in the national legislature. They are rare in developed democracies, but emerged in Russia because of official backing, and this situation is very common in sub-Saharan Africa, where non-ruling parties are short of resources (Doorenspleet, 2003: 205). Some authoritarian regimes (such as Indonesia under President Suharto) have explicitly supported the primacy of one party on the grounds that it provides opportunities for representation of different interests and groups within the constraints of a

single party, where unprincipled party competition would jeopardize social cohesion (Reeve, 1985).

2. Two-party systems (for example the US)

3. Systems with three to five parties (such as France, Germany, and the UK)

4. Systems with more than five parties (for example Belgium, Denmark, and Italy)

What is striking is that, once established, especially in liberal democracies, party systems tend to change very slowly—as in Lipset and Rokkan's (1967) 'frozen' party systems of Western Europe. They can play a big part in the successful operation of a democracy, such as a two-party system, and they can also frustrate it—for example a highly fragmented party system with many small parties, as in Italy from the Second World War to the early 1990s—yet it is almost impossible to design and impose a particular system when voters' choices are genuinely free. Then, party systems just emerge and acquire a life of their own. They are not easily changed even when reformers set out to do so because of perceived and unpopular weaknesses in them. Take the case of Japan. The Liberal Democratic Party (LDP) was in government from 1955, with the brief exception of a period in 1993–94, until 2009. In the 1990s, however, the LDP became unpopular because of its association with corruption and money politics. Apart from the general need of parties for money, this corruption was attributed to the particular electoral system of multi-member constituencies, where several candidates from the same party could compete with each other, as well as with other parties. To try to break this, the electoral system was reformed, with more first-past-the-post voting, so as to try to facilitate a more genuine two-party system. It was thought that this would reduce the incentive for escalating campaign expenses and also, as Duverger's Law would predict, favour a two-party system by strengthening opposition to the LDP (Rosenbluth and Ramseyer, 1993). Yet, despite the reforms, the LDP upset these calculations, adapted to the new circumstances, and continued to win a majority of seats in the key lower house of the Diet (parliament) until 2009 and again since 2012. Nor has campaign spending been noticeably reduced. It is a reminder of a more general warning made by Gambetta and Warner (2004: 249) after reviewing electoral reform in Italy: 'Several of the effects of introducing new electoral systems are seldom predictable.'

13

KEY POINTS

- Party systems are the product of sociological and institutional interactions.
- They cannot be designed in genuine democracies.
- Once formed, they are very durable and, again in democracies, difficult successfully to reform so that they realize different objectives.

Problems Facing Parties

As ever, serious problems now confront political parties, although they vary in nature from one region of the world to another. In Western Europe, the traditional main parties themselves and the party systems still survive (though Italy is a major exception). In general, in Western Europe, the problem is one of declining party membership. The mass parties that were typical of the inter-war and post-war eras are a thing of the past. Although parties do not always maintain scrupulous records of members, in part because of the need to appear strong to outside observers, the trend seems clear throughout Europe, as can be seen from **Table 13.5**. In the case of Spain, one of the two exceptions to this general trend, it should be noted that the base year of 1980 was only five years after the death of the dictator Franco and only two years after the promulgation of a new constitution.

This means that, by the end of the 1990s, the average share of European populations who are party members was around 5.7 per cent—only around a third of what it had been 30 years earlier (Mair, 2005: 15). By coincidence, this figure is almost exactly the same as the share of Chinese Communist Party (CCP) members in the Chinese population by 2007—though the CCP is still, at least nominally, deliberately more selective in its membership. Yet membership of the CCP is going up, while that of parties in the West is declining.

Much thought has been devoted to the reasons for this increasing apparent reluctance for party activism in Europe. In Britain, one of the objectives of the Power Inquiry held between 2004 and 2006 was to remedy this. It recommended a number of measures, including calls for 'a responsive electoral system—which offers voters a greater choice and

13

TABLE 13.5 Trends in changing membership in European parties, 1980–2009

Country	Period	Change in numbers	% change in original membership
France	1978–2009	– 923,788	– 53.17
Italy	1980–2007	– 1,450,623	– 35.61
UK	1980–2008	– 1,158,492	– 68.42
Norway	1980–2008	– 288,554	– 62.60
Austria	1980–2008	– 422,661	– 28.61
Sweden	1980–2008	– 241,130	– 47.46
Germany	1980–2007	– 531,856	– 27.20
Greece	1980–2008	+ 335,000	+ 148.49
Spain	1980–2008	+ 1,208,258	+ 374.60

Source: van Biezen, Mair, and Poguntke (2011).

diversity of parties and candidates—to replace the first-past-the-post system', a minimum voting age of 16, and state funding for parties through vouchers assigned by voters at a general election (Power Inquiry, 2006). This last principle of state funding for political parties has become much more common around the world in recent years, as a way of boosting funds for the vital functions that parties perform in democracies and also as a way of trying to reduce their dependence on corporate sponsors.

Critics, however, warn of the need to ensure that this does not protect parties from new challengers and prevent newcomers from winning seats in parliament, as did happen in Venezuela from the 1980s (**see Case Study 13.4**) (Falguera, Jones, and Ohman, 2003). State funding can encourage party fragmentation rather than consolidation, opening up the possibility of funds for dissident factions to establish themselves as new parties, as happened in Japan in the 1990s. Other critics argue that the cause of the indifference is the sense that individuals can make no impact upon government or party decisions—a variant of the public-choice argument about the 'irrationality' of membership for the party rank-and-file mentioned above. From this perspective, the only solution is to change the process of political decision-making to make it more 'relevant'. Once this happens, people will flock back to parties.

 CASE STUDY 13.4   **Venezuela and the downfall of liberal democracy**

From the time when democracy was re-established in 1958, Venezuela had a reputation as the most stable and most liberal democracy in South America. Yet recent years have seen this system pushed aside by President Chávez in favour of a more populist democracy. It is a reminder that while liberal democracy may have been presented by Fukuyama (1992) as 'the end of history', this type of regime may be vulnerable too. How did it get into this situation?

In 1958, former dictator Pérez Jiménez was overthrown in a military coup that led to the reintroduction of democracy. In October, the leaders of the three main parties signed a pact at Punto Fijo that committed them to observing the same basic rules of the political game for the sake of preserving democracy. Subsequently, this underlay the evolution of Venezuela into a state with effectively two parties: Acción Democrática (AD) and Comitida de Organización Política Electoral (COPEI). The concept of 'pacted democracy' was later cited by commentators as a model for how to establish a successful democracy, especially in Latin America, and for many years it underpinned US policy for promoting transitions to democracy there (see also Chapter 5).

The two parties extended their reach into a wide range of other organizations—professional associations, peasant federations, state enterprises—which helped both to strengthen their control and also to increase their membership. On the one hand, the two parties exercised very strict control over their members. On the other hand, they sought consensus between themselves wherever possible, though this did not prevent energetic competition for power, with the presidency changing hands regularly.

13

This system worked well for nearly two decades, reinforced by prosperity based upon oil wealth. From the mid-1970s, however, the economy began to stagnate and decline. This was partly caused by falls in the international price of oil, but partly also by corruption and waste. Popular dissatisfaction grew and the parties did not reform. They became more isolated from the public.

In 1998, former Lt Colonel Hugo Chávez (**see Figure 13.1**) won a presidential election as an outsider. He promised a 'Bolivarian' revolution, appealing to the example of nineteenth-century liberator from Spanish rule Simon Bolívar, though the latter had traditionally been seen more as a liberal and an admirer of the American Revolution. Chávez aimed at sweeping away corruption and redistributing wealth towards the ordinary people. He attacked the 'partocracy' (*partidocratia*) that kept all power

FIGURE 13.1   Hugo Chávez
© Vitoriano Junior/ Shutterstock.com

13

in the hands of the two parties and their state funding was abolished. What gradually emerged was a populist regime that promoted social polarization rather than consensus. Chávez introduced a new constitution that removed many of the checks upon the powers of the president. Attempts to overthrow him through a putsch and by holding an election to recall him from office on the grounds of misusing his position both failed. The old party system fragmented, to be replaced by a multiparty system with numerous small parties. They are overshadowed, however, by Chávez's dominant Fifth Republic Movement (now the United Socialist Party of Venezuela).

Aided by the additional wealth that came from increasing world oil prices, despite a more polarized society, Chávez won a second term of office in January 2007. Chavez pushed on with his Bolivarian socialist revolution, as did his successor Nicolas Maduro after Chávez's sudden death in 2013. But the political polarization that this provoked, exacerbated by the collapse in world oil prices after 2014, which hit the Venezuelan economy hard, led to increasingly fractious politics. In 2016, the economy fell 10–15 per cent and annual inflation reached 800 per cent. Poverty soared, with widespread shortages of basic medicines. In 2017, Maduro called a national referendum on a Constituent Assembly to establish a more 'popular' form of rule to replace the constitution that Chávez himself had introduced. The opposition boycotted it. Maduro claimed victory after winning all 545 seats. Street demonstrations increasingly turned violent. Venezuela had moved very far from the pacted consensus of 1958 (Coppedge, 2002; McCoy and Myers, 2004; Gott, 2005; Corrales and Penfold, 2007).

In the US, there is an analogous problem, though it is not one of resources. In the 2004 presidential election, the two parties declared combined expenditure of US$1.91 billion. In 2008, this amount more than doubled to $2.8 billion, over ten times more than in 1980, in large part due to the Obama campaign's success in using the Internet to mobilize small sums from large numbers of supporters. In 2012, it swelled even further to over $2.6 billion, with the two main candidates alone spending $1.2 billion. In 2016, spending on the presidential campaign did go down to $2.4 billion (of which Democratic candidates spent 55 per cent), but the spending on congressional campaigns continued its inexorable rise, reaching near $4.1 billion. On average, in 2016, candidates for House elections spent $466,000 and candidates for the Senate spent almost $1.5 million (Open Secrets, 2017). As Achen and Bartels (2016: 326) admit, 'few established democracies do as little as the United States does to limit the distorting effects of money in the democratic process'. An enormous amount of this goes on media campaigning, but there is no shortage of volunteers who help on campaigns without pay. Nevertheless, here, too, we find a trend towards declining party membership. Individuals can be motivated to join and help with the campaigns of particular candidates whom they support, but they are more fickle in their allegiance. Here, too, the party professionals play a bigger role in determining party image and appeals to the electorate. As populists complain, this can lead parties to lose contact with the rest of society, just as it did in Venezuela. For new democracies, there is no problem in forming new political parties. As of 2004,

13

Russia, for example, still had 44 political parties registered with the government—yet, as Hale (2006) has described, Russia's parties have failed to take root. In Latin America, parties and party systems are still often weaker and less institutionalized, with the consequence that, as in Peru at the end of the 1990s, an elected authoritarian leader such as Fujimori can break them down (Levitsky and Cameron, 2003). The problem for these regimes is that political parties find it difficult to become the equivalent to the national institutions that they are in established democracies. If parties in the latter are seeing an erosion of their membership, when these parties have an established image and can adapt to changing electoral circumstances, the problem of membership is much worse in new democracies, where it is extremely difficult to grow to an effective size. For them, an added complication is the lack of obvious fundamental social cleavages that can underpin a party system. With the Cold War over, socialist parties on the defensive, and the emergence of post-industrial economies where social identities are more fluid, the old divisions between capital and labour no longer underpin fundamental party divides (van Biezen, 2003: 37–8).

Taiwan is an exception that proves the rule. Since 1987, Taiwan has become one of the most successful new democracies. It has a stable party system, with two main parties and one or two minor ones. The two main parties—the Nationalist Party (KMT) and the Democratic Progressive Party (DPP)—do indeed confront each other over a vital basic political issue, but this is not one of the four traditional divides that Lipset and Rokkan (1967) identified. Rather, it is unique to Taiwan: the issue of independence from mainland China. The DPP would prefer formal independence; the KMT opposes it. In fact, there is disagreement within both parties over the best way of framing policies to achieve either of these goals, so there is not complete unanimity. Both parties have a wider range of policies to appeal to voters, some of which overlap and cut across the basic cleavage, preventing the antagonism from becoming irreconcilable. This is the fundamental difference between the core images of the two parties. It structures the party system. But other new democracies do not have the same fundamental cleavage, or an analogous one, so their party systems are more volatile.

Although there are many differences between the parties in the established democracies of Western Europe and the US and those in the newer democracies in other parts of the world, there does seem one trend of convergence. This is the enhanced importance now of party professionals in determining party 'brand' and policies to appeal to the electorate. This is the result of a combination of factors. On the one hand, it is a consequence of the reduction in rank-and-file members of previously mass parties. On the other, it results from the growing importance of state funds in financing party activities. While the two main American parties do not suffer from the same problems of financial stringency, Aldrich (1995) has argued that the same change has taken place there. Since the 1960s, the Democratic and Republican parties have both changed from mass parties to ones that are candidate-centred, with party professionals at their service (Aldrich, 1995: 254). This convergence also makes it likely that parties in various parts of the world will seek to derive lessons from the American experience on ways of winning elections, even if the electoral systems are quite different, especially where those parties also mutate into candidate-centred organizations, as in Peru.

13

There is a growing divide between party professionals and the party rank-and-file. According to Mair (2005: 20), parties in Europe 'have reduced their presence in the wider society, and have become part of the state'. They are less concerned with playing the function of opposition and more concerned with preparing for government: 'Within politics . . . the parties are either all governing or waiting to govern' (Mair, 2005: 20).

The corollary of this is that the fundamental difference between rank-and-file party members and ordinary citizens in the internal life of parties is eroding. Some attempts to revive interest in politics may exacerbate the problem. For example, theories of **deliberative democracy** (see Chapter 4) advocate new ways of consulting public opinion in policy-making by involving representative groups of ordinary citizens. One striking example came in Greece in 2006, when the PASOK Party selected its candidate for mayor of one of the municipalities of Athens through consultation between a group of randomly selected citizens rather than votes from members (*CDD*, 2006). This privileged the decision-making role of ordinary citizens over that of both party professionals and party rank-and-file in a key area of party activity. Were this to become a more common phenomenon, it would certainly erode the boundaries separating parties from the rest of society.

See also the discussion on electronic decision-making in Chapter 15.

✳ KEY POINTS

- Political parties are facing a range of new challenges.
- In various parts of the world, the balance between rank-and-file party members and party professionals is tipping towards the latter.
- Despite the lack of esteem for them, parties remain vital for the formulation and legitimation of public policies.

13

Conclusion

As ever, parties and party systems are in transition and their future shape is not clear. There seems little chance that the old mass parties will return and, across Europe, popular respect for the 'old' political parties continues to decline. In Italy, former Prime Minister Renzi came to power in 2014 on a promise to 'cull' political institutions. This was in a country where, in 2012, a public opinion survey had shown that 80 per cent of respondents had no confidence in political parties, which was even slightly greater than their lack of confidence in the country's banks, at 79 per cent (Biorcio, 2015b: 40)—though Renzi was later forced to resign after his proposed plan for constitutional reforms was rejected in a referendum. In France, Emmanuel Macron won a landslide victory in 2017, first in the presidential and then in the Assembly elections, creating a new party, *La République en marche,* which has swept aside the traditional ones. Elsewhere in Europe, populist protests against traditional parties have gathered momentum and win at least a quarter of the votes. Neverthe-less, there is no obvious organizational alternative. People are still voting for alternative parties rather than independent candidates (though see the discussion of the Five Star Movement in Italy in Chapter 16). Even in Italy, a poll in 2013 showed that, for all the disillusionment, 57 per cent of respondents agreed that there could be no democracy without parties (Biorcio, 2015b: 106). And while many parties struggle, a study by Lev-itsky, Loxton, and Van Dyck (2016: 3, emphasis original) of successful parties in South America argued that:

> Robust parties emerge not from stable democratic competition, but rather from *extraordinary conflict*—periods of intense polarization accompanied by large-scale popular mobilization and, in many cases, violence or repression. Episodes of intense conflict such as social revo-lution, civil war, authoritarian repression, and sustained popular mobilization generate the kinds of partisan attachments, grassroots organizations, and internal cohesion that facilitate successful party-building.

If this is the case, then the outlook for Venezuela might be more hopeful if it leads to party resurgence as a result of the current political clashes. On the other hand, this does not explain the failure of any political party, even ones backed by the Kremlin, to take root in Russia despite all the political, economic, and social turmoil that the country has endured since 1991.

In general, parties will continue to play an important role in the way in which policy choices are presented to citizens for approval. Indeed, where significant resources are at their disposal, they will have an increasing impact on the presentation of policies, managing a widening variety of media strategies. They will also continue to play im-portant roles in structuring the work of parliaments. They will act as recruitment chan-nels for ministerial positions and they will certainly continue to legitimize, or be used for the purposes of legitimizing, political regimes. Although parties often suffer from a bad press and they are sometimes accused of exacerbating social divisions rather than finding ways of reconciling them, attempts to devise alternative forms or organization such as 'movements' have failed to supplant them for long. Political parties are not a guaranteed solution to problems of political instability. They structure the formulation of public policies, but their leaders still have to make choices about priorities and they can change them. They make mistakes, antagonize people, and seem self-interested—but, without them, a politics dominated by narrower interest groups would be even less attractive (Fiorina, 2002: 541). It remains difficult to envisage the formulation and legitimation of public policies without parties.

Yet Savoie (2010: 214) also stresses the increasing importance of personal leadership in parties specifically and in democracies in general—it always has been crucial in au-thoritarian regimes: 'Personalism is now the key to understanding where both power and influence are located and who has it.' Presidents Obama, Chávez, and Erdogan all exemplify this trend. Donald Trump was elected as much against the Republican (as

13

well as the Democratic) Party as with its support. According to Savoie, the same trend is true of Canada. In general, he declares: 'Power today is more fluid and transient than at any time in the past' (Savoie, 2010: 227). It is one of the key factors that has contributed to the re-emergence of populism, as will be discussed in Chapter 16.

? Key Questions

- How stable is the party system in any country with which you are familiar? What might upset it?

- The land area of the Indian state is roughly one third of that of the US. The American population is roughly a quarter of that of India. Both are consolidated federal democracies. How do you explain the fact that two main parties contested the last presidential election in the US, while 464 parties contested the 2014 general election in India?

- If personal leadership is becoming more important in political parties, why did the 'team May' strategy of the Conservative Party in the UK fare so badly in the 2017 elections? Is that why the Labour Party, under Jeremy Corbyn, did so much better than expected?

- Has the Labour Party in Britain managed to reverse the long-term trend of declining party membership across Europe? How and why?

- In what ways is *La République en marche* different from the other French political parties?

- Both French President Macron and former Italian Prime Minister Renzi have styled themselves as radical youthful reformers of their countries' political systems. Compare their strategies and achievements.

- Do you take an active part in the life of a political party? How do you justify this? How rational is it?

- Is partisan extremism an inherent danger in multi party democracies? Can it be overcome? How?

- How appropriate is state funding of political parties? How valid are the objections?

- How far do American parties conform to the model of cartel parties?

- Are Chinese leaders right to fear that political parties divide societies more than they integrate them? Are there lessons from the Indian experience? Or the Mexican?

- Are parties' programmes becoming more difficult to distinguish from each other? Are they becoming less 'ideological'?

- Are parties in other parts of the world becoming more 'American'? If so, in what ways? Does it matter?

- How well does either of the two typologies of party systems fit the political systems of countries with which you are familiar?

Further Reading

Achen, Christopher H., and Bartels, Larry M. (2016), *Democracy for Realists: Why Elections Do Not Produce Responsive Government* (Oxford and Princeton, NJ: Princeton University Press).
A stimulating critique of what they term the 'folk' justification of democracy in the US, which assumes that elections effectively ensure that government conforms to citizen preferences and keep it meaningfully accountable.

Aldrich, John H. (2011), *Why Parties? A Second Look* (Chicago, IL: Chicago University Press).
A theoretically informed history of the rise of parties in the US.

Booysen, Susan (2011), *The African National Congress and the Regeneration of Political Power* (Johannesburg: Wits University Press).
The fullest and most detailed account of the evolution of the multifarious activities of the African National Congress, in power since the end of apartheid.

Dalton, Russell J., Farrell, David M., and McAllister, Ian (2011), *Political Parties and Democratic Linkage: How Parties Organize Democracy* (Oxford: Oxford University Press).
A wide-ranging survey of the practice of parties in democracies.

Elischer, Sebastian (2013), *Political Parties in Africa* (Cambridge: Cambridge University Press).
A very good introduction to party systems in several African states.

Gallagher, Michael, Laver, Michael, and Mair, Peter (2011), *Representative Government in Modern Europe: Institutions, Parties and Governments* (Boston, MA: McGraw Hill, 5th edn), chs 7–10.
A survey of parties in various European states.

Greene, Kenneth J. (2007), *Why Dominant Parties Lose: Mexico's Democratization in Comparative Perspective* (Cambridge: Cambridge University Press).
A sophisticated analysis of how one of the most durable ruling parties stayed in power for 70 years and then lost it.

Hale, Henry E. (2006), *Why Not Parties in Russia? Democracy, Federalism and the State* (Cambridge: Cambridge University Press).
A much-cited analysis of the reasons for the failure of political parties to take root in Russia.

Katz, Richard S., and Crotty, William (eds) (2006), *Handbook of Party Politics* (London: Sage).
A compendium of information on many features of political parties.

Katz, Richard S., and Mair, Peter (1995), 'Changing Models of Party Organization and Party Democracy: The Emergence of the Cartel Party', *Party Politics*, 1(1): 5–28.
A widely cited analysis of recent changes in the organization and role of parties, especially in Europe.

Levitsky, Steven, and Cameron, Maxwell A. (2003), 'Democracy without Parties? Political Parties and Regime Change in Fujimori's Peru', *Latin American Politics and Society*, 45(3): 1–33.
A study of a political system whose president attempted to rule without parties, which complements the case study on Uganda.

Levitsky, Steven, and Cameron, Maxwell A. (2005), *Parliamentary Affairs,* 58(3), special issue on 'The Future of Parties'.
A collection of articles on the challenges to political parties.

Levitsky, Steven, Loxton, James, and Van Dyck, Brandon (2016), 'Introduction: Challenges of Party-Building in Latin America', in Steven Levitsky, James Loxton, Brandon Van Dyck, and Jorge I. Dominguez (eds), *Challenges of Party-Building in Latin America* (Cambridge and New York: Cambridge University Press), 1–48.
A very good analysis of the limited number of successful new parties in Latin America and the reasons for their success.

Mainwaring, Scott (ed.) (2018), *Party Systems in Latin America: Institutionalization, Decay, and Collapse* (Cambridge and New York: Cambridge University Press).
The most up-to-date analysis of party systems in Latin America.

Mair, Peter (1997), *Party System Change* (Oxford: Oxford University Press).
A theoretical discussion of how modern parties change.

McGregor, Richard (2010), *The Party: The Secret World of China's Communist Rulers* (London: Allen Lane).
A journalist's eye-opening account of the internal life of the world's largest party.

Reeve, David (1985), *Golkar of Indonesia: An Alternative to the Party System* (Singapore: Oxford University Press).
Presents the Indonesian justification for an authoritarian ruling party as a substitute for democracy.

Ware, Alan (1996), *Political Parties and Party Systems* (Oxford: Oxford University Press).
A thorough survey of the relationship between parties and party systems.

Web Links

https://www.idea.int/data-tools/data/voter-turnout
Comprehensive source of information on voter turnout around the world.

http://www.psr.keele.ac.uk/parties.htm
Compendium to websites of political parties, social movements, and interest groups around the world.

http://www.opendemocracy.net/democracy-open_politics/article_2312.jsp
Paul Hilder's 2005 article discusses alternative possible future organizational forms.

https://escholarship.org/uc/item/3vs886v9
Peter Mair's 2005 paper discusses the changing politics of the party.

http://www.opensecrets.org
Contains a wealth of information on US party funding.

Visit the **Online Resources** that accompany this book to access more learning resources on this topic: www.oup.com/uk/ferdinand/

Executives, Bureaucracies, Policy Studies, and Governance

14

- Legislatures and Executives
- Civil Service
- 'Embedded Autonomy' and Economic Policy-Making
- Theories of Bureaucratic Policy-Making
- The Emergence of Agencies
- Governance and Good Governance

- Policy Communities, 'Iron Triangles', and Issue Networks
- Conclusion: Towards a Network State?
- Key Questions
- Further Reading
- Web Links

Reader's Guide

This chapter will first set the general framework of legislature–executive relations, focusing mainly on the competing claims of parliamentary versus presidential systems. Then, it will introduce the subject of the civil service and its traditional role in building up the effective power of the state. It will suggest that embedded autonomy is an appropriate way of characterizing its relationship with the rest of society, using examples from economic policy-making. Then, it will introduce theories of bureaucratic policy-making and, in particular, the problem of facilitating policy innovation. It will take the basic issue of relations between principals and agents as the starting point. This leads on to the more recent proliferation of agencies in government set up to implement policies devised by the political leadership, but operating at arm's length from the structures of ministries. This expands the scope of study from governments to governance and, in the case of the developing world, the related subject of good governance. The domain of policy-making spreads beyond state officials or civil servants to issue networks and policy communities. Finally, the conclusion addresses the emergence of a 'network state', what that might mean, and the implications for civil servants.

Legislatures and Executives

Parliaments and political parties are intimately connected with the executive branch of government. There are two overlapping meanings for the term executive. In the broader sense, it denotes one of the three main branches of government, alongside the legislature and the judiciary. In the narrower sense, it denotes the more explicitly 'political' elements of a government. Both legislature and executive are responsible for formulating government policy, and the executive is responsible to parliament for its implementation in democratic systems and most non-democratic ones. There are two distinct alternative principles underpinning their relationship, parliamentarianism and presidentialism, though there are an increasing number of hybrid systems that combine features of both.

Presidentialism versus parliamentarianism

In a parliamentary system, the head of the government is almost always decided by the parliament. Thus parliamentarianism denotes the principle that parliament is the final arbiter in the choice of the head of the government. The UK is one of the best-known examples. The alternative principle is presidentialism, which means that the head of state, whether elected or not, either determines the choice of prime minister, if there is one, as in France, or is personally the head of the executive branch of government, as in the US. In the latter case, the direct election of the president by the whole nation confers a powerful mandate. If there is a separate prime minister, the parliament can offer advice and ratify the decision, but it does not have the power to make the decision itself. In practice, the implication of this distinction determines the primary direction of loyalty of members of the executive. Ministers and officials are either primarily responsible for policy to the prime minister or to the president.

In parliamentary systems, the normal practice is that the prime minister is chosen because (s)he can command a majority in the parliament. Where a single party has a majority of the seats in parliament, the choice is usually easy. Where no single party has a majority, this usually involves negotiations between several parties who try to form a coalition government, as happened recently in the UK and Australia. If that fails, then sometimes minority governments are formed that hold only a significant proportion of the seats in parliament, but not a majority. In that case, the government is obviously more vulnerable to defeat if the opposition can unite against it, but sometimes minority governments can survive for quite a long time by careful selection of policies.

These general structures, of course, hide wide variations in the ways in which particular presidential and parliamentary executives operate. In the US, for example, Presidents Johnson and Carter ran their administrations in quite different ways, even though they came from the same party. Among democracies, there are widespread variations in the power of prime ministers relative to the rest of the cabinet. For example, while there is recurring comment upon the 'imperial' tendencies of British prime ministers, Japanese prime ministers still hold office on average for only one to two years, and recently often even less—though, since 2001, Koizumi and Abe have managed to stay in power for five years each.

Linz (1992) argued that parliamentarianism is more advantageous for democracy because it leads to greater stability, whereas presidentialism is more fragile (**see Key Debate 14.1**). He based most of his case upon the experience of Latin America, where there has been a high degree of political instability and where almost all regimes have been presidential. Linz identified one fundamental problem that caused this. Presidential democratic rule assumes a powerful executive based upon a mandate from the whole people, while at the same time legislators also lay claim to popular mandates. Therefore, president and parliament are driven by their respective senses of equal public legitimacy into clashes over policy, even where they agree over the basic direction in which they would like government policy to go. It makes for a 'zero-sum' approach to policy-making, with each side striving for a winner-takes-all outcome.

 KEY DEBATE 14.1   Presidential versus parliamentary systems

New democracies are confronted by a fundamental immediate choice: should they opt for a presidential or a parliamentary system? It is not a simple choice. There are numerous examples of both types in the world. Each has strengths and weaknesses. There are also more and less successful versions of each. But whichever choice is made then structures other key characteristics of the system. Linz and Cheibub outline some of the key contrasting considerations. If you were establishing a new democratic system, which type would you prefer, and why?

> Perhaps the best way to summarize the basic differences between presidential and parliamentary systems is to say that while parliamentarianism imparts flexibility to the political process, presidentialism makes it rather rigid . . . [W]hile the need for authority and predictability would seem to favour presidentialism, there are unexpected developments—ranging from the death of the incumbent to serious errors in judgement committed under the pressure of unruly circumstances—that make presidential rule less predictable and often weaker than that of a prime minister.
>
> Presidentialism is ineluctably problematic because it operates according to the rule of 'winner-take-all'—an arrangement that tends to make democratic politics a zero-sum game, with all the potential for conflict such games portend . . . [Parliamentary elections] more often give representation to a number of parties. Power-sharing and coalition-forming are fairly common . . . By contrast, the conviction that he possesses independent authority and a popular mandate is likely to imbue a president with a sense of power and mission, even if the plurality that elected him is a slender one. Given such assumptions about his standing and role, he will find the inevitable opposition to his policies far more irksome and demoralizing than would a prime minister, who knows himself to be but the spokesman for a temporary governing coalition rather than the voice of the nation or the tribune of the people. (Linz, 1992: 122–3)

14

> True, presidential democracies are more unstable than parliamentary ones, but this instability is not caused by the incentives generated by presidentialism itself. Presidential democracies die not because the institutions are such that they compel actors to seek extra-constitutional solutions to their conflicts. The conflicts themselves should take some of the blame, since they are probably hard to reconcile under any institutional framework . . . One of the advantages of presidentialism is that it provides for one office with a national government. (Cheibub, 2007: 165, 168)

Questions

1. If presidential democracies are more prone to collapse, how do you explain the longevity of the American presidential system?

2. If parliamentary democracies are more stable, why did Italy have 56 governments between 1945 and 2000?

3. How stable is Greek parliamentary democracy?

By contrast, Linz (1992) argued, parliamentary systems tend to be inherently more flexible. They encourage actors holding different political positions to negotiate compromises because they have to reconcile their own individual mandates with the potential national mandate for government. They can also keep tighter discipline among their members in parliament because they can offer the prospect of promotion to ministerial posts as an incentive to avoid challenging government policies. He found confirmation of his argument in the very successful transition to parliamentary democracy that was achieved in post-Franco Spain. This differed strikingly from the experience of many less-successful transitions to democracy in Latin America.

On the other hand, Persson and Tabellini (2007) have argued that presidential regimes have smaller governments and lower welfare expenditures than parliamentary ones. And Cheibub (2007) has argued that even if presidential systems appear less stable than parliamentary ones, the reason lies not in the different forms of government themselves, but in the political contexts in which they have to operate. He claimed that, in Latin America, there is a tendency for military authoritarian regimes to be replaced by democratic presidential ones, and if the transitions break down, then it is because of a more fundamental crisis of authority than because of the type of system adopted. Thus the balance of advantages of parliamentary systems as compared with presidential ones may be less clear-cut.

King (2015) has remarked that the British system is an exception to Linz's argument. While being parliamentary, it hoards power at the centre rather than shares it:

> The government of the UK is still meant to govern—full stop. It is not meant to, and does not, share power with others, certainly not with opposition parties. On almost every issue that arises, the government of the day is expected to take the initiative. The government of the day acts. Others react. Ministers decide. No-one else does. The political parties in coalition governments certainly share power between or among themselves, but they do not share it with anyone else. (King, 2015: 283)

In any case, in practice there are hybrid versions that synthesize these two principles. One form of this is the increasing practice of parties choosing their leader through elections that involve their wider membership rather than simply their own parliamentary members. The main British parties now normally involve all of their membership in the selection of their leaders (the election of Theresa May after the sudden resignation of David Cameron in the aftermath of the failure of the Brexit referendum was an exception). Parties in some states, for example Canada and Germany, have their prospective candidates for leader in parliament, and therefore also for becoming prime ministers, elected by conventions of all party members rather than just the representatives of those parties in parliament. As both are federal states, this allows for the possibility of a national prime-ministerial candidate being chosen who holds a post in one of the state governments rather than the national parliament. If this happens, then the same party has to find a way of enabling that person to become a member of the national parliament. In general, these reforms have the effect of strengthening the role of party members in selecting their leader, thereby weakening the power of their parliamentary colleagues.

Another hybrid system was devised in France and has subsequently been copied in other states, including Russia. Here, the president is responsible for nominating the prime minister, but the prime minister must enjoy the confidence of parliament. If the parliament passes a vote of no confidence in the prime minister, then general elections have to be called. The original reasoning behind the introduction of this system was to make the position of the prime minister quite strong and avoid the endless wrangling between small parties that was characteristic of the Fourth Republic up until 1958. On the other hand, it can also make for rivalry between president and prime minister that can divide the government, especially when the latter has ambitions to become president later and uses the post to advance those ambitions. For many years, the problem was further complicated by having different terms of office for the president and the prime minister. It was not uncommon for the president and the prime minister to come from different parties because they were elected at different times, when the relative popularity of parties had changed. This led to uneasy periods of cohabitation, when the rivalry between the two became much more intense and often paralysed decision-making. France displayed the potential issue most acutely. Between 1986 and 2002, there were three periods when the president and the prime minister were elected from different parties (Mitterrand–Chirac, Mitterrand–Balladur, Chirac–Jospin). Each of them was noted for contradictory policy-making, as the two protagonists sought to undermine each other in the hope of winning the next election. The same effect can be observed in other states where the terms of office of directly elected heads of state and of parliaments have diverged, sometimes leading to different parties controlling the two institutions (for example Taiwan and South Korea). The US has often suffered from a similar problem since the Second World War. The Democrats dominated the House of Representatives between 1954 and 1994, but the Republicans controlled the presidency for more of that time, which led to frequent 'gridlock' in Washington. Even though elected presidents have constitutionally greater powers than prime ministers and therefore ought

14

to be able to overrule them, the fact that both can claim a mandate from the people and usually take advantage of that to appeal to public opinion to support their views means that the struggle is often quite tangled and intense. Principally for that reason, the French constitution was amended in 2000 so that both president and prime minister now hold office for identical five-year terms. The same happened in Taiwan in 2008.

※ **KEY POINTS**

- Parliaments perform a number of 'governmental' functions.
- They usually play an important role in the choice of head of government in presidential systems, and in parliamentary ones, their role is decisive.
- Parliamentary and presidential systems may have different effects on the stability of democratic regimes.
- There are a number of hybrid systems that attempt to synthesize these two different forms of government.
- Cohabitation of an executive head of state and a prime minister from different parties can easily paralyse government decision-making.

Civil Service

⟩ See Chapter 10, Table 10.1, for figures on general government expenditure.

If you remember from Chapter 10 the share of gross domestic product (GDP) taken by the state in modern Western societies, you will appreciate the immense significance of ensuring that all that money is well spent—that is, allocated to the highest priority projects and managed so as to ensure successful outcomes. Misguided or mismanaged projects have wasted billions of pounds in the UK alone over the last 30 years (King and Crewe, 2013). Probably no other branch of political science offers the possibility of saving large sums of money for taxpayers as policy-making studies.

In Chapter 10, we saw how the Western-type state spread across the globe in the nineteenth and twentieth centuries. One important factor in this was that state's bureaucratic mode of operation. Weber emphasized the impact of the innovation of the large modern bureaucracy, which transformed economic organizations such as companies, but did the same for government too through the greater consistency, impartiality, and effectiveness that it brought to policy-making (**see Key Quote 14.2**).

The qualitative change that it brought is associated with what came to be known as the civil service in Britain. It was the Northcote–Trevelyan Report of 1854 that laid the basis for it. This recommended the establishment of a government service divided between those responsible for routine tasks and an administrative class responsible for policy formulation. It also recommended replacement of the previous system of recruitment of officials

See Chapter 10
for a discussion of the
rise of the modern state.

> ### Q KEY QUOTE 14.2 · Max Weber on the efficiency of modern bureaucratic organization
>
> 'The decisive reason for the advance of bureaucratic organization has always been its purely *technical* superiority over any other form of organization. The fully developed bureaucratic apparatus compares with other organizations exactly as does the machine with the non-mechanical modes of production. Precision, speed, unambiguity, knowledge of the files, continuity, discretion, unity, strict subordination, reduction of friction and of material and personal costs—these are raised to the optimum point in the strictly bureaucratic administration.' (Weber, 1968: 973)

by personal recommendation to one based upon competitive examination. In principle, under the reform, civil servants could move from one ministry to another without losing any of their entitlements, although in practice this did not happen so often. It served as a model for other states later setting up their own systems of administration and it eliminated corruption from the recruitment process. It survived more or less unchanged for a century.

It was also an important innovation in the development of a democratic state. Officials were supposed to be politically neutral. They were no longer serving at the whim of the monarch, except in the most formal sense. In return for abstaining from active political commitment, officials were assured of protection against malicious or capricious dismissal. They were guaranteed tenure as professionals. Whichever party was in power was entitled to the best impartial advice on policy and how to implement it. Officials could and should offer this even if it was unpalatable to their political masters. This objectivity reinforced the ability of democratically elected leaders to translate their ideas into the most appropriate and most effective policy.

The British version of the impartiality of the civil service laid particular stress upon the impartiality of officials even at the highest levels. However, there can be problems for leaders who wish to introduce radical changes in policy, especially after a change of government, when they feel that the officials through whom they have to work are still committed to the old policies because they have implemented them as effectively as they could in the past. Other states have been more ready to allow political appointees to hold senior administrative posts. The French system of administration allows for political appointees to hold posts in the office of ministers, including and especially the *chef de cabinet* (the head of a minister's office). The US still operates a 'spoils system' (that is 'to the victor, the spoils'), which allows newly elected political leaders at various levels of government to fire and hire large numbers of officials, although their ability to do so was much curtailed in the twentieth century. Currently, every incoming president has around 9,000 positions, as listed in the *US Government Policy and Support Positions* (the 'Plum Book'), to which (s)he can appoint supporters. This is a tiny proportion of the total number of federal employees, which stands currently at 2.75 million, but it does represent all the most senior and politically

14

sensitive posts. In continental Europe, political leaders can also appoint supporters to top posts in state corporations, which can include public broadcasting organizations—part of what is now called *lottizzazione* ('parcelling out') in Italy. In Britain, the Thatcher government also began down this road, introducing the possibility of ministers appointing political advisers who worked in the minister's private office—though not always harmoniously, if television series *Yes, Minister* was to be believed. During the Major government, there were around 35 special advisers in Whitehall. The Blair government doubled that to around 80 (Richards, 2008: 180); under May, there are 83.

Thus European states developed forms of state administration that emerged from their own particular political, legal, and historical context, with the British version of the civil service operating the most stringent separation of civil servants from political roles. In general, in continental Europe they placed greater stress upon the role of law in establishing the relationship between the state and the bureaucracy, because law had played a greater role than in the UK in curbing the powers of autocratic regimes (Lynn, 2006: 58–9). It was associated with the German concept of the Rechtsstaat (a law-based state). According to Ginsborg (2001: 217), this is most evident in the case of Italy. An official Italian government report on administrative reform in 1993 estimated that whereas in France there were 7,325 laws in force and in Germany 5,587 passed by the central government, in Italy there were 90,000 laws or regulations with legal status. Even though a later report by the Italian parliament put the figure closer to 40,000, this was still a significant excess. The effect is to place much greater constraints on the freedom of initiative of Italian civil servants and it still did not necessarily lead to a more impartial civil service. Italian officials found ways of favouring clientelistic or familial connections. Over a 15-year period in the 1980s and early 1990s, 60 per cent of the hirings of state officials were initially made on the basis of 'temporary' or 'precarious' contracts, which were not subject to the same strict regulations as permanent ones, but later these were converted into permanent employment (Ginsborg, 2001: 218).

There was also a greater tendency for administrative, political, and business elites to overlap. This is most evident in the case of France, where the École Nationale d'Administration has trained generations of administrators, some of whom have gone on to glittering careers in the state administration, others going into politics, with three (Giscard d'Estaing, Chirac, and Macron) later becoming president. Yet others have become top businessmen.

The colonial powers also transferred these forms of administration to their colonies. After independence, the new states took them over for their inaugural administration. The difference that this could make can be seen in the different experiences of India and Nigeria before and after independence. In India, the merit system of appointment by examination was introduced in 1853—that is, slightly earlier than in Britain itself—and the Indian Civil Service (ICS) continued to attract high-quality applicants from Britain until independence nearly a century later. It was quite small: around the 1930s, the colonial state employed nearly 1 million people to administer a population of 353 million, but the ICS itself only employed around 1,000 and, by then, half of the new recruits were already Indian rather than British. This relative paucity meant that its presence was uneven around the country. Nevertheless, according to Kohli (2004: 237–40), it made long-term contributions to Indian state formation for three reasons. First, it resisted provincialism and ensured consistent all-India administration. It ensured a unity that nationalists were happy to harness later. Second, its competence and efficiency enabled limited, good government. Third, it exemplified the idea that a modern state can put the public interest above private ones. All of this justified the praise that Weber had heaped upon modern bureaucratic administration.

The experience of the colonial state in Nigeria was quite different: 'In stark contrast to India, the civil service the British created in Nigeria reflected the minimal goals of British colonialism in that country and therefore was not very good. The numbers were relatively small; they were not well trained; and very few Nigerians were incorporated' (Kohli, 2004: 306). In fact, the numbers of British officials were proportionately much greater in Nigeria than in India. In the latter, there was one British official to every 353,000 in the population in the 1930s; in Nigeria, there was one to every 20,000. But the quality of the civil service in Nigeria was much lower. Recruitment continued to be on the basis of personal recommendation rather than competitive exam. Few Nigerians were recruited to the administrative service. Equally, much less emphasis was placed upon consistency of administration across the country as a whole, which meant lower resistance to division after independence (Kohli, 2004: 306–7).

KEY POINTS

- The creation of an impartial civil service first developed the effective power of the state and then, later, the stability of democracy.
- European states developed different variants of the civil service and national traditions of administration.
- Colonial powers transferred these forms of government organization to their colonies, with varying long-term success.

14

'Embedded Autonomy' and Economic Policy-Making

The notion of a civil service closed off from the rest of society is, however, an oversimplification. Rather, it would be more appropriate to borrow from developmental political economy and describe the role of the civil service with the term embedded autonomy. In other words, civil servants are insulated from pressures from the rest of society, but not completely isolated. Their position is embedded in a set of official regulations that guarantee it, but it also grows into a habit of mind, a form of political culture. Let us see how this emerged.

▶ See Chapter 2 for a description of the developmental state.

The term comes in particular from the successful development of East Asian states that is transforming the world economy. Nowadays, there is fairly widespread agreement about the contribution that the developmental state, as introduced in Chapter 2, has made to those achievements. The success of the first of these, Japan, was subsequently attributed to the coordinating role of the Ministry of International Trade and Industry (MITI) from the 1960s (Johnson, 1982). Later accounts have challenged the leading role that Johnson attributed to MITI, arguing instead that MITI provided more of a coordinating role for major actors in the economy, while ideas on the desirable direction of policy emerged from industry representatives (Calder, 1993). Nevertheless, there is a consensus that MITI played an active role in the process.

Subsequently, the lessons of the state as autonomous actor in economic policy-making were learnt by other states in the region. South Korea, Taiwan, and Singapore all achieved economic breakthroughs. Evans (1995) then generalized from this some lessons about the reasons for their success. In particular, he explained the prolonged economic success of South Korea in terms of the embedded autonomy that state economic decision-makers enjoyed vis-à-vis other economic actors. By this, he meant that they were insulated, but not completely divorced, from pressures from various economic actors. If they had been completely divorced from the rest of society, then all of their plans would have risked unreality. They had to be aware of society's current needs and priorities. They also needed some detachment to determine what was in the public interest and follow it.

Nor is the term 'embedded autonomy' only relevant to developing economies. In their path-breaking study of economic systems in Europe and the US, Hall and Soskice (2001) identified two distinct categories. On the one hand, there is the Anglo-American 'liberal' model, which does indeed prescribe a more autonomous role for both the market and the state, as private capitalist actors determine how to interact with each other on the basis of expected comparative advantage. The contrast is with the coordinated market economies (CMEs) of continental Europe, particularly France and Germany. Here, governments play a more active role in directing the economy through a substantial number of state-owned enterprises, in regulating competition (possibly making hostile takeovers more difficult), in managing labour relations, and in providing technical and professional education and training. In general, there is a more sceptical attitude in CMEs towards what Landier and Thesmar (2007) have characterized as 'the big, bad market'.

Yet such typologies are, at best, illustrative simplifications of reality. Even the category of the Anglo-American 'liberal' model is less homogeneous than this theory might suggest. Though the British and American governments often share similar perspectives on financial capital markets, this does not apply to welfare arrangements. Their respective policies have diverged as a result of different national political traditions and culture. Nowhere is this more evident than in policies governing the provision of health services, as can be seen from **Case Study 14.3**.

The importance of bureaucracies in government policy-making in all states has generated a whole range of theories to explain how they operate.

CASE STUDY 14.3   **Healthcare provision in the UK and the US**

In Britain, there is a very widely shared support for a government-run National Health Service (NHS) that does not charge for most treatments at the point of delivery. Originally founded after the Second World War, the Labour Party still proclaims that this is one of its greatest achievements and the NHS has been said to enjoy quasi-religious devotion in a secular age. According to a report from the Commonwealth Fund of New York (2013), in 2011 spending on the NHS in England accounted for 9.4 per cent of GDP, which was nearly the lowest among other European states, but it provided universal coverage. The same report showed that healthcare arrangements in Britain enjoyed the highest approval rating of 11 OECD countries. In the US, on the other hand, traditional political suspicion of 'big government' and socialism, added to lobbying from private insurance companies, means there is much greater support for private provision of health care, even though millions of Americans cannot afford serious medical procedures that would save their lives or even basic insurance. According to the Commonwealth Fund, in 2011 50 million Americans lacked health insurance and a further 30 million were underinsured. Yet the US spent almost twice as much as the UK on health care (17.7 per cent of GDP), and the Commonwealth Fund report showed that Americans had the second lowest approval rating for their system among the OECD countries, after Australia.

In practice, neither system is as internally homogeneous as the rhetoric would suggest. In the UK, adult patients of working age are expected to contribute to prescriptions for medication, to dental care, and eye care. The state will sometimes pay for medical treatment in private hospitals if public ones are full. In the US, the state provides basic health care for the very poor and the elderly through Medicaid and Medicare. In addition, health care in both countries is facing the same looming challenge of rising costs as populations age. In the UK, this has led both Labour and Conservative governments to experiment with reforms that are intended to achieve greater value for money, some of them involving quasi-market incentives. In the US, the fact that tens of millions of Americans are unable to afford either expensive medical procedures or basic insurance led the Obama administration to introduce the Affordable Care Act in 2010, which was intended to expand government-backed health insurance and reduce costs.

Such innovations might suggest gradual convergence. Both systems are facing increasingly daunting challenges. Neither can afford not to change and adapt. No country will be able to afford ever-increasing resources, for health care as for anything else. Yet governments in both countries continue to provoke fury from opponents who allege that 'their' government is planning to adopt the system of the other. In the UK, Labour and Conservative governments have found themselves repeatedly forced to deny any intention of 'privatizing' the NHS or any part of it (**see Figure 14.1**). In the US, even though the Supreme Court ultimately accepted its constitutionality,

14

'Obamacare' continues to provoke implacable hostility from many Republicans. The Trump administration announced that it would abolish it on taking office, but it has struggled to come up with an alternative that satisfies Congress. It is a striking manifestation of the way in which ideology and national political culture can still dominate debates over public policy and drown out practical alternatives.

FIGURE 14.1
© 1000 Words/ Shutterstock.com

✳ KEY POINTS

- The civil service needs a degree of embedded autonomy if it is to pursue the public interest, but it may realize this autonomy in different ways.
- Some policies, such as health care, attract considerable controversy based upon ideology and national political culture.

Theories of Bureaucratic Policy-Making

Theories of bureaucratic policy-making have always revolved around what are now often termed principal–agent issues. This is a set of situations found in micro-economic game theory where the actions of two or more actors need to be harmonized, but their interests do not necessarily converge. A set of incentives and/or rules needs to be devised so that they do converge and activity is coordinated. In the case of a civil service, this takes the form of one person (minister, 'the principal') or one group giving instructions to others ('agents') on what to do. This always involves a hierarchical relationship. Civil services (agents) are subordinated to the decisions of political leaders (principals). Of course, within the civil service, there are further nested hierarchies, with varying levels of principals having the authority to issue instructions for implementation by agents below them. Theories of bureaucratic policy-making have always sought to do two things: to clarify how bureaucracies actually implement decisions; and to identify ways that will enable principals to better ensure that policy outcomes conform to the original policy objectives.

Over time, theories of bureaucratic policy-making have evolved. Allison (1971) wrote a very influential work on the Cuban missile crisis that attempted to theorize the ways in which the executives in both the US, but especially the USSR, formulated policies and interacted. He identified three competing paradigms. The first hypothesized that government as a whole, and individual ministries, operated as a single rational actor, where outcomes corresponded to the original objectives. Research quickly showed, however, that this did not seem to be the practice, at least not uniformly. It left many uncertainties about key developments during the crisis that could not be easily explained or understood on this basis.

The second paradigm was what Allison called 'organizational process'. This hypothesized that, rather than designing new structures and practices to implement new policies, wherever possible government agencies adapted existing structures and practices to the new circumstances. In other words, a great deal of policy-making consists of what Allison termed 'standard operating procedures' (SOPs). Of course, outsiders trying to decipher policies from outcomes without knowing the underlying procedures would have great difficulty in identifying the SOPs—as sometimes happened to the Americans when puzzling over Soviet moves that needed an urgent response. It is often the case that outsiders will not be able to penetrate the rules of the civil service, so that they will not be able to decide whether particular policy outcomes are the result of SOPs. Determining how large a part this plays in the overall picture of policy-making is bound to be problematic. However, it clearly cannot be the case that all policy-making is the product of SOPs and hence Allison formulated his third paradigm.

This focused instead on bureaucratic politics—that is, the ways in which particular institutions interacted with each other that led to specific policy outcomes. This is a self-evidently reasonable thing to do, but reliably identifying this process is also as difficult for outsiders to penetrate as SOPs.

The problem of policy innovation

To some extent, Allison's third paradigm became an orthodoxy for analysts of bureaucratic politics, but at the same time it exacerbated frustrations about the responsiveness of bureaucratic institutions to the decisions of their political masters. It seemed not merely to explain, but also to legitimize the different agendas of public servants from ministers. Put together with the size of government bureaucracies and their reputation for Weberian efficiency, it seemed to pose an enormous problem for public policy innovation in general. *All* public administration seemed to be 'embedded autonomy'. How could it be reduced?

A great deal of analysis has been devoted to clarifying the extent to which policy innovation does occur. Kingdon (1995), for example, showed that there were 'windows of opportunity' for it to take place. Baumgartner and Jones (1993) introduced the notion of 'punctuated equilibrium' in US politics (that is, periods of policy continuity interrupted by bouts of change). Innovation could be the product of activity by alternative policy-makers, media pressure, or simply changing circumstances. But if one wanted to theorize ways of making change happen, how could one go about it?

One of the most influential approaches was emphasis upon the principal–agent relationship, at a time when economic game theory was becoming more influential in the social sciences. It stressed the need for clear specification of objectives by principals for agents, and an appropriate selection of incentives and sanctions to elicit the desired response. As it happened, the broader context of policy-making was also changing then. This too changed perspectives on policy-making and what it could be expected to achieve. Serious economic crises in the 1970s and 1980s concentrated the minds of Western governments on reducing their expenditure and getting better value for money. Neo-liberal ideas on economic reform gradually spread from the US and displaced Keynesian approaches to policy-making. Then, the collapse of communism opened the way for initiatives for government restructuring in new parts of the world.

What emerged was what came to be known as the New Public Management (NPM). This new paradigm of managerialism emphasized incentives, competition, and performance instead of the traditional values of rule-based hierarchies: 'The mantra has grown in volume: the bureaucratic paradigm is dead; long-live quasi-markets and quangos, flattened hierarchies and continuous improvement, competitive tendering and subsidiarity' (Lynn, 2006: 2). As will be obvious from this terminology, a lot of the ideas for reform came from economics and from business management.

For some critics, this was fundamentally mistaken. It was based upon a confusion over the different purposes of public and private institutions. New Public Management implies that 'the public sector is not distinctive from the private sector' and that its practitioners are 'self-interested, utility maximizing administrators', like corporate executives (Olsen, 2003: 511, 522). It challenged the traditional notion of the impartial, public-spirited civil service.

Nevertheless, it has been an extremely influential approach to public sector reform. Toonen (2001: 186) has identified six features, as can be seen from **Key Concept 14.4**.

There is a paradox about these reforms, however. The wave has spread from the more developed countries and international aid agencies now encourage developing countries to learn lessons from it. As Ourzik (2000: 44), a Moroccan professor of administration,

> **KEY CONCEPT 14.4**   **The features of New Public Management**
>
> - A business-oriented approach to government
> - A 'quality- and performance-oriented approach to public management'
> - An emphasis on improved public service delivery and functional responsiveness
> - An institutional separation of public demand functions (councils, citizens' charters), public provision (public management boards), and public service production functions (back offices, outsourcing, agencification, privatization)
> - A linkage of public demand provision and supply units by transactional devices (performance management, internal contract management, corporatization, intergovernmental covenanting and contracting, contracting out) and quality management
> - Wherever possible, the retreat of bureaucratic institutions in favour of an intelligent use of markets and commercial market enterprises (deregulation, privatization, commercialization, and marketization) or virtual markets (internal competition, benchmarking, competitive tendering)

said in an address to the African Training and Research Centre in Administration for Development:

> The role of the State has been shaped by a trend which is today universal, that of a State as an enabler rather than a doer, a State that regulates instead of manages. Like a genuine orchestra conductor of social and economic activities, the State is required to promote private initiative without stifling or restricting it. A State that is at once modest and ambitious, since the population still expects much of it: it must, while ensuring that overall balances are maintained, protect the environment, ensure proper land-use management, put in place new infrastructures, provide health and education services, etc.

See the discussion of the modern state in Chapter 7.

Yet the context in which these ideas were originally formulated was countries where civil services were relatively well established, with traditions of impartiality and incorruptibility. In the developing world, these traditions are not always so strong. True, the Indian Administrative Service retained the elite ethos of its colonial predecessor and, until the 1990s, maintained a firm grip upon the country and its strong public sector of the economy. Indeed, there were regular complaints about the extent of the stifling 'licence raj' of permits that they imposed upon the economy. The challenge of NPM was particularly appropriate there, as the state moved towards deregulation of the economy after an economic crisis in 1991.

In Africa, however, there were many problems. On the one hand, by the early 1990s many African states were confronted with the need to reduce what had become bloated state bureaucracies. International financial institutions such as the World Bank were advocating NPM as a coherent way of doing this (Adamolekun, 2007). On the other hand, these states were also suffering from widespread official corruption. NPM did not explicitly

14

foster an official ethic of incorruptibility. Rather, it assumed that this had already been inculcated. Nigeria can be taken as a serious, but not untypical, example. As reported by Salisu (2003: 171–2), there are problems with the internal organization of the Nigerian civil service, including overstaffing and poor remuneration of employees, poor assessment of labour needs, inadequate training, and lack of qualified technical support. In addition, there has been considerable political interference in personnel administration, which has bred apathy, idleness, and corruption. Although there have been several attempts to reorganize the structure and operation of the service so that incentives and performance are better aligned, the problem of eradicating corruption remains huge, so there is a real danger in seeking to transfer NPM here that, by treating civil servants as if they were business executives, it will undo previous efforts to inculcate an ethic of incorruptibility.

 KEY POINTS

- Policy innovation in government bureaucracies is extremely complex and often unpredictable.
- Theories of public administration have always revolved around principal–agent relations.
- New Public Management borrowed its basic principles from business studies and economics.
- It may undermine efforts to eradicate corruption in public administration in developing countries.

The Emergence of Agencies

One key element of the NPM reforms has been the hiving off of government departments and functions to newly created separate agencies—which is encapsulated in the ugly term 'agencification'. In the UK, this saw the emergence of institutions such as the Child Support Agency and the Driver and Vehicle Licensing Agency. The underlying rationale was, on the one hand, to simplify the tasks of government administration and, on the other, to more clearly establish incentives for good performance, which could lead to greater rewards for those who deliver it. In one sense, it merely extended a well-established principle of public administration, which is to separate 'policy' from 'implementation'. However, what was new was the proliferation of 'outside' agencies that were not directly under the control of those who made the policy. Most were hived off from existing administrative structures, though the extent to which some 'new' agencies were really separate from ministries was sometimes opaque. Implementation was to be the responsibility of a different principal, who established distinct rules and procedures for its own agents. This undermined the homogeneity of a civil service with common standards and operating procedures. The control over the performance of the agencies was often to be framed in the form of targets for desirable outcomes. Achievement of them was the standard by which the agencies would be judged. Thus the setting of targets became an expanding feature of administrative leadership.

Talbot (2004: 6) has concluded that there are really three dimensions to the idea of 'agency':

- structural disaggregation and/or the creation of 'task-specific' organizations;
- performance 'contracting'—some form of performance target-setting, monitoring, and reporting; and
- deregulation (or more properly reregulation) of controls over personnel, finance, and other management matters.

It represented a move towards what Rhodes (1997: 87–141) has called the 'hollowing out' of the state, and what Bevir and Rhodes (2006: 74–86) have termed the 'decentring' of governance. This reflected a trend of devolving both decision-making authority to Scotland, Wales, and Northern Ireland, and also implementation authority to agencies outside Whitehall. For them, it reflected a gradual change towards more autonomous steering of society by actors outside the government. This would mean greater policy-making from, if not below, at least lower down in the system, or possibly from outside. One type of reform that was introduced involved the creation of public–private partnerships between government agencies and private companies to provide services or infrastructure, such as hospitals. Under these arrangements, private-sector institutions would provide the finance for new projects in return for contracts ensuring profits for years ahead. This was touted as a way of expanding infrastructure without having to raise taxes or for the state to borrow more. But critics alleged that it provided an opportunity for nimble and devious entrepreneurs to extract excess profits by running rings around less agile, trusting government administrators, or, worse, for corruption through collusion. For an example, **see Case Study 14.5**.

> See also Chapter 2 for a discussion of the 'hollowing out' thesis.

14

CASE STUDY 14.5 | **The costly shambles of the public–private partnership for the London Underground**

When New Labour won the general election in 1997, the London Underground was in a dreadful mess. In their manifestos, both the Conservative and Labour parties had promised radical reforms. The Conservatives had proposed full-scale privatization; New Labour wanted to demonstrate policy originality. It also wanted to show it was business-friendly and it believed that the private sector was often more efficient than the public—certainly, the management of the Tube was, in Labour's eyes, incompetent. It wanted to rebut allegations it was a high-tax party. Secretly, New Labour leaders were afraid that the party's likely candidate in the forthcoming elections for mayor of London—Ken Livingston—would want to lavish public money on the network and they wanted to pre-empt him, in case it prejudiced their attempts to demonstrate that Labour was not obsessed by old-fashioned high-spending public ownership. The solution was the idea of public–private partnerships—a new way for private enterprise and the state to cooperate without pushing up public spending. The London Underground became a flagship project for New Labour's Third Way—between traditional capitalism and socialism. It met a whole range of policy objectives.

The idea was to sell the infrastructure rights for individual Tube lines (individual stations, etc.) to three consortia of companies, who would operate them for up to 30 years. The companies would commit to investing in infrastructure and service them in return for a guaranteed rate of profits. If they made losses, the companies would bear the cost. In theory, it should have ensured more stable funding than when the Tube was financed out of the overall local government budget, where its share could fluctuate wildly from one year to the next (Wolmar, 2002: 106).

Implementation, however, became a nightmare. Because of the novelty of the idea, lots of (expensive) consultants had to be hired to flesh out the details. The companies required detailed legal contracts to guarantee their rights, which involved large numbers of (expensive) lawyers from the City. The contracts totalled 28,000 pages. Again, because of the novelty and the importance of the project for New Labour, several ministers and politicians wanted to keep their hands on the steering wheel. It was far removed from the NPM ideal of clear and simple principal–agent relations. Accountability was far too diffuse to be effective. There was a high turnover of administrators, so expertise was constantly being undermined. The companies in the consortia, having agreed on their original bid, failed to agree on much else afterwards. When they failed to deliver to contract, they blamed each other, or factors 'beyond their control'. They claimed compensation from the government and, even though they were contractually liable for losses, the government found that the reputation of the project was so bad, no one else was willing to bid to replace the operators, so the government had to compensate them for fear of the worse nightmare of the Tube having to close.

In the end, the arrangements collapsed in 2007 and the public entity Transport for London took control. The cost to the public is difficult to quantify, but King and Crewe (2013: 221) put it anywhere between £2.5 billion and £30 billion, which makes it one of the most expensive failures in recent years.

It was a disaster that was hushed up. No minister lost their job. The Labour government was re-elected in 2001 and 2005. As one of the top people involved put it to King and Crewe (2013: 221): 'You couldn't make it up. You couldn't make it up.' (Based on King and Crewe, 2013: 201–21; Wolmar, 2002.)

As this case study shows, it certainly enabled greater policy autonomy and hindered parliamentary scrutiny and accountability. Governance meant steering society rather than guiding it and now there would be more hands on the steering wheel.

On the other hand, this was to some extent contradicted by a counter-tendency of the reforms: greater stress upon the delivery of services. One benefit of this was the focus upon the delivery of services as an activity in its own right. Trying to find ways of making the delivery of services consumer-friendly was made a higher priority. 'Delivery' became a mantra during the later years of the Blair government. Barber (2007) was the director of the Number 10 Delivery Unit, and he has produced a very insightful insider's account of the procedures that were adopted and the lessons that could be learnt for further reforms. For him, better implementation is essential if the huge sums of money spent on public services are to be politically sustainable (Barber, 2007: 294). And, according to King and Crewe (2013), misguided or mismanaged projects have wasted billions of pounds in the UK alone over the last 30 years. However, for the reforms to become permanent, civil servants would have to internalize them and make them the basis of their official behaviour. Blair believed this could only be achieved if the prime minister's office acquired greater power to supervise the implementation processes. Savoie (2010) suggests that this is common in modern democracies.

In addition, the separation of policy-making from implementation added to problems of accountability. Though an elaborate array of techniques came to be developed to clarify ways in which implementation agencies could be made accountable to the policy principals (Lynn, 2006: 139–40), accountability of policy-makers to parliament was more difficult to enforce. If particular targets were not met, was it the fault of principals who had set unrealistic ones? Was it due to lack of commitment on the part of the 'agents' (the officials)? Or were the targets contradictory or incompatible? If so, whose fault would it be and who would decide? The greater the incentives for meeting targets and also the penalties for failure to do so, the greater the danger of neglect of other work where targets were more difficult to devise, but which might still be regarded as important (for example over environmental change). It could lead to perverse effects. Meeting (quantifiable) targets could be prioritized over (qualitatively) good policies. The whole process reduced the salience of politics in policy-making and made the policy process more technocratic. It attenuated the whole notion of ministerial responsibility. Ministers were less likely to take responsibility for policy failures by resigning.

India has not seen an exception to these pressures. The Indian economy fell into a major crisis in 1991 and this focused minds on, amongst other things, improving the quality of public administration. This was not for lack of previous attempts, but they had failed because 'the administrative system . . . was rigid for most people, but very flexible for the privileged among them. Rules were flouted with impunity, privatization of public office was common, and procedures were discarded at many personal pretexts' (Mathur, 2013a: 278). One type of solution that was embraced was NPM. But it was accompanied by another reform—the establishment of democratically elected local councils (*panchayats*) below the state level, from districts to villages, to put pressure on bureaucrats to perform for the good of the people—what has been termed the 'Panchayat Raj' (Mathur, 2013b). While these institutions have faced great difficulties in getting government agencies to take them seriously, they have represented an attempt to fill the democratic deficit associated with NPM.

14

KEY POINTS

- The emergence of agencies charged with implementation of policies formulated elsewhere facilitated concentration upon delivery.
- In Britain, the Prime Minister's office became more directly involved in pushing through the reforms.
- There was a heavy reliance upon targets as performance indicators.
- This complicated the problems of ministerial accountability.
- India has been experimenting with democratizing local government as a way of increasing the accountability of government bureaucracy at the same time as adopting NPM reforms.

Governance and Good Governance

As will be clear from the above discussion, an increasing trend in political science is to blur the old distinction between state and society. Instead of focusing upon government, now there is greater stress upon governance. However, there are a variety of interpretations of its meaning. Pierre and Peters (2000: 1) use the term to focus on 'the capacity of government to make and implement policy—in other words, to steer society'. They emphasize, however, that sometimes the term is used to describe the structure of decision-making. From this perspective, people conceptualize it as hierarchies, or as markets, or as networks, or as communities, or as combinations of these. Sometimes, it is used to concentrate on processes of steering and coordinating. And sometimes it is used rather as an analytical approach, which questions the normally accepted meaning of terms such as 'government' and 'power', as well as the distinction between state and society. These diverse uses in themselves cause confusion (Pierre and Peters, 2000: 14–27).

By contrast, the UN Economic and Social Commission for Asia and the Pacific (UNESCAP, 2009) has defined governance simply as 'the process of decision-making and the process by which decisions are implemented (or not implemented)'. Actually, the term does not have to be used in a political context at all. For example, it is also used in the term 'corporate governance' (that is the processes by which companies make decisions). However, when involving the state, it stretches to cover non-governmental participants in the decision-making and implementing processes. Indeed, it can include circumstances when non-state actors may take the lead in formulating policies in a particular issue area, or even in their implementation. An example of the latter would be private security organizations that are hired to protect government offices or to provide protection for a country's nationals abroad, such as in Iraq. Because of their importance for the implementation process, this also gives them the freedom to make greater inputs into the policy that they are supposed to be implementing.

A related term that is now much used in international politics is good governance. Governments in the developing world are often encouraged to practise this, sometimes as a condition for foreign aid. Again, it emphasizes the importance of non-state actors, as well as government in decision-making. UNESCAP has identified eight features of this term (**see Key Concept 14.6**). UNESCAP accepts that few states meet all of these criteria, but emphasizes that, without progress in most of them, real sustainable development is not possible.

Kayizzi-Mugerwa (2003: 17) presents the concept of good governance in more concrete terms, focusing more explicitly on institutions. According to him, it includes:

1. an effective state that enables economic growth and equitable distribution;

2. civil societies and communities that are represented in the policy-making process, with the state facilitating political and social interaction and promoting societal cohesion and stability; and

3. a private sector that plays an independent and productive role in the economy.

This summary recapitulates the principle underlying the more general concept of governance—namely, that it involves wider sections of society. The steering of society implicit in the term 'governance', and even more so in '*good* governance', cannot be successfully performed without the active involvement of civil society and the private sector.

 KEY CONCEPT 14.6   The elements of good governance

- *Participation*—that is, encouragement for the involvement of a wide range of actors in making and implementing decisions, which would contribute to, but does not actually require, democracy

- *Rule of law*—that is, clear, legal frameworks that are enforced impartially, which implies respect for human rights, an independent judiciary, and an incorruptible police

- *Transparency*—that is, open decision-making procedures

- *Responsiveness*—that is, policies that are formulated and implemented in ways that respond to social needs

- *Consensus-oriented*—that is, decision-making through mediation between different interests

- *Equity and inclusiveness*—that is, opportunities for all, especially the most vulnerable, to improve the conditions under which they live

- *Effectiveness and efficiency*—that is, good policies to make the best use of available resources and protect the environment

- *Accountability—that is*, decision-makers, both public and private, being held responsible for all their decisions to society as a whole, and procedures for making sure that this happens

14

✳ KEY POINTS

● This change of focus reflected a broader perspective of focusing upon governance rather than just government.

● This blurs or ignores the distinction between state and society.

● Developing states are encouraged to introduce and practise good governance, which also downplays the state–society distinction.

● Good governance presumes wide societal involvement in the formulation and implementation of policies, as well as accountability to the people for their outcomes.

Policy Communities, 'Iron Triangles', and Issue Networks

▶ See Chapter 3 for an exploration of elitism.

The focus of this chapter has gradually expanded from the civil service to the totality of policy-making and steering processes. One other concept that links the two together is that of **policy communities**. This is an analytical concept drawn from elitist understandings of politics, which originated in the study of British politics in the 1970s (Thatcher, 2001: 7940). It was based upon the assumption that policy-making in a particular area emerged out of the interaction of officials responsible for policy in a certain area and **interest groups**. It argued that, out of this regular interaction, the views of officials and interest groups gradually converged. They tended to see issues and solutions to problems in congruent ways. Thus the policies that emerged were likely to enjoy greater legitimacy and have greater effectiveness because of this convergence of perspectives.

Another version of the same idea emerged from the study of US politics at about the same time. This was the notion of **iron triangles**. These are groups of officials, politicians, and outside experts who, together, formulate a set of policies towards a particular issue area. The difference from policy communities is the more explicit inclusion of politicians in them. A long-established feature of politics on Capitol Hill is the lobbying of members of Congress by business organizations and sometimes the lobbying of some members of Congress by others. This process of lobbying helps to establish a commonality of views on policy. The length of the respective sides of the triangle may vary from issue to issue. But within such communities policy entrepreneurs can emerge from any side and mobilize coalitions to bring about change, though clearly administrative and legislative support is crucial for success (Grossmann, 2014).

A variant of this process can be found in Japan, which reflects the greater organizational power of parties. There, the Liberal Democratic Party (LDP) has been in power almost continuously since 1955. Over the years, it established powerful policy committees that meet regularly with civil service counterparts to devise new policies. This has created what have been termed policy 'tribes' (*zoku*), which have had a distinctive impact upon Japanese policies because of the LDP's long hold on power. The LDP created committees for specific areas of public policy—for example welfare, construction, and agriculture—that met regularly with representatives from the sector concerned and with ministry officials to discuss the operation of existing policies and the formulation of new ones. Traditionally, they have had great opportunities to set the parameters for policy in a given area and also resist changes that were proposed from outside or above. These 'tribes' have had a great impact on policies, often obstructing change that the prime minister would wish to introduce (Kim, 2006).

There is a problem, however, about these theories. In the urge to identify the commonality of views that emerges through close interaction, their proponents sometimes exaggerated the degree of this closeness as compared with other kinds of groupings in the political system (for example political parties or more formalized structures of policy-making). Also, they did not necessarily allow for change taking place. The tighter the implied connections, the more difficult it was to identify spaces through which new or alternative ideas might penetrate. Once again, it raised the issue of how to achieve public-interest policy innovation. Clearly, policy alternatives do periodically emerge in every issue area, so there developed instead the looser concept of issue networks. As Thatcher (2001: 7940) describes it:

> An issue network consists of a large number of issue-skilled 'policy activists' drawn from conventional interest groups and sections of the government, together with academia and certain professions but also comprising expert individuals regardless of formal training. Participants are constantly changing, and their degree of mutual commitment and interdependence varies, although any direct material interest is often secondary to emotional or intellectual commitment.

Building on this insight, subsequent theorizing attempted to identify typologies of networks to identify different types and to show how they interact in the overall policy process.

One of the best-known examples of such a typology was proposed by Rhodes (1997: 38). It had five elements that represented a continuum of organizational strength, running from weak (issue networks, sharing only common ideas) to strong (policy communities that share both ideas and organization):

1. issue networks, which tend to be unstable, with large numbers of members and limited vertical interdependence (for example environmental activists);

2. producer networks, most often sharing economic interests, which tend to have fluctuating membership, limited vertical interdependence, and to serve the interests of producers (for example national associations of car manufacturers);

3. intergovernmental networks, which tend to have limited membership, limited vertical interdependence, and extensive horizontal articulation (for example intergovernmental networks on drug abuse);

14

4. professional networks, which are more stable, with highly restricted membership, vertical interdependence, limited horizontal articulation, and serve the interests of the profession (for example healthcare professionals or lawyers); and

5. policy or territorial communities, which are much more stable, with highly restricted membership, vertical interdependence, and limited horizontal articulation (for example statutory advisory groups on agricultural pest control).

In general, issue networks tend to be larger, covering a wide range of interests, with fluctuating contacts between members, with regular disagreements between members, with only limited resources as a group, and with uneven powers, resources, and access. By contrast, policy communities have much more limited membership, are more focused on economic or professional issues, have frequent, high-quality interaction of members, who share basic values and have access to common resources, and have a hierarchical leadership that can deliver support from members to government (Rhodes, 1997: 44).

> ✳ **KEY POINTS**
>
> ● Where officials and non-governmental actors are jointly involved in policy formulation and implementation, the nature of their relations can be located somewhere on a continuum stretching from issue networks to policy communities.

Conclusion: Towards a Network State?

The focus of this chapter has widened from an initial concern with civil administration to the broader context in which policy is formulated. In previous decades, civil services brought efficiencies and effectiveness to governmental policy-making, especially in Western Europe and the US. More recently, their role has come to be more questioned by people both inside and outside government, as governments have sought to reduce their own size and increase efficiency. In Africa, issues of reforming governance became a higher priority for three, not dissimilar, reasons. First, there was a recognition that weaknesses in governance were limiting the pay-offs to economic reform. Second, the collapse of communism deprived some African states of aid. Third, Western donors could become more demanding in the conditions that they expected recipients to observe, because there were no longer any rivals in the East (Kayizzi-Mugerwa, 2003: 20).

The result has been a widening of the focus in studies devoted to policy-making. They now devote much more attention to non-governmental actors, both individuals and groups. There is a changed awareness about the primacy of the state in many areas of policy, and this in turn has weakened the emphasis upon the authority of the state to impose its will and expect compliance. How far this change can be reconciled with the persistent need to

14

establish effective and clean administration where this does not already exist in developing countries remains to be seen.

Nevertheless, as was indicated in Chapter 1, there is a growing literature that envisages a hollowing out of the nation-state as a response to globalization. Though some, such as Weiss (1998), would contest the inevitability of such changes, we have seen in this chapter the emergence of converging approaches to administrative reform in various parts of the world that might further contribute to this process. The stress upon both governance and good governance implies a rebalancing of relationships between state and society in favour of the latter. Various commentators have looked forward to a state of the future that will look more like a market-based network than a traditional Weberian bureaucratic hierarchy (Bobbitt, 2003). Castells (1998) visualizes the EU as a network state of the future.

See Chapter 2 for a discussion of the 'hollowing out' thesis.

Kamarck has gone so far as to claim that we are witnessing the end of government as we have known it, at least in the US, and the emergence of a new kind of state. She looks forward to two things: (i) 'government by network'; and (ii) 'government by market'. 'Government by network' she interprets as follows:

> The state makes a conscious decision to implement policy by creating a network of nongovernmental organizations through its power to contract, fund or coerce. In government by network, the state itself decides to create, activate, or empower a network for the purpose of implementing a policy. Thus the network is a self-conscious creation of a policymaker or a group of policymakers rather than a naturally occurring part of the greater society. (Kamarck, 2007: 100–1)

As for 'government by market', here she means something broader than a government or state that just relies upon markets to run the economy, though that is subsumed in it. As she explains it: 'In . . . government by market, the work of government involves few, if any, public employees and no public money . . . the government uses state power to create a market that fulfils a public purpose' (Kamarck, 2007: 127). Here, her examples are drawn from environmental policy, where the state creates markets so as to achieve publicly desired ends (such as trading in carbon emissions and reducing pollution). It could also include the creation of markets in schooling, so as to put pressure on failing schools, or it could be used to stimulate the provision of welfare services without relying upon state providers.

This is an imaginative sketch of a future state that is very far removed from the Weberian-type bureaucracy, though Rhodes (1996) already indicated the difficulties such network organization would pose for integrated public policy. How far can networks provide **structuration** for policies, as compared with more organized institutions? Not only does it mean more hands on the steering wheel of the state, but also it means multiple steering wheels. Clearly, networks do not have the same capacity to impose or implement policies except by persuasion. And Savoie (2010) has remarked on the lowered prestige and morale of civil servants that has resulted from the reforms. How far the traditional features of civil services such as hierarchies will survive remains to be seen, as do the ways in which they interact with the new networks that they have helped to create. Certainly, the legal basis of state administration in continental Europe will not be easily eroded.

14

However, it is a strong reminder of the significance of groups and organizations outside the state and civil service in determining the way in which governance operates. A major study of policy-making in the US since the Second World War guardedly concluded, as it looked to the future, that:

> The best bet in Washington politics is always on the status quo. "Not much" is still the best answer for what might happen over the next decade . . . Most Americans will be spectators in the policymaking process. Individual activists and public constituencies can influence policy, but long-established policymakers and interest groups are likely to have much more central roles. (Grossmann, 2014: 189–90)

This difficulty in bringing about change is yet one more factor that sparks public disquiet over the effectiveness of democratic accountability if voters do not trust the 'insiders'. Chapter 16 will return to this issue.

? Key Questions

- Can a valid distinction be drawn between the values and motivations of public administration and business management?
- How would you set about trying to reform the healthcare system of the country in which you live so that it can cope with the various multiple challenges?
- Is it unrealistic to expect civil servants to be politically impartial?
- Should state security functions be devolved to private contractors? What are the dangers?
- How can civil services be made incorruptible? Will New Public Management help?
- Is good governance a Western imposition on the developing world? Did the West have it at similar levels of development? Did it matter then?
- What are the advantages and disadvantages of the 'spoils system' in the US?
- How can agencies and officials be made accountable under the New Public Management?
- Does the Trump administration's experience of trying to change government priorities so that they are more consistent with public opinion illustrate or undermine existing theories of policy-making in the US? Or do they illustrate the fundamental truth of the Arrow impossibility theorem?
- 'Most significant policy changes [in the US] expand the scope of government responsibility. Comparatively few contract government's scope' (Grossmann, 2014: 178). Why? Is that still true?
- What would a network state look like? In what ways would it differ from more traditional states?

▌▏ Further Reading

Barber, Michael (2007), *Instruction to Deliver* (London: Politico's).
A fascinating insider's account of the Blair government's Delivery Unit, illuminated by comparisons of the administrative load of the prime minister today with earlier periods.

Barber, Michael (2015), *How to Run a Government So That Citizens Benefit and Taxpayers Don't Go Crazy* (London: Allen Lane).
An update on general principles of 'deliverology'.

Grossmann, Matthew (2014), *Artists of the Possible: Governing Networks and American Policy Change since 1945* (Oxford and New York: Oxford University Press).
A wide-ranging survey of the experience of American policy-making since the Second World War and of the theories that have been advanced to explain it.

Kamarck, Elaine C. (2007), *The End of Government . . . As We Know it: Making Public Policy Work* (Boulder, CO: Lynne Rienner).
Details the prospects for state administration transformed by new technology.

King, Anthony, and Crewe, Ivor (2013), *The Blunders of Our Governments* (London: OneWorld).
A salutary collection of examples of major policy failures and miscalculations by a series of British governments

Lijphart, Arend (ed.) (1992), *Parliamentary versus Presidential Government* (Oxford: Oxford University Press).
The argument in favour of a parliamentary system.

Lynn, Laurence E., Jr (2006), *Public Management: Old and New* (London: Routledge).
An account of changing approaches to public management.

Pierre, Jon, and Peters, B. Guy (2000), *Governance, Politics and the State* (Basingstoke: Palgrave).
A good introduction to the concept of governance and its implications.

Rhodes, R. A. W. (2000), 'The Governance Narrative: Key Findings and Lessons from the ESRC's Whitehall Programme', *Public Administration*, 78(2): 345–63.
A summary of the findings of a very influential research programme on reforming public administration in the UK.

Savoie, Donald J. (2010), *Power: Where Is It?* (Montreal and Kingston: McGill-Queen's University Press).
A critical analysis of increasing difficulty in ensuring the accountability of public officials in Canada and elsewhere, stemming in part from the New Public Management reforms.

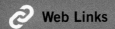 **Web Links**

http://www.civilservant.org.uk/index.html
A master site of information about the civil service in the UK.

https://www.govinfo.gov/collection/plum-book?path=/GPO/United%20States%20
Government%20Policy%20and%20Supporting%20Positions%20%2528Plum%20
Book%2529
US Government Policy and Supporting Positions is the 'spoils' list of government positions to be filled with political appointees by an incoming administration.

 Visit the **Online Resources** that accompany this book to access more learning resources on this topic: www.oup.com/uk/ferdinand/

Media and Politics

15

- Overlap of Governmental and Media Functions
- News: What Is It and Who Makes It?
- Theorizing Political Journalism
- Towards Media Globalization
- Theorizing the Media and Democracy

- The Challenge of New Technologies
- Conclusion
- Key Questions
- Further Reading
- Web Links

Reader's Guide

The term 'media' covers the means and technologies of mass communication, including TV, radio, the press, and the Internet. This chapter begins by considering the more general relationship between the media and governmental organizations, as well as the contribution made by dramatic representation to our understanding of political life. It goes on to look at ways in which journalists and media organizations make news. Next comes the contribution that the media make to political life, especially in democracies. The chapter ends with the impact of the Internet and social media upon political life, from potentially enabling stronger democracy by facilitating much wider participation in decision-making to accusations of false narratives and 'fake' news.

Overlap of Governmental and Media Functions

According to a former head of the UK home civil service, Lord Richard Wilson (2013: 23): 'Communication is a central activity of the state in the modern age. It is the bread and butter of everyday life in government.'

Traditional media organizations play a crucial role in establishing the legitimacy of a nation's political systems and ensuring the trust of citizens in their government, whether it is a democracy or an authoritarian regime. They structure the general contours of public opinion and create an attentive audience.

As journalist Andrew Marr (2004: 63–4, 60) points out:

> Suppose in an average week you are aware of a dozen news stories. It is probably many more than that, but take twelve as the number you think about, even briefly. Those stories, 600 in a year—though since stories intermingle and repeat themselves, let's cut it to 300—affect you. They colour your attitude to the world, and often condition how you take specific decisions, from holiday plans, to saving or spending, to how you look at a possible mugger . . . Your world view is altered by the news you get.

As Hay (1997) puts it, the media have 'context-shaping power'. This means that they structure popular attitudes towards political issues and thus help to frame the range of legitimate responses. They do this in three ways. First, as Marr has already suggested, they do this simply by presenting information of which citizens as a whole would otherwise be ignorant. Second, they advocate what their audiences should think about a particular issue—most obviously, in the leading articles of newspapers. Third, they 'frame' news items in a certain way that is or can be linked to a broader narrative about how the world operates and how it should do so (Iyengar, 2017). In other words, they provide the context within which lots of people see the world.

While this can enhance the power of public deliberation, because they can provide ideas and opinions that individuals would not themselves have considered, it can also mean that possible alternative responses can be screened out of popular gaze. For example, a capitalist press is unlikely to give much credence to possible socialist policies. On the other hand, the media also frame the perspective of government decision-makers on a whole range of policy alternatives, since they provide information about the factual basis on which rational policies need to be built. Even though governments can obtain information on their own, they do rely heavily upon information publicly available in the media as well.

At the same time, it is important to recognise that citizens in general form opinions about political processes and political issues from a wider range of sources than just political or current affairs reporting (Delli Carpini, 2017). Political life is sometimes the stuff of dramas, movies, and novels. Audiences do not neatly separate political entertainment from factual news. *Yes, Minister* had an iconic status in presenting to the public the relationship between politicians and civil servants, whether or not it was always accurate. *Spitting Image* contained nuggets of satire about the Thatcher government that audiences felt must be true at a deeper level, even if they portrayed scenes that never really happened. *The West*

Wing, for some people, was built around the best Democratic president that the US never had. Precisely because daily political life is often humdrum and, to most people, boring, such dramatizations can have a bigger effect upon audiences. And Orwell's novel *Animal Farm* has had a far more profound and widespread impact upon the way in which people think about political life than innumerable political tracts and academic works.

Nor are political insiders immune to such portrayals. President Putin, for example, reportedly told newly appointed Minister of Defence Shoigu that if he wanted to understand American politics, he should watch the TV series *House of Cards* (Zygar, 2016: 332). Bailey (2011) has even argued that fiction might better help us to understand the 'true' nature of 'real' politics, since politics is about drama and the clashes of alternative choices. Politicians have to 'act' as they appeal to disparate audiences. Political and artistic roles do overlap. How we 'imagine' politics cannot be totally distinguished from how it is 'represented', in art, as well as in the media.

 KEY POINTS

- Both governments and the media structure public opinion and cue possible policy responses.
- Politics and entertainment cannot be clearly separated.
- People's perceptions of politics are partly also structured by dramatic representations on TV, film, and stage.

News: What Is It and Who Makes It?

According to former political journalist and editor Andrew Marr (2004: 62):

> 'News' is not 'facts'. News is based on fact. We have to believe, at least for a while, that what is said to have happened did happen . . . But our interest comes from how effectively we can use these facts to make sense of the world and our place in it. News is a source of emotion, belonging and even morality.

News in the media is information that is potentially interesting to a significant number of people, or can be presented in a way that makes it interesting. News organizations are devoted to providing it for the audience that they seek to serve and whom they expect to pay. This generally applies to public service broadcasting too. According to a former Controller of Editorial Policy in the BBC: 'News is a way of making money. No one believes that news and journalism are simply a service to democracy' (Davies, 2009: 135). The BBC needs to demonstrate that it too has national audiences to justify the licence fee. Increasingly, news organizations devote considerable resources to identifying the core 'demographic' of their readers/listeners/viewers, to guide the search for 'news' that will keep attracting their attention.

Journalists select what is going to be reported. According to the former editor of the *Sunday Times*, Harold Evans: 'Facts may be sacred—but which facts? The media are not a neutral looking glass: we select what we mirror' (Davies, 2009: 112).

How do they choose? Again, according to Marr (2004: 56–7):

> What *is* a news story? . . . Of course there are human events which interest almost everyone. We are perpetually intrigued by the extreme, the gruesome, the outlandish. But there is not a reliable supply of these events . . .

> So journalists learn to take less extraordinary things and fashion them into words that will make them seem like news instead . . . To work the alchemy, journalists reshape real life, cutting away details, simplifying events, 'improving' ordinary speech, sometimes inventing quotes, to create a narrative which will work.

> Journalists are not taught what news is. We learn by copying. We look at what news *was*, in yesterday's paper, and the week before . . . Most of us prefer not to analyse news. We have the 'nose' for it, we say . . . News 'just is' . . . Asking a proper reporter to define a story is like asking a teenager what lust is.

Of course, journalists generally subscribe to a code of accuracy in reporting. Factual accuracy is fundamental. Making up and plagiarizing stories can end careers, as former *New York Times* reporter Jayson Blair discovered in 2003. In general terms, Harrison (2006: 2–3) characterizes core news journalism as a 'disposition towards truthfulness'—that is, not an absolute commitment to it—since, as she puts it, 'truth is impossible to attain in anything other than a forensic or scientific setting, although even here it is not guaranteed'. She lists its main values as 'accuracy, sincerity, location and contemporaneousness' (that is, focus on the here and now).

But, in addition to factual accuracy, journalists are expected to make stories 'interesting' because they need to attract readers or viewers. Sometimes, 'stories' are printed because they are *felt* to be true, or at least credible or amusing. 'Freddie Starr Ate My Hamster' (1986) is one of *The Sun*'s most iconic headlines, and though there was no truth in it, no one lost their job. Readers gulped, laughed, and moved on.

Schudson (2008: 76) confirms:

> In practice journalists are committed to much more than neutral transmission of relevant political facts. They are also committed to making news interesting—that is, to entertaining and engaging citizens as well as informing them, drawing them into politics rather than assuming that they come to the newspaper or television or webpage with interests and motives fully formed.

So, as disputes and disagreements are—or are assumed to be—more likely to pique readers' curiosity than consensus and good news, political reporting tends to prioritize and highlight the former, to the frequent chagrin of politicians. TV news bulletins have to entertain, as well as inform. They need to have variety to keep viewers watching. Personalities, especially 'celebrities', are more gripping than lengthy policy positions, let alone party manifestoes. And, when confronted by 'the anarchy of events' in real time (sequences of actions whose full significance may still not be clear), journalists fall back upon 'available cultural resources, the treasurehouse of tropes, narrative forms, resonant mythic forms and frames of their culture' (Schudson, 2008: 89).

One very common such trope is the presentation of political issues in democracies in terms of horse races for political office between rivals, which has the attraction for journalists of treating all the 'competitors' in fundamentally the same way and thus 'objectively', without obliging the reporters to analyse the merits of their individual campaign offerings (Patterson, 2017). There are often many possible alternative ways of framing a particular event or series of events. The assassination of President Kennedy attracted various typical tropes: a human tragedy, a Mafia conspiracy, a personal vendetta by a madman, a judicial cover-up, a plot by the USSR and/or by Cuba, even a plot master-minded by Vice-President Johnson (Stone and Colapietro, 2014). In choosing and developing any one of them, a journalist acts in part like a storyteller to provide overall meaning to readers. It demonstrates that the art of the journalist is not so dissimilar from that of the novelist, dramatist, or film director—with the difference that, in this case, the end of the story is fixed: President Kennedy did die.

Clarity and simplicity are prized for writers in general, journalists included. Marr (2004: 267) recounts the advice he was given when he moved to BBC television:

> Your job is to take an often confusing or complicated situation or series of events and make sense of it for the viewer . . . If your story needs to be seen more than once before it can be understood (and too many do), then it will have totally failed . . . You are distilling information, not packing it in. Get to the point, stick to it, know when it's finished, then end it.

Tabloid newspapers are generally most blamed for populist political reporting, oversimplification, and 'dumbing down' politics. But are the practices of 'quality' publications always so different? For example, an editor of *The Economist* famously urged his journalists, in writing articles, first of all to simplify (distil) and then to exaggerate (Henry, 2007). While this kind of house style certainly makes for a clear perspective—a trait valued by readers with busy schedules—it can oversimplify complex issues. When this happens, at what point does simplification and exaggeration turn into oversimplification, distortion, or even falsehood?

Of course, while journalists are on the front line of finding stories, they are not free agents. They are responsible to editors and publishers. The latter know who their readers or viewers are and what stories are likely to appeal to them, but they also operate within a political and commercial framework that 'prefers' certain types of news and certain types of reporting. The effect of such frameworks has been heatedly debated, as can be seen from **Key Debate 15.1**.

15

 KEY DEBATE 15.1 | **Chomsky versus Marr on editors, media magnates, and the impact of the political economy of Western journalism: does a capitalist press promote conformism and prevent change?**

Noam Chomsky is one of the best-known academic critics of Western media organizations. He has long argued that Western, and especially American, capitalism structures the reporting of news so as to preserve the system by 'manufacturing' its legitimacy.

Along with Herman, he argues:

> It is our view that, among their other functions, the media serve, and propagandize on behalf of, the powerful societal interests that control and finance them . . . This is normally not accomplished by crude intervention, but by the selection of right-thinking personnel and by the editors' and working journalists' internalization of priorities and definitions of newsworthiness that conform to the institution's policy . . . We believe that what journalists do, what they see as newsworthy, and what they take for granted as premises of their work are frequently well explained by the incentives, pressures, and constraints incorporated into such a structural analysis. (Herman and Chomsky, 2002: i)

Marr (2004) does not venture into the broader political economy of media ownership, but as a former editor he does have direct experience of working with newspaper owners and his view of their impact upon news reporting is more nuanced. Owners can and do fire editors, but he argues that they intervene fairly rarely in the stories carried by their papers:

> Proprietors are rich. Journalists, particularly editors, depend on their whims . . . Any decent editor will stand up to the proprietor at times, for the sake of self-respect if nothing else, and to convince the proprietor that he has chosen wisely in having someone who will speak back. Yet no editor who survives speaks back very often, or ignores the little errands and favours the proprietor requires . . .
>
> What, for the reader, are the consequences of the rule of press barons? Yes, rich men have rich men's politics. But these are not entirely predictable. Murdoch is as staunchly republican as the average Lenin-admiring student (which he once was). But if you start from the assumption that moguls are driven by the desire to remove commercial forces in their way, the politics makes sense . . . Rupert Murdoch, born into the era of American market dominance, saw European federalism as an outdated idea and a potential regulatory and taxation threat to his increasingly US-based empire. His most consistent hostility is expressed for organizations that are commercial rivals, such as the BBC, rather than for individuals in power: if he has a preference in politicians, it is simply for the ones in office. Rich newspaper proprietors with TV interests are obsessed with regulatory and competition issues; can mostly avoid paying tax, certainly at normal national rates; and are not much worried by most domestic issues, from crime to public transport, that obsess ordinary voters. The campaigns their editors run, to lock up paedophiles or force some minister to resign, are rarely of more than passing interest to the men at the top . . .
>
> The proprietors, seeing themselves as independent of party politics, and often as outsiders, are partly responsible for the strange fact that the British press is both impertinent and yet also profoundly pro-capitalist, populist. Overall, it has the personality of the insecure and self-made insider. (Marr, 2004: 240–4)

Of course, these two positions are not irreconcilable. Owners want their newspapers or TV stations to profit within the existing commercial environment, so they are unlikely to encourage their organizations to press for radical change. But they can be more open-minded about particular coverage—if it wins audiences that will translate into profits. And even if, collectively, the actions of media magnates reinforce the status quo, they are not conformists. The press in the UK still has what Marr terms a 'buccaneering' tradition. But he also believes that the existence of a public service broadcaster in the BBC, which is competing with private news organizations in its coverage of news and events, acts as a check upon the wilder excesses of journalistic standards, both in print and broadcasting media. Public service broadcasting can also promote variety and diversity of analysis and approaches. Relying exclusively upon free-market competition is not the only way of achieving this.

These two contributions show that there are still important differences between national media policies and practices, even in the same part of the world. For example, British public opinion is overwhelmingly supportive of the BBC (though it is has certainly endured torrid criticism from both Conservative and Labour governments, not to mention its rivals), but, as Freedman (2008) shows, its American counterpart, PBS, is much more subject to complaints over 'squandering' public funds on middle-class viewers who could afford to pay for its output. So national political cultures do affect the operation of public service broadcasting and the expectations of what journalists should do.

Theorizing Political Journalism

Does media reporting change political outcomes? A recurring conclusion of research on the media has been that it does not, or at most has a marginal effect (Bennett and Iyengar, 2008). However, this is not straightforward. Why do newspapers regularly bother to announce which candidates they are backing for election if it has no effect? According to Tsfati (2017: 571), while relatively few studies have been done of the attitudes of politicians towards the media, he reports that studies from the Nordic countries and the US 'all demonstrated that politicians believe that the news media are enormously influential'. Marr (2004: 186) concurs: 'There is a strong sense that the power to set the agenda and initiate the terms of national debate has passed from ministers to journalists.' When Labour won the 1997 general election, the headline of newspaper *The Sun* was 'It's *The Sun* Wot Won It', because the normally Conservative-supporting newspaper had switched sides and urged its readers to vote Labour. In fact, as Reeves, McKee, and Stuckler (2015) argue, the magnitude of the swing was too great for it to be explained by that fact alone. Voters had become too exasperated by a tired, divided, and self-serving Conservative government. There was an overwhelming national desire for a change. However, Reeves et al. also argue that, in the much closer election of 2010, *The Sun*'s endorsement of the Conservative Party quite possibly did swing the election the Tories' way, though the ultimate outcome was a coalition government with the Liberal Democrats. On the other hand, in the British general election in 2017 (**see Figure 15.1**), the Labour Party did much better than expected, despite near-universal

15

disparagement of its leader, Jeremy Corbyn, by all the mainstream media and even many of his own MPs. All this suggests that, at the margin, media reporting can sometimes have an effect, but not always in the way that media experts expect.

Davies (2009: 389–90) has no doubts about the influence of the *Daily Mail* on British politics, which he castigates:

> In the course of serving its readers, the *Daily Mail* has had a significant impact on almost every political issue of the day—Europe, crime and policing, the NHS, binge drinking, the MMR vaccine, GM foods, asylum and immigration, drugs, fuel tax, homosexuality, trade unionism, human rights. In so far as it is simply making moral judgements about what is important, its work is entirely legitimate. In so far as it allows its special relationship with inaccuracy to distort those issues, it clearly is not. In that case, the effect of the *Mail*'s professional foul is not merely to mislead its readers about the state of the world but to distort the whole political process . . .
>
> It's the aggression that makes the *Mail* powerful. I know of nothing anywhere in the rest of the world's media which matches the unmitigated spite of an attack from the *Daily Mail*.

Hart and Lavally (2017: 109) have argued that political journalism now 'more closely resembles a Second Legislature of debaters than a Fourth Estate of onlookers'. By this, they mean that political journalists act more as committed participants in the political process than as dispassionate observers. Sometimes they challenge and sometimes they bolster official authorities, just as legislators do:

> Reporters construct political events by weighing popular notions against officially preferred interpretations, by favouring local attitudes and assumptions over the distant. Their dominant story frames may isolate or overpower the same subgroups dismissed by legislators. Journalists stand guard against disorder, giving sway to institutional priorities and even sanitizing government views. (Hart and Lavalley, 2017: 117)

They identify six ways in which political journalists perform these functions on a day-to-day basis. By doing so, they extend and deepen the debate over the extent to which the capitalist media promote conformism and stifle radical challenges to the official order presented in **Key Debate 15.1**.

1. The traditional media act as 'vessels of accommodation' in that they try to balance popular interpretations of current events with official ones (for example mediating how to present international threats or terrorism).

2. They prioritize localist, rather than cosmopolitan, agendas. '[T]he news text often contains within it subtle and not-so-subtle signals of nationalism'— namely, the different reporting of international summits in different countries, or of migration issues.

3. They help to reproduce existing power dynamics within their societies: 'If read with sufficient subtlety, the news text often tells us who is influential and who is not, which views hold sway and which have gone by the board.'

4. Sometimes they challenge existing interpretations of events, but sometimes they reinforce traditionalist values.

5. The media tend to emphasize popular understandings, employing everyday metaphors to make things clear, relevant and interesting, rather than official or academic versions.

6. The media tend to focus upon current issues and narratives, at the expense of a longer view. So '[r]eading a newspaper can ... be a study in provisional biases and transitory understandings of the political order' (Hart and LaVally, 2017: 112–17).

✳ KEY POINTS

- Journalists and editors determine what 'news' is.
- News is based upon facts, but also has to be made interesting so as to catch the attention of audiences.
- Reporters operate in the interstices between official and popular understandings of events, sometimes leaning more to one side and sometimes more to the other.
- The media draw ordinary people into thinking about politics.
- They often use standard storylines to explain or make sense of facts and events.
- The stances of individual media organizations can tilt electoral outcomes and policy choices, but not always in predictable ways.

FIGURE 15.1   British Prime Minister Theresa May at a press briefing
© Frederic Legrand - COMEO/ Shutterstock.com

15

Towards Media Globalization

The standards and expectations of journalism do vary around the world. For example, the Worlds of Journalism project has shown that journalists in the developing world tend to adopt a more positive framework in reporting national development policy and a less confrontational attitude towards domestic politics than their counterparts in the developed world (Kalyango et al., 2017). The diversity is particularly true of the print media, where different national traditions of newspaper ownership persist. Hallin and Mancini (2004) identified three distinct systems in the West: (i) the Mediterranean or 'polarized pluralism' model, typically found in southern Europe, where newspapers are more partisan and where journalists are expected to be more committed to a particular party view than 'objectively' professional; (ii) the northern European or democratic corporatist model, with traditions of state intervention and state subsidies, but strong professionalism and institutionalized self-regulation; and (iii) the North Atlantic or liberal model, in the US and the UK, with strong professionalization, non-institutionalized self-regulation, and market regulation, apart from public broadcasting in the UK. When they extended the analysis, they concluded that other regions of the world tended to come closer to the 'polarized pluralist' model than to liberal America (Hallin and Mancini, 2012). All this affects the way journalism impacts political life.

Hallin and Mancini suggest, though, that the increasing commercialization of the media may be leading to greater international homogenization of media practices and gradual convergence with the liberal model, albeit very slowly. That is most evident in TV. Television has attracted widespread academic analysis for the ways in which it has transformed the practice of politics around the world. Sometimes, this is dismissed as part of a broader syndrome of changes of 'Americanization'. While the actual term is an oversimplification (the owner of the Sky and Fox TV networks, Rupert Murdoch, for example, is Australian and the BBC has also been influential), there is no doubt that programme formats that originated in the US have spread around the world. In France, for example, this trend has spawned neologisms such as *le talk-show*, *le soap opera*, *la policytainment* (that is, policy + entertainment) (Musso, 2009), no doubt to the horror of the Académie Française. And the phenomenon is not limited to the developed world. The format of current affairs programmes on the Chinese state broadcaster CCTV (though not so much of their content) would be very familiar to regular viewers of CNN. This is a complete transformation when compared with CCTV's formats in the 1980s and 1990s.

But there is one respect in which globalization has not spread as much as might have been expected. The main international news agencies are still overwhelmingly based in the developed world—Associated Press, Reuters, Bloomberg, Dow Jones, Agence France Press, etc. Most of their reporters are located in the developed world too. This matters because, as veteran BBC foreign correspondent Martin Bell remarked: 'People tend to suppose that journalists are where the news is. This is not so. The news is where journalists are' (Marr, 2004: 292). For example, Wessler et al. (2008) identified variations in the number of correspondents of newspapers from various European countries stationed in Brussels as a key factor in explaining differences in the coverage of EU affairs.

15

This has two unfortunate side effects. The first is that newspapers in the developed world increasingly rely upon reports from news agencies as their own profits and reporting staff have been cut. So it diminishes the range of stories that figure in public opinion there. The second is that news organizations in the developing world, with more meagre resources, are forced to rely heavily upon these news agencies for coverage of international affairs. So coverage in both the developed and the developing world is skewed towards events in the developed world. In the 1980s, the Non-Aligned Movement attempted to redress this imbalance with a proposed New World Information and Communication Order in conjunction with UNESCO, but it was strongly resisted by Reagan and Thatcher, in part because of bitter opposition from Western news organizations. As Nordenstreng (2012) puts it, the idea has not died, but neither has any progress been made in addressing the problem.

In the second half of the 2000s, the UN Department of Public Information published annual lists of the ten most under-reported stories of world news. The last list, in 2008, was: (i) thousands of refugees displaced by violence in the Central African Republic; (ii) the global food crisis; (iii) a novel approach to fighting crime and impunity in post-conflict Guatemala; (iv) the West African drug trade; (v) the untold story of a diplomatic breakthrough in Kosovo; (vi) global warming and climate change; (vii) trafficking in arms, drugs, and human beings through ports; (viii) the threat from orbiting debris in space; (ix) the struggle for survival of an indigenous people in Colombia; and (x) a new UN Human Rights protocol boosting economic, social, and cultural rights (UN, 2009). Most related primarily to the developing world.

Recent years have seen the emergence of new global TV news channels such as Al Jazeera, which Seib (2008) acclaimed as heralding greater diversity in international news reporting. Certainly, its Arabic service has attracted a pan-Arab and broader Islamic audience that is distrustful of Western news reporting, especially its generally sympathetic treatment of Israel. It played a key role in spreading the Arab Spring: 'Al Jazeera is loved by the Arab street but hated by entrenched governing authorities from Rabat to Gaza . . . Al-Jazeera clearly constructs itself not only as an Arab media outlet but also as the Arab media representative that contrasts with American and Western media' (Cherribi, 2012: 472, 481). Apart from that, the Russian, Chinese, and French governments have all ploughed large sums of money into starting up their own English-language news broadcasters as a way of enhancing their nations' 'soft power'. They have certainly expanded the range of comment available on TV channels globally, but whether they have significantly expanded the range of issues covered or the variety of coverage, or attracted broad new international audiences, remains to be researched.

15

✴ KEY POINTS

- Standards and expectations of journalists vary around the world.
- Styles of news presentation and reporting on television converge around the world.
- International news agencies are predominantly located in the developed world and this skews the pattern of events that are covered.

Theorizing the Media and Democracy

It is very difficult to envisage democracy without freedom of the press. This is illustrated by **Table 15.1**, which shows the 2017 ranking of the states with the greatest press freedom, as compiled by Reporters Without Borders. All would be termed democracies.

TABLE 15.1   Press Freedom Index 2017

Rank	Country
1.	Norway
2.	Sweden
3.	Finland
4.	Denmark
5.	Netherlands
6.	Costa Rica
7.	Switzerland
8.	Jamaica
9.	Belgium
10.	Iceland
11.	Austria
12.	Estonia
13.	New Zealand
14.	Ireland
15.	Luxembourg
16.	Germany
17.	Slovakia
18.	Portugal
19.	Australia
20.	Surinam
21.	Samoa
22.	Canada ...
40.	UK
43.	US

Source: https://rsf.org/en/ranking_table (accessed May 2017).

Historically, the rise of democracy in Western societies was associated with the rise of the press. One of the most influential works in the field was *The Structural Transformation of the Public Sphere* published by Jürgen Habermas in 1962. It could be distinguished from civil society, because it denoted a 'sphere' in which citizens came to debate matters of public importance, whereas civil society also encompassed private interests and the market. In it, journalists and publishers had played a key role in becoming 'the carriers and leaders of public opinion' (Habermas, 1989: 182). Garnham (2001) summarizes the notion of 'public sphere' in **Key Quote 15.2**. Thus the notion of 'public sphere' can be used both to describe a long process of historical evolution and also as a model against which to measure the actual operation of citizenship in any given society.

Schudson (1998) has written a magisterial history of civic life in the US since the American Revolution in which he emphasizes the widening evolution of the understanding and practice of citizenship. From a rather restricted concept that focused upon occasional involvement in the political life of the republic, it has swelled to encompass much more:

> Citizens still exercise citizenship as they stand in line at their polling places, but now they exercise citizenship in many other locations. They have political ties not only to elected public officials in legislatures but also to attorneys in courtrooms and organized interest groups that represent them to administrative agencies. Moreover, they are citizens in their homes, schools, and places of employment. Women and minorities self-consciously do politics just by turning up, so long as they turn up in positions of authority and responsibility in institutions where women and minorities were once rarely seen. They do politics when they walk into a room, anyone's moral equals, and expect to be treated accordingly . . . Citizenship now is a year-round and day-long activity, as it was only rarely in the past. (Schudson, 1998: 299, 311)

The notion of the legitimate sphere of democratic politics has expanded, along with the notion of openness of information. The media have both been a major factor in that change and benefited from it. It is a vital element in Keane's (2009) notion of present-day democracy as 'monitory democracy'—that is, holding public officials to account (see Chapter 5).

Q KEY QUOTE 15.2 Garnham on the public sphere

15

'The public sphere was both a set of institutional spaces—newspapers, lecture halls, coffee houses, etc.—and a set of discursive rules . . . a site within which the formation of public opinion, and the political will stemming from and legitimized by such opinion, is subject to the disciplines of a discourse, or communicative ethics, by which all views are subjected to the critical reasoning of others. At the same time, a democratically legitimate public sphere requires that access to it is open to both all citizens and all views equally, provided only that all participants are governed by the search for general agreement.' (Garnham, 2001: 12586)

Schudson (2008) has enumerated seven vital functions that the media perform for democracies and these are listed in **Key Quote 15.3**. But, as the title of his book suggests, the media are not necessarily loved, even if they do perform a vital public service. Obviously, they are resented by politicians for holding them to account. But there is another element in the relationship between the media and democracy that needs to be mentioned. At least until recently, the media also acted as gatekeepers for democratic activity. Politicians needed to enlist their cooperation in spreading their messages. This was a two-way dependency:

> Politicians need access to the communication channels that are controlled by the mass media, including the hopefully credible contexts of audience reception they offer. Consequently, they must adapt their messages to the demands of formats and genres devised inside such organizations and to their associated speech styles, story models and audience images. Likewise, journalists cannot perform their task of political scrutiny without access to politicians for information, news, interviews, action and comment. (Blumler and Gurevich, 2007: 50)

Until the 1960s, the tension in this relationship was less acute because the media still tended to behave relatively deferentially towards politicians. Gradually, however, that relationship has changed. Barnett (2002) argues that it has gone through four stages: initial deference; 'equal engagement', when politicians and journalists vigorously challenged each other; journalistic 'disdain'; and, finally, 'contempt'—the present phase, when politicians are uniformly suspected of self-interested, if not corrupt, motivations and subjected to

KEY QUOTE 15.3   **Schudson's seven key functions that the media perform for democracy**

'1. information: the news media can provide fair and full information so citizens can make sound political choices;

2. investigation: the news media can investigate concentrated sources of power, particularly governmental power;

3. analysis: the news media can provide coherent frameworks of interpretation to help citizens comprehend a complex world;

4. social empathy: journalism can tell people about others in their society and their world so that they can come to appreciate the viewpoints and lives of other people, especially those less advantaged than themselves;

5. public forum: journalism can provide a forum for dialogue among citizens and serve as a common carrier of the perspectives of varied groups in society;

6. mobilization: the news media can serve as advocates for political programs and perspectives and mobilize people to act in support of those programs;

7. publicizing representative democracy: journalists [should] cover more carefully some institutions and relationships that today they take for granted or ignore.'

(Schudson, 2008: 12, 23–4)

15

'unthinking ridicule'. Prime Minister Blair made a speech in 2007 in which he complained of the media behaving 'like a feral beast, just tearing people and reputations to bits' (Barnett and Townend, 2014: 160), though he only dared to say it just before stepping down. Expenses scandals in the UK, US, and France have fuelled this anti-politician feeling, especially as they have largely been uncovered by journalists rather than public watchdogs—though Barnett (2002) points out that MPs are now paid less than journalists on national newspapers and ministers are paid a lot less than newspaper editors.

Yet newspapers, too, in the UK and the US have since become even less 'loved' than before. They have suffered a backlash from the public, although for different reasons. In the UK, the revelation that journalists had been hacking into other people's phones caused a storm of protest. A practice that began with arguable public interest motivations—the phones of members of the royal family, politicians, and celebrities—morphed into widespread hacking of ordinary people who happened to pop up in the course of newspaper investigations. Most shockingly, it transpired that the phone of Milly Dowler, a teenager who had disappeared, had been hacked. On the basis of what they thought they found, the Murdoch empire's *News of the World* had, for a while, been running stories about her having left home to look for work when, in fact, she had already been murdered. This unleashed a flood of complaints from other people who felt that their privacy had been trampled by unscrupulous journalists—and thousands might have been involved (Cathcart, 2012). Prime Minister Gordon Brown was excoriating:

> Many, many wholly innocent men, women and children who, at their darkest hour, at their most vulnerable moment in their lives, with no one and nowhere to turn to, found their properly private lives, their private losses, their private sorrows treated as the public property of News International—their private innermost feelings and their private tears bought and sold by News International for commercial gain . . . This nexus—this criminal-media nexus—was claiming to be on the side of the law-abiding citizen but was in fact standing side by side with criminals against our citizens. Others have said that in its behaviour towards those without a voice of their own, News International descended from the gutter to the sewers. The tragedy is that it let the rats out of the sewers. (Kenski and Jamieson, 2017: 333–4)

The *News of the World* was forced to close. In the aftermath, the government set up the Leveson Enquiry to examine whether there was a need for more effective public regulation of the press. This reported in 2012 and recommended the establishment of a new independent statutory body to replace the ineffective Press Complaints Commission, in the same way that judicial freedom in the UK has statutory guarantees. However, although it promised action, the government has delayed—initially because of the legal argument that it might prejudice the prosecution of journalists who had broken the law, but also in the face of enormous hostility from the press (Thomas and Finneman, 2014). The *Daily Mail* has been particularly strident. The criminal trials have now ended and still nothing has been done, which suggests that the government is reluctant to confront the media for fear of what they might do in retaliation.

In the US, the media have also come under increasing fire in the 2000s, though not so much for misdeeds as for partisanship. This has been primarily directed at the 'vast left-wing

15

media apparatus that rigs the national narrative in the pursuit of partisan politics', allegedly just as much as the Soviet Union controlled thought through the media (Breitbart, 2012: 2), and has accompanied the rise first of the Tea Party and then Donald Trump. It portrays America as being in the middle of a 'media war' just as much as during the Cold War (Breitbart, 2012: 3). People like Breitbart blame the Clinton administration for starting this process, or making it qualitatively worse. They allege that websites like Salon.com, which claims to analyse events from 'a politically progressive viewpoint', were mobilized in a counter-attack to smear their opponents during the Monica Lewinsky disputes, and then the Obama administration patronized the Huffington Post when it wanted to get its views across. Breitbart News was set up in 2007 to counter this with online posts from the conservative right. But its biggest adversary is the traditional media, because it is alleged to be biased:

> The left is the media . . . I'm at war with the mainstream media because they portray themselves as objective observers of reality when they're no such thing—they're partisan 'critical theory' hacks who think they can destroy everything America stands for by standing on the sidelines and sniping at patriotic Americans with all their favorite slurs . . . The Democrats have the Big Three Networks and major news dailies as their offensive line, and a starting backfield of Hollywood celebrities and academia . . . Everyone is now disillusioned about the media. Nobody is fooled into believing that most reporters are objective, straight-down-the-middle truth-seekers. (Breitbart, 2012: 3, 58, 210, 222)

This line has now come to be associated with the Trump administration and Trump's tweets. There is no doubt that the rise of the Internet and social media is transforming current affairs media and politics in general.

KEY POINTS

- The rise of the press led to the emergence of a 'public sphere' in society.
- This also led to the enrichment of the concept of citizenship.
- The press performs seven functions in democracies.
- The contribution of the press is only grudgingly accepted.
- The press in the UK and the US has come in for more criticism.

The Challenge of New Technologies

In recent years, new communications technologies have begun to revolutionize the role of the media in politics again. Indeed, it can be argued that they may have a bigger impact than newspapers and TV did in the past, not least because they provide additional opportunities for ordinary citizens to take advantage of the new public space to make an impact on politics. They can provide civil society with new arenas for activity. There are three reasons for this. First, the Internet and mobile phones have transformed the ability of ordinary citizens to organize even when confronted with repression from their authorities. Second, they offer the future possibility of transforming decision-making institutions as well (for example voting and referendums). Third, they have democratized access to the media. We will consider these three dimensions in turn.

Promoting horizontal communication

Previously, communication channels within states were mainly vertical. The most influential media outlets tended to congregate in national capitals. That was especially true of TV stations. Political parties and interest groups achieved results by concentrating their efforts there. The opportunities for other groups to make themselves into significant forces were constrained by the difficulties of contacting people through landline telephones and the mail. Now, however, there are much greater opportunities for would-be political actors to mobilize support using horizontal communications—mobile phones (including SMS texting) and the Internet. It represents a new stage in the relationship between the media and political involvement, a new opening for Habermas's 'public sphere'. Gradually, it is giving voices to Scott's 'infrapolitics' (see Chapter 16). Potentially, it creates opportunities for new forms of citizenship, where a much broader range of citizens can exercise more immediate influence over policy choices in real time, when previously they could only comment from the wings at most (Allen and Light, 2015).

In the early years of the Internet, there was optimism about the possibilities that the new media offered for organizing political parties. In the US, in particular, the enormous cost of standing for office made it very difficult for outsiders to be elected. Much was made of the success of a former wrestler, Jesse Ventura, in winning election against all expectations as Governor of Minnesota in 1998 as a third-party candidate. He made widespread use of the Internet as a cheap means to get his message across, bypassing existing party and media establishments. Ventura stood out from the latter in a big way. He prefigured later unconventional 'populist' politicians, such as Italian piano-playing comedian Bepe Grillo and Donald Trump, who have also exploited the potential of online media:

> Ventura's political substance lies partly though significantly in his style—a style that is as tabloidized as any: sensationally populist, ironically playful, laughingly sceptical, wildly outrageous, sometimes self-mocking and sometimes self-satisfied, inclusive and participatory, blusterous and averse to euphemism, scandalous, offensive, and often in your face. Ventura is to 'respectable' politicians what tabloids are to 'respectable' journalism . . . Like the tabloid media, Ventura collapses the distinction between politics and entertainment. (Glynn, 2007)

The established parties quickly took note of the threat and started throwing money at their Internet strategies. They have refined the techniques of using the Internet for candidates to communicate directly with individual voters and target specific messages to their various concerns. For a long time, they outflanked the challengers. As was mentioned in the

15

FIGURE 15.2 Politicians such as Donald Trump now rely heavily on Twitter as a means to communicate directly with voters

© Bloomicon/ Shutterstock.com

previous chapter, American political parties have profited from the Internet by mobilizing far more campaign contributions than ever before. Yet the victory of Donald Trump in 2016, this time relying heavily upon Twitter (**see Figure 15.2**) to communicate directly with voters, as well as his prior exposure as host of a TV reality show, demonstrates that it is still possible for outsiders to defeat party establishments.

The new technologies can also empower groups to organize protests in new ways, by mobilizing supporters much more quickly and unexpectedly in real time (Bennett and Segerberg, 2013). This can be very effective. Not only can social media campaigns topple authoritarian regimes whose institutions have lost legitimacy (as in the Arab Spring), but they can also bring about the downfall of publicly elected officials in democracies, even if it means flouting democratic institutions in the process. The Philippines saw an important example at the end of 2000, with an explosion of SMS texting making a decisive contribution to the overthrow of the democratically elected President Estrada (**see Case Study 15.4**). It is still relevant today.

These new possibilities for self-organization will impact both democratic and authoritarian states, although in different ways. More open systems are vulnerable to the activities of what Rheingold (2002) has termed 'smart mobs'. These are technologically sophisticated groups who use their skills to organize group protests that the authorities find difficult to prevent, even if they are aware of what is planned, because of the short warning that they are given. It can be a kind of political blackmail. It certainly challenges

 CASE STUDY 15.4   **The fall of Joseph Estrada**

In 1998, Joseph Estrada was elected president of the Philippines. A former actor who had played the lead in over 100 movies and had produced 70, he entered politics in the late 1980s as mayor of a town in Metro Manila. Gradually, his political career took off as he was elected first a senator and then, in 1992, vice-president. Coming from a poor background in a country whose politics are dominated by traditional elite families, he won the support of the poorer strata of society.

By 2000, however, his administration was in trouble. His popularity in opinion polls was sliding. He launched a costly military campaign against the Moro Islamic Liberation Front on the island of Mindanao. Then, it was alleged that he had taken several million dollars in bribes from gambling and the senate moved to impeach him. In January 2001, pro-Estrada senators blocked a key piece of evidence from being presented in court. This plunged the country into crisis (Doronila, 2001).

In Manila, outraged demonstrators began to organize public demonstrations using mobile phones. In a normal week, Filipinos had been exchanging 50 million text messages per day, but, as the crisis deepened, this figure rose to 80 million. People intending to demonstrate passed on information about the location at very short notice to everyone they knew, who then cascaded it on to others. The organizers of the demonstrations quickly realized that it was this short timescale that made it extremely difficult for the authorities to respond. Hundreds of thousands of people kept gathering in flash demonstrations on or around the same street that had been the site of demonstrations of 'people power' in 1986 that had toppled the dictator President Ferdinand Marcos.

After five days of demonstrations that paralysed the capital, Estrada was forced to step down, to be replaced by Vice-President Gloria Macapagal Arroyo. He was the first political casualty of SMS texting. Three months later, he was arrested and put on trial. After proceedings lasting six years, he was found guilty in 2007 and sentenced to life imprisonment. Almost immediately afterwards, President Arroyo pardoned Estrada on the grounds that he had reached the age of 70, the age at which prisoners in the Philippines are released, and in return for a commitment that he would retire from politics.

15

the ability of the state to satisfy demands without alienating the rest of society that did not take part. Obviously, authoritarian regimes place more emphasis on controlling the freedom to organize in this way because any such protest is fundamentally more threatening (**see Key Quote 15.5**).

China, in particular, has devoted enormous efforts to frustrating the claim made in this quote through surveillance of the Internet. It has erected a firewall to limit the access of its own citizens to politically sensitive material abroad. It also has a large number of censors (nicknamed 'Internet mamas') supervising electronic message boards and requiring that politically or socially undesirable materials are deleted. This process has been further tightened under President Xi Jinping. However, the struggle continues. Technologically sophisticated netizens use mirror servers to outwit the censors. Some end up in jail.

Of course, not all the groups that use the new technologies to aid organization are benign. The Internet can be extremely useful to small extremist groups for attracting adherents. The challenge of combating groups bent on violence or terrorism has been made more serious for all governments, whether democratic or authoritarian.

Developing democracy and electronic decision-making

Evangelists for the new media have also suggested that they can be used to bring public decision-making much closer to the people than ever before. Barber (1998, 2003), for instance, has looked forward to the new technology inaugurating a new era of 'strong' democracy (that is, a modern equivalent of the democracy of ancient Athens). However, for the moment, actual proposals have focused more on two alternative strategies. The first is based on local government; the other, on the greater use of referenda.

The local government option has been based on the model of town meetings in the US (that is, meetings of citizens in a local community to debate and decide policy). The electronic variant is to arrange for citizens to be connected through cable so that they can debate and decide online (Becker and Slaton, 2000). The expectation was that this would enable a richer form of democracy to take root locally and then gradually spread throughout the nation. It assumed that the electronic meetings would themselves propose and decide on policy. The alternative was to organize regular electronic consultation of citizens about proposals that initially emerged either from representatives or from administrators. The model would be based on the referenda regularly organized in Switzerland (Budge, 1996).

KEY QUOTE 15.5   ***Rolling Stone* on the Internet and authoritarian states**

'The Internet is the censor's biggest challenge and the tyrant's worst nightmare . . . Unbeknown to their governments, people in China, Iraq and Iran, among other countries, are freely communicating with people all over the world.' (*Rolling Stone*, quoted in Swett, 1995)

This latter variant is clearly a 'weaker' form of democracy than the former, though one might lead to the other. Neither variant has yet made a great deal of progress. The same is true of online voting in Europe.

There is an important issue hanging over all such proposals: how reliable and robust is the technology, especially for voting? An American report reminded us that there are a great many potential dangers (*National Research Council of the National Academies*, 2005). These dangers are likely to be less great when the voting is confined to localities. Once voting is aggregated at higher levels, there is a serious danger of the integrity of the voting process being compromised. Votes could be secretly stolen, redirected, or simply dumped. The whole process could be disrupted by viruses. Even though the existing American system of voting in many states ran into serious criticism after the shambles of the 2000 presidential election recounts, there are still good reasons for waiting until a really secure voting system can be devised. Until that happens, the more ambitious hopes for e-democracy will have to be delayed. And the allegations about foreign hacking in the presidential campaigns in the US and France in 2016 and 2017 have reinforced the need for caution.

But although these are daunting challenges, they are not the only ones that stand in the way of politics being transformed by e-democracy. As McLean (1989) pointed out, there are other fundamental difficulties in aggregating preferences of citizens in some kind of direct democracy. They relate to the general difficulty of coming to a definitive view of the wishes of large number of people expressing preferences for a range of alternative policy proposals that they rank in quite different ways. This is another manifestation of the problem identified by the Arrow impossibility theorem presented in Chapter 12. This problem becomes even more intractable if any of the possible choices are dependent upon conditions resulting from other choices, as is almost always the case where government-spending priorities are involved. Thus the problems of e-democracy transforming traditional problems of democracy are not likely to be resolved any time soon.

From democratizing the media to 'fake' news

The new media have also made it much easier for non-journalists to publish comments and views in blogs on politics. Some have become more influential than established commentators. Politicians, whether elected or standing for election, now increasingly publish blogs to connect with voters. This further personalizes political life.

Equally, individuals can now report breaking news as quickly as news agencies if they happen to be in the right place at the right time. They can also publish alternative versions of events to 'correct' 'inaccurate' official reports—something that has happened many times in China, despite the controls.

In both these ways, the new media have begun to change the traditional media landscape creating more hybrid forms (Chadwick, 2013). At the same time, politicians are having to become more savvy in the ways in which they promote themselves and their causes. According to the Pew Research Center, already by the beginning of 2016, 62 per cent of

15

Americans were getting news from social media and 18 per cent were doing so often (Gottfried and Shearer, 2016). During the 2016 US presidential campaigns, Pew then noted a significant difference in the way in which the two campaigns organizations dealt with Twitter. Trump retweeted posts from ordinary people far more than Clinton and his own comments were retweeted much more often than Clinton's (Pew Research Center, 2016). It reinforced his image as a man of the people.

What also became a qualitatively different change was the way in which campaigns, especially Trump's, used social media to generate and disseminate news stories of their own, bypassing the conventional media (**see Key Debate 15.6**). Steve Bannon, White House chief strategist in the first months of the Trump administration and former executive of right-wing Breitbart News website, has talked openly about the need to 'weaponize' the media. Their views have been articulated as follows:

> It's time we take back our media from politically motivated puppet masters and demand the original intended purpose: to hold power accountable in an unbiased, non-partisan manner . . . Mainstream liberal media over this past decade became handmaidens to a government run by an Executive Office that was on the path to tyranny. (Donner, 2017: 4)

 KEY DEBATE 15.6 **Barber and Breitbart versus Morozov on the Internet as a liberating force for democracy**

Barber and Breitbart were at opposite ends of the political spectrum, in that Barber was a 'progressive', whilst Breitbart was a Tea Party conservative. However, they agreed on the potential of the Internet to strengthen and spread democracy. Barber (1998, 2003) looked to the Internet to provide a technological solution to the weaknesses of contemporary democracy. In particular, he looked forward to it enabling the modern-day equivalent of democracy in classical Greece, which provided a regular opportunity for all citizens to debate and decide public policy.

Breitbart was a pugnacious critic of the traditional media elites in the US, but he was a very strong believer in the way in which the Internet could enable the 'forgotten' ordinary citizens to make themselves heard: 'Millions of so-called bloggers write, report, upload their stories online, and influence the national political landscape because of the advent of the very liberating and democratic World Wide Web' (Breitbart, 2012: 3). But, echoing *Rolling Stone* in **Key Quote 15.5**, he also believed in the potential for American democracy, if rightfully redirected, to save the world:

> The people of the United States, with its First Amendment, are leading the way in combining free speech and technology. Just as Western rock and roll helped bring down the Eastern Bloc in the latter half of the twentieth century, the Internet is going to provide a similar impetus to the people of the world to grasp the possibilities of freedom . . . The big picture goes beyond America because the world is also under attack by the same anti-free market, anti-individual liberty forces. It is not just a political war, it is a cultural war, and our audacious goal is to change the big narrative . . . I want to foment their [the Tea Party]

> righteous anger. These people are *my* people. They recognize the civilizational battle under way here; they understand that the United States is *it*, the last outpost for freedom. (Breitbart, 2012: 9, 211, 205)
>
> Morozov (2012), by contrast, is much more sceptical. Given his Russian background, it is no surprise that one of his chapters is entitled 'Why the KGB Wants You to Join Facebook', warning against putting so much of one's life online for anyone to see—and the loss of privacy is not just a problem in Russia. He anticipated the way in which, in the 2016 US presidential election, Facebook was providing both sides with contextual data on individual citizens so that more precisely targeted appeals could be sent directly to them to vote for a particular candidate, without anyone else knowing what precisely was being said or, possibly, promised. Manufactured posts can flood the Web with misleading, or even false, information.

The Trump campaign in 2016 promoted Reddit, Facebook, Instagram, and Twitter as news sources, and then co-opted them as a campaign weapon. According to the political commentator Peter Oborne (Oborne and Roberts, 2017), 'Trump gave politics back to the people who vote':

> He exploited Twitter's ability to express raw sentiment instantly, without nuance or subtext, and its ability to blur, even extinguish the boundary between sentiment and fact . . . He made enemies, pursued feuds and communicated a sense of apocalyptic doom. He was very funny and often acute . . . Trump told lies, smeared and fabricated in order to destroy opponents. If the facts proved what he was saying to be untrue, Trump didn't care. He constructed a personal epistemology. His truth claims were purely instrumental. He made assertions about his own honesty—and the lies of his enemies—in order to gain power and win arguments . . . He viscerally understood the power of this new medium to simplify complex ideas, to remove nuance and subtext and, above all, to remove any boundary between assertion and fact. Donald Trump was the first modern politician . . . to create a world of belief impervious to reality. He understood that politics was entertainment. Hence the name-calling, the bullying, the public humiliation, the relish to combat.

Bannon went further and allegedly mobilized artificial intelligence to spread news and fake news through endless automated linked 'bots' to create a sense of an alternative public opinion online, which would reassure covert supporters of Trump that they were not alone and that they could come out openly. According to Anderson and Horvath (2017), organizations behind Trump made up 'a nearly impenetrable voter manipulation machine that is quickly becoming the new deciding factor in elections around the world . . . in a world of polarization, isolation, trolls, and dark posts . . . Elections in 2018 and 2020 won't be a contest of ideas, but a battle of automated behaviour change.' The lessons of their aggressive automated negative messaging about political opponents have begun to spread around the world (Bradshaw and Howard, 2017).

At the level of practical politics, the coining of the term 'fake news' has provoked a storm of controversy, and not just among the traditional media. The idea that the outcome of a democratic election might be altered by false claims of facts has generated a great deal of debate over how to overcome it.

15

As Tambini (2017) explains, the term 'fake news' has been used in six different ways: (i) falsehoods deliberately spread to undermine candidates or elections; (ii) falsehoods spread for financial gain; (iii) parody and satire; (iv) bad journalism and unsubstantiated rumour; (v) news that challenges consensus; and (vi) news that challenges orthodox authority.

One remedy comes from civil society: increasing the number of fact-checking organizations that can publicly challenge factually incorrect claims, such as FactCheck.org and Politifact.com. Media organizations like the *New York Times*, the BBC, *The Guardian*, and *Le Monde* are all doing more on this. Facebook and Google have started devoting more resources to identifying and quickly taking down false information that has appeared on their sites. The EU has funded a website to monitor and check facts. But there is no clear framework for doing this and assessments are always liable to challenge (Graves and Cherubini, 2016; Marietta, Barker, and Bowser, 2017).

However, simply putting information into the public domain that corrects mistaken facts will not be enough to win arguments and change behaviour. During the American presidential election in 2016, various organizations published factual rebuttals of factually incorrect claims made by both campaigns, and most of these referred to claims by Trump and his supporters. According to Politifact, over a five-day period Trump averaged a lie about every three minutes in five hours of speaking and tweeting. Over the same period, Clinton averaged a lie every 12 minutes in one-and-a-half hours of statements (Garvey, 2017: 260). Yet still Trump won. In his book *The Art of the Deal*, Trump claimed that 'a little hyperbole never hurts . . . I call it truthful hyperbole. It's an innocent form of exaggeration' (Trump and Schwartz, 1987: 58).

Similarly, in the Brexit referendum in the UK (**see Case Study 15.7**), both sides made graphic claims about the likely results of the UK leaving the EU or staying in. For example, the Leave campaign repeatedly implied that if the UK left, it would save £350 million per week, which would then be spent on the NHS (**see Figure 15.3**). This did not take account of the fact that the UK got back £100 million per week and, in any case, it later was admitted that this was more of 'an aspiration'. But the claim struck home despite the fact that the UK Office of Statistics, the BBC, and various other media organizations regularly highlighted how misleading it was. Nevertheless, they had little impact, in part because the claim really reflected the principle of *The Economist* mentioned earlier in this chapter: first, simplify; then, exaggerate. This message graphically encapsulated the issue of UK government control, or rather the lack of it, over its own national resources. Even though a lesser sum would have more accurately reflected the amount of money that the UK 'sent' to Brussels every week, what really was at issue was whether the UK had adequate control. Admitting that it was 'only' sending £250 million would not have made much difference. As Arron Banks from the Leave campaign recognized: 'The Remain campaign featured fact, fact, fact, fact. It just doesn't work. You've got to connect with people emotionally. It's the Trump success' (d'Ancona, 2017: 15).

FIGURE 15.3   The Leave campaign in the UK's Brexit referendum repeatedly implied that if the UK left, it would save £350 million per week, which would then be spent on the NHS
© Martyn Evans / Alamy Stock Photo

📖   CASE STUDY 15.7   **Explaining Brexit**

In 2016, the UK voted in a referendum to leave the EU after over 40 years. This was both momentous and widely unexpected. Although the turnout, at 72 per cent, was significantly higher than in a general election, the split of the vote—52:48 per cent, or around 600,000 votes—was small enough to provoke a welter of attempts to explain what happened, why, and what might have been.

Some accounts more straightforwardly recounted the important events. Shipman (2016) has provided what is still the fullest journalist's account of the events and the campaigns leading up to the vote. Clarke, Goodwin, and Whiteley (2017) have supplemented this with a more academic analysis focusing in particular upon opinion surveys to identify the reasons why people voted the way that they did and also the extent to which public opinion in the UK was similar to, or different from, that in the other EU member states. Ashcroft and Culwick (2016) have also reported on surveys that they carried out for the Leave campaign—particularly polls that they carried out on referendum day, which showed that a tenth of voters only decided which way to vote on that day (that is around 3 million people).

Others have provided alternative narratives to explain the result. For Hannan (2016), the vote reflected the long-term difference in political culture between Britain and the rest of Europe. It was not just a matter of different economies and different economic cycles. More fundamentally, it reflected the historic value that the British put upon the principles of parliamentary sovereignty and the common law, both of which contrast with the experience and principles of continental European states, not to mention the practice of the EU.

Banks (2017), one of the leaders of the Leave campaign, presented the result as the result of a political insurgency against the political establishment by the 'bad boys', who did not play by the rules of the established political game, but played to win—and did. Without their key contribution, the result would have gone the other way.

Saltiel (2017) provided another Leave insider's insight into the ways in which the Leave campaign used blogs and emails to coordinate its efforts and fight back against the opposition.

By contrast, Oliver (2017), former head of communications for Prime Minister Cameron, explained the result in terms of complacency in the Remain camp, lulled into believing that they would win right to the end by mistaken polling, but also by clear lying from the Leave campaign 'on an industrial scale'.

Hume (2017) sees the Brexit vote, like the Trump victory, as a reflection of a wider problem of widespread discontent in Western societies with existing politics and the appetite for more popular democracy.

Goodhart (2017) has located the outcome in a broader international picture, which includes the victory of Trump in the US and the rise of populist groups across Europe—namely, the reaction against two decades of neo-liberal globalization. This has led to a general bifurcation within national societies into two opposing groupings: on the one hand, the 'anywheres', who are generally content with globalization and could feel at home more or less anywhere in the world; and, on the other hand, the 'somewheres', who have stronger roots in a particular place and feel that they have been ignored by the 'anywheres'.

And, lastly, there is Cadwalladr (2017), who has alleged that the result was hijacked by dark forces linked to mysterious corporate groups in the US, and possibly elsewhere, who used the Internet and social media to create a synthetic public opinion that misled the real public about the stakes involved and the strength of the 'outers'.

The more people rely upon sources like Twitter and Facebook for information, which they can then send on to others in their networks of friends with just a click, the more difficult it is to reverse a tide of 'likes' for what is false. It is part of the general phenomenon of what Sunstein (2017: 109) calls 'cybercascades', when 'large groups of people end up believing something—whether or not that something is true or false—simply because other people in the relevant community seem to believe that it is true'. The use of bots to accentuate the apparent popularity of messages makes the problem worse.

But the problem is even more deep-seated. Hochschild and Einstein (2016) point out that the creation of false news as part of election campaigns has a long pedigree in the US—and elsewhere. They show that significant numbers of people believe things to be true that 'feel' right, though actually false, particularly when they trust those passing on the information. This was true even before the social media age, but now the problem is more acute. A survey of social media users in Michigan during the presidential campaign showed that they shared—that is, passed on—far more 'extremist, sensationalist, conspiratorial, fake . . . and junk news' than professionally researched political news (Howard et al., 2017). This overwhelmed 'real' facts.

Now, American politics has become more polarized. More facts are essentially contested. According to Mann and Ornstein, the Republican Party is 'unpersuaded by conventional understanding of facts, evidence, and science' (quoted in Hochschild and Einstein, 2016: 33). Hochschild and Einstein (2016: 33) also suggest that 'the more ideologically committed a person or party is, the more prone to accept and use misinformation.' It leads to people living in 'echo chambers' where they only hear what they already believe to be true. Though most do not seek completely to exclude other viewpoints, those who do exercise disproportionate influence because of their unshakable conviction of 'knowing' what is right (Sunstein, 2017: 112–16).

There can only be complex solutions to the problem. For Garvey (2017), a philosopher, the answer to the problem has to involve increasing the ability and willingness of people to debate honestly with others. He wants more deliberation in politics. The OECD has recommended more education: member countries should devote resources to teaching schoolchildren how to spot fake news (Siddique, 2017).

As political columnist Matthew d'Ancona (2017: 125, 128) recognizes: 'In a Post-Truth world [where objective facts are less influential in shaping public opinion than appeals to emotion and personal belief] . . . it is not enough to make an intellectual case. In many (perhaps most) contexts, facts need to be communicated in a way that recognises emotional as well as rational imperatives . . . Veracity will be drowned out unless it is resonant.' Ironically, he and Breitbart agree on the importance of narrative: 'Narrative is everything' (Breitbart, 2012: 4). But d'Ancona (2017: 134) is clear: '[N]arrative must never violate or embellish truth; it should be its most powerful vehicle.' But does that equate to first simplify and then exaggerate?

The rise of social media and their infiltration into political life pose a conceptual challenge. They might make Habermas's notion of a distinct 'public sphere', distinguishable from other 'spaces' of social life, obsolete, at least in the form suggested by its English translation, where the term 'sphere' implies a space, however abstract, distinct from other, less public 'spaces'. The problem is that, on platforms like Twitter, politics becomes intermingled with all the other minutiae of everyday social life. There is no clearly delineated distinct public space. Politics and life endlessly intermingle. On the other hand, the origi-

15

nal term in German—*Öffentlichkeit*—simply means 'public-ness' in general, which could accommodate these developments.

Theorists like Coleman and Blumler (2009) and Sunstein (2017) advocate some kind of overt political space on the Internet to aid public deliberation in democracies, precisely because it would give new substance to the notion of a 'public *sphere*', without which democratic life may well fragment. It would also give new life and meaning to the notion of citizenship.

✳ KEY POINTS

- New communications technologies may transform citizen involvement in politics by enabling outsiders and new ideas to penetrate established political systems.
- They can also enable 'smart mobs' to disrupt government and hold the public to ransom.
- Their effect is likely to be greater in states with less established, or less legitimate, political institutions, especially in times of crisis.
  - They also allow non-journalists to publish news stories and influential blogs.
  - They may enable greater participation in local decision-making.
  - Electronic voting is still subject to great risks about the integrity of the technology.
- Social media can provide alternative news to the established news channels and be exploited to challenge them.
- Fact-checking will not be enough to rebut 'fake' news.
- Alternative plausible narratives will be needed.
- Some would argue the need for a distinctive public space for online deliberation to aid democracy.
- But the rise of the social media as purveyors of news and disseminators of opinions may make this futile.

Conclusion

For all the possible benefits brought by the new social media, they have also made the practice of democracy more difficult for citizens. In addition to having to choose between the competing claims made by political parties, they now have to think more carefully about the truthfulness of things they see online. Strong democracy needs active citizens, but now they also need to be sophisticated in the ways of the media:

> The promise of the Internet is that it is a great democratizing force, allowing everyone to express their opinions, and everyone to have immediate access to all the world's information.

Combine these two, as the Internet and social media do, and you have a virtual world of information and misinformation cohabiting side by side, staring back at you like identical twins, one who will help you and the other who will hurt you. Figuring out which one to choose falls upon all of us, and it requires careful thinking and one thing that most of us feel is in short supply: time. Critical thinking is not something you do once with an issue and then drop it. It's an active and ongoing process. It requires that we all think like Bayesians, updating our knowledge as new information comes in. (Levitin, 2017: 253)

Do enough people have the time and commitment to 'read' the media and its underlying messages properly? It is yet another challenge for democracies in addition to those mentioned in Chapter 5.

? Key Questions

- Compare the treatment of a major political issue in the *Daily Mail* with that in one of the major broadsheet newspapers. What are the most important differences?
- Compare the treatment of a major international issue by the BBC, CNN, CCTV, Russia Today, and Al Jazeera. What are the differences?
- Does the press in the UK, or anywhere else, need better public regulation? If so, who should carry it out? Can statutory regulation be avoided? If not, how can it be done to avoid state suppression of undesirable news? Assess the recommendations from Cohen-Almagor (2014).
- What picture of US politics would President Putin have gained from watching *House of Cards*? How accurate would it be? How would you know?
- How, and how far, does public service broadcasting keep the rest of the media 'honest' (Marr, 2004)?
- How would you characterize digital citizenship? In what ways does it differ from earlier forms of citizenship?
- Do the techniques of a 'post-truth' age make it easier for authorities to 'manufacture consent' (Herman and Chomsky, 2002)?
- Have Facebook and Twitter smuggled in the basis for the world described in Orwell's *Nineteen Eighty-Four*?
- Which 'narrative' explaining the outcome of the Brexit referendum is most convincing?
- How should democracies combat 'fake' news? Is this more of a problem in liberal media systems, such as the US, than in more overtly partisan, polarized, pluralist ones, such as southern Europe? What should be the relationship between 'truth' and 'narrative'?
- Is the US moving away from a liberal and closer to a polarized pluralist media system? How would you measure it?

● Was the Leave claim that if the UK left the EU, it would save £350 million per week for the NHS, a lie, or 'just' truthful hyperbole? What about the Remain claim that if the UK left, it would cost every family £4,300 per year? How would you establish credible 'true' facts and persuade others to accept them?

● Do we need to create distinct spaces online for democratic deliberation? How could they work? Would they work?

Further Reading

Bailey, Matthew (2011), 'The Uses and Abuses of British Political Fiction or How I Learned to Stop Worrying and Love Malcolm Tucker', *Parliamentary Affairs*, 64(2): 281–95.
Argues that the dramatization of politics can help us to better understand it.

Cohen-Almagor, Raphael (2014), 'After Leveson: Recommendations for Instituting the Public and Press Council', *International Journal of Press/Politics*, 19(2): 202–25.
Discusses ways of making the press accountable in the UK, based upon international experience.

d'Ancona, Matthew (2017), *Post-Truth: The New War on Truth and How to Fight Back* (London: Ebury Press).
A political columnist's remedies for the rise of 'fake' news.

Hallin, Daniel C., and Mancini, Paolo (eds) (2012), *Comparing Media Systems beyond the Western World* (Cambridge and New York: Cambridge University Press).
A very stimulating collection of essays that attempts to compare media systems and their relationship to politics both in and beyond the West.

Hart, Roderick P., and LaVally, Rebecca (2017), 'Not a Fourth Estate but a Second Legislature', in Kate Kenski and Kathleen Hall Jamieson (eds), *The Oxford Handbook of Political Communication* (Oxford and New York: Oxford University Press), 109–19.
A sophisticated analysis of the ways in which political journalism sometimes challenges the existing political order and sometimes reproduces it.

Levitin, Daniel (2017), *A Field Guide to Lies and Statistics* (London: Viking).
An introduction to distinguishing statistical lies from truths in the media.

Marr, Andrew (2004), *My Trade* (London: Macmillan).
Marr's career as political journalist, editor of a broadsheet newspaper, and the BBC's political editor gives him an unusually broad perspective on how journalism operates.

Morozov, Evgeny (2011), *The Net Illusion: How Not to Liberate the World* (London: Penguin).
A sceptical look at the rise of the Internet and the social media.

Orwell, George (1949/2008), *Nineteen Eighty-Four* (London: Viking).
An iconic dystopian novel given new relevance by the rise of Facebook and Twitter.

Schudson, Michael (2008), *Why Democracies Need an Unlovable Press* (Cambridge: Polity).
A collection of very insightful, concise analyses of the importance of journalism for democracy.

Street, John (2011), *Mass Media, Politics and Democracy* (Basingstoke: Palgrave, 2nd edn).
A lucid introduction to the field.

Sunstein, Cass R. (2017), *#republic* (Princeton, NJ: Princeton University Press).
How to take advantage of the Internet and social media to improve democracy.

Tait, Richard (2012), 'Never Waste a Good Crisis: The British Phone Hacking Scandal and Its Implications for Politics and the Press', in Holli A. Semetko and Margaret Scammell (eds), *The Sage Handbook of Political Communication* (London and Los Angeles, CA: Sage), 518–26.
A very clear account of the British phone-hacking scandal and its implications for media regulation.

Waugh, Evelyn (1943/1978), *Scoop: A Novel about Journalists* (London: Eyre Methuen).
A classic satire on journalistic practices.

Woodward, Bob, and Bernstein, Carl (1974), *All the President's Men* (New York: Simon & Schuster).
A heroic story of journalism holding government to account and winning a stupendous victory.

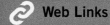 **Web Links**

https://www.youtube.com/watch?v=InPR90dJ3Gk
The first of four TV programmes on the impact of Facebook on the Arab Spring.

https://www.oii.ox.ac.uk/blog/video-is-social-media-killing-democracy-computational-propaganda-algorithms-automation-and-public-life/
An inaugural lecture from the Oxford Internet Institute that briefly surveys the evolution of studies of the Internet, asks whether social media are killing democracy, and speculates about the future direction of research on the Internet.

https://cyber.harvard.edu/research
The portal of the Berkman Klein Center for Internet and Society at Harvard.

https://www.oii.ox.ac.uk/research/
The research portal of the Oxford Internet Institute.

http://www.socialcapitalgateway.org/
Gateway to a large number of sites devoted to social capital and interest group activity.

http://www.politifact.com/
A fact-checking portal for US politics.

 Visit the **Online Resources** that accompany this book to access more learning resources on this topic: www.oup.com/uk/ferdinand/

Civil Society, Interest Groups, and Populism

16

- Introduction
- Civil Society
- Interest Groups
- Corporatism
- Infrapolitics and Subaltern Studies: The State Viewed from Below

- From Infrapolitics to Populism
- Conclusion
- Key Questions
- Further Reading
- Web Links

Reader's Guide

This chapter will cover a selection of dimensions of political life outside the state and political parties. First, it will look at the very popular and broad concept of 'civil society', which encompasses the activity of apparently non-political actors, certainly not 'politically' organized actors, in pursuing their goals. After that, it will present interest groups and also corporatism. Next, will come an introduction to 'infrapolitics'—that is, politics from below, as presented by political anthropologists, particularly with regard to politics in the developing world. Finally, we will consider the growing phenomenon of populism as a way of enhancing the status and position of previously neglected groups in democracies and also as a challenge to liberal democracies.

Introduction

Chapter 5 discussed democracies and authoritarian regimes, and it suggested that there was increasing evidence of convergence between them with the use of hybrid methods of rule. To analyse how to assess a particular system most appropriately, it is important to look beyond the top institutions and the constitution, and to consider the broader relationship between the state and other groups and institutions in society. If we just took account of constitutions, we might conclude that North Korea is as democratic as its constitution claims. If democracy is to mean 'rule by the people' in any meaningful sense, we need to look at how 'the people' actually do participate in addition to voting in elections. Indeed, an overall assessment of the way in which politics operates in any state—whether a democracy or an authoritarian regime—needs to take account of this bigger picture. It is not enough to look at the top actors, or even just elites. We must not forget about the rest of the people below them. One of the general terms used to conceptualize this broader community of citizens outside the main established political actors is 'civil society'. And one of the main ways in which members of civil society operate in politics is through 'interest groups'. These are the terms to which we first turn.

Civil Society

This term was originally mentioned in the Introduction. Robertson (1993: 69) defined it as follows:

> Civil society is the framework within which those without political authority live their lives—economic relationships, family and kinship structures, religious institutions and so on. It is a purely analytic concept because civil society does not exist independently of political authority, nor vice versa, and, it is generally believed, neither could long continue without the other; therefore, no very clear boundary can be drawn between the two.

A term originally formulated in the eighteenth century, civil society became much more widely used and contentious in the twentieth century. Italian communist theoretician Antonio Gramsci (**see Key Thinker 16.1**) paid particular attention to civil society to explain the failure of communism to triumph in Italy and the rest of Western Europe after the First World War when the 'objective' preconditions for revolution (from the Marxist viewpoint) were present. According to Gramsci, civil society was the key site of ideological control by the bourgeoisie over the proletariat. Despite the presence of objective conditions that should have led to revolution, the bourgeoisie exercised their hegemony over the rest of society through control of the ruling ideas in society. These legitimized hierarchy and domination—in the case of Italy, backed by the power of religion—which diverted the proletariat from the revolutionary liberation that was 'objectively' in their interest. Though Gramsci was an original Marxist thinker, in that he paid much more attention to the place of ideas and the superstructure of society than to the economic determinism of many of his

16

KEY THINKER 16.1   Antonio Gramsci (1891–1937)

Gramsci was a famous Italian communist leader and thinker, who wrote on politics, sociology, and linguistics. His main concern was to bring about a communist revolution, but his greatest theoretical innovation was in explaining why it had not occurred. He did so by focusing not on the classical Marxist approach of concentrating upon the economic basis of society, but on the superstructure and the role of ideas and ideology. He developed a theory of hegemony to show how the bourgeoisie used intellectuals to formulate ideas that led the proletariat (and themselves) away from revolution.

He was imprisoned and ultimately executed by Mussolini's fascist state. Gramsci's main writings—the *Prison Notebooks*—were only published posthumously, but they came to serve as one of the key sources for the Eurocommunist movement that dominated the Italian and other 'revisionist' communist parties in Europe, which sought to distance themselves from the Soviet Union after the latter crushed the 'Prague Spring' in 1968.

The notion of 'hegemony' was later taken up by neo-Gramscians in the field of international political economy to explain the power and stability of dominant ideas in global economic governance.

Marxist contemporaries, he viewed civil society essentially negatively, standing in the way of the revolution in which he believed. It could be and was dominated by the bourgeoisie. By contrast, at the end of the 1980s, a much more positive view of civil society became popular, again in response to epochal political changes—this time, the swelling tide of Huntington's third wave of democratization (see Chapter 5). Some of these changes took place in the Far East. In 1986, authoritarian President Ferdinand Marcos of the Philippines was overthrown by waves of 'people power' demonstrations in Manila supporting Corazon Aquino, the widow of one of his most famous victims, Benigno Aquino. In 1987, demonstrations in Seoul destabilized the plans for an orderly handover of power by South Korean President Chun Doo Hwan to his chosen successor, General Roh Tae Woo. This set in train a sequence of events that led to the reintroduction of democracy. In spring 1989, a demonstration in Beijing by thousands of students mourning the death of the Chinese Communist Party's former General Secretary Hu Yaobang turned into a massive challenge to the nation's leaders on Tiananmen Square and in many other cities of China that drew in hundreds of thousands of protestors and was only put down on 4 June with the loss of thousands of lives.

The biggest demonstration of the potential power of civil society, however, came in the autumn of that year in Eastern Europe. It was civil society that brought down the communist regimes there and hastened the end of the Soviet Union in 1991. This was despite the fact that those regimes had had decades to organize the repression of

16

opponents and to establish very powerful secret police forces. They had brutally suppressed demonstrations in Hungary in 1956 and Czechoslovakia in 1968, which served as enduring lessons. The victory of the demonstrators in Eastern Europe was achieved with minimal casualties. It was a striking affirmation of the potential political power of civil society, if roused.

They had achieved this despite—or more likely because—other more 'regular' political groupings such as parties had been relentlessly repressed. The communist regimes had devoted enormous resources to identifying, dispersing, and punishing organized opposition, and yet it had all been in vain. The more amorphous civil society had overcome it—for more details, **see Case Study 16.2**.

 CASE STUDY 16.2 **Civil society and the collapse of communism**

By 1989, the communist regimes in Eastern Europe were beset by mounting difficulties. Their leaderships were ageing and the economies were stagnating. The regimes themselves had been imposed by the USSR after the Second World War and lacked popular legitimacy. Attempts by individual states to extricate themselves from Soviet tutelage had provoked brutal repression in Hungary in 1956 and Czechoslovakia in 1968. All attempts at organized political opposition were crushed.

However, the Soviet Union was descending into turmoil after four years of perestroika, which was failing to deliver the promised economic revival. The new Soviet leader, Gorbachev, no longer seemed to offer the same unconditional support for Eastern European leaders in return for political loyalty as Brezhnev had done. He started pressuring them to reform their systems as he had done.

The crisis first broke out in Poland, where the regime was among those most beset by economic and political problems. There, independent trade union Solidarity, which had been challenging the regime throughout the decade despite martial law, forced the government into round-the-table negotiations over reforms. As the price for agreeing to participate in what were expected to be rigged elections, it extracted an agreement for its own legalization. However, contrary to everyone's expectations, including its own, it won all but one of the seats that it could contest in the elections in June. This fatally undermined the legitimacy of the communist rulers and, by September, Solidarity had become the dominant actor in a new government.

The ferment of expectation and resistance spread to other states. East Germans tried to flee to the West by travelling to Hungary and seeking asylum in the West German embassy. The Hungarian authorities were reluctant to suppress them when Moscow would not commit itself unequivocally to support such action. Their indecision was noted and spread to other capitals. It further encouraged hopes of change. The aged East German leader, Honecker, was deposed and his successors began also to make conciliatory noises. Demonstrations started taking place and, when they were

See Chapter 5, Case Study 5.1, for more discussion of the fall of communism in Poland.

not repressed, involved masses of people. By November, the demonstrations had spread to Prague and, there, the authorities quickly capitulated with virtually no loss of life in what came to be known as the 'Velvet Revolution'. Change was remarkably peaceful and amicable. Also in November, the new East German leadership abandoned rather feeble attempts to keep the Berlin Wall closed. With the Wall open, it was no longer possible to prevent people crossing to the West. After that, resistance in most East European regimes crumbled. The last to do so was Romania in mid-December, although it was accompanied by street fighting and the filmed execution of former dictator Ceausescu and his wife.

The regimes collapsed remarkably easily after over 40 years of repression. Through a combination of circumstances, they had become sclerotic, brittle, and weak. However, it had taken the courage and heroism of tens of thousands of demonstrators in all the states to reveal this by challenging the authorities. Although largely not organized beforehand, they quickly found ways of cooperating decisively. It was a time and movement of joyous good humour or, as one account put it, 'a carnival of revolution' (Kenney, 2002). The legend of the power of civil society was born.

After this, civil society became the focus of intense attention, as it seemed to offer the promise of an alternative, more consensual, non-coercive democratic politics. For some it acquired a normative status. It became a metaphor for the good society (**see Key Debate 16.3**).

Would-be reformers started looking at other authoritarian regimes to try to identify analogous groupings to those in Eastern Europe in the hope that they could achieve similar results. It did not matter whether these groups were well organized or agreed on their long-term goals. They contained the germ of freedom, if only some way could be found of incubating it. Policy-makers in Western governments and international charities had become disenchanted with giving aid to governments in the developing world which, had failed to reduce poverty and, in particular, they were exasperated by official corruption, so they fastened on civil society and the voluntary sector as instruments to spread good governance and democracy. Aid money was liberally dispensed to non-governmental organizations (NGOs) in the developing world in the hope that they would spread their enthusiasm and experience among fellow citizens. They had the advantage of large numbers and, unlike political parties in dictatorships, they operated at the grass roots. Even existing democracies such as Japan began to pay more attention to their NGOs as potential political actors, or at any rate as institutions with legitimate political inputs to make. The 1990s was a heroic decade for civil society. It became one of the top items on the international agenda. It was this heroic aspect of civil society that many people found so inspiring. It seemed to symbolize the possibility of the downtrodden rising up and overthrowing their oppressors.

16

KEY DEBATE 16.3   Civil society as liberation or anti-liberation

Buttigieg (1995: 6–7, 26) on Gramsci and bourgeois hegemony in civil society:

For Gramsci civil society is best described not as the sphere of freedom but of hegemony. Hegemony to be sure depends upon consent (as opposed to coercion), but consent is not the spontaneous outcome of 'free choice'; consent is manufactured, albeit through extremely complex mediums, diverse institutions, and constantly changing processes . . . The site of hegemony is civil society, in other words, civil society is the arena wherein the ruling class extends and reinforces its power by non-violent means.

Edwards (2004: 111–12) on civil society as liberation:

It is a truism that civil society is what we as active citizens make it, but it is also true that 'social energy', or 'willed action', is the spark that ignites civil society as a force for positive social change. The determination to do something because it is the right thing to do, not because we are told to do it by governments or enticed to do it by the market, is what makes associational life a force for good, provides fuel for change in the practices of states and business, and motivates people to raise their voices in the public sphere . . . Against the background of weak democracies, strong bureaucracies, corporate power, legalism and nationalism resurgent, civil society, as both concept and reality, is essential to the prospects for a peaceful and prosperous world order in the twenty-first century . . . Warts and all, the idea of civil society remains compelling, not because it provides the tidiest of explanations but because it speaks to the best in us, and calls on the best in us to respond in kind.

In addition, there was the economic appeal of voluntary associations for helping with welfare in developing world countries where a welfare state would be beyond their means. This was attractive for aid donors because it provided them with opportunities to ensure that their aid actually reached the grass roots and because often they involved women, who had previously been excluded from this. It was attractive for the governments because it helped to reduce the pressure on them to provide welfare, and it was attractive for the recipients too because it provided them with opportunities to organize and stand up more for their rights. Left-inclined local authorities in developing countries occasionally experimented with ways of drawing selected groups of citizens into active participation in the compiling of budgets, for example in Porto Alegre in Brazil (Bruce, 2004) and Kerala in India. This was blurring the distinction between civil society and elected representatives.

Of course, problems quickly emerged in trying to spread it around the world. On the one hand, the policy became a victim of its own success. Many NGOs in the developing world became dependent upon foreign funding for their activities. This meant that their leaders had to spend as much time, if not more, on devising projects that would attract foreign funding rather than ones that they themselves felt their communities needed most urgently. On the other hand, dictatorships were quickly alerted to the potential political threat from civil society and moved to hem it in. Authoritarian regimes also sought to restrict the flows of foreign aid that might be channelled their way, sometimes, like Russia, playing the nationalist card and complaining about unjustified foreign interference from organizations like the Carnegie Foundation for International Peace. Many started organizing alternative, pliant civil society organizations. This led to a plethora of new acronyms, such as GONGO (government-organized non-governmental organization). In Indonesia in 1990, for instance, one of President Suharto's ministers (and later successor as president), B. J. Habibie, created ICMI, an organization of Islamic intellectuals, so that it could have an impact upon the authoritarian political decision-making system. It was expected to act as a think tank for new ideas on furthering Islam while promoting education. By 1994, it claimed to have 20,000 members.

On the other hand, one of the strengths of the concept for the study of comparative politics was that it could open the way to integrating regimes that lacked many of the political institutions of the developed world. It brought the study of informal social politics back in, as well as political activity at the margins of institutions. Jenkins (2005: 280–1) has explained that, in India, there is a long-standing tradition of political parties, especially the Indian National Congress (INC), fostering associations that were part of the independence movement. This relationship has continued into the post-independence era, so a clear-cut division between the state and civil society would preclude consideration of important elements of Indian politics. The term certainly attracted a great deal of interest among students of Middle Eastern politics. Social institutions such as the salons in the Gulf states, where all sorts of subjects could be discussed including politics, or the informal 'circles' in Iranian society were known to play a significant part in political life (Eickelman, 1996: x–xi). Now, there was a framework that could integrate them into broader comparisons with informal politics elsewhere in the world. Traditionally, the state had played a more limited role in the lives of Muslims and non-state actors, for example charitable foundations, had provided a great deal of public services such as education and water supplies. Although their role has become more limited, it is still important. So too is the role of professional organizations of doctors, engineers, teachers, and suchlike (Ibrahim, 1995). They embody the principle of a self-organizing society separate from the state. So the concept of civil society could accommodate their activities too (Hoexter, 2002).

Not surprisingly, given the enormous interest that was generated in it, the concept of civil society remained subject to great contradictions and misunderstandings. For one thing, there was disagreement over whether it was primarily an analytical term or a normative one. The concept of 'civil society' itself was subjected to quite disparate interpretations. Did it mean that all the groups shared some kind of common perspective when they pursued political goals? In particular, was it committed to an altruistic advocacy of policies that were judged to be in the public interest? Or at least were they committed to some kind of 'civility', which meant excluding from consideration groups that pursued non-civil goals? Could it include the advocacy of interest groups? Could it include clientelistic networks,

16

See Chapter 10, Case Study 10.5, on Somalia.

mafia organizations, fundamentalist religious sects, and extreme right-wing nationalist groups? Or is it a bulwark against the **anarchy** of weak or failed states (Chabal and Daloz, 1999: 17–18)? Does some form of civil society keep Somalia together after the collapse of the state outlined in Chapter 10? Or is it simply a collective noun that designates all the activities of a wide variety of groups and organizations that are not part of the state or of political society? Finally, civil society is vulnerable to existing inequalities in society, which may privilege some groups and disadvantage or even silence others, which inhibits its normative potential.

Beyond this, there was difficulty in translating the term into foreign languages because of extra connotations that attached to the term in English and which could imply some new version of Westernization. Right-wing critics of Japanese democracy such as Saeki (1997) stigmatize civil society as a (harmful) Western implant. Islamic societies were also suspicious about the term. Some of them were unhappy about the derivation of the term from nineteenth-century European philosophy, which they associated with an Enlightenment (that is, secular) project. They condemned it as part of an intolerant Westernizing project. They wanted instead a term that was more compatible with Islamic traditions and goals—one that focused more upon organizations of the *ulama*, the body of Islamic scholars.

Analysts of African politics also complained that the term had been inappropriately transferred from a quite different European context.

> In Africa, as in other places, 'civil society' evokes otherwise inchoate—as yet unnamed and unnameable—popular aspirations, moral concerns, sites and spaces of practice; likewise it bespeaks a scholarly effort to recalibrate worn-out methodological tools, and to find a positive politics, amid conceptual confusion. (Comaroff and Comaroff, 1999: 2–3)

See Chapter 10 for a discussion of the modern state.

Not only is there ambiguity over the meaning of the concept, but also there is ambiguity over the boundaries of the phenomena that it is supposed to encompass. In simple terms, it seemed to indicate the space for social activity between the state, on the one hand, and private individuals, on the other. We have already seen from Chapter 7 that the boundaries of the state are also fuzzy, which then makes the boundaries of civil society equally fuzzy. As Chabal and Daloz (1999: 17) put it, the fundamental problem in trying to apply the concept of civil society is that there is no clear division between the state and society. Instead, there is constant interpenetration. Chandhoke (2003: 10) emphasizes that civil society is impossible without a robust legal system that can protect civil rights. On the other side, it was not always clear—or at any rate made clear—where the boundaries of 'the private' began. Did it only apply to individuals? Or did 'the private' include the family too, as has usually been the case in the West since Aristotle (Swanson, 1992)? If it did, then it would seem to exclude the very important dimension of family-based social activity that is typical of Middle Eastern, African, and Asian societies (as well as Southern European—see Ginsborg, 2001). Hahm (2004: 454–7), for instance, has argued that the traditional Confucian view could either not accommodate the public–private distinction or made it a fluctuating one. This was because Confucian doctrine

16

began with the development of virtue in the individual and then gradually widened its horizon to encompass the whole of society. The goal of a virtuous society was impossible without virtuous individual members of it, and individuals could not be virtuous unless they performed the necessary familial roles and rites. So distinctions between family and society were positively detrimental.

Lastly, the subsequent evolution of the civil society groups in Eastern Europe after 1989 weakened enthusiasm for it as a model for the future. In Eastern Europe itself, the euphoria that surrounded the unbelievable success of groups such as independent trade union Solidarity in Poland quickly evaporated. The hopes that such groups might form the basis for a new kind of consensual rule were quickly dashed, despite all the encouragement and approval from outside. The need to make radical changes and to take drastic decisions in the face of mounting economic crises quickly revealed the difficulty for civil society organizations to maintain their cohesion. They lacked the ideologies and organization forged in earlier years that would keep their members together. The crises polarized them rather than united them. Solidarity—the largest such organization, and the one with the longest and most distinguished history of struggle against the communist authorities—quickly fragmented. Instead, new political parties began to appear like mushrooms—further confirmation of their importance for democracy, however difficult the circumstances. By 1992, only three years after the collapse of the communist regime, 222 parties had been registered in Poland, although not all of them had candidates standing at elections.

All of these uncertainties have made the use of the term problematic and the unhappy experience of the Arab Spring since 2011 has also challenged belief in the natural emancipatory power of civil society. What began as a series of unorganized protests in several Arab countries and initially led to the downfall of several dictators has subsequently regressed into revived authoritarianism in Egypt, a failed state in Libya, and protracted bloody civil war in Syria. These contrasting perspectives are illustrated in **Key Debate 16.4**.

The Arab Spring has renewed questioning of the theoretical and practical utility of the term 'civil society' (Cavatorta, 2012; Härdig, 2014).

Yet 'civil society' has now acquired such widespread usage that it is impossible to abandon it. After all their criticisms, Comaroff and Comaroff (1999: 33) conclude: 'Civil society may be deeply flawed as an analytic construct . . . But it still serves, almost alone in the age of neoliberal capital, to give shape to reformist even utopian visions.' Edwards (2004) advocates positively embracing its diversity: if you use the term, you should specify clearly what you understand by it and what you do not. As Chandhoke (2003: 33) reminds us, 'civil society is not a given; it is what its practitioners make of it'. It is as much a project to be created as it is a concept to be applied. Like politics more generally, it is an arena of great contestation.

Now let us turn to a subset of institutions that are often included within the notion of civil society: interest groups.

16

KEY DEBATE 16.4   The Arab Spring

The rapid spread of the Arab Spring initially brought hopes of a repeat of the emancipatory Velvet Revolution in Eastern Europe. However, in some places, popular movements fell into chaos; in others, authoritarian opponents fought back.

Filiu (2011: 16, 32, 42, 56, 72) on emancipation and the Arab Spring:

> Arabs have been fighting for their rights as citizens for more than a generation, but cultural prejudices and political bias prevented to grasp the extent of this disaffection . . . [T]he real Arab exception is the speed with which the democratic protests sweep the regimes away . . .

> If there is an Arab exception, it is an exceptionally young population: the median age in the Arab world is twenty-two in 2009 . . . Their anger is their power and their rage could be the energy of the future. And they all echo the militant message from Tahrir [Square]: tomorrow is yours if you fight for it . . .

> Social networks . . . were crucial in nurturing a community feeling of shared grief and aspirations, mainly among the educated and urban youth. By exposing the lies and crimes of the ruling regime, they helped to bring down the wall of fear. Once this was done, their real importance in the revolutionary process became secondary . . .

> Leaderless movements . . . were able to topple entrenched dictatorships through peaceful protests, before a combination of street pressure, labour unrest and freedom activists paved the way for a democratic transition coupled with constitutional change.

Stacher (2015: 269) on the aftermath of the Arab Spring:

> While the cases [that is, regimes] travel diverse paths, the overwhelming majority have brought with them increased state violence that has militarized the governing apparatus. This is not a transitional moment of uncertainty. It is deliberate political engineering by elites who are directing violence against their citizens in order to maintain some part of the existing regime or create a new regime on the ashes on the older order . . .

> Elites are deploying state violence against those pushing for more freedoms, better economic prospects and more social justice. This popular mobilization may still one day result in democratization but for now scholarly efforts are better directed at developing more concise theories of militarizing state violence if we are to accurately portray contemporary Arab politics.

Questions

1. What were the catalysts for civil society protests in the Arab Spring (**see Figure 16.1**)?

2. Why was conservative opposition able to reform and repress their opponents?

3. Why was civil society so much less successful in bringing about lasting democratic change in the Arab Spring than in the Velvet Revolution in Eastern Europe?

FIGURE 16.1
© MidoSemsem/ Shutterstock.com

✳ KEY POINTS

- Civil society is an ambiguous term subject to a wide variety of interpretations.
- It acquired a heroic aura because of its association with the protests that brought down communist regimes in Eastern Europe.
- Subsequently, it was appropriated by policy-making elites in the West as the targets for aid that they wished to distribute to grass-roots organizations in the developing world.
- There is a big disagreement over whether it can be applied in a non-European environment, and if so, how.

Interest Groups

Interest groups represent a big component of civil society. They are an essential element of democracy: it is impossible to think of a democracy without interest groups and, to a limited extent, they may raise or enhance the level of democratic participation, especially in polities where 'cartel' political parties have become more integrated into the state (see Chapter 13).

See the discussion in Chapter 13 on the emergence of parties.

Interest groups also attract normative comment. For some writers, they exert a baleful influence on democracy because they may disproportionately privilege some interests at the expense of others, or of the public interest as a whole. This was the kind of attitude expressed by Madison about 'factions' that was mentioned in Chapter 13. For others, they are entirely desirable because they facilitate the input of new ideas into the political process. According to this view, they are a key element in the pluralism that is an essential feature of (liberal) democracy. For rational choice theorists such as Olson (1971), interest groups are the most rational form of political activity for ordinary citizens because they are smaller than parties and offer a greater likelihood of return on effort. On the other hand, group interests are not just confined to democracies. All societies are prone to them, including dictatorships, even though the opportunities for expressing them may be more restricted in the latter.

See Chapter 2 for a discussion of pluralism.

Interest groups have attracted an enormous amount of commentary and analysis, both in general and with respect to particular political systems, and they still do. There is also a long-standing argument about the term itself. What counts as a 'group'? Does it have to be a self-consciously cohesive group, like Friends of the Earth? For groups of this kind, an alternative term is pressure group, although it is less widely used. Or could it denote a disparate group of people who share common interests, but do not act in a cohesive manner (for example corporations or social classes)? There is no definitive answer to this and analysts differ over which version to employ. But, generally, interest groups are conceived as more organized elements of civil society.

According to Robertson (1993: 240), interest groups are 'associations formed to promote a sectional interest in the political system'. They differ from political parties in that they do not seek to present themselves as candidates for government. Instead, they focus on a narrower range of issues than a government does, although it does happen that interest groups turn into political parties, as environmental groups have done. One distinction often made is between insider groups and outsider groups. Insiders concentrate upon winning support through lobbying, personal contacts, etc. Outsiders rely more upon winning over public opinion through campaigning, the media, etc. While some groups may be permanently oriented towards insider or outsider roles because of their membership, the difference between the roles may also be determined by the nature of the government. For example, conservative governments are typically more inclined to treat employers' associations as insiders, giving greater attention to their views in formulating policy, while labour or socialist governments typically treat trade unions more as insiders.

Puhle (2001: 7703–4) divided interest groups into eight types: (i) professional associations; (ii) groups of business, commerce, and industry; (iii) trade unions; (iv) agricultural organizations; (v) single-interest groups, such as the National Rifle Association in the US; (vi) ideological interest groups, such as the British Humanist Association, or religious groups; (vii) public interest groups, such as Amnesty International; and (viii) welfare associations, such as the Royal National Institute for the Blind.

Interest groups operate in a great many ways, but insofar as they pursue political goals, they will adapt themselves to the structure of the institutions that they wish to influence. If they want to influence the national government, then they will turn most of their attention to the capital, appealing to public opinion, lobbying ministers, officials, and members of parliament. In federal systems, they will devote much attention to winning support in individual states. In more administratively dominant communities, interest groups will concentrate most of their efforts on lobbying officials, as happens in Brussels with the European Union. Schlozman (2001) suggests that the strong centralized French political system leads to weak interest groups. On the other hand, the traditions of 1789 continue to endorse a greater inclination towards direct action by interest groups, such as farmers, in France than is normal in other European states. Given the enormous range and diversity of interest group activity around the world, it is very difficult to generalize about it with overarching theories. It is the basic features of individual political systems that structure what interest groups do and how they do it.

✳ KEY POINTS

- There is an ambiguity in the term 'interest group'.
- It can refer to consciously organized groups promoting interests or concerns, in which case it is an essential element in any democracy.
- Alternatively, it can refer to groups of interests in society that some actors may promote, in which case it can be found in any state.
- In either case, interest groups adapted to the institutional framework of a particular regime to maximize their effect.

Corporatism

One variant of interest group theory is called corporatism, which was also discussed in Chapter 2. As mentioned, governments do not treat all interest groups equally. They will be more inclined to listen to some (that is, insiders) than to others. In this model, though, the state is still responding to ideas or pressure from outside, but some states do more to formalize this relationship. They set up arrangements for regular consultation of key interest groups that represent the views of sections of society that are politically or economically strategic—what have been termed 'peak' associations, such as the Confederation of British

 See Chapter 2 for a discussion of corporatism.

16

See Chapter 14 for a discussion on governance.

Industry and the Trades Union Congress in the UK. They do this for the sake of better policy-making, which they recognize requires regular consultation. It resonates with the tendency to focus on governance rather than government as the most appropriate framework for national decision-making, as was outlined in Chapter 14. Because this role is rather different from that of more conventional interest groups that concentrate on expressing views to the government, Schmitter (1980) coined instead the notion of 'interest intermediation'. In other words, this more select group of organizations act as channels for exchanging views between their members and the government, rather than necessarily promoting a set view.

Schmitter also identified two distinct patterns of establishing these relationships. One, which he termed the 'societal' variant of corporatism, emerged out of pressure from below (from society or economic actors). As a consequence, the choice of which of these actors the state recognizes depends partly on these pressures from below. In the alternative variant, which he termed 'state' corporatism, it was the state that took the lead in designating its preferred partners.

Lehmbruch (2001) suggests that corporatism has been more prominent at certain periods of history and in certain groups of countries than others. The practices of corporatism were particularly important at times of Keynesian economic management in the 1960s and 1970s, when government, employers, and trade unions regularly consulted over policies that made a trade-off between levels of unemployment, wage rates, and inflation rates. Although several European countries later turned away from these methods, they remain influential in others. The Nordic countries, Germany, and France all practise variants of 'organized' or 'coordinated' capitalism, as indicated in Chapter 14, which still allow significant scope for negotiations between national partners as opposed to impersonal market forces in determining socio-economic policies.

 See Chapter 14 for more on coordinated market economies.

✳ KEY POINTS

- Corporatism privileges certain national 'peak' organizations as negotiating partners for the state in determining socio-economic policies.
- There are two variants: society-led or state-led.
- It is still a common approach to governance in countries in continental Europe.

Infrapolitics and Subaltern Studies: The State Viewed from Below

The preceding sections of this chapter have focused on ways in which civil society responds to state actors and tries to manoeuvre them into cooperation. This is politics from below. It is important to realize that politics can be viewed through this lens, as well as through a lens focused on national governments and state leaders. Another manifestation of this comes from political anthropology. It is important to appreciate this because it is an important dimension of the study of politics, especially in the developing world, although their insights are not just confined to developing states.

One of the key concerns of political anthropologists is power and its disguises, to use the title of a book by Gledhill (1994). They focus on the ways in which ordinary people relate to political systems: how they view rulers, defer to them, and also manipulate the system for their own ends. One very influential work was Scott's 1990 book, *Domination and the Arts of Resistance*. What attracted his attention was the ways in which peasants among whom he had done fieldwork talked differently among themselves from the way in which they talked to their social superiors. It alerted him to the existence of a whole world that he designated as 'infrapolitics'—that is, the subtle ways in which the powerless subvert or undermine the authority of the powerful. Most often, it depended on ambiguity rather than direct expression of opinions. Individuals needed to avoid retribution: 'Infrapolitics is the realm of informal leadership and nonelites, of conversation and oral discourse, and of surreptitious resistance' (Scott, 1990: 200). Because of this ambiguity, he argued, it had often been missed, or misunderstood, by outside observers. In fact, social historians such as Hobsbawm had written about such phenomena, but it was much less commonly noted by political scientists. Infrapolitics could take various forms of covert resistance to the dominant groups in society, ranging from individual acts such as poaching, squatting on land, desertion (of slaves), evasion, and foot-dragging, through the creation of dissident sub-cultures of resistance to millenarian religions, folk myths of social banditry, and class heroes, such as Robin Hood (Scott, 1990: 198). It could include folk art and folk songs that assert the superior qualities of ordinary people and seek to unsettle, or even supplant, those above them. It would include radical religious beliefs such as those of the Levellers in the English Civil War, who wanted the unjust existing order turned upside-down either in this world or the next. Holston (2008: 34) conveys the disconcerting effect of seeing political institutions in Brazil from this perspective with his notion of 'insurgent citizenship':

> [I]nsurgence describes a process that is an acting counter, a counterpolitics, that destabilizes the present and renders it fragile, defamiliarizing the coherence with which it usually presents itself. Insurgence is not a top-down imposition of an already scripted future. It bubbles up from the past in places where present circumstances seem propitious for an eruption. In this view, the present is like a bog: leaky, full of holes, gaps, contradictions, and misunderstandings. These exist just beneath all the taken-for-granted assumptions that give the present its apparent consistency.

Banerjee (2014) has remarked that this sounds a lot like grass-roots politics in India.

One particular recent approach in political anthropology has been to try to see the politics and institutions of other regions of the world in their own context and in their own right, not in the shadow of Europe. Given the way in which the European state spread around the world, as outlined in Chapter 10, this is an understandable reaction. There has emerged a school of 'subaltern' studies, especially among academics in and studying South

See Chapter 11 for a discussion on the spread of the Western state.

16

Asia. This approach too began with social history. Again, the concern is with the underdogs in society and their relationship with lower-level officials, the 'subalterns'. As Gupta (2006) explained, there is relatively little ethnographic evidence of what lower-level officials do in the name of the state and how this impacts on the lives of ordinary citizens. These officials are differentially positioned in hierarchical networks of power, which means that they behave differently whether they are turned towards their administrative superiors or towards ordinary citizens. The consequence is, he argued, that there is no such thing as a single state. Instead, there are multiple variants of the state within the same nation, with different groups having different experiences of it.

Another concern of the subaltern school is 'decentring' or 'provincializing' Europe—that is, examining politics and society in other parts of the world in their own right and on their own terms, not as seen through a European lens (Chatterjee, 2001: 15240). Apart from trying to give a voice to the previously underprivileged in society, it also aims at challenging those who would recommend a Western path to modernity. They want equality of respect with and from the West. They recommend the search for an alternative path to modernity that is not necessarily the same as in the West and is more in tune with local circumstances.

 KEY POINTS

- Political anthropology examines the connections between political attitudes and political behaviour and their cultural contexts, especially at the grass roots.
- Subaltern studies emphasize the multiplicity of ways in which the state is perceived by people because of the disparate ways in which they are treated by local officials.
- Subaltern studies also demand consideration for development strategies that are not borrowed from the West and are better adapted to local (non-Western) conditions.

16

From Infrapolitics to Populism

The previous section has emphasized the need to take account of strategies for subverting or getting round authorities on the part of the powerless when trying to build a comprehensive picture of political life in individual countries. These operate in authoritarian regimes, as well as democracies. But democracies are supposed to take account of the interests and concerns of all their citizens, non-elites as well as elites. Do the 'weak' there have additional 'weapons' that they can use to get consideration?

One possibility is populism. This has a particular contemporary resonance. The election of Donald Trump in the US and his claim to be speaking on behalf of the forgotten or neglected Americans has highlighted its salience in changing democracy. So too has the victory of the Leave campaign in the UK referendum on EU membership in 2016, in which the populist UK Independence Party (UKIP) played a major role. Globally, populism has kept recurring over the past 150 years, sometimes rising, sometimes falling, but it has definitely been on the rise over the past 20 years. For example, at the end of the 1980s, there was only one populist party in Europe, the Front National in France, and it was relatively marginal. Now, even though their fortunes fluctuate, populist parties often win 15–20 per cent of the vote in several European countries (Biorcio, 2014).

What is populism?

Populism is a type of rule or political behaviour usually associated with minimalist forms of democracy. It exalts the will of the majority as the dominant principle and it constructs an 'imagined' image of (the overwhelming majority of) the people willing and legitimating a set of priorities—usually different from the establishment's. In practice, populist leaders have in mind a particular core constituency rather than a people or nation as a whole, but these are then elevated as surrogates for the whole people or as the core of a new, better 'people'. For French populist leader of the 1950s Poujade, it was the shopkeepers and small artisans of mainly rural France who typified the family values that were supposedly being suffocated by corrupt politicians, big business, and a rapacious state (Souillac, 2007). For President Erdogan of Turkey, it is the pious population and businesses of Anatolia who have suffered decades of discrimination from the secular Kemalist elite of Istanbul and Ankara (White, 2013). Generally speaking, populist movements are radical protests against either the existing political system, major policy failures, or both. Some direct their appeal towards the right of the political spectrum, others incline more towards the left, while yet others try to refute such stereotypes as they aim at support from broader sections of society.

An extensive literature has been written on populism, but no consensus has emerged on how it should be conceptualized. Some, for example, are wary of the whole enterprise, regarding the label 'populist' as mainly a pejorative term for political attitudes or behaviour of which one disapproves (Deegan-Krause and Haughton, 2009). They would prefer more neutral descriptive analysis. Indeed, populist politicians themselves also tend to shun the term. Nevertheless, probably the most common approach has tried to identify common normative principles of populism.

According to Mudde and Kaltwasser (2017: 9–19), there are three basic principles that underpin populism: (i) 'the people' as the core value, though it can receive varying emphases (for example the people as sovereign, the 'common people', or the nation); (ii) an elite or establishment, who actually manipulate power to their advantage and who should be confronted; and (iii) the 'general will' of the people, which should be absolute, expressed

16

through direct consultation or referendums, but which can also be appropriated by individuals or leaders who instinctively 'know' what it is.

While these values are supposed to serve as the starting point in determining political decisions, they are vague on specifics and of less help in determining particular policies. That is why Mudde and Kaltwasser term it a 'thin-centred ideology', which is usually linked to another, 'thicker', or more comprehensive ideology that situates politics in a more comprehensive framework of ideas (such as nationalism, socialism, religious belief, or secularism). This linking of populism with another ideology in practice helps to provide a tighter explanation in specific situations, but it also makes it more difficult to disentangle the particular contribution that populism makes. Generally speaking, because of its emphasis upon 'the people', particularly the ordinary people, populism is much more likely to prioritize local values and to concerns and challenge the values of (trans)national elites, which is why it is often closely associated with nationalism.

Another, more recent, approach has concentrated upon political behaviour: identifying a political style that embodies the attitudes, tastes, and values of 'the common man'. Moffitt (2016: 38) articulates it as 'the repertoires of embodied symbolically mediated performances made to audiences that are used to create and navigate the fields of power that comprise the political, stretching from the drama of government through to everyday life'. They 'perform' populism, as well as express it. Clearly, this approach is better suited to analysing the behaviour of individual leaders, or even individual parties, rather than that of whole political systems. It also enables a more sensitive analysis of the variations in appeals that political leaders may make—sometimes more populist, sometimes less so.

Both approaches pre-suppose an inherent contradiction and clash between the values and interests of 'the people' and those of 'the elite' or the establishment, with the populists on the side of the 'ordinary' people. One of the first manifestations of populism came in the second half of the nineteenth century in Russia—the *narodniki*. They extolled the moral virtues of the simple peasant over their aristocratic masters, a theme later popularized internationally by Tolstoy. This became the core value of various Russian populist movements until they were defeated by the Bolsheviks in the civil war. In the 1880s, share-cropping farmers in the Mid-West of the US mounted a political campaign against 'immoral' exploitative capitalists and bankers from New York—the 'robber barons'. Since then, populist movements have constructed—or reconstructed—images of the 'virtuous' ordinary people who are being ignored or repressed by self-interested elites. So although the notion in English of 'the people' sounds all-embracing, in practice their use of it implies a division between most of the people of a particular country and the small proportion who constitute the establishment. It always implies a 'we', opposed to some kind of 'they'. Other languages may express this in a different way. Populist Spanish party Podemos ('we can') brings out this division by appealing to *la gente* (the ordinary people, the 'we') rather than *el pueblo* (the people or nation), who are opposed to *la casta* (the caste, or elite 'them') (Errejón and Mouffe, 2016: 134–5).

Because populist movements view politics from below, they tend to be led by 'outsiders', or at any rate by people who see themselves as outsiders. They play upon their humble origins or the fact that they come from previously marginalized strata of society. President Fujimori in Peru in the 1990s stressed his poor Japanese immigrant forebears. President Morales in Bolivia stresses his indigenous, pre-Spanish ancestry, which he 'performs' on a daily basis with the traditional sweater that he wears on official occasions. Both started their campaigns in part to bring about greater social and ethnic integration. But this does not mean that all 'populist' politicians come from the lowest or most excluded strata of society. Many populist figures see themselves as outsiders as compared with the national establishment, though their own origins may not be so humble. Donald Trump demonstrates this phenomenon starkly. Despite his wealthy father and the millions that he himself made from business, Trump always regarded himself as an outsider compared with the comfortable liberal New York establishment, let alone the one in Washington, DC. Such populist politicians can be termed 'insider-outsiders'. Another example would be Nigel Farage, the former leader of UKIP—a former public schoolboy and successful commodities trader in the City of London who went into politics and 'performed' as a populist with his image of the chain-smoking 'man in the pub', the scourge of 'the establishment'.

Populist movements always represent a challenge to the existing order, a protest that things are not working as they should. They often deliberately break with the practices of 'conventional' establishment politics. Arditi (2007: 80) expresses the point colourfully in **Key Quote 16.5**. In that sense, populism aims to open the way towards the redress of previously ignored grievances. Thus, at least in theory, it can claim to be expanding or deepening democracy.

Populism can attempt to win power through three pathways: (i) by taking over an existing political party (as with Jörg Haider and the Austrian Freedom Party in the 1990s); (ii) by grass-roots civil society activism (for example the Tea Party in the US); and (iii) by creating a new movement with a dynamic leader. In practice, the third path is the most common because it exemplifies the claim to be creating a new kind of politics. However, it also ties populist movements to particular leaders and this personalism complicates the task of ensuring a long-lasting political transformation. However well intentioned they may have been on taking power, they may become reluctant to relinquish power later and try to suppress opposition. President Museveni of Uganda, mentioned in Chapter 13,

16

 KEY QUOTE 16.5 **Arditi on populism**

'Populism calls the bluff on claims that gentrified politics is politics "as such". It also shows that the "table manners" of democratic politics are often little more than props to bestow an aura of public virtue on elected officials that have none.'
(Arditi, 2007: 80)

established a democracy without parties at the end of the civil war to help reconciliation—but has shown himself since then determined to hang on to power 'for the good of the nation'. The problems for populist regimes of ensuring lasting change through institutionalization have been starkly exemplified in Venezuela after the death of President Chávez in 2013. His designated successor, President Maduro, has increasingly struggled to maintain the momentum of the Bolivarian socialist transformation of society in the face of mounting economic chaos and protests on the streets. However much he stigmatizes the opposition as 'them'—that is, elites opposed to the poor who have sold out to American neo-liberalism—his support from the 'real' people shrinks, however passionate they remain in defending the regime, with increasing confrontation on the streets.

In general, populists can accept some kinds of political institutions—and often they introduce new constitutions after taking power—but they are uneasy about institutions in general, even 'democratic' ones, which might be used to frustrate the 'sovereign will' of the people. They do not respect an independent judiciary or the rule of law. They certainly are wary of any notion of constitutional 'checks and balances' that might limit it. Mexico is the exception that proves the rule. The Mexican Revolution (1910–20) swept aside the traditional regime of Porfirio Diaz primarily in the name of the poor peasantry, but this inaugurated two decades of violence and political turbulence. In 1929, then President Elias founded the National Revolutionary Party to try to institutionalize political order after the assassination of his predecessor, which was renamed the Revolutionary Institutional Party (PRI) in 1946. It was designed as a broad grouping, with its members distributed in corporatist organizations throughout the country, but as a body it was not intended democratically to choose its leaders. The presidency was 'imperial' (Krause, 1997). Though limited to one six-year term of office, each president had almost unlimited freedom to choose his successor through the practice of the 'tap' (*dedazo*). Each party leader and national president could designate his successor by metaphorically 'tapping' him (it always was a him) on the shoulder and the Party would acclaim the choice. The people would then ratify it in an election. Until the 1980s, national leaders performed as 'populist' men of the people (Kiddle and Muñoz, 2010): in the 1920s, President Álvaro Obregón received foreign dignitaries in his pyjamas; in the 1930s, President Cárdenas ignored an official banquet in his honour, instead eating a chocolate bar next to a soft drinks stand (Knight, 1998: 236). Ultimately, what undermined this political style was the increasing economic difficulties of the regime in the 1980s and the emergence of more technocratically minded presidents to try to solve them. Nevertheless, PRI domination only ended in 2001 after 70 years in power.

Populist leaders want a direct and immediate link between decisions and their implementation—see Chávez excoriating failed officials to their face on YouTube. They also pride themselves on a direct relationship with 'their' people. As Chávez told a mass demonstration in Caracas: 'I am not an individual, I am the people. It's my duty to demand respect for the people' (News 24 Archives, 2010). They also place great emphasis upon their public image, trying to talk directly to the people. Chávez held regular and interminable phone-ins under the rubric 'Alo Presidente'. Though they usually demonstrate great concern about control over traditional media, especially television, populist leaders now espy whole new vistas to interact with their people through the Internet and social media. Indeed, this can offer opportunities for new movements of outsiders to start up, as can be seen from the emergence of the Five Star Movement in Italy, presented in **Case Study 16.6**.

 CASE STUDY 16.6   **Populism online: Beppe Grillo and the Five Star Movement**

The collapse of the Soviet Union precipitated the collapse of the post-war Italian party system. In the aftermath, the Italian Communist Party also collapsed, while coincidentally a major scandal over political corruption (*Tangentopoli*, aka Bribesville) in other parties erupted in 1992–93. The previously dominant Christian Democratic Party was dissolved, as was the Socialist Party. This removed many of the main institutional pillars of Italian democracy and opened the door to populist politics, but it has proved very difficult to create stable replacements. Several have been populist, for example the Lega Nord ('Northern League') and Berlusconi's Forza Italia ('Go Italy!'), and they have strengthened the general anti-establishment mood of Italian politics. However, the issue of corruption has not gone away—it has allegedly infected both the Lega Nord and Forza Italia—and public opinion has seethed. This lies behind the rise of the Five Star Movement (M5S) as an alternative.

In 2005, satirical clown Beppe Grillo set up his own blog—Friends of Beppe Grillo—to test its appeal. It was run in conjunction with Gianroberto Casaleggio, who had his own Internet consulting company and held a utopian view of the potential of the Internet to transform societies, including politics, through frequent online referendums (Casaleggio and Grillo, 2011). Its quirky, carnivalesque satires on Italian politics quickly attracted a broad followership. Then, followers were encouraged to get in touch with others in the same locality using the Meetup.com platform, and this laid the basis of the Movement. The way in which the Movement was formed allowed Grillo to claim that it had grown from the grass roots, unlike other parties that were created from the top down.

It was so successful that, in 2007, Grillo organized the first public mass protest event—V-day (V for *Vaffanculo*, meaning 'b****r off'—that is, what the political elite should do)—with a programme of anti-establishment protests combined with performances from sympathetic actors and musicians in Bologna. It was ignored by almost all TV channels, but broadcast online, accompanied by parallel fringe events in 179 other public squares across the country. From this mushroomed a movement of the previously politically apathetic, especially among young people. Grillo encouraged groups of them to form electoral lists and stand for local government, though he himself refuses to stand for parliament to avoid looking like other politicians. In 2009, he presented the Movement's Programme. It rejects labels of 'left' and 'right', but it proclaims a strong interest in environmental issues—the 'Five Stars' refer to the five core issues of public water, sustainable transport, sustainable development, the right to Internet access, and environmentalism.

16

The Movement encourages a spirit of anti-(conventional) politics. It aims to shake up politics in the way in which the theatre of the absurd shook up conventional drama (anarchist writer and Nobel Prize winner Dario Fo was a supporter), offering meaning for people in an absurd, alienating world. It regards political parties as historical anachronisms and it proclaims a future of genuine universal online political participation, prioritizing local participation. In this respect, it resembles the Tea Party, though its social and economic goals are quite different. It proclaims itself a movement, rather than a party, and it rejects the idea of long-term careers in politics for its activists. Its candidates can only serve two terms if elected and they have to give up a significant proportion of their public salaries. Membership only involves subscribing to Grillo's blog, with the right to add comments. It has an 'anti-rule book' rather than a rule book. It has 'local spokespersons' rather than secretaries or presidents. It refuses to accept funds from the state to support its activities, unlike other parties. It opposes the EU, but it has won seats in the European Parliament and has joined the European Freedom and Democracy grouping there. In theory, the Movement could use online media to promote a new kind of horizontal policy deliberation with much greater equality between participants than is found in traditional parties, but in practice so far it has mainly used these media to develop its organizational ties and to showcase its activities.

Grillo's position in the Movement is both high-profile and obscure. He has no formal power and he claims to be only the 'megaphone' of ordinary people, rather than imposing his views upon them: 'Folks, it works like this. You let me know and I play the amplifier' (Müller, 2016: 35). He retweets a lot of other people's posts without commentary, leaving unclear his own attitude to their content, but it makes him (and the movement) appear to be listening and inclusive. He disclaims formal leadership, but sole ownership of the trademark 'Friends of Beppe Grillo' lay with him and Casaleggio (who died in 2016), which makes local committees like 'franchises'. Grillo did use control over the name to 'expel' individuals whose views he disapproved of who attempt to win support through membership of the Movement when standing for election to public office. He has disbarred M5S candidates who have flouted his instruction not to take part in political talk shows on television. And while local groups are encouraged to compile lists of potential candidates for public office, the procedure by which the leadership selects individuals for a particular local list remains opaque.

The Movement put up a large number of candidates for the 2013 parliamentary elections and won 25 per cent of the votes, but it has refused to participate in any coalition governments. Members have won office at the local level (for example Virginia Raggi as mayor of Rome). Turning anti-politics activists into administrators is challenging both for them and their supporters. Their performance in local government has disappointed some, but they still remain a powerful political force. In the general election of March 2018, M5S won the highest number ever of seats in the lower chamber of parliament and became the largest single party there. Their success offers pointers to the emergence and evolution of populism and new party organizations more generally in the age of social media.

(Based on Biorcio and Natale, 2013; Biorcio, 2015a, 2015b; Tronconi, 2015.)

In general, populist movements find it easier to operate in political systems with lower institutional checks because they find it easier to overturn them and because they themselves are conflicted over the need for robust institutions. This explains why they have flourished more in systems that have only recently democratized, where institutions are still fragile—namely, Thaksin Shinawatra in Thailand (Phongpaichit and Baker, 2008), or more recently the increasing assertiveness of President Erdogan in Turkey (Cagaptay, 2017). Mudde (2002) commented that, at the turn of the century, populism played a much more prominent role in the recently democratized Eastern European countries than in the West. And democratic institutionalization has remained a perennial problem in Latin America, which partly explains why it has been the continent with the greatest experience of populist politics of various kinds. With their frequent mingling of democratic and authoritarian principles, populist regimes represent yet another variant of the hybrid systems identified in Chapter 5. Nevertheless, as Ware (2002: 119) pointed out, populism also remains one of the permanent elements even in American political culture: 'Populism is everywhere in American politics, but nowhere in particular'—though, for now, it has captured the White House.

The aftermath of the 2008 global financial crisis and popular reactions to austerity measures have opened the way for populist protest movements across the West, especially in southern Europe—Podemos and M5S being only two examples. They have flourished because of the discrediting of the previous elite consensus on the need for neo-liberal economic policies to spread prosperity, which downplayed the importance of fairness in distributing the rewards of that prosperity. Their grievances have been intensified by the failings of the cartelized political party systems that were explored in Chapter 13, with its tendency to encourage cooperation between party elites (the 'caste') at the expense of ordinary citizens. To the extent that populist protests have forced the grievances of the previously neglected on to the political agenda, it can be said that they have done democracy a service. On the other hand, it can also be argued that populist movements are inherently aggressive (Biorcio, 2014): they would say that they have to behave 'improperly' to get a hearing—but, in the process, they exacerbate political divisions. They make compromise solutions and reconciliation more difficult.

Yet whatever the strength of these competing assessments, populism will keep reappearing—albeit unpredictably. It appeals to the principles of sovereignty of the people and of their representatives exercising that sovereignty. If those representatives fail to live up to their perceived obligations, critics will plead the principle of popular sovereignty to get them replaced. Whether or not a particular system's political culture recognizes the principle of the autonomy of a representative to exercise their own judgement on individual issues (**see Key Quote 12.4** on Burke's attitude on the relationship between an MP and his constituents in Chapter 12), if change is long delayed or even prevented, critics will always be tempted to appeal to the higher principle of the supremacy of the will of the people as a justification for replacing that representative. If this dissatisfaction turns into a movement, it is can always take a basically populist turn, whatever tactics it adopts. This

16

is one of the key 'weapons of the weak' in a democracy. That is why sophisticated analysis identifies degrees of populism, rather than just focusing on fixed definitions.

In addition, as Canovan (2002) has pointed out, well-functioning liberal democracies recognize two basic principles as equal: constitutional rights and guarantees, and popular sovereignty. But which should take precedence if things go badly and reforms are needed? The broader the inclusion of the views and interests of various sub-sections of society in overall public decisions, the more difficult it is to see clearly how and why any particular decision comes to be made, let alone assign accountability. Apart from the difficulty for ordinary citizens of properly understanding constitutional arrangements and the way they operate (remember **Key Quote 11.2** from King in Chapter 11 on the difficulties that Americans have understanding their Constitution), the increasing cartelization of party systems in Western democracies examined in Chapter 13 intensifies suspicion of elite chicanery. The creation of arm's-length agencies to deliver government services under the New Public Management discussed in Chapter 14 has added layers of complexity to attempts to assign accountability when things go wrong. And, in Europe, these problems at the national level are exacerbated by further mystification amidst the multiple layers of EU governance. 'Crudely stated' says Canovan (2002: 25), 'the paradox is that democratic politics does not and cannot make sense to most of the people it aims to empower. The most inclusive and accessible form of politics ever achieved is also the most opaque.' People turn to ideologies to dispel the mist and help them to understand what happens, and populism, however 'thin-centred', can be enlisted to do this. It can offer a simpler and apparently more satisfying explanation for events: basically, that the elite(s) are abusing their position to hoodwink and exploit 'ordinary working people'. Populists appeal to the principle of the will of the people, rather than to constitutional and legal propriety, when they advocate remedies. The clash between the two can be seen particularly starkly in the disputes surrounding the early Trump presidency. Populism is the Cheshire cat of democratic politics. Sometimes, it is really present and active. More often, it is just a phantasmic smile. It comes and goes and it is hard to pin down, but it never vanishes completely.

KEY POINTS

- Populism has been growing around the world since the end of the 1980s.
- Populism emerges as a protest when things go wrong.
- It takes various forms and combines with various political ideologies.
- It can be seen as a style of political argument that prioritizes the 'sovereign will' of the (ordinary) people over the concerns of the elite(s).
- It can also be seen as a style of political behaviour.
- Many populist movements are led by 'insider-outsiders' rather than complete outsiders.

- Populists want a more direct and clear organic relationship between the leader(s) and the people.
- Populists are suspicious of institutions that may constrain the will of the people, whether constitutional, legal, or political.
- Populism can never be completely banished from democratic politics.

Conclusion

This chapter has concentrated on views of the state from below and attempts to influence it. It has also discussed the concept of civil society and the great impact it has had on policies of the developed world towards the developing world since the 1980s—yet, as we have seen, it also suffers from great ambiguities and contradictions, which make it another essentially contested concept. The final section considered the rise of populism around the world over the last two decades. It too provokes controversy in both real life and academic analysis. It adds a new dimension to the analysis of the relationship between politics and the media presented in Chapter 15 and the challenges facing democracies in Chapter 5. Populist politicians are particularly dependent on the media to establish a direct relationship with their supporters. The Internet and social media offer new opportunities for them to bypass more traditional media channels. Donald Trump has shown what can be done. Many liberal democracies are now facing their own disturbing challenge of Holston's 'insurgent citizenship'. Politics there is in as much flux as it is elsewhere in the world. It is both exciting and unsettling.

? Key Questions

- What are the problems involved in applying the concept of civil society to analyse the Arab Spring? Is the term any less valid there than it was during the collapse of the communist regimes in Eastern Europe?
- Is the rise of single-issue interest groups good for democracy?
- Why is there not a single model of a successful interest group that others could follow?
- Identify some of the 'weapons of the weak' with which you are familiar. How can you tell whether they are subversive of the existing order?
- In what ways can political actors 'perform' populism?
- Can rivals only beat populists by imitating them with a populist persona of their own? Why?

- How persuasive are Mudde and Kaltwasser's (2017) suggestions on ways to of combating populism and populists?
- How did Jokowi defeat Subianto to become President of Indonesia? Is Jokowi really a populist?
- If the middle classes play a key role in democratization (Chapter 5), how do they respond to populist attacks on democracy?
- Can Chavismo survive? Are there any lessons from the longevity of PRI populism in power in Mexico?
- How does the intensified populism in India affect your assessment of Indian democracy?
- Has the M5S strengthened or weakened democracy in Italy? Given the proliferation of populist parties and movements there, should Italy still be regarded as a liberal democracy?
- Has Donald Trump installed authoritarian populism in the White House?

 Further Reading

Biorcio, Roberto (2015), *Il populismo nella politica italiana. Da Bossi a Berlusconi, da Grillo a Renzi* (Passato Prossimo/Presente Italiano).
For those with Italian, a more fine-grained comparative analysis of the different populist styles and programmes in the most populist political system in Western Europe.

Cavatorta, Francesco (2012), 'Arab Spring: The Awakening of Civil Society—A General Overview' (Barcelona: IEMed) (http://www.iemed.org/observatori-en/arees-danalisi/arxius-adjunts/anuari/med.2012/Cavatorta_en.pdf, accessed January 2018).
This article and the one by Härdig are interesting attempts to apply the concept of civil society to the Arab Spring.

Edwards, Michael (2004), *Civil Society* (Cambridge: Polity Press).
Committed advocacy of the potential for civil society to transform politics by the director of the Ford Foundation's Governance and Civil Society Program.

Hamilton, Omar Robert (2017), *The City Always Wins* (London: Faber).
A fictionalized account of the Arab Spring.

Härdig, Anders C. (2014), 'Beyond the Arab Revolts: Conceptualizing Civil Society in the Middle East and North Africa', *Democratization*, 22(6): 1131–53.
To be read together with Cavatorta's article.

Hawkins, Kirk A. (2010), *Venezuela's Chavismo and Populism in Comparative Perspective* (Cambridge and New York: Cambridge University Press).
A comparative account of the internationally most famous current populist movement in South America, the region most noted for populist traditions.

Jordan, Grant, and Moloney, William A. (2007), *Democracy and Interest Groups: Enhancing Participation?* (Basingstoke: Palgrave).
An enquiry into the ways in which participation in interest groups enhances democracy.

Kenny, Paul D. (2017), *Populism and Patronage: Why Populists Win Elections in India, Asia, and Beyond* (Oxford: Oxford University Press).
Populism in the world's largest democracy.

Mény, Yves, and Surer, Yves (eds) (2002), *Democracies and the Populist Challenge* (Basingstoke: Palgrave).
An excellent collection of articles devoted to populism in the West before the rise of movements like the M5S.

Mietzner, Marcus (2015), *Reinventing Asian Populism: Jokowi's Rise, Democracy, and Political Contestation in Indonesia* (Honolulu, HI: East-West Center).
An analysis of how a 'technocratic' populist defeated a demagogic one to become president of Indonesia—but how much of a typical populist is Jokowi?

Moffitt, Benjamin (2016), *The Global Rise of Populism: Performance, Political Style and Representation* (Stanford, CA: Stanford University Press).
Argues that populism is better understood as a style of doing politics than as an ideology.

Mudde, Cas, and Kaltwasser, Cristóbal Rovira (2017), *Populism: A Very Short Introduction* (Oxford: Oxford University Press).
A very readable introduction to the phenomenon of populism.

Scott, James C. (1990), *Domination and the Arts of Resistance: Hidden Transcripts* (New Haven, CT: Yale University Press).
An influential examination of the ways in which ordinary people get around authoritarian rulers.

Tronconi, Filippo (ed.) (2015), *Beppe Grillo's Five Star Movement: Organisation, Communication and Ideology* (Farnham: Ashgate).
The most comprehensive study of the M5S in English.

Wilson, Graham K. (1990), *Interest Groups* (Oxford: Blackwell).
A well-regarded analysis of interest groups.

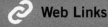 **Web Links**

https://www.youtube.com/watch?v=fpdZ7XZpT-A
An Al Jazeera video analysing the role of the social media in the Arab Spring.

http://www.beppegrillo.it/en/
Beppe Grillo's blog, in English.

https://www.youtube.com/watch?v=n7VWr4-Kpcw
The video of the first M5S V-Day. (There are also videos of later ones on YouTube.)

https://www.youtube.com/watch?v=6m-ii2-RW6w
A (fortunately relatively short) compilation video of President Chávez from 'Alo Presidente' with subtitles.

 Visit the **Online Resources** that accompany this book to access more learning resources on this topic: www.oup.com/uk/ferdinand/

Security, Insecurity, and the State

17

Reader's Guide

Security and insecurity—the two sides of the same coin—have many dimensions both within states and in the global sphere. This chapter begins by considering various conceptualizations of security and the many issue areas within which it may be applied. The next section takes a step back into the history of political thought to consider the ideas about security and insecurity developed by English theorist Thomas Hobbes and how these relate to the sovereign state. This is followed by a discussion of ideas about collective security, as embodied in the United Nations (UN). We then consider some pressing security challenges in the post-Cold-War period and the broadening of the security agenda to encompass more recent concerns such as environmental security, energy security, and the diffuse concept of 'human security'. The last part provides an overview of the 'war on terror', raising further questions concerning how best to deal with non-conventional threats.

Conceptualizing Security

'Security', like so many concepts in the social sciences, is multilayered and contested, as is its antonym, 'insecurity'. Security and insecurity possess both objective and subjective, material and ideational, dimensions and one person's perception of threat may be another's idea of opportunity. Domestic security issues range from the maintenance of law and order to food security, energy security, health security, economic security, cyber security, biosecurity, gender security, identity security, and environmental security, among others. All of these may pose issues for personal security, as well as for the security of particular groups, varying from violence against women, children, and the elderly within families to the persecution of religious groups, outbreaks of infectious diseases, financial crises, terrorist attacks, cyber attacks, and so on.

In the global sphere, security has traditionally been concerned mainly with the threats that states pose with respect to each other, but many of the issues noted already in relation to the domestic sphere overlap with those of the contemporary global sphere. Terrorism, for example, has historically taken different forms and poses problems for both the domestic and global spheres that are often difficult to disentangle.

Conceptualizing and theorizing security requires that we address three basic questions: first, what is being secured; second, what constitutes a condition of security; and third, in what circumstances do ideas about security (and insecurity) arise (Lipschutz, 1998: 1)? Looking at the first question, we could start enumerating various issues areas pertinent to security, starting with those referred to above. The problem here becomes one of an ever-expanding list with no limits on where one should draw the line. This is much the same issue that we encountered in defining 'the political' in Chapter 1. Some may consider that there should be no limits to defining security—that everything and anything to do with human well-being must be included and the interrelationships between different aspects of security identified. This is a holistic approach, the alternative to which would be to identify specific issue areas and deal with them all separately. But even if we did so, it would not resolve the general problem of limits—of just how many issues should be on a security checklist. The conventional split in the discipline between the study of politics within states and the study of politics in the global or international sphere, which maps onto a split between the study of security within the state and the study of security in the international sphere, does offer one way of managing the general field, although the spheres are often very difficult to disentangle, as we see in some of the sections that follow.

The second question concerning what constitutes a condition of security might seem more straightforward, including: being able to walk down the street, day or night, without fear of being assaulted; to be free of the same fear within the home environment; to know that if one falls ill, one can access appropriate medical care; to be confident that adequate food, water, shelter, and energy is available on an ongoing basis; to trust that the air one breathes is not polluted by toxic particles; to know that one's assets are protected by law or that the financial institutions on which one depends are adequately regulated; to be assured that one is not in danger of arbitrary arrest and detention by one's own government, or that one's own state is unlikely to be attacked or invaded by another or, just as disastrously, to fall apart and lapse into civil war—and so on. But the 'and so on' entails the same problem of limits: where does the list stop? How many different conditions must be met in order for one to be secure, or at least to feel secure?

Another issue raised by both the first and second questions introduced above entails the delimiting of responsibility—that is, who or what is responsible for providing security? In politics, the maintenance of security for both individuals and the community at large has been seen primarily as the responsibility of the state, especially when it comes to law and order. This includes the establishment of rules for human conduct in almost all spheres of life, many of which are designed to protect people from each other, as well as the detection and punishment of those who transgress those rules. Thus there are rules (laws) covering an enormous range of potentially dangerous human behaviour, from domestic violence, theft, and other forms of criminality to professional standards of health practice, financial regulation, and even the limits of government power, although the latter do not necessarily apply, or apply only weakly, in authoritarian states. The latter point raises the issue of threats to security coming from one's own government. History is replete with cases of the mass murder of citizens by governing authorities—Germany under Hitler, Russia under Stalin, China under Mao, and Cambodia under Pol Pot are among the most notorious in the twentieth century.

Beyond individual sovereign states, which by definition possess sovereign authority to act in all the above areas, there is no 'world government' as such to enforce security in the international sphere. But there is the UN and a considerable body of international law that underpins a system of global governance and plays a key role in global security. We consider the role of the UN in a later section.

The third question entails investigation of the actual circumstances in which security issues arise. For example, at what point does the flow of people from one state to another appear to pose a threat (rather than a benefit, or even just a neutral issue) to the receiving state? Who decides whether immigrants—including both regular immigrants and asylum seekers—actually pose a threat at all and on what basis? And why should 'state' or 'national' security be privileged over other types of security, including the 'human security' of those seeking refuge? Questions such as these have given rise to a distinctive field of 'securitization theory', which has been developed over the last decade or so mainly in the field of international politics, although its insights are drawn from the behaviour of national elites whose main (but not exclusive) audience is within the domestic sphere of politics.

At its most basic, securitization theory holds that an issue becomes 'securitized' when those in positions of power and influence *declare* that it poses a threat in one way or another. Thus any particular instance of securitization occurs as the result of a 'speech act' performed by an elite. It follows that securitization is a special form of politicization, and a more extreme one than those occurring in the ordinary course of politics. For example, the issue of immigration in countries like the US, the UK, and Australia, among others, is an issue that has become increasingly politicized in recent years. In the UK, in the lead-up to the Brexit referendum of June 2016, the relatively high level of immigration over the

17

previous decade or so had become increasingly politicized. In the Leave campaign, much was made by right-wing politicians of the alleged threats posed by immigrants from within the EU (and especially from Eastern Europe) to jobs for locals as well as the more diffuse threat to British national identity.

Of course, the securitization of an issue such as immigration will not work unless there is a reservoir of public feeling on the matter to be tapped. The US has, at least in the past, generally been much more tolerant of immigration. In the 2016 presidential election campaign, however, Republican candidate Donald Trump attempted to securitize immigration by Muslims, associating them with terrorism, as well as 'illegals' from Mexico, whom he depicted as murderers and rapists. In Australia, 'border security' has been an increasingly prominent buzzword in relation to asylum seekers attempting to arrive by boat. All of those intercepted at sea are now detained offshore in what is dubbed 'Operation Sovereign Borders'. In all these cases, then, certain types of immigrant have been 'securitized'. In considering this example, we return once again to the circumstances under which ideas about security (and insecurity) arise. We can gain an insight into the dynamics central to these circumstances only by asking the right questions, as illustrated by **Key Quote 17.1**.

 KEY QUOTE 17.1   On securitization

'How do ideas about security develop, enter the realm of public policy debate and discourse and, eventually, become institutionalized in hardware, organizations, roles, and practices? Do they arise, as the conventional wisdom might suggest, from objective threats and conditions inherent to an anarchic world? Are they generated within, a consequence of notions about multiple selves and feared others? Or, are they socially constructed, the worst-case result of a dialectic between what is observed and what is imagined? This process is the least-understood of all, yet it is this . . . question that may be the most important one to be asked.' (Lipschutz, 1998: 1)

 KEY POINTS

- Security is a multilayered and contested concept that once again raises problems of definition and scope.
- Splitting the study of security into intra-state and external spheres is a conventional way of managing the field, but many issues cross over into both spheres.
- Securitization theory is based on the notion that issues become 'securitized' when those in positions of power and influence declare something to be a threat and public perceptions respond accordingly.

Security and Insecurity in the State of Nature

As we saw in Chapter 2, a number of classic texts in the history of ideas have constructed an image of the state of nature as characterized by a permanent condition of anarchy, defined in terms of the absence of a sovereign authority, which we would normally understand to be a government capable of making *and* enforcing laws and punishing wrongdoers. The best-known account along these lines is that of Thomas Hobbes (1588–1679), originally published in 1651 in the last year of the English Civil War, an event that had a profound influence on his ideas. Hobbes' book, entitled *Leviathan* (Hobbes, 1651/2008), represents the state of nature as a highly dangerous environment, lacking any effective civil structure under the authority of a ruler or ruling body. In the absence of an authoritative source of political authority capable of imposing order, there is no security at all. The most powerful individuals prevail over the weaker, although even the powerful must watch their backs constantly to guard against threats from rivals. Thus the anarchic state of nature offers the most *in*secure existence imaginable.

The first part of **Key Quote 17.2** describes this situation of unrelieved insecurity, devoid of the incentives for cooperation for productive purposes and which can only be remedied by the establishment of a state with a sovereign at its head. The second part of the quotation describes relations between states, where each sovereign must exercise constant vigilance, forever watching what other sovereigns are doing lest they threaten the security of one's own state. This latter concern is a logical accompaniment to Hobbes' ideas about security *within* the state, which is at the heart of his social contract theory. In applying such ideas to the contemporary political scene, writers in the tradition of political realism argue that the security of the state itself must always come first, because if it breaks down, it can no longer provide the conditions essential for enabling basic human security to be assured—meaning, at a minimum, safe access to food, water, and shelter, and safety from each other, as well as from outsiders.

Q   KEY QUOTE 17.2   Thomas Hobbes on the state of nature

'In such condition, there is no place for industry; because the fruit thereof is uncertain; and consequently no culture of the earth; no navigation, nor use of the commodities that may be imported by sea; no commodious building; no instruments of moving and removing; such things as require much force; no knowledge of the surface of the earth; no account of time; no arts; no letters; no society; and which is worst of all, continual fear, and danger of violent death; and the life of man, solitary poor, nasty, brutish, and short. . . .

[I]n all times, kings, and persons of sovereign authority, because of their independency, are in continual jealousies, and in the state and posture of gladiators; having their weapons pointing, and their eyes fixed on one another, that is, their forts, garrisons, and guns upon the frontiers of their kingdoms; and continual spies upon their neighbours; which is a posture of war.' (Hobbes, 1651/2008: 95–6)

17

In summary, Hobbes postulated a dangerous, anarchic 'state of nature' as the original condition in which humans lived before the rise of organized political communities, and saw the sovereign state as the only real guarantor of personal security and community order. Although often depicted as a key founding figure in conceptualizing security in terms of *state* security, a closer look at his work suggests that his analysis is, first and foremost, that of a *human* security theorist concerned with the conditions under which people can not only live (that is, survive), but also thrive in peace among each other at the level of everyday life. It should also be noted that some political philosophers, including social contract theorists such as Jean-Jacques Rousseau (1712–78), see the state of nature as essentially benign, while others dismiss the concept altogether.

 KEY POINTS

- The 'state of nature'—a key concept in the history of ideas about security and the state—is taken by theorists such as Hobbes to mean a highly dangerous anarchic environment, lacking any effective political authority and therefore offering no security at all.
- A structure of civil authority within a sovereign sphere is often seen as a prerequisite for dispelling anarchy and thereby securing the safety and well-being of individuals.

Securing the State

The concept of 'national security', which encompasses more recent terms such as 'border security' and 'homeland security', has both external and internal dimensions. In conventional approaches to security, states must be on the watch for threats emanating from outside, although they must also guard against threats from within. States typically maintain both a military force oriented to external security threats (although military forces may be deployed to assist with events such as natural disasters) and a separate internal security apparatus in the form of a police force along with courts of law, prisons, etc. A conventional approach also holds that states, and only states, have the authority to operate, or at least oversee, the operations of security forces, especially of the military kind. This accords with German sociologist Max Weber's (2009: 78) famous definition of the modern state in terms of its possession of a monopoly of the legitimate use of physical force within a given territory—noting also that territoriality is one of the distinctive characteristics of a state.

There is a balance, however, between the extent to which people may be 'protected' by the state and its security apparatus, as opposed to subjugated under a regime of harsh rules and penalties that infringe on the civil and political rights of a state's citizens. Ruling elements within authoritarian states are renowned for the repression of such rights, including the right of individuals or civil society groups to even criticize the government or its policies, these often being portrayed as a security threat to the state itself (Lawson, 1993: 195). Authoritarian one-party states are especially prone to identifying both the state and the nation with the ruling party, and conceiving 'all attacks on the party as an attack on the state' and interpreting 'all proposals to change the government as an attempt to overthrow or destroy the state' (Gilly, 1990: 289). A recent commentary issued on behalf of Freedom House, a US-based watchdog organization that describes itself as dedicated to the expansion of freedom and democracy around the world, observed growing tendencies to authoritarian repression among African states, noting that countries such as Uganda, Burundi, Rwanda, and Kenya have all resorted 'to more brazen antidemocratic tactics . . . often justified on the grounds of strengthening national security, fighting terrorist threats, or preserving national unity' (Durham, 2015). As noted above, some of the worst historic cases of mass murder or genocide have been perpetrated by authoritarian dictators against their own citizens, aptly dubbed 'death by government' (Rummel, 1994).

By contrast, contenders for office in democratic systems may well depict their rivals or political enemies as representing a danger to national security in one way or another, and indeed often do, but cannot have them imprisoned or even gagged. Some may question whether this makes democratic systems less secure in some ways or whether the relatively small risks are simply part of the price one pays for democracy. **Case Study 17.3** provides some insights into the kind of issues concerning national security raised during the 2016 US presidential campaign, which have continued into the Trump presidency.

 CASE STUDY 17.3 **National security and the 2016 US presidential campaign**

A key issue during the 2016 US presidential campaign was the extent to which the leading candidates were depicted by their respective opponents as an actual or potential threat to national security. The first debate to erupt concerned Hillary Clinton's use of a private email server during the time she was Secretary of State in the Obama administration. A constant theme of her Republican opponents in general, and the Trump campaign (**see Figure 17.1**) in particular, was that she had jeopardized national security by sending classified information via an insecure email system. Although a number of emails were apparently identified as containing some classified material, there was no evidence that any had been hacked by external agents and the FBI found no case for a prosecution. Hillary Clinton later called the whole email investigation the 'biggest nothing burger ever' (quoted in Le Miere, 2017). Even so, the episode showed that State Department security was somewhat lax and it certainly gave the Trump campaign plenty of political ammunition.

In turn, Hillary Clinton made Republican nominee Donald Trump's ignorance and carelessness on issues of national security a centrepiece of her campaign—receiving strong support from some members of the Republican establishment itself in the process, as well as from figures within US national security agencies. A former deputy director of the CIA, Michael J. Morrell, wrote of Trump that, even as a candidate, he had shown himself to be undermining US national interests and security, one example being his praise of Russian President Vladimir Putin. Morrell added that Trump took 'policy positions consistent with Russian, not American, interests—endorsing Russian espionage against the United States, supporting Russia's annexation of Crimea and giving a green light to a possible Russian invasion of the Baltic States' (Morrell, 2016). The *Washington Post* concluded that, as far as security was concerned, '[a] Trump presidency would be dangerous for the nation and for the world' (*Washington Post* Editorial Board, 2016).

In the wake of his election victory, speculation about possible collusion between Russian agents and the Trump campaign team during the election also came to light, turning into a scandal equalling Hillary Clinton's 'emailgate' affair. It was now the turn of Trump's defenders to call the whole thing a 'nothing burger'. If true, however, it would indicate not merely collusion with a rather unfriendly foreign power, but also that the US election process is insecure from external interference.

FIGURE 17.1
© mikeledray/ Shutterstock.com

17

Case Study 17.3 also indicates that liberal democratic states clearly allow a great deal of freedom of speech when it comes to political contestation for elected office, even when security becomes an issue. Moreover, political contestation is itself seen not as a security threat, but as part of normal politics and certainly as a civil right. There have, however, been many instances where the civil rights of both citizens and non-citizens in democratic countries have been undermined in the name of securing the state. Prime examples include laws introduced by both the US and the UK to detain terror suspects without charge for extended periods of time. In the case of the UK, some of these laws date back to the days of Irish Republican Army (IRA) terrorism. The establishment by the US of a special detention facility in Guantanamo Bay at its military base on the island of Cuba in January 2002, for holding alleged terror suspects following the events of '9/11' on an indefinite basis, is especially notorious. In Australia, many asylum seekers have not only been detained offshore, but also a number have been detained within Australia on an indefinite basis following secret assessments by the Australian Security Intelligence Organization (ASIO), the terms of which have not been made known to those detained or to their lawyers. This means that people could possibly be imprisoned for life without charge and without trial for reasons that no one outside of an official security organization is permitted to know, let alone contest. In August 2013, Australia was found guilty on 143 counts of violation of human rights under international law. Over the next three years, a number of detainees had their security assessments reversed and were eventually released, after being held for up to six years. This illustrates that 'securing the state' may involve violating the human rights of both citizens and non-citizens, noting that human rights are universal by definition and not defined by one's citizenship, or lack of it.

KEY POINTS

- Conventional political theory holds that states, and only states, have the authority to organize or oversee the operations of security forces, which generally include both military and police forces.

- Authoritarian systems typically see threats to the government emanating from political opponents as threats to the state itself and often react with harsh punitive measures, whereas in democratic systems political opposition and contestation is part of normal politics.

- There is evidence of violations of international human rights law in the name of national security even within some democratic countries.

The Privatization of Security

Security may well be the primary responsibility of the state, but it has become a booming business in the private sector. This not only comes in the form of private companies providing additional security services for private property and private safety, but also is an increasingly significant adjunct to state security institutions across a range of areas. It is important to note that this trend has a significant political economy dimension because the privatization or 'outsourcing' of what would normally be the full responsibility of the state in terms of both funding and operating, but which is turned into a profit-making enterprise, accords with contemporary neo-liberal thought.

17

We saw in Chapter 9 that neo-liberalism is based on the notion that free markets enable individuals to maximize their own material interests and that this provides the best means for satisfying human aspirations. Markets are to be preferred over states and politics, these being depicted as far less efficient in allocating and utilizing resources. The trend to privatization in many sectors follows the same neo-liberal logic—that the private management of almost any enterprise or service will always be more efficient than management by the state and that *only* services that cannot be provided by the private sector should be provided by the state. Of course, this logic is challenged by critics of neo-liberalism and we also saw in Chapter 9 some of the adverse implications for deregulation, especially of financial markets. Critics would also suggest that the ideology of neo-liberalism has served powerful private interests for the last few decades, first under the influence of Margaret Thatcher in the UK and Ronald Reagan in the US. It was also boosted significantly by the collapse of communism, which exposed the glaring inefficiencies of centralized planning under authoritarian rule. And it continues to underpin trends to this day, including those in the security industry. A 2010 report on the situation in the US stated that:

> The private security industry is a crucial component of security and safety in the United States and abroad. Today, private security is responsible not only for protecting many of the nation's institutions and critical infrastructure systems, but also for protecting intellectual property and sensitive corporate information. U.S. companies also rely heavily on private security for a wide range of functions, including protecting employees and property, conducting investigations, performing pre-employment screening, providing information technology security, and many other functions. (Strom, Berzofsky, Shook-Sa, et al., 2010: 1–1)

Another source notes that trends worldwide have seen private security services in the commercial sector expand at a phenomenal rate. Services range from guarding property and installing alarms and other security devices to risk assessment and surveillance: 'Worldwide, the private security market is valued at over $139 billion, and its growth is forecast to continue at an annual rate of 8 per cent to reach a value of $230 billion in 2015' (Abrahamsen and Williams, 2011: 20–1). A more recent estimate by a professional marketing firm provides similar figures, with global demand increasing annually by 7.4 per cent, reaching US$244 billion in 2016. It also notes a number of factors driving the trend, including 'rising urbanization, the real and perceived risks of crime and terrorism, belief that public safety measures are insufficient, and growth of a middle class with assets to protect and the means to pay for supplementary security measures' (Freedonia, 2016a). Looking ahead, the forecast for 2018 is further growth of 6.9 per cent, to reach a total of nearly $267 billion, with much of this continued growth coming from developing countries, especially Brazil, China, India, and Mexico (Freedonia, 2016b).

A notable example of the increasing privatization of security services that the state would normally provide is both the building of prisons and their ongoing operation. One media commentary on the trend in the US noted that prisons there had become a 'cash cow for big business', whose profits depended on spending as little as possible on both the prisons and the prisoners. Thus 'the interest of private prisons lies not in the obvious social good of having the minimum necessary number of inmates but in having as many as possible, housed as cheaply as possible' (Gopnick, quoted in Whitehead, 2012). Private prisons have been established mainly in English-speaking developed countries and, in addition to the US, have been operating in the UK and Australia since the early 1990s, while US companies have been looking to expand their operations in Canada. Private companies have also been operating Australia's detention facilities for asylum seekers both onshore and offshore.

Private contracting for state security purposes, however, goes well beyond prisons. Private corporations have long been involved in supporting the military sector, especially since the world wars of the twentieth century. Key areas in the general field of defence and security contracting includes weapons and engineering, logistical support and facilities operation, and armed protection for individuals or particular events (Lucas, 2016: 121). The extent to which powerful corporate interests had become enmeshed in the entire structure of the US military led Dwight D. Eisenhower, former Supreme Commander of the Allied Forces in Europe during the Second World War and then US president from 1953 to 1961, to warn of its dangers to the fabric of American society, and the world beyond, in his famous farewell speech, as set out in **Key Quote 17.4**.

Warfare in the post-Cold-War world has seen even further expansion of private corporations into the sphere of military operations. From Africa to the Balkans and the Middle East, a variety of private companies have been involved in virtually every sphere of operations, from supply chains to on-the-ground military activity, the latter sometimes including mercenaries. A notable and ultimately successful use of a private military contract operation occurred in Sierra Leone, a country rich in diamonds, in the mid-1990s. The state was on the verge of collapse due to an insurgent rebel force that the government of the time had battled ineffectively until it resorted to bringing in a firm called Executive Outcomes, based in South Africa and with experienced personnel drawn largely from former apartheid-era security forces. Whatever one may think of the deployment of such forces, the end result, within a relatively short space of time, was the ending of one of the African continent's most vicious civil wars and the restoration of legitimate government (Singer, 2008: 3–4).

Q   KEY QUOTE 17.4   US President Dwight D. Eisenhower on the rise of the military-industrial complex

'Our military organization today bears little relation to that known by any of my predecessors in peacetime . . . Until the latest of our world conflicts, the United States had no armaments industry . . . But now . . . we have been compelled to create a permanent armaments industry of vast proportions. . . . This conjunction of an immense military establishment and a large arms industry is new in the American experience . . . In the councils of government, we must guard against the acquisition of unwarranted influence, whether sought or unsought, by the military-industrial complex. The potential for the rise of misplaced power exists and will persist.' (Eisenhower, 1961)

17

Of course, not all such operations will necessarily turn out well. And privatization and outsourcing carries with it significant risks in terms of corruption and graft—although this is hardly confined to the private sector. Transparency International, an international non-governmental organization (NGO) dedicated to the elimination of corruption in all sectors, notes that the official defence sector worldwide loses at least US$20 billion a year to corruption: 'Single source contracts, unaccountable and overpaid agents, obscure defence budgets, unfair appointments and promotions, and many more forms of corruption in this secretive sector waste taxpayer funds and put citizens' and soldiers' lives at risk' (Transparency International, quoted in Alfreds, 2014). Endemic corruption in Afghanistan since the US-led invasion in 2001 permeates all sectors, including the myriad private contractors working in the security industry and into which billions in aid has been poured (see, generally, Goodhand and Sedra, 2015). In the aftermath of the invasion of 2003, Iraq also became awash with private military contractors (PMCs), many of them ex-soldiers operating in a legal vacuum and with no regulations covering their activities. The big companies involved, often under contract to the US government, also tended to be run by former senior military personnel (Saner, 2016).

An International Code of Conduct for Private Security Service Providers (ICoC) was eventually produced in 2010 on the initiative of Switzerland, aiming to provide better governance, compliance with basic human rights standards, and an oversight mechanism (ICoC, 2016). But the code is voluntary and relies on self-regulation—another feature of neo-liberal ideology. More generally, one recently retired PMC observed: 'There are vast amounts of money to be made from private military contracting and these people have their political interests, same as any corporation. War is money, war is profit' (quoted in Saner, 2016).

 KEY POINTS

- Privatization is evident in virtually all security sectors, from guarding private and public property and undertaking risk assessment to the building and operating of prisons and key areas of the military.
- The privatization of what would conventionally be seen as the responsibility of the state in terms of security provision accords fully with neo-liberal ideology.
- Privatization raises numerous problems for regulation in many security sectors.

Security and Insecurity in Global Politics

The study of life *within* the state is regarded as the proper focus for political science, whereas for traditional scholars of global politics or international relations the principal concern is with relations *between* states. It was noted earlier that there is no world government possessing sovereign power through which the kind of order that Hobbes regarded as essential for a secure life may be imposed. This anarchic international sphere is therefore regarded by conventional theorists as the principal locus of *in*security for sovereign states and therefore, ultimately, for the people enclosed within them. Thus the concern is with how to maintain the survival of the sovereign state itself. It is only when this is assured that people can effectively work to achieve 'the good life' within the state. The logic of this position is set out in **Key Quote 17.5**.

   None of this means that the international sphere is one of perpetual chaos or warfare. The anarchic nature of the global sphere need not preclude a degree of order and stability. But, given its underlying dynamics, peace and security in this sphere at any given time are assumed to be tenuous, at least according to the more pessimistic approaches taken by political realists. The main message from this perspective is that states can ultimately depend only on their own resources. *Self-reliance* is therefore the watchword for security and the ultimate key to survival in the international sphere.

   Others, however, put greater faith in the capacity of international institutions to ameliorate the dangerous conditions inherent in the global sphere through the dynamics of *collective* security. The first major international institution of this kind was the League of Nations. Although it had many weaknesses and clearly failed to prevent the Second World War, the idea of a major institution of global governance through which collective security could be realized remained an imperative for world leaders, as we see in **Case Study 17.6**.

 KEY QUOTE 17.5   John Mearsheimer on state survival

'States seek to maintain their territorial integrity and the autonomy of their domestic political order. They can pursue other goals like prosperity and protecting human rights, but those aims must always take a back seat to survival, because if a state does not survive, it cannot pursue those other goals.' (Mearsheimer, 2010: 80)

 CASE STUDY 17.6   The United Nations, collective security, and the Security Council

As the Second World War drew to a close, a Charter for a new international organization to replace the League of Nations was approved at a meeting in San Francisco in June 1945 by representatives of 51 countries, with the United Nations Organization coming into official existence on 24 October 1945. Its membership grew steadily as decolonization created newly independent states throughout the following decades, with a further increase occurring after the collapse of the Cold War and the creation of many more sovereign states in its aftermath. Membership now stands at 193.

17

The UN Charter establishes basic principles of order in support of international peace and security to which every new member must sign up. The Security Council, set up under Chapter V, was originally composed of five permanent members (the UK, the US, the USSR, France, and China) and six non-permanent members. There are now ten non-permanent members who each serve a two-year term and Russia has replaced the defunct USSR. The five permanent members—or 'P5'—each retain veto power over any Security Council decision. This extraordinary power reflects a belief that the new UN would not function without according a special place to the most prominent states, thereby rectifying a perceived weakness of the old League. More generally, the Security Council is primarily responsible for maintaining international peace and security, and its functions and powers are set out accordingly. Thus the Security Council embodies the UN's aspirations to provide for 'collective security'—a term encapsulating the notion that true security cannot be obtained through the practice of 'every state for itself'.

The composition and functioning of the Security Council has been subject to many criticisms over the years. One is that the permanent membership, which holds such a privileged position, reflects circumstances prevailing over 65 years ago in a world where decolonization had scarcely begun. The UN's membership has almost quadrupled since then and many now see the permanent membership as skewed unfairly in favour of the developed world. Certainly, the geographic distribution of the P5 is relatively narrow, with no representation from Africa, the Middle East, South Asia, or South America.

Although lack of reform is often thought to undermine its legitimacy, this does not necessarily diminish whatever efficacy the Security Council possesses (see Hurd, 2008: 199–217). The Libyan intervention in 2011 illustrated sufficient political will among its members to authorize military intervention to establish a no-fly zone to protect civilians. Using Chapter VII of the UN Charter on 'Action with Respect to Threats to the Peace, Breaches of the Peace, and Acts of Aggression', the Security Council authorized a coalition of member states to take 'all necessary measures . . . to protect civilians and civilian populated areas . . . while excluding a foreign occupation force of any form' (United Nations Security Council, 2011). Of the P5 members, Russia and China abstained. The North Atlantic Treaty Organization (NATO) officially assumed sole responsibility for international air operations, but then exceeded the UN mandate to enforce regime change—deemed successful in October 2011 when Gaddafi was killed by insurgents. But, like Iraq, the security situation in Libya has scarcely improved. It is wracked with political factionalism and provides yet another theatre for Islamist extremism.

The Security Council has been criticized more recently for failures with respect to both the civil war in Syria and the crisis in Ukraine. The Syrian conflict erupted in 2011 when protests against the authoritarian regime of President Bashar Al-Assad were met with violent repression. As of mid-2017, the conflict had seen up to half a million casualties, while around 5 million refugees had fled to neighbouring countries and more than 6 million had been internally displaced. Both Russia and China have used their veto to block Security Council Resolutions against the Assad regime. This has been partly influenced by the experience of the Libyan intervention, with the Russian permanent envoy to the UN stating that the international community should be alarmed by claims that the NATO interpretation of Security Council Resolutions on Libya can serve as a model for the intervention (cited in Kirsch and Helal, 2014: 431). But Russia has traditionally been close to the Assad regime and is effectively an ally in the civil war.

The Ukraine crisis emerged from tensions and struggles within the Ukraine over its relationship with the EU (and, by implication, NATO), on the one hand, and Russia, on the other. Pro-Russian forces in Crimea, with Russian support, subsequently succeeded in orchestrating the annexation of Crimea by Russia in March 2014. This triggered another movement by pro-Russian separatists across other parts of eastern and southern Ukraine, resulting in widespread violence.

Critics of the UN Security Council's failure to effectively mitigate these conflicts, let alone to resolve them, highlight serious tensions within the Security Council itself where any of the five veto-wielding permanent members can prevent action being taken on a security issue if it is perceived as impacting on their own national interest. In her outgoing address in 2014, former UN High Commissioner for Human Rights Navi Pillay said that: 'Short-term geopolitical considerations and national interest, narrowly defined, have repeatedly taken precedence over intolerable human suffering and grave breaches of and long-term threats to international peace and security' (UN, 2014). However, the speech also highlighted certain UN successes in promoting positive change—for example in the ending of apartheid in Pillay's home country of South Africa.

In the light of the reasoning behind both the UN as a whole and the Security Council in particular, one might ask how different approaches to global politics are reflected. In the first instance, the practical imperatives driving its formation were based squarely on the experience of warfare and the desire to minimize international conflict. The rhetoric accompanying the various declarations was infused with optimistic visions of a better world in which security was the norm rather than the exception. Further, with membership open to all on equal terms, and a normative commitment to decolonization, the UN reflected a certain egalitarianism, while provisions for the social and economic advancement of all nations ensured a proactive role in areas outside mainstream security concerns.

This tendency was strengthened with the Universal Declaration of Human Rights (1948) and an expanded humanitarian role in later years, as well as provisions for NGO participation. In short, the UN system may be founded on the sovereign state system, but its basic principles and vision for world order extend beyond this to embrace a broader interpretation of security. Thus its wide-ranging Charter has seen it respond to significant non-military international security concerns, such as the environment, health, food, water, energy, and so on, illustrating a very broad, multidimensional security role.

17

Alternative approaches to global security have been around at least from the 1960s, although this was a time when the threat of nuclear war—which would have precipitated 'mutually assured destruction' (MAD) of the two superpowers, many of their allies, and possibly the entire world—dominated strategic thinking. Conventional approaches to the problem were encapsulated in deterrence theory, which held that a preponderance of military power—in this case, the possession of a vast array of tactical nuclear weapons by the US and key allies—would persuade the enemy that the risks and costs of starting a 'hot war' were too great to contemplate seriously. The same reasoning dominates certain approaches to North Korea today. From the early 1960s, however, the peace movement promoted the idea that genuine security was to be obtained not by threatening annihilation of one's enemies, but by working with them to resolve conflicts. A case for rethinking security along the lines of 'positive peace' was also pursued. This concept rejects peace as consisting merely in the absence of violent conflict and focuses attention on the causes of conflict and their amelioration through cooperative social mechanisms (see Galtung, 1969: 167–91). There were cross-cutting links as well to other social movements, including the women's movement and the environmental movement, both of which were to advance their own particular conceptions of security and an alternative agenda for policy-makers well before the end of the Cold War.

Feminism and gender theory have provided some challenging critiques of conventional approaches to security. Feminism, as discussed in Chapter 8, is concerned primarily with a range of inequalities and disadvantages suffered by women and girls under conditions of patriarchy. Gender theory is broader because it focuses on issues in the construction of both masculinity and femininity, and brings in sexuality as well. With respect to the latter, there is no doubt that people who identify as homosexual have suffered severe abuses in many countries around the world, including imprisonment, assault, and murder, making it a serious personal security issue. Violence against women, another personal security issue with implications for the wider society, remains a major problem even in countries that are considered highly developed in social and economic terms. One security issue with obvious gender dimensions that has received long overdue attention in recent years is the incidence of rape in war, an issue highlighted during the war in Bosnia-Herzegovina (1992–95). Before this, there was enormous reluctance to recognize the extent to which rape is used as a widespread tactic in war. The publicity surrounding the situation in the former Yugoslavia also brought long overdue attention to the widespread rape of German women at the end of the Second World War, mainly at the hands of the victorious Red Army, and of the forced prostitution of 'comfort women' used by Japanese forces during the Pacific war: instances of sexual assault in both cases ran into the millions. Rape by US soldiers during the Vietnam War has also come to light only in fairly recent years (Weaver, 2010).

These are clearly not the only historic cases. It has been going on for centuries and soldiers from many other countries have engaged in rape either en masse or individually, almost always with impunity. It has only very recently been treated seriously in international law. Indeed, the first time that rape was treated as a war crime in its own right was in 1996, when eight Bosnian Serb military and police officers were indicted in The Hague in connection with the rape of Muslim women in the Bosnian war. This has scarcely prevented the continuation of the practice in other war zones, but it provides an indication that the practice of rape in war, as something that affects women in particular (although not exclusively), is now treated as an important security issue. Various reports on conflicts in Africa in recent years, especially in Congo and the Darfur region of Sudan, have highlighted rape as a widespread phenomenon. More recently, a report from Syria indicated that rape of both men and women has been used 'as a tool of control, intimidation and humiliation throughout the conflict' (Wolfe, 2013).

Another security concern in the post-Cold-War period has been the increasing gap between 'haves' and 'have-nots'—with the former consisting largely of the prosperous, industrialized countries of the northern hemisphere and the latter, of underdeveloped countries, most of which lie in the global South, producing a 'North–South' economic–developmental divide, which is often seen as having significant security dimensions. Again, concerns about this pre-date the end of the Cold War, as the report of a UN-sponsored commission headed by former West German Chancellor and Nobel Peace Laureate Willy Brandt shows. Published in 1980, this influential report, entitled *North–South: A Programme for Survival*, examined in depth the range of problems arising from significant socio-economic disparities between countries. Its findings remain relevant today.

See Chapter 9 for more on the 'North–South Gap'.

A feature of the report was its emphasis on the fact that both North and South had a strong mutual interest in putting an end to dependence, oppression, hunger, and general human distress. It proposed vastly increased aid flows, arguing that the transformation of the global economy would be in the long-term interests of all counties. Further, its implementation was less an act of charity on the part of the North than a condition of mutual survival for all. Although some developed countries saw value in acting on its recommendations, others were not convinced. US President Ronald Reagan had little interest in development issues except where aid was seen as a counter to Soviet influence. But overall aid flows did increase. Just as importantly, the Brandt Commission opened up new public discourses on the relationship between global development and security by highlighting that narrow military concerns were insufficient in an era of increasing global interdependence. Certainly, by 1989, it was clear that the Cold War had virtually collapsed and that the time for new security thinking in an increasingly globalized world had arrived. Even so, millions remain in dire poverty in the global South and this is a major factor in contemporary global migration patterns, which better-off states very often see as threatening their border security. A 2017 report suggested that there were as many as 1 million, mainly 'economic refugees', in a migration pipeline to Europe from Africa, most coming through Libya, where there are few controls (Wintour, 2017).

In addition to the plight of millions in the global South and the multifaceted security threats they faced, attention also turned to the security issues relating to the environment. Again, concerns were raised well before the end of the Cold War and the UN had held an environmental summit in 1972. But the post-Cold-War world, when the threat of nuclear war and the massive security concerns associated with it receded, seemed more conducive to expressing concerns about the environment explicitly in terms of *security*. The UN again took a lead, organizing a World Summit in Rio de Janeiro in 1992. Three major concerns were given particular attention: the state of the world's forests, biodiversity, and climate change. All are interrelated, but the latter is now the most prominent issue.

17

The summit produced the UN Convention on Climate Change, which set up a framework for intergovernmental efforts to tackle global warming, followed by the 1997 Kyoto Protocol, which strengthened the Convention by committing its signatories to binding targets for the reduction of greenhouse gas emissions. The US under the Bush administration and Australia under the Howard government, however, subsequently pulled out, each claiming that the emissions reduction targets would damage their respective economies and both also claiming that developing countries, which included major emitters such as China and India, should not be given special treatment. Further conferences were held in Copenhagen in 2009 and Cancún in 2010, with the latter producing some progress, including the establishment of a Green Climate Fund intended to raise and disburse US$100 billion a year by 2020 to help poor nations to deal with climate impacts and assist low-carbon development (see http://www.bbc.co.uk/news/science-environment-11975470, accessed January 2018). Yet another conference in November/December 2015, known as COP21, produced the Paris Agreement, a key feature of which was to set a goal of limiting global warming to 2 degrees above the pre-industrial level and with a further commitment to attempt to keep it at 1.5 degrees. In June 2017, however, US President Trump announced that he was pulling out of the Paris Agreement on the grounds that it impacted negatively on US interests.

The consequences of global warming for security are potentially enormous. Rising sea levels—just one consequence—threaten not just the very existence of small island states, such as Tuvalu and Kiribati, and low-lying countries, such as Holland and Bangladesh, but extensive coastal regions of countries including the US, as well as other major greenhouse gas emitters such as Australia, China, India, Brazil, and many more. Climate change will also impact on food and water security, not to mention the considerable problems that will inevitably attend mass migration from low-lying areas, impacting in turn on border security with new waves of 'environmental refugees'. And while climate change sceptics have often derided the concerns voiced by environmentalists as alarmist, the scientific evidence about the extent to which the earth's climate is changing as a result of greenhouse gas emission, and the devastating effects that this is likely to have, is now beyond serious dispute. More generally, environmental security feeds directly into many other security concerns (**see Key Quote 17.7**).

Q KEY QUOTE 17.7   Why is environmental security important?

'To the extent humankind neglects to maintain the globe's life-supporting eco-systems generating water, food, medicine, and clean air, current and future generations will be confronted with increasingly severe instances of environmentally induced changes.

Such events will test our traditional concepts, boundaries, and understandings of national security and alliance politics and, if taken for granted, may lead to conflict, including violent conflict, from the global to the regional, national, local or human level.

Environmental security, broadly defined, affects humankind and its institutions and organizations anywhere and at anytime.' (http://www.envirosecurity.org/activities/What_is_Environmental_Security.pdf, accessed January 2018)

KEY POINTS

- The security and survival of the state itself is traditionally seen as a prerequisite for the security of citizens in the everyday lives.

- The UN system is founded on the sovereign state system but its vision for world order extends beyond this to embrace a much broader interpretation of security.

- Social movements, such as the peace movement, the women's movement, and the environmental movement, have all contributed to alternative conceptualizations of security.

From State Security to Human Security and the 'Responsibility to Protect'

UN intervention in the post-Cold-War world has been supported conceptually by new security thinking first articulated explicitly in the *Human Development Report 1994* (UNDP, 1994). Opening with the claim that '[t]he world can never be at peace unless people have security in their daily lives' (UNDP, 1994: 1) and a survey of the contrast between the unprecedented prosperity achieved by some and the deepening misery of so many others, the report went on to set out a case for redefining security in 'human' terms, implying a substantial shift away from security defined in terms of state/national security. The 'human' aspect here includes health security, employment security, environmental security, and security from crime as emerging global issues. Security itself was defined in the broadest possible terms as 'safety from the constant threats of hunger, disease, crime and repression' and 'protection from sudden and hurtful disruptions in the pattern of our daily lives—whether in our homes, in our jobs, in our communities or in our environment' (UNDP, 1994: 3).

As with previous UN reports, there were both supporters and critics. Among the latter, a common objection was that if virtually everything came under the rubric of 'security', then the term would be meaningless. Furthermore, the broadening of the security agenda in this way meant that the important focus on *international* or security may be lost. In theoretical terms, it is not hard to see that while realists would be concerned to maintain the international–domestic distinction as a matter of both practical and conceptual importance, those subscribing to alternative ideas about security would welcome the conceptual shift. This has resulted in efforts by policy-makers and others to tackle security at different levels. So while not neglecting traditional state security needs, more attention has been directed to the multiple levels at which security considerations operate. New security thinking has also prompted a questioning of state legitimacy when it comes to humanitarian crises, as **Key Debate 17.8** shows.

17

KEY DEBATE 17.8 **The responsibility to protect**

An important report issued by the International Commission on Intervention and State Sovereignty (ICISS) in 2001, entitled *The Responsibility to Protect*, was adopted by the UN World Summit in 2005. A central claim is that while it is the responsibility of sovereign states to protect their own citizens from avoidable catastrophe, if they are unwilling or unable to do so, then that responsibility must be borne by the international community (ICISS, 2001). Thus the 'responsibility to protect'—commonly known as 'R2P'—is, in the first instance, the responsibility of states, but may shift to the external realm—the international community—when any state fails in its essential responsibility. The 2005 UN World Summit outcome emphasized the obligations of both individual states and the international community collectively in terms of their responsibilities (**see Figure 17.2**):

138. Each individual State has the responsibility to protect its populations from genocide, war crimes, ethnic cleansing and crimes against humanity. This responsibility entails the prevention of such crimes, including their incitement, through appropriate and necessary means. We accept that responsibility and will act in accordance with it. The international community should, as appropriate, encourage and help States to exercise this responsibility and support the United Nations in establishing an early warning capability.

139. The international community, through the United Nations, also has the responsibility to use appropriate diplomatic, humanitarian and other peaceful means, in accordance with Chapters VI and VIII of the Charter, to help protect populations from genocide, war crimes, ethnic cleansing and crimes against humanity. In this context, we are prepared to take collective action, in a timely and decisive manner, through the Security Council, in accordance with the Charter, including Chapter VII, on a case-by-case basis and in cooperation with relevant regional organizations as appropriate, should peaceful means be inadequate and national authorities manifestly fail to protect their populations from genocide, war crimes, ethnic cleansing and crimes against humanity. We stress the need for the General Assembly to continue consideration of the responsibility to protect populations from genocide, war crimes, ethnic cleansing and crimes against humanity and its implications, bearing in mind the principles of the Charter and international law. We also intend to commit ourselves, as necessary and appropriate, to helping States build capacity to protect their populations from genocide, war crimes, ethnic cleansing and crimes against humanity and to assisting those which are under stress before crises and conflicts break out. (United Nations General Assembly, 2005)

Some have argued that the report did not go far enough in setting out a new framework for UN action in response to crises. A stronger framework would require, for example, limiting the veto power of P5 members when extraordinary circumstances arose and requiring the UN to do more than merely 'stand ready' to intervene, but actually oblige it to act (Bellamy, 2006). Others, however, see R2P as a crucial normative advance in the UN's development, making a significant break with the previous emphasis on the inviolability of state sovereignty (Thakur, 2011a). With respect to the Libyan crisis, Ramesh Thakur (2011b) writes that the Security Council's authorization of 'all necessary measures' to protect civilians (short of invasion and occupation) marked a historic shift. Instead of the UN merely watching 'haplessly from the sidelines', R2P acted as 'a powerful new galvanizing norm'. Such actions, however, have not produced unambiguous positive results in the global system, as exemplified by the case of Libya.

FIGURE 17.2 UN peacekeeping forces
UN Photo/Milton Grant

✳ KEY POINTS

- Traditional security paradigms have been challenged by the shift in emphasis from state security to human security and acknowledgement of the multiple levels at which insecurity occurs.
- The 'responsibility to protect' has highlighted the role that the international community (mainly through the UN) is expected to play when states cannot, or will not, protect their own citizens from harm.

Security and Insecurity after 9/11

Developments in new security thinking have taken place against the background of a 'global war on terror' (although this term was officially dropped by the US when President Obama came to power). The attacks on the World Trade Center in New York and the Pentagon in Washington by Al-Qaeda operatives on 11 September 2001 (widely referred to as '9/11') precipitated the US-led invasion of two sovereign states: Afghanistan and Iraq. The 'war on terror' is not easily analysed in terms of traditional security paradigms, even though the US response, insofar as it has involved military force and inter-state warfare, has used traditional methods. The rise of Al-Qaeda and 'militant Islam', together with the responses by the US and its allies, illustrates a number of twists and variations on the theme of security, as illustrated in **Case Study 17.9**.

17

CASE STUDY 17.9   The rise of Islamic militancy

Islamic radicalism and militancy, which is deeply intertwined with politics in the Middle East region, has been on the rise since at least the 1970s, although the essential background to these developments can be traced back much further. The current geo-political landscape has been shaped by the outcomes of the First and Second World Wars, colonialism, the authoritarianism of successor regimes in the postcolonial period, and the competing claims of Palestinian and Jewish groups to territory—claims that have acquired an increasing religiosity over the years, in turn fuelling the emergence of extremist, politically driven fundamentalism.

It was under the conditions of the Cold War, however, that Osama bin Laden's Al-Qaeda organization emerged in Afghanistan, a country with a long history of political instability and with strategic significance for the Soviet Union. It became a battleground for competing factions within the country from the early 1970s. While the Soviets supported a Marxist government, the US, along with Pakistan, Saudi Arabia, China, the UK, and other disparate regimes, generally supported an insurrection led by the Mujahidin, whose name means 'strugglers', also related to the word *jihad*, or 'holy struggle'. Initially energized by and partially united in opposition to the Soviet presence in Afghanistan, any coherence the Mujahidin possessed largely dissipated after the Soviet withdrawal in 1989.

Violent conflict between contending factions, as well as with the embattled central government, continued until the strongest faction, the Taliban, gained control in 1996, imposing an uncompromising version of Islamic rule. Afghanistan thereafter became a haven for Al-Qaeda, originally formed in Afghanistan during the struggle against the Soviets, but for a time with its main base in Sudan. In 1996, bin Laden shifted to Afghanistan, from where he planned attacks on two US embassies in East Africa in 1998 and a US Navy vessel in Yemen in 2000. The most spectacular attacks, and those with the most far-reaching consequences, however, were those of 9/11, which sparked the 'war on terror'.

Related organizations operating in the contemporary period include Boko Haram, which emerged in Nigeria in 2002. Although undoubtedly inspired and supported by Al-Qaeda, the origins of Boko Haram are also to be found in a sense of alienation and deprivation among Islamic communities in Nigeria's north. The organization achieved particular notoriety for its abduction of more than 200 schoolgirls in April 2014. Another Al-Qaeda-related organization in Africa is Somali-based Al Shabaab, which made headlines when it killed almost 70 people in an attack on a shopping mall in Nairobi in September 2013 and again, in April 2015, with its attack on Garissa University College in which 147 people were killed. Both organizations are dedicated to the establishment of Islamic states and enmity against 'the West' and non-Muslims, as well as any rival and/or moderate Muslim groups.

17

Even more infamous in recent time, especially in light of its gruesome execution of hostages, is the organization known variously as ISIL (Islamic State in Iraq and the Levant), ISIS (Islamic State in Iraq and Syria), or simply Islamic State (IS), which originally formed as an offshoot of Al-Qaeda in Iraq. It has attracted both Islamist enemies of the Syrian regime, as well as Iraqi Sunnis, repressed under a Shi'a-dominated regime since the overthrow of Saddam Hussein. However, its targets also include Kurds and Christian minorities. It is well known for attracting foreign militants from around the world, including Australians, Canadians, North Americans, Britons, and other Europeans willing to fight, as well as Chechens, Jordanians, and Saudis, among others. Its activities in Iraq have drawn the US and certain allies back to military engagement in the country.

Al-Qaeda, known to be based in Afghanistan with the blessing of the Taliban government, was the prime suspect in the 9/11 attacks. The US demanded that its leader, Osama bin Laden (**see Figure 17.3**), be handed over by the Taliban government. When it refused to do so, the US and allies attacked just four weeks after. NATO invoked Article 5 of its founding Charter, which declares that an armed attack against one member is an attack on all. 'Operation Enduring Freedom', as the initial intervention was called, eventually gave way to NATO's International Security Assistance Force (ISAF). Efforts in political reconstruction then saw elections held, a new government put in place, and a programme of infrastructure development commenced. Afghanistan, however, still barely functions as a state and insecurity at multiple levels is the order of the day, while corruption is endemic. It took almost a decade to track bin Laden down.

The war in Iraq, launched in March 2003 by the Bush administration as part of the 'global war on terror', was supported strongly by the UK's then Prime Minister Tony Blair. This intervention, however, lacked the support of either the UN Security Council or NATO. In the Security Council, French opposition to the war was backed by Russia and China. Nonetheless, support for intervention was forthcoming from a 'coalition of the willing', which at one stage included almost 50 countries around the world, although only Poland, Denmark, and Australia sent token military contingents.

By almost any measure, the aftermath of the invasion went badly. The years that followed saw Iraq teetering on the brink of civil war between Shi'a and Sunni factions. And while Al-Qaeda had virtually no presence in Iraq before March 2003, the chaos opened the country up to its operatives, and indeed it became another recruiting ground for both criminal and terrorist organizations. Almost a decade on, one highly critical report noted that the US had suffered casualties of 4,400 soldiers dead and more than 32,000 seriously wounded—figures that nonetheless pale alongside an estimated 1 million Iraqi civilian deaths as a result of the invasion. The cost to the US economy had reached around US$3 trillion (more than 60 times the initial estimate), while the cost to Iraq in terms of infrastructure, environmental damage, and human

17

FIGURE 17.3 Osama bin Laden
ROPI / Alamy Stock Photo

capital is incalculable. In a 'liberated' Iraq, millions of Iraqis remain displaced, in both Iraq itself, as well as around the region, and ordinary citizens remain politically oppressed in the post-war order (see Benjamin and Davis, 2011). The emergence of so-called IS has also contributed to the worst refugee crisis in any region since the Second World War, although the Syrian government is no doubt the root cause of the problem there. As of October 2016, the EU estimated that the total number of Syrians needing humanitarian assistance both within Syria and in neighbouring countries was 13.5 million (European Commission, 2017).

Another major lesson from the 'global war on terror' to date is that the use of conventional military tactics against a non-conventional enemy may not only be ineffectual in defeating that enemy, but also create many new problems. While bin Laden was finally killed in May

2011, Al-Qaeda and the Taliban have not only *not* been destroyed, but also have now been joined by other militant groups, including IS; a seemingly never-ending supply of suicide bombers continues to pose a threat to civilian populations in countries around the world; and the prospects for peace and security for the people of both Afghanistan and Iraq remain bleak.

Military force is always a very blunt weapon and its consequences are often both unpredictable and uncontrollable. This led one of the most famous commentators on war, Prussian military strategist Carl von Clausewitz (1780–1831), to observe that the planning and execution of war necessarily takes place in a kind of twilight where the effects of fog distort and obscure what is going on (see Clausewitz, 1993). The phrase 'the fog of war' is based on this observation and has become an increasingly common theme as the outcome for the countries ensnared in the conflicts discussed above remains shrouded in uncertainty. Chinese Taoist thinker and strategist Sun Tzu advised, more than 2,000 years ago, that the best victory of all is gained without fighting and outlined various strategies for achieving this end (Sun Tzu, 1963). These observations point to the fact that much subtler instruments of politics may be needed to achieve desirable security outcomes in the longer term, especially against highly unconventional threats.

 KEY POINTS

- The 9/11 attacks prompted what may be seen as a conventional military response, but against a highly unconventional enemy.
- Although regime change was achieved in both Afghanistan and Iraq through military force, the long-term security outcomes for both countries, as well as the region more generally, remain highly problematic.
- Islamist claims, although superficially religious in nature, are essentially political claims.

Conclusion

The terms 'security' and 'insecurity' clearly signify multifaceted conditions both conceptually and in practical terms, and have been at the heart of political thought about the state and state sovereignty since the early modern period. More recently, securitization theory has offered insights into how security threats emerge, while highlighting that securitization is a special, rather extreme form of politicization. Various institutions, practices, and policies have been developed over the years to cope with different security challenges both within the state and in the global sphere. These challenges range from those that pose a threat to international peace and security in conventional terms—that is, in terms of armed aggression by one or more states against others—to other kinds of challenges, including civil conflict, environmental security, health security, food, water and energy security, cybersecurity, biosecurity, and threats from non-state actors such as terrorist organizations. These latter non-conventional threats are among the most serious today and we may well ask what alternative policy approaches, attuned to the specific dynamics of these threats, are possible. The extent to which security resources have been privatized has also raised concerns not just with respect to the consequence of turning insecurity into a source of profit-making, but also in terms of the abrogation of state responsibility with respect to some of its most basic functions.

? Key Questions

- How does securitization theory help to explain or interpret the emergence of security threats?
- How does the Hobbesian approach to security and insecurity relate to images of the 'state of nature'?
- Should the sovereign state remain central to how security is conceptualized in the present period with respect to both traditional and newer security issues?
- What issues does the privatization of security raise for the role and responsibilities of states?
- To what extent does the UN play an effective role in global security?
- How have social movements such as the peace movement and the environmental movement challenged traditional militarist approaches to security?
- In what ways does a gender perspective illuminate non-traditional security issues in international relations?
- Does the concept of 'human security' offer a superior framework for addressing issues in the contemporary period?
- In what sense does the R2P doctrine set up a tension between the responsibilities of individual states and the international community?

Further Reading

Abrahamsen, Rita, and Leander, Anna (eds) (2015), *Routledge Handbook of Private Security Studies* (Abingdon: Routledge).
Essays by leading scholars from around the world offer a wide-ranging overview of current research on private security and military companies.

Balzacq, Thierry (ed.) (2011), *Securitization Theory: How Security Problems Emerge and Dissolve* (Abingdon: Routledge).
Provides a new framework for analysing not just 'security', but also the processes by which security issues emerge, evolve, and dissolve.

Bellamy, Alex J. (2014), *The Responsibility to Protect: A Defence* (Oxford: Oxford University Press).
The latest book-length study of the doctrine and the complex of issues driving the R2P agenda by a leading expert on the subject.

Dodds, Felix, and Pippard, Tim (eds) (2005), *Human and Environmental Security: An Agenda for Change* (London: Earthscan).
An edited collection by leading (mainly non-academic) commentators produced in advance of the UN's 2005 World Summit, illustrating the complex links between human and environmental security.

Hudson, Natalia Florea (2010), *Gender, Human Security and the United Nations* (Abingdon: Routledge).
A critical gender analysis focusing on the relationship between women and the global security agenda, including the strategies of the global women's movement.

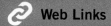 **Web Links**

https://www.cfr.org
Website of the US-based Council on Foreign Relations, containing numerous articles and commentary on contemporary security concerns around the world.

https://theglobalobservatory.org/about/
Website published by the International Peace Institute, providing expert contemporary analyses of peace and security issues across many different dimensions.

http://www.terrorism-research.com
A useful general website containing articles and information about terrorism.

http://www.un.org
This is the general UN website through which an enormous number of subsites with important documents and other interesting material can be accessed.

 Visit the **Online Resources** that accompany this book to access more learning resources on this topic: www.oup.com/uk/ferdinand/

18

Governance and Organizations in Global Politics

- What Is an International Organization?
- The Emergence of International Organizations
- Intergovernmental Organizations
- Non-Governmental Organizations
- Social Movements and Global Civil Society

- Conclusion
- Key Questions
- Further Reading
- Web Links

Reader's Guide

This chapter looks first at the nature of governance and organizations and the way in which they are generally understood as participants in the global political arena. It then reviews the rise of organizations in the global sphere—usually called international organizations (IOs)—from a historical perspective, with particular reference to developments from the nineteenth century onwards. The chapter goes on to discuss the major intergovernmental institutions that emerged in the twentieth century and which have played such an important role in shaping global order. We look briefly at the League of Nations, but most attention is given to its successor, the United Nations (UN), and its various appendages. Then, there is the world of non-governmental organizations (NGOs), populated with a bewildering variety of bodies. Some possess significant status in the global sphere, while others have little relevance and still others pose dangers. Finally, we consider ideas about social movements and civil society, and their relationship with contemporary governance and organizations.

What Is an International Organization?

International organizations, from the UN down to voluntary organizations with constituent members in just a few countries, operate in a sphere that transcends states and the state system in one way or another. This does not mean that they are necessarily more powerful or more important than states. But, like states, these organizations exist as tangible institutional products of social and political forces. Beyond that, they comprise clusters of ideas and coalitions of interest at a transnational level and generate purposeful activities in pursuit of certain desired outcomes.

International organizations may be public or private organizations, depending on whether they are set up by state actors or by non-state actors. Most are permanent, or at least aspire to an ongoing existence, even if many fall by the wayside. They invariably possess constitutional structures, although the extent to which they possess a legal personality is often unclear. Their power varies enormously, depending on their size and the resources at their disposal. And they come in such diverse forms that it is difficult to pin them down to one clear description. The term 'international organization' also overlaps with international regime. The latter concept originated as a way of understanding international cooperation. As Keohane (1993: 23) explains, highly organized and systematic cooperation characterizes much of global politics, yet there are few rules that are, or can be, enforced. Rather, they are followed voluntarily and cooperatively, becoming embedded in relations of reciprocity. An international regime, though not itself an organization as such, usually incorporates one or more international organizations whose interests centre on a particular issue or theme. A prime example is the 'international human rights regime', which revolves around a cluster of important norms and principles that give it its focus. It encompasses many organizations, including—but not limited to—the UN, and operates through processes and rules set up to promote and protect human rights at both national and international levels (see Rittberger and Zangl, 2006: 6–7).

Some definitions encompass multinational corporations and these do fit a broad conception of what constitutes an international organization. However, multinationals are often treated separately from government and non-profit actors. The 2015 edition of the *Yearbook of International Organizations*, which lists about 67,000 active bodies, as well as several thousand inactive or near-dead entities, does not include for-profit organizations such as multinationals (http://www.uia.be/yearbook, accessed January 2018).

Another category of IO, also excluded from most standard definitions, encompasses transnational criminal organizations (TCOs). They are included here because they are becoming increasingly important actors. They have been implicated very clearly in the 'new wars' described by Kaldor (2006) as combining traditional aspects of war with organized crime and involving actors at many levels. Whereas organized crime was very largely a concern for domestic policing agencies in earlier periods, the development of TCOs has required increased policing cooperation in the international sphere to deal with their various activities, which include drugs, money laundering, people smuggling, and weapons smuggling. One author notes that the emergence of TCOs results at least partly from the

18

same underlying changes in the global sphere that have proved conducive to the success of transnational corporations. Thus increased interdependence between states and the permeability of boundaries, developments in international travel and communications, and the globalization of international financial networks 'have facilitated the emergence of what is, in effect, a single global market for both licit and illicit commodities' (Williams, 1997: 316).

In addition to their sheer criminality, TCOs are also increasingly seen as threats to both national and international security, especially in the post-9/11 world. It has been suggested that, even though they are primarily economic actors, they may facilitate the business of terror networks through the provision of money-laundering facilities, false documents, and the procurement of weapons or other material for terrorist purposes. There may also be a growing convergence between some terrorist organizations and organized crime networks (see Sanderson, 2004: 49–61; Dishman, 2005: 237–52).

For the remainder of the chapter, we focus mainly on those IOs that are more conventionally recognized as such—namely, those set up by states through multilateral agreements, sometimes called intergovernmental organizations (IGOs), and those set up by non-state or non-government actors whose primary business is not strictly commercial (or illicit)—that is, the ubiquitous non-governmental organizations (NGOs). An important theme here is the interaction between different organizations in the international sphere that make a model of global governance based almost exclusively on individual sovereign states acting on their own initiative and in their own interest seem very inadequate. At the same time, those who lean heavily in the other direction by exaggerating the importance of IOs can too easily dismiss the crucial role that states play not simply in organizing their own affairs, but in creating the very world of IOs, which may seem to make states less important in many areas. **Key Quote 18.1** suggests an approach that balances these views.

Q KEY QUOTE 18.1 International organizations

'There are two predominant views of international organizations among the general public. The first is a cynical view that emphasizes the dramatic rhetoric and seeming inability to deal with vital problems that are said to characterize international organizations generally and the UN in particular. According to this view, international organizations should be treated as insignificant actors on the international stage. The other view is an idealistic one. Those who hold this view envisage global solutions to the problems facing the world today, without recognition of the constraints imposed by state sovereignty, and they view most of the naive calls for world government as products of this view. An understanding of international organizations and global governance probably requires that neither view be accepted in its entirety, nor be wholly rejected. International organizations are neither irrelevant nor omnipotent in global politics. They play important roles in international relations, but their influence varies according to the issue area and situation confronted.' (Diehl, 2005: 3)

> ### ✳ KEY POINTS
>
> - International organizations come in such a variety of forms that they are difficult to define, with respect to both their relationship with states and the organization of global governance, as well as in terms of their constituent elements.
> - Scholars interested in the contribution that IOs make to global governance as a whole tend to focus on IGOs and NGOs.
> - Although multinational corporations and terrorist and other criminal organizations operating in the international sphere do constitute IOs of a kind, they are usually treated separately.

The Emergence of International Organizations

'History, prior to the nineteenth century, affords relatively few examples of international organizations' (Gerbet, 1981: 28). Although this is a widely accepted view, the myriad IOs of the present era do have important precursors. The earliest known examples appear to have been defensive leagues set up among small, neighbouring states. This was the case in at least one part of China between the seventh and the fifth centuries BC where assemblies met to organize their defences, while in ancient Greece rudimentary IOs were established to arbitrate on issues of mutual concern to a number of city-states (see, generally, Harle, 1998).

Examples of IOs in late medieval Europe include the Hanseatic League, which operated between the fourteenth and sixteenth centuries and in which some 50 towns joined forces for the mutual protection of their trading interests, with representatives meeting in a general assembly to decide policy by majority voting. The Swiss Confederation, dating from the late 1200s, and the United Provinces of the Netherlands, which emerged in the sixteenth century, although limited territorially, effectively started out as IOs (Gerbet, 1981: 28–9; Klabbers, 2003: 16).

We may also consider the question of whether some of the major religions have come to constitute IOs, although not of the conventional kind. For example, the Catholic Church, which held sway throughout much of Europe in earlier historic periods and exercised considerable political, as well as cultural, power, became one of the first organizations to establish a near-universal presence in the modern period to match its name—'catholic' meaning universal in the sense of 'all-embracing'. This may also be read as part of the more general pattern of globalization.

It is obvious that the scale of IOs in earlier times was necessarily constrained by limitations on mobility and communications, as was the phenomenon of globalization itself. But as communications and transport technologies developed, so too did the

18

capacity to form ongoing associations, which eventually gave rise to formal organizations on a much broader, more inclusive, scale and which were intended to have a more or less permanent existence. The rise of the modern state system, together with technological advances in transport and communications, therefore saw not only the enhancement of diplomatic networks and practices among states, but also an accompanying growth of organizations designed to facilitate the business of international relations as such. State actors may well have looked first to their own interests, but on a very wide range of matters those interests were likely to be enhanced by cooperation with other states, especially on issues concerning trade. And, in turn, international cooperation was best achieved through certain kinds of organizations set up for particular purposes and through which rules and procedures agreed on by member states could be operationalized.

Post-Napoleonic Europe had seen the rise of a 'Concert system', which started with the 1815 Congress of Vienna (**see Figure 18.1**). This provided a benchmark for inter-state cooperation on setting international boundaries and managing waterways (vital for trade) on the continent, as well as establishing certain diplomatic protocols. Subsequent conferences generated as part of the Concert system established a pattern of interaction that

FIGURE 18.1 The Congress of Vienna
© DEA / G Cigolini/ Age Fotostock

nurtured important ideas about collective responsibility and a mutual commitment to 'concert together' against threats to the system. Most importantly, it established the idea that states' representatives should meet not merely to sign peace treaties at the end of a war, but also during peaceful periods to prevent war (Archer, 1983: 7). The 'Concert of Europe' was not what we would call an IO, since it lacked a constitution, a permanent secretariat, and a headquarters, and did not meet on a regular basis (see Gerbet, 1981: 32). Even so, it can be seen as a precursor to other major European developments in later years.

Although the Concert system virtually ceased to exist after the mid-nineteenth century, the second half of the nineteenth century did see further ad hoc conferences held on important matters of mutual interest. For example, the 1878 Congress of Berlin met to settle issues in the Balkans following the Russo-Turkish War of 1877–78 and included delegates from the major European powers and observers from several smaller European states with interests in the region, as well as representatives of the Ottoman Empire. With the inclusion of the latter, the international element of such conferences was expanded beyond Europe into West Asia. Other treaties and conventions that reached beyond Europe were applied in relation to colonial territories and the US, often with respect to the navigation of waterways to facilitate trade. The Hague Conferences of 1899 and 1907 established the principle of compulsory arbitration of disputes, giving the development of international law a significant boost. Most importantly, the conferences were not just European events. Apart from the US and Russia, participants included Brazil, Uruguay, Mexico, China, Japan, Turkey, and Persia, among others.

It is noteworthy that the Congress of Vienna was the first significant international forum that took a stand on a broad humanitarian issue by condemning the slave trade as contrary to universal morality (Butler and MacCoby, 2003: 353). This was quite an unusual step for such a conference. But it is no coincidence that it occurred around the time that private organizations, many with a specific philanthropic mission, started to make their presence felt on the international scene as well. The anti-slavery movement in Britain, already active domestically and a prime force behind the Congress resolution, gave rise to an early NGO when its supporters coalesced into the Society for the Mitigation and Gradual Abolition of Slavery Throughout the British Dominions in 1823. Anti-Slavery International, which operates today, was originally founded in 1839, and in 1840 a World Anti-Slavery Convention was held in London (see http://www.antislavery.org, accessed January 2018). Anti-Slavery International is also associated with the International Labour Organization (ILO), established by the Treaty of Versailles in 1919 with the status of an autonomous institution, but in association with the League of Nations. It survived the demise of the League and is now a UN agency. The early anti-slavery efforts were underpinned by concerted activism on the part of British women who had formed their own local anti-slavery societies and went on to forge international links, especially across the Atlantic. So in these activities we also see an emergent women's movement, which spread nationally and internationally to take up various causes, including their own liberation (see, generally, Midgley, 1992).

Transport and communications technologies, so essential to both globalization and the emergence of functioning IOs, were themselves among the most important subjects

18

of international agreements and formal associations. For example, 1865 saw the foundation of the International Telegraph Union (now the International Telecommunications Union), followed in 1874 by the Universal Postal Union and in 1890 by the International Union of Railway Freight Transportation (see Klabbers, 2003: 18). The two former organizations are now UN specialized agencies, again illustrating continuities in the system of IOs despite the massive disruption of two world wars in the twentieth century. But improvements in transport technologies brought with it other problems, including the more rapid spread of disease, and so concerns about international public health were reflected in the 1853 International Sanitary Convention and subsequent conventions and international offices. Equally, the rapid development of industry and trade saw the introduction of an International Bureau of Weights and Measures in 1875, while on the intellectual property front the Union for the Protection of the Rights of Authors over their Literary and Artistic Property was established in 1884.

Private associations at an international level began to outstrip intergovernmental ones in this period, accelerating the trend in internationalism. Such associations were set up in connection with every kind of activity, including the humanitarian, religious, ideological, scientific, and technological (Gerbet, 1981: 36). At the first World Congress of International Organizations held in Brussels in 1910, convened under the auspices of the Union of International Associations, 132 international bodies and 13 governments were represented. A second World Congress in Ghent and Brussels in 1913 gathered 169 international associations and 22 governments. The last World Congress of this type (the seventh) was held in 1927, after which the League of Nations assumed responsibility (http://www.uia.org/ta, accessed January 2018).

The overall trend to internationalism in the century before the outbreak of the First World War might have indicated that a new era of peaceful international relations was about to dawn. But other forces, including those of nationalism, were also at work (see Chapter 6). The death and destruction of 1914–18 was, for a number of key actors, the clarion call for a permanent IGO supporting a strong framework for international law and designed above all to prevent further international conflict—a need reinforced, rather than undermined, by the Second World War.

✳ KEY POINTS

- Although forms of IO existed before the nineteenth century, the Congress of Vienna in 1815 acted as a catalyst for their rapid growth in the nineteenth century.

- Private organizations also achieved a significant international presence in the nineteenth and early twentieth centuries, those with philanthropic aims contributing to the development of humanitarian principles and the idea of international morality.

- Developments in transport and communications technologies provided a boost to the growth of IOs and themselves became the subject of international agreements and associations along with a host of other agreements.

Intergovernmental Organizations

The supremo of all IGOs is the UN—officially, the United Nations Organization—with near-universal membership of the world's states. Its founding commitment is to 'maintaining international peace and security, developing friendly relations among nations and promoting social progress, better living standards and human rights' (http://www.un.org/en/about-un/, accessed January 2018). The early development of the UN and the role of the Security Council have already been set out in Chapter 17, so we focus here on other aspects of the UN's history, structure, and mission. But, first, it is useful to recall the key ideas behind the development of its predecessor organization, the League of Nations. These ideas were to come under attack from political 'realists' in later years for their vision of a peaceful global order founded on strong institutions of global governance and an explicit emphasis on the place of morality in the international sphere, rather than naked self-interest. The preface to US President Woodrow Wilson's famous Fourteen Points address to the US Congress in January 1918 stands as one of the clearest statements of the idealist vision of global order in that period. The preface was followed by a 'program of the world's peace', the fourteenth point of which proposed the formation of a general association of nations, an idea given substance by the formation of the League of Nations in the immediate aftermath of the war. Interestingly, although President Wilson was a leading figure in the foundation of the League of Nations, the US Congress declined to join the organization (**see Key Thinker 18.2**).

 KEY THINKER 18.2   Woodrow Wilson (1856–1924)

Thomas Woodrow Wilson was born in Staunton, Virginia, just five years before the start of the Civil War, in which his father served as a pastor on the Confederate side. Wilson showed little early promise, failing to learn to read before he was 10 or 11 years old and experiencing difficulties all his life, probably because of dyslexia. His later achievements as both a scholar and a politician, becoming first a professor at Princeton University and then US President for two terms from 1913 to 1921, therefore stand out as representing a triumph over personal adversity.

As a Democrat, Wilson gained a reputation for promoting an expanded role for government and pursued progressive liberal policies on a number of fronts, reflecting the abandonment of nineteenth-century laissez-faire dogma. Reforms included the abolition of child labour, the introduction of an eight-hour day in the private sector, a graduated income tax, and the establishment of the Federal Reserve to steer the economy. Other innovations saw regular press briefings—previously unheard of in US presidential politics. Wilson was also the first Southerner to be elected president since the Civil War. Unfortunately, he proved to be very much a product of his time and place when it came to race issues, supporting segregation and other regressive policies within his administration.

Internationally, Wilson is best known for his role in bringing the US into the First World War in 1917, 'to make the world safe for democracy', and later for his efforts at the Versailles Peace Conference and in bringing the League of Nations into being.

18

Despite failing to persuade an isolationist US Congress to join the new international institution, in which hopes for a more stable and peaceful world order were invested, he was nonetheless awarded the Nobel Peace Prize in 1920 in recognition of his leading role in promoting world political organization.

The League of Nations has sometimes been described as a failed experiment because it did not prevent the Second World War. It could also be argued, however, that the Second World War illustrated just how important it is to have a strong, functioning IGO to provide for collective security, as well as many other matters requiring international support and coordination. In any event, a number of key institutions and practices set up under the League's auspices survived and are enshrined in the present UN system. Certainly, the latter owes much to the previous experiment in global governance, which, in turn, drew on the earlier experiences of the Concert system, thus demonstrating continuity over almost two centuries. It also drew intellectual inspiration from liberal political ideas about the possibility of building a more peaceful world order through intergovernmental institutions—ideas that had emerged over the same time period and which were underpinned by a more optimistic approach to problems of war and peace. As suggested earlier, these stood in contrast to the pessimistic outlook characterizing political realism, which highlighted the inevitability of conflict in a global sphere where no sovereign power capable of enforcing order existed.

The UN (**see Figure 18.2**) emerged from the wartime cooperation between the major allied powers of the time, with many other states then joining in to create a more truly

FIGURE 18.2   The headquarters of the United Nations
© Drop of Light/ Shutterstock.com

international body operating under a formal charter setting out the rights and obligations of members. The Preamble to the Charter states the general principles and ideals on which the organization is based (**Key Quote 18.3**). The main organs of the UN comprise the General Assembly, Security Council, Economic and Social Council (ECOSOC), Trusteeship Council, International Court of Justice (ICJ), and Secretariat (http://www.un.org/en/sections/about-un/main-organs/index.html, accessed January 2018).

The business of the Trusteeship Council, set up for the purpose of dealing with 11 non-self-governing trust territories, which had formerly been League of Nations mandate territories, was terminated in 1994 when the last trust territory, administered by the US, chose self-government and became an independent state. The most powerful of the UN's organs is, of course, the Security Council, discussed earlier. Some may say the weakest, as well as being the largest, is the General Assembly. A common criticism is that it produces little but endless Resolutions, which are largely ineffective because there is no mechanism for enforcing them. This illustrates the fact that the UN General Assembly cannot be compared directly to a legislature because although its resolutions may carry normative force and guide policy, they cannot have the same legal status as legislation produced by a parliament within a national sphere. However, it would be a mistake to dismiss the significance of the General Assembly as a debating forum. It is the one place where representatives from all states can meet on a more or less equal footing, express views, and debate the full range of issues in international politics. It

 KEY QUOTE 18.3   **Preamble to the Charter of the United Nations**

'We the peoples of the United Nations determined

- to save succeeding generations from the scourge of war, which twice in our lifetime has brought untold sorrow to mankind, and
- to reaffirm faith in fundamental human rights, in the dignity and worth of the human person, in the equal rights of men and women and of nations large and small, and
- to establish conditions under which justice and respect for the obligations arising from treaties and other sources of international law can be maintained, and
- to promote social progress and better standards of life in larger freedom,

And for these ends

- to practice tolerance and live together in peace with one another as good neighbours, and
- to unite our strength to maintain international peace and security, and
- to ensure, by the acceptance of principles and the institution of methods, that armed force shall not be used, save in the common interest, and
- to employ international machinery for the promotion of the economic and social advancement of all peoples.' (http://www.un.org/en/sections/un-charter/preamble/index.html, accessed August 2017)

18

is, moreover, a key forum for both formal and informal diplomacy and strategic alliances on issues that come up for a vote. This does not necessarily produce desirable outcomes, let alone outcomes that satisfy everyone, but that is in the nature of any political body.

The Economic and Social Council has a mandate to initiate studies and reports and to formulate policy recommendations extending over an enormous range of economic and social issues, covering: living standards; full employment; international economic, social, and health problems; facilitating international cultural and educational cooperation; and encouraging universal respect for human rights and fundamental freedoms. Some of the best-known UN agencies, such as the World Health Organization (WHO), the Food and Agricultural Organization (FAO), the United Nations Educational, Scientific and Cultural Organization (UNESCO), and the World Bank group all fall under ECOSOC's rubric. It has a major role in organizing the many international conferences initiated by the UN and oversees the functional commissions, regional commissions, and other special bodies set out in the organizational chart. ECOSOC is by far the largest of the UN's principal organs and expends more than 70 per cent of the human and financial resources of the entire UN system (see https://www.un.org/ecosoc/en/about-us, accessed January 2018).

One of ECOSOC's most difficult and controversial functional commissions has been that dealing with human rights, and a brief account of developments in this area illustrates just how problematic it is to achieve coherence in regimes of global governance. The establishment of a Human Rights Commission (HRC) was mandated by the UN's Charter and reflected the abhorrence at the atrocities of the Second World War. Past wars throughout much of human history had produced some appalling cases of cruelty and ill-treatment, but the nature of the genocidal policies of Nazi Germany was unprecedented. Beginning with the Universal Declaration of Human Rights (UDHR), which was adopted by the General Assembly in 1948 (**Key Concept 18.4**), the Commission produced a raft of human rights documents and treaties over a period of almost 60 years. The behaviour of many governments around the world over that period, however, demonstrates clearly that the existence of the Charter, or the fact that all members of the UN must endorse the UDHR, is no guarantee that basic human rights will be respected or protected.

 For further discussion of human rights, see Chapters 11 and 17.

 KEY CONCEPT 18.4   **The Universal Declaration of Human Rights (UDHR)**

The UDHR was adopted by the General Assembly of the United Nations on 10 December 1948, reflecting a moment in international history when all member states could agree, at least in principle, to a substantial list of human rights ranging from the basic right to life to a host of economic and social goods. All new members joining the UN must sign up to the UDHR.

The Preamble highlights ideals that recognize 'the inherent dignity' and the 'equal and inalienable rights of all members of the human family', regarding these as 'the foundation of freedom, justice and peace in the world'. It further notes the extent to which 'disregard and contempt for human rights have resulted in barbarous acts which have outraged the conscience of mankind' and heralds 'the advent of a world in which human beings shall enjoy freedom of speech and belief and freedom from fear and want has been proclaimed as the highest aspiration of the common people'.

The Declaration itself contains 30 Articles, the first ten of which are set out below:

'**Article 1.** All human beings are born free and equal in dignity and rights. They are endowed with reason and conscience and should act towards one another in a spirit of brotherhood.

Article 2. Everyone is entitled to all the rights and freedoms set forth in this Declaration, without distinction of any kind, such as race, colour, sex, language, religion, political or other opinion, national or social origin, property, birth or other status. Furthermore, no distinction shall be made on the basis of the political, jurisdictional or international status of the country or territory to which a person belongs, whether it be independent, trust, non-self-governing or under any other limitation of sovereignty.

Article 3. Everyone has the right to life, liberty and security of person.

Article 4. No one shall be held in slavery or servitude; slavery and the slave trade shall be prohibited in all their forms.

Article 5. No one shall be subjected to torture or to cruel, inhuman or degrading treatment or punishment.

Article 6. Everyone has the right to recognition everywhere as a person before the law.

Article 7. All are equal before the law and are entitled without any discrimination to equal protection of the law. All are entitled to equal protection against any discrimination in violation of this Declaration and against any incitement to such discrimination.

Article 8. Everyone has the right to an effective remedy by the competent national tribunals for acts violating the fundamental rights granted him by the constitution or by law.

Article 9. No one shall be subjected to arbitrary arrest, detention or exile.

Article 10. Everyone is entitled in full equality to a fair and public hearing by an independent and impartial tribunal, in the determination of his rights and obligations and of any criminal charge against him.' (http://www.un.org/en/universal-declaration-human-rights/index.html, accessed January 2018)

Since the Charter was first drawn up, there has been a strong tendency to divide the broad concept of human rights into two distinct cluster concerns: civil and political rights, on the one hand, and economic, social, and cultural rights, on the other. The division between the two groups, and whether one group is more important than the other, has been the subject of much debate in international politics, as illustrated in **Key Debate 18.5**, along with recurrent issues of sovereignty and non-intervention.

KEY DEBATE 18.5   The politics of human rights in the UN

Civil and political rights are sometimes seen as possessing a typically 'Western' liberal character unsuited to the cultural context of non-Western countries. The most vocal proponents of this view have come from a number of Middle Eastern and African countries and parts of South East and East Asia, especially China. In addition, economic, social, and cultural rights are often regarded as more urgent for poorer, underdeveloped countries than the right to vote (although human rights activists in such countries generally do not support these kinds of 'culturalist' or 'developmentalist' arguments).

An early division of opinion on the two different clusters of rights gave rise to the development of separate covenants for each and so, in 1976, the International Covenant on Civil and Political Rights (ICCPR) and the International Covenant on Economic, Social and Cultural Rights (ICESCR) entered into force. Apart from representing two broad approaches to rights, the covenants also represent a significant attempt to advance the codification of human rights as such and to introduce an international legal framework to support their advancement. Member states are not obliged to sign up to the covenants, but those that do so agree to accept their provisions as legal obligations, as well as moral obligations.

The history of human rights issues in the UN has also been plagued by competing conceptions of what the UN can and cannot, or should and should not, do to advance the protection of human rights around the world. On the one hand, the UN is committed to respect for state **sovereignty** and therefore to the notion that each state is entitled to conduct its own affairs free from external interference. On the other hand, it is committed to the universality of human rights, which implies that it is not only entitled, but also actually enjoined, to act to promote and protect human rights wherever and whenever such action is needed. But any action—even mere criticism of state practices—can be construed as a violation of state sovereignty. The HRC itself was frequently caught between these imperatives and contradictions. Apart from issues of state sovereignty versus universal principles, some countries represented on the Commission at any one time were themselves countries where human rights abuses—often perpetrated by the government—were being carried out. However, countries with poor human rights records—mainly outside 'the West'—complained of being unfairly singled out for criticism. This also led to accusations of attempted interference in the internal affairs of sovereign states. By 2006, the HRC was seen as an ineffectual and largely discredited body. It was replaced by a new Human Rights Council, which has revised terms for membership and functions. Whether it can avoid past problems remains to be seen and can only be tested over the longer term (see Freedman, 2013).

Questions

1. Can human rights really be divided into different categories?

2. Under what circumstances, if any, should state sovereignty be violated to protect human rights?

Another main organ of the UN is the International Court of Justice (ICJ), located in The Hague. As with other parts of the UN system, its origins can be traced to much earlier periods and linked to the gradual development in the modern era of methods of mediation and arbitration of disputes between states. Its immediate predecessor, the Permanent Court of International Justice (PCIJ), was part of the League of Nations system and operated from 1922 until it was dissolved in 1946 to make way for the new UN court. The 15 judges of the ICJ are elected for nine-year terms by both the United Nations General Assembly and the Security Council. The ICJ functions as something of a world court, with the jurisdiction to decide legal disputes submitted to it by states and to give advisory opinions on legal questions at the request of UN organs or authorized agencies. Between May 1947 and August 2007, 136 cases had been entered into its General List.

A notable case was brought with respect to the *Application of the Convention on the Prevention and Punishment of the Crime of Genocide (Bosnia and Herzegovina v Serbia and Montenegro)* on which judgment was delivered in February 2007. The 171-page judgment dealt with a number of issues in general, and the case of Srebrenica in particular. This village was the scene of the single biggest massacre in Europe since the end of the Second World War when Serb forces killed approximately 8,000 Bosnian Muslim men and boys. While the Court found Serbia and Montenegro not guilty of deliberately perpetrating a genocide, it found the state guilty of failing to prevent a genocide and therefore in breach of its obligations in international law. This case was separate from the trial of former Serb President Slobodan Milošević, which was conducted by a special tribunal, the International Criminal Tribunal for the Former Yugoslavia (ICTY), which was established by a UN Security Council Resolution. Milošević's trial ended prematurely with his death in 2006 (although the trial had already run for four years by then), but was nonetheless seen as a landmark case because it was the first time a former head of state had been put on trial before an international criminal tribunal. More recently, former Bosnian Serb military leader Ratko Mladić was extradited from Serbia in June 2011 to face a war crimes tribunal in The Hague in relation to the Srebrenica massacre. His trial commenced in 2012 and in 2017 he was found guilty of genocide, war crimes, and crimes against humanity.

For background to the conflict in former Yugoslavia, see Chapter 6.

The final organ comprises the UN Secretariat and the office of the Secretary-General. The organizational map of the General Assembly alone, which currently brings together 193 member states at least annually, as well as running important offices and conferences and providing services in six official languages (English, French, Arabic, Chinese, Russian, and Spanish), makes clear how extensive the demand for the services of a secretariat are (Gordenker, 2005: 16). The Secretary-General also seems to be expected to be everywhere at once and to possess an encyclopedic knowledge not only of the UN system itself, but also of all the world's troubles, both current and potential. In practice, the Secretary-General will often appoint a representative for much routine committee work. One particularly important role for the Secretary-General is to bring matters likely to affect international peace and security to the attention of the Security Council and to report regularly on operations that the UN is involved in. Although the Secretary-General has no authority beyond issuing formal warnings of trouble and delivering information, including

18

anything gleaned from informal discussions, the importance of this function should not be underestimated. In some ways, the Secretary-General has become the voice of moral authority in a world still plagued by conflict, poverty, natural disasters, and other tragedies.

The UN has also populated the sphere of IOs with a plethora of agencies and special programmes; WHO, the FAO, UNICEF, and UNESCO have already been mentioned above there are many more. Some, like UNICEF, are well known, but others, such as the United Nations Population Fund (UNFPA), are unlikely to register immediately in the minds of the general public. Others have emerged in more recent years to deal with problems unheard of in earlier periods. These include the joint United Nations Programme on HIV/AIDS (UNAIDS). Then there are regional commissions dealing with all the major regions of the world: Africa, Europe, Latin America and the Caribbean, Asia and the Pacific, and Western Asia (more commonly called the Middle East).

The UN and its agencies do not have the IGO field entirely to themselves. There are also a growing number of regional organizations, many with an economic function, as mentioned in Chapter 9 in relation to regionalization. Here, we may note that this trend, which has been gathering pace over the last few decades, is likely to have a significant impact in the future, but one that complements, rather than undermines, the role of the UN. More generally, this points to a future in which IGOs are likely to play an increasingly important role in international order rather than a diminishing one.

 KEY POINTS

- The League of Nations is often seen as a failure, but it was nonetheless an important forerunner to the UN and a number of its institutions have been maintained as part of the latter system.

- The UN is the largest single IGO, with five functioning main organs and a plethora of programmes, agencies, commissions, funds, courts, and tribunals involved in different aspects of global governance.

- Although the UN is the principle organ of global governance, it does not possess the characteristics of a 'world government' insofar as its constituent members maintain sovereign authority within their own realms and do not form a 'world state'.

Non-Governmental Organizations

The non-state variety of IO sometimes goes by the acronym INGO—which simply stands for international non-governmental organization—but, for present purposes, we shall make do with the more common term NGO. Like IOs in general, NGOs cannot be defined in a completely straightforward way. Generally speaking, however, they share the following characteristics: they are formal, rather than ad hoc, entities; they aspire to be self-governing according to their own constitutional set-up; they are private, in the sense that they operate independently from governments; and they do not make or distribute profits. This describes both national and international bodies, so for those that operate outside of the national sphere, we need to add that they obviously have formal transnational links (see Gordenker and Weiss, 1996: 20).

There are other types of organization that fall somewhere between the government and non-government spheres, and although they often claim to be NGOs, they do not really conform to the description above. Gordenker and Weiss identify three significant deviations. The first are 'government-organized non-government organizations' (GONGOs)— entities created by governments usually as front organizations for their own purposes. These were typically produced by communist countries during the Cold War, but the US and other Western countries sponsored some as well. Today, there is a wide variety of GONGOs, many of which serve dubious causes. The excerpt from an article in **Key Quote 18.6** on the subject of GONGOS and the dangers that some of them pose, is highly instructive as to their role in the sphere of IOs.

Another special type of organization is the quasi-autonomous NGO (QUANGO), which is typically funded largely by governments, but operates autonomously. Unlike GONGOs, the relationship to government is a transparent one and no subterfuge is intended. The variety of functions covered by QUANGOs is enormous, ranging from the UK's British Council, which has a 'soft diplomacy' role in promoting cultural relations around the world, to the US Federal Reserve, which oversees the operation of the US economy. Another type is the donor-organized NGO (DONGO). In this case, agencies such as the United Nations Development Program (UNDP) might organize and fund NGOs to coordinate or carry out particular projects (Gordenker and Weiss, 1996: 20–1). A significant number of other NGOs enjoy consultative status with the UN or, more specifically, one of its coun-

---

Q KEY QUOTE 18.6   How government-sponsored groups masquerade as civil society

'Behind this contradictory and almost laughable tongue twister [GONGO] lies an important and growing global trend that deserves more scrutiny: governments funding and controlling nongovernmental organizations (NGOs), often stealthily. Some gongos are benign, others irrelevant. But many . . . are dangerous. Some act as the thuggish arm of repressive governments. Others use the practices of democracy to subtly undermine democracy at home. Abroad, the gongos of repressive regimes lobby the United Nations and other international institutions, often posing as representatives of citizen groups with lofty aims when, in fact, they are nothing but agents of the governments that fund them. Some governments embed their gongos deep in the societies of other countries and use them to advance their interests abroad . . . The globalization and effectiveness of nongovernmental organizations will suffer if we don't find reliable ways of distinguishing organizations that truly represent democratic civil society from those that are tools of uncivil, undemocratic governments.' (Naím, 2009)

18

cils or agencies. The UN's ECOSOC for example, accords consultative status of some kind to more than 3,000 NGOs, ranging from the Adventist Development Relief Agency to the World Press Freedom Committee. These are allied in turn to specific UN agencies such as UNESCO, the FAO, and WHO.

The practice of according UN consultative status to NGOs dates back to 1946, when ECOSOC granted such status to just over 40 NGOs. Growth was steady over the next 45 years and, by 1992, there were more than 700 NGOs with consultative status. As indicated above, that number has since increased to more than 3,000. There are various rules and criteria governing eligibility. Among the most basic are the following.

1. The organization must have been in existence (officially registered with the appropriate government authorities as an NGO/non-profit) for at least two years.

2. It must have an established headquarters.

3. It must possess a democratically adopted constitution, authority to speak for its members, a representative structure, appropriate mechanisms of accountability, and democratic and transparent decision-making processes.

4. Its basic resources must be derived mainly from contributions of the national affiliates or other components or from individual members.

5. It must not have been established by governments or intergovernmental agreements (see http://csonet.org/index.php?menu=30, accessed August 2017).

Many NGOs have a specific philanthropic or humanitarian purpose. Sometimes, these are underpinned by religious beliefs, but they are just as likely to be secular. Many are aligned with broader movements such as the environmental movement, the labour movement, the ecumenical movement, the peace movement, the indigenous rights movement, and the women's movement. More will be said about the role of these broader movements later in this chapter.

Examples of some of the better-known NGOs reflecting the ideals of one or other of these movements, or sometimes two or more of them, are the Worldwide Fund for Nature, Greenpeace, the World Council of Churches, the World Peace Council, the International Women's Health Coalition, Doctors Without Borders, and Amnesty International, to name just a few. A brief account of the Red Cross/Red Crescent Movement in **Case Study 18.7** provides an interesting account of how one of the earliest NGOs operating in the international sphere has grown to be the largest humanitarian organization in the world.

 CASE STUDY 18.7 **The origins and development of the Red Cross/Red Crescent Movement**

In 1859, Henry Dunant, a travelling Swiss businessman, witnessed one of the bloodiest battles of the nineteenth century in northern Italy when Napoleon III joined with local forces to drive Austrians from the country. Dunant subsequently published a small book, which depicted, among other things, the battlefield after fighting had ceased, describing not just the dead, but also the plight of the wounded and their desperate need for care. He went on to devise a plan for national relief societies to aid the wounded of war. In February 1863, the Société Genevoise d'Utilité Publique (Geneva Society for Public Welfare) appointed a committee of five, including Dunant, to consider how the plan could be put into action. This committee, which effectively founded the Red Cross, called for an international conference to pursue Dunant's basic objectives. Dunant put his own time and money into the project, travelling throughout much of Europe to persuade governments to send representatives. The conference was held in October 1863, with 39 delegates from 16 nations. Just under a year later, 12 nations signed the International Convention for the Amelioration of the Condition of the Wounded and Sick in Armed Forces in the Field, otherwise known as the Geneva Convention of 1864. The Convention provided for guaranteed neutrality for medical personnel and officially adopted the red cross on a field of white as the identifying emblem (the red crescent was adopted in most Muslim countries). Three other conventions were later added to cover naval warfare, prisoners of war, and civilians. Revisions of the Geneva Conventions have been made periodically, the most extensive being in 1949 relating to the treatment of prisoners of war. The International Committee of the Red Cross remains based in Geneva and the International Federation of Red Cross and Red Crescent Societies has a presence in every country (**see Figure 18.3**). The Red Cross has been associated with four Nobel Peace Prizes, with the very first Nobel Peace Prize being awarded to Henry Dunant himself in 1901 (http://www.nobelprize.org/nobel_prizes/peace/laureates/1963/red-cross-history.html, accessed July 2017).

FIGURE 18.3 A worker for the Red Cross/Red Crescent movement
© ChameleonsEye/ Shutterstock.com

18

In addition, it was the prime mover behind the original Geneva Convention, which has become the most important international convention relating to the conduct of warfare.

It is also worth emphasizing the role that NGOs have been playing in international development efforts over the last 50 years or so and the extent to which they have become integral to governance in poor countries where the state sector has been unable to deliver essential basic services. The latter problem was exacerbated from the 1980s when structural adjustment programmes (SAPs) were imposed by the World Bank, as described in Chapter 9. These programmes encouraged the privatization of state functions, which left significant gaps in service provision. Because no private actors moved in to fill gaps in such vital areas as health, education, and infrastructure, NGOs tended to fill the vacuum, subsequently becoming a vital part of the more general governance structure within the state (Brass, 2017: 121). This suggests that although NGOs are indeed non-*government* organizations, any theorization of the broader concept of *governance* cannot ignore their important role.

 KEY POINTS

- International governmental organizations, especially the UN and its agencies, often have a close working relationship with NGOs and have established structures supporting much of their work.
- Not all NGOS are 'good' in the sense that they make a positive contribution. Some are merely fronts for nefarious activities by dictatorial governments and may work actively to undermine the efforts of other organizations with respect, for example, to human rights issues.
- Many NGOs are also allied with broader movements, thus contributing to a complex web of relationships between different kinds of actors, both state and non-state, in the international sphere.

Social Movements and Global Civil Society

The foregoing discussion indicates that many NGOs are involved in philanthropic or humanitarian causes, some of which are embedded in broader social movements, along with other kinds of civil society organizations such as interest groups, professional associations, think tanks, charitable groups, and so on. The term 'social movement' is generally understood to denote some kind of collective action, driven by a particular set of social concerns and emerging from society at large rather than through the governmental institutions of the state. Indeed, a feature of many social movements is an oppositional posture vis-à-vis certain aspects of state or governmental activity. In this respect, they are often seen as a manifestation of grass-roots democracy expressing or articulating non-mainstream issues and agendas. As we have seen, social movements often transcend the domestic sphere, an early example being

18

the anti-slavery movement. When a movement achieves a transnational profile and popular following, it obviously achieves the status of an international or global social movement. The development of such movements often reflect the development of coalitions of interests around issue-oriented activities. But what social movements and the NGOs associated with them usually represent in one way or another is a 'cause', very often in relation to what is perceived as an injustice and/or a danger: Third World poverty, environmental degradation, the oppression of indigenous communities, the proliferation of nuclear weapons, and so on.

These broad social movements and the world of NGOs are said to constitute a kind of global civil society that has an important role in the general sphere of global governance. The idea of global civil society can also be understood initially in terms of its domestic counterpart discussed in Chapter 16 along with the role of NGOs and interest group politics. 'Civil society' signifies a space allowing for the activities of individuals as participants in groups or collectivities that have a private purpose—private in the sense that they are not part of the realm of formal state or governmental activity. But they do not include the business sector either. However, some may receive grants or some other form of funding from either government or business, or both.

See Chapter 16 for a discussion of civil society.

The freedom of organization of such groups and their articulation of interests is widely regarded as another important manifestation of democracy, and so the repression of civil society organizations and activities is seen as characteristic of authoritarian systems. Many civil society groups are obviously NGOs, but some do not fall easily into the definition of the latter. Also, not all NGOs are connected to social movements. It follows that although we can often connect NGOs to social movements and in turn class these as part of civil society, we cannot simply conflate the lot into one seamless whole.

Civil society, whether in the domestic or global arena, not only names a sphere that is autonomous of direct government control, standing apart from the formal structures of governance controlled by states, but is also sometimes positioned in opposition to the realm of formal state-based or state-generated activities. It is, therefore, another avenue through which critical democratic expression can take place. Certainly, those who look for democratic transformations in the global sphere and promote a form of 'cosmopolitan democracy'—a project involving the extension of democratic accountability to the global sphere, as discussed in Chapter 4—are broadly supportive of the positive critical role that global civil society has to play in such a process.

But whether social movements and the broad sphere of global civil society, and the NGOs that are the principle vehicles of activity in these arenas, really do present a serious challenge to the traditional structures generated by state sovereignty and the state system is an open question. As we have seen, many NGOs have a close association with the UN and its programmes and agencies. So although we may distinguish NGOs from the UN as such, they have come to form an important part of the UN system as a whole. Social movements and global civil society are, therefore, at least partly enmeshed in the web of relations created by IOs, including the more formal intergovernmental institutions of global governance.

One kind of social movement that has stood out in recent years is the so-called anti-globalization/anti-capitalist movement discussed in Chapter 9. As noted there, many of

18

the participants in this movement are associated with various NGOs concerned with social justice and environmental issues and engage in peaceful activities and protests at events such as meetings of the G8, the G20, the WTO—or any other meeting of powerful world leaders. However, media reports of the protests at the 2017 G20 meeting in Hamburg, at which some 100,000 protesters gathered, were dominated by scenes of criminal violence and destruction by small groups apparently associated with left-wing political extremism and whose aim was not merely to protest, but to disrupt the Summit (http://www.bbc.com/news/world-europe-40534768, accessed August 2017).

Various theoretical perspectives have been advanced to explain or interpret the complex world of global civil society and the social movements and groups of which it is composed. **Key Quote 18.8** provides a concise summary of four distinct approaches, each of which critically highlights a different dimension of the phenomenon.

Q KEY QUOTE 18.8 Interpreting global civil society

'Liberals may understand [global civil society] as the actor that provides a bottom-up contribution to the effectiveness and legitimacy of the international system as a whole. In essence, it is democracy in action as power is being held to account by the populace. Realists, however, may interpret global civil society as a tool used by the most powerful states to advance their ultimate interests abroad, often promoting and popularising ideas that are key to the national interest. Marxists may see global civil society as political vanguards that can spread a different world view that challenges the dominant order. Finally, some even argue that the concept of civil society as a sphere distinct from the family, state and market remains a Western concept that does not apply easily to societies where the boundaries between these spheres are more blurred.' (Marchetti, 2016)

✳ KEY POINTS

- Social movements reflect particular sets of concerns coalescing around issues such as the environment, indigenous rights, arms control, and so on, and which often engender collective action on a global scale.

- Global civil society, as a sphere of action and interaction standing apart from formal intergovernmental structures and sometimes in opposition to it, constitutes the space within which both international NGOs and social movements more generally operate.

- Both social movements and global civil society are often regarded as enhancing the space and substance of democratic activity at a supranational level, although the same space also affords opportunities for displays of violence by minority protest groups.

Conclusion

Conventional views of how the international or global sphere is organized see states and the state system as the standard units around which almost everyone and everything else revolves, with international activity of any real consequence being generated by state actors and with state interests firmly in mind. It follows from this view that the role of virtually all other institutions and actors is subordinate, including any form of IO. Indeed, some may dismiss the whole project of global governance, composed of the efforts of both state and non-state actors, as of little relevance in the 'real world' of power politics. For others with more liberal views, it is largely through IOs that the dangerous aspects of international anarchy can be ameliorated, and all states have an interest in this. (Note that, in this context, 'anarchy' refers to the fact that there is no world sovereign authority or government as such.) Both the League of Nations and the UN represent a practical manifestation of liberal ideas in world politics. As for the fluid realm of NGOs, social movements, and civil society, these may be seen as an important complement to the more formal sphere of IO and global governance, often acting in concert with it, but sometimes opposing and resisting their policies and practices. However we may regard them, IOs have become such an integral part of the international system that it is difficult to imagine a world without them.

? Key Questions

- What are the key characteristics of IOs?
- How and why did IOs emerge in the modern period?
- To what extent has there been a continuity of IOs over the last two centuries?
- Was the League of Nations a complete failure?
- On what general principles is the UN founded?
- Is it possible for the UN to reconcile respect for state sovereignty and respect for universal human rights?
- Could the UN do more as an IO, or is it expected to do too much as it is?
- What role do NGOs and social movements play in the global system?
- How can global civil society enhance opportunities for democratic expression?
- Can the global political sphere actually be 'governed'?

Further Reading

Davies, Michael, and Woodward, Richard (2014), *International Organizations: A Companion* (Cheltenham: Edward Elgar).
This very useful book covers not only the theory and practice of international organizations, but also details specific institutions, including the UN, the EU, scientific organizations, and transport, as well as alliances and security.

Karns, Margot P., Mingst, Karen A., and Styles, Kendall W. (2015), *International Organizations: The Politics and Processes of Global Governance* (Boulder, CO: Lynne Rienner, 3rd edn).
This book covers a wide range of IGOs and NGOs, as well as norms and rules, issues of legitimacy and accountability, and problems of human rights, development, and the environment relating to IOs. Included are case studies focusing on contemporary concerns such as conflict in the Congo and attempts to combat human trafficking.

Murdie, Amanda (2014), *Help or Harm: The Human Security Effects of International NGOs* (Stanford, CA: Stanford University Press).
This is an interesting exploration, with numerous case study illustrations, of the extent to which international NGOs such as Oxfam or Human Rights Watch make a difference to the cause of promoting human security around the world.

Ruggie, John (1998), *Constructing the World Polity: Essays on International Institutionalization* (London: Routledge).
Ruggie has made his name as a leading constructivist and this book brings together a number of his essays, surveying the field of post-war international relations theory and how constructivist theories of IOs and institutions contribute to it. It remains a key text in the field.

Walker, James W. St G., and Thompson, Andrew Stuart (eds) (2011), *Critical Mass: The Emergence of Global Civil Society* (Waterloo, ON: Wilfred Laurier University Press and the Centre for International Governance Innovation).
This edited collection focuses on the apparent demand for citizen participation in global decision-making and the role of civil society organizations at the global level. Contributors include both academics and leaders of influential global civil society organizations.

 Web Links

https://uia.org
Website of the Union of International Associations, which publishes the *Yearbook of International Organizations*. It is self-described as a non-profit, apolitical, independent

NGO, which has been 'a pioneer in the research, monitoring and provision of information on international organizations, international associations and their global challenges since 1907'. It also contains a link directory to major organizations.

http://www.un.org/en/
Official website of the UN, providing the initial point of navigation for the entire range of the organization's functions.

http://www.crwflags.com/fotw/flags/int.html#world
Another useful directory of IOs, which provides direct links to UN-linked websites, as well as those of many regional organizations and NGOs.

 Visit the **Online Resources** that accompany this book to access more learning resources on this topic: www.oup.com/uk/ferdinand/

19 Conclusion: Politics in the Age of Globalization

- The Study of Politics in Context
- The Impact of Globalization
- Decentring the West?
- Politics in a Globalizing World
- Key Questions
- Further Reading
- Web Links

Reader's Guide

This concluding chapter brings together some of the major themes and the threads of various arguments that have run throughout the book. It first highlights the complexity of the field and emphasizes the close connection between political philosophy and the empirical study of politics. It also stresses that the study of politics cannot be neatly separated from the study of other disciplines—economics, philosophy, law, sociology, psychology, and history—and the fact that policy-making often involves the natural sciences as well. The chapter goes on to consider the impact of globalization on political studies, emphasizing the importance of international and comparative perspectives. In addition, although much of the analysis in the book centres on the state, it notes other important actors and forces at work, as well as the limits of 'methodological nationalism' in political analysis. As for the future, this chapter suggests that we cannot automatically assume the pre-eminence of Europe and the US, or the West more generally, and take for granted that they serve as exemplars for others to follow. Different cultural contexts produce different conceptions of the good life and the political means of achieving it. As for the study of politics, it remains the case that more works have been written on political systems in the West than in other parts of the world, and scholars located in the West have tended to dominate academic publishing to date. Looking to the future, however, there is no doubt that there will be shifts in the major centres of power that will produce new trends in these and other respects.

The Study of Politics in Context

This book began with a discussion of the problem of defining both the nature and scope of politics, and outlined various approaches to studying the political. Subsequent chapters have explored many dimensions of the subject, from basic concepts and theories to processes and institutions, together with a variety of examples and cases. From the start, the book has sought to demonstrate that the study of normative political philosophy—of how the political world ought to be arranged—cannot be kept apart from the empirical study of political institutions as they actually exist in particular contexts, no matter where and how they operate. Furthermore, both normative and empirical approaches are deeply implicated in the most basic and long-standing concern of politics—that is, the conditions under which people can achieve the 'good life' in terms of security, prosperity, and general well-being. For many students of politics, following Aristotle, the good life can be achieved only within the bounds of a well-ordered political community—a stable and functioning state. And it is indeed the basic function of the state to provide the conditions for enabling it. As we have seen, the nature of states has varied according to time and place, from the *polis* of the ancient Greeks to the sovereign state of the modern period. For better or worse, the latter is now the template on which all 193 formal members of the United Nations is based and to which national groups still seeking statehood aspire. It is, of course, within the context of the modern, sovereign, nation-state that the study of politics has largely occurred, although the study of politics in a global context is essential to a more holistic grasp of the field.

We have also seen that there are opposing views about the state—negative views that see the state as an impediment to the good life rather than a structure through which it is enabled. The empirical study of certain authoritarian states certainly supports the view that some states have bought great suffering to their people. Germany under Adolf Hitler, Russia under Joseph Stalin, Cambodia under Pol Pot, and China under both Chiang Kai-shek and Mao Tse Tung: all were responsible for the mass murder of their own citizens or, as we saw in Chapter 17, 'death by government'. Other states have obviously done much better, delivering a high standard of living in societies marked by the relative freedom of citizens to pursue their own conception of the good life within a certain framework of rules for living together. The UN Human Development Index, which uses indicators for life expectancy, education, and gross national income per capita ranks the top ten countries in the world in the following order: Norway, Australia, Switzerland, Germany, Denmark, Singapore, Netherlands, Ireland, and Iceland, with Canada and the US ranked equal tenth. The UK comes in at 16th place. The bottom 19 countries are all in sub-Saharan Africa, where poorly functioning states appear to correlate with abject poverty, severely limiting longevity, social goods such as education, and life choices (http://hdr.undp.org/en/data#, accessed January 2018). With the exception of Singapore, which has a semi-authoritarian one-party state, all countries in the top group are liberal democracies. Indeed, we do not encounter any non-liberal democracies until we start striking oil-rich states such as Brunei

19

at number 30 and Qatar at number 33. This is the kind of empirical data that leads political analysts to conclude that, by and large, liberal democracy is a major factor in producing the conditions for the good life.

On a related theme, various cases and examples throughout the book have also shown that states and societies, or more especially the political systems under which they operate, are dependent for their stability on their legitimacy. This is reflected in the extent to which members of the society believe them to be appropriate and acceptable. Where sufficient members of a society perceive the political system to be illegitimate, political rulers will need to employ a significant degree of coercion to remain in power. This also occurs when sub-state national groups challenge the very legitimacy of the state itself and seek a state of their own. Suppressing dissent and maintaining power through coercion is generally inefficient and costly. At worst, it can lead to civil war, as the case of Syria so clearly demonstrates. Of course, most states explicitly set out to educate and/or socialize their people into supporting them, which is yet another argument in favour of seeing the connection between the normative and empirical dimensions of politics.

This book is also based on the assumption that the study of politics overlaps with other disciplines in terms of subject matter, theories, and methods. In other words, the study of politics often takes place in an interdisciplinary context. These overlaps occur mainly in the social sciences, but they also include history and philosophy, as well as mathematics (especially statistics) and the natural sciences. In the social sciences, economics, is a discipline with a high degree of formal abstraction, yet there is an increasing recognition that institutions play a key role in determining many economic outcomes—exemplified by the New Institutionalist school. The study of political economy, examined in Chapter 9, is based on methods and forms of analysis drawn from both politics and economics and highlights the relationship between states and markets in national and global contexts. In addition, economic abstractions form the basis of rational choice theories of politics, such as the economic theory of democracy examined in Chapter 4. Here, it is assumed that political parties and voters have the utility-maximizing characteristics of actors—businesses and consumers—in the economic sphere. Parties will therefore be preoccupied with winning political power and voters will be concerned with exercising electoral choice in a way that will further their interests. More generally, however, the 2008 global financial crisis has reinforced the view that economic modelling, however sophisticated, cannot provide a complete picture of how economies actually operate.

The overlap between sociology and politics is equally apparent. For example, social stratification clearly plays a major role in the emergence of politicians and in voting patterns. The study of power, examined in Chapter 3, employs concepts and models of society developed by political sociologists, while Chapter 12 emphasized the overlap between law and politics in determining the rules that decide who gets what, when, and how in society. Historical studies also contribute enormously to both empirical and normative studies in politics, from locating the origins and thought processes involved in earlier state forms through to the rise of the modern sovereign state, as well as how ideas about democracy,

19

justice, legitimacy, authority, and a range of ideologies from liberalism to nationalism have developed in various contexts. Psychology, too, overlaps with the study of politics. For example, Chapter 12 illustrated ways in which it can contribute to our understanding of voting behaviour and many themes in political philosophy are dependent on assumptions made about human nature. And, in many of these disciplines, statistics often features as an indispensible element in analysis, although data produced in quantitative studies always require interpretation.

Studies of various forms of policy-making may also draw on the natural sciences, as well as technical expertise in disciplines such as engineering. Policy on energy security, climate change, genetically modified organisms (GMOs), public health, and so on, all depend on the interaction of scientists, technical experts, and policy-makers. So too does policy relating to the medical sciences and pharmaceuticals. Challenges to scientific knowledge can also become major issues in political debates. Again, climate change and GMOs are just two major areas that have figured prominently in recent debates. An interesting historical case is the resistance by tobacco companies to accepting evidence of the adverse effects of smoking on human health, which featured heavily in policy debates from the 1960s through to the 1990s, with the companies involved spending huge sums on political campaigns and lobbying. In more recent years, oil companies have funded studies in an attempt to counteract the science of anthropogenic global warming, as noted in Chapter 3. The food industry, and the fast food industry in particular, is often blamed for excessive consumption of sugar, fat, and salt, and therefore implicated in the significant increase in diseases such as diabetes, as well as obesity and ill-health more generally, which have seen national economies bear huge costs in terms of public health spending, as well as lost productivity. The political debates on these issues are often between liberal opponents of the 'nanny state', who support the view that individuals should be allowed to make up their own minds, and those who see a vital role for state regulation on the other, as illustrated in **Key Debate 19.1**.

 KEY DEBATE 19.1   The 'nanny state'

Debates over the proper role of the state in protecting the well-being of their citizens arise frequently in relation to public health issues such as the consumption of drugs, tobacco, and alcohol, and the safety and nutritional value of food, as well as, more specifically, medical issues such as vaccination. The state also requires the compulsory education of children and legislates for their protection in other ways. Building standards and numerous product safety regulations are now commonplace. Beyond these particular examples, the state regulates numerous aspects of our daily lives, as well as the way in which companies run their affairs. Not surprisingly, there is often resistance to state regulation—sometimes from consumers themselves, but more often from businesses or industries whose freedom to pursue profits is limited by such regulation and who often claim that they are capable of self-regulation to maintain appropriate standards. On the other hand, state regulations protect private property and individual rights in many other ways. Getting the right balance may seem obvious, but, as with so many other things in politics, getting broad agreement over where that balance lies is not easy. Below are two excerpts from media sources from opposite sides of the debate.

One great, long-standing British tradition has been that governments wherever possible left people alone to get on with their lives.

Provided you broke none of the sensible laws that existed to keep the peace, interference in your life by any agent of the state was almost unheard of . . .

The state has long since decided that it knows what is best for us, and our opinions on the matter are not deemed remotely relevant.

This approach to governance, in which our political leaders stop us from doing what they decree is bad for us, robs people of the ability to think for themselves; it also vastly increases the power of the state.

Armies of advisers are now employed at our expense to dream up new ways of protecting us from ourselves, which means their tentacles penetrate further and further into every aspect of our existence—and with a zealotry that verges on the totalitarian. (Heffer, 2012, published in the *Daily Mail*)

[A]nyone who supports rules and regulations that make products safer or improve public health can expect to come under attack from critics arguing they're restricting freedom and turning the country into a 'nanny state'.

These 'nanny state' critics are everywhere and they're superficially persuasive. After all, who wants government to tell them how to live their lives? But scratch the surface and you'll discover nanny state critics are frequently backed by powerful vested interests, like the tobacco industry arguing against plain packaging on cigarettes . . .

Nanny state critics are almost always self-interested. They're rarely motivated by the freedoms they purport to defend. And invariably their arguments crumble under scrutiny . . . Changes to laws, regulations, mandatory product standards and public awareness campaigns have saved countless lives over the years. (Chapman, 2013, published online at *The Conversation*)

To summarize this section, it is evident that a sophisticated understanding of political processes at all levels and in different contexts will often require insights derived from other disciplines and fields of expertise. This should not be taken to imply, however, that politics is simply a hybrid discipline, made up of concepts, modes of analysis, and methods borrowed from other disciplines. It clearly has its own specific preoccupations—most notably, political obligation, political ideologies, political institutions, and political behaviour at all levels, focusing on recurring regularities in political thinking and action. This is in addition to deeper, normative considerations arising in political philosophy. Taken together, these provide a very broad context for the study of politics in all its forms.

19

KEY POINTS

- Normative political philosophy and the empirical study of political institutions cannot be properly considered in isolation from each other.
- The study of politics overlaps with other disciplines in terms of subject matter, theories, and methods, but nonetheless maintains a distinctive emphasis on the way in which societies are governed.

The Impact of Globalization

Although this book has focused largely on politics within states, thereby maintaining the common distinction between the domestic and international spheres of politics, we have stressed that the phenomenon of globalization and its impact on national politics cannot be ignored. Some key examples for students of politics to consider are as follows.

1. It is very difficult to prevent economic crises in individual states from spreading to others. The most recent example is the global financial crisis, discussed in Chapter 9, when the 'sub-prime' mortgage crisis in the US triggered worldwide consequences. The Eurozone was subject to similar 'financial contagion' in 2011, spreading fears of economic collapse in Greece, Ireland, Portugal, Spain, and Italy. The renewed Greek financial crisis in 2015 posed a new existential threat to the euro, which has combined with simultaneous fears of a serious slowdown in the Chinese economy to unsettle markets. All of this clearly has a serious effect on the economic policies of governments around the world and raises questions about to the extent to which we can speak of discrete 'national economies'.

2. There have been increasing flows of people across national borders in search of work or refuge. In Britain, for instance, we noted in Chapter 6 the extent to which the population is made up of immigrants from other countries, a trend that has been increasing in recent years. The 2011 Census showed that 11.9 per cent of the population had been born abroad, as compared with 6.7 per cent in the 1991 Census. Migrant workers and their families play a significant role not only in the political life of their new countries, but also as diasporas of the countries from which they came. This is especially well documented for politics in the US and is an increasingly frequent phenomenon within the EU, but it can be found elsewhere around the world too. As China develops into a global economic and political power, its diaspora in Australia and New Zealand, South East Asia, and Africa may become increasingly relevant to its foreign policy.

3. Concern for the environment has also become pre-eminently a global issue, especially since problems such as pollution and climate change can scarcely be confined

19

within national borders. The northern summer of 2017 saw extreme heat and wildfires across Europe, while other parts of the world were subject to extremes of flooding. India, Nepal, and Bangladesh suffered well over 1,000 dead following catastrophic monsoonal rain, with millions evacuated, while in the US Hurricane Harvey brought with it an unprecedented deluge, devastating large swathes of Texas in particular. States increasingly accept the need to move jointly towards policies of sustainability that will constrain the domestic policy choices of individual states, as outlined in Chapter 3 in relation to climate change policies. Acceptance of the need for joint action was behind the UN Paris Agreement of December 2015 when a consensus was reached by world leaders to adopt policies to limit global warming. Although the US under President Trump has since pulled out, the Agreement nonetheless stands as an example of global cooperation in the face of an unprecedented challenge for policy-makers that transcends individual states. Interestingly, a number of state governors, mayors, and US-based companies are pledging to bypass their own national government and make a direct commitment to the UN to reduce greenhouse gas emissions to the levels promised in Paris.

4. There has been an increase in regional organizations where states agree to pool elements of their sovereignty in exchange for the promise of coordinated policies and action. For centuries, states have done this in the form of military alliances. In more recent decades, however, this has spread to organizations with economic and non-military political objectives. The best example of this is the EU, which has the closest ties between its members of all regional organizations, but there has been a proliferation of regional organizations elsewhere—for example the Association of Southeast Asian Nations (ASEAN), the Southern Common Market (Mercosur), the North American Free Trade Agreement (NAFTA), the Asia-Pacific Economic Cooperation (APEC), and so on—as discussed in Chapter 9. Brexit has no doubt been a setback for the regionalist project in Europe but to date there has been little evidence that the apparent retreat into nationalism by a majority of British voters (albeit an extremely narrow one) will be emulated elsewhere.

5. As discussed in Chapter 5, there have been two waves of democratization spreading around the world since the 1970s. The collapse of one authoritarian regime sometimes encourages opponents in others—the 'demonstration effect'—as happened in Eastern Europe, followed by the former Soviet Union, between 1989 and 1991, and in the Arab Spring of 2011; hence the 'wave-like' phenomenon. Political actors within states also look elsewhere for ideas on political organization, for example constitutional provisions, models for federal systems, electoral arrangements, ways of running electoral campaigns, the reorganization of civil services, and so on. Equally, democratic states also sometimes seek to promote the spread of democracy through various forms of external assistance, ranging from training in the techniques of political professionalism to outright intervention, while authoritarian states may also cooperate to try to stay in power.

6. Ideas for the reform of policies in specific areas spread through international epistemic communities of professionals who share common orientations towards the most effective ways of delivering their policy objectives, irrespective of the particular state in which they live. Ideas of reforms to welfare policies, for example, spread from the US to Western Europe. Ideas on educational policies have spread around the EU as individual states have been confronted with the evidence from league tables of the relative achievements of their pupils in mastering basic skills. The internationalization of higher education has also seen more convergence on standards and procedures in universities around the world. Equally important has been the role of the Intergovernmental Panel on Climate Change (IPCC)—a group of climate scientists drawn from around the globe who have played a significant role in getting the issue of global warming on the political agenda.

7. The proliferation and globalization of media institutions and sources of information, accelerated by the rise of the Internet and other forms of electronic communication, as outlined in Chapter 18, have facilitated the emergence of a global civil society—that is, transnational organizations of political activists. Whether it is organizations such as Greenpeace, Doctors Without Borders, Amnesty International, Oxfam, Caritas, the Red Cross/Crescent, the World Wide Fund for Nature, or events such as the Live Aid concerts, all raise concerns above the level of the nation-state.

It is evident, then, that globalization presents particular challenges to conventional academic approaches to the study of politics based, as it has been, on the domestic–international divide. It is also increasingly difficult for students of politics and the social sciences more generally to maintain the approach known as 'methodological nationalism', the subject of **Key Quote 19.2**, which is based on the assumption that the nation-state, as the prime container of social and political processes, provides the 'natural' unit of analysis, whether one engages in the analysis of domestic politics within a single state or comparative analysis across two or more states. Even traditional international relations approaches have usually taken the sovereign nation-state as the only political actor that, in the final analysis, really counts. Critics of these traditional approaches therefore emphasize state-transcending dynamics and the fact that transnational structures, linkages, identities, movements, and so on, cannot be ignored.

Political philosophers, too, will have to reorient their focus from the modern nation-state, the character of which, since the sixteenth century, they have helped to shape. Debates over the last few decades have seen increasing attention to the concept of cosmopolitanism as a normative orientation to questions concerning issues such as democracy and justice in the global sphere, as we have seen in Chapters 4 and 7. If we subscribe to the general principles of human rights, we obviously cannot justify confining our concerns for human well-being to our fellow citizens alone. Cosmopolitan justice requires

19

> **Q**   KEY QUOTE 19.2   **Questioning methodological nationalism**
>
> 'Methodological nationalism considers nation-states as the basic unit of all politics. It assumes that humankind is naturally distributed among a limited number of nations, which organize themselves internally as nation-states and delimit themselves externally from other nation-states . . . In addition, it assumes that the external delimitation and the subsequent competition between nation-states are the most fundamental concepts of political organization . . . Methodological nationalism sees self-determination as ontologically given and as the most important cleavage in the political sphere. This double premise pre-determines empirical observations, as can be seen in the case of aggregate statistics, which are almost exclusively categorized in national terms. It locates and restricts the political sphere to the national level.'
> (Zürn, 2002: 248)

that we look beyond national borders to the plight of people elsewhere who are subject to severe abuses or material deprivation.

Globalization has also increased the pressures on the state, complicating the activities of national governments in a number of ways. According to economist Rodrik (2011), it is impossible for states simultaneously to pursue all three goals of democracy, national self-determination, and economic globalization—they have to choose two—and, in recent years, the tendency in Western states has been to pursue economic globalization and democracy, thereby eroding the capacity to control their national economies. In the present period, US President Trump has been attempting to reassert control over the national economy through the adoption of economic protectionism, as mentioned in both Chapters 6 and 9 in the context of nationalism and political economy, respectively. With Brexit, too, many arguments in favour of leaving the EU were premised on the assumption that the UK would regain control over certain national economic issues.

Another trend challenges governments from the opposite direction, from below, in the form of decentralization or sub-state nationalisms demanding greater autonomy or independence, as noted in Chapter 6. The declaration of independence by Kosovo from Serbia is a recent example. It was preceded by the disintegration of the former Soviet Union and the former Yugoslavia, which, as we saw in Chapter 8, gave rise to many new sovereign states, or in some cases restored sovereignty to previously independent countries. Elsewhere in the world, we have seen successful bids for independence in East Timor and South Sudan, while there are continuing demands for independence for the Basque country, Northern Cyprus, and the Kurds, and secessionist movements in Tibet, the Philippines, and Thailand, to name just a few. A referendum on independence for Scotland in 2014 failed, but in the wake of the Brexit referendum of 2016, in which a clear majority of Scots opposed leaving the EU, a second referendum on independence appears to be on the cards.

At the same time, the state is being eroded at another level through the spread of neo-liberal market ideas, which advocate a clearer separation of the state from market operations, exemplified by the increasing trend towards establishing the independence of central banks from government intervention, which makes state control of the national economy less direct. Chapter 9 also noted the extent to which neo-liberal ideas strongly supported the privatization of state resources and the deregulation of financial and other institutions. Also discussed here was the problem of tax avoidance by companies operating globally and which have often managed to by pass virtually all nationally based taxation regimes, much to the detriment of public goods.

Another interesting development has been the role of criminal gangs in carving out and controlling 'statelets' of neighbourhoods that coexist in delicate, 'often symbiotic' relationships with nation-states. Examples include the *favelas* in Brazil, the ganglands of Kingston, Jamaica, and several cities in northern Mexico, not to mention the drug lords of Afghanistan and Myanmar. Often, these gangs are linked with broader networks of transnational crime, challenging the traditional state from both within and without as noted in Chapter 18.

All of this has sometimes been seen as the 'hollowing out' of the state evoked in Chapters 2, 6, 9, and 14, with forces both above and below national governments practically sucking the vitality out of the state. Certainly, as Savoie (2010) notes, it has eviscerated traditional expectations of democratic accountability. It is now much more difficult to know who to blame for policy failures in Western democracies, let alone to punish them in elections. Some commentators, such as Scholte (2005), have even gone so far as to identify 'globalization' with the deterritorialization of social, economic, and technical processes, which flow around the globe without significant obstacle.

Others counter this by pointing to a different form of state activity at the international level—namely, transnationalism. Slaughter (1997), for instance, has pointed to the rise of new networks of nodes of cooperation between branches of national governments. She points to the increasing webs of relations that link the courts and ministries of justice of individual states. This leads them to cooperate in new approaches to solving problems and sometimes to convergence. Certainly, judges in one jurisdiction are often more aware now of the thinking of judges in others on similar issues—and this applies not just to the EU, which has the greatest integration of a supranational court with national ones. According to Slaughter (1997: 184), '[t]he state is not disappearing; it is disaggregating into its separate, functional distinct parts'. Yet the protracted Eurozone crisis since 2011 is a stark reminder that network arrangements may find decisive, quick decision-making problematic. International markets move rapidly and national political decision-makers are expected to keep up. Failure to do so invites speculation against currencies. So while globalization may now mediate the way in which states conduct their affairs, they may not be in decline as such, but rather in a situation of adjustment to changing circumstance. Certainly, it is difficult to see the demise of the sovereign state any time soon, although the extent to which it exercises untrammelled sovereign power may be increasingly limited in some areas.

> ## ✳ KEY POINTS
>
> - Globalization presents particular challenges to traditional approaches to the study of politics, especially in terms of maintaining 'methodological nationalism', based as it is on the assumption that the nation-state provides the 'natural' unit of analysis.
> - The weakening of the sovereign state is often seen as a result of certain neo-liberal elements of globalization, but there are also pressures from sub-state sources.

Decentring the West?

Much of the discussion in this book has been informed by modes of analysis developed almost entirely in Western political and social thought. Virtually all of the methods examined in earlier chapters and the concepts associated with them, including empiricism, positivism, behaviouralism, comparativism, interpretivism, and so forth, are the product of Western scholarship. So too are the ideologies, and the theories that arise from them, as discussed in Chapter 8, as well as the intellectual tools used in developing frameworks for analysis in fields such as political economy, the media, civil society, and security, as examined in Chapters 9, 15, 16, and 17, respectively. Much the same general point can be made about most academic disciplines. This is the result of the fact that the modern university system, in which so much of our intellectual activity has taken place over the last few centuries, is itself a product of the rise of the more general phenomenon of modernity in the West.

Historically, we should note that modernity is associated with intellectual movements beginning in Europe with the Renaissance, followed by the Reformation and the Enlightenment, as well as the Industrial Revolution. Accompanying these was the rise of capitalism, democracy, and an increasingly secular social and political sphere. The French and the American revolutions are also key events that have had a decisive influence on intellectual developments, as well as practical outcomes, in terms of institutions and practices. We should also note, however, that important elements contributing to modernity and European culture more generally come from other parts of the world, especially from across the Asian continent. Many of these contributions have been in science and technology—gunpowder and the magnetic compass came from China, while key developments in mathematics (including our system of numbers) came from South Asia and the Arab world of scholarship. Ancient philosophies from these regions have also had an impact. All have contributed to what is generally called 'Western civilization'. We have not discussed these historical phenomena in detail in this book, but they do constitute an important background for understanding contemporary politics, and students pursuing the field at a more advanced level will no doubt encounter them in due course.

19

One point arising from this is that the theories and methods through which the study of politics, as set out in this book, are often criticized for being largely ethnocentric or more especially Eurocentric. *Ethnocentrism* is usually defined as the tendency to view one's own culture, and its members, as superior to others. A milder interpretation might suggest that it simply describes the tendency to view the world through the lens of one's own cultural experiences—certainly a common enough predisposition. *Eurocentrism* is a particular form of the phenomenon. It refers not just to Europeans as such, but more generally to a world view emanating from the West. The latter is a geo-political construct that, in addition to Europe, includes North America, Australia, and New Zealand—countries dominated by the descendants of Europeans and their culture, which includes not just literature and the arts, but also language (with English dominating) and systems of knowledge (including scientific and industrial knowledge).

The term 'Eurocentrism' came into increasing usage in critical scholarship from around the 1980s to call attention to the fact that many of the assumptions underpinning knowledge in the social sciences, including politics, were based on 'false universals'—that is, assumptions were derived from the particular experiences of Western societies and then projected onto the rest of the world as universal truths. Thus what may be considered in Western societies to constitute 'the good life' was often projected as good for everyone else as well. But 'the good life' may, in fact, be viewed very differently in other societies according to their own cultural contexts.

Debates around such issues, especially after the end of Cold War, saw the concept of cultural relativism rise to prominence as a counter to what was seen as the (false) universalism implicit in much Western social science. Cultural relativism, as a concept, was first developed in early twentieth-century anthropology and referred to the idea that values, beliefs, and practices originate within cultural groups and cannot be judged according to the standards of another culture. This leads to a form of moral or ethical relativism which, taking as its primary reference point the evident fact that different societies or 'cultures' have different moral or ethical systems, holds that, as a consequence, there is no basis for claiming that any one is better or worse than any other. In other words, all are equally valid. One irony of this, however, is the fact that the idea of cultural relativism, and the particular concept of culture on which it is based, is itself a product of Western scholarship (Lawson, 2006).

The concept of cultural relativism also has serious implications for the basic principles of human rights, which are by definition universal. In essence, these principles hold that one cannot be more or less human and that one does not bear rights only according to the precepts of any particular culture, or indeed any particular state. This reflects a cosmopolitan world view that focuses on a common humanity, as mentioned in Chapters 2 and 6, and to which cultural relativism appears to stand opposed. Many criticisms have, of course, been directed at some of the implications of cultural relativism for human rights outcomes. How could 'Nazi culture', for example, be seen as morally equal to liberal democratic culture when it permitted the Holocaust? Would anyone nowadays want to defend human sacrifice as a morally worthy cultural practice? These are rather extreme examples, but they

19

illustrate the limits of cultural relativism in ethical terms. On the other hand, we know that we live in a culturally plural world and that different cultural backgrounds and experiences lead people to develop different conceptions of 'the good life' and the means for pursuing it. We also know that encounters with cultural difference are often very enriching experiences—intellectually, socially, and in other ways. Moreover, while mainstream political scholarship is likely to remain largely Eurocentric in the short term, the rise of other centres of knowledge and power around the globe, embedded in quite different cultural contexts, is likely to see shifts and changes in the longer term.

Even though the US continues unchallenged as the sole superpower, with an economy that will remain the most powerful in the world for at least the next two decades, with conventional and nuclear military resources that still dwarf all others, and with a significant claim to soft power too, one cannot ignore the fact that the balance is shifting elsewhere. There has been much speculation that, under President Trump's administration, the US is fast losing its status as a world leader. Trump's campaign pledge to put 'America First' signalled that 'the world' would quite definitely come in a poor second. This has been reflected in his apparent disdain for US-led alliance systems, with organizations such as the North American Treaty Organization (NATO) coming in for much criticism during the campaign. His withdrawal from the Paris Agreement and his arguable lack of interest in the G20, which he attended in Germany in July 2017, has seen a sharp decline in general international confidence in the ability of the US to exercise any productive kind of leadership in key areas of contemporary concern. According to a report issued by the Washington-based, non-partisan Pew Research Center in June 2017, only months after taking office, 'Trump and many of his key policies are broadly unpopular around the globe, and ratings for the U.S. have declined steeply in many nations' (Wike et al., 2017). It is possible, however, that Trump's successor, whoever that may be, may take a very different approach, with the US's position in global politics adjusting accordingly.

Until recently, the EU appeared to be emerging as a powerful and cohesive economic and political power on the world stage. It sometimes seeks to offer a different approach to international politics—one based more on diplomacy and on establishing standards for law-based international behaviour. Despite some of its failings and difficulties, the EU has achieved the most basic objective of banishing inter-state war from the European continent, at least since 1945, and with good prospects of that continuing into the future. Given the experience of three major Franco-German wars between 1870 and 1945, with the two latter wars enveloping much of the world outside Europe as well, this is a significant achievement. Furthermore, the gradual integration that has taken place has led to much greater prosperity. All this has made the EU a standard against which regional integration projects in other parts of the world have often been measured, although we must be careful not to assume it is a model that other regional projects can, and must, follow, especially given the Eurozone crisis of 2011 and the Brexit vote in 2016.

Despite problems with both the US and the EU, the 'West' still appears as powerful now as at any time since the end of the Second World War and a Western model of modernity could seem as influential and attractive as ever. But other actors in the world are gaining in

19

confidence, as is illustrated in **Key Debate 19.3**, which summarizes the contrasting views, first, of a former Singaporean diplomat turned academic, Kishore Mahbubani, second, of the head of the STRATFOR consulting firm in the US, George Friedman, and third, of a senior long-time State Department official and academic, Joseph Nye. Even the US National Intelligence Council (2008) recognized the heavy probability of increasing multilateralism and multipolarity over the next 15 years, which it had downplayed only four years earlier. The updated version of its 2012 report confirmed the continuing diffusion of global power in the world to 2030.

 KEY DEBATE 19.3   Is the West in decline?

Mahbubani (2008: 127–31, 237–8) on the rise of the East over the West:

Sometimes the hardest things to see are the largest things.

At the height of Western power, when Western influence extended into virtually every corner of the world, the West essentially wrapped the globe with several layers of Western influence. The enormity of Western power made the world believe that there was only one way forward . . .

The unraveling of Western influence is a complex process. It has many different strands. The West has to understand that this is the major historical trend of our time, that it defines our era . . .

The process of de-Westernization is much deeper than the story of anti-Americanism . . . Many in the West want to believe that this bout of anti-Americanism is just a passing phase caused by the harsh and insensitive policies of one administration . . .

This is a mirage. The mindsets of the largest populations within Asia—the Chinese, the Muslims, and the Indians—have been changed irrevocably. Where once they may have happily borrowed Western lenses and Western cultural perspectives to look at the world, now with growing cultural self-confidence, their perceptions are growing further and further apart . . .

History teaches us that leadership in any era is provided by emerging powers. For example, when America replaced the UK as the world's leading power, it moved naturally to providing global leadership. By the same logic, China should eventually take over the mantle of global leadership from America. In its own way it is providing global inspiration, if not leadership.

Friedman (2010: 14) on the new 'American century':

We are now in an America-centric age. To understand this age, we must understand the United States, not only because it is so powerful but because its culture will permeate the world and define it. Just as French culture and British culture were definitive during their times of power, so American culture, as young and barbaric as it is, will define the way the world thinks and lives. So studying the twenty-first century means studying the United States.

If there were only one argument that I could make about the twenty-first century, it would be that the European century has ended and that the North American age has begun, and that North America will be dominated by the United States for the next hundred years. The events of the twenty-first century will pivot around the United States. That doesn't guarantee that the United States is necessarily a just or moral regime. It certainly does not mean that the United States has yet developed a mature civilization. It does mean that in many ways the history of the United States will be the history of the twenty-first century.

Nye (2015: 116–17, emphasis original) on the durability of American power:

Any effort to assess American power in the coming decades should recall how many earlier efforts have been wide of the mark. It is chastening to remember how wildly exaggerated were American estimates of Soviet power in the 1970s and of Japanese power in the 1980s . . .

As an overall assessment, describing the twenty-first century as one of American decline is likely to be inaccurate and misleading . . . America has many problems, but it is not in absolute decline, and even in relative terms, it is likely to remain more powerful than any single state in the coming several decades. The real problem for the United States is not that it will be overtaken by China or another contender, but that it will be faced with a rise in the power resources of many others—both states and non-state actors. This diffusion of power will make the United States relatively less able to control others. Entropy [that is, increasing disorder] may become a greater challenge than China. Moreover, the world will face an increasing number of new transnational issues which will require power *with* others as much as power *over* others.

Questions

1. Is the global rise of Asia credible? Likely? Coordinated?
2. Does it matter if Asia becomes more dominant? To whom, and why?
3. How should the US respond? How should people outside the US respond?

The global financial crisis that broke in the US in the second half of 2007, discussed in Chapter 9, has accelerated the trend. What it revealed is that the increasing role of the state in Western societies in providing public goods, as highlighted by the rise in state finance as a share of national gross domestic product (GDP) throughout the twentieth century, has become fiscally unsustainable. In recent years, the US and other Western states have relied on borrowing from global financial markets to provide the scale of financing for activities for which their taxpayers were apparently unwilling to pay directly. The problem was further exacerbated by the mushrooming US deficit in foreign trade (Reinhart and Rogoff, 2009). Ironically, many states had been reducing their fiscal share of GDP before the crisis broke (Tanzi, 2011: 95), but they were caught out by events in 2007–08. This dependence on external borrowing turned toxic when large financial institutions such as banks ran into their own liquidity and credibility crisis and needed state bailouts. The consequence, according to Gagnon and Hinterschweiger (2011), is that Western states will need to do much more over the next 25 years to reduce this level of public debt to avoid another, even bigger crisis. As a consequence, Western states will find their freedom of manoeuvre much more restricted for years to come.

The anticipation of a fundamental shift in global power is reinforced by the trend in basic demographic data, as shown in **Table 19.1**. This table cites the current UN median projection of world population growth over the period to 2030. What it shows is that, in the period 2010–30, the world population is expected to grow by 1.3 billion, but within that overall figure the European population will shrink both absolutely and relatively by roughly 35 million, so that it will be roughly equal with the population of South America and the Caribbean. While the population of North America is expected to rise by 59 million, the population of Africa will rise both absolutely and relatively by 414 million—that is, a fifth more than the entire North American population of 348 million in 2010, while the population of Asia is expected to rise by 739 million, with the Indian population beginning to overtake China's.

The rise of powerful states in Asia and of the region as a whole is graphically demonstrated by the change in foreign exchange reserves held there. Whereas, in 1980, Pacific Asia held 12.37 per cent of global reserves, by the end of 2009 this figure had risen to 56.57 per cent. Japan has been an economic giant for some decades, but now China and, more recently, India have come into focus as both economic and military contenders for great power status. China is sometimes presented in the US as the country most likely to challenge American ascendancy in the coming decades. Whether or not this turns out to be the case, there is no doubting the significance of the change compared with the twentieth century and, indeed, the second half of the nineteenth, when China was so preoccupied with internal disorder that it was unable to play a leading role in world affairs. Now, the 'rise' of China has become a standard topic of discussion and debate, including inside China itself. Books are written with eye-catching titles such as *When China Rules the World* (Jacques, 2012). India's economic take-off since the early 1990s adds further to the challenge to the West. According to a US National Intelligence Council (2012: 15) report, 'by 2030, Asia will have surpassed North America and Europe combined in terms of global power, based upon GDP, population size, military spending, and technological investment'.

TABLE 19.1   Regional distribution of world population, selected years

	1990	2010	2030
Africa	11.8	14.4	17.2
Asia (including Middle East)	60.2	60.7	60.1
Europe (including Russia to the Urals)	13.7	10.5	8.4
Latin America and the Caribbean	8.4	8.7	8.7
North America	5.4	5.1	5.0
Oceania	0.5	0.5	0.5
World (in millions)	5,264	6,830	8,130

Source: http://www.un.org/esa/population/publications/longrange2/WorldPop2300final.pdf (accessed 9 January 2018).

19

A second significant change is the increasing self-confidence of the Islamic world. Throughout the nineteenth and twentieth centuries, the Islamic world declined significantly vis-à-vis the West. The dissolution of its most powerful grouping—the Ottoman Empire—led to both military occupation by Western countries and, equally importantly, a sense of inferiority in the face of Western modernity, as exemplified by the Ataturk secularist revolution of the 1920s, mentioned in Chapter 10. Even the use of the oil 'card' by Saudi Arabia and others in the 1970s, did not essentially change this. Now, things are different. Younger generations of Muslims, it seems, feel more self-assured and less deferential towards the West. The same is true of various Islamic governments. Having said that, we must remain very careful not to draw a simplistic dividing line between the 'Islamic world' and 'the West'. The Islamic world is not united. Turkey is a member of NATO—a largely 'Western' alliance—as well as a candidate for EU membership (although that has been set back, given recent developments in Turkey, which have seen a reversion to a more authoritarian mode of politics). Many Islamic countries are allies of the US in the war on terror. There are many overlapping interests, and even alliances, between the Islamic world and the West, but there are also many between the Islamic world and the East.

The third big change is the resurgence of Russia. In one sense, this does not represent such a significant break with recent history. After all, the Soviet Union, dominated by Russia, was the rival superpower from the end of the Second World War until the Union's collapse in 1991. Russia's reappearance as a global player should not, then, be so surprising. What is significant about Russia's resurgence is the regime's greater disdain for supposed Western superiority, even as it continues sometimes to proclaim itself as of the West—and this is in spite of the fact that the West lavished considerable resources, both financial and advisory, on Russia to try to smooth its transition from a communist regime to, hopefully, democracy and a market economy. The intervention by Russia and Russians in Crimea and Eastern Ukraine in 2014 has further widened the rift with the West and stimulated greater official enthusiasm for a 'Eurasian', rather than Western, identity.

A fourth factor is the increasing international prominence of the BRICS states (Brazil, Russia, India, China, and South Africa). Originally highlighted as a disparate group with the potential for dramatic returns on foreign investment, it has gradually evolved into a forum that now holds annual summits for foreign policy cooperation and to provide international leadership, especially for developing states in their dealings with the developed world. Their most recent innovation was the establishment of a BRICS Development Bank that might compete with the World Bank. All these new actors demand greater respect and attention.

These changes also signal a broad shift in attitudes towards the 'West'. This entity no longer attracts the same deference as it did during most of the nineteenth and twentieth centuries. While its levels of economic development and technological prowess remain undisputed, the West is no longer seen as embodying the only path to 'modernity'—a path that nations in other parts of the world are obliged to follow if they are going to achieve the same levels of development. Indeed, there is an increasing body of people who argue that the Western style and level of development is out of keeping with the new priority of an ethic of environmentally friendly, sustainable development. They advocate a search for alternative solutions.

19

China is often presented as the state most likely to challenge the West and it is true that books now appear there that look forward to a dominant China that embodies different (and superior) civilizational values (Zhang, 2012, 2014). Indian writers too promote their country as a source of alternative, more genuinely plural, global values and receive endorsement from Prime Minister Modhi (Malhotra, 2013). Equally, the developing world's resistance to agree to binding commitments on reducing carbon emissions until they are given the resources to cope with the consequences reveals a much more confident persona. This behaviour is predicated on the developing world's insistence that developed countries have been largely responsible for climate change and therefore should take much of the responsibility for dealing with it.

This inclination resonates with the emergence of two other schools of political analysis. The first is the 'subaltern studies' school, described in Chapter 16. This rejects the idea of automatically assigning superiority and paying greater attention to the 'winners' of development. These 'winners' include both elites within individual states and also, internationally, the developed world. Instead, from this perspective, analysts should pay more attention to the 'subalterns'—that is, the 'underdogs'. The latter point is encapsulated in the title of an article by American academic and black activist Cornel West (1991), 'Decentring Europe', as well as a book by Indian anthropologist Dipesh Chakrabarty (2000), *Provincializing Europe*—that is, treating Europe 'merely' as the equal of other regions of the world.

To some extent, this approach resonates with postmodernism, as briefly outlined in Chapter 8. The orientation underlying it is the rejection of deference to 'god-like' scientific authorities. Rather, it encourages and advocates pluralism. It has been criticized, with some justice, for taking this too far, for excessive relativism. Postmodernists are more noted for seeking to undermine the claims to objectivity of particular academic authorities than for establishing the validity of alternative claims. Yet much of this book is compatible with their critical outlook. We do not believe that Western political systems should automatically enjoy greater esteem than those in other parts of the world and, certainly, politics in other parts of the world is equally worthy of study.

It is certainly true that, as emphasized in the comparative chapters of this book, Western ideas and institutions have spread around the world and, in many ways, set the standard for what could be regarded as 'modern' political systems. It is a historical fact that the sovereign state model along with democracy, for example, spread from Europe and the US to other parts of the world in the twentieth century. 'Political science' is often seen as primarily a Western academic discipline—and although critics continue to argue that 'Western' political institutions such as political parties, as discussed in Chapter 13, are not necessarily appropriate for non-Western societies with different traditions, it is striking that viable alternative forms of political activism and political organization have proved remarkably limited. In the 1960s and 1970s, for instance, leaders of Third World states such as Sukarno in Indonesia and Nyerere in Tanzania advocated forms of political organization and decision-making that were more in keeping with the traditions of village societies, yet these alternative forms have not prospered. To some extent, this was the result of other dimensions of modernization. Increasing urbanization, for example, has undermined the appeal of traditional rural forms of decision-making.

It is worth reiterating, however, that there is no obvious logical reason why forms of political organization found in the West should acquire automatic pre-eminence. Nor is it obvious that political institutions in the West are all in rude health. One of the arguments underlying Chapter 13 was that political parties in the West suffer from great problems, not least the lack of esteem in which they are held by their potential supporters. Concepts underlying such forms are not always easily translated from Western, especially Anglophone, contexts to other parts of the world. Chapter 16, for example, showed how the concept of 'civil society' was based on assumptions derived from Western experience that were not easily translated into Islamic or Asiatic societies. Chapter 5 referred to the increasing disconnect between politicians and voters across most of the Western world. Yet we all tend to assess political institutions in other countries through lenses that were fashioned in our own societies. The state, political parties, interest groups, and federalism—these are just some of the key terms of political discourse that look and behave differently from one political system to another. Just because we think we know what they mean in systems with which we are familiar does not mean that they are identical elsewhere.

 KEY POINTS

- The formal study of politics, including its methods and modes of analysis, have been developed largely within a Western intellectual context and, for that reason, may be seen as essentially Eurocentric.
- Although the concept of cultural relativism raises difficult issues for human rights, it nonetheless gives us an appreciation of the fact that different cultural experiences may lead to different conceptions of 'the good life' and the means for pursuing it.
- In the longer term, the rise of other centres of knowledge and power around the globe is likely to see challenges to dominant Western conceptions of politics.

Politics in a Globalizing World

All of this suggests that the forms and modes of politics with which we are familiar are evolving. According to Naim (2013), power in general has become more difficult to exercise, whether by governments, political leaders, or business leaders. Government within the national or domestic sphere has become more fraught as authorities face more challenges than ever before. The regional shifts in global power outlined above represent another key facet of a challenge to contemporary political forms. Another is the constraint on national governments posed by the need to attract foreign capital. Already, at the end of the 1990s, American commentator Thomas Friedman identified the challenge of the

19

'golden straitjacket'—that is, the need for governments to appeal to international markets and investors. His idea, which resonates with the discussion of neo-liberalism in Chapter 9, is encapsulated in **Key Quote 19.4**.

Friedman remarked that the consequence of governments adopting such a golden strait-jacket is that the economy grows, but politics shrinks. In other words, the range of policy alternatives is narrowed to technocratic ones, even in democracies. Citizens in democracies find their preferences ever more subordinated to financial markets. The global financial crisis has intensified that trend, as heavily indebted governments impose austerity to satisfy lenders, whether domestic or foreign, even if it means savage cuts in living standards. Most countries have experienced this challenge, but in the Eurozone it is best exemplified by Greece. If Gagnon and Hinterschweiger (2011) are right, dealing with this problem will continue to define the parameters of political debate in many countries for at least another decade.

All of this means that it will become even more important to understand such challenges, to incorporate them into the analysis of how politics operates around the world, and to devise ways of coping with them. Moreover, contemporary political philosophers will have to engage more than they have done previously with the ideas underlying non-Western political practices and institutions. To reiterate, we have emphasized the declining importance of the sovereign state, as well as the growing significance of non-Western parts of the world, both of which present enormous challenges for the political analyst. This does not mean that the state has, or is likely to, become a peripheral concern of the political analyst. Nor does it mean that politics in Europe or the US will become unimportant. The evolution of these political systems and the ideas underlying them will still attract wide interest and offer important lessons for observers of politics everywhere,

---

 KEY QUOTE 19.4   Friedman on the neo-liberal 'golden straitjacket'

'To fit into the Golden Straitjacket a country must either adopt, or be seen as moving toward, the following golden rules: making the private sector the priority engine of its economic growth, maintaining a low rate of inflation and price stability, shrinking the size of the state bureaucracy, maintaining as close to a balanced budget as possible, if not a surplus, eliminating and lowering tariffs on imported goods, removing restrictions on foreign investment, getting rid of quotas and domestic monopolies, increasing exports, privatizing state-owned industries and utilities, deregulating capital markets, making its currency convertible, opening its industries, stock, and bond markets to direct foreign ownership and investment, deregulating its economy to promote as much domestic competition as possible, eliminating government corruption, subsidies and kickbacks as much as possible, opening its banking and telecommunications systems to private ownership and competition, and allowing its citizens to choose from an array of competing pension options and foreign-run pension and mutual funds. When you stitch all of these pieces together you have the Golden Straitjacket.' (Friedman, 1999: 86–7)

19

and what happens on both sides of the Atlantic will also have a major impact on world affairs for decades to come. The rise of other centres of power, however, appears inevitable. It also makes it difficult to predict the outcomes. But, because of this, the study of politics in the twenty-first century will continue to be exciting and challenging.

? **Key Questions**

- What makes the study of politics distinct from other disciplines?
- Can human prosperity and well-being be achieved only within the bounds of a stable and functioning state? Is there a viable alternative political structure?
- What evidence is there for the greater efficacy of liberal democracies in delivering the good life?
- What role has Western modernity played in shaping the global political system?
- What does recognition of cultural differences around the globe mean for the study of political issues?
- How has globalization impacted on traditional approaches to the study of politics?
- Is it possible or desirable to abandon methodological nationalism in the study of politics?
- Is political power becoming more diffuse and therefore more difficult to exercise, and if so, is this necessarily a bad thing?
- Is a shift of global power from the West to the East inevitable?
- What factors are likely to shape the politics of the future?

║** **Further Reading

Ehteshami, Anoushiravan (2007), *Globalization and Global Politics in the Middle East: Old Games, New Rules* (London and New York: Routledge).
A thoughtful survey of the impact of globalization on the Middle East.

Friedman, Thomas (1999), *The Lexus and the Olive Tree* (London and New York: HarperCollins).
A widely quoted analysis of the impact of globalization around the world and some of the resistance that it has engendered.

Mahbubani, Kishore (2008), *The New Asian Hemisphere: The Irresistible Shift of Global Power to the East* (New York: PublicAffairs).
Passionate advocacy of the Asian century.

Malhotra, Rajiv (2013), *Being Different: An Indian Challenge to Western Universalism* (Noida, Uttar Pradesh: HarperCollins).

Presents traditional Indian ways of thinking as a more appropriate basis for genuinely plural global values.

Naim, Moises (2013), *The End of Power: From Boardrooms to Battlefields and Churches to States—Why Being in Charge Isn't What It Used to Be* (New York: Basic Books).
A thought-provoking commentary on the way in which power—especially political power—is becoming increasingly hobbled.

Nye, Joseph S. (2015), *Is the American Century Over?* (Cambridge and Malden, MA: Polity).
A well-balanced analysis of the opportunities and challenges facing what is still the world's most powerful nation.

Poirson, Timothy, and Oprisko, Robert (eds) (2015), *Caliphates and Islamic Global Politics* (Bristol: E-International Relations).
Updates Ehteshami with more recent developments in the Middle East, including the rise of ISIS/ISIL.

Shambaugh, David (2014), *China Goes Global: The Partial Power* (New York: Oxford University Press).
A wide-ranging, persuasive analysis by one of America's foremost China-watchers.

US National Intelligence Council (2012), *Global Trends 2030: Alternative Worlds* (Washington, DC) (http://www.dni.gov/files/documents/GlobalTrends_2030.pdf, accessed January 2018).
The most recent set of scenarios for global trends, as seen from Washington, DC.

Zhang, Weiwei (2012), *The China Wave: Rise of a Civilizational State* (Hackensack, NJ: World Century).
Portrays the rise of China as a civilizational challenge to the West.

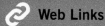 **Web Links**

http://ifg.org/
The International Forum on Globalization is a site devoted to research, advocacy, and activism.

http://sociology.emory.edu/faculty/globalization/organizations.html
A university site with lots of links to other sites focusing on globalization.

https://agenda.weforum.org/
The World Economic Forum analyses global issues primarily from the perspective of global business.

http://www.brics.utoronto.ca/
A site publicizing cooperation between the BRICS states.

 Visit the **Online Resources** that accompany this book to access more learning resources on this topic: www.oup.com/uk/ferdinand/

Glossary

Agency In social science literature, denotes the fact of something happening or existing because of an actor's action. The contrast is with a state of affairs that is chiefly determined by impersonal factors (historical, economic, etc.) over which human actors have little control. Hence the frequent use of the combined term structure–agency to pose the question whether background factors or human action were the primary causes.

Alternative member model A hybrid voting system that combines strengths of both majoritarianism and proportional representation, in which votes are cast both for individual candidates within a constituency and for a general list of candidates from separate parties.

Amoral familism The exaltation of family interests above all other moral considerations, originally coined by sociologist Banfield to describe social relations in Sicily.

Anarchy In its simplest sense, denotes an absence of political rule or sovereign authority. In traditional international relations theory, states are said to exist in an anarchic international sphere because there is no sovereign authority standing above individual states.

Anthropocentric An ethic that prioritizes the interests of humans over all other forms of life.

Anti-politics A phenomenon associated largely with the dissatisfaction felt in many contemporary Western countries with professional career politicians, party politics, and liberal democracy more generally.

Arrow's impossibility theorem A mathematical theorem formulated by economist Kenneth Arrow, which shows the impossibility of determining the 'optimal' ranking of preferences by members of a society when no alternative choice receives an absolute majority.

Authoritarian Refers to rule that is unaccountable and restrictive of personal liberty.

Authority A situation whereby an individual or group is regarded as having the right to exercise power and is thereby acting legitimately.

Balance of payments Refers to a country's international economic transactions over a certain period, showing the sum of all ingoing and outgoing sums between individuals, businesses, and government agencies in that country in relation to those in the rest of the world.

Behaviouralism An approach that stresses the importation of the scientific method in the study of social phenomena. Objective measurement of the social world is the goal, other values to be completely jettisoned from social enquiry.

Bicameralism The principle of having two separate chambers of a national parliament.

Bourgeoisie Term appearing frequently in Marxist analysis and referring to a merchant and/or propertied class possessing essential economic power and control.

Bretton Woods system Refers to an international system of monetary management, which includes the International Monetary Fund (IMF) and the World Bank, established following a meeting of Allied powers at Bretton Woods, New Hampshire, in 1944.

Cartel parties A type of party that has evolved from the mass party, with more limited membership and dominated by professional politicians.

Citizenship The granting of social and political rights to enable individuals to participate in state decision-making.

Civic culture A variety of political culture, where citizens predominantly feel capable of taking an active part in politics.

Civic nationalism Refers to loyalty to the institutions and values of a particular political community; sometimes presented as a more moderate form of nationalism.

Civil society Consists of institutions, such as interest groups, which stand in an intermediary position between the individual and the state. See also International civil society.

Class analysis Associated with traditional Marxism, which places socio-economic class (e.g. proletariat, peasantry, bourgeoisie, aristocracy) at the centre of virtually all political analysis.

Classical liberalism Emphasizes that the state's role should be limited to ensure internal and external security and to ensure that private property rights are enforced.

Cohabitation Occurs when a country's president comes from one party and the prime minister from a different one.

Cold War A description of the states system existing between the end of the Second World War in 1945 and the collapse of Soviet communism by the early 1990s. On the one side was the US, the dominant power in the West; on the other was the Soviet Union, the dominant power in the East.

Colonialism A mode of domination involving the subjugation of one population group and their territory to another, usually through settling the territory with sufficient people from the colonizing group to impose direct or indirect rule over the native population and to maintain control over resources and external relations. It is a common manifestation of imperialism, but is not identical with it.

Communitarianism A strand of thought which argues that individuals gain their rights and duties within particular communities. It is often contrasted with cosmopolitanism.

Consociational democracy A means whereby the elites of different parts of a heterogeneous community can share power and integrate society.

Consociationalism The principle that, in societies divided into major 'pillars' (ethnic, linguistic or religious), elites from each pillar should cooperate to devise acceptable national policies.

Constituency An electoral district.

Constitution The complex of relations between a state's governing institutions and the people, including the understandings that are involved. Most of these relations are usually codified in a single document.

Constitutionalism The principle that assigns a special significance to constitutions and rule of law in national life.

Constructivism Sometimes called *social* constructivism, refers to the notion that the 'reality' of the world around us is constructed intersubjectively through social interaction, which gives meaning to material objects and practices; thus 'reality' is not simply an objective truth detached from a social base.

Coordinated market economies Where firms depend more heavily on non-market relationships to coordinate their activities than in liberal Anglo-American economies; more typically found in continental Europe.

Corporatism Traditionally, referred to the top-down model where the state, as in the fascist model, incorporates economic interests in order to control them and civil society in general. Modern societal or neo-corporatism, on the other hand, reflects a genuine attempt by governments to incorporate economic interests, trade unions, and business interests into the decision-making process.

Cosmopolitan democracy A system of popular control of supranational institutions and processes.

Cosmopolitanism A position which holds that humans ought to be regarded as a single moral community to which universal principles apply irrespective of national boundaries.

Cultural pluralism The descriptive fact of the existence of different norms of behaviour determined by culture. Can be regarded as normatively desirable or undesirable.

Deliberative democracy A model of democracy emphasizing the role of discussion and debate as a means of reaching rational, legitimate, and altruistic decisions.

Democracy A political system in which 'the people' rule, or at least hold ultimate political authority.

Democratic elitism An attempt, most associated with Joseph Schumpeter, to reconcile elitism with democracy. According to this model, voters have the opportunity to choose between competing teams of leaders.

Democratization Denotes two overlapping processes: (i) the transition from non-democratic to democratic regimes; (ii) the expansion of democratic rule in basically democratic regimes to cover new areas of public decision-making.

Deontological An ethical theory which holds that certain end states (as in the case of a natural right) are to be upheld because they are right in themselves, irrespective of the consequences that accrue from them in particular circumstances.

Developmental state A state, such as Japan, which prioritizes economic resources for rapid development, and which uses carrots and sticks to induce private economic institutions to comply.

Dichotomy A division into two mutually exclusive or contradictory entities or groups such as 'the West' and the 'non-West'.

Direct democracy Refers to a system whereby the people rule directly and not through representatives.

Distributive justice Refers to the equitable distribution of goods in society and the means by which it is achieved.

Duverger's Law The conclusion by the French political scientist Maurice Duverger that first-past-the-post electoral systems lead to two-party systems.

Ecocentric An ethic that removes humans from the centre of the moral universe and accords intrinsic value to non-human parts of nature.

Ecological modernization A version of sustainable development that seeks to show how liberal capitalist societies can be reformed in an environmentally sustainable way.

Ecologism An ideology that stresses the interdependence of all forms of life and which is often used to denote the moral dethroning of humans.

Elitism In a normative sense, refers to the rule of the most able. From an empirical perspective, it refers to the existence of a ruling group beyond popular control in all societies of any complexity.

Elitist theory of democracy See Democratic elitism.

Emancipation A common theme in critical theory, which denotes a normative aspiration to liberate people from unfair economic, social, and political conditions.

Embedded autonomy The insulation of state economic policy-makers in developmental states from short-term political pressures.

Empire Shares a common etymology with imperialism and denotes a system in which one country or centre of power dominates and controls other, weaker, countries either directly or indirectly using either force, the threat of force, or some other means of coercion.

Empirical analysis Refers to the measurement of factual information—of what is rather than what ought to be.

Enlightenment A seventeenth- and eighteenth-century intellectual and cultural movement that emphasized the application of reason to knowledge in a search for human progress.

Epistemic communities Groups of specialists in various countries who share a common approach to a policy area that transcends national differences.

Epistemology Refers to the task of establishing what can be known about what exists.

Ethnic cleansing A term that emerged during the break-up of the former Yugoslavia and which referred to attempts to physically rid (i.e. 'cleanse') a particular area of people from a certain ethnic group by either driving them out or murdering them.

Ethnic nationalism Refers to loyalty to a shared inheritance based on culture, language, or religion.

Ethnocentrism The tendency to see and interpret the world primarily from the perspective of one's own cultural, ethnic, or national group. It often entails elements of hierarchy in that one tends to regard one's own culture as superior, or at least preferable, to others.

Ethnosymbolism The manipulation of mainly cultural symbols to strengthen national identity.

Eurocentrism The tendency to see the world only from the standpoint of Europe or the West and, in a stronger sense, to regard European or Western culture, politics, and society as superior to others.

Executive The branch of government responsible for the execution of policy. It is conceptually separate from the other two branches of government—legislative and judicial—and it comprises ministers (whether elected or not) and all government officials.

Federalism The principle that, within a state, different territorial units have the authority to make certain policies without interference from the centre.

Fordism Refers to a form of large-scale mass production that is homogeneous in terms of both the products made and the repetitive jobs that came with it.

Game theory A form of strategic theory that seeks to predict how people will act rationally vis-à-vis others to ensure or advance their own interests in particular circumstances.

General will A concept, associated with Rousseau, which holds that the state ought to promote an altruistic morality rather than the selfish interests of individuals.

Global governance This term extends the concept of governance to refer loosely to the 'architecture' constituted by various authoritative political, social, and economic structures and actors that interconnect and interact in the absence of actual 'government' in the global sphere.

Global justice The application of principles of justice at a global, rather than a national, level.

Global South Corresponds more or less to what was once commonly referred to as the 'Third World'; designates poorer, underdeveloped countries, most of which lie geographically south of the equator. Correspondingly, it requires a 'North', which is sometimes used as an alternate designation for 'the West'.

Globalization A term used to describe the process of increasing economic, political, social, and cultural interdependence, which has, for good or ill, reduced the autonomy of sovereign states.

Good governance A set of principles formulated by international financial institutions to make the government of developing states fair, effective, and free from corruption.

Governance A term often preferred now to government, since it reflects the broader nature of modern government, which includes not just the traditional institutions of government, but also the other inputs into decisions that steer society, such as sub-national and supranational institutions, the workings of the market, and the role of interest groups.

Harm principle A position, associated with John Stuart Mill, that actions are to be allowed unless the effect of them is to harm others.

Human nature Refers to innate and immutable human characteristics. Hobbes, for instance, regards the competitive and self-serving nature of humans as necessitating an all-powerful state. Other strands of thought either regard human nature in a more positive light or, as with Marx, suggest that human character depends upon the social and economic structure of society.

Humanitarian intervention This term implies direct intervention by one country, or a group of countries, in the internal affairs of another country, on the grounds that such intervention is justified by humanitarian concerns relating, for example, to genocide. See also Intervention.

Ideational Refers to the formation of ideas, concepts, or schemes that are not perceived simply as objects by the sense.

Illiberal democracy Describes states where competitive elections are held, but in which there is relatively little protection of rights and liberties, and state control over the means of communication ensures that governing parties are rarely defeated at the polls.

Imperialism Literally, 'to command', and denoting the exercise of power by one group over another. It is sometimes used synonymously with colonialism, but is broader in its application because it does not necessarily involve actual physical occupation of the territory in question or direct rule over the subjugated people.

Insider groups Interest groups enjoying a privileged relationship with government.

Institutions Regular patterns of behaviour that provide stability and regularity in social life; sometimes, these patterns are given organizational form, with specific rules of behaviour and of membership.

Interest groups Political actors who seek collectively to press specific interests upon governments (sometimes also called pressure groups).

Intergenerational justice Principles of justice relating to non-contemporaries, i.e. between those living now and those yet to be born.

International civil society Refers broadly to the realm of non-state actors, including interest groups and voluntary associations, in the international sphere.

International society Associated with the English School of international relations, denotes a world in which states attenuate international anarchy and establish greater predictability based on commonly recognized norms and rules.

Internationalism Refers to both a belief in the benefits of international political and economic cooperation and a movement that advocates practical action in support of these objectives.

Intragenerational justice Principles of justice relating to contemporaries, i.e. those who are living at the same time.

Iron triangles Groups of politicians, officials, and outside experts who regularly formulate government policy in particular issue areas to the exclusion of wider social groups.

Issue networks Looser groups of officials and outsiders who regularly share ideas in particular policy areas.

Legal positivism A form of legal theory that asserts that law is simply what the state says it is.

Legislature Institutions of government that have the power of making, amending, and repealing laws in a society. The term is often used interchangeably with 'parliament', but whereas the latter term focuses upon the role of the chamber(s) as an arena for debates over laws and policies, the term 'legislature' focuses more upon its law-making role.

Liberal democracy Describes states—such as the US, the UK, and India—which are characterized by free and fair elections involving universal suffrage, together with a liberal political framework consisting of a relatively high degree of personal liberty and the protection of individual rights.

Liberal institutionalism Closely associated with liberal internationalism, this concept focuses more attention on the ability of international institutions to ameliorate the negative effects of anarchy in the international system.

Machtpolitik See Power politics.

Marxism A set of ideas associated with German scholar and activist Karl Marx (1818–83). He wrote on an enormous range of subjects, but is associated above all with the idea that capitalism is not only unjust, but will be replaced by an egalitarian communist regime based on the principles of equality and common ownership. Since his death, Marxism has been adopted by numerous scholars, movements, and regimes. It was seen as the main ideological alternative to liberalism, but, since the collapse of the Soviet Union, its influence has waned somewhat.

Marxist See Marxism.

Mass parties Political parties, typically in the first half of the twentieth century, that attracted millions of grass-roots members.

Meritocratic theory of justice Advocates distributing resources to those who display some merit, such as innate ability, and therefore deserve to be rewarded.

Metanarrative Sometimes called a 'grand narrative', refers to a total philosophy or historical explanation of the social and political world presented as an ultimate truth.

Methodology Refers primarily to the particular way(s) in which knowledge is produced. Methodologies vary considerably depending on the type of research being carried out to produce knowledge in different fields—historical, anthropological, linguistic, biological, medical, etc. Different methodologies invariably incorporate their own assumptions and rationales about the nature of knowledge, although these are not always stated explicitly.

Modernity A temporal and cultural phenomenon linked not only to the rise of industrialization in Europe and North America, but also to profound changes in social and political thought that are closely associated with the intellectual movement known as the Enlightenment.

Monism The view that there are no fundamental divisions in phenomena.

Multiculturalism A philosophy that promotes respect for cultural, ethnic, religious, or other such differences within a society.

Nation A named community, often referred to as 'a people', usually occupying a homeland and sharing one or more cultural elements, such as a common history, language, religion, customs, etc. Nations may or may not have a state of their own.

National interest A concept closely associated with *raison d'état* and power politics. It suggests that the interests of the state (or at least of one's own state) are paramount over any other consideration in the international sphere. Although regarded as a foundational concept in realist approaches, it is as easily used to justify idealist approaches as well, indicating that what is actually in the national interest may be highly contested.

Nationalism A doctrine or ideology which generally holds that 'the nation' is entitled to political autonomy, preferably in a state of its own.

Natural law Law conceived as both universal and eternal, applying to all people in all places and at all times, because it derives either from 'nature' or God, as distinct from local laws arising within specific communities.

Natural rights Rights that humans are said to possess irrespective of the particular legal and political system under which they live.

Negative liberty Holds that liberty can be increased by removing external obstacles, provided by physical incarceration or law, to it.

Neo-liberalism A form of liberal ideology that reasserts the fundamental principles of the free market and private sector activity, while seeking to minimize government regulation and public sector activity.

Neo-medievalism A system of governance resembling Europe in the Middle Ages where authority belongs to an overlapping array of local, national, and supranational institutions.

New liberalism A version of liberalism that advocates a more positive role for the state than classical liberalism. Argues that the state, in correcting the inequities of the market, can increase liberty by creating greater opportunities for individuals to achieve their goals.

New Public Management An approach to the reform of government bureaucracies in the 1990s that sought to introduce methods of business administration.

Night-watchman state A model in which the state concentrates on ensuring external and internal security, playing little role in civil society and the economy, where the economic market is allowed to operate relatively unhindered.

Non-governmental organization (NGO) A term applying to almost any organization that operates independently from government, whether at the local, national, or international level.

Normative analysis Refers to analysis that asks 'ought' rather than 'is' type questions, therefore forming the basis of political philosophy. It does not seek to ask, therefore, whether democracy, or freedom, or a pluralist state exists, but rather whether these outcomes are desirable ones.

Ontology Relates to what exists. It asks: what is there to know? Is there, for instance, a political world out there capable of being observed, or is the reality, to at least some degree, created by the meanings or ideas we impose upon it?

Original position A device used by John Rawls to denote a position where individuals meet to decide the rules of justice governing the society in which they are to live.

Outsider groups Interest groups that enjoy no special relationship with the government and thus seek to press their case from the outside.

Parliamentarianism The principle that governments are formed by prime ministers, rather than heads of state, who are primarily responsible to parliament.

Paternalism The practice, often associated with conservatism, of restricting the liberty of individuals in order to benefit them.

Patriarchy A system of male domination and corresponding female subordination.

Perestroika The policy of attempted restructuring of the Soviet political system under President Gorbachev in the late 1980s.

Pluralism Originated as a normative argument against monism or sameness. In political theory, it is most associated with a theory of the state which holds that political power is diffuse, all organized groups having some influence on state outputs. In international relations, it is associated with one of two main approaches adopted by the 'English School', as well as with neo-liberal theory, which highlights the multiplicity, or plurality, of forces at work in the international system.

Pluralist See Pluralism.

Plurality A simple majority in voting (sometimes also known as first-past-the-post), as distinct from an absolute majority (i.e. 50 per cent plus one).

Policy communities Groups of officials and experts in particular policy areas who regularly consult each other.

Political culture The aggregate attitudes of members of a society towards the institutions of rule and how they should operate.

Political obligation A central preoccupation of political theorists asking why, if at all, individuals ought to obey the state. There have been a variety of different answers to this question ranging from the divine right of kings to rule to the modern claim that democracy is the basis for authority.

Political party A group of political activists who aspire to form or be part of the government on the basis of a programme of policies.

Political system The totality of institutions within a state and all the connections between them.

Polyarchy A term coined by Robert Dahl; refers to a society where government outcomes are a product of the competition between groups. The rule of minorities, not majorities, is postulated as the normal condition of pluralist democracies.

Populism A political approach that appeals to ordinary people who feel that their concerns are disregarded by established elite groups (*Oxford Living Dictionary*).

Positive discrimination Refers to the practice of discriminating in favour of those disadvantaged groups who, it is argued, will remain disadvantaged unless affirmative action is taken in their favour.

Positive liberty A theory which holds that liberty can be increased either by state action or by removing internal obstacles, such as immorality or irrationality.

Positivism An approach that believes it is possible to generate empirical statements without any evaluative connotations. At an extreme level, so-called logical positivists argue that only empirical statements, together with those that are true by definition, are meaningful, thereby ruling out the value of normative statements.

Positivist See Positivism.

Postmodernism A multifaceted theoretical approach that challenges the certainties and dualisms of modernism. It therefore promotes pluralism and difference.

Post-politics Refers to the notion that there is such a convergence of ideas and attitudes around key themes and issues, at least in Western societies, that real political differences no longer exist or are increasingly irrelevant.

Power The ability to make others do something that they would not have chosen to do.

Power politics A view of politics associated with realism, which generally takes morality and justice to be irrelevant to the conduct of international relations—a view predicated in turn on the notion that 'might is right'.

Presidentialism The principle that the president of a republic is the head of the government.

Principal–agent relations Identifies the differentiation of roles between the giver of instructions, usually in government administration, and the implementer.

Procedural justice The distribution of goods according to a set of rules, irrespective of the outcome.

Proportional representation A family of voting systems that make their highest priority a close approximation between the votes given to all the parties putting up candidates and the number of seats into which this is translated in parliament.

Protectionism An economic strategy, usually associated with a national policy of trade restriction in the form of tariffs and quotas, which attempts to protect domestic industries, businesses, and jobs from competition from abroad.

Public space The arena (real or virtual) in which any member of society is free to express views on any issue of interest to the public. Sometimes associated with German philosopher Habermas, who stressed its key importance for democracy and the difficulty of maintaining it under capitalism.

Realism Denotes a complex array of theories and ideas that emphasize the competitive and conflictual aspects of political behaviour, with power as the principal dynamic.

Reason of state (*raison d'état*) See National interest.

Rechtsstaat Literally, a law-based state, as distinct from a state where the ruler or executive is free to adopt policies and change them as they see fit.

Regionalization A process in which a number of states in a given geographical area come together for mutually beneficial purposes, often forming a regional association. Some, like the EU, are highly institutionalized and have myriad economic, social, and political interconnections, while others may have minimal rules and less ambitious purposes.

Religious fundamentalism A particular type of ideology. To be a fundamentalist is to be convinced of the truth of the doctrine one is professing (in the case of religious fundamentalism, based on an interpretation of a sacred text) and to seek to ensure that these truths are adopted by the state, even through the use of force and violence.

Representative democracy Refers to a system whereby the people choose others to represent their interests, rather than make decisions themselves.

Rule of law The principle that everyone in a state, the executive included, is subject to the same impersonal laws.

Secularism Reflects the basic principle that the institutions of government and the state should operate independently of any and all religious institutions and, conversely, that religion is a matter of individual choice and is not to be dictated by the state.

Self-determination A doctrine that emerged in the early twentieth century in relation to the right of 'peoples' (nations) to determine their own political future, thus embodying elements of both democracy and nationalism.

Social capital The aggregate set of attitudes and networks that enable members of a society to cooperate willingly in pursuit of joint projects.

Social constructivism See Constructivism.

Social contract A device used by a number of political thinkers, most recently John Rawls, to justify a particular form of state. It is conceived as a voluntary agreement that individuals make in a state of nature, which is a society before government is set up.

Social Darwinism The application of Darwin's theory of natural selection to social life. It was used by the social theorist Herbert Spencer to justify a laissez-faire approach to social policy to ensure that only the fittest survive.

Social democracy An approach that, after the Russian Revolution in 1917, became associated with liberal democracies that engaged in redistributive policies and the creation of a welfare state.

Social democratic See Social democracy.

Social justice The principle that goods ought to be distributed according to a principle based on need, merit, or pure equality.

Social movement Refers to largely informal broad-based movements composed of groups and individuals coalescing around key issue areas on a voluntary and often spontaneous basis. Examples include the environmental movement, women's movement, peace movement, and anti-globalization movement.

Sovereignty Refers to self-government either at the level of the individual or at the level of the state. To say that a state is sovereign is to claim that it has a monopoly of force over the people and institutions in a given territorial area.

State A two-level concept: (i) the government executive of a country, sometimes also known as a nation-state; (ii) the whole structure of political authority in a country.

State of nature A concept with a long history in political and social thought that posits a hypothetical vision of how people lived before the institution of civil government and society. There are various competing versions of the state of nature, some portraying it as dangerous, while others see it in a more positive light.

Statecraft The skilful conduct of state affairs, usually in the context of external relations.

Structural adjustment Used in application to economic policies imposed on countries—usually poor and underdeveloped—by the World Bank and the International Monetary Fund as a condition for obtaining loans, so as to reduce fiscal deficits. Specific policies have included privatization, cuts in government expenditure on public services, devaluation, tariff cuts, and so on.

Structuration A concept derived from sociologist Anthony Giddens, which here designates all of the factors that both constrain and provide resources for the functioning of a political system.

Sustainable development A term that seeks to denote the compatibility between environmental protection and economic growth.

Totalitarian Refers to an extreme version of authoritarian rule, in which the state controls all aspects of society and the economy.

Totalitarianism See Totalitarian.

Unicameralism The principle of having a single chamber of a national parliament.

Utilitarianism A consequentialist ethical theory which argues that the behaviour of individuals and governments should be judged according to the degree to which their actions maximize pleasure or happiness.

Utopia Refers to an ideal state of affairs that does not exist, but which can be aimed for. The search for utopias is seen by some as a worthwhile exercise to expand the limits of human imagination and by others as a recipe for illiberal, authoritarian, and even totalitarian societies.

References

Abi-Saab, Georges (ed.) (1981), *The Concept of International Organization* (Paris: UNESCO).

Abord de Chatillon, Renaud (1994), *La Politique des transports en France* (Paris: Eds Eska).

Abrahamsen, Rita, and Leander, Anna (eds) (2015), *Routledge Handbook of Private Security Studies* (Abingdon: Routledge).

Abrahamsen, Rita, and Williams, Michael C. (2011), *Security beyond the State: Private Security in International Politics* (Cambridge: Cambridge University Press).

Achen, Christopher H., and Bartels, Larry M. (2016), *Democracy for Realists: Why Elections Do Not Produce Responsive Government* (Oxford and Princeton, NJ: Princeton University Press).

Adamolekun, Ladipo (2007), 'Africa: Rehabilitating Civil Service Institutions—Main Issues and Implementation Progress', in Jos C. N. Raadschelders, Teho A. J. Toonen, and Frits M. Van der Meer (eds), *The Civil Service in the 21st Century: Comparative Perspectives* (Basingstoke: Palgrave), 82–99.

Aldrich, John H. (1995), *Why Parties? The Origin and Transformation of Political Parties in America* (Chicago, IL: Chicago University Press).

Alfreds, L.-A. (2014), 'A Killer in More Ways than One', *Corruption Watch*, 7 March (http://www.corruptionwatch. org.za/a-killer-in-more-ways-than-one/, accessed January 2018).

Ali, T. (2002), *The Clash of Fundamentalisms* (London: Verso).

Allen, Danielle, and Light, Jennifer S. (eds) (2015), *From Voice to Influence: Understanding Citizenship in a Digital Age* (London and Chicago, IL: University of Chicago Press).

Allison, Graham T. (1971), *Essence of Decision: Explaining the Cuban Missile Crisis* (Boston, MA.: Little, Brown).

Alston, Philip (2006), 'Reconceiving the UN Human Rights Regime: Challenges Confronting the New UN Human Rights Council', *Melbourne Journal of International Law*, 7(1): 185–224.

Anderlini, J. (2015), '"Western Values" Forbidden in Chinese Universities', *Financial Times*, 30 January (https://www. ft.com/content/95f3f866-a87e-11e4-bd17-00144feab7de, accessed January 2018).

Anderson, Benedict (1990), *Language and Power: Exploring Political Cultures in Indonesia* (Ithaca, NY: Cornell University Press).

Anderson, Benedict (2006), *Imagined Communities: Reflections on the Origins and Spread of Nationalism* (London: Verso, rev edn).

Anderson, Berit, and Horvath, Brett (2017), 'The Rise of the Weaponized AI Propaganda Machine' (https://scout.ai/ story/the-rise-of-the-weaponized-ai-propaganda-machine, accessed May 2017).

Anderson, James (1988), 'Nationalist Ideology and Territory', in R. J. Johnston, D. Knight, and E. Kofman (eds), Nationalism, Self-Determination, and the World Political Map: An Introduction (London: Croom Helm), 18–39.

Arblaster, A. (1984), *The Rise and Decline of Western Liberalism* (Oxford: Basil Blackwell).

Arblaster, A. (2002), *Democracy* (Milton Keynes: Open University Press).

Archer, Clive (1983), *International Organizations* (London: Allen & Unwin).

Archibugi, D. (1995), 'From the United Nations to Cosmopolitan Democracy', in D. Archibugi and D. Held (eds), *Cosmopolitan Democracy: An Agenda for a New World Order* (Cambridge: Polity Press), 121–62.

Arditi, Benjamin (2007), *Politics on the Edges of Liberalism: Difference, Populism, Revolution, Agitation* (Edinburgh: Edinburgh University Press).

Arora, Balveer (2003), 'The Indian Parliament and Democracy', in Ajay K. Mehra and Gert W. Kueck (eds), *The Indian Parliament: A Comparative Perspective* (Delhi: Konarck), 14–37.

Asa-El, Amotz (2008), 'Israel's Electoral Complex', *Azure*, 31 (Winter) (http://www.azure.org.il/magazine/magazine. asp?id=419, accessed January 2018).

Ashcroft, Michael, and Culwick, Kevin (2016), *Well, You Did Ask … Why the UK Voted to Leave the EU* (London: Biteback).

Aspinall, Edward (2015), 'The New Nationalism in Indonesia', *Asia and the Pacific Policy Studies*, 3(1): 72–82.

Assiter, A. (1996), *Enlightened Women: Modernist Feminism in a Postmodern Age* (London and New York: Routledge).

Avineri, S., and de-Shalt, A. (eds) (1992), *Communitarianism and Individualism* (Oxford: Oxford University Press).

Axiarlis, Evangelia (2014), *Political Islam and the Secular State in Turkey: Democracy, Reform and the Justice and Development Party* (London: I.B. Tauris).

Ayer, A. J. (1971), *Language, Truth and Logic* (Harmondsworth: Penguin, 2nd edn).

Bachrach, P. (1967), *The Theory of Democratic Elitism* (Boston, MA: Little, Brown).

Bachrach, P., and Baratz, M. (1963), 'Decisions and Non-Decisions', *American Political Science Review*, 57: 632–42.

Bachrach, P., and Baratz, M. (1970), *Power and Poverty: Theory and Practice* (New York: Oxford University Press).

Bailey, Matthew (2011), 'The Uses and Abuses of British Political Fiction or How I Learned to Stop Worrying and Love Malcolm Tucker', *Parliamentary Affairs*, 64(2): 281–95.

Bajpai, R. (2011), *Debating Difference: Group Rights and Liberal Democracy in India* (New Delhi: Oxford University Press).

Baktiari, Bahman (1996), *Parliamentary Politics in Iran: The Institutionalization of Factional Politics* (Gainesville, FL: Florida University Press).

Balaam, David N., and Veseth, Michael (2005), *Introduction to International Political Economy* (Upper Saddle River, NJ: Pearson Education, 3rd edn).

Balibar, Etienne (1991), 'Racism and Nationalism' in Etienne Balibar and Immanuel Wallerstein (eds), *Race, Nation, Class: Ambiguous Identities* (London: Verso), 37–68.

Balzli, Beat (2010), 'How Goldman Sachs Helped Greece to Mask Its True Debt', *Spiegel Online*, 2 August (http://www.spiegel.de/international/europe/0,1518,676634,00.html, accessed June 2011).

Banerjee, Mukulika (2014), *Why India Votes?* (New Delhi: Routledge).

Banks, Arron (2017), *The Bad Boys of Brexit: Tales of Mischief, Mayhem and Guerrilla Warfare in the EU Referendum Campaign* (London: Biteback).

Barber, Benjamin (1998), 'Three Scenarios for the Future of Technology and Strong Democracy', *Political Science Quarterly*, 113: 573–89.

Barber, Benjamin (2003), *Strong Democracy: Participatory Politics for a New Age* (London and Berkeley, CA: University of California Press, 2nd edn).

Barber, Michael (2007), *Instruction to Deliver: Tony Blair, Public Services and the Challenge of Achieving Targets* (London: Politico's).

Barnett, Steven, and Townend, Judith (2014), '"And What Good Came of It at Last?" Press–Politician Relations Post-Leveson', *Political Quarterly*, 85(2): 159–69.

Barnett, Steven (2002), 'Will the Crisis in Journalism Provoke a Crisis in Democracy?', *Political Quarterly*, 73(4): 400–8.

Barnett, Vincent (2013), *John Maynard Keynes* (Abingdon: Routledge).

Barrett, M. (1988), *Women's Oppression Today* (London: Verso).

Barry, B. (1970), *Sociologists, Economics and Democracy* (Basingstoke: Collier Macmillan).

Barry, B. (2001), *Culture and Equality: An Egalitarian Critique of Multiculturalism* (Cambridge: Polity Press).

Barry, J. (1999), *Rethinking Green Politics* (London: Sage).

Barry, N. (2000), *An Introduction to Modern Political Theory* (Basingstoke: Macmillan, 4th edn).

Barry, N. (2006), 'Defending Luck Egalitarianism', *Journal of Applied Philosophy*, 23(1): 89–107.

Bartash, Jeffry (2017), 'Trump Calls US–Mexico Trade One-Sided—And Here's the Reality', *Market Watch*, 27 January (http://www.marketwatch.com/story/trump-calls-us-mexico-trade-one-sided-heres-the-reality-2017-01-26, accessed January 2018).

Barton, Dominic, Chen, Yougang, and Jin, Amy (2013), 'Mapping China's Middle Class', *McKinsey Quarterly*, June (http://www.mckinsey.com/insights/consumer_and_retail/mapping_chinas_middle_class, accessed April 2015).

Baumgartner, Frank R., and Jones, Bryan D. (1993), *Agendas and Instability in American Politics* (Chicago, IL: Chicago University Press).

Bayart, Jean-François (1993), *The State in Africa: The Politics of the Belly* (London: Longman).

BBC (2017), 'Brexit: Race to Host EU Agencies Relocated from London', 31 July (http://www.bbc.co.uk/news/uk-40772332, accessed January 2018).

Becker, Ted, and Slaton, Christa Daryl (2000), *The Future of Teledemocracy* (Westport, CT: Praeger).

Beetham, David, Bracking, Sarah, Kearton, Iain, and Weir, Stuart (2002), *International IDEA Handbook on Democracy Assessment* (London: Kluwer).

Beitz, C. (1979), *Political Theory and International Relations* (Princeton, NJ: Princeton University Press).

bell hooks (1981), *Ain't I a Woman? Black Women and Feminism* (London: Pluto Press).

Bell, D. (1960), *The End of Ideology* (Glencoe, IL: Free Press).

Bell, Daniel A., Brown, David, Jayasuriya, Kanishka, and Jones, David Martin (1995), *Towards Illiberal Democracy in Pacific Asia* (Basingstoke: Macmillan).

Bell, Daniel (2006), *Beyond Liberal Democracy: Political Thinking for an East Asian Context* (Princeton, NJ: Princeton UP).

Bellamy, Alex J. (2006), 'Whither the Responsibility to Protect? Humanitarian Intervention and the 2005 World Summit', *Ethics and International Affairs*, 20(2): 143–69.

Benjamin, Medea, and Davis, Charles (2011), 'A Look back at Eight Years of War in Iraq', (http://english.aljazeera.net/indepth/opinion/2011/03/201132173052269144.html, accessed April 2011).

Bennett, Owen (2017), *The Brexit Club: The Inside Story of the Leave Campaign's Shock Victory* (London: Biteback).

Bennett, W. Lance, and Iyengar, Shanto (2008), 'A New Era of Minimal Effects? The Changing Foundations of Political Communication', *Journal of Communication*, 58: 707–31.

Bennett, W. Lance, and Segerberg, Alexandra (2013), *The Logic of Collective Action: Digital Media and the Personalization of Contentious Politics* (Cambridge: Cambridge University Press).

Bentham, J. (1948), *An Introduction to the Principles of Morals and Legislation* (New York: Hafner Press).

Berggruenn, Nicolas, and Gardels, Nathan (2013), *Intelligent Governance for the 21st Century: A Middle Way between East and West* (Cambridge: Polity).

Berlin, I. (1969), *Four Essays on Liberty* (Oxford: Oxford University Press).

Bevir, Mark, and Rhodes, R. A. W. (2006), *Governance Stories* (London: Routledge).

Bevir, R., and Rhodes, R. A. W. (2002), 'Interpretive Theory', in D. Marsh and G. Stoker (eds), *Theory and Methods in Political Science* (Basingstoke: Palgrave), 131–52.

Bingham, Tom (2011), *The Rule of Law* (London: Penguin).

Biorcio, Roberto (2014), *L'aggresività dei populismi* (Milan: Casa della Cultura).

Biorcio, Roberto (ed.) (2015a), *Gli attivisti del Movimento 5 Stelle: Dal web al territorio* (Milan: FrancoAngeli).

Biorcio, Roberto (2015b), *Il populismo nella politica italiana: Da Bossi a Berlusconi, da Grillo a Renzi* (Milan: Passato Prossimo/Presente Italiano).

Biorcio, Roberto, and Natale, Paolo (2013), *Politica a 5 stelle: Idee, storia e strategia del movimento di Grillo* (Milan: Feltrinelli).

Blom-Hansen, J. (2000), 'Still Corporatism in Scandinavia?', *Scandinavian Political Studies*, 23(2): 157–78.

Blowers, A. (1984), *Something in the Air: Corporate Power and the Environment* (London: Harper & Row).

Blumler, Jay, and Gurevich, Michael (2007), 'Politicians and the Press: An Essay on Role Relationships', in Ralph Negrine and James Stanyer (eds), *The Political Communication Reader* (London and New York: Routledge), 49–53.

Bobbitt, Philip (2003), *The Shield of Achilles: War, Peace and the Course of History* (London: Penguin).

Boix, Carles, and Stokes, Susan (2003) 'Endogenous Democratization', *World Politics*, 55(4): 517–49.

Bonnett, Alastair (2004), *The Idea of the West: Culture, Politics and History* (Basingstoke: Palgrave).

Bookchin, M. (1971), *Post-Scarcity Anarchism* (Berkeley, CA: Ramparts).

Booysen, Susan (2011), *The African National Congress and the Regeneration of Political Power* (Johannesburg: Wits University Press).

Borchert, J. (2003),'Professional Politicians: Towards a Comparative Perspective', in J. Borchert and J. Zeiss (eds), *The Political Class in Advanced Democracies* (Oxford: Oxford University Press), 1–25.

Boucher, David (1998), *Political Theories of International Relations: From Thucydides to the Present* (Oxford: Oxford University Press).

Boundary Commission for England (2007), *Fifth Periodical Report, Vol. 1* (London: HMSO, CM7032).

Bradshaw, Samantha, and Howard, Philip N. (2017), *Troops, Trolls and Troublemakers: A Global Inventory of Organized Social Media Manipulation* (Oxford Internet Institute Working Paper 2017.12) (https://www.oii.ox.ac.uk/blog/video-is-social-media-killing-democracy-computational-propaganda-algorithms-automation-and-public-life/, accessed January 2018).

Bramwell, A. (1989), *Ecology in the Twentieth Century* (New Haven, CT: Yale University Press).

Brandt, R. (1992), *Morality, Utilitarianism, and Rights* (Cambridge: Cambridge University Press).

Brass, Jennifer N. (2017), 'Development Theory', in Christopher Ansell and Jacob Torfing (eds), *Handbook on Theories of Governance* (Cheltenham: Edward Elgar), 115–25.

Breitbart, Andrew (2012), *Righteous Indignation: Excuse Me While I Save the World!* (Boston, MA: Grand Central).

Breuilly, John (1993), *Nationalism and the State* (Manchester: Manchester University Press, 2nd edn).

Breuilly, John (ed.) (2013), *The Oxford Handbook of the History of Nationalism* (Oxford: Oxford University Press).

Brinded, Lianna (2016), 'The 17 Countries with the Highest Level of Government Debt', *Business Insider* (http://www.businessinsider.com/wef-countries-highest-level-of-government-debt-vs-gdp-2016-4?IR=T/#17-iceland–902-prior-to-the-credit-crisis-in-2007-government-debt-was-a-modest-27-of-gdp-at-the-time-of-wefs-rankings-its-debt-was-still-super-high-1, accessed January 2018).

Britten, S. (1977), *The Economic Consequences of Democracy* (London: Temple Smith).

Brooker, Paul (2014), *Non-Democratic Regimes* (Basingstoke: Palgrave, 3rd edn).

Brown, David (2000), *Contemporary Nationalism: Civic, Ethnocultural and Multicultural Politics* (London: Routledge).

Brown, Melissa J. (2004), *Is Taiwan Chinese? The Impact of Culture, Power and Migration on Changing Identities* (Berkely, CA: University of California Press).

Bruce, Iain (ed.) (2004), *The Porto Alegre Alternative: Direct Democracy in Action* (London: Pluto Press).

Bryson, V. (1999), *Feminist Debates* (Basingstoke: Macmillan).

Budge, Ian (1996), *The New Challenge of Direct Democracy* (Cambridge: Polity Press).

Bugre, Ayse, and SavasKan, Osman (2014), *New Capitalism in Turkey: The Relationship between Politics, Religion and Business* (Cheltenham: Edward Elgar).

Burke, Edmund (1790/1968), *Reflections on the Revolution in France* (Harmondsworth: Penguin).

Burke, Edmund (1996), *The Writings and Speeches of Edmund Burke, Vol. III*, ed. W. M. Elofson, with John A. Woods (Oxford: Clarendon Press).

Burnell, Peter (2012) 'Democracy, Democratization and Climate Change: Complex Relationships', *Democratization*, 19(5): 813–42.

Burnham, J. (1941), *The Managerial Revolution* (New York: Day).

Butler, Geoffrey G., and MacCoby, Simon (2003), *Development of International Law* (Union, NJ: Lawbook Exchange).

Buttigieg, Joseph A. (1995), 'Gramsci on Civil Society', *boundary 2*, 22(3): 1–32.

Buxbaum, R. M. (2004), 'Law, Diffusion of', in Neil J. Smelser and Paul B. Baltes (eds), *International Encyclopedia of the Social and Behavioral Sciences* (Amsterdam: Elsevier), 1–7.

Buzan, Barry (1991), *People, States and Fear* (London: Harvester Wheatsheaf, 2nd edn).

Cadwalladr, Carole (2017), 'The Great British Brexit Robbery: How Our Democracy Was Hijacked', *The Observer*, 7 May (https://www.theguardian.com/technology/2017/may/07/the-great-british-brexit-robbery-hijacked-democracy, accessed May 2017).

Cagaptay, Soner (2017), *The New Sultan: Erdogan and the Crisis of Modern Turkey* (London and New York: I.B. Tauris).

Calder, Kent E. (1993), *Strategic Capitalism: Private Business and Public Purpose in Japanese Industrial Finance* (Princeton, NJ: Princeton University Press).

Callahan, Mary P. (2003), *Making Enemies: War and State-Building in Burma* (Ithaca, NY: Cornell University Press).

Caney, S. (2008), 'Human Rights, Climate Change and Discounting', *Environmental Politics*, 17(4): 536–55.

Canovan, Margaret (2002), 'Taking Politics to the People as the Ideology of Democracy', in Yves Mény and Yves Surel (eds), *Democracies and the Populist Challenge* (Basingstoke: Palgrave), 25–44.

Caplan, Bryan (2007), *The Myth of the Rational Voter: Why Democracies Choose Bad Policies* (Oxford and Princeton, NJ: Princeton University Press).

Carbaugh, Robert (2016), *International Economics* (Boston, MA: Cengage Learning, 16th edn).

Carothers, Thomas (2002), 'The End of the Transition Paradigm', *Journal of Democracy*, 13(1): 5–21.

Carothers, Thomas (2006), *Confronting the Weakest Link: Aiding Political Parties in New Democracies* (Washington, DC: Carnegie Endowment).

Carruthers, P. (1992), *The Animals Issue* (Cambridge: Cambridge University Press).

Casaleggio, Gianroberto, and Grillo, Beppe (2011), *Siamo in guerra: Per una nuova politica* (Milan: Chiarelettere).

Castells, Manuel (1998), *The End of Millennium, the Information Age: Economy, Society and Culture, Vol. III* (Oxford: Blackwell).

Cathcart, Brian (2012), *Everybody's Hacked off: Why We Don't Have the Press We Deserve and What to Do about It* (London: Penguin).

Cavatorta, Francesco (2012), *Arab Spring: The Awakening of Civil Society—A General Overview* (Barcelona: IEMed) (http://www.iemed.org/observatori-en/arees-danalisi/arxius-adjunts/anuari/med.2012/Cavatorta_en.pdf, accessed 29 May 2015).

CDD (Centre for Deliberative Democracy) (2006), *First Deliberative Polling® for Candidate Selection in Marousi, Greece: A Summary*, 15 June (http://cdd.stanford.edu/2006/results-of-the-first-deliberative-polling-for-candidate-selection-in-marousi-greece/, accessed January 2018).

Chabal, Patrick, and Daloz, Jean-Pascal (1999), *Africa Works: Disorder as Political Instrument* (Oxford: International African Institute, in association with James Currey).

Chadwick, Andrew (2013), *The Hybrid Media System: Politics and Power* (Oxford: Oxford University Press).

Chakrabarty, Dipesh (2000), *Provincializing Europe* (Princeton, NJ: Princeton University Press).

Chandhoke, Neera (2003), *The Conceits of Civil Society* (New Delhi: Oxford University Press).

Chapman, Malcolm, McDonald, Maryon, and Tonkin, Elizabeth (2016), 'Introduction: History and Social Anthropology', in Elizabeth Tonkin, Maryon McDonald, and Malcolm Chapman (eds), *History and Ethnicity* (Abingdon: Routledge), 1–21.

Chapman, Simon (2013), 'One Hundred and Fifty Ways the Nanny State Is Good for Us', *The Conversation*, 1 July (http://theconversation.com/one-hundred-and-fifty-ways-the-nanny-state-is-good-for-us-15587, accessed January 2018).

Chappell, Hilary M. (2016), 'Introduction: Ways of Tackling Diversity in Sinitic Languages', in Hilary M. Chappell (ed.), *Diversity in Sinitic Languages* (Oxford: Oxford University Press), 3–12.

Chatterjee, P. (2001), 'Subaltern History', in Neil J. Smelser and Paul B. Baltes (eds), *International Encyclopedia of the Social and Behavioral Sciences* (Amsterdam: Elsevier), 15237–41.

Chatterjee, Partha (2010), 'The Poverty of Western Political Theory: Concluding Remarks on Concepts Like "Community" East and West', in Aakash Singh and Silika Mohapatra (eds), *Indian Political Thought: A Reader* (London: Routledge), 287–99.

Cheibub, Jose Antonio (2007), *Presidentialism, Parliamentarianism and Democracy* (Cambridge: Cambridge University Press).

Chen, Jie (2013), *A Middle Class without Democracy: Economic Growth and the Prospects for Democratization in China* (Oxford and New York: Oxford University Press).

Cherribi, Sam (2012), 'Al-Jazeera Arabic, Transnational Identity and Influence', in Holli A. Semetko and Margaret Scammell (eds), *The Sage Handbook of Political Communication* (Los Angeles, CA: Sage), 472–83.

Chew, Jonathan (2016), '7 Corporate Giants Accused of Evading Billions in Taxes', *Fortune International*, 11 March (http://fortune.com/2016/03/11/apple-google-taxes-eu/, accessed January 2018).

Christoff, Peter (2005), 'Out of Chaos, a Shining Star? Toward a Typology of Green States', in John Barry and Robyn Eckersley (eds), *The State and the Global Ecological Crisis* (Cambridge, MA: MIT Press), 25–52.

CINIC (China Internet Network Information Center) (2014), *34th Statistical Report on Internet Development in China'* (2014) (https://cnnic.com.cn/IDR/ReportDownloads/201411/P020141102574314897888.pdf, accessed April 2015).

Clapham, Christopher (1996), *Africa and the International System: The Politics of State Survival* (Cambridge: Cambridge University Press).

Clark, Ian (2005), *Legitimacy in International Society* (Oxford: Oxford University Press).

Clarke, Harold D., Goodwin, Matthew, and Whiteley, Paul (2017), *Brexit: Why Britain Voted to Leave the European Union* (Cambridge: Cambridge University Press).

Clarke, Michael (2014), 'China's West Bank: The Alienation of the Uyghur', *Asian Currents*, August (http://asaa.asn.au/chinas-west-bank-the-alienation-of-the-uyghur/, accessed January 2018).

Clift, Ben (2014), *Comparative Political Economy: States, Markets and Global Capitalism* (Basingstoke: Palgrave Macmillan).

CNN (2017), 'Inaugural Address: Trump's Full Speech', 21 January (http://edition.cnn.com/2017/01/20/politics/trump-inaugural-address/index.html. accessed January 2018).

Cobham, Alex, and Jansky, Petr (2017), *Global Distribution of Revenue Loss from Tax Avoidance* (UNU-WIDER Working Paper 2017/55, March) (https://www.wider.unu.edu/sites/default/files/wp2017-55.pdf, accessed January 2018).

Cohen, G. (1979), 'Capitalism, Freedom and the Proletariat', in A. Ryan (ed.), *The Idea of Freedom* (Oxford: Oxford University Press), 8–25.

Cohen-Almagor, Raphael (2014), 'After Leveson: Recommendations for Instituting the Public and Press Council', *International Journal of Press/Politics*, 19(2): 202–25.

Cohn, Theodore H. (2005), *Global Political Economy: Theory and Practice* (New York: Pearson Longman, 3rd edn).

Coleman, Stephen (2017), *Can the Internet Strengthen Democracy?* (Cambridge: Polity Press).

Coleman, Stephen and Blumler, Jay (2009), *The Internet and Democratic Citizenship* (Oxford: Oxford University Press).

Collier, D., and Levitsky, S. (1997), 'Democracy with Adjectives: Conceptual Innovation in Comparative Research', *World Politics*, 49(3): 430–51.

Colomer, Josep M. (ed.) (2004), 'The Strategy and History of Electoral System Choice', in Josep M. Colomer (ed.), *Handbook of Electoral System Choice* (Basingstoke: Palgrave), 1–73.

Colomer, Josep M. (2007), *Great Empires, Small Nations* (London: Routledge).

Comaroff, John L., and Comaroff, Jean (eds) (1999), *Civil Society and the Political Imagination in Africa: Critical Perspectives* (Chicago, IL: Chicago University Press).

Commonwealth Fund (2013), *International Profiles of Health Care Systems, 2013* (New York) (http://www.commonwealthfund.org/publications/fund-reports/2013/nov/international-profiles-of-health-care-systems, accessed May 2015).

Cooper, Ian (2013), 'Bicameral or Tricameral: National Parliaments and Representative Democracy in the European Union', *Journal of European Integration*, 35(5): 531–46.

Coppedge, Michael (2002), 'Venezuela: Popular Sovereignty Versus Liberal Democracy', in Jorge I. Dominguez and Michael Shifter (eds), *Constructing Democratic Governance* (Baltimore, MD: Johns Hopkins University Press, 2nd edn), 165–92.

Corbett, Richard, Jacobs, Francis, and Neville, Darren (2016), *The European Parliament* (London: John Harper, 9th edn).

Coronel, Sheila S., Chua, Yvonne T., Cruz, Boomba B., and Rimban, Luz (2004), *The Rulemakers: How the Wealthy and Well-Born Dominate Congress* (Quezon City: Philippine Center for Investigative Journalism).

Coronil, Fernando (1997), *The Magical State: Nature, Money, and Modernity in Venezuela* (Chicago, IL: Chicago University Press).

Corrales, Javier, and Penfold, Michael (2007), 'Venezuela: Crowding out the Opposition', *Journal of Democracy*, 18(2): 99–113.

Council of Europe (2004), *The Future of Democracy in Europe: Trends, Analyses and Reforms* (Strasbourg) (http://www.europarl.europa.eu/RegData/etudes/note/join/2008/408339/IPOL-AFCO_NT(2008)408339_EN.pdf, accessed January 2018).

Cowley, Philip, and Ford, Robert (eds) (2014), *Sex, Lies and the Ballot Box* (London: Biteback).

Cox, Robert (1981), 'Social Forces, States and World Orders: Beyond International Relations', *Millennium*, 10(2): 126–55.

Cracknell, Richard (2005), *Social Background of MPs*, (Houses of Parliament Standard Note 1528, London).

Crenshaw, K. (1989), 'Demarginalizing the Intersection of Race and Sex: A Black Feminist Critique of Antidiscrimination Doctrine, Feminist Theory, and Antiracist Politics', *University of Chicago Legal Forum*, 140: 139–67.

Crenson, M. (1971), *The Un-Politics of Air Pollution* (Baltimore, MD: Johns Hopkins University Press).

Crewe, Emma (2015), *The House of Commons: An Anthropology of British MPs at Work* (London: Bloomsbury).

Crick, B. (1962), *In Defence of Politics* (London: Weidenfeld & Nicolson).

Crouch, Colin (2011), *The Strange Non-Death of Neo-Liberalism* (Cambridge: Polity).

Crutzen, P., and Stoermer, F. (2000), 'The Anthropocene', *Global Change Newsletter*, 41: 17–18.

Cunningham, F. (2002), *Theories of Democracy* (London: Routledge).

d'Ancona, Matthew (2017), *Post-Truth: The New War on Truth and How to Fight back* (London: Ebury Press).

Dahl, R. (1958), 'A Critique of the Ruling Elite Model', *American Political Science Review*, 52(2): 463–9.

Dahl, R. (1963), *Who Governs?* (New Haven, CT: Yale University Press).

Dahl, R. (1971), *Polyarchy* (New Haven, CT: Yale University Press).

Dahl, R. (1989), *Democracy and Its Critics* (New Haven, CT: Yale University Press).

Dahl, R. (1991), *Modern Political Analysis* (Englewood Cliffs, NJ: Prentice-Hall, 5th edn).

Dahl, R. (2001), *How Democratic Is the American Constitution?* (New Haven, CT: Yale University Press).

Dahlerup, Drude (2005), 'Increasing Women's Political Representation: New Trends in Gender Quotas', in Julie Ballington and Azza Karam (eds), *Women in Parliament: Beyond Numbers* (Stockholm: International IDEA, rev edn), 141–53.

Daniels, N. (1975), *Reading Rawls* (New York: Basic Books).

Davies, Anjuli, and MacAskill, Andrew (2017), 'Brexit: Banks Planning to Move 9,000 Jobs from Britain to Mainland Europe', *The Independent*, 8 May, http://www.independent.co.uk/news/business/news/brexit-latest-news-banks-move-9000-jobs-britain-mainland-europe-eu-european-union-jpmorgan-hsbc-a7724231.html, accessed January 2018).

Davies, Nick (2009), *Flat Earth News: An Award-Winning Reporter Exposes Falsehood, Distortion and Propaganda in the Global Media* (London: Vintage).

Dawisha, Karen (2014), *Putin's Kleptocracy: Who Owns Russia?* (New York: Simon & Schuster).

De Tocqueville, Alexis (1994), *Democracy in America* (London: Everyman).

Dearlove, J., and Saunders, P. (2000), *Introduction to British Politics* (Cambridge: Polity Press, 3rd edn).

Deegan-Krause, Kevin, and Haughton, Tim (2009), 'Toward a More Useful Conceptualization of Populism: Types and Degrees of Populist Appeals in the Case of Slovakia', *Politics and Policy*, 37(4): 821–41.

Della Porta, Donatella (2013), *Can Democracy Be Saved?* (Cambridge: Polity).

Delli Carpini, Michael X. (2017), 'The Political Effects of Entertainment Media', in Kate Kenski and Kathleen Hall Jamieson (eds), *The Oxford Handbook of Political Communication* (Oxford and New York: Oxford University Press), 851–69.

deSouza, Peter Ronald, and Sridharan, E. (eds) (2006), *India's Political Parties* (New Delhi: Sage).

Diamond, Larry (2002), 'Consolidating Democracy', in Lawrence LeDuc, Richard G. Niemi, and Pippa Norris (eds), *Comparing Democracies 2: New Challenges in the Study of Elections and Voting* (Los Angeles, CA: Sage), 210–27.

Diamond, Larry (2008), *The Spirit of Democracy: The Struggle to Build Free Societies Throughout the World* (New York: Henry Holt).

Diehl, Paul F. (ed.) (2005), *The Politics of Global Governance: International Organizations in an Interdependent World* (Boulder, CO: Lynne Rienner, 3rd edn).

Dishman, Chris (2005), 'The Leaderless Nexus: When Crime and Terror Converge', *Studies in Conflict and Terrorism*, 28(3): 237–52.

Dobson, A. (1996), 'Democratising Green Theory: Preconditions and Principles', in B. Doherty and M. de Geus (eds), *Democracy and Green Political Thought* (London: Routledge), 132–48.

Dobson, A. (2007), *Green Political Thought* (London: Unwin Hyman, 4th edn).

Dobson, William J. (2012), *The Dictator's Learning Curve: Inside the Global Battle for Democracy* (New York: Doubleday).

Donner, Paige (2017), *The Audacity of Despotism: How the U.S. Liberal Mainstream Media Tried to Swing the 2016 Presidential Election and Failed* (CreateSpace Independent Publishing Platform).

Doorenspleet, Renske (2003), 'Political Parties, Party Systems and Democracy in Sub-Saharan Africa', in M. A. Mohamed Salih (ed.), *African Political Parties* (London: Pluto), 169–87.

Doronila, Amando (2001), *The Fall of Joseph Estrada: The Inside Story* (Pasig City: Anvil and Philippine Daily Inquirer).

Downs, Anthony (1957), *An Economic Theory of Democracy* (New York: Harper & Row).

Dryzek, J., and Dunleavy, P. (2009), *Theories of the Democratic State* (Basingstoke: Palgrave).

Dryzek, J. (2010), *Foundations and Frontiers of Deliberative Governance* (Oxford: Oxford University Press).

Duncan, G., and Lukes, S. (1964), 'The New Democracy', in S. Lukes (ed.), *Essays in Social Theory* (London: Macmillan), 30–50.

Dunleavy, P. (2005), 'Facing up to Multi-Party Politics: How Partisan Dealignment and PR Voting Have Fundamentally Changed Britain's Party System', *Parliamentary Affairs*, 58(3): 503–32.

Dunleavy, P., and O'Leary, B. (1987), *Theories of the State* (Basingstoke: Macmillan).

Dunleavy, P., and Ward, H. (1981), 'Exogenous Voter Preferences and Parties with State Power: Some Internal Problems of Economic Theories of Party Competition', *British Journal of Political Science*, 11: 351–80.

Dunn, Bill (2014), *The Political Economy of Global Capitalism and Crisis* (Abingdon: Routledge).

Durham, Jennifer (2015), 'East Africa's Authoritarian Drift', *Freedom House*, 2 February (https://freedomhouse.org/blog/east-africa-authoritarian-drift, accessed January 2018).

Duverger, Maurice (1964), *Political Parties* (London: Methuen, 3rd edn).

Dworkin, A. (1981), *Pornography: Men Possessing Women* (London: Women's Press).

Dworkin, R. (1978), *Taking Rights Seriously* (London: Duckworth).

Dye, T. (2000), *The Irony of Democracy* (London: Harcourt Brace).

Eckersley, R. (1992), *Environmentalism and Political Theory* (London: UCL Press).

Eckersley, R. (2004), *The Green State* (Cambridge, MA: MIT Press).

Economist (2012), 'The Rise of State Capitalism', 21 December (http://www.economist.com/node/21543160, accessed January 2018).

Edelman, Murray (1964), *The Symbolic Uses of Politics* (Urbana, IL: University of Illinois Press).

Edwards, Michael (2004), *Civil Society* (Cambridge: Polity Press).

Egan, Timothy (2016), 'The Sore Loser Uprising', *New York Times*, 5 August (http://www.nytimes.com/2016/08/05/opinion/the-sore-loser-uprising.html, accessed January 2018).

Eickelman, Dale F. (1996), 'Foreword', in Augustus Richard Norton (ed.), *Civil Society in the Middle East, Vol. II* (Leiden: E. J. Brill), ix–xiv.

Eisenhower, Dwight D. (1961), *Farewell Radio and Television Address to the American People*, 17 January, (https://www.eisenhower.archives.gov/all_about_ike/speeches/farewell_address.pdf, accessed January 2018).

Ekeli, K. (2009), 'Constitutional Experiments: Representing Future generations through Submajority Rules', *Journal of Political Philosophy*, 17(4): 440–61.

Elischer, Sebastian (2013), *Political Parties in Africa: Ethnicity and Party Formation* (Cambridge: Cambridge University Press).

Elstub, S., and McLaverty, P. (eds) (2014), *Deliberative Democracy: Issues and Cases* (Edinburgh: Edinburgh University Press).

End Poverty Initiative (2015), 'Current US Poverty Statistics', February (https://kairoscenter.org/wp-content/uploads/2015/02/Poverty-Fact-Sheet-Feb-2015-final.pdf, accessed January 2018).

Epp, Charles B. (1998), *The Rights Revolution: Lawyers, Activists, and Supreme Courts in Comparative Perspective* (Chicago, IL: Chicago University Press).

Eriksen, Thoma Hylland (2016), *Ethnicity and Nationalism: Anthropological Perspectives* (London: Pluto Press, 2nd edn).

Errejón, Iñigo, and Mouffe, Chantal (2016), *Podemos: In the Name of the People* (London: Soundings).

European Commission (2017), *Syrian Crisis*, ECHO Factsheet, September (https://ec.europa.eu/echo/files/aid/countries/factsheets/syria_en.pdf, accessed January 2018).

Evans, Peter B. (1995), *Embedded Autonomy: States and Industrial Transformation* (Princeton, NJ: Princeton University Press).

Falguera, Elin, Jones, Samuel, and Ohman, Magnus (eds) (2003), *Funding of Political Parties and Election Campaigns* (Stockholm: International IDEA).

Faludi, S. (1991), *Backlash: The Undeclared War against American Women* (New York: Crown).

Farrell, David M. (2001), *Electoral Systems: A Comparative Introduction* (Basingstoke: Palgrave).

Farrelly, C. (2007), 'Justice in Ideal Theory: A Refutation', *Political Studies*, 55: 844–64.

Fergusson, James (2013), *The World's Most Dangerous Place* (Boston, MA: Da Capo Press).

Festenstein, M., and Kenny, M. (2005), *Political Ideologies* (Oxford: Oxford University Press).

Field, Catherine (2011), 'High Hopes for Rich Nation's G8 Talkfest', *NZHerald*, 26 May (http://www.nzherald.co.nz/world/news/article.cfm?c_id=2&objectid=10728035, accessed June 2011).

Fielding, Steven (2014), *A State of Play: British Politics, Screen, Stage, and Page from Anthony Trollope to* The Thick of It (London: Bloomsbury).

Filiu, Jean-Pierre (2011), *The Arab Revolution: Ten Lessons from the Democratic Uprising* (London: Hurst).

Finer, S. E. (1997), *The History of Government from the Earliest Times, Vol. III: Empires, Monarchies and the Modern State* (Oxford: Oxford University Press).

Fiorina, Morris P. (2002), 'Parties, Participation, and Representation in America: Old Theories Face New Realities', in Ira N. Katznelson and Helen V. Milner (eds), *Political Science: State of the Discipline* (New York: Norton, for the American Political Science Association), 511–41.

Firestone, S. (1972), *The Dialectic of Sex* (London: Paladin).

Fish, M. Steven, and Kroenig, Matthew (2011), *The Handbook of National Legislatures: A Global Survey* (Cambridge: Cambridge University Press).

Fishkin, J., Jowell, R., and Luskin, R. (2002), 'Considered Opinions: Deliberative Polling in Britain', *British Journal of Political Science*, 32: 455–87.

Flinders, M. (2012), *Defending Politics: Why Democracy Matters in the Twenty-First Century* (Oxford: Oxford University Press).

Forster, Katie (2016), 'Hate Crimes Soar by 41 Per Cent after Brexit Vote, Official Figures Reveal', *The Independent* 13 October, (http://www.independent.co.uk/news/uk/crime/brexit-hate-crimes-racism-eu-referendum-vote-attacks-increase-police-figures-official-a7358866.html, accessed January 2018).

Foucault, M. (1977), *Discipline and Punishment* (Harmondsworth: Penguin).

Fox, W. (1995), *Toward a Transpersonal Ecology: Developing New Foundations for Environmentalism* (Totnes: Resurgence).

Frantz, Erica, and Ezrow, Natasha (2011), *The Politics of Dictatorship: Institutions and Outcomes in Authoritarian Regimes* (Boulder, CO: Lynne Rienner).

Freeden, M. (1996), *Ideologies and Political Theory* (Oxford: Oxford University Press).

Freedman, Des (2008), *The Politics of Media Policy* (Cambridge: Polity Press).

Freedman, Rosa (2013), *The United Nations Human Rights Council: A Critique and Early Assessment* (Abingdon: Routledge).

Freedom House (2014), *Freedom in the World 2014* (https://freedomhouse.org/report/freedom-world/freedom-world-2014, accessed July 2014).

Freedom House (2015), *Freedom in the World 2015* (https://freedomhouse.org/sites/default/files/01152015_FIW_2015_final.pdf, accessed July 2014).

Freedonia (2016a), 'World Security Services, as Quoted in *Stealth Monitoring*', (http://www.freedoniagroup.com/industry-study/2978/world-security-services.htm, accessed January 2018).

Freedonia (2016b), 'World Security Services, as Quoted in *ISHN Industrial Safety & Hygiene News*', (http://www.freedoniagroup.com/industry-study/3201/world-security-services.htm, accessed January 2018).

Frey, R. K. (1983), *Rights, Killing and Suffering* (Oxford: Clarendon Press).

Friedan, B. (1963), *The Feminine Mystique* (Harmondsworth: Penguin).

Friedman, Milton (1968), 'The Role of Monetary Policy', *American Economic Review*, 58(1): 1–17.

Friedman, Thomas (1999), *The Lexus and the Olive Tree* (London and New York: HarperCollins).

Fukuyama, F. (1992), *The End of History and the Last Man* (Harmondsworth: Penguin).

Fulbrook, Mary (2005), *The People's State: East German Society from Hitler to Honecker* (New Haven, CT: Yale University Press).

Fuller, Lon L. (1969), *The Morality of Law* (New Haven, CT: Yale University Press, rev edn).

Gagnon, Joseph E. and Hinterschweiger, Marc (2011), *The Global Outlook for Government Debt over the Next 25 Years: Implications for the Economy and Public Policy* (Washington, DC: Peterson Institute for International Economics, Policy Analysis No. 94).

Gagnon, V. P., Jr (1994–5), 'Ethnic Nationalism and International Conflict: The Case of Serbia', *International Security*, 19(3): 130–66.

Galbraith, J. K. (1984), 'Comment', *National Review*, 36(6): 39–42.

Galbraith, John Kenneth (1998), *The Affluent Society* (Boston, MA: Houghton Miflin).

Gallagher, Michael, and Marsh, Michael (2011), *How Ireland Voted 2011: The Full Story of Ireland's Earthquake Election* (Basingstoke: Palgrave).

Gallagher, Michael, Marsh, Michael, and Mitchell, Paul (eds) (2003), *How Ireland Voted* (Basingstoke: Palgrave).

Gallie, W. (1955/6), 'Essentially Contested Concepts', *Proceedings of the Aristotelian Society*, 56(1): 167–98.

Galtung, Johan (1969), 'Violence, Peace, and Peace Research', *Journal of Peace Research*, 6(3): 167–91.

Gambetta, Diego, and Warner, Steven (2004), 'Italy: Lofty Ambitions and Unintended Consequences', in Josep M. Colomer (ed.), *Handbook of Electoral System Choice* (Basingstoke: Palgrave), 237–52.

Gamble, A. (1994), *The Free Economy and the Strong State* (London: Macmillan, 2nd edn).

Gamble, A. (2000), *Politics and Fate* (Cambridge: Polity Press).

Gamm, Gerald, and Huber, John (2002), 'Legislatures as Political Institutions: Beyond the Contemporary Congress', in Ira Katznelson and Helen V. Milner (eds), *Political Science: State of the Discipline* (New York: Norton for the American Political Science Association), 313–41.

Gandhi, Jennifer (2008), *Political Institutions under Dictatorship* (Cambridge: Cambridge University Press).

Gandhi, Jennifer, and Przeworski, Adam (2007), 'Authoritarian Institutions and the Survival of Autocrats', *Comparative Political Studies*, 40(11): 1279–301.

Garner, R. (2005), *The Political Theory of Animal Rights* (Manchester: Manchester University Press).

Garnham, N. (2001), 'Public Sphere and the Media', in Neil J. Smelser and Paul B. Bailes (eds), *International Encyclopedia of the Social and Behavioral Sciences* (Amsterdam and New York: Elsevier), 12585–90.

Garvey, James (2017), *The Persuaders: The Hidden Industry That Wants to Change Your Mind* (London: Icon Books).

Geddes, Barbara, Wright, Joseph, and Frantz, Erica (2014), 'Autocratic Breakdown and Regime Transitions: A New Data Set', *Perspectives on Politics*, 12(2): 313–31.

Gellner, Ernest (1964), *Thought and Change* (London: Wiedenfeld & Nicholson).

Gellner, Ernest (1983), *Nations and Nationalism* (Ithaca, NY: Cornell University Press).

Gerbet, Pierre (1981), 'Rise and Development of International Organizations', in Georges Abi-Saab (ed.), *The Concept of International Organization* (Paris: UNESCO), 27–49.

Gerth, H., and Wright Mills, C. (1946), *From Max Weber: Essays in Sociology* (London: Routledge & Kegan Paul).

Giddens, Anthony (1979), *Central Problems in Social Theory: Action, Structure and Contradiction in Social Analysis* (Basingstoke: Macmillan).

Gill, Graeme (2003), *The Nature and Development of the Modern State* (Basingstoke: Palgrave).

Gilly, Adolfo (1990), 'The Mexican Regime in Its Dilemma', *Journal of International Affairs*, 43(2): 273–90.

Gilpin, Robert, and Gilpin, Jean M. (1987), *The Political Economy of International Relations* (Princeton, NJ: Princeton University Press).

Ginsborg, Paul (2001), *Italy and Its Discontents* (London: Allen Lane, The Penguin Press).

Glaister, Stephen, and Burnham, Jane (2006), *Transport Policy in Britain* (Basingstoke: Palgrave, 2nd edn).

Glaister, Stephen, Burnham, Jane, Stevens, Handley, and Travers, Tony (1998), *Transport Policy in Britain* (Basingstoke: Macmillan).

Gledhill, John (1994), *Power and Its Disguises: Anthropological Perspectives on Politics* (London: Pluto).

Glynn, Kevin (2007), 'Cultural Struggle, the New News, and the Politics of Popularity in the Age of Jesse "The Body" Ventura', in Ralph Negrine and James Stanyer (eds), *The Political Communication Reader* (London and New York: Routledge), 245–9.

Godbole, Madhav (2009), *The Judiciary and Governance in India* (New Delhi: Rupa).

Goodhand, Jonathon, and Sedra, Mark (eds) (2015), *The Afghan Conundrum: Intervention, Statebuilding and Resistance* (Abingdon: Routledge).

Goodhart, David (2017), *The Road to Somewhere: The Populist Revolt and the Future of Politics* (London: Hurst).

Goodin, R. (1992), *Green Political Theory* (Cambridge: Polity Press).

Goodin, R. (2007), 'Enfranchising All Affected Interests and Its Alternatives', *Philosophy and Public Affairs*, 35(1): 40–68.

Goodman, H. A. (2014), 'Illegal Immigrants Benefit the US Economy', *The Hill*, 23 April (http://thehill.com/blogs/congress-blog/foreign-policy/203984-illegal-immigrants-benefit-the-us-economy, accessed January 2018).

Goodwin, B. (2014), *Using Political Ideas* (Chichester: John Wiley & Sons, 6th edn).

Gordenker, Leon (2005), *The UN Secretary-General and Secretariat* (London: Routledge).

Gordenker, Leon, and Weiss, Thomas G. (1996), 'Pluralizing Global Governance: Analytical Approaches and Dimensions', in Thomas G. Weiss and Leon Gordenker (eds), *NGOs, the UN and Global Governance* (Boulder, CO: Lynne Rienner), 17–47.

Goss, Joss, and Lindquist, Bruce (1995), 'Conceptualizing International Labor Migration: A Structuration Perspective', *International Migration Review*, 29(2): 317–51.

Gott, Richard (2005), *Hugo Chavez and the Bolivarian Revolution* (London: Verso).

Gottfried, Jeffrey, and Shearer, Elisa (2016), *News Use across Social Media Platforms 2016* (Pew Research Center) (http://assets.pewresearch.org/wp-content/uploads/sites/13/2016/05/PJ_2016.05.26_social-media-and-news_FINAL-1.pdf, accessed May 2017).

Gramsci, A. (1971), *Selections from Prison Notebooks* (London: Lawrence & Wishart).

Grant, W. (2004), 'Pressure Politics: The Changing World of Pressure Groups', *Parliamentary Affairs*, 57(2): 408–19.

Graves, Lucas, and Cherubini, Federica (2016), *The Rise of Fact-Checking Sites in Europe* (Oxford: Reuters Institute for the Study of Journalism).

Greene, Kenneth F. (2007), *Why Dominant Parties Lose: Mexico's Democratization in Comparative Perspective* (Cambridge: Cambridge University Press).

Greer, G. (1970), *The Female Eunuch* (New York: McGraw-Hill).

Grossmann, Matthew (2014), *Artists of the Possible: Governing Networks and American Policy Change since 1945* (Oxford and New York: Oxford University Press).

Gunther, Richard, and Diamond, Larry (2003), 'Species of Political Parties: A New Typology', *Party Politics*, 9(2): 167–99.

Guo, Yingjie (2015), *Language, National Identity and Nationalism in China* (China Policy Institute) (https://cpianalysis.org/2015/06/17/language-national-identity-and-nationalism-in-china/, accessed January 2018).

Gupta, Akhil (2006), 'Blurred Boundaries: The Discourse of Corruption, the Culture of Politics and the Imagined State', in Aradhana Sharma and Akhil Gupta (eds), *The Anthropology of the State: A Reader* (Oxford: Blackwell), 211–42.

Gutmann, A., and Thompson, D. (1996), *Democracy and Disagreement* (Cambridge, MA: Harvard University Press).

Habermas, Jürgen (1969), *Strukturwandel der Öffentlichkeit* (Neuwied and Berlin: Hermann Luchterhand Verlag, 3rd edn).

Habermas, Jürgen (1989), *The Structural Transformation of the Public Sphere: An Enquiry into a Category of Bourgeois Society* (Cambridge: Polity Press).

Haggard, Stephan (1997), 'The Political Economy of Regionalism in Asia and the Americas', in Edward D.

Mansfield and Helen V. Milner (eds), *The Political Economy of Regionalism* (New York: Columbia University Press), 20–49.

Hague, R., and Harrop, M. (2007), *Comparative Government and Politics* (Basingstoke: Palgrave, 7th edn).

Hahm, Chaihark (2004), 'Disputing Civil Society in a Confucian Context', *Korea Observer*, 35(3): 433–62.

Hajer, M. (1997), *The Politics of Environmental Discourse* (Oxford: Clarendon Press).

Hale, Henry E. (2006), *Why Not Parties in Russia? Democracy, Federalism, and the State* (Cambridge: Cambridge University Press).

Hall, Peter A., and Soskice, David (eds) (2001), *Varieties of Capitalism: The Institutional Foundations of Comparative Advantage* (Oxford: Oxford University Press).

Hallaq, Wael B. (2005), *The Origins and Evolution of Islamic Law* (Cambridge: Cambridge University Press).

Hallin, Daniel C., and Mancini, Paolo (2004), *Comparing Media Systems: Three Models of Media and Politics* (Cambridge and New York: Cambridge University Press).

Hallin, Daniel C., and Mancini, Paolo (eds) (2012), *Comparing Media Systems beyond the Western World* (Cambridge and New York: Cambridge University Press).

Handler, Richard (1988), *Nationalism and the Politics of Culture in Quebec* (Madison: University of Wisconsin Press).

Hannan, Daniel (2016), *Why Vote Leave* (London: Head of Zeus).

Hanusch, Folker, and Hanitzsch, Thomas (2017), 'Comparing Journalistic Cultures across Nations', *Journalism Studies*, 18(5): 525–35.

Härdig, Anders C. (2014), 'Beyond the Arab Revolts: Conceptualizing Civil Society in the Middle East and North Africa', *Democratization*, 22(6): 1131–53.

Hardin, G. (1968), 'The Tragedy of the Commons', *Science*, 162: 1243–8.

Harle, Vilho (1998), *Ideas of Social Order in the Ancient World* (Westport, CT: Greenwood Press).

Harrison, Jackie (2006), *News* (Abingdon: Routledge).

Hart, Roderick P., and LaVally, Rebecca (2017), 'Not a Fourth Estate but a Second Legislature', in Kate Kenski and Kathleen Hall Jamieson (eds), *The Oxford Handbook of Political Communication* (Oxford and New York: Oxford University Press), 109–19.

Harvey, David (2007), *A Brief History of Neoliberalism* (Oxford: Oxford University Press).

Hawkins, William R. (1984), 'Neomercantilism: Is There a Case for Tariffs?', *National Review*, 36(6): 25–39.

Hay, C. (1997), 'Divided by a Common Language: Political Theory and the Concept of Power', *Politics*, 17(1): 45–52.

Hay, C. (1999), 'Marxism and the State', in A. Gamble, D. Marsh, and T. Tant (eds), *Marxism and Social Science* (London: Macmillan), 152–74.

Hay, C. (2002), *Political Analysis* (Basingstoke: Palgrave).

Hay, C. (2007), *Why We Hate Politics* (Cambridge: Polity).

Hay, C., Lister, M., and Marsh, D. (eds) (2006), *The State: Theories and Issues* (Basingstoke: Palgrave).

Hay, C., and Lister, M. (2006), 'Introduction', in C. Hay, M. Lister, and M. D. Marsh (eds), *The State: Theories and Issues* (Basingstoke: Palgrave), 1–20.

Hayward, T. (2005), *Constitutional Environmental Rights* (Oxford: Oxford University Press).

Heater, D. (1999), *What Is Citizenship?* (Cambridge: Polity Press).

Heffer, Simon (2012), 'A Nanny State That Dictates What We Drink Will Soon Be Telling Us How to Think', *Daily Mail*, 28 November (http://www.dailymail.co.uk/debate/article-2240118/A-nanny-state-dictates-drink-soon-telling-think.html, accessed January 2018).

Heilbroner, R. (1974), *An Inquiry into the Human Prospect* (New York: Norton).

Held, D. (1989), *Political Theory and the Modern State* (Cambridge: Polity Press).

Held, D. (2006), *Models of Democracy* (Cambridge: Polity Press, 3rd edn).

Held, D., Barnett, A., and Henderson, C. (2005), *Debating Globalization* (Cambridge: Polity).

Held, D., and Leftwich, A. (1984), 'A Discipline of Politics?', in A. Leftwich (ed.), *What is Politics? The Activity and Its Study* (Oxford: Blackwell), 139–59.

Henry (2007), 'Simplify and Exaggerate' (http://crookedtimber.org/2007/01/19/simplify-and-exaggerate/, accessed May 2017).

Herb, Guntrum H., and Kaplan, David H. (eds) (2008), *Nations and Nationalism: A Global Historical Overview* (Santa Barbara, CA: ABC-Clio).

Héritier, Adrienne, and Knill, Christoph (2001), 'Differential Responses to European Policies: A Comparison', in Adrienne Héritier, Dieter Kerwer, Christoph Knill, Dirk Lehmkuhl, Michael Teutsch, and Anne-Cécile Douillet (eds), *Differential Europe: The European Union Impact on National Policy-Making* (Lanham, MD: Rowman & Littlefield), 257–94.

Herman, Edward S., and Chomsky, Noam (2002), *Manufacturing Consent: The Political Economy of the Mass Media* (New York: Pantheon).

Hewitt, C. (1974), 'Policy-Making in Postwar Britain: A National-Level Test of Elitist and Pluralist Hypotheses', *British Journal of Political Science*, 4(2): 187–216.

Heyck, Thomas William (2002), *A History of the Peoples of the British Isles, Vol. 3* (London: Routledge).

Heywood, A. (2007), *Political Ideologies* (Basingstoke: Palgrave).

Heywood, A. (2013), *Politics* (Basingstoke: Palgrave Macmillan, 4th edn).

Heywood, A. (2015), *Political Theory: An Introduction* (Basingstoke: Palgrave Macmillan, 4th edn).

Hirst, P. (1996), *Associative Democracy: New Forms of Economic and Social Governance* (Cambridge: Polity Press).

Hirst, Paul, and Thompson, Graeme (1999), *Globalization in Question* (Cambridge: Polity Press, 2nd edn).

Hitler, A. (1926/1969), *Mein Kampf* (London: Hutchinson).

Hobbes, Thomas (1651/1992), *Leviathan* (Cambridge: Cambridge University Press).

Hobbes, Thomas (1651/2008), *Leviathan*, ed. Michael Oakeshott (New York: Simon & Schuster).

Hobsbawm, E. J. (1992), *Nations and Nationalism since 1780: Programme, Myth, Reality* (Cambridge: Cambridge University Press, 2nd edn).

Hochschild, Jennifer L., and Einstein, Katherine Levine (2016), *Do Facts Matter? Information and Misinformation in American Politics* (Norman, OK: University of Oklahoma Press).

Hoexter, Miriam (2002), 'The Waqf and the Public Sphere', in Miriam Hoexter, Shmuel N. Eisenstadt, and Nehemia Levtzion (eds), *The Public Sphere in Muslim Societies* (Albany, NY: State University of New York Press), 119–38.

Hoffman, J. (1995), *Beyond the State* (Cambridge: Polity).

Hoffman, J., and Graham, P. (2006), *Introduction to Political Theory* (Harlow: Pearson).

Holston, James (2008), *Insurgent Citizenship: Disjunctions of Democracy and Modernity in Brazil* (Oxford and Princeton, NJ: Princeton University Press).

Horton, J. (1984), 'Political Philosophy and Politics', in A. Leftwich (ed.), *What is Politics? The Activity and Its Study* (Oxford, Blackwell), 106–23.

House of Commons Library (2016), *Number of Commons Sitting Days by Session since 1945* (House of Commons Briefing Paper 04653) (http://researchbriefings. parliament.uk/ResearchBriefing/Summary/ SN04653#fullreport, accessed January 2018).

Howard, Philip N., Bolsover, Gillian, Kollanyi, Bence, Bradshaw, Samantha, and Neudert, Lisa-Maria (2017), *Junk News and Bots During the U.S. Election: What Were Michigan Voters Sharing over Twitter?* (Oxford: Comprop Data Memo 26 March) (http://comprop.oii.ox.ac.uk/wp-content/uploads/sites/89/2017/03/What-Were-Michigan-Voters-Sharing-Over-Twitter-v2.pdf, accessed May 2017).

Howell, Chris (2003), 'Varieties of Capitalism: And Then There Was One?', *Comparative Politics*, 36(1): 103–24.

Hueglin, Thomas, and Fenna, Alan (2015), *Comparative Federalism: A Systematic Enquiry* (Toronto: University of Toronto Press).

Hume, Mick (2017), *Revolting! How the Establishment Are Undermining Democracy and What They're Afraid of* (London: Collins).

Hunter, Paul, and Holden, Dan (2015), *Who Governs Britain: A Profile of MPs in the 2015 Parliament* (https:// smithinstitutethinktank.files.wordpress.com/2015/05/ who-governs-britain.pdf, accessed January 2018).

Huntington, Samuel P. (1991), *The Third Wave: Democratization in the Late Twentieth Century* (Norman, OK: University of Oklahoma Press).

Huntington, Samuel P. (1996), *The Clash of Civilizations* (New York: Simon & Schuster).

Hurd, Ian (2008), 'Myths of Membership: The Politics of Legitimation in UN Security Council Reform', *Global Governance*, 14(1): 199–217.

Hutchinson, John, and Smith, Anthony D. (eds) (1994), *Nationalism* (Oxford: Oxford University Press).

Hyams, K. (2015), 'Political Authority and Obligation', in C. MacKinnon (ed.), *Issues in Political Theory* (Oxford: Oxford University Press, 3rd edn), 8–29.

Ibeanu, Okechukwu, and Kuna, Mohammad J. (2016), *Nigerian Federalism: Continuing Quest for Stability and Nation-Building* (Sebastopol, CA: Safari).

Ibrahim, Saad Eddin (1995), 'Civil Society and Prospects of Democratization in the Arab World', in Augustus Richard Norton (ed.), *Civil Society in the Middle East, Vol. I* (Leiden: E. J. Brill), 27–54.

ICISS (2001), *The Responsibility to Protect* (Ottawa: International Development Research Centre) (http:// responsibilitytoprotect.org/ICISS%20Report.pdf, accessed January 2018).

ICoC (International Code of Conduct Association) (2016), 'History' (http://icoca.ch/en/history, accessed January 2018).

Inglehart, Ronald, Basáñez, Miguel, Díez-Madrano, Jaime, Halman, Loek, and Luijkx, Ruud (eds) (2004), *Human Beliefs and Values: A Cross-Cultural Sourcebook Based on the 1999–2002 Values Surveys* (Mexico, DF: Siglo XXI Editores).

Institute for Research on Poverty (2014), 'Who is Poor'?, (http:// www.irp.wisc.edu/faqs/faq3.htm, accessed January 2018).

Inter-Parliamentary Union (1997), *Universal Declaration on Democracy* (http://www.ipu.org/cnl-e/161-dem.htm, accessed January 2018).

Inter-Parliamentary Union (2017), 'Parliaments at a Glance: Structure' (http://www.ipu.org/parline-e/ ParliamentsStructure.asp?REGION=All&LANG=ENG, accessed January 2018).

Iyengar, Shanto (2017), 'A Typology of Media Effects', in Kate Kenski and Kathleen Hall Jamieson (eds), *The Oxford Handbook of Political Communication* (Oxford and New York: Oxford University Press), 59–68.

Jackson, Robert H. (1990), *Quasi-States: Sovereignty, International Relations and the Third World* (Cambridge: Cambridge University Press).

Jacobson, Gary C. (1997), *The Politics of Congressional Elections* (New York: Longman, 4th edn).

Jacobson, Gary C. (2013), 'Partisan Polization in American Politics: A Background Paper', *Presidential Studies Quarterly*, 43(4): 688–708.

Jacques, Martin (2012), *When China Rules the World: The Rise of the Middle Kingdom and the End of the Western World* (London: Penguin).

Jaggar, A. (1983), *Feminist Politics and Human Nature* (Lanham, MD: Rowman & Littlefield).

Jakobsson, Sverrir, and Halfdanarson, Gudmundur (2016), *Historical Dictionary of Iceland* (Lanham, MD: Rowman & Littlefield, 3rd edn).

James, A. (1986), *Sovereign Statehood* (London: Allen & Unwin).

Jenkins, Rob (2005), 'Civil Society: Active or Passive? India', in Peter Burnell and Vicky Randall (eds), *Politics in the Developing World* (Oxford: Oxford University Press), 275–85.

Jessop, B. (1990), *State Theory* (Cambridge: Polity Press).

Johnson, Chalmers A. (1982), *MITI and the Japanese Miracle* (Stanford, CA: Stanford University Press).

Johnson, Chalmers A. (1995), *Japan: Who Governs? The Rise of the Developmental State* (New York: Norton).

Johnson, R. W. (2015), *How Long Will South Africa Survive? The Looming Crisis* (New York: Jonathan Ball).

Jones, Daniel Stedman (2014), *Masters of the Universe: Hayek, Friedman and the Birth of Neoliberal Politics* (Princeton, MJ: Princeton University Press).

Jones, Martin, Jones, Rhys, and Woods, Michael (2004), *An Introduction to Political Geography: Space, Place and Politics* (London: Routledge).

Jones, P. (1994), *Rights* (Basingstoke: Macmillan).

Juncker, Jean-Claude (2017), 'There Can Be No Place for Economic Nationalism in Europe of the Future', *Sunday Herald* (Scotland), 9 March (http://www.heraldscotland.com/opinion/15143011.Jean_Claude_Juncker__There_can_be_no_place_for_economic_nationalism_in_Europe_of_the_future/, accessed January 2018).

Kaldor, Mary (2006), *New and Old Wars: Organized Violence in a Global Era* (Cambridge: Polity Press, 2nd edn).

Kalyango, Y., Jr, Hanusch, F., Ramaprasad, J., Skjerdal, T., Saraf Hasim, M., Muchtar, N., Sahid Ullah, M., Zeleza Manda, L., and Bomkapre Kamara, S. (2017), 'Journalists' Development Journalism Role Perceptions', *Journalism Studies*, 18(5): 576–94.

Kamarck, Elaine C. (2007), *The End of Government … As We Know It: Making Public Policy Work* (Boulder, CO: Lynne Rienner).

Kamminga, M. (2008), 'The Ethics of Climate Politics: Four Modes of Moral Discourse', *Environmental Politics*, 47(4): 673–92.

Karl, Terry Lynn (1990), 'Dilemmas of Democratization in Latin America', *Comparative Politics*, 23(1): 1–21.

Katz, Richard S., and Mair, Peter (1995), 'Changing Models of Party Organization and Party Democracy: The Emergence of the Cartel Party', *Party Politics*, 1(1): 5–28.

Katz, Richard S., and Mair, Peter (2009), 'The Cartel Party Thesis: A Restatement', *Perspectives on Politics*, 7(4): 753–65.

Kayizzi-Mugerwa, Steve (2003), 'Introduction', in Steve Kayizzi-Mugerwa (ed.), *Reforming Africa's Institutions: Ownership, Incentives, and Capabilities* (Tokyo: UNUP and UNU WIDER), 1–12.

Keane, John (2009), *The Life and Death of Democracy* (London and New York: Simon & Schuster).

Kenney, Padraic (2002), *A Carnival of Revolution: Central Europe, 1989* (Princeton, NJ: Princeton University Press).

Kenski, Kate and Jamieson, Kathleen Hall (eds) (2017), *The Oxford Handbook of Political Communication* (Oxford and New York: Oxford University Press).

Keohane, Robert O. (1993), 'The Analysis of International Regimes: Towards a European–American Research Programme', in Volker Rittberger and Peter Mayer (eds), *International Regime Theory* (Oxford: Oxford University Press), 23–48.

Keohane, Robert O. (2001), *After Hegemony: Cooperation and Discord in the World Political Economy* (Princeton, NJ: Princeton University Press).

Keynes, J. M. (1926), *The End of Laissez-Faire* (London: Hogarth Press).

Keynes, J. M. (1936), *The General Theory of Employment, Interest and Money* (London: Macmillan & Co).

Khilnani, Sunil (2004), *The Idea of India* (London: Penguin, rev edn).

Kiddle, Amelia M., and Muñoz, Maria L. O. (eds) (2010), *Populism in Twentieth-Century Mexico: The Presidencies of Lázaro Cardenas and Luis Echeverría* (Tucson, AZ: University of Arizona Press).

Kim, Oliver W. (2014), 'Meet Homo Economicus', *The Harvard Crimson*, 19 September (http://www.thecrimson.com/column/homo-economicus/article/2014/9/19/Harvard-homo-economicus-fiction/, accessed January 2018).

Kim, Wangsik (2006), 'Government Executive and Policy Reform in Japan', *International Review of Public Administration*, 10(2): 21–35.

King, Anthony (2001), 'Distrust of Government: Explaining American Exceptionalism', in Susan J. Pharr and Robert D. Putnam (eds), *Disaffected Democracies: What's Troubling the Trilateral Countries?* (Princeton, NJ: Princeton University Press), 74–98.

King, Anthony (2007), *The British Constitution* (Oxford: Oxford University Press).

King, Anthony (2015), *Who Governs Britain?* (London: Penguin).

King, Anthony, and Crewe, Ivor (2013), *The Blunders of Our Governments* (London: Oneworld).

Kingdon, John W. (1995), *Agendas, Alternatives and Public Policies* (New York: Longman, 2nd edn).

Kirsch, Philippe, and Helal, Mohamed S. (2014), 'Libya', in Jared Genser and Bruno Stagno Ugarte (eds), *The United Nations Security Council in the Age of Human Rights* (Cambridge: Cambridge University Press), 396–433.

Kitchen, M. (1976), *Fascism* (Basingstoke: Macmillan).

Klabbers, Jan (2003), *An Introduction to International Institutional Law* (Cambridge: Cambridge University Press).

Knight, Alan (1998), 'Populism and Neo-Populism in Latin America, Especially Mexico', *Journal of Latin American Studies*, 30(2): 223–48.

Koelble, Thomas A., and LiPuma, Edward (2008), 'Democratizing Democracy: A Postcolonial Critique of Conventional Approaches to the "Measurement of Democracy"', *Democratization*, 15(1): 1–28.

Kohli, Atul (2004), *State-Directed Development: Political Power and Industrialization in the Global Periphery* (Cambridge: Cambridge University Press).

Kornhauser, W. (1960), *The Politics of Mass Society* (Glencoe, IL: Free Press).

Krämer, Gudrun (2015), 'Pluralism and Tolerance', in Gerhard Bowering (ed.), *Islamic Political Thought: An Introduction* (Oxford and Princeton, NJ: Princeton University Press), 169–84.

Krause, Enrique (1997), *La presidencia imperial: Ascenso y caída del sistema político mexicano* (Mexico City: Tusquets).

Krugman, Paul (2007), 'Who Was Milton Friedman?', *New York Review of Books*, 15 February (http://www.nybooks.com/articles/2007/02/15/who-was-milton-friedman/).

Kukathas, C., and Pettit, P. (1990), *Rawls: A Theory of Justice and Its Critics* (Oxford: Polity Press).

Kurlantzick, Joshua (2013), *Democracy in Retreat: The Retreat of the Middle Class and the Worldwide Decline of Representative Government* (London and New Haven, CT: Yale University Press, for the Council on Foreign Relations).

Kymlicka, W. (1995), *Multicultural Citizenship: A Liberal Theory of Minority Rights* (Oxford: Oxford University Press).

Kymlicka, W. (2002), *Contemporary Political Philosophy* (Oxford: Oxford University Press, 2nd edn).

Landier, Augustin, and Thesmar, David (2007), *Le Grand méchant marché* (Paris: Flammarion).

Lasswell, H. (1936), *Politics: Who Gets What, When, How?* (New York: McGraw-Hill).

Law Society of Australia (2016), 'Indigenous Imprisonment Fact Sheet' (http://lawcouncil.asn.au/lawcouncil/images/LCA-PDF/Indigenous_Imprisonment_Fact_Sheet.pdf, accessed January 2018).

Laws, David (2017), *Coalition: The Inside Story of the Conservative–Liberal Democrat Coalition Government* (London: Biteback).

Lawson, Stephanie (1993), 'Conceptual Issues in the Comparative Study of Regime Change and Democratization', *Comparative Politics*, 25(2): 183–205.

Lawson, Stephanie (2006), *Culture and Context in World Politics* (Basingstoke: Palgrave Macmillan).

Lawson, Stephanie (2016), *Theories of International Politics: Contending Approaches to World Politics* (Cambridge: Polity).

Le Miere, Jason (2017), 'Hillary Clinton Calls Email Scandal Fake News and "Biggest Nothing Burger Ever"', *Newsweek*, 31 May (http://www.newsweek.com/hillary-clinton-emails-fake-news-618557, accessed January 2018).

Leftwich, A. (ed.) (1984), *What is Politics? The Activity and Its Study* (Oxford: Blackwell).

Lehmbruch, Gerhard (2001), 'Corporatism', in Neil J. Smelser and Paul R. Baltes (eds), *International Encyclopedia of the Social and Behavioral Sciences* (Amsterdam: Elsevier), 2813–6.

Leopold, A. (1949), *A Sand County Almanac* (Oxford: Oxford University Press).

Lerner, Daniel (1958), *The Passing of Traditional Society: Modernizing the Middle East* (Glencoe, IL: Free Press).

Levitin, Daniel (2017), *A Field Guide to Lies and Statistics* (London: Viking).

Levitsky, Steven, and Way, Lucan A. (2002), 'Elections without Democracy: The Rise of Competitive Authoritarianism', *Journal of Democracy*, 13(2): 51–65.

Levitsky, Steven, and Cameron, Maxwell A. (2003), 'Democracy without Parties? Political Parties and Regime Change in Fujimori's Peru', *Latin American Politics and Society*, 45(3): 1–33.

Levitsky, Steven, Loxton, James, and Van Dyck, Brandon (2016), 'Introduction: Challenges of Party-Building in Latin America', in Steven Levitsky, James Loxton, Brandon Van Dyck, and Jorge I. Dominguez (eds), *Challenges of Party-Building in Latin America* (Cambridge and New York: Cambridge University Press), 1–48.

Lewis, Bernard (2005), 'Freedom and Justice in the Modern Middle East', *Foreign Affairs*, 84(3): 36–51.

Lieberman, J. K. (2001), 'Legalization', in Neil J. Smelser and Paul B. Baltes (eds), *International Encyclopedia of the Social and Behavioral Sciences* (Amsterdam: Elsevier), 8693–7.

Lieven, Anatol (2011), Pakistan: *A Hard Country* (New York: Public Affairs).

Lijphart, Arend (1977), *Democracy in Plural Societies: A Comparative Explanation* (New Haven, CT: Yale University Press).

Lijphart, Arend (ed.) (1992), *Parliamentary versus Presidential Government* (Oxford: Oxford University Press).

Lijphart, Arend (1999), *Patterns of Democracy: Government Forms and Performance in Thirty-Six Countries* (New Haven, CT: Yale University Press).

Lijphart, Arend (2001), 'The Puzzle of Indian Democracy', in Niraja Gopal Jayal (ed.), *Democracy in India* (New Delhi and Oxford: Oxford University Press), 326–57.

Lijphart, Arend, and Crepaz, Markus M. L. (1991), 'Corporatism and Consensus in Eighteen Countries: Conceptual and Empirical Linkages', *British Journal of Political Science*, 21: 235–46.

Lindblom, C. (1977), *Politics and Markets* (New York: Basic Books).

Linklater, A. (2008), 'Globalization and the Transformation of Political Community', in J. Baylis, S. Smith, and P. Owens (eds), *The Globalization of World Politics* (Oxford: Oxford University Press), 617–33.

Linz, Juan J. (1992), 'The Perils of Presidentialism', in Arend Lijphart (ed.), *Parliamentary versus Presidential Government* (Oxford: Oxford University Press), 118–27.

Lipschutz, Ronnie (1998), 'On Security', in Ronnie Lipschutz (ed.), *On Security* (New York: Columbia University Press), 1–23.

Lipset, S. M. (1959), 'Some Social Requisites of Democracy: Economic Development and Political Legitimacy', *American Political Science Review*, 53(1): 69–105.

Lipset, Seymour Martin (1960), *Political Man: The Social Bases of Politics* (London: Heinemann).

Lipset, Seymour Martin, and Rokkan, Stein (eds) (1967), *Party Systems and Voter Alignments: Cross-National Perspectives* (New York: Free Press).

List, Frederich (1991), 'Political and Cosmopolitical Economy', in George T. Crane and Abla Amawi (eds), *The Theoretical Evolution of International Political Economy: A Reader* (Oxford: Oxford University Press), 48–54.

Little, Peter D. (2003), *Somalia: Economy without State* (Oxford: International African Institute, in association with James Currey).

Lively, J. (1975), *Democracy* (Oxford: Blackwell).

Locke, J. (1690/1988), *Two Treatises of Government* (Cambridge: Cambridge University Press).

Lombardi, Clark Benner (1998), 'Islamic Law as a Source of Constitutional Law in Egypt: The Constitutionalization of the Sharia in a Modern Arab State', *Columbia Journal of Transnational Law*, 37(1): 81–123.

Lucas, George R., Jr (2016), *Military Ethics: What Everyone Needs to Know* (New York: Oxford University Press).

Lukes, S. (2005), *Power: A Radical View* (Basingstoke: Palgrave Macmillan, 2nd edn).

Lynn, Laurence E. (2006), *Public Management: Old and New* (Abingdon: Routledge).

Máiz, Ramón (2000), 'Democracy, Federalism and Nationalism in Multinational States', in William Safran and Ramón Máiz (eds), *Identity and Territorial Autonomy in Plural Societies* (London: Frank Cass), 35–60.

MacIntyre, A. (1985), *After Virtue: A Study in Moral Theory* (London: Duckworth, 2nd edn).

Macpherson, C. B. (1962), *The Political Theory of Possessive Individualism* (Oxford: Oxford University Press).

Macpherson, C. B. (1966), *The Real World of Democracy* (Oxford: Oxford University Press).

Macpherson, C. B. (1977), *The Life and Times of Liberal Democracy* (Oxford: Oxford University Press).

Macpherson, C. B. (1980), *Burke* (Oxford: Oxford University Press).

Magaloni, Beatriz (2006), *Voting for Democracy: Hegemonic Party Survival and Its Demise in Mexico* (Cambridge and New York: Cambridge University Press).

Mahbubani, Kishore (2008), *The New Asian Hemisphere: The Irresistible Shift of Global Power to the East* (New York: Public Affairs).

Mainwaring, Scott (2006), 'State Deficiencies, Party Competition, and Confidence in Democratic Representation in the Andes', in Scott Mainwaring, Ana María Bejarano, and Eduardo Pizarro Leongómez (eds), *The Crisis of Democratic Representation in the Andes* (Stanford, CA: Stanford University Press), 295–345.

Mair, Peter (2005), *Democracy beyond Parties* (UC Irvine Center for the Study of Democracy Working Paper) (https://escholarship.org/uc/item/3vs886v9, accessed January 2018).

Mair, Peter, and van Biezen, Ingrid (2001), 'Party Membership in Twenty European Democracies, 1980–2000', *Party Politics*, 7(1): 5–21.

Malhotra, Rajiv (2013), *Being Different: An Indian Challenge to Western Universalism* (Noida, Uttar Pradesh: HarperCollins).

Mandelbaum, Michael (1999), 'The Future of Nationalism', *The National Interest*, 57: 17–26.

Manow, Philip, and Ziblatt, Daniel (2015), 'The Layered State: Pathways and Patterns of Modern State Building', in Stephan Leibfried, Evelyne Huber, Matthew Lange, Jonah D. Levy, Frank Nullmeier, and John D. Stephens (eds), *The Oxford Handbook of Transformations of the State* (Oxford: Oxford University Press), 75–98.

Marchetti, Rafelle (2016), 'Global Civil Society', in Stephen McGlinchey (ed.), *International Relations* (E-International Relations) (http://www.e-ir.info/2016/12/28/global-civil-society/).

Marcovitz, Hal (2009), *Nancy Pelosi: Politician* (New York: Chelsea House).

Marcuse, H. (1964), *One-Dimensional Man: Studies in the Ideology of Advanced Industrial Society* (Boston, MA: Beacon).

Marietta, Morgan, Barker, David C., and Bowser, Todd (2017), 'Fact-Checking Polarized Politics: Does the Fact-Check Industry Provide Consistent Guidance on Disputed Realities?', *The Forum*, 13(4): 577–96.

Marquand, D. (1988), *The Unprincipled Society* (London: Jonathan Cape).

Marr, Andrew (2004), *My Trade* (London: Macmillan).

Marschall, Stefan (2015), *Parlamentarismus* (Baden-Baden: Nomos, 2nd edn).

Marsh, David, Smith, Nicola J., and Hothi, Nicola (2006), 'Globalization and the State', in Colin Hay, Michael Lister, and David Marsh (eds), *The State: Theories and Issues* (Basingstoke: Palgrave), 172–89.

Marshall, T. H. (1950), *Citizenship and Social Class, and Other Essays* (Cambridge: Cambridge University Press).

Martell, L. (1994), *Ecology and Society* (Cambridge: Polity Press).

Marx, Karl, and Engels, Friedrich (1846/1970), *The German Ideology* (London: Lawrence & Wishart).

Marx, Karl, and Engels, Friedrich (1848/1976), *The Communist Manifesto* (Harmondsworth: Penguin).

Marx, Karl, and Engels, Friedrich (1848), *Manifesto of the Communist Party* (available at: (https://www.marxists. org/archive/marx/works/download/pdf/Manifesto.pdf, accessed February 2018).

Mather, R., and Jefferson, K. (2016) 'The Authoritarian Voter? The Psychology and Values of Donald Trump and Bernie Sanders' Support', *Journal of Scientific Psychology*, May: 1–8.

Mathur, Kuldeep (2013a), *Public Policy and Politics in India: How Institutions Matter* (New Delhi and Oxford: Oxford University Press).

Mathur, Kuldeep (2013b), *Panchayati Raj* (New Delhi and Oxford: Oxford University Press).

Matland, Richard E. (2005), 'Enhancing Women's Political Participation: Legislative Recruitment and Electoral Systems', in Julie Ballington and Azza Kazam (eds), *Women in Parliament: Beyond Numbers* (Stockholm: International IDEA, rev edn), 93–111.

McCarthy, Julie (2017), 'Why Do So Few People Pay Income Tax in India?', *NPR*, 22 March (http://www.npr.org/ sections/parallels/2017/03/22/517965630/why-do-so-few-people-pay-income-tax-in-india, accessed January 2018).

McCarty, Nolan, Polle, Keith T., and Rosenthal, Howard (2009), 'Does Gerrymandering Cause Polarization?', *American Journal of Political Science*, 53(3): 666–80.

McCoy, Jennifer L., and Myers, David L. (eds) (2004), *The Unravelling of Representative Democracy in Venezuela* (Baltimore, MD: Johns Hopkins University Press).

McDonald, Ian M. (2009), 'The Global Financial Crisis and Behavioural Economics', *Economic Papers*, 28(3): 249–54.

McElroy, W. (1995), *A Woman's Right to Pornography* (New York: St Martin's Press).

McGregor, Richard (2010), *The Party: The Secret World of China's Communist Rulers* (London: Allen Lane).

McGuinness, Feargal (2010), *Social Background of MPs* (House of Commons Standard Note SG/1528, London).

McIntosh, M. (1978), 'The State and the Oppression of Women', in A. Kuhn and A. Wolpe (eds), *Feminism and Materialism* (London: Routledge & Kegan Paul), 254–89.

McLean, Iain (1989), *Democracy and New Technology* (Cambridge: Polity Press).

McLellan, D. (1980), *The Thought of Karl Marx* (Basingstoke: Macmillan).

Meadows, D. H., Meadows, D. L., Randers, J., and Behrens, W. W. (1972), *The Limits to Growth* (New York: Universe).

Mearsheimer, John J. (2010), 'Structural Realism', in Tim Dunne, Milja Kurki, and Steve Smith (eds), *Theories of International Relations: Discipline and Diversity* (Oxford: Oxford University Press, 2nd edn), 77–94.

Medema, Steven G., and Samuels, Warren J. (2013), *History of Economic Thought Reader* (Abingdon: Routledge, 2nd edn).

Mellor, M. (1997), *Feminism and Ecology* (Cambridge: Polity Press).

Menkhaus, Ken (2007), 'Governance without Government in Somalia', *International Security*, 31(3): 74–106.

Menon, Anand (2006), *Comparative Federalism: The European Union and the US in Comparative Perspective* (Oxford: Oxford University Press).

Menski, Werner (2006), *Comparative Law in a Global Context: The Legal Systems of Asia and Africa* (Cambridge: Cambridge University Press).

Mezey, Michael (1990), 'Classifying Legislatures', in Philip Norton (ed.), *Legislatures* (Oxford: Oxford University Press), 149–76.

Midgley, Claire (1992), *Women against Slavery: The British Campaigns, 1780–70* (London: Routledge).

Miliband, R. (1972), *Parliamentary Socialism* (London: Merlin).

Miliband, R. (1978), *The State in Capitalist Society* (New York: Basic Books).

Mill, J. S. (1844/1972), *Utilitarianism, On Liberty, and Considerations on Representative Government* (London: Dent).

Miller, D. (1976), *Social Justice* (Oxford: Clarendon Press).

Miller, D. (1990), *Market, State and Community: Theoretical Foundations to Market Socialism* (Oxford: Clarendon Press).

Miller, David (ed.) (1991), *The Blackwell Encyclopaedia of Political Thought* (Oxford: Blackwell).

Miller, Vaughne (2010), *How Much Legislation Comes from Europe?* (House of Commons Briefing: Research Paper 10/62) (http://researchbriefings.parliament.uk/ ResearchBriefing/Summary/RP10-62#fullreport, accessed January 2018).

Millett, K. (1971), *Sexual Politics* (New York: Granada).

Minford, P. (2010), 'The Banking Crisis: A Rational Interpretation', *Political Studies*, 8(1): 40–54.

Mitchell, J. (1971), *Woman's Estate* (Harmondsworth: Penguin).

Mitra, Subrata K. and Pehl, Malte (2010), 'Federalism', in Niraja Gopal Jayal and Pratap Bhanu Mehta (eds), *The

Oxford Companion to Politics in India (New Delhi and Oxford: Oxford University Press), 43–60.

Mock, Steven J. (2012), *Symbols of Defeat in the Construction of National Identity* (Cambridge: Cambridge University Press).

Moffitt, Benjamin (2016), *The Global Rise of Populism: Performance, Political Style and Representation* (Stanford, CA: Stanford University Press).

Mohanty, Manoranjan (2004), 'Theorizing Indian Democracy', in Rajendra Vora and Suhas Palshikar (eds), *Indian Democracy: Meanings and Practices* (New Delhi, London, and Thousand Oaks: Sage), 99–126.

Møller, Jørgen, and Skaaning, Svend-Erik (2013), 'Regime Types and Democratic Sequencing', *Journal of Democracy*, 24(1): 142–55.

Montada, L. (2001), 'Justice and Its Many Faces: Cultural Concerns', in Neil J. Smelser and Paul B. Baltes (eds), *International Encyclopedia of the Social and Behavioral Sciences* (Amsterdam: Elsevier), 8037–42.

Moore, Barrington (1966), *The Social Origins of Dictatorship and Democracy: Lord and Peasant in the Making of the Modern World* (London: Penguin).

Morozov, Evgeny (2012), *The Net Illusion: How Not to Liberate the World* (London: Penguin).

Morrell, Michael J. (2016), 'I Ran the CIA–Now I'm Endorsing Hilary Clinton', *New York Times*, 5 August (http://www.nytimes.com/2016/08/05/opinion/campaign-stops/i-ran-the-cia-now-im-endorsing-hillary-clinton.html, accessed January 2018).

Morrison, Ken (2006), *Marx, Durkheim, Weber: Formations of Modern Social Thought* (London: Sage, 2nd edn).

Morriss, P. (1975), 'The Pluralist Case Not Proven: Hewitt on Britain', *British Journal of Political Science*, 5(3): 385–89.

Mosse, George L. (1995), 'Racism and Nationalism', *Nations and Nationalism*, 1(2): 163–73.

Moten, Abdul Rashid (1996), *Political Science: An Islamic Perspective* (Basingstoke: Macmillan).

Mouffe, C. (2005), *On the Political* (London: Routledge).

Mudde, Cas (2002), 'In the Name of the Peasantry, the Proletariat, and the People: Populism in Eastern Europe', in Yves Mény and Yves Surel (eds), *Democracies and the Populist Challenge* (Basingstoke: Palgrave), 214–32.

Mudde, Cas (2007), *Populist Right Parties in Europe* (Cambridge: Cambridge University Press).

Mudde, Cas, and Kaltwasser, Cristóbal Rovira (2017), *Populism: A Very Short Introduction* (Oxford: Oxford University Press).

Mugaju, Justus, and Oloka-Onyango, J. (eds) (2000), *No-Party Democracy in Uganda: Myths and Realities* (Kampala: Fountain).

Mulhall, S., and Swift, A. (1996), *Liberals and Communitarians* (Oxford: Blackwell).

Müller, Jan-Werner (2016), *What is Populism?* (Philadelphia, PA: University of Pennsylvania Press).

Musso, Pierre (2009), *Télépolitique: Le sarkoberlusconisme à l'écran* (La Tour d'Aigue: éds de l'Aube).

Mutz, D. (2008), 'Is Deliberative Democracy a Falsifiable Theory?', *Annual Review of Political Science*, 11: 521–38.

Naím, Moisés (2009), 'What is a GONGO?', *Foreign Policy* , 13 October (http://foreignpolicy.com/2009/10/13/what-is-a-gongo/, accessed January 2018).

Naím, Moisés (2013), *The End of Power: From Boardrooms to Battlefields and Churches to States—Why Being in Charge Isn't What It Used to Be* (New York: Basic Books).

Nathan, Andrew J. (2016), 'The Puzzle of the Chinese Middle Class', *Journal of Democracy*, 27(2): 5–19.

Nathan, Andrew J., Diamond, Larry, and Plattner, Marc F. (eds) (2013), *Will China Democratize?* (Baltimore, MD: Johns Hopkins University Press).

National Research Council of the National Academies (2005), *Asking the Right Questions about Electronic Voting* (https://www.nap.edu/catalog/11449/asking-the-right-questions-about-electronic-voting, accessed January 2018).

Neate, Rupert (2016), 'Panama Papers: US Launches Criminal Inquiry into Tax Avoidance Claims', *Guardian*, 19 April (https://www.theguardian.com/business/2016/apr/19/panama-papers-us-justice-department-investigation-tax-avoidance, accessed January 2018).

Neiertz, Nicolas (1999), *La coordination des transports en France: De 1918 à nos jours* (Paris: CHEEF).

Neuberger, Benyamin (2006), 'African Nationalism', in Gerard Delanty and Krishan Kumar (eds), *The Sage Handbook of Nations and Nationalism* (London: Sage).

New York Times (2009), 'Adding up the Government's Total Bailout Tab', 4 February (http://www.nytimes.com/interactive/2009/02/04/business/20090205-bailout-totals-graphic.html, accessed June 2011).

News 24 Archives (2010), 'I Am the People, Says Chavez', 24 January (http://www.news24.com/World/News/I-am-the-people-says-Chavez-20100124, accessed June 2017).

Nichols, D. (1994), *The Pluralist State* (Basingstoke: Palgrave, 2nd edn).

Niemeyer, S. (2004), 'Deliberation in the Wilderness: Displacing Symbolic Politics', *Environmental Politics*, 13(2): 347–72.

Niskanen, W. (1971), *Bureaucracy and Representative Government* (Chicago, IL: Aldine).

Nordenstreng, Kaarle (2012), 'The New World Information and Communication Order', in Angharad N. Valdivia (ed.), *The International Encyclopedia of Media Studies* (New York: Wiley, six volumes) (DOI: 10.1002/9781444361506.wbiems023, accessed May 2017).

Norton, Philip (ed.) (1998), *Parliaments and Governments in Western Europe, Vol. I* (London: Frank Cass).

Norton, Philip (2013), *Parliament in British Politics* (London: Palgrave, 2nd edn).

Nozick, R. (1974), *Anarchy, State and Utopia* (Oxford: Blackwell).

Nye, Joseph S. (2015), *Is the American Century Over?* (Cambridge and Malden, MA: Polity).

O'Donnell, Guillermo (2003), 'Horizontal Accountability: The Legal Institutionalization of Mistrust', in Scott Mainwaring and Christopher Welna (eds), *Democratic Accountability in Latin America* (Oxford: Oxford University Press), 34–54.

O'Hara, Phillip Anthony (ed.) (2014), *Encyclopedia of Political Economy* (Abingdon: Routledge).

O'Leary, Brendan (1988), 'Ernest Gellner's Diagnoses of Nationalism: A Critical Overview, Or, What is Living and What is Dead in Ernest Gelner's Philosophy of Nationalism?', in John A. Hall (ed.), *The State of the Nation: Ernest Gellner and the Theory of Nationalism* (Cambridge: Cambridge University Press), 40–88.

Oakeshott, M. (1962), *Rationalism in Politics and Other Essays* (New York: Routledge, Chapman & Hall).

Oborne, Peter (2007), *The Triumph of the Political Class* (London: Simon & Schuster).

Oborne, Peter, and Roberts, Tom (2017), *How Trump Thinks: His Tweets and the Birth of a New Political Language* (London: Head of Zeus).

Ohmae, Kenichi (1993), 'The Rise of the Region State', *Foreign Affairs*, 72(2): 78–87.

Ohmae, Kenichi (1995), *The End of the Nation State* (London: Harper Collins).

Oliver, Craig (2017), *Unleashing Demons: The Inside Story of Brexit* (London: Hodder & Stoughton).

Olsen, Johan P. (2003), 'Towards a European Administrative Space?', *Journal of European Public Policy*, 10(4): 506–31.

Olson, David M. (1994), *Democratic Legislative Institutions: A Comparative View* (New York: M. E. Sharpe).

Olson, Mancur (1971), *The Logic of Collective Action: Public Goods and the Theory of Groups* (Cambridge, MA: Harvard University Press).

Open Secrets (2017), 'Election Overview 2016' (https://www.opensecrets.org/overview/index.php?display=T&cycle=2016, accessed February 2018).

Ophuls, W. (1973), 'Leviathan or Oblivion', in H. Daly (ed.), *Toward a Steady State Economy* (San Francisco, CA: Freeman), 215–30.

Orwell, George (1945/2014), *Notes on Nationalism* (Adelaide: ebooks@Adelaide, University of Adelaide Library, web edn).

Orwell, George (1949/2008), *Nineteen Eighty-Four* (London: Viking).

Ourzik, Abdelouahad (2000), 'Public Service in Africa: New Challenges', in UN/CAFRAD (eds), *African Public Service: New Challenges, Professionalism and Ethics* (New York: United Nations), 43–9.

Özkirimli, Umut (2010), *Theories of Nationalism: A Critical Introduction* (Basingstoke: Palgrave Macmillan, 2nd edn).

Page, E. (2006), *Climate Change, Justice and Future Generations* (Cheltenham: Edward Elgar).

Pai, Sudha, and Kumar, Avinash (2014), 'Introduction', in Sudha Pai and Avinash Kumar (eds), *The Indian Parliament: A Critical Appraisal* (Hyderabad: Orient BlackSwan), 1–32.

Paley, Julia (2002), 'Towards an Anthropology of Democracy', *Annual Review of Anthropology*, 31: 469–96.

Parekh, B. (2000), *Rethinking Multiculturalism: Cultural Diversity and Political Theory* (Cambridge, MA: Harvard University Press).

Parkinson, J. (2006), *Deliberating in the Real World* (Oxford: Oxford University Press).

Parry, G. (1969), *Political Elites* (London: Allen & Unwin).

Pateman, C. (1970), *Participation and Democratic Theory* (Cambridge: Cambridge University Press).

Pateman, C. (1988), *The Sexual Contract* (Oxford: Polity Press).

Pateman, C. (1989), *The Disorder of Women* (Oxford: Polity Press).

Paterson, M. (2000), *Understanding Global Environmental Politics* (Basingstoke: Palgrave).

Patterson, Samuel C., and Mughan, Anthony (eds) (1999), *Senates: Bicameralism in the Contemporary World* (Columbus, OH: Ohio State University Press).

Patterson, Thomas E. (2017), 'Game versus Substance in Political News', in Kate Kenski and Kathleen Hall Jamieson (eds), *The Oxford Handbook of Political Communication* (Oxford and New York: Oxford University Press), 377–90.

Pavković, Aleksandar, and Radan, Peter (2016), *Creating New States: Theory and Practice of Secession* (Abingdon: Routledge).

Pepper, D. (1993), *Eco-Socialism: From Deep Ecology to Social Justice* (London: Routledge).

Persson, Torsten, and Tabellini, Guido (2007), *The Economic Effects of Constitutions* (Cambridge, MA: MIT Press).

Peterson, Scott (2000), *Me against My Brother: At War in Somalia, Sudan, and Rwanda* (London and New York: Routledge).

Petsoulas, Christina (2001), *Hayek's Liberalism and its Origins: His Idea of Spontaneous Order and the Scottish Enlightenment* (Abingdon: Routledge).

Pew Research Center (2016), *Election 2016: Campaigns as a Direct Source of News* (http://www.journalism.org/2016/07/18/election-2016-campaigns-as-a-direct-source-of-news/, accessed May 2017).

Phillips, A. (1995), *The Politics of Presence* (Oxford: Clarendon Press).

Phongpaichit, Pasuk, and Baker, Chris (2008), 'Thaksin's Populism', *Journal of Contemporary Asia*, 38(1): 62–83.

Pierre, Jon, and Peters, Guy B. (2000), *Governance, Politics and the State* (Basingstoke: Macmillan).

Plamenatz, J. (1963), *Man and Society, Vol. II* (London: Longman).

Plant, R. (1991), *Modern Political Thought* (Oxford: Basil Blackwell).

Plaut, Martin, and Holden, Paul (2012), *Who Rules South Africa?* (London: Biteback Publishing).

Pogge, T. (1989), *Realizing Rawls* (Ithaca, NY: Cornell University Press).

Pollak, Joel B., and Schweikart, Larry (2017), *How Trump Won* (Washington, DC: Regnery).

Polsby, N. (1980), *Community Power and Political Theory* (New Haven, CT: Yale University Press, 2nd edn).

Popper, K. (1962), *The Open Society and its Enemies, Vol. II: Hegel and Marx* (London: Routledge & Kegan Paul).

Poulantzas, N. (1973), *Political Power and Social Classes* (London: New Left Books).

Poulantzas, N. (1976), 'The Capitalist State: A Reply to Miliband and Laclau', *New Left Review*, 95: 63–83.

Power Inquiry (2006), *Power to the People* (http://www.jrrt.org.uk/sites/jrrt.org.uk/files/documents/PowertothePeople_001.pdf, accessed January 2018).

Przeworski, Adam, Alvarez, Michael E., Cheibub, José Antonio, and Limongi, Fernando (2000), *Democracy and Development: Political Institutions and Well-Being in the World, 1950–1990* (Cambridge and New York: Cambridge University Press).

Puhle, H.-J. (2001), 'History of Interest Groups', in Neil J. Smelser and Paul B. Baltes (eds), *International Encyclopedia of the Social and Behavioral Sciences* (Amsterdam: Elsevier), 7703–8.

Rajamani, Lavanya, and Sengupta, Arghya (2010), 'The Supreme Court', in Niraja Gopal Jayal and Pratap Bhanu Mehta (eds), *The Oxford Companion to Politics in India* (New Delhi and Oxford: Oxford University Press), 80–97.

Ramet, Sabrina P. (2005), *Thinking about Yugoslavia: Scholarly Debates about the Yugoslav Breakup and the Wars in Bosnia and Kosovo* (Cambridge: Cambridge University Press).

Rauchway, Eric (2008), *The Great Depression and the New Deal: A Very Short Introduction* (Oxford: Oxford University Press).

Rawls, J. (1971), *A Theory of Justice* (Cambridge, MA: Harvard University Press).

Rawls, J. (1993), *Political Liberalism* (New York: Columbia University Press).

Reeve, David (1985), *Golkar of Indonesia: An Alternative to the Party System* (Singapore: Oxford University Press).

Reeves, Aaron, McKee, Martin, and Stuckler, David (2015), '"It's the Sun Wot Won It": Evidence of Media Influence on Political Attitudes and Voting from a UK Quasi-Natural Experiment', *Social Science Research*, 56: 44–57.

Reid, Anthony (2010), *Imperial Alchemy: Nationalism and Political Identity in Southeast Asia* (Cambridge: Cambridge University Press).

Reinhart, Carmen M., and Rogoff, Kenneth S. (2009), *This Time is Different: Eight Centuries of Financial Folly* (Princeton, NJ: Princeton University Press).

Reynolds, Andrew, Reilly, Ben, and Allis, Andrew (2007), *Electoral System Design* (Stockholm: International IDEA).

Rheingold, Howard (2002), *Smart Mobs: The Next Social Revolution* (Cambridge, MA: Perseus).

Rhodes, R. A. W. (1996), 'The New Governance: Governing without Government', *Political Studies*, 44(4): 652–67.

Rhodes, R. A. W. (1997), *Understanding Governance: Policy Networks, Governance, Reflexivity and Accountability* (Buckingham: Open University Press).

Ricardo, David (1821), *On the Principles of Political Economy and Taxation* (London: John Murray, 3rd edn).

Richards, David (2008), *New Labour and the Civil Service: Reconstituting the Whitehall Model* (Basingstoke: Palgrave).

Richardson, J., and Jordan, A. (1979), *Governing under Pressure* (Oxford: Martin Robinson).

Riker, William H. (1982), *Liberalism against Populism: A Confrontation between the Theory of Democracy and the Theory of Social Choice* (San Francisco, CA: Freeman).

Ringen, Stein (2007), *What Democracy Is For: On Freedom and Moral Government* (Oxford and Princeton, NJ: Princeton University Press).

Ringen, Stein (2013), *Nation of Devils: Democratic Leadership and the Problem of Obedience* (London and New Haven, CT: Yale University Press).

Rittberger, Volker, and Zangl, Bernhard (2006), *International Organization: Polity, Politics and Policies* (Basingstoke: Palgrave).

Rizzo, Sergio, and Antonio Stella, Gian (2007), *La casta: Così i politici italiani sono diventati intoccabili* (Milan: Rizzoli).

Roach, Steven C., Griffiths, Martin, and O'Callaghan, Terry (2014), *International Relations: The Key Concepts* (London: Routledge, 3rd edn).

Robertson, David (1976), *A Theory of Party Competition* (London: Wiley).

Robertson, David (1993), *The Penguin Dictionary of Politics* (Harmondsworth: Penguin).

Robertson, R. (1992), *Globalization: Social Theory and Global Culture* (London: Sage).

Rocke, Anya (2014), *Framing Citizen Participation: Participatory Budgeting in France, Germany and Britain* (Basingstoke: Palgrave).

Rodrik, Dani (2011), *The Globalization Paradox: Why Global Markets, States, and Democracy Can't Coexist* (Oxford: Oxford University Press).

Rose, R., and Peters, B. (1978), *Can Government Go Bankrupt?* (New York: Basic Books).

Rosen, Lawrence (1989), *The Anthropology of Justice: Law as Culture in Islamic Society* (Cambridge: Cambridge University Press).

Rosenbluth, Frances, and Ramseyer, Mark (1993), *Japan's Political Marketplace* (Cambridge, MA: Harvard University Press).

Rossi, E., and Sleat, M. (2014), 'Realism in Normative Political Theory', *Philosophy Compass*, 9/10: 689–701.

Rotberg, Robert I. (ed.) (2004), *When States Fail: Causes and Consequences* (Princeton, NJ: Princeton University Press).

Rousseau, J. (1913), *The Social Contract and Discourses* (London: Dent).

Roy, Olivier (1994), *The Failure of Political Islam* (London: I.B. Tauris).

RSF (Reporters sans Frontières) (2015), 'World Press Freedom Index' (https://rsf.org/en/ranking/2015, accessed April 2015).

Ruggie, John Gerard (1998), *Constructing the World Polity: Essays on International Institutionalization* (London: Routledge).

Rüland, Jürgen (2003), 'Constitutional Debates in the Philippines: From Presidentialism to Parliamentarianism?', *Asian Survey*, 43(3): 461–84.

Rüland, Jürgen, Jürgenmeyer, Clemens, Nelson, Michael H., and Ziegenhain, Patrick (2005), *Parliaments and Political Change in Asia* (Singapore: ISEAS).

Rummel, R. J. (1994), *Death by Government* (New Brunswick, NJ: Transaction).

Runciman, David (2013), *The Confidence Trap: A History of Democracy in Crisis from World War I to the Present* (Oxford and Princeton, NJ: Princeton University Press).

Russell, B. (1938), *Power: A New Social Analysis* (London: Allen & Unwin).

Rÿser, Rudolph C. (2012), *Indigenous Nations and Modern States: The Political Emergence of Nations Challenging State Power* (New York: Routledge).

Saari, Donald G. (2001), *Chaotic Elections! A Mathematician Looks at Voting* (Providence, RI: American Mathematical Society).

Saeki, Keishi (1997), *Gendai minshushugino byōri* (Tokyo: NHK Books).

Salisu, Mohammed (2003), 'Incentive Structure, Civil Service Efficiency and the Hidden Economy in Nigeria', in Steve Kayizzi-Mugerwa (ed.), *Reforming Africa's Institutions: Ownership, Incentives, and Capabilities* (Tokyo: UNUP and UNU/WIDER), 170–98.

Saltford, John (2003), *The United Nations and the Indonesian Takeover of West Papua, 1962–1969: The Anatomy of Betrayal* (London: Routledge).

Saltiel, Miles (2017), *The Brexit Blogs: What Insiders Saw, March to October 2016* (Kindle edn).

Sanderson, Thomas M. (2004), 'Transnational Terror and Organized Crime: Blurring the Lines', *SAIS Review*, 24(1): 49–61.

Saner, Emine (2016), 'The Return of the Dogs of War: What's It Like to Be A Soldier for Hire?', *Guardian*, 6 February (https://www.theguardian.com/uk-news/2016/feb/06/the-return-of-the-dogs-of-war-whats-it-like-to-be-a-soldier-for-hire, accessed January 2018).

Sartori, Giovanni (1976), *Parties and Party Systems: A Framework for Analysis* (Cambridge: Cambridge University Press).

Sassoon, Joseph (2012), *Saddam Hussein's Ba'ath Party: Inside an Authoritarian Regime* (Cambridge: Cambridge University Press).

Savigny, H., and Marsden, L. (2011), *Doing Political Science and International Relations: Theories in Action* (Basingstoke: Palgrave).

Savoie, Donald J. (2010), *Power: Where Is It?* (Montreal and Kingston: McGill-Queen's University Press).

Saward, M. (2001), 'Reconstructing Democracy: Current Thinking and New Directions', *Government and Opposition*, 36(4): 559–81.

Schain M., Zolberg, A., and Hossay, P. (eds) (2002), *Shadows over Europe: The Development and Impact of the Extreme Right in Western Europe* (Basingstoke: Palgrave Macmillan).

Schedler, Andreas (ed.) (2006), *Electoral Authoritarianism: the Dynamics of Unfree Competition* (Boulder, CO: Lynne Rienner).

Schlozman, K. L. (2001), 'Interest Groups', in Neil J. Smelser and Paul B. Baltes (eds), *International Encyclopedia of the Social and Behavioral Sciences* (Amsterdam: Elsevier), 7700–3.

Schmitter, Philippe (1980), 'Modes of Interest Intermediation and Models of Societal Change in Western Europe', in Philippe Schmitter and Gerhard Lehmbruch (eds), *Trends towards Corporatist Intermediation* (Beverly Hills, CA: Sage), 63–94.

Schmitter, Philippe C., and Karl, Terry Lynn (1991), 'What Democracy Is ... and Is Not', *Journal of Democracy*, 2(3): 75–88.

Scholte, Jan Art (2005), *Globalization: A Critical Introduction* (Basingstoke: Palgrave, 2nd edn).

Schudson, Michael (1998), *The Good Citizen: A History of American Civic Life* (New York: Free Press).

Schudson, Michael (2008), *Why Democracies Need an Unlovable Press* (Cambridge: Polity).

Schumacher, E. (1973), *Small is Beautiful: Economics as if People Mattered* (London: Blond & Briggs).

Schuman, Michael (2011), 'What the US Debt Problem Means for the Global Economy', *TIME*, 19 April (http://business.time.com/2011/04/19/what-americas-debt-problem-means-for-the-global-economy/, accessed June 2011).

Schumpeter, J. (1961), *Capitalism, Socialism and Democracy* (New York: Harper & Row).

Scott, J. (1990), *Domination and the Arts of Resistance* (New Haven, CT: Yale University Press).

Scruton, R. (2001), *The Meaning of Conservatism* (Basingstoke: Palgrave Macmillan, 3rd edn).

Seib, Philip (2008), *The Al Jazeera Effect: How the New Global Media Are Reshaping World Politics* (Washington, DC: Potomac).

Sen, Amartya (1999), 'Democracy as a Universal Value', *Journal of Democracy*, 10(3): 3–17.

Shadbolt, Peter (2013), 'Pakistan hatches scheme to claw back tax', *CNN*, 11 February (http://edition.cnn.com/2013/02/11/world/asia/pakistan-tax/index.html, accessed January 2018).

Shahin, Emad El-Din (2015), 'Government', in Gerhard Bowering (ed.), *Islamic Political Thought: An Introduction* (Oxford and Princeton, NJ: Princeton University Press), 68–85.

Shambaugh, David (2008), *The Chinese Communist Party: Atrophy and Adaptation* (Washington, DC, and Berkeley, CA: Woodrow Wilson Center Press and University of California Press).

Shankar, Shylashri (2010), 'India's Judiciary: Imperium in Imperio?', in Paul R. Brass (ed.), *Routledge Handbook of South Asian Politics* (London and New York: Routledge), 165–76.

Shapiro, I. (2003), *The Moral Foundations of Politics* (New Haven, CT: Yale University Press).

Shearman, D., and Wayne-Smith, J. (2007), *The Climate Change Challenge and the Future of Democracy* (Westport, CT: Praeger).

Shipman, Tim (2016), *All-Out War: The Full Story of How Brexit Sank Britain's Political Class* (London: Collins).

Shorten, A. (2016), *Contemporary Political Theory* (London: Palgrave).

Siddique, Haroon (2017), 'Teach Schoolchildren How to Spot Fake News, says OECD', *The Guardian*, 18 March (https://www.theguardian.com/media/2017/mar/18/teach-schoolchildren-spot-fake-news-says-oecd, accessed January 2018).

Singer, P. (1973), *Democracy and Disagreement* (Oxford: Oxford University Press).

Singer, P. (2002), *One World: The Ethics of Globalization* (Melbourne: Text).

Singer, Peter W. (2008), *Corporate Warriors: The Rise of the Privatized Military Industry* (Ithaca, NY: Cornell University Press).

Sivaramakrishnan, K. C., and Joshi, Bhanu (2014), 'Bicameralism in India: The Centre and the States', in Sudha Pai and Avinash Kumar (eds), *The Indian Parliament: A Critical Appraisal* (Hyderabad: Orient BlackSwan), 100–11.

Slaughter, A. (2003), *A New World Order* (Princeton, NJ: Princeton University Press).

Slaughter, Anne-Marie (1997), 'The Real New World Order', *Foreign Affairs*, 76(5): 183–97.

Smith, Anthony D. (1998), *Nationalism and Modernism* (London: Routledge).

Smith, Anthony D. (2000), *The Nation in History: Historiographical Debates about Ethnicity and Nationalism* (Cambridge: Polity).

Smith, Anthony D. (2009), *Ethnosymbolism and Nationalism: A Cultural Approach* (Abingdon: Routledge).

Smith, G. (2003), *Deliberative Democracy and the Environment* (London: Routledge).

Smith, M. (1993), *Pressure, Power and Policy: State Autonomy and Policy Networks in Britain and the United States* (Hemel Hempstead: Harvester Wheatsheaf).

Smith, M. (2006), 'Pluralism', in C. Hay, M. Lister, and M. D. Marsh (eds), *The State: Theories and Issues* (Basingstoke: Palgrave), 21–38.

Smith, N. (1990), *The Politics of Agricultural Support in Britain* (Aldershot: Dartmouth).

Smits, K. (2016), *Applying Political Theory: Issues and Debates* (London: Palgrave, 2nd edn).

Soros, George (2010), 'Remarks Delivered at the INET Conference at King's College: Anatomy of a Crisis', 9 April (https://www.georgesoros.com/2010/04/09/anatomy_of_a_crisis_-_the_living_history_of_the_last_30_years_economic_theo/, accessed June 2011).

Souillac, Romain (2007), *Le movement Poujade: De la défense professionnelle au populisme nationaliste (1953–1962)* (Paris: Presses de Sciences Po).

Souza, Celina (2014), *Constitutional Engineering in Brazil: The Politics of Federalism and Decentralization* (London: Palgrave Macmillan).

Spencer, Phillip, and Wollman, Howard (eds) (2005), *Nations and Nationalism: A Reader* (New Brunswick, NJ: Rutgers University Press).

Spero, Joan E., and Hart, Jeffrey A. (1997), *The Politics of International Economic Relations* (New York: St Martin's Press, 5th edn).

Sridharan, E. (2010), 'The Party System', in Niraja Gopal Jayal and Pratap Bhanu Mehta (eds), *The Oxford Companion to Politics in India* (Oxford and New Delhi: Oxford University Press), 117–35.

Stacher, Joshua (2015), 'Fragmenting States, New Regimes: Militarized State Violence and Transition in the Middle East', *Democratization* 22(2): 259–75.

Starr, June (1992), *Law as Metaphor: From Islamic Courts to the Palace of Justice* (Albany, NY: State University of New York Press).

State Council Information Office (China) (2005), '*Building of Democracy in China*' (http://www.china.org.cn/english/2005/Oct/145718.htm, accessed January 2018).

Steger, Manfred B., and Roy, Ravi K. (2010), *Neoliberalism: A Very Short Introduction* (Oxford: Oxford University Press).

Steiner, J., Bächtiger, A., Spörndli, M., and Steenbergen, M. R. (eds) (2004), *Deliberative Politics in Action: Analysing Parliamentary Discourse* (Cambridge: Cambridge University Press).

Steinmo, S. (2001), 'Institutionalism', in Neil J. Smelser and Paul Baltes (eds), *International Encyclopedia of the Social and Behavioral Sciences, Vol. XI* (Amsterdam: Elsevier), 7554–8.

Stepan, Alfred (2004), 'Federalism and Democracy: Beyond the US Model', in Ugo Amoretti and Nancy Bermeo (eds), *Federalism and Territorial Cleavages* (Baltimore, MD: Johns Hopkins University Press), 441–56.

Stepan, Alfred, Linz, Juan J., and Yadav, Yogendra (2011), *Crafting State-Nations: India and Other Multinational Democracies* (Baltimore, MD: Johns Hopkins University Press).

Stockwin, J. A. A. (1999), *Governing Japan* (Oxford: Blackwell, 3rd edn).

Stoker, G. (2006), *Why Politics Matters* (Basingstoke: Palgrave).

Stoker, G., and Marsh, D. (2002), 'Introduction', in D. Marsh and G. Stoker, *Theory and Methods in Political Science* (Basingstoke: Palgrave), 1–16.

Stone, Roger, and Colapietro, Mike (2014), *The Man Who Killed Kennedy: The Case against LBJ* (New York: Skyhorse).

Street, John (2011), *Mass Media, Politics and Democracy* (Basingstoke: Palgrave, 2nd edn).

Strom, Kevin, Berzofsky, Marcus, Shook-Sa, Bonnie, Barrick, Kelle, Daye, Crystal, Horstmann, Nicole, and Kinsey, Susan (2010), *The Private Security Industry: A Review of the Definitions, Available Data Sources, and Paths Moving Forward* (Document No. 232781) (Research Triangle Park NC: RTI International).

Suberu, Rotimi T. (2004), 'Nigeria: Dilemmas of Federalism', in Ugo M. Amoretti and Nancy Bermeo (eds), *Federalism and Territorial Cleavages* (Baltimore and London: Johns Hopkins University Press), 327–54.

Sun Tzu (1963), *The Art of War*, tr. Samuel B. Griffith (Oxford: Clarendon Press).

Sunstein, Cass R. (2017), *#republic* (Princeton, NJ: Princeton University Press).

Sutherland, Keith (2004), *The Party's Over: Blueprint for a Very English Revolution* (Exeter: Imprint Academic).

Suwannathat-Pian, Kobkua (1988), *Thai–Malay Relations* (Oxford: Oxford University Press).

Swanson, Judith A. (1992), *The Public and the Private in Aristotle's Political Philosophy* (Ithaca, NY: Cornell University Press).

Swett, Charles (1995), *Strategic Assessment: The Internet*. Paper prepared for the Department of Defence, July 17, 1995. (Available at: https://powersthatbeat.wordpress.com/2011/07/18/strategic-assessment-the-internet-1995/, accessed February 2018.)

Tait, Richard (2012), 'Never Waste a Good Crisis: The British Phone Hacking Scandal and Its Implications for Politics and the Press', in Holli A. Semetko and Margaret Scammell (eds), *The Sage Handbook of Political Communication* (London and Los Angeles, CA: Sage), 518–26.

Talbot, Colin (2004), 'The Agency Idea: Sometimes Old, Sometimes New, Sometimes Borrowed, Sometimes Untrue', in Christopher Pollitt and Colin Talbot (eds), *Unbundled Government: A Critical Analysis of the Global Trend to Agencies, Quangos and Contractualisation* (Abingdon: Routledge), 3–21.

Talmon, J. (1952), *The Origins of Totalitarian Democracy* (London: Secker & Warburg).

Talos, E., and Kittel, B. (2002), 'Austria in the 1990s: The Routine of Social Partnership in Question', in S. Berger and H. Compston (eds), *Policy Concertation and Social Partnership in Western Europe* (New York: Berghahn Books), 35–50.

Tambini, Damien (2017), *Fake News: Public Policy Responses* (London: LSE Media Policy Brief 20) (http://eprints.lse.ac.uk/73015/1/LSE%20MPP%20Policy%20Brief%2020%20-%20Fake%20news_final.pdf, accessed May 2017).

Tanner, Lindsay (2009), 'Combating the GFC: An Australian Perspective', 15 October (http://www2.financeminister.gov.au/speeches/2009/sp_20091015.html, accessed June 2011, now defunct).

Tanzi, Vito (2011), *Government versus Markets: The Changing Economic Role of the State* (Cambridge: Cambridge University Press).

Tanzi, Vito, and Schuknecht, Ludger (2000), *Public Spending in the Twentieth Century* (Cambridge: Cambridge University Press), 6–7.

Taylor, A. J. P. (1965), *English History, 1914–1945* (Oxford: Clarendon Press).

Taylor, Robert H. (2009), *The State in Myanmar* (London: Hurst, 2nd edn).

Teets, Jessica C. (2014), *Civil Society under Authoritarianism: The China Model* (Cambridge: Cambridge University Press).

Thakur, Ramesh (2011a), *The Responsibility to Protect: Norms, Laws and the Use of Force in International Politics* (Abingdon: Routledge).

Thakur, Ramesh (2011b), 'UN Breathes Life into "Responsibility to Protect"', *The Star* (Toronto), 21 March (https://www.thestar.com/opinion/editorialopinion/article/957664—un-breathes-life-intoresponsibility-to-protect, accessed May 2011).

Thatcher, M. (2001), 'Issue Networks: Iron Triangles, Subgovernments, and Policy Communities', in Neil J. Smelser and Paul B. Baltes (eds), *International Encyclopedia of the Social and Behavioral Sciences* (Amsterdam: Elsevier), 7940–2.

Thomas, G. (1993), *An Introduction to Ethics* (London: Duckworth).

Thomas, Ryan J., and Finneman, Teri (2014), 'Who Watches the Watchdogs?', *Journalism Studies*, 15(2): 172–86.

Tierney, Stephen (2007), *Multiculturalism and the Canadian Constitution* (Vancouver: University of British Columbia).

Tilly, Charles (1975), 'Reflections on the History of European State-Making', in Charles Tilly (ed.), *The Formation of National States in Western Europe* (Princeton, NJ: Princeton University Press), 3–83.

Tilly, Charles (1990), *Coercion, Capital and European States, AD 990–1990* (Oxford: Blackwell).

Tolstoy, Leo (2017), 'Patriotism and Government', in Robert Hoffman (ed.), *Anarchism as Political Philosophy* (London: Routledge), 70–85.

Toonen, Theo A. J. (2001), 'The Comparative Dimension of Administrative Reform: Creating Open Villages and Redesigning the Politics of Administration', in B. Guy Peters and Jon Pierre (eds), *Politicians, Bureaucrats and Administrative Reform* (Abingdon: Routledge), 183–201.

Townley, Cynthia (2007), 'Patriotism: Problems at Home', in Aleksandar Pavković and Igor Primoratz (eds), *Patriotism: Philosophical and Political Perspectives* (Aldershot: Ashgate), 163–81.

Trevor-Roper, H. (1947), *The Last Days of Hitler* (London: Macmillan).

Tronconi, Filippo (ed.) (2015), *Beppe Grillo's Five Star Movement: Opposition, Communication and Ideology* (Farnham: Ashgate).

Trump, Donald J. (2017), 'Inaugural Address', 20 January (https://www.whitehouse.gov/briefings-statements/the-inaugural-address/, accessed February 2018).

Trump, Donald J., and Schwartz, Tony (1987), *Trump: The Art of the Deal* (New York: Ballantine).

Tsebelis, George, and Money, Jeannette (1997), *Bicameralism* (Cambridge: Cambridge University Press).

Tsfati, Yariv (2017), 'Public and Elite Perceptions of News Media in Politics', in Kate Kenski and Kathleen Hall Jamieson (eds), *The Oxford Handbook of Political Communication* (Oxford and New York: Oxford University Press), 565–79.

Twining, William (2000), *Globalisation and Legal Theory* (London: Butterworth).

United Nations (2009), 'Ten Stories the World Should Hear More About 2008' (http://www.un.org/en/events/tenstories/08/index.shtml, accessed May 2017).

United Nations Department of Economic and Social Affairs (2010), *Rethinking Poverty: Report on the World Social Situation 2010* (http://www.un.org/esa/socdev/rwss/docs/2010/fullreport.pdf, accessed June 2011).

United Nations Development Program (1994), *Human Development Report 1994* (New York: United Nations).

United Nations Economic and Social Commission for Asia and the Pacific (2009), *What is Good Governance?*, (http://www.unescap.org/sites/default/files/good-governance.pdf, accessed January 2018).

United Nations General Assembly (2005), *2005 World Summit Outcome* (Draft Resolution) (http://responsibilitytoprotect.org/world%20summit%20outcome%20doc%202005%281%29.pdf, accessed May 2011).

United Nations Office of the High Commissioner for Human Rights (2014), 'Statement by the UN High Commissioner for Human Rights, Navi Pillay to the Security Council Open Debate on Maintenance of International Peace and Security', (http://www.ohchr.org/EN/NewsEvents/Pages/DisplayNews.aspx?NewsID=14958&LangID=E, accessed February 2015).

United Nations Security Council (2011), *Resolution 1973 (2011)* (SRES/1973) (https://www.nato.int/nato_static/assets/pdf/pdf_2011_03/20110927_110311-UNSCR-1973.pdf, accessed April 2011).

US National Intelligence Council (2008), *Global Trends 2025: A Transformed World* (Washington, DC: National Intelligence Council).

US National Intelligence Council (2012), *Global Trends 2030: Alternative Worlds* (Washington, DC: National Intelligence Council).

Usui, Chikako, and Colignon, Richard A. (2004), 'Continuity and Change in Paths to High Political Office: Ex-Bureaucrats and Hereditary Politicians', *Asian Business and Management*, 3(4): 395–416.

Vaishnav, Milan (2017), *When Crime Pays: Money and Muscle in Indian Politics* (London and New Haven, CT: Yale University Press).

van Biezen, Ingrid (2003), *Political Parties in New Democracies: Party Organization in Southern and East-Central Europe* (Basingstoke: Palgrave).

van Biezen, Ingrid, Mair, Peter, and Poguntke, Thomas (2011), 'Going, Going, … Gone? The Decline of Party Membership in Contemporary Europe', *European Journal of Political Research*, 51: 24–56.

van Creveld, Martin (1999), *The Rise and Decline of the State* (Cambridge: Cambridge University Press).

van den Berghe, Pierre (1978), 'Race and Ethnicity: A Sociobiological Perspective', *Ethnic and Racial Studies*, 1(4): 401–11.

Vanderhill, Rachel (2013), *Promoting Authoritarianism Abroad* (Boulder, CO: Lynne Rienner).

Varshney, Ashutosh (2002), *Ethnic Conflict and Civic Life: Hindus and Muslims in India* (London and New Haven, CT: Yale University Press, 2nd edn).

Varshney, Ashutosh (2013), *Battles Half-Won: India's Improbable Democracy* (New Delhi and London: Penguin/Viking).

Vincent, A. (1995), *Modern Political Ideologies* (Oxford: Blackwell, 2nd edn).

Viner, Jacob (1949), 'Power versus Plenty as Objectives of Foreign Policy in the Seventeenth and Eighteenth Centuries', *World Politics*, 1(2): 1–29.

Vogler, J. (2005), 'In Defence of International Environmental Cooperation', in J. Barry and R. Eckersley (eds), *The State and the Global Ecological Crisis* (Cambridge, MA: MIT Press), 229–54.

von Beyme, Klaus (1985), *Political Parties in Western Democracies* (Aldershot: Gower).

von Clausewitz, Carl (1993), *On War*, tr. Michael Howard and Peter Paret (New York: Alfred A. Knopf, rev. edn).

von Hayek, Friedrich (2001), *The Road to Serfdom* (Abingdon: Routledge).

Wæver, Ole (1998), 'On Securitization and Desecuritization', in Ronnie Lipschutz (ed.), *On Security* (New York: Columbia University Press), 46–87.

Walzer, M. (1990), 'The Communitarian Critique of Liberalism', *Political Theory*, 18(1): 6–23.

Ware, Alan (1996), *Political Parties and Party Systems* (Oxford: Oxford University Press).

Ware, Alan (2002), 'The United States: Populism as Political Strategy', in Yves Mény and Yves Surel (eds), *Democracies and the Populist Challenge* (Basingstoke: Palgrave), 101–19.

Washington Post Editorial Board (2016), 'Donald Trump is a Unique Threat to American Democracy', *Washington Post*, 22 July (https://www.washingtonpost.com/opinions/donald-trump-is-a-unique-threat-to-american-democracy/2016/07/22/a6d823cc-4f4f-11e6-aa14-e0c1087f7583_story.html, accessed January 2018).

Watson, Alison M. S. (2004), *An Introduction to International Political Economy* (London: Continuum).

Watt, W. Montgomery (1968), *Islamic Political Thought* (Edinburgh: Edinburgh University Press).

Waugh, Evelyn (1978), *Scoop: A Novel about Journalists* (London: Eyre Methuen).

Weale, A. (2007), *Democracy* (Basingstoke: Palgrave, 2nd edn).

Weaver, Gina Marie (2010), *Ideologies of Forgetting: Rape in the Vietnam War* (Albany, NY: State University of New York Press).

Weber, Max (1968), *Economy and Society: An Outline of Interpretive Sociology, Vol. III*, ed. Guenther Roth and Claus Wittich (New York: Bedminster Press).

Weber, Max (2009), *From Max Weber: Essays in Sociology*, ed. H. H. Gerth and C. Wright Mills (Abingdon: Routledge).

Weiss, Linda (1998), *The Myth of the Powerless State: Governing the Economy in a Global Era* (Cambridge: Polity Press).

Welsh, Bridget, and Chang, Alex (2015) 'Choosing China: Public Perceptions of Choosing "China as a Model"', *Journal of Contemporary China*, 24(93): 442–56.

Welzel, Christian (2013), *Freedom Rising: Human Empowerment and the Quest for Emancipation* (Cambridge: Cambridge University Press).

Wessler, Hartmut (ed.) (2008), *Transnationalization of Public Spheres* (Basingstoke: Palgrave).

West, Cornel (1991), 'Decentring Europe: A Memorial Lecture for James Snead', *Critical Quarterly*, 33(1): 1–19.

Westergaard, J., and Resler, H. (1975), *Class in a Capitalist Society* (London: Heinemann).

White House (2017), 'The Inaugural Address' (https://www.whitehouse.gov/briefings-statements/the-inaugural-address/, accessed January 2018).

White, Jenny (2003), *Islamist Mobilization in Turkey: A Study in Vernacular Politics* (London and Seattle, WA: University of Washington Press).

White, Jenny (2013), *Muslim Nationalism and the New Turks* (Princeton, NJ: Princeton University Press).

Whitehead, John W. (2012), 'Jailing Americans for Profit: The Rise of the Prison Industrial Complex', *Huffington Post*, 10 June (http://www.huffingtonpost.com/john-w-whitehead/prison-privatization_b_1414467.html, accessed January 2018).

Wighton, David (2009), 'Efficient Market Hypothesis is Dead—for Now', *Sunday Times*, 29 January (https://www.thetimes.co.uk/article/efficient-market-hypothesis-is-dead-for-now-kzqx8slf8vf, accessed January 2018).

Wike, Richard, Stokes, Bruce, Poushter, Jacob, and Fetterolf, Janell (2017), 'US Image Suffers as Publics around World Question Trump's Leadership', *Pew Research Center*, 26 June (http://www.pewglobal.org/2017/06/26/u-s-image-suffers-as-publics-around-world-question-trumps-leadership/, accessed September 2017).

Wilkinson, Rorden (2000), *Multilateralism and the World Trade Organisation: The Architecture and Extension of International Trade Regulation* (London: Routledge).

Williams, Colin, and Smith, Anthony D. (1983), 'The National Construction of Social Space', *Progress in Human Geography*, 7(4): 502–18.

Williams, Phil (1997), 'Transnational Criminal Organizations and International Security', in John Arquilla and David Ronfeldt (eds), *In Athena's Camp: Preparing for Conflict in the Information Age* (Santa Monica, CA: Rand Corporation), 315–37.

Williamson, John (2009), 'A Short History of the Washington Consensus', *Law and Business Review of the Americas*, 15(1): 7–26.

Wilson, Lord Richard (2013), 'Public Sphere and Political Experience', in Christian J. Emden and David Midgley (eds), *Beyond Habermas: Democracy, Knowledge, and the Public Sphere* (Oxford and New York: Berghahn), 1–16.

Wintour, Patrick (2017), '1m African Migrants May Be En Route to Europe, Says Former UK Envoy', *The Guardian*, 2 April (https://www.theguardian.com/uk-news/2017/apr/02/1m-african-migrants-may-be-en-route-to-europe-says-former-uk-envoy, accessed January 2018).

Wissenburg, M. (1993), 'The Idea of Nature and the Nature of Distributive Justice', in A. Dobson and P. Lucardie (eds), *The Politics of Nature: Explorations in Green Political Thought* (London: Routledge), 3–20.

Wolfe, Lauren (2013), 'Syria Has a Massive Rape Crisis', *The Atlantic*, 3 April (https://www.theatlantic.com/international/archive/2013/04/syria-has-a-massive-rape-crisis/274583/, accessed January 2018).

Wolff, J. (1996), *An Introduction to Political Philosophy* (Oxford: Oxford University Press).

Wolff, R. P. (1970), *In Defence of Anarchism* (New York: Harper & Row).

Wolff, R. P. (1977), *Understanding Rawls* (Princeton, NJ: Princeton University Press).

Wolmar, Christian (2002), *Down the Tube: the Battle for London's Underground* (London: Aurum).

Woods, K. (2014), *Human Rights* (Basingstoke: Palgrave Macmillan).

Woodward, Bob, and Bernstein, Carl (1974), *All the President's Men* (New York: Simon & Schuster).

Woolstonecraft, M. (1792/1978), *A Vindication of the Rights of Women* (Harmondsworth: Penguin).

World Bank (2005), *Economic Growth in the 1990s: Learning from a Decade of Reform* (Washington, DC: IRBD/World Bank).

World Commission on Environment and Development (1987), *Our Common Future* (Oxford: Oxford University Press).

Wright, A. (1979), *G. D. H. Cole and Socialist Democracy* (Oxford: Clarendon Press).

Wright, A. (1996), *Socialisms* (London: Routledge).

Wright, Mills, C. (1956), *The Power Elite* (New York: Oxford University Press).

Wyatt, Andrew (2015), 'India in 2014: Decisive National Elections', *Asian Survey*, 55(1): 33–47.

Wyplosz, Charles (2015), *The Centralization-Decentralization Issue* (Brussels: Directorate-General for Economic and Financial Affairs, EU Commission Discussion Paper 14) (https://publications.europa.eu/en/publication-detail/-/publication/b0865d0b-8907-11e5-b8b7-01aa75ed71a1/language-en, accessed January 2018).

Yilmaz, Ihsan (2005), *Muslim Laws, Politics and Society in Modern Nation States: Dynamic Legal Pluralisms in England, Turkey and Pakistan* (Aldershot: Ashgate).

Young, I. (2000), *Inclusion and Democracy* (Oxford: Oxford University Press).

Zakaria, F. (2003), *The Future of Freedom: Illiberal Democracy at Home and Abroad* (London: Norton).

Zakaria, Fareed (1997), 'The Rise of Illiberal Democracy', *Foreign Affairs*, 76(6): 22–43.

Zhang, Weiwei (2012), *The China Wave: Rise of a Civilizational State* (Hackensack, NJ: World Century).

Zhang, Weiwei (2014), *Zhongguo chaoyue: yi ge 'wenmingxing guojia' de guangrong yu mengxiang* [*China passing: The Glory and Dream of a 'Civilizational State'*] (Shanghai: Renmin chubanshe).

Zürn, Michael (2002), 'From Interdependence to Globalization', in Walter Carlsnaes, Thomas Risse, and Beth A. Simmons (eds), *Handbook of International Relations* (London: Sage), 255–74.

Zygar, Mikhail (2016), *Vsia kremliovskaia rat'* (Moscow: Intellektual'naia literatura).

Index

Note: Tables, figures, and boxes are indicated by an italic *t*, *f*, and *b* following the page number.